Footnotes to Plato

An Introduction to Philosophy

Kevin K. Durand

University Press of America,® Inc.
Lanham · Boulder · New York · Toronto · Plymouth, UK

Copyright © 2009 by
University Press of America,® Inc.
4501 Forbes Boulevard
Suite 200
Lanham, Maryland 20706
UPA Acquisitions Department (301) 459-3366

Estover Road
Plymouth PL6 7PY
United Kingdom

All rights reserved
Printed in the United States of America
British Library Cataloging in Publication Information Available

Library of Congress Control Number: 2009927839
ISBN-13: 978-0-7618-4681-9 (paperback : alk. paper)
ISBN-10: 0-7618-4681-6 (paperback : alk. paper)
eISBN-13: 978-0-7618-4682-6
eISBN-10: 0-7618-4682-4

∞™ The paper used in this publication meets the minimum
requirements of American National Standard for Information
Sciences—Permanence of Paper for Printed Library Materials,
ANSI Z39.48-1992

Contents

Preface	v
Introduction	1
Chapter 1 – Ancient Philosophy	15
Section 1: Heraclitus – *Fragments*	15
Section 2.1: The Search for the Historical Socrates	25
Section 2.2: Trial Trilogy, Part 1 – *Euthyphro*	31
Section 2.3: Trial Trilogy, Part 2 – *Apology*	45
Section 2.4: Trial Trilogy, Part 3 – *Crito*	63
Section 3.1: Plato and the Virtue of Socrates	75
Section 3.2: Socrates, Philosophy's Martyr	83
Section 3.3: Plato and Justice	99
Section 4.1: Reading Aristotle	119
Section 4.2: Aristotle – *Categories*	125
Section 4.3: Aristotle and the Highest Good	139
Section 4.4: Aristotle and the Human Function	153
Section 4.5: Aristotle and Virtue	169
Chapter 2 – Medieval Philosophy	183
Section 5: The Advent of Medieval Philosophy	183
Section 6.1: Reading St. Augustine	189
Section 6.2: St. Augustine, Doctor of the Church	193
Section 7: Boethius, Medieval Metaphysician	205
Section 8.1: Reading St. Anselm	217
Section 8.2: St. Anselm and the Ontological Argument	219
Section 9.1: Reading St. Thomas of Aquinas	231
Section 9.2: St. Thomas, Doctor of the Church	233
Section 10: William of Ockham: Ockham's Razor	249
Chapter 3 – Modern Philosophy	257
Section 11: The Birth of the Modern Era	257
Section 12.1: Descartes and the Method of Doubt	263
Section 12.2: Descartes and the Nature of the Mind	269
Section 12.3: Descartes, and the Existence of God	277
Section 12.4: Descartes and theory of Truth	289
Section 12.5: Descartes, Father of Modern Philosophy	299
Section 13.1: Reading David Hume	307
Section 13.2: Hume and the Origin of Ideas	313
Section 13.3: Hume and the Association of Ideas	327
Section 13.4: Hume and Substance	337
Section 13.5: Hume and Causation	345
Section 13.6: Hume and Religion	355
Section 14.1: Reading Immanuel Kant	371
Section 14.2: Kant and the Good Will	375
Section 14.3: Kant and the Metaphysics of Morals	385

Contents, continued

    Section 14.4: Kant and the Categorical Imperative   395
    Section 15: Mary Wollstonecraft, Forgotten Philosopher   417
Chapter 4 – Middle/Late Modern Philosophy   431
    Section 16: The Fragmentation of Philosophy   431
    Section 17.1: Reading John Stuart Mill   435
    Section 17.2: Mill and the Principle of Utility   439
    Section 17.3: Mill and *The Subjection of Women*   449
    Section 17.4: Mill and the Benefits of Liberty   465
    Section 18.1: Reading Karl Marx   475
    Section 18.2: Marx and the Philosophy of History   485

work of considering the views of great thinkers, struggling with our own views, and engaging the scholarship, the conversation moves to our peers. What insights have they gleaned in their work? How can our own views contribute to their understandings of the great philosophical questions, and vice versa? In preparing this work, I envision groups talking about these questions. To that end, the Guided Reading questions can help the reader engage the primary text and can also guide the group in using the primary text as a jumping off spot for their own explorations.

Finally, the conversations never take place in a vacuum or ivory tower. Philosophy is the most interdisciplinary of all disciplines. Biology, mathematics, chemistry, sociology, anthropology, psychology, aesthetics, ethics, geology, grammar, literary criticism – all of these have their birth in the philosophical quest for knowledge and truth. Throughout the text, these connections are often quite obvious. Care has been taken to drawing out both the obvious and the somewhat more obscure connections. Likely, the careful reader will see many, many more. It is precisely this sort of conversation that motivates philosophical investigations.

This text could never have come to its current state without the conversations I have enjoyed with class after class of quite capable and insightful students, with supportive colleagues and friends who have offered helpful critical reflections, and with a family that has a somewhat bemused look, at times, at all that philosophical inquiry entails. All have been very patient and helpful. I would especially like to thank Mary Leigh, Kathryn Zawisza, Roman Briggs, Kenny Shields and Brent Linsley for their care in reading, commenting, and being patient with draft after draft. The philosophical conversations I have had with each of them have inspired much of this work. Of course, all errors and sins of omission and commission are mine and mine alone.

Dr. Kevin K. J. Durand
Arkadelphia, Arkansas
February, 2009

Preface

Philosophy is best learned by doing. And, philosophy is best done in conversation. To that end, this text is designed to foster as many conversations as possible on a variety of levels. These conversations are nested within each other, in a sense, though they are rather clearly demarcated within the various sections of the text.

The first set of conversations encountered in these pages is the conversation between the reader and great philosophers of the past; men and women who have set the course of Western thought and culture. These conversations begin with primary texts, translated and edited to be readable and accessible. Reading primary text allows the reader to enter into conversations with great philosophers of the past over questions that are timeless. For example, what is the good life? How do we live the good life? What is the world really like? How do we know? These are the questions confronting Socrates and Plato, and they are the questions confronting the 21st century.

The second set of conversations is with current scholarship examining carefully the works of the past with the tools of the present. Since the questions Aristotle addressed are questions we face, it stands to reason that current scholarship exploring Aristotle's work on the nature of virtue, for example, helps the ongoing conversation the contemporary reader of Aristotle has with him.

The third conversation is personal. Philosophers enter into conversations with themselves, reflecting on what they have read, what they know, what their new questions are. Serious reflection will inevitably affect the way the careful thinker understands the world in which he or she lives, his or her views about the nature of the good life, and the understanding of the world. Having reflected, the careful thinker is likely to have a different perspective on the questions than previously held. This will enliven the earlier conversations and prepare the philosopher for the next set.

The fourth conversation is that with one's peers. Having done the reflective

Introduction: What is Philosophy?

> The Greek philosopher who laid the foundation of all our finer thoughts ended his most marvellous dialogue with the reflection that the ideal state could never arrive till philosophers are kings. Today, in an age of democracy, the kings are the plain citizens pursuing their various avocations. There can be no successful democratic society till general education conveys a philosophic outlook.
>
> Philosophy is not a mere collection of noble sentiments. A deluge of such sentiments does more harm than good. Philosophy is at once general and concrete, critical and appreciative of direct intuition. It is not - or, at least, should not be - a ferocious debate between irritable professors. It is a survey of possibilities and their comparison with actualities. In philosophy, the fact, the theory, the alternatives, and the ideal are weighed together. Its gifts are insight and foresight, and a sense of the worth of life, in short, that sense of importance which nerves all civilized effort. Humankind can flourish in the lower stages of life with merely barbaric flashes of thought. But when civilization culminates, the absence of a coordinating philosophy of life, spread throughout the community, spells decadence, boredom, and the slackening of effort.
>
> Alfred North Whitehead, *Adventures of Ideas*

~

What is philosophy? The word has clearly been used to mean many different things – from guiding principles ("My philosophy of life is…") to pithy sayings ("Live free or die!") to sales pitches ("Here at Wreck 'Em Used Cars, our sales philosophy is…").. This is not philosophy. During the 20th century, the scope of the discipline has often been reduced to angry arguments between ivory tower residents over esoteric principles of logic, meanings of words, and disconnected abstractions that have seemed to have little, if any, connection to the actual world. Again, this is not philosophy. And, oftentimes, philosophy has been portrayed as merely one discipline among many, alongside Chemistry, Mathematics, Finance, and the like. Once more, this fails to capture the activity that is philosophy. So, what is it?

Lord Alfred North Whitehead, among the most renowned mathematicians and philosophers of the late 19th and 20th centuries, captured quite nicely the meaning of *philosophy*. In the passage from *Adventures of Ideas* that begins this chapter, Whitehead notes that things have changed substantially since Plato wrote the *Republic*. In the *Republic*, Plato makes his famous argument that in the ideal city, the one who should rule is the philosopher – that is, not the politician who knows nothing of life, nor the craftsman who knows nothing beyond his craft, nor the artist who knows nothing beyond the inspiration at the core of his art, nor anyone who has not been carefully trained to see the interconnection of all of life and the truth that lies at the very core of all that is. This rare person, this Philosopher-King (or Philosopher-Queen even), is the one who is most fit to rule the polis.

The age of monarchy is past, however. The hope of a benevolent despot is precisely that, a vain hope that causes more harm than benefit. In an age of participatory democracy (either direct or representative), the necessary condition of its success is a public of philosophers – those whose education, from the earliest years, has been crafted to aid people in the development of well-rounded character, of broad knowledge, and of intellectual capacity to thoughtfully analyze and critique the many competing ideals, circumstances, and possibilities that comprise everyday life. Thus, the very success of the Western experiment of democracy depends on the cultivation of a society of philosophers capable of thinking carefully and acting in accordance with the conclusions of that thorough reflection.

If nothing less than the success of democracy is at stake, it becomes somewhat imperative that we understand what it is that we are to pursue. The first approach to determining the nature of philosophy is to say what it is that philosophy is *not*. As suggested, philosophy is not lists of catchy sayings, bumper stickers, or simple answers to complex questions. If the world is frightfully complex, it would be strange indeed if the answers to the world's questions were not at least similarly thorough. As Whitehead points out, considerable damage has been done by those who have managed to boil an entire world view down into a slogan. Perhaps less harmful, but only because of its limited scope, has been the professionalizing of the discipline, with Ph.D.s arguing ever smaller points of interpretation in obscure journals read only by other Ph.D.s who want to make even more narrow critiques. That the public at large, or students in particular, should find these discussions impenetrable and frightfully dull should come as no surprise to anyone.

Whitehead suggests that we return to the ancients, to examine the ways in which Socrates, Plato, and Aristotle approached philosophy. In them, we see philosophy coming into contact with the actual world, engaged, enlightening, and beneficial. Philosophy as they did it, and as Whitehead would say – as it is properly done, is both abstract *and* concrete. That is, it is concerned with experience, with experiments and the like, but also concerned with the big picture, the concept of the universe in which those experiences, experiments, etc., fit. Philosophy is a comparison of the things one might suppose at the outset to be possible with the things one already has determined to be true about the actual world in order to determine which of those apparent possibilities are actually possible and which are but chimeras. As Whitehead puts it, "in philosophy, the fact, the theory, the alternatives, and the ideal are weighed together." Philosophy is a comprehensive, interdisciplinary approach to understanding the world around us, the place of humans in the world, and the relations between all aspects of the universe. That is, it is a development of insight into the amazing variety of things, systems, and structures that comprise the world and the foresight into the possibilities for the world going forward – given what is, what might be. From this analysis comes a deeper understanding of the value of life – the "sense of the worth of life." And it is this sense, along with the gifts of insight and foresight, that make civilization itself possible.

Without these, and hence, without the philosophic work that is their foundation, the decay of civilization is inevitable. Laziness, boredom, hopelessness, and despair are the byproducts of ignoring the big questions. Narrowness of vision and shortsightedness become the order of the day and in the process, the sense of the worth of life, all life, fades. The only preventive for this slow descent into barbarism is a commitment to the search for truth, for a love of wisdom – for philosophy.

The Branches of Philosophy

If we understand philosophy to be a comprehensive, interdisciplinary approach to understanding the world around us, the place of humans in the world, and the relations between all aspects of the universe, then we have anticipated the three most common internal divisions within philosophy – metaphysics, epistemology, and ethics. Philosophy has often been divided into several branches and sub-branches, but for the most part, it is possible to group all philosophical investigations into one of these three.

Metaphysics is generally the branch most often misunderstood and parodied as everything from pointless speculation to blind faith in the supernatural and fantastical. In truth, metaphysics is a disciplined approach to attempting to understand the world as it actually is. This is a profoundly difficult process. From the very earliest philosophical investigations, it has been obvious that human senses are deceptive with regard to communicating to the human mind the actual structure of the universe around us. Simply put, our senses make all sorts of mistakes with regard to their apprehension of the actual world. To make matters more difficult, we have come to understand, particularly during the Modern Period, how very completely it seems that each person is locked up inside his or her own mind, able to infer how another might experience the world, but fundamentally incapable of seeing the world from any perspective but his or her own. As a result, all metaphysics becomes rather speculative from the outset, depending on inferences from at times faulty sources of data. Difficult and speculative though metaphysics may be, it is still a central aspect of the traditional approach to philosophy. Further, it seems impossible to abandon metaphysics altogether, no matter how difficult it may be. From Immanuel Kant, we have the following ethical principle, colloquially put as "ought implies can." That is to say, if it makes sense to say that someone *ought* to do something, then it must be a fact of the universe that it is actually possible for them to do it. If this is the case, then the world must be such that the course of action can be taken. And, if this be so, then it makes some sense to try to understand what the structure of the universe is like such that we can act in ethically praiseworthy or blameworthy ways. Thus, while it may be impossible to access the reality of the actual world directly through our own perceptions, it seems possible to make reasonable inferences from experience. This conjoining of rational and empirical techniques is paradigmatic of philosophical investigations.

As difficult as metaphysics may be, ethics is likely even more problematic. The philosophical branch that is ethics designates a careful attempt to understand how human beings should live life. However, it is quite difficult to decide the scope of the claim that a person ought to do some action or other. Is "good" determined by cultural norms? Is it, rather, a matter of the structure of the universe itself? Must ethics be a matter of religious inspiration and command or can there be a wholly naturalistic approach to ethics? Is the ethical analysis of an action a matter of the consequences of the action or the motives/intentions that give rise to the action or the sort of character possessed by the person who acts? Because ethical principles are so very difficult to justify beyond the ethical intuitions that give rise to them, some philosophers suggest that we have long since come to the point where ethics should be eliminated from the umbrella of philosophy. However, this may be more the result of Modern focus on the next branch of philosophy rather than something inherently problematic with the study of ethics itself. Since ethics is the primary way in which the biggest questions of philosophy come to the mind of the inquirer, it is probably premature to consign it to the dustbin of the history of ideas.

Epistemology, or the science of human knowledge, has been the primary branch of philosophy to receive considerable study during the Modern Period of philosophy, capturing the attention of some modern philosophers to the elimination of all else. The central questions of epistemology concern the ways in which human knowledge is founded, involving theories of truth, theories of justification, and theories of belief and ideas along with investigations into the nature of logic and logical systems.

Most of the greatest philosophers throughout history have approached the three branches of philosophy as intimately interconnected, to the extent that claims in one branch (for example, ethics) will have direct and indirect implications for claims in others. For example, to say that "ought implies can" makes certain claims about metaphysics necessary (as we shall see) and suggests that one of the questions to address in epistemology is how one comes to know what is actually possible and to justify that knowledge accordingly. One of the more intriguing approaches to philosophy, however, is to suppose that one can investigate each of the fields separately, completely independent of the others. One of the most important philosophers of the 19th century, Henry Sidgwick, and his 20th century disciple, G. E. Moore, serve as examples of this Exclusivist school of thought. On Sidgwick's view, one echoed by Moore, each of the branches of philosophy is a wholly independent science, completely removed from the others – as different, for example, as astronomy is from literature. Thus, commitments in one field of inquiry need not influence ruminations in another, on their view. While not an uncommon approach, it is clearly the minority view. It is the minority view, in large part, because the philosophical intuitions that give rise to the philosophical imperative are deeply interrelated, with a rather common sense view that beliefs about the structure of the world will necessarily have some relation to beliefs about the way in which one should live in that world and to beliefs about how human beings can both know the world and know how to live in it. Thus, at the prephilosophical level, it is clear that the branches are conceived of as different and yet related.

That prephilosophical intuitions suggest that the fields are related is not sufficient evidence to conclude that they are. The differentiation of the branches is a development of the specialization that marks the progression of human knowledge in the humanities, sciences, and technology. Greater and greater specialization with less and less interaction between disciplines was the order of the day from generally the middle of the 19th century through the end of the 20th. However, this is a very recent development in human knowledge – from the period of ancient philosophy through at least the Renaissance and again toward the end of the 20th century, the emphasis has been on the many ways in which human knowledge and beliefs form webs of interrelated concepts; concepts that are fundamentally impossible to extract and examine in isolation from all of the others, not just the others within generally related field, but from the majority of the others which form the architecture of the human mind and human perception. Thus, perceptions of the actual world, ruminations about how one ought live life in that world, and reflections on the ways in which the actual world and the living of life can be known seem impossible to abstract one from the other. A much more profitable approach is the interdisciplinary one in which no potential data is excluded from reflection and the full breadth of philosophy is surveyed, albeit from at least three different perspectives.

Within the three main branches of philosophy are subfields, many of which we will discuss at great length. Among the subfields of Metaphysics, for example, are inquiries into the nature of reality (or Ontology), investigations of cause and effect (or Causation), and speculations on Space and Time. Questions of Truth and Logic fall more under the heading of Epistemology. Ethics is generally divided into three main types, Virtue, Deontology, and Utilitarianism; although some would add Ethical Egoism as a fourth. With the greater specialization in these fields, it is not surprising that internecine squabbles among professional philosophers might ensue. For example, some have excluded metaphysics as a purely speculative and scientifically unverifiable endeavor. An even narrower view would be to reduce philosophy to merely the handmaid of the sciences, plowing the fields of logic and theoretical minutiae in the service of empirical science. Thus, there have been those thinkers who, while being committed to deeply held ethical and moral views, hold at the same time that ethics is not properly a part of philosophy as it fails to be as exacting a discipline as formal logic. This view, held by some of the most famous philosophers of the 20th century (Bertrand Russell, for one), fails to grasp the most fundamental questions asked by the ancients philosophers like Plato and Aristotle. This even narrower view, popular within some circles in the 20th century, is fortunately a minority opinion regarding the nature of philosophy as well.

Everyone is a philosopher. The only question is whether a person will do philosophy well or poorly. The best way to learn philosophy is to actually do philosophy, focusing on critical thinking, ethical commitments, structures of knowledge, and perceptions of the actual world. And, the best way to do philosophy is in conversation. This volume invites the reader to do philosophy by entering into conversations with great philosophers of the past, thinkers who have explored the big questions of philosophy and have come to, at times, wildly divergent conclusions. Over time, ideas have been mulled, rejected, resurrected, and mulled again. By entering into conversations with great philosophers of the past, the reader will be also invited to mull these ideas him or herself, entering into conversations within ourselves. So, conversations with great philosophers and within ourselves are two important aspects of the philosophical journey. The other conversation that is important to enter is the conversation with contemporary philosophers, both professional and lay. In doing this, we reenact the model of philosophical investigation of the great philosophers themselves. To this end, this volume includes considerable primary text from a variety of styles – dialogues, treatises, meditations, newspaper serials, and propaganda. It also includes commentary on those primary texts that encourages the reader to read again the primary text and also to challenge both the conclusions of the philosopher in question as well as the commentary. Finally, through various guided reflections, the reader is encouraged to engage in self-reflection. All of these primary texts, commentaries, and reflections range across all three branches of philosophy, embodying the underlying premise of the author that all of human experience is interrelated and that the best avenue to becoming a lover of wisdom is to seek not only facts but relations, not merely knowledge but wisdom.

Logic Blurb
Introduction to Logic

While it is true that logic is not the whole of philosophy, it is also true that it is an essential part. Logic is among the most fundamental tools in the philosopher's toolbox – like a tape measure or ruler to an architect or carpenter. As an architect or carpenter takes the measure of some aspect of their work, so the philosopher uses the principles of logic to measure arguments, to determine validity of construction, and to evaluate soundness of reasoning.

Introduction: What is Philosophy? 7

Throughout the text, we will examine different aspect of logical thinking as they pertain to the topic under consideration. For example, as we explore *The Euthyphro Problem*, an understanding of the "Disjunctive 'or'" and "Contradiction" will prove helpful. Here, however, we shall briefly examine some basics.

Any argument is comprised of two kinds of statements – premises and conclusions. The premises are those things agreed upon by the participants, definitions, formal statements of relationships, and the like. Conclusions are those statements that validly follow from the premises. For example:

```
P1:     All bachelors are unmarried males.
P2:     Tom is a bachelor.
-----
C:      Tom is unmarried.
```

The first two sentences are premises and the last is the conclusion. Premises do not stand on their own. Each needs some justification. For example, the justification of P1 is that it is a definition. The justification of P2 is an observation. For example, if Tom were not a bachelor, then P2 would be false. If even one of the premises is false, then the entire argument fails.

The justification of premises need not be purely external; e.g., P1 is a definition, P2 is an observation. In most cases, the justification of a premise is internal – that is, it follows from other, earlier premises. Consider the following example:

```
P1:     All unmarried men are bachelors.         Definition
P2:     Tom is a man.                            Observation
P3:     Tom is unmarried.                        Observation
P4:     Therefore, Tom is an unmarried man.      From P2 and P3
-----
C:      Tom is a bachelor.                       From P1 – P4
```

P4, here, follows from P2 and P3. In essence, P4 is itself a conclusion (of premises P2 and P3) and also a premise (of the ultimate conclusion of the argument).

These are but a few of the forms of argument we will examine and this is but a brief taste of the smorgasbord that is formal logic. The ability to see the arguments in the works of great thinkers is often a precursor to developing the ability to think critically and develop valid and sound arguments of one's own. It also serves as a guard against being baffled by inelegant, inarticulate, or straightforwardly misleading rhetorical flourishes. The popular media is awash in rhetorical devices that purport to argue some point or other when in fact they exhibit merely specious claims for highly questionable products. Political debate, journalistic license, and advertising/marketing provide innumerable examples of sloppy logic designed to sway the masses with sleight of hand. Informal fallacies such as appeals to emotion, *ad hominem*, appeals to authority, slippery slopes, and others are common and will be examined at various points within the text where appropriate to the larger context of the arguments at hand. By becoming comfortable both with the philosophical conversation with great thinkers and questioners of the past and with the tools of analytical and critical thought, students of philosophy are more capable of discerning where truth lies behind or within the welter of data that is increasingly mountainous and inescapable. In this development of philosophical acuity lies the path to an examined, thoughtful, and worthwhile life.

Before we turn to arguments, though, it would be best if we begin our investigation of formal logic by looking at the foundational concepts and first principles. Some of the first elements of logic may seem quite elementary. Indeed, they are. Yet often the most deceptive practices trade on these most elementary of principles. The very first tool in the logic toolbox is the statement or proposition. Statements may be collected with others as premises for a larger argument (as demonstrated above) or they may stand alone. For example, "Benny has apples and oranges." This, too, is a proposition. This proposition, like those serving as premises in arguments, bears *truth value*. That is, they are either true or false. The statement "Benny has apples and oranges" is true just in that case where Benny actually has apples and oranges. This quite rudimentary and common-sensical approach to a theory of truth is a good example for a start because it allows us to explore two more essential elements of formal logic; the logical operators, "not," "and," and "or."

To begin the discussion of the logical connectors, let us write our first statement more formally.

---

p: Benny has apples and oranges.

The first logical operator we encounter, then, is the conjunction, "and," which we will represent in formal sentences by "&." The "and" operator conjoins two distinct objects, in the exemplified sentence above, apples and oranges.

The next operator that we should examine is the negation or the "not" operator. We commonly use the tilde (~) as the formal symbol for negation or "not." The negation of simple sentences is quite straightforward. A simple sentence is one for which there is only a single predicate. For example, "The book is red." We would negate this simply by writing, "The book is *not* red." However, when we negate a complex proposition by applying the "not" operator, the result is not nearly so straightforward. A complex sentence is one in which there are at least two predicates. The sentence, "Benny has apples and oranges," is an example of a complex sentence. Let us alter the sentence slightly, adding parentheses to clearly group the objects in the predicate. By doing this, we can see the force of the "not" operator, and in the complexity of it, gain some insight into the "or" one. Suppose that the statement, "Benny has apples and oranges" were not true; which is to say, suppose it was a false statement. That would mean that we have negated the sentence. What might it mean for us to know that it is false? We can re-write the statement thus:

> ~p: It is not the case that [Benny has (apples and oranges).]

A common mistake here is to assume that if the statement is false, then Benny must not have apples and oranges. In other words, upon learning that the statement is false, one might conclude that Benny has neither apples nor oranges. This would be the wrong conclusion to draw. The reason is simple. Benny might well have apples, but not oranges; or he might have oranges, but not apples. In both of these cases, the proposition, p, is false because Benny does not have apples **and** oranges, he has one or the other. Now, to be sure, it is true that in the case where the statement, "Benny has apples and oranges," is false, it might be false because he has neither, be we cannot conclude that, nor do we need to. This is because of the relationship between the other two logical operators, "and" and "or." Let us look at this more formally.

Suppose, p = A & B, where A and B are variables and "&" is the logical operator "and." The negation of p, then, would be represented as follows: ~p = ~(A & B). If, however, we take the negation of an "and" relation, we get the following expansion of ~p; ~p = ~A ∨ ~B, where "∨" is the logical operator "or." Thus, it is important to realize that the negation of (A & B) is not actually ~A & ~B. While it is true, in the case of Benny, that he may have neither apples nor oranges (~A & ~B), it is also true that he might have apples and not oranges (A & ~B) or he may have oranges and not apples (~A & B). Thus, we might write ~p in the following way: ~p = (~A & ~B) ∨ (A & ~B) ∨ (~A & B). However, this is bulky, cumbersome, and unnecessary. All that is required for the proposition, p, to be false is if one or the other (A or B) is false. Hence, we can simply write that if p = (A & B), then the negation of p, or ~p = (~A ∨ ~B). In the case of Benny, then, we have the following:

> ~p: Benny either does not have apples or he does not have oranges.

Given that the negation or "not" operator turns an "and" relation into an "or" relation, it might be supposed that it would have a similar effect on an "or." This supposition would be correct. Suppose we have the following proposition:

> p: Wayne has a softball or a baseball.

If we were to negate that proposition, we would have the following:

> $\sim p$: Wayne does not have a softball and he does not have a baseball.

The negation of an "or" statement, p = (A or B), results in the following: $\sim p$ = $\sim A$ & $\sim B$. The reason for this is obvious. If we ask ourselves when the statement, "Wayne has a softball or a baseball," is false, we discover that the only time it is false is when Wayne has neither a softball nor a baseball. If he had a softball, but not a baseball, then the statement, p, would be true because it says that he has one **or** the other. Similarly, if he had a baseball but not a softball, then the statement would still be true. Thus, only in the case when he has neither is the negation of the statement true. Thus, any time we negate an "or" statement, it is transformed into an "and" statement in which both related objects are themselves negated.

While the "and" operator conjoins to statements or objects and the "not" operator negates a proposition, oftentimes in rather complex ways, the "or" relation is a bit more complex yet. There are essentially two different forms of the "or" operator, despite the fact that we have but one word for them in both ordinary, prephilosophical language and more technical, philosophical terms. We will return to this topic and expand it in the next section, *Socrates – Euthyphro*, here we treat it in a very formal method. The two sorts of "or" are the *inclusive or* and the *disjunctive or*. It is perhaps best to discuss these two forms of the "or" operator by use of Venn diagrams. The first diagram, of the *inclusive or*, follows:

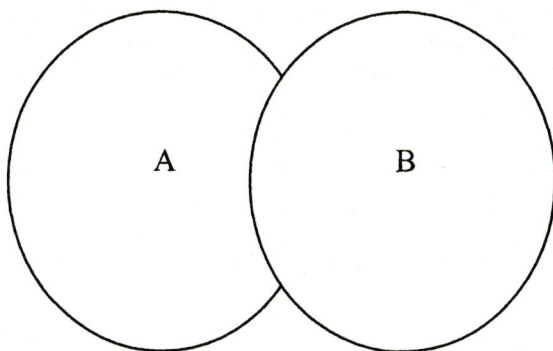

If we use the sentence "*x* is an A or B" here, the statement will be true in the cases where the element, *x*, is an A, is a B, or is both an A and a B. The only time the sentence would be false is when *x* is neither an A nor a B. This is an example of an *inclusive "or"*. The *inclusive "or"* is the broadest of the logical operators because it is the least restrictive. And, often, the *inclusive "or"* reflects the world quite well. One common misuse of the "or" operator in arguments is to use it as a *disjunctive "or"* when, in fact, the inclusive one is required. For example, an angry diplomat, dealing in absolutes, might say to a mediator in a dispute, "You are either with us or you are against us." This would seem very much like an either/or proposition. However, one could easily imagine, in the case, say, of mediation between conflicting parties, that the mediator would respond to the ultimatum by saying, "No, I am with both of you and against neither." Looking at the Venn Diagram of the *inclusive "or,"* we see that the angry diplomat is ignoring the shaded middle region in which the mediator actually resides. The mediator is the bridge between A and B, occupying a position in both; hence, with both and against neither.

We can see this again in another example. Suppose Sharon is looking to buy a new car. Two car dealerships are located side by side. At A Dealership, the salesman says, "You can buy a car from here or you can buy a car from there." Suppose she is told the same thing at B Dealership. And, suppose further that each of the salespeople is framing the statement in the same way; that is, "You can buy a car from us, but not from them." However, this is obviously not strictly the case. Sharon, who is independently wealthy, could well buy a car from both. Hence, she need not fall victim to the pressure of "Buy this *or* buy that" with the understood "but not both" attached to it.

As the *inclusive "or"* is the least restrictive of the logical operators, it is also the least interesting. Generally, we want to be as clear as possible in distinguishing elements and the *inclusive "or"* does not discriminate between A or B. In the logical mistakes discussed immediately above, the *inclusive "or"* was mistaken for a *disjunctive "or."* The nature of that type of "or" is expressed in the diagram below.

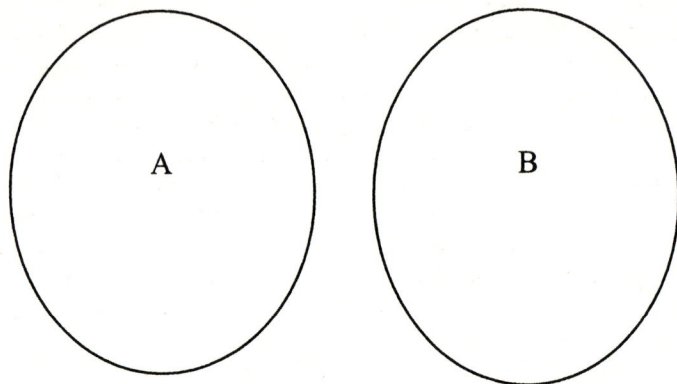

Here, we see that it is impossible for an element, x, to be both an A and a B. Since there is no intersection between the two sets, there are no elements in common between them. The *disjunctive "or"* is particularly helpful in arguments from elimination. Arguments from elimination collect all of the possibilities available to us and then systematically examine each possibility, rejecting all of them until only one remains. If we have truly collected all of the possibilities and rejected each in turn for the proper reasons, then whatever is left, must be the case. As Sherlock Holmes said, "When you have excluded the impossible, whatever remains, however improbable, must be the truth." (Sir Arthur Conan Doyle, *The Adventure of the Beryl Coronet*) Or, more formally, if A and B are the only two possible sets and we know that x must be in one or the other, but not both, then if we assume that x is in A and discover that it is not, then it must be that x is in B, and vice versa. However, there is a pitfall here as well. It is often the case that we will be presented with two options, A and B, for example, with the supposition that A and B exhaust all of the possibilities. For example, someone could say, "You may have either an apple or an orange, but not both; and further, that you may only have fruit if you choose the apple or orange." This would clearly be an example of a *false dichotomy*.

A false dichotomy is a logical fallacy that is quite popular in arguments that depend on rhetorical flourishes of one sort or another. A politician will say, "You must either pass this bill or fail it." Or, a coach might tell a player, "You must either shoot the ball or pass it." While it is true that each of these is an example of a *disjunctive "or"* because one cannot both pass and fail a bill and one cannot both shoot the ball and pass it at the same time, it is also the case that these options do not exhaust all of the possibilities and thus are examples of false dichotomies. In the first case, the bill could be tabled, amended, or sent to committee, among the wide varieties of parliamentary options apart from "pass" and "fail." In the second case, the options are slightly more limited. To be sure, the player could shoot the ball or pass it. She could also dribble it, turn it over, or fumble it out of bounds. In both cases, we have been presented with only two options as if these were the only options. Since there are more than simply these two, it might not be surprising that the proper action is something other than the options offered. The misuse of the *disjunctive "or"* is among the most pervasive logical fallacies committed. It is quite easy to be taken in and to be convinced that the only options are the ones presented. Indeed, this may not be the case and it may require considerable attention on our part to make sure that we have exhausted all of the actual possibilities, not merely those offered.

So, in brief, then, we have statements or propositions, and logical operators that connect or modify those propositions in such ways as to reflect either relationships between the propositions themselves or relationships between the propositions and the world. It is important that we have this relationship between "and" and "or" very clear as we turn to arguments which consist of sets of premises and a conclusion or conclusions. In a sense, every set of premises represents an "and" relationship. Take the following, very simple argument as an example.

P1:	All bachelors are unmarried males.
P2:	Tom is a bachelor.
C:	Tom is unmarried.

What is actually being expressed by this argument is a set of propositions united by an "and." That is, we are given to believe that "All bachelors are unmarried males" **and** "Tom is a bachelor" **and** "Tom is unmarried." Thus, the argument about Tom can be recast in the following formal way:

S: Tom is P1 & P2 & C.

What we have seen in the discussion of formal logic to this point is that this proposition about Tom is only true if each of the three propositions that make it up is true. Since C follows from P1 and P2, then we know that it is true if P1 and P2 are true. However, we also know that if someone told us that the proposition is false, that we would understand how the negation of the proposition would go. If S is false, then ~S must be "Tom is either not a bachelor or all bachelors are not unmarried males or Tom is not unmarried." As it happens, this is easily subject to examination by elimination. Since we know that P1 must be true (as it is a definition), and that C must be true if both P1 and P2 are, then we can focus our attention on P2. If it turns out that Tom is actually a bachelor, then S is, in fact, true. If it turns out that Tom is not a bachelor, then ~S must be the case. Thus, careful attention to the elementary principles of logic, simple though they may be, provides us with a powerful tool for evaluating arguments and for preventing our deception by invalid, if compelling, ones. Throughout the text, we will explore these basic elements further as well as examining more and more sophisticated valid arguments and invalid pretenders.

Chapter 1 – Ancient Philosophy

Section 1: Heraclitus, *Fragments*

Fragment 32
    There is but one cosmic order –
        neither gods nor men have created anything.
    Everything that is,
        always has been, is now, and will forever be.
    It is fire,
        igniting and extinguishing,
        always in like proportion.

Fragment 39
    It is impossible to enter twice
        into the same river.
    Both it and we are changed.

Fragment 54
    When a soul/mind becomes water, it dies.
    When water becomes earth, it dies.
    From earth comes water.
    From water comes soul/mind.

Fragment 56
    The death of earth is fire.
    The death of fire is air.
    In the death of air lives water.
    In the death of water lives earth.

Fragment 72
    Fire is the trade for everything;
        just as merchandise is traded for gold.

~

The 20th century, marked by scientific achievements from harnessing the power of the atom to space flight to cell phones, has also see a curious renaissance of the study of a relatively obscure ancient Greek, Heraclitus. As it happens, it is not nearly as strange as it might first appear. Heraclitus's conceptualization of the universe bears a striking resemblance to the physics of Einstein and his successors. His metaphysical view that the universe is constantly in flux and that change is the principle form reality takes is compatible with certain conceptions of relativity and quantum mechanics. However, scholars should approach these apparent similarities between a philosopher of the fifth century BCE and the height of modern science with a great deal of care and more than a bit of skepticism.

One of the most deceptive intellectual practices is to read back into the work of the ancients a vision of the universe that is thoroughly modern. There are quite often the philosophical and scientific equivalents of false cognates within the ancient world – ideas that seem similar to modern ones but whose advocates had not the first clue about the world that is understood by modern science. Often, it has been an acceptable practice to ignore the radical shifts in the intervening years and to see in the ancients some justification for one's current view. Thus, for example, appeals to Aristotle were made by those arguing against the right of women to vote while appeals to Plato have been made by those arguing for a radical egalitarianism. The blatant appeals to authority commit one of the most widely used informal logical fallacies. An appeal to authority is only as credible as the authority to which one appeals, at best. To appeal to an authority that is literally thousands of years removed from the current debate is to expose oneself to derision and ridicule. At the same time, it is also true that the modern world owes a considerable debt to the philosophers of the ancient period and have inherited a great deal of the conceptual framework for exploring the world around us from them. It is in this way that the work of Heraclitus is important to study – not to justify or to support or to provide authoritative voice to some contemporary view, but rather to provide a different perspective into the philosophical framework that undergirds and supports our view of the universe and, thus, the context into which contemporary investigations fit.

Before turning to a contemporary context for the work of Heraclitus, it is perhaps important to set him into his own historical and philosophical context. Heraclitus is part of the broad category of the history of philosophy known as the PreSocratics. The PreSocratics are so known for the rather obvious reason that they predate Socrates, philosophy's first martyr, but not philosophy's first champion. Grouping all of the PreSocratics into a single category is both artificial and potentially quite distracting. Within this group are represented such a vast variety of philosophical views that only such an arbitrary name like "PreSocratics" could be used to group them all together, a name that has no philosophical import whatever.

Among the PreSocratics are to be found several schools of thought. Perhaps chief among these are the Natural Philosophers; philosophers like Thales and Anaximander who tried to explain the happenings in the world through means of natural causes rather than supernatural ones. These explanations involved metaphysical speculations as well, particularly into the nature of the building blocks of the universe. Thales, for example, argued that the primary substance of the universe, and indeed, the only substance, was water. While this may seem odd at first glance, it should be noted that water is one of the few readily observable features of the world that can fairly easily assume three distinct states – solid, liquid, and gas. One could imagine the view arising from this observation, that water itself is somehow the substance of all things, albeit in differing states and arrangements from one object to the next.

Thales was a precursor, in some ways, to another Greek school of thought, the Atomists. On the metaphysical view of the atomists, there is, at the bottom of the universe, a single kind of thing. These objects are all exactly alike and are completely simple. To say that these building blocks of the universe are completely simple is to say that they are without parts or that they are *atoms*. The word *atom* literally means, "without parts." The most famous of the early atomists was the philosopher, Democritus. Here is a cautionary tale about reading to much modern scientific theory into the work of the ancients. Soon after the first "atoms," like oxygen, hydrogen, helium, et al, were discovered, they were thought to be the fundamental and absolutely simple building blocks of the universe. Although there were clearly different sorts, it seems that each of the different kinds was, in fact, indivisible. Since scientists thought they had finally arrived at the foundational level of physical existence, they gave to these particles the name, "atom." They then argued that it was ultimately impossible to split an atom because if it does not have parts then it is clearly indivisible. Only those things that have parts can be partitioned, on their view. Thus, the modern "atom" was seen to be the smallest and simplest of all physical substances and the arguments of Democritus and the rest of the atomists were used to speculate on the nature of these fundamental particles.

Unfortunately, the modern scientists were more than a bit premature. Within a few years, it was demonstrated that "atoms" are also composite entities, made up of protons, neutrons, electrons, and other sub-atomic particles. Further, within the 20th century, it was demonstrated irrefutably that "atoms" could indeed by split, with devastating effects. So, despite the fact that the word "atom" has entered the vocabulary as a word that refers to entities like oxygen, uranium, and carbon, it is not used in the way that Democritus and the atomist PreSocratics use it. To read into their work the modern conception of an "atom" would be to commit oneself to fundamental errors of interpretation at the very outset.

Other PreSocratics present the contemporary reader with interpretive difficulties as well. One of the most famous is Zeno. Zeno's paradoxes are intriguing to contemplate. Zeno uses the paradoxes to demonstrate what he takes to be a metaphysical truth, similar to Atomism, that is at the foundation of the universe. On Zeno's view, not only are things eternal, but they are also absolutely static. That is, motion is an illusion and the actual world is completely and utterly still – at least those things that are truly real. This claim that the fundamental metaphysical principle of the universe is stillness or stasis is justified, on his view, by appeals to the paradoxes. One of the most famous is the paradox of the archer and his target. For the arrow of the archer to strike the target, it must first traverse half the distance between the two. However, before it can reach that midpoint, it must first reach the midpoint between the archer and the midpoint between the archer and the target. However, before it can reach that midpoint, it must first reach the intermediate midpoint between the archer and this second point, and so on. Since the distance between the midpoint of the distance between the archer and the target is infinitely divisible, the result of our rational ruminations is the conclusion that the arrow never actually moves from the bow. Yet the arrow appears to move from the bow and the target is struck by it. How might we account for this radical difference between our theoretical calculations and our empirical observations? On Zeno's view, the latter is a matter of illusion – the world does not actually move, it only appears to do so. The rational mind is the human faculty that has the best chance of discerning the truth and the conclusion of the rational mind, here, is that the arrow can never move at all.

There have been several attempts to incorporate Zeno's work into other metaphysical schemes. One of the most common is to envision the universe as a series of static images, one immediately after another, such that, just as the pictures in a movie do not actually move but rather form an optical illusion, so too, the universe is static at any given moment and the things that are really real are the ones that are eternal and unchanging. So, underneath the illusion of motion and change there is actually stasis and immutability.

One of the main attractions of this sort of view is that it can account for the pre-philosophical intuition that I am, in some meaningful way, the same person that I was yesterday, last week, and ten years ago. The view is that the truly important part of me, my essence or my being, exists through time as an unchanging feature of the universe. Thus, my *personal identity* is that part of me that does not change over time, whatever other changes seem to occur.

Both Plato and Aristotle adopt something very much like this view. For Plato, the really real objects of the universe are the unchanging and eternal Forms. For Aristotle, that which is really real is Substance and all apparent changes or developments are just the matter of that static thing acquiring different properties at different moments. The essence of the natural object, however, stays exactly the same. Thus, the PreSocratic notion that all of the true reality of the universe is absolutely still becomes, through Plato and Aristotle, the main track of Western Philosophy, particularly with regard to both metaphysics, and later, science.

However, the views of the PreSocratics are not without variation and Heraclitus differs radically from those whose view of the universe is one in which reality is fundamentally static. Approaching Zeno's paradox, for example, Heraclitus might well have said that the truth of the matter is the observable event; namely that the arrow left the bow and traveled the distance from bow to target. The paradox gets its power from a misconception of the experience through artificial rationalistic means. The truly rational person need not agree that the rational mind would hold that the arrow did not move. Rather, one could just as easily say that the arrow was, indeed, in motion and that that motion reflects the true status of the universe at its most basic level. Thus, Heraclitus advances the perspective that the fundamental metaphysical principle of the universe is not stasis, but rather flux, or change.

The image Heraclitus uses most often to discuss this flux principle is fire. Although it is not his most famous example, the image of fire captures best his understanding of the world as continually in motion, continually in a state of becoming, of coming to be and perishing. "Everything that is... is fire, igniting and extinguishing." While the opening of that fragment suggests a similarity to philosophers of stasis like Parmenides, Plato, and Aristotle, with its assertion that "Everything that is always has been, is now, and will forever be," the fact that "everything" is akin to a fire, whose only constancy is the nature of flux that it exhibits, it is clear that Heraclitus envisions the universe quite differently from those in the larger stream of Western philosophy.

Speaking of streams, Heraclitus's most famous example is from Fragment 39 and has primarily to do with personal identity. "It is impossible to enter twice into the same river. Both it and we are changed." One of the most important and complicated philosophical topics is that of personal identity. Suppose Jennifer is showing a new friend pictures of her taken at her third birthday party. She says something like, "That's me." The 21-year old Jennifer is clearly not the same as the girl pictured in the photograph. This intuition is extended to the conclusion that, from instant to instant, she is not the same person. At the very least, the person that she is at time T_0 is different from the person that she is at time T_1 because the latter Jennifer includes the experience of the former Jennifer, but the former does not include the experiences of the latter. This is so even if the time differential between the first and second moment is infinitesimally small. As Heraclitus points out, this is true both of the individual person and of the river into which the person steps. As a conclusion, both the river and the person being different entails that every single instant of every human life (and indeed, of the existence of every entity in the universe) is completely and utterly unique. The entirety of those things that exist exist within this cosmic order and have no control over this fundamental metaphysical feature of the universe.

This notion of metaphysical flux and variable personal identity has some immediate implications for ethical matters. If a person is truly a different person from one instant to the next, then could he not claim, when arrested and put on trial for shoplifting, that he is not the same person that committed that act and therefore should be treated as an entirely unique person? After all, it is true that he is a different person. Heraclitus might respond to this implication of his metaphysical view in something like the following way. The John who is on trial for shoplifting is the only individual in the world who has as part of his past the stepping into that particular store at that particular instant and stealing that particular item. Indeed, all of these have changed in the flux of the progression of the cosmic order, but that progression does not eliminate from John's actual experiences the experience of having taken the item. Only he has that experience as part of his past. Thus, although he has clearly changed, part of the composition of his *self* is the earlier counterpart of his current *self* having shoplifted. This compositional and fluid notion of the self has increasingly become a central feature of the debate over personal identity and responsibility.

To be sure, Heraclitus's work does not answer all of the difficult questions that plague Western Philosophy. The question of how things change is a question upon which much of Western Philosophy founders given that its fundamental metaphysical principle is stasis. If the fundamental order of the cosmos is stasis, how does one account for the appearance of change? From a Heraclitean point of view, that question is easily eliminated. The fundamental feature of the cosmos is flux, thus explaining change is quite simple. However, addressing that question raises a different one – if the fundamental feature of the universe is flux and change, then how does one account for identity (personal or otherwise) over time? Does one not have to reject the notion of *identity* altogether, and if so, can one do without a notion of *identity*? The Heraclitean scholar would respond that, indeed, the notion must be surrendered, but this surrender opens up many potentially fruitful avenues for addressing problems that have so far proven to be insoluble to those philosophical approaches who take the opposite metaphysical view.

The work of Heraclitus, though it was not to form the primary track of Western Philosophy, is nevertheless a helpful counterpoint to that track. As more and more has come to be known about the workings of the universe, it has seemed more profitable to return to the work of Heraclitus as a way of understanding a world that seems radically mutable and in flux rather than static and still. Such a shift in metaphysical, epistemological, and ethical speculations is evident in the late 19th and early 20th century philosopher, Alfred North Whitehead, among others. While this metaphysical turn presents the philosopher and the seeker after truth with an entirely different set of problems and puzzles, it also provides him with a fresh, and yet ancient, model for conceptualizing the cosmos.

Guided Reading Questions
1. For Heraclitus, what is the fundamental metaphysical principle? How does the assumption of this principle cause Heraclitus's work to differ from that of later philosophers like Plato and Aristotle.
2. What problems does the basic notion that all things are in flux cause for views of personal identity? What problems does it solve?
3. How does Heraclitus differ from other PreSocratic philosophers?

Logic Blurb
Basic Valid Logical Forms – Modus Ponens and Modus Tollens

Among the earliest discussions of logic are descriptions of the forms of argument that are always valid. These related forms are still recognized by their Latin names – *modus ponens* and *modus tollens*.

Modus ponens is a form of direct argument. It begins with a statement of implication: If *p*, then *q*. This is written as "p → q". This formal implication is known as the major premise. The second premise of this direct argument is "p". The conclusion is "q". Thus, formally, this argument is written as

$$p \to q \quad \text{(major premise)}$$
$$p \quad \text{(minor premise)}$$
$$\overline{}$$
$$q \quad \text{(conclusion)}$$

An example of an argument that fits the *modus ponens* form is:

If I drop the ball, it will fall.   (p → q)
I dropped the ball.   (p)

The ball fell.   (q)

The other form, *modus tollens*, is similar. It is formally represented as follows:

$$p \to q \quad \text{(major premise)}$$
$$\sim q \quad \text{(minor premise)}$$
$$\overline{}$$
$$\sim p \quad \text{(conclusion)}$$

The major premise of both *modus ponens* and *modus tollens* can be read in several ways. It can be read "If *p*, then *q*" or "*p* implies *q*" or "*p* is necessary for *q*." The formalized "p → q" reflects each of these. The minor premise of *modus tollens*, ~*q*, is read "not *q*"; that is, ~*q* reflects the negation of *q*. We can revisit the earlier example to see how *modus tollens* would work.

If I drop the ball, it will fall.	(p → q)
The ball did not fall.	(~q)

I did not drop the ball.	(~p)

Modus ponens and *modus tollens* are examples of valid arguments. Any argument that can be framed in one or the other form will be a valid argument. This is not to suppose that the argument will necessarily be true (one of the premises could be false or meaningless or completely irrelevant). For example, if we supposed that the major premise was something like this, "If I drop the ball, the dog will roof his house with pancakes," then we have a premise that makes the minor premise of the *modus tollens* example irrelevant and the conclusion of the *modus ponens* argument meaningless. Thus, while the argument forms are valid, the soundness of the argument depends on the content of the premises. It is a sound argument if the premises actually entail the conclusion, or alternatively, if the conclusion is relevant and meaningful given the statement of the premises.

While it is true that the content of the premises is exceptionally important for assessing the truth of an argument, it is also important to note that the argument form itself is crucial to that assessment as well. In the midst of an argument, should one interlocutor (Sadie) grant the other (Kat) all of the premises, then she is incapable of arguing against any logically valid conclusion that those premises entail. It is here that many novices to the practice of critical thinking go astray. Finding a conclusion with which he disagrees, the novice will rail against the conclusion, ignoring both the premises and the fact that his rejection of the conclusion is meaningless insofar as he grants the premises. There are really only two ways of engaging in a true dispute over an argument. The first of these is to reject at least one of the premises, or to say that it is not a sound argument; the other is to demonstrate that the argument is logically flawed. If it is the case that the argument fails to violate any of the rules of logic, then the novice is left to either argue against a particular premise or to concede defeat.

Not all arguments are logically valid, of course. Indeed, one of the most deceptively tricky invalid argument forms resembles *modus ponens and modus tollens*. This argument is known by several names, but here we will call it the Denial of the Antecedent. The *antecedent* of an argument is the first half of the major premise. Thus, the antecedent in the formal major premise "p → q" is "p". The structure of this invalid logical form is as follows:

$p \rightarrow q$ (major premise)
$\sim p$ (minor premise)

The untrained logician might well conclude that there is a conclusion for this argument and that that conclusion is $\sim q$. However, let us examine this argument form with the example used already.

If I drop the ball, it will fall. $(p \rightarrow q)$
I did not drop the ball. $(\sim p)$

If we conclude that, in virtue of me not dropping the ball that ($\sim q$) "the ball did not fall" we have fallen into a logical trap. Suppose that I fell. I have not dropped the ball, but the ball has, indeed, fallen. Thus, in any argument of this form in which the antecedent is rejected, there is no deductively valid conclusion that can be said to follow. Because this argument form is so very close to both *modus ponens* and *modus tollens*, it is a simple mistake to make and one against which philosophers learn to guard.

Modus ponens and *modus tollens* are called *syllogisms* after the name given to the valid argument forms that Aristotle develops in the *Organon* (Aristotle's philosophical toolbox of works, the first of which, *Categories*, is included in this volume). There are several other logical argument forms (and both formal and informal fallacies) that will be investigated through the course of the text. Mastery of these first two will suffice to be going on with.

Section 2.1: The Search for the Historical Socrates

Socrates never wrote anything down. This, of course, makes the job of figuring out who Socrates was a particularly difficult task. At the same time, there are few philosophers in history who have had more written about them. Rather than make our task easier, this increases the difficulty. Even if we limit the scope of the investigation to those things written about Socrates in antiquity, by contemporaries, followers, and historians, the task of finding the historical Socrates remains problematic. However, given the profound influence Socrates has had on the history and development of Western thought, the task is an important one. So, like good detectives, we sift through the evidence in hopes that a coherent picture of the philosopher appears.

Our first job will be to collect the resources – those pieces of information that have survived the nearly two and a half millennia since his execution in 399 BCE. Fortunately, there is quite a lot. We will examine the three most important of those collections. In each case, the writer is a contemporary of Socrates. Aristophanes, the great playwright, wrote a comedy in which Socrates is the primary character. It has been suggested that perhaps Aristophanes and Socrates were friends and Aristophanes was using his run of the stage to poke fun at Socrates. The "Socrates" of *The Clouds* is quite an interesting character, bawdy and ribald, clumsy and distracted. Inquiring into the things of the heavens and the earth, "Socrates" goes about making a great nuisance of himself as the youth flock to him to the shock and dismay of their elders.

Aside from Thucydides (author of *The Peloponnesian War*), there is probably not a more significant historian of ancient Greece than Xenophon. Xenophon was an early student of Socrates and the teacher apparently made a significant impression on him. From Xenophon we have a somewhat little explored perspective of the Peloponnesian War. Although he was an Athenian, he fought alongside the Spartans. Xenophon's *Apology*, not to be confused with Plato's *Apology*, is a scathing indictment of the Athenian court that convicted and executed Socrates. The "Socrates" of Xenophon is a very likeable, if somewhat distracted and at times boring chap. He is definitely not portrayed as a menace or threat, but a rather harmless thinker.

Our last contemporary of Socrates is like Xenophon in that he, too, was a student of Socrates. Unlike Xenophon, however, Plato was much younger than

Socrates, not quite thirty years old when Socrates died. A discussion of Plato and his mentor, Socrates, would be incomplete without a brief examination of the world of ancient Athens and their places in it. Plato (428 – 348 BCE) was born into an aristocratic family that had connections to the greatest events in Athenian history. Plato's mother, Perictione, was a direct descendent of Solon, "the Law-Giver," founder of Athens. His father, Ariston, or "the Best," was a well-known aristocrat during the Golden Age of Athens. After his father's death, his mother remarried another noble, Pyrilampes. Pyrilampes was best known as one of the closest advisors to Pericles. Pericles, of course, was the great general and statesman who ushered in the Golden Age of Athens with his military exploits, governance of the city, and extensive building campaigns (including the Parthenon). Thus, Plato was of noble birth; an aristocrat closely tied to the best and most favored of Athens and Athenian history.

In the Platonic dialogues, often thought to be the best picture available of the historical Socrates, we come across some potential difficulties. First of all, given that Plato was a student of Socrates and clearly in disagreement with the findings of the Athenian court, there is the very real potential for bias in his rendering of his mentor. Second, since Socrates is the primary character in nearly all of Plato's dialogues, it is difficult at times to distinguish when Plato is writing for Socrates and when he is putting his own words in the mouth of the character, "Socrates." There is the further difficulty that in some dialogues, in which "Socrates" appears, he does not say anything (or at least very little); the *Sophist*, for example. And finally, there are some dialogues in which it is not clear whether "Socrates" speaks for Plato or some other character does. In the next chapter, we will discuss these later difficulties in some length, as we explore the development of Plato's thought from the Early through the Middle to the Late dialogues. Here, suffice it to say, if we are to find the historical Socrates in the writings of Plato, and I think we are, then it will be in the Early dialogues (also called the "Socratic dialogues"). Therefore, we will pay particular attention to three of them – *Euthyphro*, *Apology*, and *Crito*.

Before examining the textual sources in depth, we should collect first the pieces of evidence that are not in dispute. First, Socrates was executed in 399 BCE following a trial by the citizens of Athens in which he was convicted of impiety and corrupting the youth. Second, we know that the conviction has been roundly criticized as unjust from nearly all quarters. Aristotle, student of Plato, when faced with a similar prospect, fled the city, "lest Athens sin twice against philosophy." Xenophon inveighed against the decision. So, too, did Plato. So, whatever interpretation of Socrates is developed, it must be consistent with the fact of Socrates's conviction and with the view that the conviction was unjust.

To understand the trial, the conviction, and the various commentaries on Socrates and his fate, we need also to understand the context in which all these are situated. The dominant feature of the 5th century BCE in Athens was the conflict known as the Peloponnesian War. The great historian, Thucydides, in *The Peloponnesian War*, describes the time leading up to the great war between Sparta and Athens. Athens, under Pericles, provoked the conflict that lasted nearly thirty years. Pericles died during one of the plagues that swept through Athens and ultimately crippled the city. Of his replacements, two were considered the most apt – Nicias and Alcibiades. Alcibiades was strongly in favor of continuing the campaign, confident that the great naval might of Athens would prevail. This confident stance was in line with that of the democrats of Athens. Nicias, on the other hand, advanced a different view. He was unsure of victory and thought the better course of action was to sue for peace and come to terms with the Spartans and their allies. Alcibiades's view, not surprisingly, won the day as the democrats in the Assembly voted to put the confident general in charge. Unfortunately for Athens, charges were soon brought to the Assembly against Alcibiades. Because the Athenian court system required the plaintiff and the defendant to personally present arguments, Alcibiades could not both defend himself in court and lead the troops in battle. This system was rife with the possibility of corruption. The only thing it took to be able to win a case before the Assembly was great oratorical skill. Suppose one person, whose case was unjust, had the ability to weave wonderful, spellbinding tales and play upon the emotions of the jury, while his opponent, though his case was just, was unable to speak eloquently. Further, one could imagine, since the people of the jury were citizens and those charged and bringing charges were citizens and there were no rules about contact outside the hearing, the possibility for a contaminated jury was considerable. Into this court, Alcibiades was recalled and Nicias sent to the front. Eventually, after great hardship, sickness, and destruction, the Athenian forces were defeated and the city fell to the Spartans. While this may not immediately seem like a problem for Socrates, personally, it was. Alcibiades and Nicias had both been students of Socrates's. And while neither survived the war, Socrates did. Thus, the anger of the defeated citizens of the city found no refuge in those actually blamed for the ignominious defeat. Instead, much of the anger was directed at Socrates.

If defeat at the hands of the hated Spartans was not enough, there were more setbacks to follow. To prevent the city of Athens from regrouping, gathering its strength again from its considerable economic advantages, the Spartans installed a group of Athenian nobles who had collaborated with the Spartans to rule the city for them. A group of thirty was chosen to serve as the masters of Athens, ruling as the law, judge, and jury over the city. A city that had taken great pride in citizen self-determination found itself at the whim of thirty of their own brothers who seemed to like power quite a bit. Indeed, the reign of the Thirty Tyrants turned out to be more trouble for the Spartans than it was worth. Eventually, after only a couple of years of the experiment, the Tyrants were overthrown and a sort of armistice fell between the two cities.

Within the city of Athens, however, something had to be done with the Thirty and their supporters; all considered traitors of the worst sort. It was decided that for the sake of peace in the city that an amnesty should be given; that none of the Thirty should be tried for any crimes they may have committed and that none of those associated with the defeat in the Peloponnesian War should be tried either. This had two direct effects on Socrates. First of all, among the Thirty Tyrants were two of Socrates's students – Critias and Charmides. As it happens, Critias and Charmides were renowned even among the Thirty for their ruthlessness and bloodthirstiness. If the Tyrants were the worst Athens had to offer, Critias and Charmides were the worst of the worst. As Socrates had been their teacher as well (although apparently for a very short time), and since Critias and Charmides did not survive the overthrow of the Thirty, again the true target for the anger of the Athenians was removed. Again, their gaze fell on Socrates. The second effect of the overthrow and amnesty was that Socrates could not be prosecuted for any crimes, real or imagined, because of his association with Nicias, Alcibiades, Critias, or Charmides. Any charges brought against him would have to be independent of the War, the reign of the Thirty, and the overthrow.

So, these are the pieces of evidence that we have as we approach the question of the historical Socrates. We have a fairly good grasp of the background, the political intrigue and structure of the system of justice in Athens; we know that Socrates was convicted of impiety and corrupting the youth by the Athenian court and ultimately executed; we know that this conviction was widely decried at the time, in the immediate aftermath, and for many years following; and we have at least three disparate pictures of the man from contemporaries – Aristophanes, Xenophon, and Plato. So, which is the nearest picture to the man called Philosophy's Martyr?

It seems that the easiest and perhaps most productive way of addressing this question is to pose another. Of the characters presented by Aristophanes, Xenophon, and Plato, which is the one most likely to be sentenced to death by a court of his peers? Simply put, it seems unlikely that the buffoon of Aristophanes is worthy of execution. Even Athens did not make it a habit to kill the mentally unstable; banishment or confinement were the generally accepted practices. An "enlightened" society does not execute the crackpots. Similarly, the boring and harmless "Socrates" of Xenophon is not one likely to find himself subject to execution. Those who do not raise the ardor of their opponents rarely find themselves with opponents at all, much less with opponents who want them dead.

Having said this, however, one need only read a bit of one of the early dialogues of Plato to encounter a thoroughly frustrating individual. If one can imagine being subject to the sort of inquiry to which Socrates subjects Euthyphro, for example, one can quickly begin to understand the tenor of the jury as they listened to Socrates's arguments. One can easily imagine how being made to feel foolish, being shown to be less wise than one's reputation "warranted" would quickly make one very unwilling to suppose that Socrates was innocent of the charges. Having been subjected to the examination and cross-examination (the elenchus) that exposed one's false beliefs and showed that one did not have nearly the knowledge one thought would be a thoroughgoing annoyance. Now, suppose that this examination had not been private, but quite public; word of it traveling quickly to all one's friends, acquaintances, business partners, etc. The embarrassment would be enough to want to rid oneself forever of this gadfly. Further, imagine now that it was not just one or two people who had been on the receiving end of this questioning, but each and every person with a reputation for wisdom and for knowledge. Many of those in the jury had been such people, examined publicly by Socrates and found to be wanting. It was a hostile jury that Socrates faced; a hostile jury quite ready to convict him of anything simply to rid themselves of the annoyance. It is fairly easy to see how this Socrates might find himself convicted and awaiting execution. This is a picture of a man consistent with the evidence we have already established. Given this, it seems reasonable to conclude that the Socrates found in the early dialogues (the Socratic dialogues) of Plato is indeed the historical Socrates (or at the very least, the closest it is possible to get to him).

Section 2.2: Trial Trilogy, Part 1 – *Euthyphro*

Euthyphro

Setting: The porch of the king-archon's court.

Euthyphro: Socrates, what brings you here? Why are you here and not at the Lyceum like normal? Are you prosecuting someone here? Surely not.

Socrates: It's not a prosecution. I believe it's called an indictment.

Euthyphro: What?!? Since you could not possibly have brought an indictment against another, then you must be the one indicted.

Socrates: Yes, indeed.

Euthyphro: Who?

Socrates: A young man, not well-known. In fact, I hardly know him. He is called Meletus.

Euthyphro: I don't know him. So, what's the charge?

Socrates: A most shameful one. Apparently he has discerned how the young men of Athens are corrupted, and further, who it is that is corrupting them. I'm sure he is a wise young man and is offended that my ignorance corrupts his fellow citizens.

Euthyphro: How does he allege that you corrupt the youth?

Socrates: Apparently I create new gods and do not believe in our old gods.

Euthyphro: Ah, I see, Socrates. That's because you are always talking about that sign from god. ... Maybe it won't amount to anything.

Socrates: What brings you here, Euthyphro? Defending or prosecuting?

Euthyphro: I am prosecuting.

Socrates: Whom?

Euthyphro: My father.

Socrates: Oh my! Your father?!?

Euthyphro: Indeed.

Socrates: On what charge?

Euthyphro: Murder.

Socrates: Heavens! Not many people would know how to do this and be sure that they did it right. Truly, this is a job for one who has become quite wise, not just for anyone.

Euthyphro: By Zeus, yes.

Socrates: Whom did he kill? One of your kin? Surely you would not prosecute your father for killing a stranger.

Euthyphro: That makes no difference. The only thing that matters is whether the killer acted rightly or wrongly. If he acted rightly, or justly, then he should not be prosecuted; but if he killed unjustly, then he must be prosecuted. As it happens, the victim was a servant; mine, in fact. He got drunk and in a rage, he killed one of the house servants. My father caught him, tied him up – hand and foot, and left him in a ditch. My father dispatched a messenger to the priest for guidance in what to do and in the interim, he neglected the servant in the ditch. Before the messenger came back, the servant in the ditch had died from hunger and exposure – it was quite cold. Actually, my kin are quite angry with me for prosecuting my father, since the servant had killed a man and they say that my father did not even kill the servant, but merely neglected him as he was himself a killer and deserved no regard. They say I am not behaving piously because I prosecute my father. Unfortunately for them, they are wrong on the matter of piety and impiety; they don't know what piety is Socrates.

Socrates: My, my. You are confident enough in that assessment and in your own grasp of piety that you are not afraid of acting impiously by prosecuting your father? I must become your student, Euthyphro, for I have been charged with being impious myself. If I were your student, then Meletus would either have to charge you as well, as my teacher, or would have to accede that his indictment is flawed because if you know the pious and teach it to me then I shall not be impious, but pious, and Meletus will have been proven wrong.

So, tell me now Euthyphro, what sort of thing is piety; not just about murder, but about all things – what are the pious and the impious? Is not piety the same everywhere, regardless of the particular action? And isn't impiety just the opposite? Does not everything that is pious present one form (ειδος) and the same for impiety?

Euthyphro: Definitely.

Socrates: So, then, what is piety, or the pious? I did not ask you to tell me some one thing that is pious. There are presumably many pious actions. Listing some does not tell me what *piety* is. What is the form (*eidos*) that makes all pious things pious. You said that all impious things are impious because of one form (*eidos*) right? So what is the form (*eidos*) that makes all pious things pious? If I know that, then I can test any action by comparing it to that form and determine if the action is pious.

Euthyphro: Okay, Socrates. The pious is whatever is loved by the gods. What is not loved by the gods is impious.

Socrates: Very good! Now that's what I was looking for. I do not know if this is the right answer or not, but it is the right kind of answer. I'm sure you will be able to show me whether it is the right answer or not. Let us figure this out. Something or someone loved by the gods is pious; something or someone not loved by the gods is not pious? Right? The pious and the impious are opposites, right?

Euthyphro: Of course.

Socrates: But is it not true that the gods are in disagreement with one another. And about what? It must be something important to cause hatred among them. For example, if it were numbers about which we were in disagreement. Could we not count and thereby remove the difference? And the larger and the smaller are resolved by measuring. The heavier and the lighter also, right? So, what would cause us to war with one another? Is it not those subjects that deal with the good and the bad, the just and the unjust, the beautiful and the ugly? Are these not the subjects that, failing to come to agreement, cause people to become angry with one another?

Euthyphro: Certainly.

Socrates: So, different gods think different things to be just and they would not be at war with themselves if they didn't differ about these topics?

Euthyphro: Right.

Socrates: So, each likes what each likes (and these are different things) and despises what each does not like.

Euthyphro: Certainly.

Socrates: So, since they like different things and hate different things, then the same things are both loved and hated by the gods — what one loves, another hates, and so forth. Some something could be both loved by the gods and hated by the gods.

Euthyphro: It would seem so.

Socrates: So these would be both pious and impious. They would be the opposite of each other.

Euthypho: I fear so.

Socrates: So, it seems as if you have not answered my question after all. You surprising young man, I did not ask you for the things that are both pious and impious; but only the thing that makes all pious things pious.

Euthyphro: Well, let us refine the answer a bit. What all the gods love is pious and what all the gods despise is impious. Those things where there is no disagreement; where all the gods love something, that is pious and where all the gods despise something, that is impious.

Socrates: Good, Euthyphro. Let us examine (*elenchein*) this answer as well. Consider this question. Is something loved by the gods because it is pious or is it pious because it is loved by the gods? (*Stephanus page 10a*)

Euthyphro: What do you mean, Socrates?

Socrates: Consider. Isn't it true that we sometimes talk of being carried and at other times talk of carrying and we mean something different in each case? Or, leading and being led; seeing and being seen? These are all different, right?

Euthyphro: Of course.

Socrates: So, something is not being seen because it is a thing seen. Rather, it is a thing seen because it is being seen, right? And if something is changed; it is changed because it is a thing undergoing change, it is not a thing undergoing change because it is a thing changed, right? So, the same applies to piety and the pious. It is not loved by its lovers because it is something loved; but instead is something loved because it is being loved by its lovers. So, is the pious loved because it is pious?

Euthyphro: Yes, that's the reason.

Socrates: It is loved because it is pious, not pious because it is loved?

Euthyphro: Yes.

Socrates: So, it is both loved and loved by the gods because it is loved by the gods?

Euthyphro: Of course.

Socrates: Then the pious and that loved by the gods cannot be the same thing – they must be different from each other.

Euthyphro: Why?

Socrates: We agreed that the pious was loved because it is pious, but not pious because it was loved. Right?

Euthyphro: Yes.

Socrates: And that which is loved by the gods is loved by the gods because it is being loved. It is not being loved because it is loved by the gods.

Euthyphro: Okay.

Socrates: If that which is loved by the gods and the pious are the same, then the pious is being loved because it is pious; that which is loved by the gods is loved because it is that which is loved by the gods. Further, that which is loved by the gods was so because it was being loved by the gods. If that were so, then the pious would be pious because it was loved by the gods. But these are opposites. One is that which is loved because it is being loved and the other is being loved because it is that which is loved. So, that which the gods love cannot be the pious. Perhaps the pious has as one of its qualities "that which is loved by the gods" but that cannot be what makes it pious. It is clear to me now, Euthyphro, that you are not trying to make the nature of the pious known to me.

Euthyphro: Socrates, I'm confused. Every statement we make seems to go round and round in circles and never comes to rest anywhere. It's not my fault, because I want them to stay put.

Socrates: That's my wish as well. I am quite hopeful that you can teach me about piety, as I said at the outset. Let us not give up now. How about this: is the pious also just?

Euthyphro: I suppose.

Socrates: If the pious is also the just, is the opposite also true? Is the just also pious? Or are only some just things also pious and some are not while all pious things are just?

Euthyphro: I don't understand, Socrates.

Socrates: This is what I'm asking: in those cases where there is piety, is there justice as well. But, perhaps where there is justice there is only sometimes piety – that is, piety is a part of justice, but not all.

Euthyphro: That seems so. That's it, Socrates. Piety is part of justice – the part concerned that has to do with taking care of the gods.

Socrates: Do you meant that taking care of the gods is similar to taking care of other things. For instance, don't we say that only the trainer of horses "takes care" of horses and most people don't know how to do so?

Euthyphro: Yes.

Socrates: So the horse trainer is "taking care" of horses. In the same way, most people do not know how to take care of dogs, but the hunter does. That would mean that hunting is the science that takes care of dogs. Ranching or raising cattle is the science that takes care of cattle. And, by extension, piety is the science of taking care of the gods. Do you mean this, Euthyphro.

Euthyphro: That is what I mean, Socrates.

Socrates: In each of these cases, "taking care" has the same result – each aims at the benefit of the thing taken care of? Horses are benefited by training; dogs by hunting; cattle by ranching; and so on. So, piety, if it is "taking care" of the gods would also benefit the gods and make them better?

Euthyphro: No, not that. That's not the kind of care I mean.

Euthyphro: Let me put it simply. Piety is knowing what to say and do in such a way that it is pleasing to the gods – like sacrifice and prayer – those are pious things. The opposite of these is then impious.

Socrates: So, piety is knowing how to sacrifice and pray?

Euthyphro: Most definitely, Socrates.

Socrates: So, to begin the right way (to pray) is to ask the gods for the things we need and to give to the gods in the right way (to sacrifice) is to give the gods the things they need from us.

Euthyphro: Yes, Socrates.

Socrates: So, piety is a kind of commerce between humans and the gods. Like trading.

Euthyphro: If that's what you want to call it.

Socrates: What I want is of little concern. I am most concerned with what is actually the truth. So, tell me, what is it that the gods receive from us; what benefit do we give them?

Euthyphro: Honor, reverence, gratitude. Things that are pleasing to them.

Socrates: So, the pious is what is pleasing to the gods, but not what is beneficial to them or loved by them, then?

Euthyphro: I think these are loved most by them.

Socrates: Are we back to piety is what is loved by the gods?
Euthyphro: Yes.
Socrates: So, it seems that it is your arguments that go round and round in circles and do not stay put. Surely you remember that we ruled this possibility out earlier in our investigation. Don't you remember?
Euthyphro: Yes, Socrates.
Socrates: So, either we were wrong before when we were in agreement, or we are wrong now. So, we must begin again.

Euthyphro: Socrates, I am in quite a hurry to be somewhere else. It is time for me to go. Maybe some other time, Socrates.

~

Poor Euthyphro. He is convinced that he knows what Piety is. He is so convinced, in fact, that he is willing to charge his own father with impiety. When he encounters Socrates on the steps of the porch of the court, he is surprised to discover that Socrates has been charged with precisely the indictment that he brings against his father. Socrates, struck by his good fortune to encounter someone who knows enough about piety to charge his own father with violating its dictates, strikes up a conversation with Euthyphro to determine the meaning of "piety".

A brief aside here may serve our purposes well. Nearly all of the Socratic dialogues begin in much the same way. Socrates encounters someone who claims to know something. Socrates shortly poses a question of the form, "What is F?" where "F" is the thing that Socrates's interlocutor claims to know. So, for example, in the *Euthyphro*, Euthyphro claims to know what piety is and so Socrates asks "What is piety?" The *Laches*, for another example, addresses the question, "What is courage?" The first book of the *Republic* concerns the question "What is justice?" In each case, the "What is F?" question launches the discussion. Euthyphro makes at least five attempts to answer Socrates's question; we will walk through each in turn. One question to keep in mind during the investigation of Euthyphro's responses is whether or not there are actually five distinct answers or merely four.

Euthyphro first responds to the "What is piety?" question by saying that what he is currently doing is pious; that is, prosecuting wrongdoers is a pious action. Socrates responds that this is not what he had asked. Here we hit upon a principle that is of considerable importance in Platonic epistemology – the Priority of Definition principle. Simply put, to know something is to be able to define it or to spell out what the essence of a thing is. Given this, it is clear that Euthyphro's first attempt is insufficient. Suppose for the moment that prosecuting wrongdoers was pious. Is it the only thing that is pious? Might there not be other pious actions? By pointing out a particular case and saying that it is an example of a pious action, Euthyphro has not answered the question. He has not said what *piety* is; he has given an example.

Recognizing the error of his ways, Euthyphro tries again. His second attempt satisfies the requirement that the answer actually be something like a definition, rather than an example, but it too falls short. Euthyphro says that piety is whatever is loved by the gods. This is indeed something that can be applied to any number of actions to determine whether or not those actions satisfy the condition it spells out. However, Socrates points out that the gods are not actually in agreement about very many things. Perhaps Apollo loves one thing while Aphrodite despises it. This would mean that something was both loved and not loved and thus, that it was both pious and impious. Such a position is untenable.

Euthyphro then refines the answer. Piety is not simply what some gods love, piety is what is loved by *all* the gods. This very subtle distinction – between being loved by the gods and being loved by *all* the gods – is extremely important. No longer can Socrates point out that the gods disagree, since by hypothesis, they do not. Indeed, they are all in agreement. This response deserves longer and more in depth treatment. Rather than address it in depth here, we will return to this response a bit later.

Having thus far failed to satisfy Socrates's question, Euthyphro tries again. Piety is a part of justice that it has to do with looking after the gods. The Greek word, *therapeia*, that is translated "looking after" is the same word that would be used if one was asking a neighbor to "look after" one's pet while away on a trip. This suggests a need for "looking after" on the part of the gods, as Socrates points out. This strikes Euthyphro as strange since if the gods needed looking after, then they are probably not gods after all. He then abandons this approach.

With four responses tried, Euthyphro offers a final response to the question. Piety is knowledge of sacrifice and prayer. Sacrifice, he agrees, has to do with giving things to the gods and prayer has to do with asking for things from the gods. Thus, sacrifice and prayer are a kind of transactional relationship wherein people receive things they need and the gods receive that which they need. However, similar to the fourth attempt, this would suggest that the gods need something from their human worshippers. This, too, is rejected. Rather than remain to pursue the inquiry further, Euthyphro begs off with claims of pressing engagements elsewhere.

With the exposition of the elenchus before us, it is now possible to discuss whether or not there are five distinct attempts or only four. It would be easy to suppose that attempt three and four (what the gods love, what *all* the gods love) are indeed the same definition (or at least sufficiently close together to group). However, this would be a significant misstep. Although there is but a three-letter difference between the two, it is quite a distinction. The former is dismissed with the recognition that the gods disagree. Socrates does not have that avenue open to respond to the latter because Euthyphro has eliminated the possibility of the disagreement. If the gods all agree, then it is not possible that they disagree. Thus, if the "what all the gods love" definition is to fail, it will fail for some reason other than the now impossible disagreement of the gods. As a result, it becomes clear that these two definitions, although quite similar in form, are quite different.

We should not conclude, however, that simply because the two attempts closest in form fail to be extensionally equivalent that there are five attempts rather than four. If we look carefully at the Socratic responses to the last two attempts, we will notice some striking similarities. In the case of the "part of justice that has to do with looking after the gods" offering, the conclusion is that the gods do not need "looking after". In the "sacrifice and prayer" attempt, the same conclusion is reached. The gods do not need anything from their human followers, whether that be "looking after" or trinkets of one sort or another. Thus, the same response defeats both of these potential definitions for piety. Given this, it is relatively safe to assume that there are four potential definitions among Euthyphro's five responses. This brings the discussion to the Socratic response to the third response – piety is what *all* the gods love. The response Socrates makes here has come to be known as the Euthyphro Problem.

The Euthyphro Problem

The Euthyphro Problem is not merely a problem because of the polytheistic nature of the Athenian religion. In fact, it is not clear whether Socrates thought there were many gods or just one. It is fairly clear that he at least thought that one god existed, Apollo. However, the Euthyphro Problem is a problem whether there is an infinitely large pantheon or merely a single deity. This is because of the shift in the question at 12a. Instead of saying that piety is what is pleasing to the gods, Euthyphro amends this answer by saying that piety is what is pleasing to *all* the gods. Now, if all the gods agree, then that means they are of *one mind*. If they are of one mind, then it does not matter if there are fifty gods or just one – there is only the one opinion. Hence, if the Euthyphro Problem is a problem for a religion with many gods, it is equally a problem for a religion with but one. Indeed, it is one of the more pernicious problems in all of the philosophy of religion.

Let's look at the question that gives rise to the problem. "Is something loved by the gods because it is pious or is it pious because it is loved by the gods?" Since we have established that it is the same problem whether one is thinking of a pantheon of many gods or a single one, we can restate the question to make it easier to address. "Is something loved by god because it is pious or is it pious because it is loved by god?" Also, this problem is most often rendered as a problem of holiness because the word translated I have translated as piety is often translated as holiness. For the sake of clarity, let us make a substitution – "holy" for "piety".

At first glance, these two options do not seem to be direct contradictions, perhaps contraries. That is, perhaps it is the case that only one of the options could be true, but both could be false. Instead, if the two options define contradictory propositions, then we are left with the result that one of them must be true and one must be false. To see how this might work, it is best if we restate the question as the two propositions that underlie it. They are as follows:

> Proposition 1: God loves x because x is holy.
> or
> Proposition 2: x is holy because God loves x.

If we suppose that the first proposition is true, that God loves something because it is holy, we are left with the question, "What is it that makes x holy?" There are two possible responses to that question – God and Something other than God (or ~God). If the response we want is "God," then we have not actually affirmed Proposition 1, but rather Proposition 2. We will come to that option presently. If the response is "~God," then we are left with the conclusion that there is something independent of God that has a considerable power – namely, the power to make things holy. If this is so, then we are left with the conclusion that God is not omnipotent (or all-powerful). This is a result that is often rejected by orthodox believers of every major monotheistic religion. Since this is the case, we will turn to Proposition 2.

Suppose Proposition 2 is true. If something is holy because God loves it, we are left with the question, "Why does God love it?" Again there are two possible responses – there is some reason or there is no reason. If we select the first of these responses, there is some reason for God to love x, then we have not actually affirmed Proposition 2, but rather Proposition 1 and are right back with the conclusions that we found distasteful there. Suppose, then, that we take the second response. If the response is that God has no reason for loving x over, say, ~x, then we are left with the conclusion that God is irrational. This is not such a big problem for the ancient Greeks whose pantheon of gods was renowned for its caprice. However, for most orthodox religious traditions within the western world, this result is unacceptable as well.

So, it has now become clear that the two propositions actually do form a contradictory set of propositions – the first entails "God" or "~God" and the second entails "reason" or "~reason". In both cases, the positive response forces one into affirming the other proposition, only to be faced with a set of clearly contradictory choices. Further, the only two possible properties that survive as being true about God (or the gods who are all of one mind) are that God is not omnipotent or God is irrational. Hence, the problem.

Guided Reading Questions:
1. Who is Euthyphro prosecuting and why?
2. What are Euthyphro's definitions of the "holy"? Why does each fail?
3. What is the Socratic question at 10a? What do you think of it? (Remember,

10a is a Stephanus page designation.)
4. What is the Euthyphro Problem? (hint: it has something to do with what makes things good)

Logic Blurb
The Disjunctive "or"

The word "or" has at least three standard meanings, each of which plays an important function in formal logic, not to mention informal conversation. The two most common uses of the word "or," as either a logical operator or as a simple part of speech, are the *disjunctive "or"* and the *inclusive "or."* The third "or" is a descendent of the Greek epexigetical *kai*. *Kai* is a transliteration of the Greek word that can mean either "and" or "or," or, at times, both. The *epexigetical "or"* is used rather rarely, but at times is quite important. We shall treat each of these in turn.

The *disjunctive "or"* is perhaps the assumed use of "or" unless otherwise marked by context and it is the one with the simplest description as a logical operator. Consider the following example: John can go to the lake or he can go to class. Since the opportunity to go to class conflicts directly with the opportunity to go to the lake, we can see that the "or" here actually means that he can go to the lake or he can go to class, **but not both**. This "or" is called *disjunctive* because it designates a disjunction between to possibilities. In other words, to do one is to rule out the possibility of doing the other, and *vice versa*. The relationship between objects, options, possibilities, et al, described by this sort of "or" can be shown visually by means of Venn diagrams. Note that in the figure below, the two sets of options are completely distinct from each other. There are no points of contact between the two circles, demonstrating that should one select circle A, for example, it would rule out B and so forth.

Section 2.2: Trial Trilogy, Part 1 – *Euthyphro*

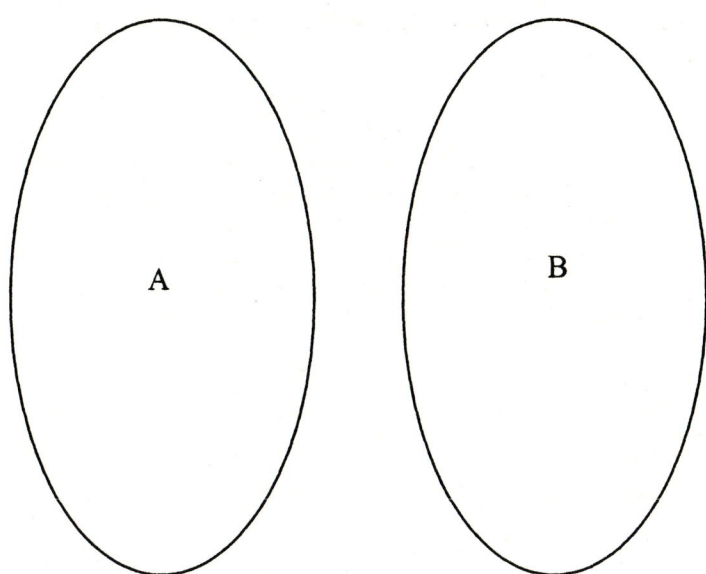

In the *Euthyphro Problem*, for example, the *disjunctive "or"* describes a relationship between two propositions that are *contradictions*. That is, one of the propositions must be true, one must be false and both cannot be true and both cannot be false. Thus, when faced with the situation of choosing between one or the other, one is restricted to choosing *only* one and not both.

The second common usage of "or" is the *inclusive "or."* The *inclusive "or"* is similar to the *disjunctive* one in that one can choose only one option or the other. One is not forced to select both. However, unlike the *disjunctive*, the *inclusive "or"* does not restrict the philosopher to *only* one. Indeed, when one says, "Sally can have an apple or an orange for breakfast," one does not generally mean to restrict her choices to only an apple or an orange, but rather to say that she can have an apple, an orange, or both. Presumably, neither is also an option, but that is not explicitly captured by the "or." This relationship can also be represented by Venn diagrams as described below.

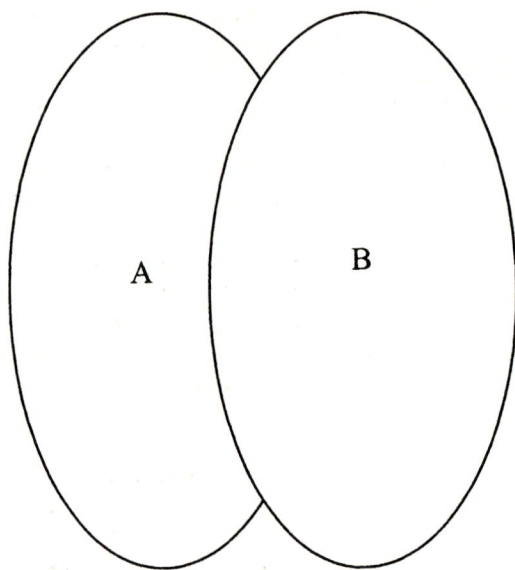

Thus, one could select only A or only B *or* one could select those options that are both part of A **and** part of B. So, the *inclusive "or"* actually presents the observer with three options, although it appears to only explicitly suggest two. While offering A or B, the *inclusive "or"* also offers both. The *inclusive "or"* is a statement of this or that or both.

Considerably less common than either of the foregoing meanings, the *epexigetical "or"* is still an important use of "or." The *epexigetical "or"* is used to elaborate or refine a feature of the subject under consideration. Consider the following statement, "A critical thinker can make important fine or subtle distinctions." It is not the case that the critical thinker can make fine distinctions or subtle distinctions, but not both. Use of the *disjunctive "or"* here would lead to all manner of confusion. It is not the case that the critical thinker can make fine **and** subtle distinctions, which would be the implication of use of the *inclusive "or"* here. While it is true that the critical thinker can make both fine distinctions and subtle ones, interpreting the statement that way would miss the important relationship that it is intended to convey. There is a relationship between "fine" and "subtle" that the *epexigetical "or"* captures. Rewriting the statement can bring this relationship out more clearly. Rather than writing it as above, let us consider this reformulation, "A critical thinker can make fine, that is to say, subtle, distinctions." Here, the word "subtle" modifies "fine" in such a fashion as to convey to the reader what sort of fine distinctions are at issue. Thus, the *epexigetical "or"* can be used to restrict the meaning of the first concept by contextualizing it in a particular way. In another way, it can be used to emphasize the meaning of the first term by means of a synonym that may be more familiar than the first term. For example, "John is a bachelor or unmarried male." While the definition of bachelor is "unmarried male," the use of the "or" here focuses the reader's attention to the aspect of bachelor on which the author means to focus.

So, the critical thinker will do well to pay close attention to the use of "or." In all three of its primary uses it conveys different implications and, as a result, can present particular difficulties when assessing arguments. Clearly careful attention to use of "or" can enhance one's analysis of philosophical argument.

One of the clearest examples of the use of the *disjunctive "or"* is to denote a logical contradiction, often symbolized by the phrase, "*p* or ~*p*." A *contradiction* is a proposition that designates two incompatible properties or states of affairs. Thus, for example, to say, as in the *Euthyphro Problem*, that either God has some reason for acting or that God does not have a reason for acting is to express two contradictory states set apart by "or". It is impossible to affirm both propositions. That is, it cannot logically be the case that God acts for a reason and that God does not act for a reason at the same time and in the same respect. Or, suppose that when considering whether or not to call Socrates a good person we make the assumption that "Socrates is wise." In the course of the argument, that assumption leads directly to the implication that "Socrates is both wise and not wise." This is clearly a contradiction. Socrates cannot be both wise and not wise; he is either one or the other.

A contradiction is different from a set of contrary propositions as well. Within a set of contradictory propositions, one of the propositions must be true and the other must be false. It is not the case that both could be true nor is it the case that both can be false. This is different from the case of contrary propositions. In the case of contraries, both of the propositions might be false. For example, here are a set of contrary propositions: "The flower is red" and "The flower is green." While it might be the case that one of the two propositions is true, it could not be the case that both are. In this sense, contraries are somewhat like contradictions. However, they differ in this respect. Both parts of contrary propositions could be false. The flower might well be blue and hence is neither red nor green. Thus, both contrary propositions are false. So, while contradictory propositions present the reader with two propositions, one of which must be true and one of which must be false, contrary propositions present us with propositions both of which might be false, but at most one is true.

Section 2.3: Trial Trilogy, Part 2 – *Apology*

Apology

Setting: The court of Athens. The citizens of the jury sit in rows of seats that surround the plaintiffs and the defendant, theater-style. Socrates's accusers have presented their case against him first. Now, it falls to Socrates to present his defense.

Socrates: My accusers are quite persuasive. Indeed, I was nearly carried away myself by the eloquence of their presentation. How you, the jury, was affected, I do not know. Though, even as I was moved by their words, almost none of those words were true.

I am not practiced in the art of speaking before court, so I beg the court's indulgence. I will make my case as I am generally accustomed to speaking since I am not a trained orator. This is my first time before the court, I am seventy years old, and unaccustomed to the procedures for argument here. Even though I am a stranger to this place, and though my words will scarcely match theirs in accomplishment, my words will be the whole truth.

I have but one request – and it is that you, people of Athens and of the jury, will not be distracted by my way of speaking, but rather to focus on whether my words are just or not.

I shall defend myself first against the first set of false accusations made against me and then turn to the later accusations for my later defense. Many have made accusation against me in the past, although not in the formal way of the court. Though completely untrue, these more informal accusations frighten me much more greatly than those formal ones made by Anytus and his friends. This is not to discount the formal charges at all – they are quite impressive – but to say that the earlier ones are much more dangerous. These earlier accusations influenced many of you in childhood; you were persuaded by others saying that there is this man, Socrates, a "wise" man, who inquires into things in the heavens and beneath the earth. [ed. note: That is to say, that Socrates is a Natural Philosopher.] Further, this Socrates goes about making the worse argument appear the stronger, and teaching others to do the same. The ones making accusation in rumor are by far the most dangerous because those that hear these rumors believe that those who inquire into the things of the heavens and the earth do not believe in the gods of the city. Not only that, these rumormongers are many and they told you these stories when you were young so that you would believe them without counterargument.

Most absurd in these indictments is that I know not the names of those making these claims – save, perhaps, one – a writer of comedies, Aristophanes. You must know that my accusers fall into two camps – those who bring indictment now and the old ones I've just been discussing. To defend myself, I must address both; though I must deal with those brought in rumors first, since you have heard these accusations first and more often than those written and brought today.

If the rumormongers were actual accusers, their indictment would be: Socrates is guilty of wrongdoing because he inquires into the things of heaven and beneath the earth; makes the weaker argument appear the stronger; and teaches the young to do the same thing. You of the jury know these things to be true for you have seen Aristophanes' play just as we have.

Not a single one of these claims is true. Have you ever heard from even one of my students that I ever have charged even the smallest fee for my teaching? I'm sure not, for I have never charged a fee. Not to discredit those who do charge fees – a fine thing it is to be able to teach something worthy of receiving compensation – those like Gorgias of Leontini, Prodicus of Ceos, and Hippias of Elis. [ed. note: These three were well-known Sophists and it seems that the rumormonger accusation is that Socrates is both a Natural Philosopher and a Sophist.] Each of these go about from city to city and collect to themselves young men who gladly pay to join themselves to them.

So, you might ask, if you, Socrates, are not like these, then where could these rumors and slanders possibly come from? What is it that you do? To this, I would respond that what has caused the rumors and slander to attach themselves to my reputation is a certain sort of wisdom that I do possess; a sort of human wisdom, perhaps. Divine wisdom, on the other hand, I truly do not have and anyone who disputes this claim is simply lying. I invoke the god at Delphi as witness to the truth of my statements – and to the kind of wisdom, if it is wisdom at all, that I have.

All of you remember Chaerophon. He is dead now but his brother is among us still and can verify all that I say here. Chaerophon traveled to the oracle – please, members of the jury, do not raise a commotion – and he inquired whether any person was more wise than his friend, Socrates. The Pythian replied that none was wiser. When I heard this, I asked myself, "What could this possibly mean?"

For a long time, I could not understand this reply. Finally, I decided I must investigate. I went to one with a reputation for great wisdom. I thought, if there is any way to refute the oracle, surely this would be it. I shall not reveal the name of the man I examined since he is one well known to the public. But when I examined him, I discovered that he seemed wise, particularly to himself, but was really not. I tried to show him the shortcoming – that he was mistaken about being wise – but instead of being grateful, he came to hate me. And not only him, but many of those who witnessed our interchange. So, I left that place and thought, "I am wiser than he; it seems neither of us knows anything of note, but unlike me, he thinks he knows things that he does not know. On the other hand, when I do not know something, I do not suppose that I do. So, I must be wiser than he, at least in this very small way." Then, I went to another, and then another, and discovered the same thing, and I was hated by them as well – and by others.

And so it went, members of the jury. Again and again, in serving the god through my investigations, I discovered that those who had the greatest reputations for wisdom were almost always the most lacking and that those widely reputed for lack of wisdom were far more knowledgeable. After the politicians, I went to the poets. I discovered that, not unlike the politicians, the poets were talented, indeed, inspired like prophets and seers. But they did not compose their poems from knowledge nor could they explain what they wrote. Still, because of the reputation acquired from popular reception of their poetry, the poets thought they knew many things which they in fact did not, and thought they possessed wisdom concerning things they did not. Again, I left with much the same conclusion as before, that I possessed some small measure of wisdom not possessed by the poets.

Finally, I went to the craftspeople. There I discovered they had much more technical knowledge than did I. In this way, it was clear that they were wiser. But the same error of the politicians and poets was found here as well. The successful builder imagined himself to have wisdom regarding things other than building, and the fault here far outweighed the knowledge he did have, for he thought himself wise about many quite important things. As it is, I possess neither the knowledge of politicians, poets, craftspeople, or indeed, any of those reputed to be wise. At the same, I possess none of their ignorance. All things considered, I would prefer to be as I am and that this must be what the oracle meant.

Because of my examinations, many people came to dislike me quite a lot. Since I performed my examinations in public, there were often many bystanders. These often thought I knew what I said I did not know or that I had the wisdom that I had shown my interlocutor not to have. And they too became angry with me.

To this day, I continue. I go about, looking for anyone with a reputation for wisdom. If I discover that he is not wise, I aid the god and show that he is not wise.

Then, I was attacked by Meletus. Along with Anytus and Lycon. Meletus, because of the poets; Anytus, because of the craftspeople and politicians; Lycon, for the sake of the orators.

This must suffice as a defense against the rumormonger slander. I turn now to the charges of Meletus, the self-described good patriot, and the others. Since this is a different group, let us look at the indictment itself. It reads something like this: Socrates is guilty of wrongdoing by corrupting the youth and by failing to believe in the gods of the city. This is the indictment. We shall examine it.

Come, Meletus, tell me something. Is it important that the youth of the city become as good as they can be?

Meletus: Yes.

Socrates: So, what is it that makes them better.

Meletus: The laws.

Socrates: Ah. But that's not the question. Who is it that has the knowledge to craft the laws at the outset?

Meletus: These gathered here, Socrates.

Socrates: All of these benefit the youth? Or just some?

Meletus: All of them.

Socrates: What a good thing for the city to have so many people who perform so vital a service. So, all the people of Athens benefit the youth of the city; except for me, of course. I alone corrupt them. Is that it?

Meletus: Yes, it is.

Socrates: What a great tragedy. Does the same sort of thing apply to, say, horses as well? That all people, or perhaps all people save one, benefit horses and only that one corrupts them? Isn't the opposite the case? Isn't it so that only a few people are of benefit to horses and the majority of people are of no benefit or are harmful? Or, tell us this, Meletus. Is it better for a person to live with good people or with evil ones? Isn't it so that evil people harm those closest to them while good people help them?

Meletus: Of course.

Socrates: So, is there some person who would prefer harm to aid from his friends? Does any person wish harm to himself?

Meletus: No.

Socrates: So, is it the case that you are accusing me of harming the youth deliberately?

Meletus: Yes.

Socrates: Oh my! You agree that evil people bring harm to those close to them while good people bring good. I must be quite ignorant if I corrupt my associates I run the great risk of being harmed in return. I can not believe you, Meletus and I cannot imagine anyone else believing you either. It's either the case that I do not corrupt the youth deliberately or I do not corrupt the youth at all. In both cases, you have been caught in a lie.

Nevertheless, Meletus, tell us how it is that I corrupt the youth. According to your indictment, it seems that you believe that I corrupt the youth by teaching them not to believe in the gods of the city and teaching them to believe in other spiritual beings. Isn't that how you say I corrupt them?

Meletus: Most definitely.

Socrates: Do you mean that I don't believe in gods at all?

Meletus: Yes, that's it.

Socrates: Oh my! Do you think you are prosecuting Anaxagoras? Consider this. Is there anyone who believes in the actions of humans who does not also believe in human beings? For example, is there anyone who does not believe in horses but believes in the activities of horses? Or playing the flute, but not players of the flute? I cannot imagine such a person. So, does anyone who believes in divine actions that does not believe in divine beings?

Meletus: No.

Socrates: Well, even though the jury forced you to answer, I appreciate your answer nonetheless. So, do we not believe divine beings are either gods or the children of god?

Meletus: Yes.

Socrates: So, if I believe in divine beings (and I do, as you yourself admit), and if divine beings are gods, then you must be joking with me and the jury if you think that I both believe in gods and do not believe in gods. If divine beings are children of gods, then who could believe that children of gods exist but not the gods of whom they are children? That would be like saying that colts exist, but not the horses from whom they come. This is sufficient, I think, to show that I am not guilty of the charges Meletus brings. It shall not be Meletus, Anytus, or Lycon who bring about my demise, if it is to be brought about, but rather the rumormongers of before.

Some might ask, "Socrates, aren't you ashamed to have pursued this course, this path that has brought you to this moment when you are in peril of death?" But I would justly reply, "You are wrong if you suppose that a person who has good in him at all should consider life or death; instead, he should look only to his actions, whether they are just or unjust, whether he is acting as a good person or an evil one."

If some say, "Socrates, you have made your case and we are not persuaded by your accusers. Therefore, we will acquit you – but on one condition. You are to cease from this philosophy and investigate and examine no longer. If you fail in this condition, you will die." If this was the term of my acquittal, I would be compelled to respond, "Members of the jury, I appreciate you and value your friendship. However, I cannot obey you and the god, and I will obey the god. I shall not cease from philosophy; nor from encouraging all that I meet, greeting them: Sir, you are of Athens, the greatest city possessed of the greatest reputation for wisdom and power; are you not ashamed at your avarice, your rush to gain money and power and honor at the expense of best state of your soul? Do you care nothing for your soul; do you not ignore wisdom and truth?" If there is argument and a claim that he cares nothing for these things, I will not let him leave me, but will examine him. If I think he does not have the goodness he claims, I will chastise him because he places to little emphasis on that which is truly important and too much on that which has little real importance. This I shall do to any and all I meet, young or old, citizen or foreigner; although more for the citizen because you are my family. This is how I have been directed by the god. And I believe this to be a blessing for the city and for you. I do nothing but persuade all among you, young and old, to long for the best state of your soul and to give less time to wealth and body. I say again and again, "Money does not bring excellence (*arete*). Excellence brings wealth and all other things that are good for human beings, both the individual and the city."

If this counsel corrupts the youth, then it is harmful counsel. But if there is anyone who claims I say anything but this, then he is either mistaken or a liar.

This may all seem very odd to some of you. I interfere in private business, giving counsel privately, and do not go to the assembly and advise publicly. Many of you have heard my reason for this. Meletus has made fun of it, but my divine sign guides me. From childhood, I have heard the voice and when it speaks it counsels me to turn from some course or another. Never does it provoke me to follow some course, but rather prevents me from taking one. This is why I have not participated in public activity, and I believe it right to have prevented me from doing so. One who strives for justice must live a private, not a public life. One who fights for justice and does not lead a private life will not likely survive long.

I leave the decision to you. You and the god will judge as is best for you and for me.

The jury returns a guilty verdict and Meletus asks for the death penalty.

Socrates: Here is the difficult point. Suppose I were to say that it is impossible to be silent, since that would mean that I must disobey the god. You would not believe me and say I am being ironic. On the other hand, if I were to say that the greatest good is to speak, talk, discuss, and investigate virtue each day (and all the other topics you have all heard me talk about) and say even that the unexamined life is not worth living, you would not believe me any more and likely less. You have given me the option of proposing a countersentence. This is my proposal. I do not think I deserve any penalty whatever. Since I do not have money, at least not much, I assess a penalty I could conceivably pay – one mina of silver.

Wait. Plato here, and Crito and Critoboulus and Appolodorus have made an offer of thirty minae.

The jury returns with judgment of death.
Socrates: The time has come. I go to die. You go to live. Only the god knows which of us has the better part.

~

Given the political intrigue that surrounded Socrates during and following the Peloponnesian War, it is not surprising that he was not the most popular person in Athens. Having taught two of the generals thought to be responsible for Athens's ignominious defeat at the hand of the Spartans and two of the traitors who were installed as a puppet regime by the Spartans following the War, he was viewed with suspicion by a great many of the Athenian citizens. However, it was not only a sort of guilt by association that swirled around Socrates. Simply put, many people did not understand what he was doing nor why he was doing it. As a result, Socrates found himself charged with corrupting the youth and with impiety. However, it is not these charges with which Socrates is most worried.

Recalling the comedy by Aristophanes, *The Clouds*, Socrates is convinced that a general prejudice pervaded the city's view of him. Though *The Clouds* was a comedy, and as such, portrayed Socrates as a comedic figure, the image of him as one who took very weak arguments and twisted them in such a way as to entrap his conversation partners and make them look foolish was easily remembered. Think of Socrates in this way, it was easy to imagine him as a Sophist, concerned with winning arguments and embarrassing those who were unfortunate enough to find themselves on the wrong end of an episode of Socratic questioning. *The Clouds* also portrayed Socrates as one who completely ignored the gods, looking instead for natural explanations for natural events, inquiring into the heavens to the point of ignoring everyday life – in other words, Socrates was one who had his head in the clouds. But, for Socrates, these two unstated prejudices, let's call them the Unofficial Charges, were far more dangerous for him than the Official ones. Simply put, Socrates was sure that those who sat in judgment of him viewed him as a Natural Philosopher and as a Sophist; that they had viewed him this way from early in their lives (having been told stories of Socrates by their parents); and that these prejudices would so taint the jury that they would convict him even if he refuted the Official Charges.

Socrates's accusers were not ignorant of these prejudices in the Athenian picture of Socrates. Meletus, Anytus, and Lycon knew full well the way in which Socrates was perceived, in no small part because they themselves had this view of him. And while Socrates could not be charged with conspiracy or collusion with either Alcibiades or Nicias, nor could he be accused of being connected with the Thirty Tyrants because of the Amnesty, he could be indicted in such a way that the prejudices of the people would do most of their work for them. The Official Charges are not divorced from the Unofficial Charges.

The Natural Philosophers, Thales, Anaxagoras, Democritus, and others, are the predecessors of modern scientists. They sought natural explanations for natural events. For example, suppose we were trying to explain why lightning flashed across the sky and thunder followed closely behind it. One possible explanation for such an event would be that Zeus is hurling lightning bolts and that, concurrently, Hephaestus is pounding away on his forge. Another explanation could be that in the midst of atmospheric turmoil, distinct regions of the sky become charged, one positively and the other negatively. As the differential becomes so great as to be unstable, electricity is discharged from the one to the other. As the electricity is discharged, the air surrounding it is expanded, causing a sound wave that is perceived as thunder. In the former explanation, we have a supernatural explanation for a natural event. In the latter, we have a natural explanation. Suppose someone believed that all natural events could be explained by natural causes. In such a case, there would be nothing left for the gods to do. Thus, the gods could be seen as useless or impotent. It is a small step from there to the view that there are no gods at all. And this is precisely how Meletus accuses Socrates in the *Apology*. It is fairly easy to see how someone holding the view that there are no gods (or that the gods have very little to do) could be considered impious. Thus, there is a close connection between the Official Charge of impiety and the Unofficial Charge of Natural Philosophy.

Similarly, Socrates is easily confused with the Sophists. The confusion is tied directly to the way in which he conducts his investigations. For a more complete understanding of the distinction between Socrates and the Sophists, we examine the much-discussed "Socratic Method"?

What is the Socratic Method? In some senses, it looks very much like the method practiced by the Sophists. However, upon closer examination, it is quite different. For the sake of argument, let's consider the modern pedagogical practice that is often called the "Socratic Method." Dr. Bob has prepared his lesson plans and has come to class with a set of objectives including the content he hopes for his students to take with them at the close of the day. Rather than putting a series of facts on the board, he begins with a question. "What is F?" he asks. The students, ideally, will respond from their own store of facts. Then, by guiding the students through a series of leading questions, Dr. Bob directs the students to "discover" the answer for themselves. Whatever the merits of this method of pedagogy, one might well imagine the frustration of the students of a teacher who never led them to an answer. Before long, the frustration of those students might well become unbearable. So much the worse would be the lot of those students who, having been thoroughly confused, were at the same time convinced that the teacher had played unfairly with them, had known the answer for which he was "questioning," but had deliberately withheld the information in a perverse game of question and confusion, taking pleasure in their inability to grasp the illusive bit of knowledge. This is essentially the accusation Socrates thinks has been leveled at him; a charge that, if true, entails that Socrates is indeed a Sophist.

Standing as rebuttal, and perhaps refutation, of this charge are Socrates's repeated disavowals of knowledge. Again and again, Socrates says that he does not have wisdom. In the *Apology* alone there are several disavowals. Among them are these: "Divine wisdom, on the other hand, I truly do not have and anyone who disputes this claim is simply lying." (20d) "I possess neither the knowledge of politicians, poets, craftspeople, or indeed, any of those reputed to be wise" (22d)

However, why should we believe these disavowals to be sincere? If Socrates is practicing the "Socratic Method" and is indeed a sophist, then lying about the content of his knowledge seems little enough a surprise. One recourse is to examine carefully Socrates's method as we find it in the dialogues. It is to that we now turn.

Comparing Socrates to Dr. Bob, one distinction becomes readily apparent. Unlike Dr. Bob, who arrives with facts to impart and questions the students, Socrates does not ask questions of students, but rather of those who put themselves forward as teachers. It is Euthyphro who makes a claim to knowledge of piety and who never disclaims that position throughout the dialogue. It is Meletus who claims to know who it is that is beneficial to the youth of Athens and who corrupts them and who does not waver in alleging positive knowledge despite the full force of the elenchus brought to bear. Socrates is not the teacher, but the student. His interlocutors are not students, but those who allege themselves to be teachers. Perhaps the following graphic can make the distinction more clear.

"Socratic Method"	Socratic Method
Teacher has knowledge	Teacher alleges his knowledge
Student does not have knowledge	Student does not have knowledge
Teacher asks questions	Student asks questions

It is rather clear that these methods differ significantly. Further, Socrates's disavowals of knowledge place him squarely in the role of the student without knowledge rather than the teacher withholding knowledge from his suffering charges.

So, given the close connection between the Official Charges and the Unofficial ones, and given that Socrates's method, even at this late date, could easily be confused with that of the Sophists, Socrates realizes at the outset that he must defend himself against both. Given that one set of charges is part of the commonly held picture of Socrates, it is these that will be the most formidable.

Before moving to examine the charges in particular, it would help to understand who it is that is charging Socrates and how Plato sees them. Meletus, Anytus, and Lycon are each democrats. Following the deposing of the Thirty

Section 2.3: Trial Trilogy, Part 2 - *Apology*

Tyrants, the democrats were returned to power in Athens. Athens is generally considered to be the birthplace of democracy and Plato has sometimes been thought of as a proponent of democracy. Unfortunately, this is quite simply a fallacy of juxtaposition. For Meletus, Anytus, and Lycon, the ideal form of government is one in which every citizen has a right, and indeed, a responsibility, to participate in the means of government. The citizens are to gather and, having heard arguments about what the best course of action in some particular situation facing the city would be, are to vote. Whichever view prevails in the course of the vote is the one the city should support.

This sort of direct democratic process is fraught with peril, on Socrates (and Plato's view). It is susceptible to all sorts of manipulations by unscrupulous characters. Even under the best of circumstances, the many will likely give undue weight to the arguments of one side or the other not because it is the best course of action, but because it is the one presented with rhetorical flourish, or by a person of high station or great reputation, or both. Imagine a situation in which a person who has made a great career as an actor in the theater becomes, on the basis of his acting, thought to be capable of making great decisions as a leader of the city. His training as an actor has not prepared him in any meaningful way to make decisions about fiscal policy or foreign policy or education. Yet, because of his rhetorical ability, his view is given greater weight in the assembly than the person who is, perhaps, an expert in the field of education. Plato is not hopeful that this sort of system will bring about the best possible state. In fact, in the *Republic*, Plato argues that the democratic constitution is the worst constitution of government except for that government in which there is no government at all (that is, an anarchy). The case of Socrates before the court is a case in point. His accusers fail to prove their case and yet they win a democratic vote. The tyranny of the majority ends ultimately in the death of Socrates, the first martyr of philosophy.

So, how did Socrates find himself in this position? Socrates's friend, Chaerophon, took it upon himself to make a trip to the Oracle at Delphi. The result of this trip was a cryptic comment that "Socrates was the wisest of all the Athenians." This was confusing to Socrates. He knew that he did not have much knowledge – for example, there were many craftsmen who knew their craft far better than Socrates did. In fact, there were many in Athens with great reputations for wisdom. Given this, how could it be that Socrates was the wisest. And so, Socrates set out to test the Oracle; not to prove that it was wrong (after all, the Oracle was the mouthpiece of the god, Apollo), but to understand how the statement could possibly be true. Greek oracles were renowned for their cryptic comments and the Oracle at Delphi was no different. Thus, the recipient of an oracular proclamation was oftentimes no better off than if he had not received one at all. In fact, it was particularly difficult at times to understand what an oracle meant at any given moment.

In testing the oracle, Socrates sought out those renowned for wisdom. He went to poets, to politicians, to craftsman, indeed, to any with a reputation for wisdom. And then he questioned them. It was true that the craftsmen had factual knowledge that Socrates did not have, but it was also true that they thought they had much more widespread knowledge about a great many things when they did not. Thus, each of the craftsmen questioned turned out to have many true beliefs, but also many false beliefs.

Socrates came to similar conclusions when he questioned the poets and the politicians. In the case of the poets, he concluded that they were inspired but that they were incapable of explaining their poetry. Like the craftsmen, the poets also had false beliefs about the extent of their knowledge. The politicians come off even worse than the craftsmen and poets. While both the craftsmen and poets are commended for some gift they have, the politicians do not receive such recognition. However, they too, are filled with false beliefs covering a great many things. In the same way, all those with a reputation for wisdom are discovered to have many false beliefs. As Socrates has gone through the city and questioned any he meets, he has come to the same conclusion – everyone else has a set of false beliefs – they may have some factual knowledge, but they all believe they know more than they do.

It is precisely here that Socrates realizes what the Oracle's pronouncement had meant. Socrates does not have false beliefs. Simply put, Socrates knows what he doesn't know and he does not pretend to know those things that he does not know. While all those around him have many false beliefs, Socrates has none. In virtue of this one advantage, Socrates is the wisest.

However, we should not conclude from this that Socrates is actually wise. Simply being the best of a particular group does not make one excellent. For example, an intermediate algebra student may have the best grasp of the material of all of his classmates. In virtue of this, we could say that he is the best mathematician of the bunch. However, it would not be reasonable to conclude further that he was a good mathematician. Or, similarly, a person may be the best pitcher in the AA minor leagues, but that would in no way suggest that he was actually a good pitcher, much less the best pitcher in baseball. Thus, the oracle's pronouncement is true – Socrates is the wisest – but this is only in a limited way. He is the wisest because he has no false beliefs.

While we have come to this conclusion, those he questioned came to a different one. In their view, Socrates was a menace. His constant questioning caused aggravation, frustration, and an abiding desire to be rid of this gadfly stinging the city. Thus, the charges of Meletus, Lycon, and Anytus found a receptive audience in those who had been questioned by Socrates, or who had heard many of the stories of Socrates since their youth, or both.

Thus having painted the backdrop against which Socrates found himself before the court, it is important now to turn and address the actual charges, and the unofficial, if more formidable ones as well. We shall address them as Socrates does, first discussing Impiety and then Corrupting the Youth.

Meletus advances an extremely untenable position. On his view, Socrates believes that there are no gods whatsoever. The charge originally is that Socrates has encouraged the youth of the city to believe in different gods, gods that Socrates himself had created. But, under questioning from Socrates, he revises his charge to "You believe in no gods at all". To this charge, Socrates has a very quick and easy response, although he does not take advantage of it. In the first place, it was the Oracle at Delphi that in some sense launched Socrates on this quest to discover whether or not he was the wisest in all of Athens. Given that he gives the Oracle's pronouncement considerable weight is itself evidence that Meletus is wrong. Since the Oracle is the Oracle *of Apollo*, it is reasonable to suppose that Socrates believes in at least one god, and further, that he believes in a god recognized by the city of Athens. Further, Socrates has apparently an annoying habit of generally doing the thing that he thinks is right (or at least, appearing to do so). This gives people the view that Socrates really does know the answers to the questions that he keeps asking, and is simply being obnoxious in not tipping his hand. Socrates gives an account of this. Whenever he is faced with a decision, and one of the options would be the wrong thing to do, he hears a little voice – a divine sign sent from Apollo – that instructs him not to do it. The voice never tells him to do something, but only restrains him from doing something that would be the wrong thing to do. On the basis of these two pieces of evidence, one would think Socrates might point out that Meletus could not possibly be correct in his accusation since Socrates admits of, and depends on, the guidance of a god.

However, Socrates does not avail himself of this defense. Instead, he turns to an argument from analogy. Meletus agrees that Socrates thinks that there are divine activities. Thus, we have the beginnings of an analogy. Since human activities imply the existence of humans, so, too, divine activities must imply the existence of divinities. So, we have the following structure to the argument.

> Humans are to Human activities
> as
> Divinities are to Divine activities

Given this agreement, the next question becomes, what is the identity of the divinities. A 21st century thinker might jump immediately to the conclusion that divinities are clearly gods. Not so for a 4th century Athenian. Divinities be one of two things – gods or children of gods. The source of this distinction is rooted in the anthropomorphic theology of ancient Greece. Gods were known to have relationships that resulted in the birth of demigods, heroes, and other divine sorts of creatures. Given this picture of divine/human interaction, Socrates must address each of these possibilities to fully refute his accusers. So, Socrates explores each of these options with Meletus. In the first case, if divinities are gods, then clearly Socrates, who believes in divine activities, believes in gods. Thus, Meletus is thwarted. In the second case, if divinities are children of gods, then they must have come from either gods or from an relation between a god and a human. Thus, if divinities are children of gods who come from gods, then it follows that there are gods. Once again, Meletus is thwarted.

Having refuted the charge of Impiety, as presented by Meletus, Socrates turns to address the charge that he corrupts the youth. Again, the argument proceeds from an analogy. Consider the case of horses, Socrates says. For horses, who is most likely to be of benefit to the animals – the many or the select few. Clearly, the view of the people is that most people are either of no benefit or of harm to horses while only a few, well-trained people are of benefit to them. This seems to be the case not just with horses but with the crafts as well. Thus, in every case, the relationship between the few and the many towards the object of benefit or harm is this: the many harm (or at least do not benefit) the object and the few benefit it. So, Socrates says, in this one case, perhaps the most important, namely the upbringing and training of the youth, the entire city of Athens are beneficial to the youth and I, alone, corrupt them. While his accusers agree to this, the implausibility of the conclusion is palpable.

Having refuted, or at the very least rebutted, the official charges of his accusers, Socrates turns to the Unofficial Charges. The charge of Natural Philosophy is given very little attention. This could be for two reasons. First, given the refutation of the charge of Impiety, the charge that Socrates does not believe that the gods are useful or that he does believe that they are impotent is unreasonable. After all, at least one god, Apollo, plays a central role in the very core of Socrates's life. His second reason is straightforward – he doesn't do what the natural philosophers do. He points out that no one could ever confuse him with someone like Anaxagoras. Their methods are completely different. Thus, we can dismiss this charge as well. While this may seem overly quick, it is supported by the appeal to the various witnesses who could testify to this difference.

The second approach to the charge of Natural Philosophy is a place to start to address the charge of Sophistry. As we have already discussed, the method of Socrates and the method of the Sophists are quite different. To be sure, it is easier to mistake Socrates as a Sophist than to mistake him for a Natural Philosopher. The Socratic and Sophistic methods are similar enough that they are easily confused. The proceeding by questions/answers/refutations is common to both. However, the roles played by the Sophists and by Socrates differ greatly (as we have already discussed). Thus, the first reason to suppose that Socrates is not a Sophist is that their methods are very different, even though on first glance they seem similar.

Section 2.3: Trial Trilogy, Part 2 - *Apology*

Given that their methods are easily confused, Socrates discusses another reason to think they are different. In making a distinction between two groups of people, it is helpful to know what it is that they are doing. For example, within a corporation, one of the things that distinguishes the Board of Directors from the Human Resources Department is the mission that each is given to fulfill. While it may be the case that there is some similarity to their activities, perhaps even in their methods, their differing missions are sufficient cause to conclude that they are different groups. From this viewpoint, it will be helpful to examine what Socrates and the Sophists see as their missions.

For Socrates, the mission is clear. At *Apology* 30b, he is addressing how he would respond if, perhaps, the Athenian court decided to acquit him on the condition that he cease his philosophizing. He responds that while some might find that an attractive option, he would not quit philosophy, even on pain of death, or from questioning those he meets until the people of the city of Athens come to care more for truth, wisdom, and the perfection of their souls than they care for wealth, reputation, and honor.

> Sir, you are of Athens, the greatest city possessed of the greatest reputation for wisdom and power; are you not ashamed at your avarice, your rush to gain money and power and honor at the expense of best state of your soul? Do you care nothing for your soul; do you not ignore wisdom and truth?" ... I do nothing but persuade all among you, young and old, to long for the best state of your soul and to give less time to wealth and body. I say again and again, "Money does not bring excellence (*arete*) brings wealth and all other things that are good for human beings, both the individual and the city."

In this passage, we have perhaps the clearest statement of the Socratic Mission in the entirety of the Platonic corpus. Socrates mission is simple – he is out to help the people of Athens, a city renowned for wisdom and power of mind, to put away their misplaced concern with transient things and to focus instead on that which endures – truth, wisdom, and the care of the soul. Each of these is of little consequence to the Sophists. From our earlier encounter with the Sophists (in the preceding sections) it should be clear now that Socrates's Method and the Method of the Sophists are distinct and further that each has a very different mission. Thus, even though Socrates's method may be confused with that of the Sophists, it is evident now that they are different. The two methods each have different aims – and as such, would be clearly seen as fundamentally different even if the particulars were the same. For example, suppose two drivers were setting out from Chicago to travel to their own destinations. Suppose that the first went south and the second west. Even if they used the same method of driving, drove the same model car, and obeyed all the rules of the road in precisely the same sorts of ways, it would be obvious that they arrived at different places – one in Atlanta, for instance, and the other in Denver. Thus, even if their methods were the same in all particulars, their different destinations are sufficient to distinguish them. So, too, Socrates and the Sophists. Even if the Athenian court was confused about the methods of Socrates and the Sophists, the fact that those methods were aimed at different goals should be sufficient to show that Socrates was not a Sophist. While Socrates's mission is truth, wisdom, and care of the soul, the Sophists' mission was honor, reputation, and wealth.

Incidentally, though Socrates thinks he is unofficially being charged with Sophistry, in his defense he fairly straightforwardly calls those sitting in judgment of him Sophists themselves. While the methods may be different (and since Meletus, Anytus, and Lycon are using the method of those trained by the Sophists to prosecute Socrates it is not clear that the methods are different), the ends of the Athenians sitting in judgment and the Sophists are similar. Though Socrates has called each of those he questions to care more for transient things like honor, reputation, and power, Socrates says that is precisely why he finds himself on trial. Thus, in substance, Socrates explicitly accuses his jury of being precisely what they will ultimately, and wrongly, convict him of being – Sophists.

Having examined both the Socratic Method and the Socratic Mission in depth, it is clear that there should be no confusion regarding the methods. In both method and mission, Socrates differs from the Sophists. Thus, though he is convicted of impiety and corrupting the youth (and probably, primarily of being a Sophist), Socrates is not guilty.

Guided Reading Questions

1. To whom did Socrates go to test the Oracle? What did he discover? What effect did Socrates's questions have on those whom he questioned?
2. What is Socrates special form of knowledge?
3. According to Socrates, what is the only thing one ought to consider when performing an action? What reasons does he give for this position?
4. What does Socrates see as the goal of all his pestering? How does he support this goal?
5. What is it that keeps Socrates from doing things that are wrong?

Questions for Reflection

1. Is Socrates virtuous? Explain.
2. Why does Socrates think that the unofficial charges are more of a problem for him than the official ones?

Logic Blurb
The Argument from Analogy

One of the most common arguments overheard from student unions to executive boardrooms is the Argument from Analogy. The reason for this is simple. The argument form is quite simple and, in the hands of a skillful rhetorician, very powerful and persuasive. Why do such proofs work and when do they fail? At its heart, an analogy is a way of expressing a complex relationship by way of referring to something more commonplace or something simpler. For example, when concerned about "corrupting the youth," Socrates makes an analogy to something much more mundane – namely, the care and treatment of horses. While it is difficult to figure out what corrupting the youth amounts to (some things may be obvious, but some are less so), it is easier, or at least more generally accepted, what benefits horses and what does not. Let's look at another analogy that Plato uses quite often, especially when discussing virtue. Virtue or living as a good person is notoriously difficult to define with precision. So, for example, suppose we are trying to understand the nature of virtue. As we have already seen in the difficulty with establishing the definition of *piety*, virtue is a very difficult concept to understand. Because of this, the argument that virtue is better than vice is going to be a difficult argument to make; yet it is clearly the case in the *Apology* that Socrates thinks virtue is better for the soul than vice is. So, how might he make this argument, even with the understanding that it is very difficult to understand the nature of virtue, and perhaps, along the way, shed light on that very difficult topic as well? Plato chooses an Argument from Analogy. The Argument from Analogy to establish that virtue is good for the soul/mind begins with a relationship that is familiar to the listener – health and the body. It is commonly known that health is good for the body and that sickness is bad for it. Thus, Plato argues that Health is to the Body as Virtue is to the Soul. Or, we can represent that formally in this way:

Virtue : Soul
: :
Health: Body

"Virtue" and "Soul" are called *relata* – that is, the things related to one another. Similarly, "Health" and "Body" are *relata*. An analogy works if the relationship between the first set of *relata* (in this case, "Virtue" and "Soul") is the same or relevantly similar. However, if the related things do not express a similar relationship, the analogy fails. In the Virtue/Soul and Health/Body analogy, Plato is arguing that just as health benefits the body and poor health harms the body, so too does virtue benefit the soul while vice harms it. If the *relata* bear the same relationship to each other in each pair, and if the relationship is preserved from the first pair to the second, then the Argument from Analogy is considered to be valid. However, Arguments from Analogy are notoriously weak. For example, if it is the case that Virtue is good for the Soul as the argument suggests, then we do have some further insight into the nature of virtue. However, the argument does not establish either that virtue is good for the soul or that the relationship between virtue and the soul, on the one hand, is the same as the relationship between Health and the Body, on the other. So, if one accepts that Health and Virtue stand in the same relation to the Body and the Soul, respectively, then the argument will be convincing. However, if one argues, for example, that virtue is not necessarily good for the soul, or that vice is not necessarily bad for it, then the analogy fails. Few would argue that disease is potentially beneficial or neutral with respect to the body, so, if the argument commits one to the view that virtue is good for the soul and therefore vice is bad for it, then the *relata* are not in the same relationship. Thus, while the argument is quite an attractive one, it is only as strong as the three relationships that comprise it – the relationship between the first pair, the relationship between the second pair, and the relationship between the first and second pairs.

The difficulties with this form of argument, however, do not keep it from being among the most commonly used even by the most sophisticated of philosophers. René Descartes's uses the argument form to try to explain the way in which the mind and the body are related: a sailor is to a ship, he says, as the mind is to the body. Similarly, John Stuart Mill uses the Argument from Analogy twice to argue for his Principle of Utility. He argues that visibility is to being seen as audibility is to being heard as desirability is to being desired. From there he argues that since individual's desire their own happiness, that the general populace will desire its own happiness (which is another formulation of the Greatest Good for the Greatest Number). Thus, whether in the informal arena of the coffee house or the most formal of published philosophical works, the Argument from Analogy is a ubiquitous tool of the critical thinker.

Section 2.4: Trial Trilogy, Part 3 – *Crito*

Crito

Setting: The cell of Socrates. The time has come for the sentence of death to be carried out.

Socrates: Isn't it quite early, Crito? Or perhaps I'm mistaken.//
Crito: It's early. Around dawn.//
Socrates: Has the ship from Delos arrived?//
Crito: Not yet. But today, I believe. Listen, Socrates, it is not too late for you to escape. Your death would not be only a single grief; I would lose a friend – one as I should never have again, that is true. However, people who don't know us will say that I should have spent some of my money to help you escape. They will think I didn't care about you at all. Is there any reputation worse than being thought to value money over friends. After all, most people will think you wanted to escape, but that we did not want you to, when the opposite is true.//
Socrates: Dear Crito, have we ever concerned ourselves with what "most people" think?//
Crito: But Socrates, we must concern ourselves with what "most people" think! Don't you think that your current imprisonment is evidence enough of that. "Most people" can produce great evil upon one who is slandered in their midst.//
Socrates: Perhaps it would be good if the masses could produce such evil – would that not also mean they were capable of similarly great good? But, in reality, the masses or "most people" are incapable of both, It is beyond them to make a person wise or to make a person a fool.//
Crito: But Socrates, it won't even take much money. We don't even have to pay big bribes – they're cheap. I'm quite sure I have enough money. And, if it's not, Simias and Cebes stand ready to supplement the funds. Others too. Besides, Socrates, staying in prison under such circumstances is clearly unjust. It is wrong to die when you could save your life. And think of your children. You are betraying them. You are depriving them of the education you could give them. You are choosing the easiest course. The courageous person (and the good person) would choose the other course. That's even

more true if that person has claimed to live their entire life in pursuit of virtue.

Come, Socrates, if you delay much longer, it will be too late. Listen to my counsel, let us take action and go.

Socrates: Mercy Crito. If you are on target, then your passion is not at all wasted. So, we must see if your target is right – this will tell us whether we should act on your view or not. As you know, I am the sort of person who can be persuaded by reasonable argument, one that seems right as we reflect on it. After all it would be inconsistent to behave differently and ignore our arguments simply because this fate has befallen me. So, Crito, I look forward to this investigation. Consider this. Is it true that one must ignore all human opinions or just some and not others; that is, shouldn't we pay attention to good views?

Crito: Yes.

Socrates: So, must we listen to the views of the masses, or should we despise them. Or, on the other hand, suppose there is a person who knows about these things or is an expert. Isn't it the case that if we ignore the expert's view, we cause injury to ourselves because we are more likely to be harmed by injust actions rather than be made better by just ones. Is it worth it to live life when the body is ruined?

Crito: Not at all.

Socrates: So, is it worth it to live life with the soul ruined? It is, of course, the part of us that is improved by justice and ruined by injustice.

Crito: Of course not.

Socrates: That part is worth more than the body, right?

Crito: Most definitely.

Socrates: Then we shouldn't concern ourselves overmuch with the views of the masses, but instead with the view of the one of us that knows what justice and injustice are, and also the truth. Think about this: Living a good life is much better than simply living. Further, is it not the case that the good life, the fine life, and the just life are indeed the same?

Crito: It is.

Socrates: Thus far, we agree. So, next let us consider what is the just thing for me to do. Is it just to escape even though I have not been acquitted by the people of Athens? If it is, then we shall escape. However, should it prove unjust, we should then put the idea away. Besides, the questions raised before – about children, money, and reputation – these questions are not matters of justice. The only thing one should consider is whether or not one is acting justly, like a good person or bad one.

Crito: That is beautiful, Socrates. What should we do?

Socrates: So, we are agreed that a person should never intentionally do the wrong thing?

Crito: Yes.

Socrates: Even when we have ourselves been wronged, we should not harm in return – the masses hold a different view, that we should return wrong for wrong or injury for injury or harm for harm – but we do not because it is never permitted to do the wrong thing?

Crito: This is so.

Socrates: So, if a person has an agreement with another and the agreement is itself just, should he honor it or not?

Crito: It should be honored.

Socrates: Well then; if I were to escape, wouldn't it be the case that I would be harming those I should not harm? Isn't it the case that we are bound by a just covenant?

Crito: I don't understand.

Socrates: Consider this. If we were to escape, as you suggest, and the laws opposed us asking, "Socrates, what are your intentions?" How would the answer go? Could I say that the city has done me an injustice and the verdict was incorrect?

Crito: Yes, by Zeus. Precisely!

Socrates: So, what if the response of the city and the laws was something like this: "But what of our agreement, Socrates? Are you trying to destroy us? Why is that? Isn't it true that your parents were married through us and you were brought to life? Did you find fault in that? What of your upbringing and your education? Your parents were directed to see that you were educated. In us, you were born, raised, and educated. So, are we equals, you and we? You, who claim to care for virtue, is it not also part of your understanding that your country should be respected, nay revered, even above your own mother? To take up this accusation against us is no more than retaliation. You have lived among us all your days and not brought complaint. You must either persuade your country or, failing that, obey its directives – even if that means going to war where you could be injured or slain. Failing persuasion, obedience is right. It would be the height of impiety to war against your parents; it is much worse to make war against the country of your birth and upbringing." Do the laws speak truly?

Crito: Yes.

Socrates: Might they not continue, "Socrates, you know our law – when a person reaches adulthood and has seen how things work here – our customs, laws, and the workings of the city – we allow that person to take all that he has and to leave us if we are not to his liking. There are no obstacles to this – he can even retain all his goods. But, if he stays, having seen all these things, he has given consent to obey us. If we find ourselves in disagreement, if he thinks we have done wrong, he then has two options – persuade us or obey. These are your options. What if he does neither? That would be like you, Socrates – not the least guilty in the city, but the most." Suppose I asked why. Might they not say, "We have been agreeable to you these many years. Have you ever even left the city? Even to attend a festival? No. Except for a stint in the military, you have always been here. Other people travel to other cities. You do not. And we have always been satisfactory before. Even at your trial, you had the opportunity to suggest a counter-penalty that could have been exile. Now you are thinking about doing what you refused to do at trial, only this time, going into exile unlawfully, when you could have done so lawfully." How should we respond, Crito? Have they said anything untrue?

Crito: No. We must agree.

Socrates: They might say, "Think. Suppose you went to Megara or Thebes. These are reasonable cities. Suppose you went there – would you not get there as their enemy? Everyone who saw you would know that you had no regard for the laws of your own city. They would look on you with suspicion as a destroyer of laws. Further, you would prove that the Athenian jury was right all along – anyone who could so easily disregard the laws might just as easily corrupt the youth, teaching them to do the same. If you escape, if you leave having been wronged by the men of Athens, not by us, if you return evil for evil, breaking covenant, and doing wrong – if you do these things (and escaping is surely to do them all) then we shall be angry while you live and the laws of the underworld will be angry with you upon death. After all, you have tried to destroy us, why should they expect better from your hand."

Crito, my friend, my good friend, I hear these words as surely as if the laws were here to speak them. If you would oppose them, you may speak – but, in my present view, it would accomplish nothing.

Crito: I have nothing to say.

Socrates: Then it shall be as it is, Crito. Let us behave as we are, since this is the way we are guided by god.

~

Socrates was convicted by a jury of his peers. After the conviction, came the penalty phase. In Athenian jurisprudence, each side of a dispute was to propose a resolution or a punishment in the case of a conviction. Socrates's accusers were in favor of death. Socrates was given the opportunity to propose a counter-punishment. Rather than banishment or life in prison without the possibility of parole, Socrates proposes what he thinks is the proper recompense for what he has been doing. Since it is his view that he has been providing a great service to Athens, he says that it would be fair for him to be supported by the city for the rest of his life. But, failing that, he proposes a very minimal fine (all he can afford) that is enhanced somewhat by that of his friends gathered. The jury takes little time in dismissing Socrates's offer and imposes the penalty requested by his accusers. Socrates is taken away to await the day the ship from Delos arrives to signal the end of the religious festival during which executions were forbidden.

Section 2.4: Trial Trilogy, Part 3 - *Crito*

Early one morning, the day the ship is scheduled to arrive, Crito comes to visit Socrates in the cell where Socrates will drink the hemlock and bring an end to his life in the prescribed method of capital punishment of ancient Athens. Crito and his friends are apprehensive, but they have one more plan to try to save Socrates's life. Since the jury has convicted him, unjustly, of impiety and corrupting the youth, and since the jury has imposed a sentence of death rather than the alternative proposed by Socrates (with the backing of Crito, Simmias, and Cebes), Crito tries to persuade Socrates that it would be justifiable for him to escape the judgment of the Athenian court and flee to another city in Greece. Crito points out that he has family in Thessaly and that Megara and Thebes are also well-governed cities that would welcome a person of Socrates's stature to their gates. But, Crito is also aware that such temptations – to save his life and to live in a place where he might be better received – are not likely to sway Socrates from his commitment to stay and endure his sentence, even a sentence of death. So, he makes several appeals to Socrates.

"Consider your family, Socrates. And your friends. And your reputation. And the comfort given to your enemies because of your death." All these and more, Crito pours out in a rush to seemingly try to overwhelm Socrates with the reasons that escape would be the most beneficial for him. However, unlike Euthyphro, Crito knows Socrates personally and not just as a teacher in Athens or by reputation. Crito knows Socrates as *his* friend and one who relentlessly pursues truth, wisdom, and the care of the soul. Thus, Crito knows that none of these appeals are likely to sway Socrates. Each would fall to the elenchus just as each definition of Piety fell in the *Euthyphro*. Socrates has said again and again, both in the *Apology* and elsewhere, that it is never appropriate to do something unjust (or wrong). Rather than create an excuse to be elsewhere, Crito offers the one reason for Socrates to escape that Socrates has to address: "Socrates, it would be unjust *not* to escape."

In Crito's final justification for his plan to help Socrates escape, he puts the onus on Socrates to show how he could avoid doing something wrong by remaining in Athens, in jail, and awaiting death. Simply put, the argument would seem to be something like this:

> Crito 1. One should never do anything that is unjust.
> Crito 2. Remaining in Athens (not escaping) is unjust.
> -----
> Conclusion. Therefore, Socrates should escape.

Socrates, perhaps recognizing that in this rare circumstance one of his interlocutors has actually been paying attention to the sorts of arguments that Socrates has himself made, proposes a counterargument to Crito's. Socrates's view can be cast as follows.

> Socrates 1. One should never do anything that is unjust.
> Socrates 2. Escaping is unjust.
> -----
> Conclusion. Therefore, Socrates should not escape.

By putting the arguments into these forms, we can see clearly where Socrates and Crito agree and where they disagree. Socrates and Crito agree on the first point, namely that doing something that is unjust is never justifiable. The issue, then, is the contradictory second premises: "Remaining in Athens is unjust" and "Escaping is unjust." In each case, the second premise forces the conclusion concerning what Socrates should do. Thus, the rest of the *Crito* is an effort by Socrates to discover which of the second premises, Crito 2 or Socrates 2, is the right one.

At this point in the dialogue, a rather strange scene unfolds. Up to this point, Socrates and Crito have been participating in a kind of abbreviated elenchus. After coming to the two competing premises, Socrates turns to a different interlocutor, the "Laws." Some translations will refer to Socrates's interlocutor as the Laws; others as the laws. The distinction is an important one, as we will see after discussing Plato's Theory of Forms in the next section. At this point, suffice it to say, that those scholars of ancient philosophy who think that Plato, or perhaps Socrates, has a Theory of Forms in the early Socratic dialogues will often translate the Greek word refers to Socrates's interrogator, *nomoi* as "Laws" while those who think that the Theory of Forms is found exclusively in the middle Platonic dialogues and later will translate *nomoi* as "laws." Whatever the case, whether the *nomoi* are the laws of Athens or the Laws of the Forms, the odd thing here is that they assume the role that Socrates normally plays – inquisitor.

To be sure, this elenchus is an imaginary one – what Socrates thinks the Laws would say if they could come into his cell and examine him as he has examined others. To this point, Socrates has been the one asking the questions; now it is his turn to answer them. Again, the point is made that Socrates thinks it is never appropriate to do the wrong thing (that is, the thing contrary to justice). It cannot be the case that Socrates is being chastised for breaking (or thinking of breaking) the law, however. Legality or illegality does not seem to be the issue. Socrates has broken the law previously and is not called to task for that. In his trial, Socrates reminded the court that he had refused to follow the directions of his own group when they had held the high office in Athens. This was because they made a decision that was both illegal and unjust. Immediately after his telling of this story, he tells another; of a time during the reign of the Thirty Tyrants when he was directed, along with four others, to go and bring Leon of Salamis in for summary execution. Rather than follow the lawful order of the rulers of Athens, Socrates went home. He, himself, acknowledges that this was an action that went contrary to the law and that could have resulted in his own death had the Thirty not been overthrown shortly thereafter.

So, in the first case, it might be thought that Socrates is in the unenviable position of being unable to keep one law without breaking another. If that is the case, then the breaking of some law or other is inevitable. In such cases, one should side with justice, on Socrates's view. In the second case, however, there is no such possibility and the distinction between law and justice is drawn more sharply. In order for Socrates's to behave in accordance with justice, he must act contrary to the law. Thus, when Socrates's refuses to go and bring Leon to the Thirty, he violates the law and yet acts justly.

The question facing Socrates in his imaginary elenchus with the Laws is not one of legality or illegality. It is a question of justice; of acting like a good person or a bad one. The questioning of Socrates by the Laws is fairly straightforward. Socrates is directed to reflect on all that the Laws and the city have provided him – birth, nurture, education, all the good things that the Laws and the city could provide. Further, because Socrates is an Athenian citizen, he had the option to leave the city, taking with him all of his possessions and suffering no ill consequences earlier in his life. All Athenian citizens of a certain age were given this opportunity to decide whether or not they agreed with the laws of the city and its customs and whether or not they could abide by them. If, upon reflection, the decision was "no," then the citizen could depart the city at no penalty, either of goods or reputation. This explicit acceptance of the agreement between Socrates and the Laws is the starting point of the elenchus. It does not end here, however. After Socrates has reflected on this agreement, the Laws come to the crux of the matter. Much like with the earlier elenchus with Crito, the simple fact of an agreement does not stand as a reason for Socrates to accept the judgment of the Athenian court and remain. After all, only if the agreement is itself just should Socrates adhere to it. If the agreement runs counter to justice, then it would not be just to uphold it. There is further reason to suppose that Socrates holds this to be true. In *Republic*, Book One, Socrates considers the possibility that the definition of Justice is the keeping of one's promises and returning to someone that which he had lent. But, he wonders, suppose a perfectly sane person loaned him a knife. Suppose further that the person loaning the knife then went insane and demanded the knife back so that he could kill himself and others. In such a case, it would be unjust to return the knife to him. So, simply because there *is* an agreement does not make it a binding one. Agreement alone does not entail justice.

Like Crito before them, the Laws turn from the first proposition (agreements) to the central question – whether it would be just for Socrates to escape. Here, the argument that Socrates seems to hear goes something like this:

> Laws 1. One should never do anything unjust.
> Laws 2. It is unjust to wrong someone who has not wronged you.
> Laws 3. The Laws have not wronged Socrates.
> Laws 4. By escaping, Socrates would wrong the Laws.
> -----
> Conclusion 1: By escaping, Socrates would do something unjust.
> Conclusion 2: Therefore, Socrates should not escape.

Again, the first premise is one with which Socrates clearly agrees – as does Crito. The second is a direct implication of Socrates's own view that it is never appropriate to do something unjust. Even in the case of an injustice being done to Socrates, it is not appropriate for him to return wrong for wrong. One way of putting that is in the famous saying, "Two wrongs don't make a right." That is somewhat applicable here, but not precisely. Generally, the old saying refers to doing harm to the person who has first done harm. This is not the situation in which the Laws say that Socrates is. In Socrates's case, he would be harming one who had not harmed him at all. The Laws do not disagree that Socrates has been treated unjustly and that his conviction is an unjust one. However, it was not they, the Laws, who convicted Socrates. The court convicted Socrates, perhaps using the Laws unjustly, but nevertheless, it was the courts doing. Having been harmed by men, Socrates would now harm the Laws – and thus, not return harm for harm, but actually harm an innocent to make up for the harm he has received from the hand of another. This is the justification for premises 3 and 4. From these four premises, the conclusions follow rather quickly. Since one should never do anything unjust, and since it is unjust to wrong someone who has not wronged you, and since the Laws have not wronged Socrates, and since by escaping Socrates would be harming the Laws, then by escaping, Socrates would be doing something unjust. Since one should never do something unjust and by escaping, Socrates would be doing something unjust, then Socrates should not escape. Socrates closes the dialogue by saying that this is precisely the words that he seems to hear in his imagined elenchus with the Laws. Crito assents.

Guided Reading Questions

1. What does Crito want Socrates to do and how does he try to convince him to do it?
2. Why does Socrates feel that he should not try to escape?

3. Are there any circumstances in which Socrates feels it would be right to do wrong?

Questions for Reflection:
1. Can the Laws of a state or country be wrong? Why or why not?
2. Is it ever okay to break a law? Why or why not? Under what circumstances?
3. Do you think Socrates did the right thing? Why or why not?

Logic Blurb
Validity

At the heart of the charge of "sophistry" against Socrates was the view that he was somehow taking weak or poor arguments and through tricks of rhetoric and sleight of hand overthrowing stronger ones. Oftentimes, the person who finds himself on what he takes to be the losing end of an argument will attribute his poor showing not to an inherently weak position or an indefensible view or simply his own failure to think clearly and analytically. Instead, he will cling to his position, all evidence and argument to the contrary. For example, as Euthyphro took leave of Socrates at the conclusion of the *Euthyphro*, we have no reason to suppose that he recognized that his arguments had failed and that he had been shown for the puffed up fraud that he was. Rather, one can imagine Euthyphro ruminating over the slights of being misunderstood, thinking to himself that if he had only said this or that other thing that Socrates would have been cowed by his erudition. What Euthyphro failed to see, and what so many interlocutors, ancient and contemporary fail to see, is that their arguments themselves are not merely weak, but invalid.

Valid arguments can be distinguished from *invalid* ones in several ways. The first, and most objective, is an application of the rules of formal structure to the argument. For example, if the conclusions proceed directly and deductively from the premises, then the argument is valid. Take the following as an example.

> Major Premise: All bachelors are unmarried males.
> Minor Premise: Tom is a bachelor.
> -----
> Conclusion: Tom is an unmarried male.

In this argument, the conclusion is completely contained within the preliminary premises. Insofar as the premises are true, the conclusion is inescapable. This argument would be considered a valid one.

Arguments that adhere to this formal structure may be invalid for several reasons. There are three possibilities – the premises are themselves false, the conclusion does not follow from the premises, or the conclusion is ampliative. Arguments that fall victim to informal fallacies (e.g., the Fallacy of the Beard) are also invalid, but these are treated in later blurbs. Let us treat the formal invalidities in order.

Invalid arguments where the premises themselves are false can be quite compelling, although they are relatively easy to spot. For example, the if the minor premise of the foregoing example, ("Tom is a bachelor") is false because Tom is, in fact, married, then the conclusion will also be false. Thus, the argument is invalid.

Another form of invalid argument is one in which all the premises are true, but the conclusion is disconnected or only tenuously connected to the premises. Often deeply emotionally held beliefs are propped up by this sort of argument. These arguments are only compelling because of the emotional tenor of the premises. The conclusions are likely to be held, even in the face of great evidence to the contrary, not because of the premises themselves, but because of the emotional commitment to the conclusion. This sort of fallacy is closely related to informal fallacies like the *Appeal to Authority*, *Irrelevant Reason*, and *Slippery Slope*. These informal fallacies are likely to commit this formal one as well and so during the reading in those sections, reference can be made to this one. For simplicity's sake, however, we will treat a strictly formal example here. An invalid argument in which all of the premises are true but the argument is invalid might be something like the following.

> P1: All Irish Setters are dogs.
> P2: All dogs are mammals.
> -----
> C: Frank is a mammal.

On the face of it, this argument could be valid under certain circumstances. If Frank is an Irish Setter, for example, then the conclusion would follow from the premises. However, let us suppose that Frank is a chimpanzee. In that case, all of the premises are true, but the argument is invalid.

An *ampliative* argument is one in which the premises are connected to the conclusion, but the conclusion extends beyond what the premises themselves support. This sort of invalid argument often involves a mistake with universal or existential quantifiers. For example, suppose we have an argument like this. Three scientists have undertaken the task of finding and cataloguing ravens. So far, they have isolated 312 ravens and all of them have been black. So, we have an iteration of experiments as our premises.

Section 2.4: Trial Trilogy, Part 3 - *Crito*

> P1: Raven 1 is black.
> P2: Raven 2 is black.
> ...
> P312: Raven 312 is black.

Let us suppose that from these trials, they come to the conclusion, then, that "all ravens are black." This is clearly an ampliative argument because the conclusion about "all ravens" is so far supported by only a small number of actually observed ravens. Here we have a possibility of demonstrating that the conclusion is false because if, with the 313th observation, they discovered a green raven, then the conclusion would be rejected. That there is space, then, between the premises and the conclusion as demonstrated by the potential counterexample demonstrates that the conclusion goes beyond what can be supported by the premises.

The evaluation of arguments is at times a difficult process. Careful analysis of premises and conclusions is essential, but not sufficient. One must also strictly observe the relationships between those premises and conclusions in order to grasp the strength or weakness of an argument. Determining whether an argument is valid or invalid is a first step in developing the analytical tools necessary to find success as a critical thinker.

Section 3.1 – Plato and the Virtue of Socrates

While Socrates was philosophy's first martyr, he is generally considered to have been eclipsed by a considerable margin by his student, Plato. Plato's work is quite compelling, both as work in philosophy and as work in literature. Indeed, it is its great readability and literary significance that sometimes make it difficult to fully grasp the philosophical work being done within it. There is considerable scholarly debate about the precise role that the dialogues played within Plato's Academy, but what is beyond serious dispute is that the dialogues were, in fact, crucial not only to the educational programme of the Academy, but also as works within which serious philosophical arguments are being made. New readers of Plato often find themselves swept away by the conversation within the text, riding the ebb and flow of the interaction, and in the process, find themselves sliding past important premises of arguments lost in the intrigue of the interchange between Socrates and his interlocutors. Thus, both a strength and a weakness of the dialogue style, at least in the hands of a masterful writer like Plato, is the literary genius that is expressed there.

Works of literature though they are, the Platonic dialogues are up to more than presenting compelling conversations. The careful reader of the dialogues will turn the conversations over and over in her mind, returning again and again to them and discovering extraordinarily sophisticated arguments about ethics, metaphysics, and epistemology. This is somewhat easier in the later dialogues as the literary style of Plato's earlier ones gives way slightly to a more obvious set of philosophical investigations. However, this does not really help the reader overmuch. The reason for this is that the character "Socrates" plays less and less of a role in the later dialogues, sometimes not appearing at all and at times being present merely as a silent, or mostly silent, observer. Thus, while premises and conclusions of arguments are slightly more easily found, often right at the very surface of the interlocutor's conversations, the question becomes which of those interlocutors speaks for the Platonic view. Perhaps more than one does. Perhaps none. Whatever the case, it is a difficulty that is not found in the earlier dialogues. In the middle dialogues, like the *Republic*, it is generally accepted that "Socrates" is a mouthpiece for Plato and Plato's views. The early dialogues share this feature, but as they are considerably more readable than the late work, the difficulty of becoming enthralled by the style and missing the arguments is more pronounced. However, it is a fruitful project to read carefully the early dialogues and tease out the premises and conclusions from the text. A prime example of this sort of process is the examination of the relationship between knowledge and virtue, between epistemology and ethics, that Plato explores in the Trial Trilogy, in general, and within the *Apology*, in particular.

Was Socrates wise? In the *Apology*, Socrates recognizes that the "old charges," or the prejudices of the jury, are the most serious threats to his case. Those charges, that he is a Natural Philosopher and a Sophist (and most importantly, that he is a Sophist), are summarized briefly at the outset of the dialogue in this way, "there is this man, Socrates, a 'wise' man, who inquires into things in the heavens and beneath the earth." Given that Socrates is clearly thought by Plato to have been unjustly convicted, it is easy to suppose that Socrates is, indeed, wise. After all, in addition to being the protagonist of the *Euthyphro/Apology/Crito* trilogy, the Oracle at Delphi has made the pronouncement that Socrates is the wisest in all of Athens. After questioning the craftspeople, the poets, politicians, and all those with a reputation for wisdom, and having shown that they are overcome with false beliefs while he is not, surely we can conclude that Socrates is not only the wisest in Athens, but also possesses wisdom.

To come to this conclusion would be to ultimately interpret the trilogy and the historical Socrates in a way foreign to Plato. For Plato, there is a very real distinction between being the wisest and actually being wise. To discuss this question in depth, we must first examine three Platonic doctrines that are involved. The first of these is the Priority of Definition discussed in earlier sections (See *Euthyphro*). By way of review, the Priority of Definition is the epistemological principle that to have knowledge is to be able to give the definition of some concept. Thus, to know what *piety* is is to be able to proffer a definition of *piety* that survives elenctic testing.

The second of the doctrines is somewhat more controversial, or at least more counterintuitive, than the first. Part of the motivation for the search for definitions has to do with the Theory of Forms (Section 3.3). However, given that Socrates is at pains to get the Athenians to care for truth, wisdom, and the perfection of the soul (Section 2.3 – *Apology*), it is not surprising that the majority of the definitions he seeks are the definitions of the virtues, or the ethical character traits. Keeping in mind the Priority of Definition in addition to this emphasis on knowledge of the virtues, it is almost to be expected that Socrates would think that there exists an intimate relationship between knowledge and virtue. To be sure, Socrates's view turns out to be somewhat controversial, but it does capture an important intuition. The relationship between knowledge and virtue, on Socrates's view, is as follows: To know the good is to do the good. Or, formally,

> *Epistemological Principle of Ethics*
> If X knows the good, then X will do the good.

Now, at first glance, this view may seem quite counterintuitive. A common experience is that a person knowing what he ought to do, knowing what duty required, knowing the good, and perhaps even telling himself that he would do it, and then, next thing he knows, not only has he not done it, he has followed precisely the opposite course. This weakness of will, or *akrasia*, is a phenomenon to which Aristotle gives considerable attention; Plato considerably less. On Plato's view, to fail to follow the good course of action is a failure of knowledge. While the person thought he knew what the good was, because he did not do it, it indicates that he, in fact, did not know the good. However, that the experience of *akrasia*, or weakness of will, is fairly common would seem to suggest to us that Socrates's Epistemological Principle of Ethics is perhaps misguided. However, to discount it totally is to make, at the same time, a similar mistake. In this case, the mistake is ignoring or rejecting a very important ethical intuition.

Suppose that Frank does not know the good, does not know what he ought to do at some given moment. The odds that he will then do whatever is required, that he will do the good, are quite poor. If, by some accident, he does the good, it will only be because he stumbled upon it. He will not possess virtue simply because he accidentally performed one good action. Thus, it seems that knowledge of the good is at least necessary for virtue, even if it is not sufficient. Thus, the rejection of Socrates's principle, if it is to be rejected at all, is a rejection of the notion that knowledge of the virtues is *sufficient* for virtue and not that knowledge of virtue is *necessary* for virtue.

The third, and last, of these doctrines is the much more controversial Unity of Virtues doctrine. There is a cottage industry in Ancient philosophy around the question of the Unity of Virtue. For Plato, in both the early Socratic works and the later Platonic ones, the virtues are unified. Simply put, the doctrine is that if one possesses one virtue (e.g., *courage*), then one must necessarily possess all of them. The converse holds as well. To fail to possess all of the virtues together is to fail to possess even a single one. Thus, on Socrates/Plato's view, it is not possible for a person to have the virtue *piety* and fail to have the virtue *courage*. While this is somewhat counterintuitive, perhaps, it follows directly from positions to which Socrates/Plato is committed in the Socratic dialogues. At the conclusion of the *Euthyphro*, while all attempts at defining *piety* have failed, one aspect of one definition remains on the table. In the fourth attempt, Euthyphro claims that piety is "part of justice concerned with looking after the gods." While the latter part of that definition is refuted, the former part (the "part of justice"), is not. Later, when Plato is discussing the ideal city in *Republic*, we discover that *piety* is subsumed totally into *justice*. Thus, from the

Euthyphro forward, the notion that *piety* is intimately related to *justice* is present. In the *Protagoras*, Socrates argues again that *piety* is a part of *justice*. However, here he goes further. He also argues that *sophrosune* (moderation, temperance, control of self) is part of *wisdom*, that *sophrosune* is part of *justice*, and that *wisdom* is a part of *courage*. Simply put, if we continue to hold that Socrates Epistemological Principle of Ethics, namely that "to know the good is to do the good," it follows that if one knows *piety* and, by extension, that *piety* is a part of *justice*, then one must also know what part of *justice* that it is. Since *justice* is related to *sophrosune*, *sophrosune* to *wisdom*, and *wisdom* to *courage*, then to know any one virtue is to know how that virtue fits within the web of the virtues. Further, if one has this knowledge, then one will possess all of the virtues because one possesses the definitions of them; that is, one knows them. Similarly, to fail to know how all of the virtues are related to one another is to fail to know how even one of them fully. Such a failure entails a failure to possess the virtue. Thus, from Socrates/Plato's commitments, the Unity of Virtues doctrine seems to follow rather straightforwardly.

This returns the conversation to the very important question about the wisdom of Socrates. Recall that there is a distinction, at least on Plato's view, between being the wisest among a group and actually possessing wisdom. This distinction is more important than simply noting the difference between the best of a mediocre bunch and actually possessing the virtue. Answering the "Is Socrates wise?" question actually has implications for understanding the Socratic mission discussed in previous sections. As we explore this question, the importance of the distinction will become more evident. Let us begin to explore the question by first supposing that the answer is "yes."

To begin, we note the Epistemological Principle of Ethics, that is, "If a person is wise, then he has knowledge of the virtues." Since we have assumed that Socrates is, in fact, wise, then, by Modus Ponens, we have that Socrates must have knowledge of the virtues. If Socrates has knowledge of the virtues, then he has been lying every time he has claimed to have no knowledge of them. When he told Euthyphro that he did not know what *piety* was, or Laches that he did not know *courage*, or the court assembled to hear his defense that he did not have knowledge of the things about which he continued to ask, he was, in fact, practicing the sort of rhetorical gamesmanship that was common to the Sophists. That is, he was being ironic, or in fact, lying, in order to trip up his opponent in the argument. Thus, if Socrates truly has knowledge of the virtues, then he is lying when he says he does not. Since, we have assumed that Socrates does know the virtues, it must follow that we are committed to the implication that Socrates is indeed lying. Thus, not only is Socrates lying, but he is playing the Sophist as he lies in order to compromise his interlocutors. Thus, Socrates is guilty of Sophistry (which clearly Plato is trying to argue against).

Nevertheless, if Socrates is a Sophist, then he cannot be virtuous. This is because the Sophists are portrayed, by Plato and by the crowd gathered to try

Section 3.1: Plato and the Virtue of Socrates

Socrates, to be the opposite of virtue, or to be vicious. If this were not so, then it would not be nearly as pressing that the Sophists be tried, convicted, and eliminated from Athenian life. So, we can safely conclude that in being a Sophist, Socrates is likewise excluded from virtue. If this is so, however, we know by implication that Socrates cannot be wise. From the Unity of Virtues, it follows that if one is virtuous, then one is wise and, conversely, that if one is wise, one is also virtuous. Given that Socrates is not virtuous, then it follows that he is not wise. However, if he is not wise, as we have concluded, then we have reasoned to a contradiction. Since our assumption was that Socrates *was* wise and since this assumption led us directly into a contradiction, it must be concluded that our assumption was false. Whenever an assumption forces a contradiction, it is safe to jettison the assumption in favor of its negation. Thus, the negation of our assumption must be "Socrates is *not* wise." Thus, we have a conclusion to the question of the wisdom of Socrates; namely that Socrates is not wise. This argument can be reflected in a much more formal way. Below is the formally rendered proof.

Question: Is Socrates wise?
Assumption: Socrates is wise.

	Statement		Justification
1.	If X is wise, then X has knowledge of the virtues.	1.	Epistemological Principle of Ethics
2.	Socrates is wise.	2.	Assumption
3.	Therefore, Socrates has knowledge of the virtues.	3.	Modus Ponens (1,2)
4.	If Socrates has knowledge of the virtues, then his professions of ignorance are lies.	4.	Definition of Lying
5.	Socrates is lying.	5.	Modus Ponens (4,3)
6.	If Socrates is lying, then Socrates is a Sophist.	6.	Definition of Sophist
7.	Socrates is a Sophist.	7.	Modus Ponens (6,5)
8.	If Socrates is a Sophist, then Socrates is not virtuous.	8.	Definition of Sophist
9.	Socrates is not virtuous.	9.	Modus Ponens (8,7)
10.	If Socrates is not virtuous, then Socrates is not wise.	10.	Unity of Virtues
11.	Socrates is not wise.	11.	Modus Ponens (10,9)
12.	Therefore, Socrates is wise and not wise	12.	2 & 11
13.	Therefore, the assumption (2) is false.	13.	Contradiction

14.	Therefore, Socrates is not wise.	14. 1-13

As it happens, there is another way to approach this question of the wisdom of Socrates. Since the assumption that Socrates is wise has led us to the conclusion that he is indeed not, perhaps it would be helpful to begin with that assumption. So, if we begin with the assumption that Socrates is not wise, it would follow from the Epistemological Principle of Ethics and Socrates's own professions of ignorance, by Modus Tollens, that he is not wise. Recall again the Epistemological Principle of Ethics, that if Socrates is wise, then Socrates has knowledge of the virtues. Accepting Socrates's professions of ignorance at face value, we have that Socrates does not know the virtues. Thus, by Modus Tollens, we conclude that Socrates is not wise. This can be represented formally as follows:

Question: Is Socrates wise?
Assumption: Socrates does not know the virtues

	Statement		Justification
1.	If X is wise, then X has knowledge of the virtues.	1.	Epistemological Principle of Ethics
2.	Socrates does not know the virtues	2.	Professions of Ignorance
3.	Therefore, Socrates is not wise.	3.	Modus Tollens (1, 2)

Thus, we can conclude that Socrates is indeed not wise. Whether we assume at the outset that he is wise or that he does not know the virtues, then the conclusion is the same. Thus, Plato's defense of Socrates, a defense that rests heavily upon the outcome of the Socratic Wisdom question, is preserved. Socrates is not a Sophist because he neither possesses wisdom nor the knowledge of the virtues.

Logic Blurb
The Method of Hypothesis

Socrates was famous, or perhaps infamous, for his use of the *elenchus* to test the beliefs of his interlocutors, showing which of them were necessarily false; or at the very least, demonstrating that the sets of beliefs were contradictory. There is great scholarly debate among scholars of Ancient philosophy concerning whether or not it is possible to glean any positive conclusions from the *elenchus* or if, instead, it serves merely the negative function of cleansing the mind of false beliefs but leaving nothing in its wake. There are two reasons for this "negative only" view. First, all of the interlocutors at the conclusion of the *elenchus* either concede that they have no definitions left to offer, that they are confused, or that they must leave, threaten Socrates with bodily harm, or think more on the matter. Given this lack of positive formulation of a proposition, there is reason to think that the "negative only" view is the right one. Second, while Plato does not abandon the *elenchus* as his writings progress, he does supplement the *elenchus* with other forms of argument that clearly do advance positive claims. As Plato moves from the early, Socratic dialogues into a set of transitional dialogues (e.g., *Meno*, *Phaedo*, *Protagoras*), he introduces a different form of argument, the Argument from Hypothesis.

The Method of Hypothesis is a very common approach to problems that require a bit of critical thinking. A hypothesis is a provisional claim the truth value of which an investigator proposes to determine. So, for example, a hypothesis could be "The sun revolves around the earth." Setting out to discover whether or not such a proposition is true, the investigator appropriates the evidence available. Since the sun rises in the east, makes its track across the sky and sets in the west while the earth remains perfectly still under our feet, it seems clear that the hypothesis is supported. However, the hypothesis, while supported in the mind of the investigator at the time, is not straightforwardly endorsed as true. A careful thinker always admits that the hypothesis under which she is working could, with the appearance of further evidence, turn out to be false. Thus, when it is discovered that the earth actually spins on an axis and that, relative to the earth, the sun is stationary while the earth does the revolving, then the investigator recognizes that the initial hypothesis has been defeated and thus is to be rejected. In the process, a new hypothesis arises, "The earth revolves around the sun." This new hypothesis is then subject to the same sort of evidential scrutiny that the former one was. This sort of hypothesis is an *empirically* testable hypothesis. All conclusions of empirically testable hypotheses are necessarily provisional and constantly subject to revision and refinement. This is not to suggest that a refining of a hypothesis is a rejection of the hypothesis. For example, Darwinian evolutionary theory is constantly refined by careful observation of biologists of all sorts. That the theory is refined and, in the process, elements of Darwin's own view are rejected, is not a rejection of the foundational hypothesis. It is merely evidence of the progression of scientific knowledge from hypothesis to hypothesis. The distinction between the Method of Hypothesis and the *elenchus* should be clear. While evidence may serve to discredit one hypothesis, the rejection of the initial hypothesis will, necessarily, give rise to a new one. Thus, while a false belief may be rejected, a replacement arises for testing.

The empirically testable hypothesis is not the only sort of hypothesis in the Method of Hypothesis. A famous hypothesis that is not empirically testable is Fermat's Last Theorem. In the margin of one of the books of his library (the *Arithmetica* by the ancient Greek mathematician, Diophantus) Fermat wrote that he had discovered a proof of one of the propositions of Diophantus. However, he never wrote a proof down nor did he make mention of it beyond this one intriguing citation. Thus, for centuries mathematicians of various gifts attempted to discover a proof of the proposition. Not until Andrew Wiles demonstrated that Fermat's Last Theorem was, in fact, true did the hypothesis gain the status of a theorem of mathematics. Here, a hypothesis is tested through deductive means and is not falsifiable by some later experiment. This is similar to Plato's famous Slave-Boy example in the *Meno*. Presented with a geometric problem, Plato walks the young slave boy through a sort of geometric deduction. The conclusion of that argument is a rationally verifiable hypothesis. In both of these cases, many trial hypotheses were employed and rejected before a deductive argument supporting the final conclusion was put forward.

The Method of Hypothesis, then, is a useful argument tool. Coupled with an elenctic rejection of false beliefs, careful empirical testing, and reflective rational verification, the Method of Hypothesis can supply the investigator with positive formulations of doctrines and propositions in addition to the negative elimination of false ones.

Section 3.2 – Socrates, Philosophy's Martyr

Phaedo

Setting: Phlius (on the Peloponnese). Phaedo is telling some of his friends of the last hours of Socrates.

Echecrates: Phaedo, were you with him, with Socrates, the day he drank the hemlock? Did you hear of it, or were you really there?

Phaedo: I was actually there.

Echecrates: What did he say? Did he have any last words?

Phaedo: I will tell everything I know.

"Socrates" to Simmias and Cebes: If I did not believe I was going to the good gods and to the wise, I should indeed resent death, and I am wrong not to. But know this, I am sure I will be with the good. For this reason, I have no resentment at my fate. I know there is a better future ahead, one after death. We've heard this for years. And it is a better future for the good than it is for the evil. Don't we think death exists?

"Simmias": Yes.

"Socrates": What is death? Isn't it the separation of the soul from the body? Is there anything more to death than that?

"Simmias": No.

"Socrates": So, a person's foremost concern should be for the soul, right? And, don't you believe that it is the philosopher who is most capable of freeing the soul from the body as much as possible in this life?

"Simmias": I do.

"Socrates": So, what about knowledge? Is the body a hindrance or a help in the pursuit of knowledge? If the soul is the part of a person that attains the truth, doesn't the body become a hindrance, deceiving the soul at every point?"

"Simmias": This is so.

"Socrates": Is it not the case that in the action of reasoning that the soul comes most close to the way things really are? And further, that the soul is most able when it is free from the troublesome nature of the bodily senses – withdrawing from sight and sound, pain and pleasure – alone with itself in its quest for truth. Isn't it so that the philosopher's soul longs to be free from the body and alone with itself?

"Simmias": Yes.

"Socrates": And what about these – don't we say that there is the Just itself; and the Beautiful; and the Good? But, these no one has actually seen. Indeed, no senses of the body apprehends these. Things like Shape, Health, Strength, and, to be sure, the real essence of every single thing – these are beyond our senses as well.

"Simmias": True.

"Socrates": If this is so, then the person who approaches these most closely is the one who does so by reasoning alone – apart from sight, sound, taste and the others – these serve only to hinder thought. The person who does this best is the one who uses pure reason alone, since this is the only way to acquire truth and in turn wisdom. That is the person most likely to understand reality, right?

"Simmias": This seems true.

"Socrates": So, the only way to acquire true knowledge is to be free of the body and to see things as they are in themselves. And the ones who engage in philosophy properly are those who wish to be free of the body and to liberate the soul. This liberation is the intent of philosophers. In fact, the ones who do philosophy properly who are actually in the practice of dying and fear death the least. In fact, wouldn't it be unreasonable to fear death? Even the masses agree that moderation (σωφροσυνη) is the control of passion, the control of self, the treating of one's passions dispassionately. But this is not the way of the masses, but is the life of philosophy. Consider, then, courage. The masses think death a great evil. The brave among the masses face death, but they do it because of fear of an even greater evil. Thus, it is fear that makes them brave? Is it not odd to suppose that we become brave through cowardice? And moderation (σωφροσυνη) the same. For fear of the control of pleasure over their lives, they avoid those pleasures. But being in the thrall of pleasure is called license. So, moderation (σωφροσυνη) is gained through its opposite? I do not think this is right. The only method for attaining these virtues is wisdom. With wisdom, Courage, Σωφροσυνη, Justice, indeed all Virtue, is attained. It does not matter if pleasure is there or not.

I have no regrets and have left nothing undone. If we have had any success, I think we will know it shortly when we have arrived in the underworld. My defense is done, Simmias and Cebes. I am right to depart without complaining, indeed, with eagerness, knowing that there, like here, I shall find worthy friends. Hopefully, I have convinced you beyond my convincing of the jury.

"Cebes": You have spoken well and convincingly. But, I know it is hard to believe your view on the soul. Most people think that when the soul leaves the body that it doesn't exist any longer, that is decays and dissolves and is destroyed just as the body is, only it happens in the very instant that it leaves the body when a person dies; that it flies away like smoke and is dispersed just as surely. It would be good if what you say about the soul is true, Socrates, but I think much persuasive argument must be brought to bear if people are to be convinced that the soul continues to live after the body has died.

"Socrates": You are right, Cebes. Shall we investigate whether it is true.

"Cebes": I would love to hear your view, Socrates.

"Socrates": How shall we proceed? Let us begin in this way – do the souls of the people who have died continue to exist in the underworld or do they not. There is a very old view that the souls that inhabit that place come from here and that they return and are reborn here. Let us think for a moment. Many things have opposites and necessarily arise from those opposites. For example, isn't it true that if we look at something that it larger, it must have arisen from that which was smaller? And, similarly, that which is smaller must have come from that which was larger?

"Cebes": Yes.

"Socrates": So, too, the weaker arises from the stronger and the stronger from the weaker? Also the faster from the slower and the slower from the faster?

"Cebes": Yes.

"Socrates": So, is there something that is the opposite of living, then? In the same way that waking is the opposite of sleeping?

"Cebes": Yes.

"Socrates": And it is…?

"Cebes": Why, being dead, of course.

"Socrates": So, if these are opposites, living and being dead, then they must each come from the other, like the process of going to sleep and waking up. Do you buy that?

"Cebes": Yes.

"Socrates": So, this must be true about life and death; that like sleeping and waking, they each come from the other; that being dead comes from having been alive and that being alive must come from having been dead."

"Cebes": So it seems.

"Socrates": Thus, if the living arise from the dead and the dead from the living, then the soul must continue to exist and exist in the underworld.

"Cebes": This must be our conclusion.

"Socrates": So, we must conclude, then, that if the living come from the dead and the dead from the living, that the souls must exist somewhere or else they could not return to enliven the dead.

"Socrates": Let us inquire, now, what are the kinds of things that can be broken into pieces? What are the sorts of things that one might worry would break and what things would be immune from such a worry? From this, we can then inquire as to which of these sorts of things a soul is. Now, anything that has a complex nature, that is comprised of parts, this sort of thing can suffer breakage and be divided?

"Cebes": I would say that this is true, Socrates.

"Socrates": So, isn't it so that things that are in one state of being and that will stay in that state are not going to be comprised of parts, but will be simple; and only those things that change over time will be comprised of parts?

"Cebes": Yes.

"Socrates": Let us think again about the Forms, the reality that is in constant existence. Are they immutable or do they change? Can the Equal or the Beautiful, every thing as it truly is, the real thing, can it ever suffer change? Or, instead, are they always exactly the same, immutable in all ways?

"Cebes": They must be immutable, Socrates.

"Socrates": So, what of beautiful things? Whether the beautiful thing is a person, a horse, clothes, or anything that is particular? What of things that are equal to each other? Are these always the same or do they change, especially with relation to each other?

"Cebes": They are never the same from one moment to the next, so it must be that they change.

"Socrates": These, then, are the things that are perceived through the senses?

"Cebes": Yes.

"Socrates": So, there are two types of existence – there is the visible and the invisible; the visible suffering changes and the invisible existing immutably?

"Cebes": This seems so.

"Socrates": So, one of these corresponds to our body and the other to our soul. Which of the types is more like our body and which more like the soul?

"Cebes": The body is more like the visible and the soul, the invisible.

"Socrates": So, the soul then is like the invisible reality and the body is like the visible reality.

Consider this. If the soul and the body are together, then one is subordinate to the other because nature dictates that it should be so, and the other is the master, again because of nature. So, which, then, is the part that is similar to the visible and which the invisible? Isn't it so that nature would be ordered so that the intelligible part is the master and the visible part is subordinate?

"Cebes": This is so.

"Socrates": So, which part, the intelligible or the visible, is like the soul?

"Cebes": That's easy. It must be that the soul is like the intelligible and the body is like the visible.

"Socrates": So, what follows from that? If the soul is like the intelligible, then it is more closely kin to the divine; to that which is uniform, unchanging, immortal, and self-same. On the other hand, the body most resembles the visible; that which is multivariate, unintelligible, susceptible to division, decay, and death, never identical to itself over time. If this is so, then the natural course of things will see the body break down, decay, and dissolve while the soul will remain do none of these things. So, if a person dies, the body, being the part that participates in the visible world, will also break down, decay, and dissolve. This may take some time. Indeed, if the body is preserved as they are in Egypt, the body may take quite a long time to suffer this fate. Even though it be embalmed, it eventually deteriorates. However, the soul participates with the Forms and, at death rejoins them in that sphere that is pure and honorable, to Hades, where I, if the god is willing, my soul will go. Thus, is it to be destroyed, dissolved, and decayed? By no means. It is really much more like this, my good Cebes and Simmias. If the soul is pure, it is not dragged down by earthly things; since it does not associate with the body and the visible during life and rather engaged in philosophy properly, contemplating the pure, eternal, and true, then philosophy is the training in how to die well. Thus, a soul so trained will travel to the intelligible, the immortal, and the wise. There it will achieve happiness without confusion, violence, ignorance, and/or fear. Isn't this what we should say about the matter, or should we say something else?

"Cebes": By Zeus, this is it!

"Socrates": So, we must conclude that the body is heavy and tends toward earth. Because of it, the soul is bound to the visible world. Those souls that are immersed in the earthly things – wealth, sexual desires, power, and the like – will, after death, remain tied to the earthly realm, and perhaps even visible, like ghosts or shades. These are not the souls of good folk, but of the lesser ones. They became accustomed to the body and continue to long for it. On the other hand, we most excellent people will be those who are happiest and these, who have attained the highest destination. They are called *sophron* and just; and they have come to this through practice in philosophy and knowledge. None shall keep company with the gods if he has not philosophized and through this become pure at the point of death. Only those with a care for the soul and a rejection of the body shall have this end. These are those who will follow wisdom and their love of wisdom will guide them. It is philosophy that allows the soul to understand that it can depart the body to a better realm, to not become encumbered by the body and dragged back to the visible world. The soul of the philosopher welcomes death rather than opposing it; he keeps from transient pleasures, from evil, and does not dwell on them. So, the soul of the philosopher would approach the question in this way. The soul will achieve calm and balance, following reason and always pondering the truth and not that which is like opinion or mere belief. In this manner, it will continue after physical death and shall not fear dissolution when it leaves the body at death.

~

Plato's *Phaedo*, despite the fact that its dramatic date is shortly after the conclusion of the trial trilogy – *Euthyphro*, *Apology*, and *Crito* – is quite clearly a middle dialogue, roughly contemporaneous with Books II-X of the *Republic*. There are some markers within the text that suggest that its authorship should be dated prior to that of the *Republic*, but while that is a bit controversial, placing it within the middle, Platonic dialogues is generally less so. The influence of the *Phaedo* is quite wide-ranging, appealing to both scholars of Ancient Philosophy and students of pre-Christian influences on early Christian doctrines, the early Church and its successors. We will explore these in order and points of commonality will be highlighted along the way.

The centerpiece question of the *Phaedo* is whether or not a philosopher ought to fear or welcome death. This is likely the reason that Plato returns to the Trial Trilogy of the trial, conviction, and sentencing of Socrates to explore this ultimate question – is death to be feared or welcomed? Socrates, clearly facing his end, is a reasonable person to have explore this question. However, *Phaedo* also illustrates a transition within the Platonic works. Here, Plato's voice becomes dominant in the mouth of "Socrates." No longer is it the historical Socrates whose views are being expressed. Rather, the views of Plato are now those that are encountered. Lest the reader miss this distinction, Plato employs a dramatic device that makes it clear that the words are not exactly those of his mentor. This dialogue is unique among the early and middle ones in that while Socrates is the chief interlocutor, he is not actually present for the dialogue. This is not nearly so strange as it seems. Two friends of Socrates, Phaedo and Echecrates are talking about their mutual friend and his last days. As Echecrates was not present for the end, he asks Phaedo, who was, to recount the conversation that took place. Phaedo says that he will tell everything that he knows, but Echecrates, and we, are given to understand that this will be at best a second-hand account of a conversation of which Phaedo was merely a hearer, and not a participant. Thus, it will be better than a sketch but less than a transcript of Socrates last hours. Thus, a transition from the historical Socrates to a character "Socrates" into whose words we can now more confidently read the words of Plato is signaled by use of a rather elegant literary device.

Before turning to the particulars of the *Phaedo* itself, it will be helpful to discuss the placement of this dialogue within the context of the complete works of Plato. One of the tragedies of the progressions of centuries and the political, economic, and social turmoil that marks it is that a great many works of the ancient period are lost forever. While there is a great deal of the work of Plato extant, we have good reason to suppose that there is much more that has been lost to us. Aristotle, for example, tells of writings of Plato that are not dialogues but more in line with the thesis/argument style that he himself employs. A later scholar, Diogenes Laertius, recounts that Plato wrote voluminously on a wide variety of subjects and in a wide variety of styles. Further, there is a rather substantial fragment of a letter by Plato extant, sometimes called the *Seventh Letter*.

That so much of Plato's work is lost to history is a tragedy of considerable proportion. Scholars are left to speculate, from the pieces of his work that endure, about the content of those lost works. While such speculation may be fruitful, in one degree or another, another technique for interpretation of the extant works themselves is to puzzle out the chronology of those dialogues that we do have.

The ordering of the dialogues into a reasonable chronological list is a task that is itself fraught with several pitfalls. For example, there is within some of the dialogues clear dramatic dating. The Trial Trilogy has a dramatic date of 399 BCE The *Laches* has a dramatic date of between 424 BCE and 415 BCE It is fairly easy to establish the dramatic dates because of the characters involved and historical information we have about those characters. For example, we know from other sources that Socrates's trial and death took place in 399 BCE, thus fixing the dramatic date of the Trial Trilogy. We also know that the retreat from Delium, of which Laches speaks in the *Laches* was in 424 BCE and that Nicias died in 415. Since these are the two primary interlocutors in the *Laches*, we can fix that dramatic date, although not with as much precision as the Trial Trilogy. However, fixing the dramatic date of a dialogue does little to assure us of the compositional date of the work. For example, it is reasonably clear that the *Laches* and the Trial Trilogy were composed about the same time, yet their dramatic dates differ considerably. Further, it is reasonably clear that the *Phaedo* was composed quite a long time after the Trial Trilogy, yet its dramatic date is the same. So, appeal to dramatic date will be of little help is ordering the dialogues chronologically by composition.

One possible solution to this problem is to order the dialogues by reference to the character Socrates. Of those dialogues in which convincing reason can be given that the character Socrates speaks for the historical Socrates, we can say that they are early or Socratic dialogues. Of those dialogues where the character Socrates speaks for Plato, we can say that they are Platonic dialogues. However, this strikes upon two difficulties rather quickly. To what extent can we discern whether the character Socrates is speaking for his historical counterpart and not functioning as a mouthpiece for Plato's own views? The second difficulty is that there are a few dialogues in which it is clear that Socrates is *not* the voice of Plato. In some dialogues that are generally considered to have been written late in Plato's career, the character Socrates either is absent or has so limited a role as to be a peripheral character hardly capable of advancing Plato's own views. Thus, this approach to the chronological ordering of the dialogues, while helpful in some ways, is only partly effective.

Several 20th century scholars have recognized that it is likely to be impossible to provide a complete accounting for an ordering of the dialogues, choosing instead to group them into categories divided by more or less clear lines of demarcation. Arguments for those divisions are then offered on a variety of bases, because it is also clear that it is unlikely that a single principle of division would be sufficient for such a complicated task. Among the scholarly tools that have been used are stylometry, doctrinal grouping, and length. Stylometry is the practice of charting the frequency of usage of words within each dialogue and comparing that frequency across the extant works, grouping those works where particularly important notions are present with similar frequency. Thus, those dialogues that speak often of Forms, for example, are grouped together while those that speak rarely or none of Forms are excluded from that group. The doctrinal grouping method is the practice of collecting those dialogues that seem to advance a particular principle or explore a particular topic and excluding those that do not. This results in several sets of trilogies and as a result seems to be quite promising, except that there are several trilogies that are either incomplete or whose third member is lost. Given that some of these incomplete trilogies are within what is generally considered the middle period of Plato's career, this is a difficult model for which to argue. Perhaps the simplest of the methods is to group the dialogues according to length. This will provide a helpful demarcation between the early, Socratic dialogues and all the others as the later dialogues tend to be much longer than the earlier ones. But, again, we are left with little in the way of dividing the later dialogues into groups of their own.

One might wonder why a chronological ordering of composition is important at all, given that the attempts to do so are particularly troublesome. This is actually quite an easy puzzlement to answer. Plato's life was fairly long and extraordinarily full, especially by the standards of his day. Over a long career of thinking and writing, it would be strange indeed to suppose that the views of a mature Plato were the same as those of his much younger self. To suppose that Plato's mind would remain static is to expect from him something that would be anathema to the pursuit of truth and the love of wisdom. Further, such a stasis of thought, even if it were possible in anyone, would clearly not be beneficial. Thus, we can safely suppose that Plato's line of investigation develops over time, shifting and changing, sometimes drastically and sometimes far more subtly.

We have textual reasons to suppose that Plato's thought changes. Indeed, from the *Phaedo* to the *Republic*, we see a progression from a conception of the soul as a simple, undifferentiated entity to a complex, tripartite one. Obviously, some shift has been made. Thus, it is important to take seriously the development that occurs throughout the course of Plato's career in order to better understand the nature of the concepts, principles, and doctrines he is putting forward and the arguments he advances for them. Given that this is a rather crucial interpretive tool, it will be helpful if it is actually possible, and to the extent that it is possible, that we have understood that development. Hence, the efforts to chronologically order the dialogues, incomplete though they may be, are important efforts in the attempt to develop a comprehensive view of this most important philosophical mind of the Western world.

There are several models for ordering the dialogues, although three have come to be the touchstones for this method of interpreting the development of

Section 3.2: Socrates, Philosophy's Martyr

Plato's work. The first of these is generally called the Traditional View and it orders the dialogues into three categories – early, middle, and late. The division is something like this:

Early: *Apology, Charmides, Crito, Euthydemus, Euthyphro, Gorgias, Hippias Major/Minor, Ion, Laches, Lysis, Menexenus, Meno, Protagoras, Republic I.*

Middle: *Cratylus, Phaedo, Phaedrus, Republic II-X, Symposium*

Late: *Critias, Laws, Parmienides, Philebus, Politicus, Sophist, Theaetetus, Timaeus*

The Traditional View has been defended by a number of scholars, mostly during the 19th century. The difference in inclusion of some dialogues here that are not included elsewhere, and vice versa, reflects some scholarly debate concerning the Platonic authorship of certain of the dialogues that are traditionally attributed to him.

Gregory Vlastos is generally considered one of the great scholars of Ancient Philosophy of the 20th century. He puts forward a differing view that adds a fourth category, the Transitional dialogues as well as changing the designation of the Early ones to reflect the method of argument most often found there. Vlastos is concerned with taking into account stylometric analysis and doctrinal analysis to argue that in the early dialogues, Socrates puts forward questions that go unanswered, in the middle dialogues, Plato puts forward doctrines and principles that are attempts to answer those questions, and in the late dialogues, Plato returns to the questions and his earlier answers and gives them further revision.

Elenctic: *Apology, Charmides, Crito, Euthyphro, Gorgias, Hippias Minor, Ion, Laches, Protagoras, Republic I.*

Transitional: *Euthydemus, Hippias Major, Lysis, Menexenus, Meno*

Middle: *Cratylus, Parmienides, Phaedo, Phaedrus, Republic II-X, Symposium, Theaetetus*

Late: *Critias, Laws, Philebus, Politicus, Sophist, Timaeus*

Vlastos argues that one can detect within the transitional dialogues the development of different philosophical methods that form a bridge from the early dialogues *elenctic* character to the greater methodological diversity of the middle and late dialogues.

Kahn puts forward a different model, suggesting that there are divisions within the traditionally conceived Early dialogues that is similar to Vlastos, although Kahn's model tends to suggest that there are dialogues within which the historical Socrates is most likely to be found. These, he calls the Pre-Systematic dialogues. The next section is comprised of the Socratic dialogues; this section is, for the most part, quite similar to Vlastos's Elenctic section. He then divides the Middle and Late categories into three – the Middle, the Post-Middle and the Late. The Post-Middle dialogues occupy a position similar to the Transitional ones in the Vlastos model, forming a sort of bridge between the generally accepted Middle dialogues and the last ones of Plato's career. His ordering is something like this:

Pre-Systematic: *Apology, Charmides, Crito, Euthyphro, Gorgias, Hippias Minor, Ion, Laches, Protagoras, Republic I.*
Socratic: *Euthydemus, Hippias Major, Lysis, Meno*
Middle: *Cratylus, Phaedo, Phaedrus, Republic II-X, Symposium*
Post-Middle: *Parmienides, Theaetetus*
Late: *Critias, Laws, Philebus, Politicus, Sophist, Timaeus*

All of these are helpful. And all of them conclude that while it would be helpful to be able to more fully distinguish between the dialogues, but that a more conservative approach to the final categorization of the dialogues is to be preferred. While I tend to agree with that position, a further distinction can be made that will be helpful is discerning the development of the Platonic work throughout his career. In one sense this is the descendent of the other views expressed above in that it takes seriously the use of Platonic argumentation styles, doctrinal developments, and textual shifts that the others employ, with little in the way of deviation from them. However, the separation can be made a bit more explicit and the dialogues ordered a bit more fully. The suggestion for chronologically ordering the dialogues that seems to take into account current scholarship is something like the following:

Trial Trilogy: *Euthyphro, Apology, Crito,*
Socrates Exemplar: *Charmides, Euthydemus, Gorgias, Hippias Minor, Ion, Laches, Republic I, Lysis*
Transitional: *Hippias Major, Phaedo, Protagoras, Menexenus, Meno*
Middle: *Cratylus, Parmienides, Phaedrus, Republic II-X, Symposium,*
Late: *Critias, Laws, Philebus, Politicus, Sophist, Theaetetus Timaeus*

In the early or Socratic dialogues, the argument style is almost exclusively *elenctic*. While this is not completely true of all of the elements of the Trial Trilogy, it is clearly present in the *Euthyphro* where Socrates performs an elenchus on Euthyphro, at times within the *Apology*, and again within the *Crito* where Socrates imagines the Laws performing an elenchus on him. However, this is where the historical Socrates begins to fade and the Platonic voice begins to appear.

The connection between the *Euthyphro* and the other early, Socratic dialogues has been noted several times. All of these dialogues end with the interlocutors having failed to advance a definition of the concept, generally a moral virtue, in question. Thus, these dialogues are all marked with a sense of *aporia*, or confusion. Something else marks them, however. In the Trial Trilogy, the primary example of the Socratic elenchus is found in the *Euthyphro*, a dialogue whose interlocutor is not historically verifiable. However, Euthyphro provides a very good example of Socrates's treatment of those puffed up with their own importance and assured in their own beliefs. At the same time, he is not an historical character like Laches, Nicias, Charmides, and Critias are. When Plato is using historical characters, it certainly seems as if he is trying to remain true to either the views or character of those characters. At the same time, it is also the case that more is going on that Socratic refutation of some people with a reputation for wisdom or virtue. One can interpret the *Euthyphro* as not merely the

Section 3.2: Socrates, Philosophy's Martyr

refutation of a single person's successive views of a virtue, but rather as a collection of the common views of the people of Athens, a collection which is refuted one piece at a time. If this is so, then the pedagogical function of the *Euthyphro*, and perhaps the other early dialogues, is to clear the decks of common misconceptions of the notion in question in order to facilitate a conversation within the Academy or in the mind of the reader concerning what the virtue might be, unfettered now by the clutter and baggage of false common opinions.

All of the early dialogues seem to be of this form, but there is a distinguishing feature in the later dialogues of this period from the Trial Trilogy. In dialogues like the *Laches* and the *Charmides* for example, we encounter historical personages of Athens who had reputations counter to the notion discussed in the dialogues that bear their names. Laches and Nicias, the primary interlocutors of the *Laches*, were known for military debacles that led, ultimately, to the defeat of Athens in the Peloponnesian War. Since the Laches is about the Cardinal Virtue, *courage*, the alleged experts on the matter are known to be anything but experts before the dialogue even begins. Similarly, Charmides and Critias, from the *Charmides*, were among the worst of the Thirty Tyrants and as such clearly not examples of *sophrosune* or balance or self-control. Indeed, in each of these dialogues, the interlocutor and the common notions of courage and control of self are refuted in the elenchus. However, at the same time, the reader is presented, not with a definition of the virtue in question, but with an example of the virtue. In the *Laches*, Socrates is commended for his virtuous actions on the battlefield and is held up, by Plato, as an exemplar of the virtue. Even more clearly in the *Charmides*, where Socrates is threatened with bodily harm by those who claim to be the most virtuous in virtue of their balanced natures, he is shown to be the one truly possessed of balance and control rather than the vicious interlocutors. Thus, we can divide the early Socratic dialogues into two groups – the Trial Trilogy in which the argument for Socrates's innocence (among other views) is put forward and the Moral Exemplar dialogues in which while refuting his interlocutors and leaving the group apparently in a sense of confusion at the end, Socrates is put forward as the example of the virtue under investigation.

It is fairly straightforward to accept the division into Transitional dialogues and Theoretical ones that generally divide the middle dialogues. These dialogues present Plato's attempts to develop methods of investigation that go beyond the *elenchus* of Socrates and which result in more clear conclusions regarding the nature of the topic in question. For example, within the *Meno* and the *Phaedo*, Plato puts forward an initial rendition of a Method of Hypothesis in which a proposition is put forward and then something like a positive argument is put forward for it. The elenchus is still used as a method of clearing away debris, but the method conjoined with it is seen as responsible for developing a positive argument for the view. Thus, in the *Phaedo* we see Plato arguing, through his Socratic mouthpiece, that the soul is immortal and that in virtue of this immortality, the true philosopher should not fear death but should welcome it.

The transitional period then moves into the Theoretical one, in which Plato advances sophisticated theories that are supposed to be thoroughgoing systems in which the various virtues and pedagogical questions of the earlier dialogues are organized. The Divided Line in the *Republic* is perhaps the clearest example of this systematizing move. There, Plato advances a Theory of Forms through the example of the Divided Line which shows how the primary branches of philosophical inquiry – metaphysics, epistemology, and ethics – are all related to each other. This comprehensive theory marks a first full attempt to address all that has come before it.

One of the commonalities between the *Phaedo* and the *Republic* is the Platonic Theory of Forms that is found within each. Given that the Theory of Forms is present in both, one might reasonably ask why the *Phaedo* would be put forward as an example of a Transitional dialogue and the *Republic* as a Theoretical one. The answer here is rather quick and also provisional, demonstrating how fine a distinction can at times be made. Within the *Phaedo*, as Socrates argues that the soul is immortal, the nature of the soul is presented as a simple or undifferentiated entity. It has no parts, no divisions, and no variation within it. By the time we have come to the middle of the *Republic*, however, the soul is presented as a tripartite entity, with considerable variation as part of its nature. As it is clear from other dialogues that Plato maintains the view of the tripartite soul in his later works, we can argue, then, that in virtue of this clear development from one to the other, we put the *Phaedo* prior to the *Republic*.

The Late dialogues are the most difficult to interpret at times, in no small part because the character, Socrates, tends to fade from center stage. There is a distinctiveness in Plato's method in these later dialogues, however. The primary method that Aristotle will use to great effect in his own work is here developed by Plato. Collection and Division is a reasonably self-explanatory name for this method. Simply put, one collects together all of the relevant or potentially relevant objects for study, whether these be insects or ideas, and through some selected means of filtering sifted until the item in question or the property in question is isolated. One Platonic example of the method can be found in the *Phaedrus*. There, while discussing the nature of rhetoric, Plato, through Socrates, argues that one aspect of rhetoric is the assessment of the variety of souls that populate an audience and the crafting of a speech that will appeal to those souls. The view here is that some souls are persuaded by one sort of speech while others are persuaded by different sorts. Thus, having collected all of the different types of souls together, one can then divide them out into the sorts that correspond to the differing kinds of speeches.

It will be noted that the *Phaedrus* is not a late dialogue, but rather is generally considered either a middle or Transitional one. However, this is not problematic for this rendering of the ordering of the dialogues. Just as there are seeds of a Theory of Forms as early as the *Euthyphro* despite the fact that it is quite some time before a thoroughgoing theory is developed, so, too, the seeds of the Method of Collection and Division are sown earlier as well. What is quite illustrative here, though, is the extent to which the Method of Collection and Division is encountered in the later dialogues. In the earlier ones, like the *Phaedrus*, it is used alongside the others, often in a secondary place in the overall sweep of the dialogue. In the later dialogues, however, the method takes center stage. In the *Sophist*, for example, the interlocutors are considering the nature of sophistry and collect six of the general models for the art. Moving through each one, they outline each, pointing out its commonality with the others, but more importantly, the distinctiveness of each. As it happens, there is good textual reason to think that Plato holds that the Sixth Sophist is not a sophist at all but a philosopher as the description of the Sixth Sophist is strikingly reminiscent of the Socrates of the *Euthyphro* and the *Apology*. Since Socrates does not appear as a central character in this dialogue, the method of argument takes center stage and the Method of Collection and Division isolates one model of sophistry, philosophy, from the collection of harmful models. Similarly, in the *Laws*, the interlocutors evaluate a number of constitutions from a variety of cities in an effort to isolate from among them the excellent constitution. Thus, in the later dialogues, the Method of Collection and Division is the argument form through which the voice of Plato is heard and by which he attempts to put forward arguments for positive doctrines.

With the understanding that within the Transitional dialogues that Plato begins to pose answers to questions raised from the earlier ones, it is time to turn to one of the most influential doctrinal developments in the *Phaedo*. When the Trial Trilogy ended, Socrates had been convicted and argued that it would be unjust for him to flee Athens, thus ensuring that he would indeed be executed by order of the council's sentencing. The question before him, then, becomes one of the manner in which death is welcomed; with fear and trembling or with a warm embrace? Simply put, should the philosopher fear death?

That Plato decides to treat this question by returning to the setting of the Trial Trilogy is instructive. In the *Apology*, Socrates argues that the proper life for any person is one lived in striving to care for the soul by pursuit of truth and wisdom. This is in direct opposition to the way in which he believes the Sophists behave, a behavior in which the Athenians share, on his view. He says he will not forego philosophy because it is important that his fellow Athenians turn from pursuit of wealth, honor, and power. At least part of the reason that Socrates seems to hold this view is that like Plato and Aristotle who follow him, Socrates believes that the pursuit of wealth, honor, and power will not lead to a life of virtue and health for the soul, but to one that will cause damage to the soul, and perhaps do so irreparably. In the *Gorgias*, another Socratic dialogue, Socrates argues that it is possible, through vicious actions, to damage the soul beyond repair.

Unargued in the *Apology* is the underlying reasoning for this view. Fairly simply put, wealth, honor, and power are goods external to a person, if they are goods at all. They are outside the control of the person and they are inherently transient; here one moment and gone the next. On the other hand, the soul is the essence of a person; insofar as there is something that Socrates is, it is his soul. Further, truth and wisdom, on Plato's view, are eternal things, immutable and unchanging. Since the care of the soul is placed alongside truth and wisdom as the opposing triad to three transient things, it is reasonable to conclude that Socrates thinks that the soul, too, is immortal.

In the *Phaedo*, we have that argument. It is an amazingly simple and straightforward argument. If the soul is a simple and undifferentiated substance, then it is impossible for it to be broken into parts. If it is impossible for the soul to be broken into parts, then it is likewise impossible for the soul to decay. If it is impossible for the soul to decay, then it is impossible for it to die. Anything that cannot die is, of course, immortal since what it is to be immortal is to be beyond the possibility of death. Thus, Socrates argues that the soul is immortal.

Since the soul is immortal, it is clear that the philosopher, who has sought to care for the soul by pursuit of truth and wisdom, ought not to fear bodily death since the soul will continue and will be reunited with the Forms. The Sophist, on the other hand, or anyone else who has failed in this noble pursuit and has instead chased transient things may well have damaged their very essence and thus may have some justification for a fear of death.

This argument for the immortality of the soul has far-reaching implications; well beyond the bounds of ancient Athens. This is the first argument in the western tradition for the immortality of the soul. In the Hellenistic period that follows the death of Socrates and is initiated by the conquest of an empire by Alexander, this notion of the immortality of the soul is transmitted throughout the Middle East and recurs in some interesting ways upon the birth of the Christian movement, particularly in the writings of St. Paul. As a good Platonist, St. Paul employs Platonic arguments to his own purpose, to argue that this new religious sect has a mission quite similar to that of Socrates – to urge people to think more of eternal things than transient ones and to care for the soul through the pursuit of wisdom and truth rather than to allow one's very essence to be corrupted by pursuit of wealth, honor, and power. While it is clear that St. Paul has a very different conception of the nature of wisdom and truth than his pre-Christian counterparts, it is also clear that his arguments are beholden to the Platonic notion of the soul and its care. Thus, the theology of the early Christian movement, rather than exhibiting a particularly Semitic character that one might expect of a middle eastern religious system, is instead, very Greek. This Platonic influence becomes more and more clear in the work of the early Medieval philosophers like St. Augustine and St. Anselm who go so far as to adopt the Theory of Forms, theorize that within the realm of the Forms there is a hierarchy of Forms, identify the highest Form as the Form of the Good, and then suggest that God is the Form of the Good. The details of this metaphysical view become clearer as we examine the way in which Plato discusses the relationship between metaphysics, epistemology, and ethics in a dialogue complementary to and contemporaneous with the *Phaedo*, the *Republic*.

Guided Reading Questions:
1. How does Socrates argue that the soul is immortal?
2. On Socrates view, why should the philosopher not fear death?
3. Why can it be concluded that the *Phaedo* is not an early Socratic dialogue?

Logic Blurb
The Dialectic

While Plato employs the Method of Hypothesis as a supplement to the Socratic *elenchus*, it is not the only additional form in his argumentation arsenal. Indeed, likely the most famous of the Platonic argument forms is the *dialectic*. Part of the reason for the fame of Plato's dialectical method is its quasi-adoption by Georg Hegel in the 19th century. While Hegel's dialectic is not identical to Plato's, it is a helpful introduction to the sort of argument that is generally given the name, *dialectic*.

A *dialectical* argument is an argument of opposition. In Hegel's hands, this dialectic is generally presented as a series of propositions. An initial proposition, a *thesis* or *hypothesis*, will give rise to its negation. So, for example, if the thesis is "The sun revolves around the earth," the very existence of that proposition suggests its opposite, "The sun does not revolve around the earth." This negation of the thesis is called the *antithesis*. Clearly, both of these propositions cannot be true. It may be that neither true. For example, as some point, the expansion of the sun is anticipated to consume all of the innermost planets of the solar system. In that even, neither of the propositions would be true because there would be nothing to which "earth" refers. Thus, while the propositions are not both true, it is the case that they could both be false.

With a thesis and an antithesis, there is inherent conflict. Evidence for one and evidence for the other is weighed. In the end, it could well be that a new hypothesis arises from the examination of the first two. This new hypothesis could be, for example, that "The earth revolves around the sun, but from the perspective of a person on the ground, the opposite seems true." This new hypothesis incorporates both antecedent propositions, although one more than the other. This new hypothesis is called the *synthesis*.

The dialectic of Plato is clearly the ancestor of the Hegelian one, but it does not proceed, necessarily from one hypothesis to the other. As we will see in the Divided Line in the next section, Plato's conception of the dialectic is a process of reasoning by which one moves from hypothesis to first principles; from "mathematicals" and ratios to the Forms. Plato does not offer an algorithmic method like Hegel's. Instead, Plato argues that the mind moves from contemplation of hypotheses and construction of new hypotheses to an epiphany or a deep insight into the structure of the universe, and breaks through to contemplate the first principles that underlie all of the hypotheses and which give rise to them. These first principles are, in one sense, not reducible to more basic principles because they are the first principles and thus are a matter of the essences of things and thus beyond proof. So, the *Chair* itself and the *Triangle* itself are Forms from which hypotheses about triangles and chairs are formed. Ultimately, the contemplation of the Forms themselves will lead one to understand that there exists a hierarchy even within the Forms, the highest of which is the Form of the Good.

Section 3.3 – Plato and Justice

Republic 2: Glaucon's Challenge and the Ring of Gyges

Glaucon: Those who are just are not so voluntarily, but only because they cannot be unjust without being caught. If they could have both the appearance of justice and the power to act in whatever ways they wanted, how might they react? Let us imagine how their desires might lead them. Let us imagine two men who are following their own desires and only constrained to justice by force of law. Indeed, let us suppose that they have such freedom as the power of Gyges, ancestor of Croesus of Lydia.

      As the tale goes, Gyges was once a shepherd who watched flocks in the kingdom of Lydia. One day there was a tremendous storm and an earthquake. Following the storm and earthquake, there was a great chasm in the ground right in the pasture where he watched his sheep. He was shocked at the sight of it and went down into the crevasse and discovered an amazing treasure trove. There was a hollow horse made of brass. It was so large as to have doors through which he could go and when he had entered the horse he saw a dead man, one who appeared greater than human and who had on his hand a ring. Gyges took the ring and left the opening.

      As was the tradition, the shepherds from surrounding fields often met together to compile a monthly report that they may send it to the king. While in this assembly, he was idly playing with the ring and when he turned it upon his finger, suddenly he was invisible. They spoke about him like he wasn't with them. He was shocked and turned the ring again and again became visible. He tried this several times and discovering that it worked every time, he made sure that he was chosen to take the monthly report to the king. As soon as he got to the palace, he seduced the queen and with her help he killed the king and took over the kingdom.

      Now, let us imagine two rings, one worn by a just man and the other by an unjust man. Can a man be thought to have such a strong constitution that he would hold to justice even in this great power? Surely, no person could keep from taking whatever he liked or killing whomever he pleased or releasing from prison whomever he wanted. He would be like a god. If this is so, then the just man and the unjust man would soon come to act exactly in the same ways. If this is so, we can conclude that a man is only just because he thinks justice will benefit him and because he cannot act unjustly with impunity. It is clear that all people believe that injustice is much more profitable than just behavior. Indeed, to even imagine a person who would possess this power and fail to use it would be to imagine a fool. While he might be lauded and praised by others, it would only be so in public and to keep up appearances.

Socrates: The others asked me to continue the examination rather than to let it falter. We were interested to know the truth about two questions – the nature of justice and its opposite, injustice, and following that, the benefits of each. This investigation would require fine sight, but since I do not think we are particularly gifted, perhaps we should construct a method to take into account our less than precise vision. After all, imagine that a person who was short-sighted was asked to read small words at some distance from him. Wouldn't it be fortunate for him if he knew of another place where the same words were only written much larger?

Adeimantus: Indeed. But how is that relevant to what we are doing here?

Socrates: Let me tell you. Justice is the object of our investigation, is it not? Well, sometimes, we speak of Justice in the individual and at other times in the *polis*.

Adeimantus: Again, true.

Socrates: So, isn't it true also that the *polis* is larger than the individual?

Adeimantus: Yes.

Socrates: Since the *polis* is considerably larger than an individual, the quantity of Justice is greater as well and thus more easily discerned. Thus, if we are going to ask about the nature of Justice and its opposite, then we should find them first in the *polis* and only then in the individual person. Thus, we will have gone from the greater to the smaller. Further, if we think of the *polis* as a work in progress, we should even more easily discover the object of our inquiry, justice in the individual.

Republic 6: The Divided Line

Socrates: Imagine the mind this way. If it is focused on the realm of truth and reality, then it knows them and is in possession of reason, but if it is focused on the lower realm, then it is merely in the thrall of opinion and is shifts back and forth without any strength. Reality lends truth to object of knowledge and power to the mode of thought of the one who knows. Let us imagine that there are two regions or worlds – intelligible world and the visible one. Do you have this distinction in mind?

Glaucon: Yes.

Socrates: Now, take a line and cut it into unequal parts. The one part should be twice as large as the other. Now divided each of these two parts into two with the same proportion preserved. The first set of divisions correspond to the intelligible and visible world; the larger to the intelligible and the smaller, the visible. Then, take the subdivisions and imagine them in terms of their clarity and lack thereof. In the lowest rank will be shadows and reflections and so on. Is this clear?

Glaucon: Yes

Socrates: Now, imagine in the next section exist all of the animals and all of the other things that grow and/or are made. Isn't it so that each of these divisions has a different level of truth and that the original is to the reflection as the division of belief is to opinion?

Glaucon: Certainly.

Socrates: Then, let us move on to the way in which the intelligible division is divided. Again, this division is divided in two parts. The bottom of these two is occupied by things analogous to images or shadows in the lower division. Here, though, the investigation is hypothetical only. In the intelligible world, the mind addresses these hypotheses, but moves from them ultimately to the Forms themselves.

Glaucon: I'm not sure I understand.

Socrates: Let's approach it again, then. Perhaps something of a preface will help. Think of students who study geometry, arithmetic, and other similar fields. Those students make certain assumptions – about the *odd*, the *even*, and *shapes*; about the three angles, and so on. These are the hypotheses that they use and since everyone is supposed to know these, at least within these groups, they do not take the time to explain them. Then start with them and argue deductively until they arrive at a conclusion.

Glaucon: That much I know.

Socrates: So, you also know that they will at times draw figures of various sorts and will use them to guide their thinking. They are not actually arguing about the figures they have drawn but about the absolutes – the Square, the Diameter, and so on – the Forms about which they are talking are represented by the figures they draw or construct and those figures can very well have a reflection in clear water or may cast a shadow. But, while they are using figures they have drawn, they are really trying to understand the things that can only be perceived by the mind.

Glaucon: Okay. That's true.

Socrates: So, if we are discussing the intelligible world, but in that division where the mind is forced to proceed from hypothesis to hypothesis rather than applying some first principle, then the mind is ultimately incapable of moving from this penultimate division to the ultimate and is using shadows and images, albeit mental ones, of the greater reality that is above it. Because that higher reality is the ultimate, it has greater value than the lower.

When we are discussing that ultimate division of the intelligible world, then we are discussing the kind of knowledge that reason, through the dialectic, obtains. It is the realm of first principles, not hypothesis. So, in stepwise manner, we move from hypothesis to first principles and then to the first principle of the entirety of the all; then, from this height, the mind moves back down the stages without having to make reference to figures or images or shadows. Thus the mind comes to focus on the Forms, through Forms and this is where it ends.

Since these are the four segments, there must be modes of thought that correspond to these objects; true reason or wisdom is connected to the highest, thinking to the penultimate, belief to the third section (and higher of the visible segments), and opinion is connected to the last. This will be a scale and we can suppose that the clarity and certainty of each mode of thought will correspond to the clarity and certainty (and lack thereof) of the objects with which they are connected.

Glaucon: I can agree to this model.

Republic 7: The Analogy of the Cave

Socrates: Now, then, let's think of an example to discern how close to being enlightened or not is human nature. Imagine people trapped in a cave that has a wide mouth that opens to the light so that the light can strike upon the whole of the cave. Imagine also that these people have been trapped here since they were children and further that they are completely bound, hand, foot, and neck, so that they cannot move but can only face the wall at the back of the cave. There is a fire burning behind them and in front of them there is a screen so that their captors can dangle puppets and cast shadows with them.

Glaucon: Okay.

Socrates: Not only this, there would likely be people who walked back and forth with all sorts of objects to cast an even greater variety of shadows on the wall.

Glaucon: These are very strange prisoners, indeed.

Socrates: Perhaps, but they are us. They see only their shadows or other shadows. Let us imagine that they can talk to each other. Wouldn't they give names to the things they saw and, if the cave echoed at all, they would not even be sure which of their fellow prisoners spoke? So, for these prisoners, truth is only shadows and illusions, right?

Glaucon: That's true.

Socrates: Okay, then, lets imagine further. Suppose one of them is freed and forced to get up and turn and walk out in the direction of the light. Won't he be in considerable pain; the light will blind him horribly and he'd be even unable to see the shadows he'd seen before because his eyes would have been troubled by the glare. However, as he moves forward and approaches the light more closely, his vision will clear and he will perceive the more real existence. Suppose someone is with him, asking him to name these new objects he has seen. Wouldn't he think the shadows with which he was accustomed to be more real than these strange new things?

Section 3.3: Plato and Justice   103

Glaucon: By a large margin.
Socrates: So, let us compel him further toward the light. His eyes will be pained again yet he will look to those newer objects noting the greater reality of those things that he now can perceive. Let us imagine even further that he is compelled to struggle to exit the cave until he beholds the sun itself. Won't the pain in his eyes be redoubled? Indeed, won't it be that he can't see anything at all?
Glaucon: Not at the moment, for certain.
Socrates: But, he will become acclimated to the light and the vision of this higher world. So, first he saw shadows best, then reflections, then objects themselves, then the very light of the celestial bodies like stars and the moon and then, ultimately, the sun. In this, he will now think about these things as they are. And, he will conclude that these greater realities are the cause of the things to which he was accustomed before.
Glaucon: Surely. He sees the sun now and would think about it.
Socrates: And, thinking back to where he once lived, wouldn't he think himself fortunate for seeing things as they are and pity his former state?
Glaucon: Certainly.
Socrates: Suppose those who were in the cave had a game and gave congratulations to one another when they were quick to identify shadows and to note which went before and which came after and to best predict which would come next. He would likely not envy them, right?
Glaucon: Absolutely. He would rather be tortured than to be trapped back into these falsehoods and to live in such a miserable state without any understanding of the way things actually are.
Socrates: Good. Let us imagine this person who has been in the sunlight coming out of the light and being put back into his earlier circumstance. Isn't it so that he would be completely blind in the darkness, completely incapable of playing their game? Wouldn't he be the worst at the exercise, since his sight would still be overwhelmed by its presence in the light? Eventually, he would become better able to play the game as his eyesight became accustomed to the dark because he would know the true causes. Till then, he would be ridiculous. People would say that he left and lost his sight, that it is best to not even think about going out. If he tried to release any of his former fellow captives and help them toward the truth, wouldn't they try to capture him and kill him?
Glaucon: No question.
Socrates: Now, take this example and attach it to the foregoing discussion. The cave/prison is the visible world. The journey from the darkness toward the light is the journey of the mind from the visible to the intelligible world. True or false, in that highest world, it seems to me that the Form of Good is the last to arrive and thus the highest of all. It is grasped only with the

greatest effort and, when we contemplate it, we understand it as the author and source of all reason, thinking, truth and reality.

Further, you shouldn't be surprised that those who have come into the light and seen the blessed truth do not want to leave it and go back down into the cave and human troubles. Their minds are always pulled toward the upper realm and this is exactly what we should expect if our allegory is accurate.

Glaucon: It certainly seems to be.

~

Many, if not all, of the early Socratic dialogues end with all of the participants in a sense of *aporia*, or confusion. One of the aspects of the Middle and Later Platonic dialogues that set them apart from their Socratic counterparts is that Plato is advancing arguments for positive views. The great majority of these positive arguments are directed at trying to address the confusion left from the Socratic dialogues. The *Republic* is perhaps the best example of this.

Book I of the *Republic* is clearly an example of an early dialogue. The centerpiece of Book I is an elenctic examination of Thrasymachus. Thrasymachus's view that *justice* is "the will of the stronger," or a proto-Machiavellian "might makes right," is systematically and thoroughly discredited. At least so it appears to the participants in the dialogue. Unfortunately, at the end of Book I, we are left without any positive view of the nature of *justice*. The *aporetic* ending of the dialogue serves as refutation of Thrasymachus's view, but not as an advancement of Socrates's own positive view. We are given to believe that it is not "the will of the stronger," but that is of small comfort. At most, we know something that *justice* is not. Indeed, even this is controversial. While it appears that the view of Thrasymachus has been abandoned at the conclusion of *Republic 1*, Glaucon (one of Plato's brothers) takes up the case again as *Republic 2* opens.

One of the first things any reader should keep in mind when approaching the *Republic* is that it is not only a massive and complicated work, but it is also a work written during at least two very distinct periods in Plato's career. *Republic 1* is an early dialogue, in the *Socrates Exemplar* period. The rest of the dialogue is from at least two periods later, from the *Middle* period. As such, this presents an interesting interpretive puzzle. It also serves as a model for understanding the development of Platonic thought from early Socratic apologist to mature philosopher putting forward his own views. That Plato revisits his earlier work is fortuitous because it provides us a glimpse of a common philosophical occurrence – philosophy is not a task that is completed, it is an ongoing wrestling with important matters and our conclusions at one moment are often no more than interim resting points that must be taken up again.

Since the later work takes up the topic of the earlier one, we are immediately confronted with an interpretive difficulty for the vast majority of social/political philosophers of the last few centuries. Plato's *Republic* is most often considered a work in political philosophy – an attempt to envision the ideal state and how that state might be constructed in the actual world. The majority of scholars of ancient philosophy do not interpret it in this way. To be sure, there is considerable discussion of the construction of a state, from the rulers to the farmers to the educational and political system. However, it is critical to realize that this discussion of the ideal state is in the service of a much bigger project; indeed, the construction of the ideal state is no more than a thought experiment in which Plato is trying to develop an analogy to suit his true purpose. The underlying point of the *Republic* is to understand what justice in the individual soul is like. Thrasymachus, Glaucon, and Adiamantus all argue that it is better to be unjust, but thought just, than it is to be just and thought unjust. But this is a matter of the state of the individual soul. Since Plato, in Socrates's voice, argues that it is best to be just, even if one is thought unjust, he must be able to say what justice is and then to show that it is truly best to have this state of the soul. Thus, *Republic 2-8* form a treatise on the nature of Justice, a state that the individual soul has. In *Republic 9*, he turns to argue that Justice is good for itself and in *Republic 10*, that it is good for its consequences. Thus, the course of the dialogue is an attempt to argue that Justice is itself a good and that it is better to be just than unjust whatever other consequences obtain.

So, one might ask, why has the *Republic* been taken to be a work in political philosophy, then? This is quite simple. It is true that the majority of the dialogue seems to focus on the development of the ideal state. However, in context, this is easily dismissed. As will be discussed in greater depth in the course of this section, the *Republic* turns on a single analogy – Justice in the individual soul is like Justice in the ideal city. The reason for the thought experiment in which the ideal city is constructed is given as a forensic tool. Since an individual soul is small and hidden, it will be difficult to isolate Justice within it or to say what Justice is like for it. On the other hand, since a city is quite large and easily visible, it will be easier to say what Justice in the city is like. By analogy, then, if we can isolate Justice in the ideal city, then the analogue of Justice in the individual soul will become obvious. Thus, the *Republic* is an examination of the nature of the virtue, Justice, within the individual soul. This suggests that the social/political discussion is not to be taken as the Platonic word on construction of the state.

There is further reason to suppose that Plato is not primarily interested in social/political philosophy within the *Republic*. There are several works in the Platonic corpus whose focus is on politics; the *Crito* and the *Laws* come immediately to mind. In both the *Crito* and the *Laws*, Plato advances very similar notions of ideal jurisprudence and politics. There, the Laws are the proper guideline for ordering the legislation of a city. Appeal to the Laws will determine whether or not individual ordinances are, in fact, laws or merely meaningless statements. Thus, the constitution of the ideal city will be one that attempts to emulate, in the everyday world, the Laws, of the world of the Forms. This view is consistent with the metaphysical and epistemological claims that Plato makes in the *Republic* in the Divided Line and Analogy of the Cave. However, in those examples, Plato is discussing the education of the individual, not the construction of the ideal city. The construction of the ideal city is a bottom-up process, rather than a top-down one. Given Plato's metaphysics, this is yet another indication that the *Republic* is not strictly a political work or even centrally one. To conclude the point about its place in the larger Platonic corpus, the political views expressed in the early *Crito* and the late *Laws* are similar to one another but both are quite different from the political views that seem to be expressed in the *Republic*. Thus, we are left to conclude that either Plato had one view in his early work, changed his mind rather drastically in the *Republic*, before returning to his earlier view in his later work, or, alternatively, that the *Republic* is not a work in political philosophy at all. If we take the former view, then the importance of the *Republic* is marginalized because it does not reflect Plato's mature view and indeed reflects a view he clearly rejects. This is untenable given the quite obvious importance of the text and its place in the Platonic corpus. To take the latter view is to commit to an interpretation that is at first counterintuitive, but at the same time to attend closely to the text. After all, Plato says that the point of the construction of the thought experiment ideal city is to isolate Justice in the individual soul. Thus, while holding the latter view will entail that we should not turn to the *Republic* for Plato's political views, it also will entail that we should examine the *Republic* to understand his theory of virtue and human good.

If the *Republic* is a work of moral philosophy, particularly focused on the nature of the virtue Justice, then it will be important to be very clear what the framework for Plato's argument is. To develop that context, it is important, as always, that we attend closely to the text. Confronted, in *Republic 2*, by Glaucon and Adiamantus over the question of whether it is better to actually be just or to simply strive to appear so, Plato's "Socrates" sets out to show that Justice is desirable not only for its consequences but also for its own sake. Here, Glaucon takes up the position of Thrasymachus from *Republic 1*; namely that Justice is merely the advantage of the stronger. Or, as Glaucon reimagines the question, suppose one can act unjustly and be thought just at the same time. Is it not the case that this would be better than acting justly and thus having our desires bounded in some ways. While it is true that satisfaction of desires is commonly called "good," it seems that it is but one kind of "good." In other words, the label "good" is often used in different ways in different circumstances. Socrates's suggests that there are three types of good: (1) Goods welcomed for their own sake (or desires satisfied which are themselves pleasurable), (2) Goods desired for their own sake and for their consequences (things desired because of the pleasantness of the thing or act itself and for the benefits that are a consequent of it), and (3) Goods accepted for their consequences (or, things desired not because they are themselves pleasant but because they bring about good benefits). An example of a Type-1 good would be something like happiness.

Happiness is itself desired and when asked if it is desired for some other end, the answer is likely to be "no." It is simply desired as an end in itself. A Type-2 good might be something like health. Indeed, this is the primary analogue that Plato uses to speak of good and virtue because it is something that is desired for itself and because it brings good consequences as well. The thesis of the *Republic*, after demonstrating what Justice is and where within the soul it is found, is to argue that Justice is a good desired for itself and desired for its consequences. The third sort of good, a Type-3, is desired only for the consequences it brings about, but not necessarily for itself. One could imagine a tetanus shot in this category. It is wholly unpleasant in itself, but it is to be desired because it can bring about health and prevent certain diseases. Glaucon's position is that Justice is good for its consequences, for in seeming just, one can receive great benefit (especially if one is actually unjust and behaving so). On his view, it is an onerous burden that one simply must endure in order to avoid negative consequences – imprisonment, banishment, death – and to acquire what meager positive consequences might accrue. The distinction between the views of Socrates and Glaucon are fairly clearly drawn, then, and the stakes of the argument are rather high.

Plato employs the Myth of the Ring of Gyges to sharpen the horns of the dilemma on which Socrates sits. The myth is a powerful one from the hazy era of Greek mythology that significantly predates Plato. It is a myth that has captured the imagination of such diverse artists as Richard Wagner (*The Ring of the Nibelung*) and J. R. R. Tolkien (*The Hobbit, The Lord of the Rings*). Plato introduces the myth as a way of demonstrating how precarious the position of Socrates seems in comparison to Glaucon's. Glaucon's challenge to Socrates is to demonstrate that it is better to be just and to be thought unjust and treated as if one were unjust than it is to be unjust and be thought and treated as if one were just. If Glaucon's view is right, that it is better to truly be unjust and yet to appear as if one is virtuous, then the Socratic mission itself is in jeopardy. On Glaucon's view, those who act justly do so unwillingly and only because they fear punishment if they decided to act in the ways they truly desired. So, Socrates sets up the problem by recalling the myth.

In the myth, a young shepherd of Lydia named Gyges encounters a ring in a deep crevasse opened by a tremendous earthquake during the course of a powerful thunderstorm. This confluence of events shakes the young shepherd who has protected the sheep throughout these happenings. In the midst of the great opening in the earth, Gyges sees many things, but a ring catches his eye and he puts it on. He discovers, during a meeting, that when he turns the ring toward himself, he becomes invisible, and when he turns it away, he becomes visible again. After experimenting with the ring to discover whether or not it truly had this power, he begins to utilize it. He manages to become appointed as a messenger to the king, and while there, he seduces the queen, assassinates the king (with her help), and takes over the kingdom. This seems to be an account of one who could act without fear of repercussion and consistent with Glaucon's view of how any person would act in such circumstances, freed from the constraints of fear of discovery and punishment.

However, the tale is altered a bit. Suppose that there were two such rings and that one was worn by a just person while the other worn by an unjust person. On Glaucon's view, both of these people would act in the same way, although perhaps it would take the just person longer to become corrupted by the ring than it would take the unjust one. Yet, Socrates is in the position of arguing that even in the case such as this one, where it is possible to act unjustly and according to whatever desires one has with impunity, it is still better to act justly rather than unjustly. The argument turns on a conception of the seat of virtue and vice, namely the soul. The soul of the one who acts unjustly is damaged by further unjust actions, whether that one began as a just soul or an unjust one. This damage, in the *Gorgias*, is even thought to be irreversible, even in the afterlife. Thus, the destruction of one's soul is the ultimate negative result of injustice and is a necessary consequent of it. Thus, even if there is no temporal repercussion, the structure of the universe is such that unjust actions ultimately breed self-destruction.

In answering Glaucon, Socrates believes himself to have refuted Thrasymachus more strongly than in *Republic 1* and to have shown, as opposed to Glaucon and the rest, that the practice of Justice is not an onerous imposition, practiced only reluctantly, but a Type-2 good, that is, a good loved for its own sake and for its consequences. This he does by drawing Glaucon, Adiamantus, and the others about him into a conversation concerning the Just City, for they agree that if Justice can be found in the city then its analogue will be more easily found in the individual. The reason for looking to the city as an analogy is because it is larger and more easily observed than the individual soul. He writes,

> Since the *polis* is considerably larger than an individual, the quantity of Justice is greater as well and thus more easily discerned. Thus, if we are going to ask about the nature of Justice and its opposite, then we should find them first in the *polis* and only then in the individual person. Thus, we will have gone from the greater to the smaller. Further, if we think of the *polis* as a work in progress, we should even more easily discover the object of our inquiry, justice in the individual.

So, in the course of their conversation, Socrates and his interlocutors develop a number of aspects of the city with the belief that since the imagined city which they are founding is founded rightly, then it is completely good. Since the city is completely good, it then possesses all of the virtues; that is, it is wise, temperate, courageous, and just. Socrates suggests that after they have fixed the locus of wisdom, temperance, and courage in the city, then the only "good-making" thing that will be left will be justice.

Wisdom is located in the persons of the guardian/ruler class. As such, wisdom is seen to be the knowledge of guardianship. Courage is located in the soldier class and as such is seen to be the true belief about what is to be feared and what is not to be feared. Moderation, or temperance, is discovered to suffuse the entirety of the city, adapting itself to the various classes with one unchanging aspect held by all; that is, the harmony and agreement about who should rule. Having located the first three virtues of the good city, the Socrates-led explorers have only to discover what "good-making" thing is left. This remainder will be justice.

At first the "remainder" is not immediately apparent to the participants in the conversation. At which point Socrates realizes that it has been there all along, but they had just missed it. The remaining "good-making" thing in the good city (after the subtraction of the other virtues) is the performance, by each class of citizens, the tasks appropriate for them, no more and no less. This, then, is Justice.

Having discerned the nature and location of Justice in the city, it is then appropriate to ask where in the individual soul it resides. One of the most famous Platonic examples is that of the Tripartite Soul characterized by the charioteer example. The human soul, on Plato's view, is divided into three parts – the appetitive part, the spirited part, and reason. The appetitive part of the soul is the part that contains all of our basic desires, urges and drives. The spirited part of the soul contains all of our desires and drives toward the "finer" things, like honor and good reputation. Reason, then, is supposed to govern the other two parts. Plato's charioteer example shows the importance of each of these parts playing its proper role.

The Charioteer example has three parts – the charioteer himself, a dark horse and a light horse. The dark horse represents the appetitive part of the soul, the light horse represents the spirited part, and the charioteer personifies reason. As a historical sidenote, Sigmund Freud appropriates this tripartite soul for his own psychoanalytical theorizing, labeling them as the id, the ego, and the superego respectively. Unfortunately for those looking to interpret Plato through a Freudian lens, Freud was a poor scholar of ancient philosophy. The only analogous parts of the two models are the first sections – the appetites and the id are roughly analogous. However, the other two features of the Charioteer example do not coincide at all with ego and superego, at least not in the sense that Plato develops them.

Finding Justice in the tripartite soul is rather straightforward. Imagine a chariot and its team of horses where the dark horse is in control. Driven by desires, it pursues them unthinkingly, dragging the rest of the system behind it, ultimately leading to its destruction. Thus, if the dark horse is not restrained, it will result in the destruction of the soul. Similarly, the light horse will also pursue its desires if left to its own devices and while it will not tend to lead to the destruction of the system as quickly as the hard-charging dark horse, it will nevertheless cause the same destruction. Only if the charioteer is in control of the system will the chariot thrive and flourish. This is not to say that the light horse and the dark horse are unnecessary. Quite to the contrary, without the horses, the chariot does not go anywhere. The charioteer himself cannot motivate the system. And a charioteer that is ruthless and micromanaging will thwart the development of the team and ultimately destroy it just as surely as either unchecked horse. Rather, there must be a balance within the system – each part doing what it is supposed to do and doing it well. Thus, the horses provide the motive force for the soul while the charioteer, with a light and even touch, guides the soul forward. Balance is the key and only the balanced soul is excellent. Thus, Justice is a matter of each part doing what it is supposed to do and only what it is supposed to do. This notion of balance also goes under the heading, *sophrosune*, or control of self.

Thus, the analogy from the tripartite soul to the tripartite city is complete. The *sophron* city (the city in which everything does what it is supposed to do and does it well) and the *sophron* soul (the soul in which everything does what it is supposed to do and does it well) are alike. Each has very specialized components that are necessary to its continued function and possible flourishing. And in each, the components must be guided by reason that understands the universe, guides the system as a whole, and drives it toward excellence and virtue.

The analogy of the city to the individual soul and the understanding of the connection between reason and virtue sets the stage for Plato to put forward an example that serves to unite the three main branches of philosophy into a single, comprehensive model. At the conclusion of *Republic 6*, Plato offers the model of the Divided Line. In this model, Plato's metaphysical, epistemological and ethical commitments are all combined in such a way that the interconnections between the three branches are made clear.

Section 3.3: Plato and Justice

Intelligible World

Forms	Wisdom, True Knowledge
(Mathematicals, Ratios)	Thinking
Physical Objects	Belief
Shadows, Reflections	Opinion

{Objects of Knowledge}   {Modes of Thought}

Visible World

One of Plato's overarching concerns throughout the dialogues is to show that the true philosopher is a very different animal from two other sorts of people who are often mistaken for being wise: Sophists and *Philotheamenes*. The Sophists concern Plato because Socrates was mistaken by many to be a Sophist – a teacher of rhetoric (among other things) who cared little for the truth and less for the state of the soul. Since the Socratic mission was to get the people of Athens to care most about truth, wisdom, and the state of the soul, Plato goes to great lengths to show that Socrates was not a Sophist. The other group, the *Philotheamenes*, or "lovers of sights and sounds," are most analogous to what are today called critics – either of the movie or literary sort. They practice the art of rhetoric in such a way that they seem to know a great many things about the art forms they criticize. Their opinions were highly sought and greatly prized. However, Plato's view is that they knew little about what they said. They were highly practiced in using language, but had no grasp of the truth. Because of this, they were lumped with Sophists as those who seem wise but are not. It is this latter group with which Plato is concerned in the discussion of education that makes up the middle of the *Republic*.

The Divided Line is used in the context of describing how a philosopher is educated. The description of the education of the philosopher is the foundation for what later becomes known as the Liberal Arts. In the course of that description, Plato distinguishes between two types of people – true philosophers and people who seem to be philosophers but are not (e.g., the lovers of sights and sounds). Plato is trying to demonstrate the difference between those who grasp the truth and focus on the things of the higher realm and those who may think they know the truth, but who are, in fact, mistaken and focused on the lower realm. The double horizontal line separates the objects of thought (metaphysics) and the modes of thought (epistemology) of the two groups, with philosophers attending to the higher and pseudo-philosophers being caught in the lower. The vertical line, between objects of thought and modes of thought, shows the relationship between metaphysics. For each sort of object that exists, there is a particular way in which that object is apprehended by the mind. Thus, not only are the different objects made distinct, but the different ways in which people think are also distinguished.

The relationship between the classes of object in the Divided Line analogy is something like this: every class is the shadow of the class immediately higher on the line (except, of course, for the Forms which are the ultimate class of object). A similar relationship exists on the other side of the Divided Line; each mode of thought is related to a class of objects and each mode of thought is related hierarchically to every other, until the ultimate mode of thought – *noesis* or True Knowledge – is achieved. Briefly, the objects of the lowest section are related to the lowest mode of thought – *eikasia* or Opinion – and are shadows of the objects of the second section. The objects of the second section are related to the next highest mode of thought – *pistis* or Belief – and are the shadows of the objects of the penultimate level. The objects of the third section are in turn shadows of the objects of the highest level (and thus shadows of the Forms). These objects at the penultimate level are related to the mode of thought – *dianoia* or Thinking.

The object/shadow relationship on the object of thought side of the Line illustrates a symmetric relationship between the knowledge states on the mode of thought side of the Line. As a student moves from the Visible World filled with sensible objects toward the Intelligible World of the Forms, the student experiences a number of paradigm shifts as she graduates from each preceding stage. Mathematicians, for example, use hypotheses to argue about the abstracted objects of which the objects of *pistis* are shadows.

While the mathematician has made the shift from beliefs tied to particular objects – drawn diagrams and the like – to, with the help of hypotheses, thinking about the relationships those diagrams symbolize (that is, from looking at the right triangle drawn in the sand to thinking about the relationship between the hypotenuse and the lengths of the other two sides), the true philosopher has put away the hypotheses and contemplates the Form *triangle* which is neither right, nor scalene, nor isosceles, but is the essence of *triangle*. At most, the paradigm shift made by the "lovers of sights and sounds" is from *eikasia* to *pistis*, from *opinion* to *belief*. And it is precisely the higher paradigm shift that distinguishes dianoetic mathematicians from the "lovers of sights and sounds." Thus, they do not possess the same epistemic state, or state of mind, but qualitatively different ones. On the one hand, while not grasping the Forms completely, the mathematician has experienced a paradigm shift in the way she looks at the world and reasons systematically about it. She is thus prepared for the next shift in perspective, from hypothesis to the dialectic in which the hypotheses are destroyed and the Forms are viewed directly. On the other hand, the "lovers of sights and sounds" have not made this first shift and so remain "unable to discuss anything of a serious nature."

So, what of the objects of the third section of the line? One of the difficulties of interpreting the Divided Line passage is that Plato never explicitly says what the penultimate object of knowledge is. Aristotle says that Plato called them "mathematicals," but it is not completely clear what a "mathematical" is. So, what should we conclude about them? Since we have seen that there exists a symmetric relationship between the objects of thought on the one side of the Divided Line and the modes of thought on the other, and further since we have seen that each class of objects is related to a particular mode of thought, the objects of the third section must be the sort of object that is not a sensible particular (since it resides above that level) and not a Form (since it resides below that level). Here, I think Plato's use of the mathematician is particularly apt. The mathematician (or the mathematical mind) can be understood to grasp something like ratios. The reasons for this are apparent from Plato's description of the Divided Line.

In laying out the Divided Line analogy, Plato clearly claims that each section bears a particular mathematical relationship to the one below. The line is divided into two unequal portions that stand in a ratio of 2:1 – the larger portion being the top part of the line. The larger portion of the line is the world of intelligible objects, the smaller portion of the line is the world of visible or sensible things. Each of these sections of the line is further subdivided, with the subdivisions of each bearing the same ratio of 2:1. In describing the occupants of the sections of the line (as discussed earlier), Plato is somewhat vague about the object of the third section. Instead of specifically naming that group of objects, he refers to the activity of the one who occupies the third section of the mode of thought side of the Divided Line. Plato writes, "So, you also know that they will at times draw figures of various sorts and will use them to guide their thinking. They are not actually arguing about the figures they have drawn but about the absolutes – the Square, the Diameter, and so on – the Forms about which they are talking are represented by the figures they draw or construct and those figures can very well have a reflection in clear water or may cast a shadow. But, while they are using figures they have drawn, they are really trying to understand the things that can only be perceived by the mind."

Plato's use of mathematics is instructive. Consider a mathematician considering the Pythagorean Theorem. For the sake of reference, she draws a triangle with a small box in the corner of the angle formed by the two shorter legs of the triangle to indicate that it is a right triangle. Clearly, it is not a perfect triangle, as it is drawn by human hands and so cannot possibly be absolutely a right triangle. Further, as it is constructed of "lines" that have three dimensions while, by definition, lines have but two, it cannot be even an actual triangle. But the mathematician uses the observable, sensible object to guide her thought – not measuring the angles of the drawn triangle, but considering the mathematical relationships of the sides to one another, the angles to one another, the sides to the various angles, and so forth. In fact, each of these relationships can be represented by a ratio. And, these relationships will be static. In a right triangle of given dimensions, the ratios that define that triangle will be precise. As a further note, one could then use those ratios to determine the quality of the drawn triangle – it would be better or worse insofar as the ratios it exemplified matched these ideal ratios. However, the true philosopher would be able to make the further distinction, understanding that the Form of *triangle* is what gives rise to the shadow of the ratios in the mind of the mathematician. Thus, through careful analysis of the text and the competing interpretive views of it, it seems reasonable to conclude that dialectic and mathematics are clearly distinct modes of thought, that the true philosopher and the mathematician are distinct, that mathematicians occupy a higher epistemic state than the "lovers of sights and sounds," and that the objects of the third section of Plato's Divided Line are mathematical ratios.

Having offered an argument for that interpretive difficulty, and shown the connection between metaphysics and epistemology that is exemplified in the Divided Line, there is only left to show how the Divided Line connects metaphysics and epistemology to ethics. Let us recall the Cardinal Virtues – Justice, Courage, *Sophrosune*, Piety, and Wisdom. If one also recalls the early dialogues, in which Plato asks for the one form by which all pious things are pious, for example, then one could conclude that perhaps the Cardinal Virtues are Forms. This would be an accurate conclusion, for the most part. Which is to say, most of the Cardinal Virtues are Forms. However, one is not. Wisdom, or true knowledge, is a mode of thought or an epistemological state. It will be noted, of course, that Wisdom is the highest mode of thought and it contemplates the Forms, including the highest Form, the Form of the Good. Thus, the truly virtuous person is the person who is wise; and wisdom consists, in large part, in apprehending the Forms, in knowing the actual world as it is, including the actualities that are virtues. Thus, epistemological concerns form the right-hand side of the Line, metaphysical ones the left, and ethical concerns are at the pinnacle of both. As *Republic 6* ends, Plato is prepared to move from a systematic treatment of these issues to an allegorical illustration of them, further enhancing the understanding of the structure of the actual world, the way in which it is known, and the sort of life that is required.

Plato's Allegory of the Cave is one of the most enduring, discussed, and debated analogies in all of philosophy to say nothing of the philosophy of Plato. The Allegory serves several purposes for Plato within the *Republic*. The first is a return to his view of the metaphysical and epistemological model expressed in the Divided Line example. There, Plato is concerned to show the relationship between his metaphysical commitments – a view of the reality of the world – and his epistemological commitments – a view of how the world is known. The world of objects of knowledge is divided into two parts which are each subdivided into two more. The upper segment of this division of knowledge is the Intelligible World, or the world apprehended by the mind. The lower segment of the division is the Visible World, or the world apprehended by the senses. Reality trickles down from the Forms, at the top, to the shadows or images of physical objects at the bottom. The mode by which the mind apprehends these objects, on the other hand, moves from the lowest form of cognition – Opinion – which is the mode of thought whose object is the image of physical objects, or shadows, through Belief, Thinking, and ultimately to True Knowledge or Wisdom at the top. The one with Wisdom knows the Forms. This very helpful model is also somewhat dry. Hence, Plato has Socrates tell the story of the cave as an allegory to explain it more fully.

A man is chained in the dark along with all his fellows. They can see nothing but the dance of shadows on the wall. These shadows are all they know and they develop elaborate systems of explaining the apparent relations between the shadows. They are certain that what they observe is real.

One day, the chains fall from the arms of one of the captives and he stands and turns. The glare of the opening of the cavern blinds him. As his eyes adjust, he sees physical objects. He comes to realize that there exists a relationship between the object and the shadows on the wall. What is striking is that he sees the shadows not as the cause of the objects, but the objects as the cause of the shadows. As he approaches the opening of the cave, and as his eyes adjust ever more to the increasing light, he comes to realize that the physical objects are not the cause of the shadows, but rather the Sun is the ultimate cause of them.

One of the aims of Plato's Allegory is to explain, by analogy, the very controversial view that the immaterial Forms are the cause of the material objects and the images of perception. The Sun in the Allegory stands to the shadows on the cave wall as the Forms stand to the perceptions of physical objects in the world. The philosopher, who now has true knowledge of the actual structure of the world, returns to the depths of the cavern to guide his fellow captives to true knowledge as well. However, he finds them resistant to abandon their comfortable and familiar shadows and opinions. Ultimately, they grow frustrated as the philosopher continues to pester them to leave the opinion of the shadows to turn to the true knowledge of the Forms. To rid themselves of this Socratic gadfly, they come together and kill him.

The Allegory stands as a striking critique of the contentment in ignorance of the Athenian democrats who unjustly convicted and executed Socrates. This view continues consistently from the early dialogues. More importantly, as a matter of philosophy, the Allegory takes the rather complicated and dry example of the Divided Line and explains by analogy the relationship between the Intelligible World of the Forms and the Visible World of particular physical objects.

Guided Reading Questions:

1. How does the Allegory of the Cave reflect Plato's continuing concern with the Socratic Mission – namely, to get the Athenians to care more for their souls than for power, reputation, and wealth?
2. How are the Allegory of the Cave and the Divided Line related?
3. How do the Allegory of the Cave and the Divided Line show the interrelations between Plato's metaphysics and epistemology?
4. How does the Ring of Gyges myth make Glaucon's point?
5. What must Socrates demonstrate in order to show that Glaucon's view about the benefits of injustice and the tendency of human nature toward injustice is false?
6. What is justice?
7. How does Plato use the analogy of the city to the individual to develop his conception of Justice?
8. What are the possible kinds of good? What are the conditions of the highest good?

Logic Blurb
The *Reductio Ad Absurdum*

If we return briefly to an examination of Plato's *elenchus*, another very important class of logical arguments can be discerned. The *elenchus* proceeds from a question by Socrates to an answer, generally a definitional answer, offered by his interlocutor and supposed expert on the topic at hand. From that answer, implications are drawn and in the ebb and flow of the argument, the interlocutor is reduced to some blatantly false conclusion. For example, after Euthyphro offers the definition of piety saying that "piety is looking after the gods." This notion of looking after the gods is shown to be something like looking after cattle or looking after dogs and cats. At the same time, Euthyphro believes that the gods have no need of looking after. Thus, his argument is reduced to a contradiction or to an absurdity.

If we are given some premise and this premise inevitably leads us to contradictory statements, then the premise results in absurd conclusions; that is, to conclusions that cannot possibly be so. Any premise that results in such contradictions is thus properly discarded. The genius of this logical insight is that it allows one to argue a point indirectly, by making an assumption – e.g., A (often, precisely the opposite of the assumption that one hopes to be true) – and by demonstrating that A leads to, for example, C and ~C (or contradictions), we know that A must be false. Hence, ~A (the premise for which we are truly arguing) is shown to be true through the use of the *reductio*.

Section 4.1: Reading Aristotle

Reading Aristotle is much different from reading Plato. That much is clear to even the most unpracticed eye. However, the differences between Aristotle and Plato go far beyond stylistic ones. The stylistic ones are not inconsequential. Neither are the historical and cultural differences between the two great philosophers. We will first address these before turning to the perhaps more obviously substantive philosophical differences.

The works of Plato that survive are far from complete. Many dialogues seem to have been lost to history. Almost the entirety of his work in any form other than dialogue have been lost as well. Thus, we are left to piece together arguments from fragmentary evidence with the dialogues and from bits and snatches in the work of others, particularly Aristotle. It is estimated that the extant works of Plato make up less than half of his complete works. The textual integrity of Aristotle is considerably worse. It is known that Aristotle, like Plato, composed dialogues. Unfortunately, none of them survive. It is also known that he wrote treatises, fragments of which have endured. The vast majority of the extant works of Aristotle, however, is in the form of notes; notes preserved from the Lyceum almost entirely by students and followers of Aristotle. To make matters more complicated, the extant work of Aristotle was essentially lost to the West for the better part of the first millennium of the Common Era, preserved, for the most part, by Arab scholars of the Middle East. The difficulties, then, in working with the philosophical contributions of Aristotle is considerably more difficult than with those of Plato.

Aristotle's work, fragmentary though it is, is still among the most important philosophic works in human intellectual history. While it is, in many ways, much less readable than the dialogues of Plato, it is also true that, at least at points, it is easier to detect the line of the argument. Further, it avoids the difficulty attendant in the scholarly work with Plato in that while at times it is difficult to discern which of the interlocutors speaks for Plato, if any, it is not difficult to discern who speaks for Aristotle, as the work is in a single voice. It is also clear that Aristotle develops arguments in one place, e.g., *Metaphysics*, that he then makes reference to, but does not redevelop, in others, e.g., *Nicomachean Ethics*. The Four Cause Doctrine is but one example of this, and an example that will be discussed at length in the first section of the discussion of the *Nico-*

machean Ethics. Given that Aristotle references and cross-references arguments and views expressed in other places within his work, it is sometimes difficult to tease out a single argument or concept without succumbing to the daunting and likely impossible task of trying to acquire the entirety of the work at once. Throughout the sections on Aristotle, we will walk carefully through some of his most important arguments, going afield for the more comprehensive support for some premises within those arguments as necessary.

One non-philosophical difference between Plato and Aristotle that has import on their contributions to the philosophical conversation is a matter of citizenship. As discussed in the foregoing section, Plato was an Athenian citizen, but not only that, he was an Athenian aristocrat with intimate ties to both the best and worst of Athenian government. Aristotle, on the other hand, was not an Athenian citizen. Aristotle joined Plato's Academy soon after its founding and is generally thought to have distinguished himself rather quickly. Diogenes Laertius, a later chronicler of ancient thought, estimated that Aristotle was recognized then, as he is now, as the greatest of Plato's students.

Whether Aristotle was recognized at the time as the greatest of Plato's students is unclear, however. It is clear that the two did not have the idyllic teacher/student relationship. Evidence of this is the succession to leadership of the Academy. Traditionally, the death of a great teacher who had established a following was followed by the succession to the position of leader by that teacher's foremost disciple and student. However, Plato took some pains to make sure that Aristotle did not become the leader of the Academy at Plato's death. Indeed, Speucippus, Plato's nephew, was elevated to the post and Aristotle took his leave of the Academy and of Athens.

For all their immediate, and later, philosophical differences, Plato and Aristotle had quite similar experiences in practical politics. Both deeply concerned with proper organization of the polis, Plato and Aristotle both made forays into practical politics that ended less spectacularly than they hoped. Plato visited Syracuse at the request of the monarch there with the aim of cultivating in him the Philosopher-King of the *Republic*. That project ended in the king's rejection of Platonic tutoring and the fortuitously failed attempt to sell Plato into slavery. Aristotle's venture into politics was somewhat less ill-fated, but only by degree. Summoned by Philip of Macedon to tutor his young son and heir apparent, Alexander, Aristotle spent quite some time with the soon to be great conqueror. However, though the project did not end with an enslavement attempt against Aristotle, it was less than successful, in Aristotle's estimation, and he returned to Athens.

The several years that followed Aristotle's departure from Athens saw him embark on a quite different methodological path from his mentor. Aristotle traveled widely and recorded extensive notes, categorizing flora and fauna from throughout the Greek world. While the elenchus, the method of hypothesis, and the dialectical method of collection and division are all features of Platonic thought, Aristotle is more known for his more empirical method of collection and division. In the *Categories*, while collecting words and dividing them into types and parts of speech and the like, he also uses the Category Map to divide the great collection of all things that exist into distinct groups based on the various differentiae that they exhibit. Thus, all mammals and birds and reptiles are grouped together under the "animate" heading with the Substance category, and then each of these groups is subdivided until each of the particular instances of each head is enumerated. Again, in the *Nicomachean Ethics*, Aristotle employs the method to great effect. In one case, he uses it to first collect all of those things people commonly call "good" in an effort to then divide those things with the goal of determining whether or not a highest good exists and what that might be. Similarly, too, he uses the method in his physical and political works. Again and again, Aristotle collects all of the particulars within one heading or another and examines them based on the differentiae they exhibit, all the while gaining greater and greater insight into the workings of the world; grammatical, biological, political, physical, and ethical.

Beyond their differences in methodology, Aristotle and Plato have commonly been held up as exemplars of two very different schools of philosophical method. Plato, with his Theory of Forms and its ontological primacy attached to Forms or universals rather than particulars, is cited as an early example of Rationalism. Rationalism, simply put, is the philosophical method that holds that the best and most effective means of apprehending truth (about the world, about knowledge, about actions) is through the power of the mind; often, and perhaps always, the mind freed of attachment to the senses which can be deceptive. On the other hand, Aristotle flatly rejects both the Theory of Forms and the ontological superiority of universals, instead arguing that human perception is the ultimate source of knowledge and that particular objects have a greater share of reality than the ideas about them. However, drawing a sharp distinction between Plato and Aristotle on this matter is both artificial and counter to their actual methodologies.

While there is a very sharp distinction between rationalism and empiricism in the Early Modern period (and subsequently), such does not exist in the Ancient period, at least not in the same way and definitely not as exemplified by Plato and Aristotle. Plato and Aristotle both exemplify that Whiteheadian conception of the practice of philosophy discussed in the introductory section. Philosophy is both general and concrete, abstract and particular. Philosophy, properly done, has both a rationalistic pole and an empirical one. Thus, the difference in methodologies of Plato and Aristotle is more a difference in emphasis, one giving greater weight to one pole and one to the other, than a radical difference. Indeed, the stylistic differences between the two thinkers are greater than their methodological ones.

The commonalities between Plato and Aristotle, and indeed, Socrates, are often overlooked in the move to demonstrate the distinctions between them.

Both Plato and Aristotle are concerned with what might be called, "The Big Questions" – what is the nature of humanity, what is the good life, how is it lived? For Plato and Aristotle, the centerpiece of the good life is a live of virtue that is productive of *eudaimonia*, or well-being; both body and soul. It is a reasonably safe characterization of ancient philosophy that the dominant philosophical system is a eudaimonistic one. In other words, the metaphysical, epistemological, and ethical questions revolve around a notion of character, its development, and the happiness (*eudaimonia*) this is understood to be the consequence of a good or excellent life.

In addition to this broad philosophical shared commitment, it is interesting to note a similarity of fate. Having already discussed the practical political difficulties encountered by both Plato and Aristotle, it is perhaps less philosophically important, but quite historically interesting and perhaps ironic to note the similarity of situations in which Aristotle and Socrates found themselves. Athenians were none too keen to be conquered by outsiders, either by the Spartans during the time of Socrates or by Alexander the Great during Aristotle's era. After the death of Alexander, Athenians reacted much the way toward Aristotle that they had toward Socrates. Unable to take out frustrations and exact vengeance upon their conqueror, they turned their wrath toward the teacher upon whom they could heap the blame for the instability of their existence. Like Socrates, Aristotle became a scapegoat, in an official way, charged and likely to be convicted, and thus, likely to encounter the same fate as Socrates before him. Rather than meet his fate as Socrates had, Aristotle abandoned Athens, "lest Athens sin twice against philosophy." Unfortunately, some ten months after abandoning his adopted hometown, Aristotle took ill and died. His school, the Lyceum, established upon his return to Athens to be a competitor to Plato's school, the Academy, did not survive his flight from Athens.

Returning to the philosophical examination of the similarities and differences between Plato and Aristotle, one encounters an important consequence of the methodological difference between them that is quite clear and strikingly simple. While Socrates, at least in the words of Plato, strictly rejects the accusation that he is a Natural Philosopher, and Plato would seem to reject such an ascription to himself as well, Aristotle would be much more amenable to such a description. Simply put, Aristotle is a Natural Philosopher. His close observation of the natural world and careful attention to natural explanations for natural events marks him as a descendent of the PreSocratic natural philosophers like Heraclitus and Thales. In this, we see perhaps the clearest distinction between Plato and Aristotle. While Plato reasons that reality and truth flow downward from a heaven of eternal and immutable Platonic Forms, Aristotle observes that the things bearing the greatest reality are those that are encountered in the particulars of the actual world.

It is good now to turn from the distinctions between Plato and Aristotle to a more particular preview of Aristotle's own work. The relationship between metaphysics, epistemology and ethics that has been discussed at some length in previous sections is of even greater importance here, if possible. At various times, Aristotle's work has been interpreted as primarily the work of an empiricist, an epistemologist, a metaphysician, a Natural Philosopher, a scientist, a dramatist, and a grammarian. However, it seems a better interpretation to read Aristotle as essentially an ethicist, concerned with the nature of the good, the nature of the good life, and the ways in which the good life is acquired and lived. Aristotle's rigorous approach to topics in anthropology, logic, mathematics, biology, grammar, and physics, to name but a few, provide the foundation for his discussion of ethical matters. For example, in the work of Aristotle, one finds a commitment to the notion that certain facts about the world are necessary of nature. After these have been discerned through careful analysis, they are included in the scope of human knowledge. That knowledge, then, is the basis for practical reason in the evaluation of the good or the fine. This is particularly clear in an evaluation of Aristotle's most well known ethical work, the *Nicomachean Ethics*.

Careful examination of the *Nicomachean Ethics* reveals that Aristotle relies on other of his writings to complete the arguments. That arguments in the *Nicomachean Ethics* are compressed is relatively uncontroversial. The Function Argument, for example, that concludes that all natural objects have necessary natural functions, is not fully elaborated in the *Ethics*. Instead, Aristotle makes use of propositions found in other of his works, particularly the *Metaphysics* and the *Physics*. The Function Argument, however, is a lynchpin in the argument in the *Ethics*. Virtue is a matter of fulfilling one's natural function excellently. Thus, without the Function Argument the arguments in the *Nicomachean Ethics* falter.

Beyond this, the implications for the views Aristotle develops in the *Nicomachean Ethics* and elsewhere are rather extensive. In the *Politics*, Aristotle discusses the nature of various constitutions, dividing them into those that are better and worse. In the midst of that discussion, he makes an analogy to the nature of men and the differing nature of women. The discussion of the difference in virtue that men and women are capable of possessing is used to discuss the differing natures of those governed by the various constitutions. In addition, his arguments about the nature of women in the *Politics* depends on his understanding of the nature of the human soul as having both a rational and an irrational part, on the structure of reproduction from *Generation of Animals*, and the function of human beings discussed at several points ranging from the *Categories* to the *Metaphysics* to the *Nicomachean Ethics*. The point of this discussion is to demonstrate briefly that without a working understanding of the Aristotelian material (metaphysics, epistemology, anthropology, etc.) developed in other works, one is hard pressed to make complete use of the arguments in the *Ethics*. Thus, as we discuss the *Categories* and the *Nicomachean Ethics*, as prime examples of Aristotle's work in metaphysics, epistemology, and ethics, we will digress from time to time to include his arguments and principles developed in other sections of his work.

As we work through the works included here, it becomes clear that Aristotle's non-ethical works serve to provide support for his ethical views and his ethical views are reflected in his non-ethical works. Within the *Categories*, we encounter perhaps the first systematic discussion of grammar, one that explores not merely how words are used but the ways in which words refer to actual objects in the actual world. From this foundational document, we turn to read significant portions of the first two books of the *Nicomachean Ethics*, in which some of the most famous of all of Aristotle's work is included.

Section 4.2: Aristotle – *Categories*

Categories

Chapter One

Objects are named equivocally when the definition for each of them is different and yet they are called by the same name. For example, an actual person and an image of a person are both reasonably called "animal." However, calling them each "animal" is an equivocation. Objects are named univocally when the name and the definition are held in common. For example, a person and an ox are both properly called "animal" because the name and the definition are the same. Objects are named derivatively if the name by which they are called is derived from some other name. For example, the grammarian is derived from "grammar"; the courageous from "courage."

Chapter Two

Parts of speech are simple or complex. For example, "a person runs" is complex; "human" is simple. Some qualities are *said-of* predicates; others are *present-in* predicates. For example, "human" is *said-of* some particular person. It is never *present-in* one.

Present-in does not mean present as a part is to a whole. If something is *present-in* something else, it means that it cannot exist without the subject. Similarly, some qualities are *present-in* predicates. A bit of knowledge (of grammar, perhaps) is *present-in* in mind, but it is not *said-of* that mind. Similarly, a particular shade of white could be *present-in* a body, but that particular shade of white is never *said-of* something.

Chapter Three

If one quality is *said-of* another quality, all of those things that are properly *said-of* the first are also *said-of* the subject. For example, "human" is *said-of* a particular individual; "animal" is *said-of* "human"; therefore "animal" is also *said-of* the particular individual.

Chapter Four

Certain categories are never composite. These refer to Substance, Quantity, Quality, Relation, Place, Time, Position, State, Action, and Affection. Here are some examples – "person" and "horse" fall under the heading Substance. Quantity refers to number; Quality to qualities like "white"; Relation to notions like "greater than" and "less than"; Place to expressions like "in the Lyceum"; Time refers to "yesterday"; Position to things like "sitting". "To burn" refers to an action; "to be burned" to an affection.

None of these expresses a positive or negative claim of its own. Only by combining these sorts of things can we create sentences that are then either true or false. Every sentence, clearly, is either true or false. Those things that are simple, and not complex, can be neither.

Chapter Five

The primary use of "substance" is to refer to that which is neither *said-of* nor *present-in* anything else; for example, the individual person or a particular horse. It can be used in a secondary sense to refer to all those things of the species and genera in which the primary substance is included. For example, the individual person is of the species "human", the species belongs to the genus "animal". "Human" and "animal" are thus called secondary substances.

All things that are not primary substances are either *present-in* or *said-of* some particular primary substance. For example, "animal" is *said-of* "human" which is *said-of* some particular person. However, if no people existed, then "animal" could not be *said-of* "human" because "human" does not exist. Without primary substances, nothing else exists.

If we consider secondary substances only, the one closest to the primary substance is the one that is most real. For example, if one were to explain what some particular primary substance (say, an individual person) was, he would give a more precise account by saying that the individual was a "human" than by saying he was an "animal." "Animal" is far too general to be a precise account. Similarly, explaining the nature of an individual tree will be better and more precise if one calls it "tree" rather than "plant."

All substance signifies individuals. This is irrefutable with respect to primary substances since the primary substance is a single thing. With respect to secondary substances, these are called substances because we are referring to a particular kind that possesses a specific quality. "Human" and "animal" are *said-of* many more things than a single subject.

Another indication of a substance is that it admits of no contrary. For instance, what could possibly be the contrary of an individual human being or a particular horse? There are none. Similarly, species and genera do not have contraries. This is not only true of those things within the Substance category, it is also true of some others – Quantity, for example.

Substance does not vary. Now, we have already seen that some things are more substance than others and some less. However, no individual substance possesses varying degrees of itself. For example, a particular person can not be more himself or less himself; nor can he be more human than another; as for example, a white object may be whiter or less white than some other object.

All this said, the most distinctive trait of substance is that it can possess contrary qualities within itself while remaining a single entity. This is not the case with any other category. For example, the same color cannot be white and black. No action can be both good and bad at the same time. However, a substance may retain its identity, its singularity, while possessing contraries. For example, an individual is at once white and later black; at one time cold and at another hot; at one time good and at another bad. Some might suggest an exception – that statements can be both true and false – "he sits" is true only while he is sitting. Upon his getting up, "he sits" is now false. The distinction is this. The substance itself changes and thus possesses contrary qualities. The statement does not. It is by changing the facts about the world that a statement that once was true becomes false and vice versa.

Chapter Six

Quantity is discrete or continuous. Some express a part-to-whole relation while others do not. An example of a discrete quantity is something like number; an example of a continuous quantity is something like a line. For numbers, there is no common point at which they are connected. For example – five plus five is ten, but the two fives have nothing in common; they are distinct. Similarly, the parts specified by three and seven also together make ten but have no common point of contact. Numbers are always separate from one another, and thus always discrete.

A line is a continuous quantity. When examining its parts, it is clear that there is a common point between them. Space and time are quantities of this sort as well.

Quantities also have no contraries. One might object that "a lot" is the contrary of "a little", for example. However, these are not quantitative terms; they are relations. Things are not absolutely "little", but relatively so. For example, a mountain may reasonably be called "small" and a grain of sand may reasonably called "large" without pain of contradiction.

The clearest and most distinctive trait of quantity is that equality and inequality are *said-of* it. For example, one solid is "equal" or "unequal" to some other; likewise number and time. If something is not a quantity, it cannot be called "equal" to something else.

Chapter Eleven

That good is contrary to evil is a matter of induction. For example, the contrary of health is illness; the contrary of courage is cowardice, etc. Further, an evil may have several contraries, only one of which may be good. Evil is a defect and so has as a contrary excess. This excess is also evil. The mean between excess and defect is a good and is the contrary to both of the instances of evil.

With contraries, it is not necessary that if one of two contraries exists that its contrary does as well. For example, all people could gain health. In that event, all would be healthy and none would be ill. Similarly, if everything became suddenly white, there would be nothing but white and no black. Further, since "Socrates is ill" and "Socrates is well" and because we cannot have both of these true at the same time and in the same respect, these contraries cannot both exists. If Socrates is well, then "Socrates is ill" is false.

~

Among Aristotle's most enduring contributions to the philosophical discourse is his systematic treatment of logic – from the meaning of atomic pieces (*Categories*) through the examination of the proper conjunction of the words into well-formed sentences (*On Interpretation*) to the discussion of the relation of those sentences in a formal argument structure (*Prior Analytics*) to an exploration of proofs (*Posterior Analytics*) to an overview of informal arguments (*Topics*) and concluding with lists of bad arguments and fallacies (*Sophist Elenchoi*). This set of works is most commonly referred to as Aristotle's *Organon*.

None of this should be taken to suggest that the philosophical works prior to Aristotle were bereft of logic, argument, or sophisticated treatment of these topics. Indeed, Plato explores many of these issues himself. The key distinction here is that Aristotle's *Organon* marks a high-water point in the exploration of logic and argument. It is not until the late 19th century that another philosopher is accorded the accolade of rising to Aristotle's level. Alfred North Whitehead has been called the greatest logician since Aristotle. That 2400 years passed in the interim suggests the greatness of Aristotle's work.

Communication, songs, plays, directions, and a great many other forms of human expression are dependent, at least in some way, on words and the use of words. To tell a person, "I love you" or to call a group of people to arms, "The British are coming! The British are coming!" depends on the use, and proper use, of words. Given that there are different uses of words, different kinds of words, it is not at all surprising that the way words are put together would add to the complexity. That is, if one puts a word in the wrong place in a sentence, the sentence no longer makes sense. With this observation about language, Aristotle builds from an understanding of individual words to an examination of how those words are combined.

When looking at a sentence, certain features are immediately clear. Before turning to features of sentences – words put together properly – it is perhaps important that we examine the individual building blocks of sentences; words, themselves. Suppose two people (Kathryn and Sarah) each offered Grace the opportunity to go with them to the bank. In fact, let us suppose that Kathryn and Sarah uttered exactly the same sentence – "Meet me at the bank." However, in Kathryn's case, she was inviting Grace to meet her at that place where money is kept while in Sarah's case, the invitation was to go fishing. Each of these is a proper use of the word "bank". Words that have this sort of feature, i.e., the same word with two different meanings, are called equivocations. Such examinations of the meanings of words is reasonably important given that Grace might well expect to meet Sarah downtown at a building with a vault and Kathryn down by the creek and would have precisely the opposite experience. Aristotle opens the *Categories* with an examination of several kinds of words – equivocal ones, univocal ones, homonyms, synonyms, etc.

Turning to the construction of sentences from the building blocks of words, Aristotle notes that any proper sentence has at least two features – a subject and a predicate. For example, the sentence "Bossie is a cow." has "Bossie" as the subject, and "is a cow" as the predicate. Understanding this, however, leads directly to a recognition that not all predicates are of the same kind. Take the following two sentences:

> Bossie is a cow.
> Bossie is brown.

At first, these predicates may not seem different at all. However, suppose we substitute the properties specified in each of the predicates so that we have the following two sentences.

> Bossie is a brown.
> Bossie is cow.

It becomes immediately obvious that something has gone awry. There is now clearly a difference between the two predicates. It is precisely this sort of observation that Aristotle explains early in the *Categories*, designating the first sort of predicate the *said-of* predicate and the second the *present-in* predicate. For example, "cow" is *said-of* Bossie, but not *present-in* her. "Brown" is *present-in* Bossie, but not *said-of* her.

So, if there are at least two sorts of predicates, might there not be very many more. As it turns out, there are only the two kinds of predicates, on Aristotle's view, although there are many varieties of the two kinds. Aristotle, through careful observation of the world and language, which is a natural feature of the world, developed a scheme with which to understand that amazing variety. His system of classification divides all the possible predicates into ten categories: Substance, Quantity, Quality, Time, Action, Affection, Relation, Place, Position, State.

Thus, with this approach, the very grammar of a language can be seen to connect directly to the world around us in such a way that better understanding of language will yield better understanding of the world and vice versa.

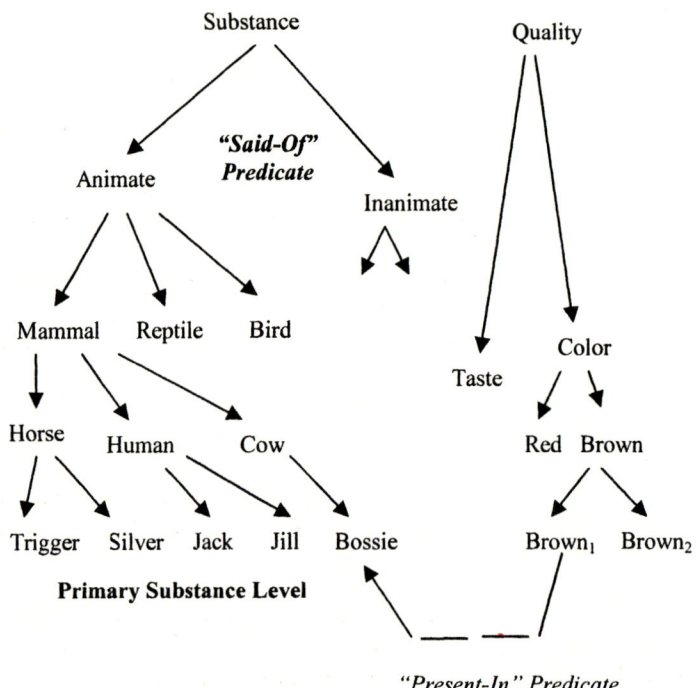

"Present-In" Predicate

The Category Map represented here is a quick rendering of the Aristotelian view, much more simple and imprecise than his own system entails. However, it also captures the central features of his view. At the lowest level, or the Primary Substance level, we find every particular in the world – all individual people, horses, cardinals, etc. Each of these is a proper subject. All of the levels of abstraction above the primary substance level are proper *substantial* predicates of those primary substances and related to them only insofar as one can trace the tree up from the primary substance to the secondary ones. So, for example,

Section 4.2: Aristotle - *Categories* 131

Bossie the Cow is a Cow, is a Mammal, is an Animate thing, and is a Substance. Or, in a more Aristotelian manner, Cow, Mammal, Animate, and Substance are properly *said-of* Bossie. Note, however, that Bird is not properly *said-of* Bossie. Thus, Bird is not a *substantial* property of Bossie. In using the Category Map to determine the proper substantial predicates, we can establish a set of properties that Bossie the Cow and some other primary substance, perhaps Ted the Cardinal, have in common and the ways in which they differ, as regards their essential or substantial properties.

In a very similar way, distinctions can be made between the accidental properties that Bossie and Ted have in common and those that they do not share. For example, Ted is red while Bossie is brown. Or, "red" is *present-in* Ted and "brown" is *present-in* Bossie. More to the point, Ted is a particular shade of red while Bossie is a particular hue of brown. So, we can discuss them having differences in their accidental properties. At the same time, if we move up the Quality tree just a bit, we find that Color is *present-in* both Bossie and Ted. Thus, they share a more abstract property than particular color because both of them have Color.

But these are not essential properties, they are, instead, accidental ones. Indeed, all non-Substance properties are non-essential, or accidental. For example, we could change Bossie's color rather easily simply by dyeing her to match Ted. However, we have not changed anything essential about her. She is still a Cow, a Mammal, an Animate thing, and a Substance. She still differs from Ted in precisely the same substantial ways that she did before they dyeing incident. Thus, an important distinction is captured by the Category Map. Those properties that are the essential properties of primary substances can be found in the Substance Category while all of the other, accidental properties, can be found in the other nine. The distinction is important because it lets us come to understand those properties of an entity that cannot be changed without changing the entity itself (the essential properties) and those properties that can and do change regularly but do not affect the nature or essence of an entity (the accidental properties).

We can go further here. Far beyond making grammatical observations or even rudimentary metaphysical ones regarding essential and accidental properties, Aristotle is of the view that even the quite complex structure of the universe might be divined by close examination of language and of the objects to which words refer. By carefully attending to the proper predication of particular substances, one might well discern the essential differences between them. For example, by examining the Substance category, one can observe the relationship between two entities, for example, Bossie the Cow and Rocky the Rat. The formal, and essential, difference between Bossie and Rocky is that Bossie is a *Cow* and Rocky is a *Rat*. Whatever it is to be a cow and whatever it is to be a rat, it cannot be denied that Bossie fails to have the essential property of a rat and vice versa. At the same time, Bossie the Cow and Rocky the Rat are more closely related to each other than either of them is to Bossie the Cardinal. This can be seen by tracing the Substance tree up from the primary substance level (where we encounter Bossie, Rocky, and Bossie) to the levels immediately preceding them in levels of abstraction – to Cow, Rat, and Cardinal. However, proceeding further in abstraction (and up the Substance Tree), one discovers, finally, that Bossie and Rocky are both Mammals and thus fall under that heading while Bossie does not. One must move to yet another level of abstraction to find some substantial feature that all three have in common. Thus, since one comes to a common substantial feature shared by Bossie and Rocky prior to one shared by either with Bossie, it is clear that Bossie and Rocky are more closely related than either is to Bossie.

The noting of all of these distinctions and similarities is an outgrowth of perhaps the most common Aristotelian method of examination, the Method of Collection and Division. Throughout the Aristotelian corpus, this method is constantly used to shed light on subjects from politics to geology to biology to ethics. The Method of Collection and Division is quite simple, in theory, and likely derives much of its analytical power through its very simplicity. It consists of two stages. The first is to collect all of the relevant objects into one group. In the case of politics, for example, this may be a collection of all of the various constitutions that one might find or imagine as the governing document of a city-state. In the case of the *Categories* and the Category Map, the objects to be collected are all of those that exist. Thus, the nature of the inquiry determines what objects are to be collected for survey.

After collecting all of the relevant objects or concepts, one then begins to look for those ways in which they are similar, and more importantly, those ways in which they are different. Like elements will be grouped with like and different with different. Thus, one begins to understand what the essential are and what the accidental properties of any particular set of objects are.

Part of the power of the Method of Collection and Division is that the dividing need not be along any particular set of lines each time. Take, for example, the six primary forms of constitution of a state – Monarchy, Aristocracy, Democracy, Anarchy, Oligarchy, and Tyranny. Having collected these, we can then divide them in different ways and in so doing, different aspects of the particular constitution will come to light. For example, we could divide the six in terms of the nature of the ruling class; that is, all those that have the good of the city-state as the motive of the ruler or rulers. In this way, we would group Monarchy, Aristocracy, and Democracy in one group and the other three in the group whose ruler or rulers have their own self-interests as the motive. Or, we could group them in terms of the number of rulers. In this way, Monarchy and Tyranny would be grouped, Aristocracy and Oligarchy, Democracy and Anarchy. Or, we could rank them, in terms both of the number of rulers and their natures. Thus, for Aristotle, the Monarchy (or the rule of one for the sake of the society as a whole) would come first, followed by the Aristocracy (the rule of a small group of aristocrats for the sake of the society as a whole), followed by the Democracy (or the rule of the citizens for the sake of the society as a whole). These would be considered the best, the better, and the good constitutions. Their counterparts, the bad, the worse, and the worst, would be as follows. An Anarchy (or the situation in which the citizens rule but are each out for his own interests) would be followed by an Oligarchy (the rule of a small group of oligarchs for the sake of themselves) followed by a Tyranny (the rule of a single despot for his own good or self-interest). Thus, but turning the various constitutions first this way and then that by way of the division part of the Method of Collection and Division, we attain a deeper understanding of the particulars in question.

While the Method of Collection and Division is exceptionally useful and, in many ways, allows Aristotle to begin the first truly systematic examination of political science, it is also intriguing to note that Aristotle's work in *Categories* essentially lays the foundations for much of the current work in many of the classical physical sciences. By looking at particular branches of the Substance category, for example, and reflecting on the work of biologists, one sees the direct inheritance they have from Aristotle. Collecting the living things on earth and dividing them into genera, species, and the like, modern biologist carry on the work of Aristotle's own empirical science, filling in branches of the Substance map along the way. Similarly, more specialized fields of zoology, botany, herpetology, etc. Each has, as one of its many functions, the collection and classification of the various genera and species particular to it. Thus, by examining particular instances of each of these creatures and plants, the scientist enumerates accidental properties characteristic of them, establishes their respective places on the Category Map, and thus continues the Aristotelian empirical project.

Returning then to the metaphysical commitments Aristotle expresses in the *Categories*, we discover that through the method of collection and division, we can discern another characteristic trait of the things that have independent existence (substances) and the properties that exist only insofar as they have something in which to inhere. Something is an actual particular object, and thus a substance, if it has independent existence. That is, if it is disconnected from other objects and yet maintains its own properties, it exists without the aid of another. Thus, Bossie the Cow is independent of the particular blades of grass that she eats. Now, it is clear that there is a sort of dependence here. Bossie depends on the food she ingests to continue to live, and one might say, roughly, to continue to exist. However, this is not strictly so and is not the sort of substantial independence that Aristotle is noting here. Even if Bossie perishes from lack of sustenance, she is still an existent thing, independent of the ground upon which she lies.

There is a potential equivocation regarding the word "independence" here. The sense in which Aristotle is suggesting that substances have independent existence is the sense in which each substance is a discrete entity, capable of being examined as an entity wholly separate from any of the particular surroundings in which it exists and from any properties that may belong to it. This is a *primary independence*. This is, perhaps, the more colloquial and common use of the word. For example, one might well declare independence from one's parents and colonies might declare independence from their colonial ruler. In this way, the individual or the colonies are separating themselves and demonstrating that they are distinct from some other discrete entity.

Here, however is the oddity of this particular "independence" equivocation. The notion opposite "independence," obviously, is "dependence." Given that the most common use of "independence" is as reference to a state of discrete existence, distinct from other objects, it might seem that the most common sense of its opposite should be a reference to a state of integrated existence, intertwined with other objects. Yet, this does not seem at all the most common use of "dependence." "Dependence," it seems, most commonly refers to a state of what is more precisely called "contingent" existence. That is, without air, a human being dies. Thus, a person is dependent upon air. Aristotle, with his assertion that the notable feature of existent objects is that they are independent, is not suggesting that human beings are independent of air or Bossie independent of food. Rather, he is pointing out that the food Bossie eats and Bossie herself are distinct entities which exist without the blessing or forbearance of the other. Thus, while Bossie is dependent on food, she is also independent of it. Hence, we see again the importance of the Aristotelian discussion of the equivocation as it relates to communication about and understanding of the actual world.

The other feature distinctly possessed by existent objects (by substances) is that they "admit of contraries." Here, Aristotle is making a distinction, not between two different substances, each independent of the other, but between a particular substance, say Bossie, and non-substantial properties of Bossie. For example, the quality "color" cannot be both black and white. It is either one or the other, or perhaps neither. Bossie, on the other hand, can be black in one moment and white in the next. Thus, substances can possess contrary properties, albeit not at the same time and in the same respect; while non-substantial properties (or *accidental* properties) cannot.

It is this latter feature of substances that leads us back to an examination of sentences, and more particularly, to the truth value of them. Despite the fact that substances can possess contraries, or perhaps because of it, Aristotle is faced with a quick and straightforward complaint about the nature of truth. If truth is a relation between some sentence and the things to which the sentence refers such that the sentence is true if the facts about the world are borne out by it, then what are we to make of sentences like "Bill is sitting." For example, "Bill is sitting" and "Bill is standing" are clearly contraries; Bill could be neither sitting nor standing and so both sentences could be false. However, suppose the sentence "Bill is sitting" is true. If it is true, it is true only because Bill is, in fact, sitting.

If Bill stands up, though, then the sentence "Bill is sitting" is false and the sentence "Bill is standing" is true.

The difficulty faced here is that truth is generally conceived to be an either/or proposition. Either a sentence is true or it is false. If sentences can change their truth values, then making an argument or giving directions or putting forward a claim of one sort or another are all constructed on quicksand. Thus, truth is often envisioned as inviolate. If this is true, however, then how can both sentences, given that they are contraries, be both true and false? While this is a reasonably difficult obstacle for Aristotle to overcome, it is not insurmountable. Indeed, Aristotle appeals fairly directly to a survey of common sense, although he adds a level of sophistication dependent upon the Category map. On Aristotle's view, the substance (in this case, Bill) changes. The sentences do not change, nor do **they** change their truth value. Bill, himself, admits of contraries, and thus sentences *about* Bill can be either true or false depending on the actions of Bill. It is not the case that the sentence is "Bill is standing and the statement 'Bill is standing' is true." To say that some sentence about a particular substance is true is just to say that the sentence accurately reflects what it purports to claim about the particular substance in question. The sentences simply are and true and falsity, while related to the sentences, are actually dependent upon the substance, itself. Given, then, that substances can admit of contraries, then this difficulty is overcome.

This leads the conversation to a final discussion within the *Categories*, and one that receives considerable prephilosophical discussion. It is often said that to understand what good is, evil must exist; or to understand light, there must also be dark. This notion picks up a metaphysical position that whatever exists must, of necessity, entail the actual existence of the things opposite. As appealing as this notion may be, it is, on Aristotle's view, a rather unsophisticated one and one that runs quite counter to the metaphysical commitment that particular objects are the things with the greatest ontological status. For example, here are two contrary sentences – "Socrates is ill." and "Socrates is well." Suppose that the latter sentence is true. Thus, there exists within the world a man, Socrates, and he is well. For the contrary sentence to be true (and for the notion that for any existent thing, its opposite also exists to be true), it must be the case that there exists within the world a man, Socrates, and he is ill. This is fairly straightforwardly nonsense. The truth of the latter sentence in no way entails the truth of the latter or the existence of the contrary object that that is the subject of the latter.

Or, suppose that in an instant, everything was suddenly the same shade of white. While a fantastical notion, to be sure, it is not strictly impossible. In such a world in which everything was the same shade of white, the color black not only need not exist, but it does not exist. Thus, the presence of one property does not entail the existence of its contrary property.

From careful observation, Aristotle set out to examine all the things that actually exist, to collect them together and through different lenses, divide them. By careful attention to the nature and structure of language, to the at times very fine distinctions between essential properties and accidental ones, and to the pitfalls that await inattentive, prephilosophical views of the world, Aristotle establishes the foundation for grammar, most of the classical physical sciences, and logic.

Guided Reading Questions:
1. Describe the two types of predicates.
2. What is the difference between a primary substance and a secondary one?
3. What role does the *Categories* play in Aristotle's *Organon*?

Logic Blurb
Fallacy of Equivocation

The *Fallacy of Equivocation* is among the most difficult to catch. This is because often there is a philosophical term that has several different meanings and when used in one part of the argument seems to work completely well and when used in another, works well again. Only, in the first part and in the second part, the philosopher equivocates. That is, he uses one meaning in one place and another meaning in another place without making clear that the word means something different in each place.

There are several words that have equivocal meanings. One of the most common is the word *natural*. We can see the different meanings of *natural* by carefully considering the context where the word is used and the proper opposite of the word as it is used there. So, suppose Socrates is accused of being a Natural Philosopher. There, the word *natural* is used in such a way that the proper opposite of the word is *supernatural*. Thus, the sort of arguments being made by a natural philosopher are arguments that depend on natural explanations, rather than supernatural ones. However, suppose we said that sugar is a *natural* sweetener, as opposed to saccharine, which is an *artificial* one. Here, we use the word *natural* to designate something that occurs in nature rather than something that is constructed by humans.

Now, let us imagine an argument in which Socrates is accused of being a Natural Philosopher. Let us suppose that Meletus argues that Socrates is a natural philosopher because he is clearly not an artifact (that is, he is not made by human hands like a statue or a ship). Socrates is a naturally occurring entity. Thus, Meletus might argue that Socrates is therefore a Natural Philosopher. However, this would be quite disingenuous since what Meletus is accusing Socrates of doing is actually a matter of impiety, and thus would depend on the meaning of *natural* whose opposite is *supernatural*. So, Meletus has equivocated on the word *natural* to advance his argument. The careful and reflective thinker will pay close attention to words that have several possible meanings and will insist that the argument presented to them be free of equivocations.

Section 4.3: Aristotle and the Highest Good

Nicomachean Ethics, The Good

Every craft, every investigation, every action, is directed toward some good – so, it seems right when it is commonly said that all things aim at the good. But, there is a quite obvious difference in the ends of these many things. Sometimes, the end is the exercise of some capacity or other; sometimes it is beyond that exercise. In those times, when the end is beyond the exercise undertaken at the moment, that end is said to be finer than the exercise itself.

Since there are many actions and crafts and sciences, it is reasonable to suppose that there are a variety of ends as well. For example, health is the end of medicine, triumph is the end of warcraft, etc. Suppose, though, these are secondary to some greater end – for example, the craft of bridle-making and the art of horsemanship and all of the things that make the act of soldiering possible and thus, these then to warcraft, etc. – the ultimate end is much more to be desired than the secondary ones. The secondary ones are pursued for the purpose of achieving the greater.

Suppose there was an end desired for itself and not desired for anything further; something that is wished for and that all other things desired are desired for this end. It could not be the case that this would go on forever, or else desire is pointless. Whatever this ultimate end is, this would be the highest good of the finest of all. So, it behooves us, then, to know this good.

To find it, we first consider what craft, science, or art to which it belongs. Which science deserves the title of the finest or highest art? Since politics is the science that examines what people need, what people shall study, and to which extent, and to which all the other arts and sciences (economics, rhetoric, warcraft) are subjected, then politics seems to fulfill our requirements. What then is the target of this investigation?

What is the scope of our inquiry? We must accept that it is not done with the precision of mathematics. Our investigation will be to achieve the level of precision possible in this subject. It is obvious that the same level of accuracy is not possible in every kind of thinking. Those things that are noble (the things examined in Politics) are multivarious and quite uncertain. They are so much so that some people deem them to be merely matters of convention and not distinctions growing from nature. Given the complexity of subject, we must content ourselves with describing the truth roughly, sketched, and in outline form. We must reason from plausibilities and thus arrive at conclusions that are similarly plausible.

Who, then, is capable of this sort of study of such a demanding science? The one who is young is excluded from the ranks of the students of Politics because he is immature in the experience of life. These experiences are the starting point for the study of Politics. In addition, because the young are driven by passions, he will gain nothing from this study; a study that is about practical reason rather than abstract speculations. Further, youth of years and youth of character amount to the same – disqualification for youth is not a matter of age. Rather, this disqualification is on the basis of being ruled by the passions/emotions. Those, on the other hand, who can guide their desires on the basis of rationality/reason will benefit from this study.

So, what is the highest good? Regarding the name by which it is called, all people, I think, would agree. It is happiness (*eudaimonia* – to live well). Even though all would agree to the name, there is much less agreement about what the name means. On this point, the general public and the philosophers disagree.

The common sense is that *eudaimonia* is pleasant or pleasurable; or perhaps money or reputation. Indeed, *eudaimonia* often means different things to the same person at different times – health after long illness, money in the face of poverty, lofty words that sound meaningful. Many philosophers have argued that, in addition (or besides these), there is something like Goodness that makes all these other things good. In this discussion, we must take care to maintain an important distinction – that between beginning with principles and working down, on the one hand, and beginning with what is known and working up to the principles. Plato often used the former method. However, we must start with what we know.

[1095b] "What we know" (*gnosimon* – root: *gnosis*) can have at least two meanings. The first is what is familiar to us; the second is what is familiar, or commonly known. Thus, we start with what *we* know, with what is familiar *to us* – what *we* observe.

Given this, only good moral training can equip a person for studying the noble and the just. The well-trained person will recognize that the fact that we must start here is clear without needing further justification.

Let us return to the subject at hand. The views of common folks about good and *eudaimonia* derive from the lives they live and witness. Given this, it is clear why the majority of people, the ones least well-trained, think that *eudaimonia* is pleasure and further, why they seek nothing more than a life of pleasure. Observing the lives of people, they can safely be divided into three kinds – a life of pleasure, a life of honor/reputation, and a life of contemplation.

The majority of people are completely consumed by their desire for the life of animals – but their opinions are noted because many in the highest places share their appetites. Those of refinement tend rather toward honor/reputation.

However, this is also too transient and fickle to be the highest good. It is determined by those who bestow honor rather than on the one receiving it; but the highest good must be something particular to the individual who is good, must be stable, and cannot be given to and taken from him. Further, those who pursue honor do so in order that they may be thought to be men of rationality, of excellence (*arete* – excellence, virtue). Thus, even in their own minds, they value *arete* above reputation.

[1096a] The life of contemplation is one to which we will return.

There is a fourth sort of life, one of attention to money. It is clearly contrary to the dictates of nature; money is merely useful, it is not good of itself. It is a means and not an end. It is clear that either pleasure and honor and *arete* are all higher than money since they are at least desired for themselves.

Having eliminated all these views, we can now evaluate the "ultimate good". The investigation is not particularly pleasant as it will bring us into conflict with those friends who advocate a theory of forms. However, this is the correct path as we ought give up even those closest to us in pursuit of the truth; that is, if we call ourselves philosophers. While we love both, it is a sacred duty to pursue truth above all.

[1096b] Some might object because the theory of forms does not mean to address all manner of goods without distinction. Instead it holds that there are two kinds of goods – those desired for themselves (and these are grouped under one form) and those desired as a means to some further end (and these are grouped under a different form). We should separate, then, those things that are good in themselves (inherent goods) from those that are merely useful (instrumental goods).

Which are those that we might call inherently good? These must be the ones that are good in themselves and desired independent of their effects – even if these be wisdom, sight, pleasures, honor. If these are not inherently good, then there is no particular that is good, apart from perhaps the idea, and then the form is empty. If a form is empty, then it has no meaning. Thus, good is not said of all these things in the same way and does not pick out some particular form that makes each of them good.

[1097a] Further, let us consider practical matters. How, for example, would a carpenter benefit from this "ideal good"? Or a soldier? Or a physician? Even the physician in his healing art does not aim at some abstraction, but rather strives for the health of the particular person under his care.

There are a great many ends. Some are instrumental only, desired merely for some end beyond themselves. Clearly, these are not ultimate ends. The ultimate end, the finest end, must be a final end (*telion*).

[1097b] Something desired for itself only, without regard to its effects, is more final than something desired for itself and as a means to something else. This is more final than something that is instrumental only, desired not at all for

itself but only for its effects. Something is the final end if it is desired only for itself and never as a means.

Eudaimonia, of all the things discussed, most meets these requirements. It is always desired for itself and only for itself. All the others – honor/reputation, pleasure, *arete* – are all things desired for themselves in part and for their effects – that is, they contribute to *eudaimonia*. *Eudaimonia* is not desired for these, they are desired for *eudaimonia*.

If we consider the notion of self-sufficiency, we find that *eudaimonia* again meets the test. If, by self-sufficiency, we mean whatever is required to make life desirable and lacking in nothing, then *eudaimonia* alone meets this requirement.

Further, *eudaimonia*, even among the common, is thought to be the finest of all goods, not merely one among many. Adding other ends to *eudaimonia* does not make it more desirable. So, *eudaimonia* is final, self-sufficient, and the end of all human action.

~

"The End" is a strange way to start a book. After all, we have become accustomed to seeing "the End" at, well, the end – of books, of fairy tales, of films. "The End" sounds somewhat final, as if we have come to the conclusion of something rather than merely finding ourselves at the outset. Before turning to a discussion of why Aristotle might begin one of his most influential works in this strange way, it would be instructive to note that this is but the first stylistic oddity that we will encounter in the *Nicomachean Ethics*. Rather than opening with a statement of his thesis about ethics and the development of the character that is intrinsic to becoming a good person and living a good life, Aristotle instead walks his reader through a process of discovery. The point seems to be to lead the reader to the End suggested at the outset.

About that End, there is, of course, an explanation of this seeming oddity. It will be recalled that in the *Categories*, we first encountered the notion of an equivocation. It is because of the equivocal meanings of "end" in English that we might find it strange to open a book with it. Aristotle is not concerned with the conclusion or termination of something, that moment at which something ends. The Greek word commonly translated "end" is *telos*. It is here we begin to understand that connection Aristotle sees between the way the world is (metaphysics), the way we know the world (epistemology), and the way humans should act (ethics).

Aristotle's approach to explaining his theory of ethics begins with an application of his Method of Collection and Division. An ethical system will require some explanation of the notion of "the good," and particularly, "the highest good." So, Aristotle begins by collecting all those things that the citizens of Athens commonly call "good." It is not a given that there will be some highest or greatest good among these many things. Indeed, at the outset of the examination, there is no particular reason to think that a highest good exists. However, for the living of a truly good life, it seems a requirement that some standard or some aim or some *end* or *telos* must be the highest good for human beings, or the end at which the ethical human life exemplifies. To determine whether or not a highest good actually exists, Aristotle employs a three-fold method of paring off those things that are called good but cannot logically be the highest good. If any good(s) remain after this process, then that good or goods will be the highest good.

The first step in ridding the collection of good things of all those that cannot possibly be a candidate for the highest good is to apply criteria by which the highest good can be established. That is, what are the necessary conditions that any good would have to meet in order to be considered the highest good. Anything called "good" that fails to meet these criteria will be discarded from the collection. This is not to say that something that fails to meet the criteria of the highest good will not be something good; only that it will not be the highest good. Those criteria that Aristotle thinks are the necessary conditions of the highest good are *self-sufficiency* and *independence*. Or, in the words of Aristotle, the highest good must be both desired for itself and not desired for anything further.

It is important to understand why these two criteria are necessary conditions for establishing the highest good and Aristotle goes to a bit of trouble to argue for them. We will expand that argument here a bit further. Aristotle says that if the highest good is desired for something further, then it will be desired for something beyond itself. If this is so, then that thing beyond the "highest good" would, in fact, be greater. But, it too would be desired for something beyond itself. If the highest good is desired for something beyond itself then the quest for the highest good is an infinite journey and, as such, ultimately futile and doomed even from the start. However, we can examine the criteria of the highest good set forth by Aristotle and see, at least through example, why it seems right to conclude that the highest good must be both self-sufficient and independent, desired for itself and not desired for anything further.

The notion of desire is at least a binary notion. That is, something may be desired for itself (or intrinsically desirable) or it may be desired for its consequences (or instrumentally desirable). However, given the binary nature of desire, it is possible to pair the two off, along with their respective negations, to create four categories, at least three of which correspond to a common use of the word "good." The first of these good things is something that is desired for itself and desired for its consequences. Let us call these Type 1 goods. The second is something desired for itself and not desired for its consequences. These we will call Type 2 goods. The third is something that is not desired for itself but that is desired for its consequences. These we will call Type 3 goods. The fourth category is likely not to be called good, but it is a fourth potential construction resulting from the binary nature of desire and so, for the sake of being thorough, we include it here – something that is not desired for itself nor is it desired for something further.

If we imagine plotting the objects in these four categories along a gradient, we would clearly place those things that are neither intrinsically nor instrumentally desired at the bottom and would scarcely be likely to call them "good" in the first place. At the other end of the spectrum, we encounter a philosophical difference between Plato and Aristotle. On Plato's view, the highest good is something that is desired both for itself and its consequences. For more of his argument concerning this, see the preceding section over the first book of the *Republic*. An example of a Type 1 good would be perhaps the most common Platonic example, health. Again and again, Plato makes analogies between the health of the body and the health of the soul to argue that a virtuous soul is both good for itself and good for its consequences. Health clearly meets both of these criteria. If one is asked why one desires health, it is perfectly reasonable to respond that, "I want to be healthy" and to leave it at that. Health is desired for itself and thus is intrinsically desired. At the same time, one might also answer that question with, "I want to be healthy because it makes life more enjoyable and I can do more things and play more games and live a more exciting life." Each of these is a good beyond the good of health, per se, but which health makes possible. Thus, health is also desired for its consequences and therefore is instrumentally desired.

However, such instrumental desire leads ultimately to an infinite series of desires, each aimed at for the consequences it would bring. Faced with such an infinite path, it follows that there would be no highest good because the infinite string would simply continue, each good aimed at, in part, because of some successive higher good. Though this is a progression rather than a regress, it is an example of Aristotle's commitment to a particular solution to the logical difficulty posed by infinite series of explanations. For Aristotle, any infinite regress is inherently negative; indeed, he commonly refers to them as vicious regresses. Any assumption that issues in an infinite regress can as surely be discarded as an assumption that issues in a contradiction, on Aristotle's view. So, Type 1 goods are rejected as candidates for the highest good because they would lead, inevitably, to an infinite series. Aristotle is not suggesting that health, for example, is not good, only that it is not the highest good.

Type 4 goods are not goods at all and so can safely be discarded. Type 2 goods are ultimately going to be the candidates for the highest good, but to show this, we need first examine why Type 3 goods can be discarded. A Type 3 good would be something that is not desired for itself (that is, is not intrinsically good), but is desired for its consequences. A possible example of a Type 3 good would be something like Brussels sprouts. In the main, Brussels sprouts are not desired for themselves. However, it is universally recognized that they possess particular nutrients that promote good health. Hence, one might decide to eat them, despite an aversion to them, because of the benefits that they bring with them. However, even in this case, a Type 3 good, while clearly good, is also subject to the same sort of infinite series that fells the Type 1 good. Thus, since we can rather straightforwardly eliminate Type 1, 3, and 4 goods, we are left, by process of elimination, with Type 2 goods as the only possible candidates for being the highest good.

Rather than rely purely on the eliminative process, let us look particularly at the criteria that define Type 2 goods. Type 2 goods are desired for themselves, and thus are intrinsically desirable. This would place them above both Type 3 and 4 because those goods are not desired for themselves. As a good that is intrinsically good, it is a self-sufficient good; that is, it does not require appeal to something beyond itself to be called "good." Type 2 goods are not desired because of consequences beyond themselves, and thus are independent of such appeals. Because they are not instruments to greater goods, Type 2 goods do not resolve into infinite series and thus render the quest for the highest good impossible. Thus, Type 2 goods will be the highest goods because they are desired for themselves but not desired for anything further.

It is important to note here that no assumption is being made about the number of goods that might qualify as Type 2 goods (there might be one, two, or two thousand). To assume that there was but a single Type 2 good, at this stage, would be to beg the question. Instead, the prospect of multiple Type 2 goods is left open. To this point, then, having collected all the things that people commonly call "good," Aristotle has whittled that list down to only those that satisfy the criteria of being self-sufficient and independent.

Having pared the collection of good things down to only those that meet the criteria of self-sufficiency and independence, Aristotle now applies a different lens to the collection with the intent of paring it down further. There are many different approaches to problems. For example, one might decide that taking up the violin is the method one will use to come to understand particle physics. Such a choice would likely be fruitless as it would be the wrong tool for the task at hand. The highest good or the proper end (or *telos*) for human beings is going to be the subject of a particular type of investigation or science. The science of the highest good is not likely to be something like shipbuilding. Rather, Aristotle claims that the science of the highest good is Politics.

That the science of the highest good is politics may seem a rather odd claim to modern ears. Indeed, politics and politicians seem, oftentimes, little interested in the highest good for human beings and more interested in the acquisition, cultivation, and maintenance of power. However, this is not the sort of politics Aristotle has in mind. Unfortunately, one will not divine this notion of politics from the *Nicomachean Ethics*. Instead, one must turn to the *Politics* for a more complete discussion of why politics is the science of the human good. We will mention that argument in brief here.

In the *Politics*, Aristotle is concerned to show what sort of government, structured within which sort of constitution, would bring about a polis or city in which the citizens have the most opportunity and guidance toward becoming fully flourishing human beings. There are several forms of government in which the good of the ruler or the good of a small group of people is the actual aim. But, the good governments and the excellent constitutions are those where the polis is structured to cultivate lives of well-being and virtue. Politics, then, is the study of how human beings live and interact with one another, fashioning systems by which they will be governed. Human beings are essentially social creatures, living best, as a general rule, in community with their fellows. How that living is organized is the subject of politics. While there may well be an applied side to this study, that is, while one might strive to tutor a king or a ruling class to aim properly at the well-being of all, political science is essentially the study of how human beings can aim at and ultimately achieve the highest human good.

If politics is the science of the highest good for human beings, then the goods studied primarily by any other science will be safely excluded from this conversation. For example, one might imagine that a particular mathematical system, say Euclidean geometry, was inherently desired and, because of the esoteric nature of some of its proofs, instrumentally void. Thus, some theorem derived from the Euclidean elements might be the highest mathematical good. However, as mathematics is not the science of the highest good for human beings, whatever goods might meet the self-sufficiency and independence criteria within the scope of that science are safely discarded from the collection of things people commonly call "good."

Having whittled that collection down through two filters, Aristotle applies a third. One who sets out to explore the science of the highest good must himself meet certain criteria. That is, some potential students are not yet ready for the study as there are certain qualifications that must be met before one can properly begin the study.

The first and foremost among these qualifications of the student of the highest good is that the student cannot be young. Here, Aristotle means two things. "Youth" applies both to chronological age and to the level of maturation of the student. To say that the student of the highest good cannot be chronologically young is just to say that, generally speaking, there is a developmental curve that cannot be abridged. For example, it is the rare 7 year old that is ready for the study of calculus. This is not to say that no 7 year old could study calculus, only that, as a general rule, 7 years of age is too young to begin that study. Similarly, the study of the highest good requires a bit of age and the experience that goes with it as preparation for the study itself.

That "youth" applies to maturity level is also fairly straightforward and uncontroversial. Immaturity is sufficient to disqualify a potential student. One who is not of sober mind and possessed of at least a measure of self-control will clearly be incapable of the work that is required to pursue the highest good. For the most part, only those people with at least moderate, if not considerable, control of self are proper students. That control of self is a manifestation of the rule of reason over the passions. Those who are young are those who, regardless of chronological age, have not yet mastered the passions and have not brought them under the rule of reason.

With the further refinement of the sort of student proper for the science of the highest good, it is reasonable to suppose that the collection of goods has been narrowed sufficiently that that highest good might be identified. On Aristotle's view, the sole good that meets the critieria of the highest good, that has politics as its proper science and the rational, self-controlled individual as its student is *happiness*. If one asks why happiness is desired, it is quite clear that one might reasonably respond that happiness is desired simply because people want to be happy. That is, it is desired for itself and, thus, is intrinsically desirable. At the same time, if one asks a person why happiness is desired hoping for some answer beyond happiness itself, one will be disappointed. Happiness is desired for itself and for itself alone. Thus, it meets the criteria set forth.

There is a very important Aristotelian distinction that must be made at this juncture. When Aristotle is interpreted as arguing for happiness as the highest good for humans, it is quite important to be clear that by *happiness*, he does not mean *pleasure*. The Greek that lies behind the "happiness" is *eudaimonia*. *Eudaimonia* is commonly translated "happiness" and this translation can lead to rather significant misinterpretations of the Aristotelian view. Pleasure cannot be the highest good because, among other things, pleasure is transient and, more, fleeting. One might be quite happy, in the sense of experiencing pleasure, one day and just as down or miserable the next. Such pleasures are clearly not the basis for a stable life of goodness, although they may be individually quite desirable. Further, the pleasures are often the result of satisfactions of one passion or another, of a great and consuming desire. However, a life consumed by the passions is precisely the life of an individual whom we have already seen to be unfit for the pursuit of the life of the highest good. Thus, if the student of the highest good could not possibly be the one in pursuit of pleasure, then it is quite impossible that Aristotle should mean to equate "happiness" with "pleasure." Aristotle actually takes great pains to say that such an equating is foreign to his view.

How then should we translate *eudaimonia*? It might be most helpful to simply divide the word into its component parts and rebuild it. The Greek prefix *eu* is commonly added to a root to express goodness or wellness; so "eu" can be translated "well." The Greek *daimon* refers to being or spirit. Thus, *eudaimonia* can be translated rather literally as "well-being." This seems to capture what Aristotle has in mind. For example, the highest good is not something transient, but is something stable. Happiness, in the sense of pleasure, is likely to be quite transient, indeed. Suppose Lee's team wins the National Championship in College Football. She is likely to be quite happy. Suppose immediately following that moment of happiness, it is learned that her team committed several violations in the process of the season and is forced to forfeit every game and surrender the national championship. The pleasure of the first moment is likely wiped out by the second, perhaps even making the aftermath of the forfeiture worse than it would have otherwise been. Thus pleasure is fleeting and can leave in its wake distress of greater magnitude that the initial pleasures. *Eudaimonia*, on the other hand, is a stable state of the soul, however. One who has well-being might experience pleasure and distress, but will be ruled by neither and will be overwhelmed by neither. The person with well-being is one who is balanced, neither taken up by great pleasure nor devastated by great loss. This stable state of character is the nature of happiness that Aristotle holds out as the highest good.

In his discussion of the highest good Aristotle distinguishes the life of virtue or the life in pursuit of the highest good from the life of pleasure. Again, Aristotle employs his method of collection and division to pull together all of the kinds of lives that are commended as the best life to be lived. Among these are four in particular – the life of contemplation, the life of honor, the life of pleasure, and the life of wealth.

Aristotle says that the life of wealth is safely discarded without much argument in support of its dismissal. However, given some of the characteristics of the good person and the good life it is easy to see why this dismissal will be so swift. The life of wealth is a life directed at the acquisition and holding of material goods, particularly money. Indeed, some scholars have translated what Aristotle says here simply as the "life of money," rather than the "life of wealth." The broader translation captures more fully Aristotle's meaning, however. The life of virtue is going to be a life that supports the life of the highest good.

The life of pleasure is clearly rejected as pleasure is not the highest good. A life lived with the *telos* of pleasure would be a life ultimately lived on a rollercoaster of highs and lows, finally dissolving into disappointment, futility, and frustration. As a life that cannot exhibit the sort of stability of character that is the hallmark of the good life, the life of pleasure is safely rejected as well.

It would not seem strange to suppose that Aristotle might hold that the life of honor would be the life of virtue. After all, honor, more than wealth, seems likely to hold a place higher in the estimation of virtue. However, paying careful attention to the nature of honor is instructive. Aristotle does not mean to suggest that the life of honor is to be equated with an "honorable life." Here, Aristotle imagines someone like Achilles, the great Greek hero of the Trojan War. Far from being an honorable person, Achilles is represented by Homer as one who demands honor (or recognition) that he feels is due him and is scarcely willing to recognize the contributions of others. Indeed, when feeling slighted, he abandons his own kinsmen to certain defeats until his wounded honor is salved. If this sort of honor and esteem is the *telos* of action, then a life lived in pursuit of such will again be one of instability and, perhaps, vice. Such a life cannot then be considered as the life of the highest good or the life of virtue.

By process of elimination, then, it is the life of contemplation that will be the life of the highest good. Here, we must be careful not to limit our notion of "contemplation" to merely thinking, meditating, or otherwise participating in mental gymnastics of one sort or another. Contemplation has to do with coming to understand the world, the particulars of any given situation, the right course of action to take, and the execution of that action in ways consistent with that judgment of the proper course of action. Further support for the life of contemplation as the life of virtue is discussed in the next section, particularly as related to Aristotle's discussion of the natural function of human beings and the process by which the right course of action is discerned and the virtuous character cultivated.

Even with further elaboration on the nature of the highest good and the life aimed at it, the theory of ethics will, at best, be a sketch rather than a fully developed portrait, explicit in all detail. This might well disappoint those in search of a system by which each course of action is spelled out in considerable detail. Aristotle, however, argues that such disappointment would actually be a product of unreasonable expectations and indicative of a fundamental misunderstanding of the subject. Many people want ethics to be as clear and precise as deliberations within disciplines like mathematics. There, answers can be quite precise and are the culmination of thought processes that are equally rigorous and precise. If one takes mathematical reasoning, for example, as the model, or any other model that would require a similar precision, then one is likely to mistake ethical reasoning as either less than rigorous or hopelessly fraught with error. Neither is the case, at least on Aristotle's view. He writes,

> This is a general outline, and, I think, the proper and useful approach. First we draw an outline and then fill in detail. With this framework, one can adjust to fit whatever circumstances present. This is how all of the sciences develop, and it will not require an extraordinary intellect to fill in. At the same time, we cannot require the same precision as in some areas of knowledge. Indeed, we must not require the same precision in all fields. Both the carpenter and mathematician will approach a right triangle, but only as is required for its use in his work. By demanding overmuch precision, we will waste time on irrelevancies rather than the core of our investigation.

That ethics should be different from mathematics is strikingly obvious. Mathematics, and many other sciences, proceeds from axioms and postulates and theorems to come to deductive conclusions that are certain, given the initial premises from which those conclusions are deduced. Ethics, however, is a completely different sort of subject. It is not a discipline that is easily reduced to a small set of axioms and postulates from which all possible conclusions about behavior in any given situation might be derived. This ought not be shocking. In a similar way, mathematics is dissimilar to the empirical sciences. There, after taking into consideration a set of experimental data, provisional hypotheses are developed and then tested through the use of more experiments. No statement of science is considered to carry the same certainty as a proof within mathematics. The empirical sciences are, by their very nature, less precise than mathematics. Thus, it is clear, from a survey of the various sorts of sciences, that each science admits of a particular level of precision, and that those levels of precision need not be identical across disciplines.

With regard to the notion that less precision entails less rigor, it is quite clear that anyone paying even scant attention to the work of Aristotle would be disabused straightaway of the notion that ethical reasoning is anything less than gruelingly rigorous. Indeed, because of the great number of variables and the fluidity of any situation in which an ethical agent finds himself or herself, ethical reasoning is likely to be more demanding than that of other sciences where greater precision is possible.

Despite the rather odd opening of the work, beginning a work of ethics by first discussing "ends," Aristotle systematically addresses those things that are commonly called good, dividing and discarding those things that cannot be the highest good, narrowing the focus again and again until the highest good for human beings, *eudaimonia*, comes into focus. From that foundational notion of the good, Aristotle turns to questions concerning the acquisition of the sort of character that possesses this well-being.

Guided Reading Questions:

1. Aristotle thinks that there is a highest (or chief) good. What conditions must this good satisfy?
2. What is the science of the highest good?
3. What qualifications are required for the student of this study?

Logic Blurb
Syllogism/Formal Logic

In the *Prior Analytics*, Aristotle turns his attention to the construction of formal logical arguments from the building blocks of sentences. The most famous of these formal arguments is the syllogism. The syllogism will be much more thoroughly addressed in the *Posterior Analytics* as Aristotle turns his attention to proofs. Here, though, he is primarily concerned with what amounts to valid inferences. These are sometimes called "pure syllogisms". If we say, "p implies q," there are presumably conditions under which such a proposition constitutes a valid inference. Just as in the *Categories* where Aristotle is concerned with the proper reference of discrete words like "horse" and "human," here he is concerned for the proper joining of sentences into inferential statements that form the basis of a logical argument. A premise for such arguments will always be a statement that makes a claim that something is the case, that something may be the case, or that something is an attribution or property of something else. For example, "Bob is human" is a statement claiming something to be the case; "If Bob is a bachelor, then Bob is unmarried" suggests a possibility – it may be the case that Bob is unmarried, but it may be the case that he is not. Finally, if one said "Cardinals are red," then the property "red" has been attributed to the subject "Cardinals."

Section 4.3: Aristotle and the Highest Good

Two of the central features of the *Prior Analytics* are the discussions at the outset of the work covering the notion of universal quantification and possibility. Here, Aristotle is making the first steps toward a sophisticated modal logic of necessity and contingency. Before such a system can be developed, and it remains undeveloped, finally, in Aristotle's work, a strong notion of universal quantification and syllogisms relating to it must be put forward. After putting forward a premise, a universal quantifier ranges over all premises of that sort. For example, to say that "All bachelors are unmarried" is to say that for everything that it exists, if it can properly have the name "bachelor" attached to it, then it is "unmarried." Thus, if Bob is a bachelor, then we have an example of the following formal structure – All As are Bs, Bob is an A; therefore, Bob is a B. Or, in other words, All bachelors are unmarried; Bob is a bachelor; therefore, Bob is unmarried.

The other logical notion with which Aristotle is concerned is the concept of possibility. If it is the case that some B is A, then it will also be possible that some A is B. However, it is not necessary that that all of A will be B. For example, some cardinals are red. However, it is not the case that all things that are red are cardinals. At the same time, if we suppose that all B is A, then it still not necessary that all A is B. For example, all squares are rectangles. However, not all rectangles are squares. Here we have a situation where all of one class of things belongs to the second, but the converse is not true. Thus, Aristotle has developed two critical types of major premises for syllogistic arguments – the universally quantified premise and the premise of possibility. These are topics that are addressed more extensively in later Logic Blurbs.

Section 4.4: Aristotle and the Human Function

Nicomachean Ethics, The Function Argument

However, perhaps we need to approach this in another way. So, what is the end of a human being; that is, the function (*ergon*) of a human being? Why should we ask this question in this way? Well, we say that a good sculptor is good because of the function or activity that he does; indeed, this is true for any practice or trade. So, if this is so, then the good of a human being must be a description of the function of human beings. At the same time, it is clear that a carpenter has a particular function and a cobbler another. Perhaps this is so of human beings, generally, that each has a particular function but there is no function *qua* human. We can reject this. As each person is composed of several parts – eyes, ears, hands, feet – and each of these clearly has a function particular to it, we can suppose, then, that there is some overarching human function independent of any particular craft or trade in which he engages himself. So, what is it, this human function?

There are several possibilities. If we suppose it is the process of life itself (taking in nutrition, growing, etc.), then we can reject that as the human function because it is held in common with even the plants. Thus, since this is not unique to humans, it cannot be the *human* function. Similarly, we can exclude the next possibility, the life of sense-perception. This, also, is held in common with all of the animals. This being the case, there is but one possibility remaining – the life of action; which is to say, the life of the mind, or reason. It is through reason that the two parts of this life are governed; the first as the side of the soul that is obedient to reason and the second that is engaged in the exercise of reason. The function of human beings, then, is to engage the soul in obedience to reason and in exercise of reason.

Now, we can expand our concept of *eudaimonia*. *Eudaimonia* or happiness will be an *arete* (excellence) that meshes with our analysis. So, *eudaimonia* must be a stable state of the soul that expresses virtue. However, there is an important distinction – it makes a difference whether we conceive this excellence as a mere possession or as something that is utilized and practiced. For example, one may have an ability that lies dormant and is used. However, if the ability is used, then it cannot be dormant. Let us consider the Olympics. It is not the most beautiful nor is it the strongest who awarded the wreath. Only those who actually participate can be triumphant. It is the same in life. Those who are triumphant are those who both have the excellence as a possession and practice it throughout.

How might we acquire this *eudaimonia*? It is clear that the acquisition of *eudaimonia* must require the possession of some goods, external to the soul. It is impossible to act without some means by which to act, some wealth and the like. Indeed, many things can only be accomplished by use of some external thing, some instrument – political power, influence, wealth, friends, connections of one sort or another. At the same time, the lack of certain good things will certainly detract from the pursuit of *eudaimonia*. One is unlikely to achieve the good life if he is alone, if he is without children, if he is of low birth, or if he is rather ugly. Even more, if his children are worthless or he has evil friends or has lost good ones. Thus, *eudaimonia* requires more than simply strength of soul and reason, but depends on some external aids as well.

The person with *eudaimonia*, then, can be understood as the one with requisite property and practice who throughout life maintains his excellent character. He will always be employed in *arete*, both in reason and in the actions that flow from the dictates of reason. Whatever befalls him, he will meet honorably and virtuously, and he will do all this because he is good indeed. He will do the right things at the right times in the right ways and for the right reasons.

The good person is stable and will not be swayed from *eudaimonia* during the regular course of events and misfortune. Only heavy misfortunes, falling quickly upon him, will topple him. After such bombardment, *eudaimonia* is not easily regained, nor quickly.

Given that *eudaimonia* is a stable state of the soul expressing virtue, we should examine virtue. This will surely shed light on the understanding of *eudaimonia*.

The virtue to be examined is the one we isolated before, the virtue of a human being *qua* human. Since it is the highest good for humans in which we are interested, we must mean the virtue of the soul, and not the body.

We can distinguish two distinct parts of the soul – one rational and the other irrational. How this distinction is established – whether actually (like the parts of a body are actually distinct) or whether only conceptually, but not actually (like the convexity or concavity of an arc of a circle) is irrelevant for our purposes here. All that matters is that the two parts can be distinguished. If we look at the irrational part of the soul (or emotional part), this too is not unique to humans but shared even by plants as this is the part of the soul wherein the function of nutrition – of taking in food and growing – takes place. All things have this capacity. Therefore, since it is not unique to humans, it cannot be peculiarly human and thus not the human *ergon* (function).

Another aspect of the irrational or emotional part of the soul comes to mind. This is a part that has a share of reason because it is obedient to reason. Consider two cases, the continent person and the incontinent person. The continent soul is praised because the rational part controls the irrational part, or at least guides it toward the best. However, it is a struggle and not an easy relation between the irrational and the rational, and the irrational fights reason. So, there is clearly something other than reason that lives within the soul. Thus, we say the continent person has a soul where the irrational part submits to the governance, if unwillingly, of the rational part. In the person who is *sophron* or brave, all the more so and without as great a struggle.

So, there must be two parts to the irrational part of the soul. In the first place, there is the nutritive or vegetative part that is wholly excluded from reason. In the second, there is a faculty of desire that either submits to reason (in the continent person) or does not (in the incontinent one). Similarly, we can see that the rational part will have two divisions as well – one that has reason or possesses reason and one that attends to or pays attention to reasonable argument.

This being the case, we can describe different kinds of excellence – intellectual *arete* (excellence) like wisdom, knowledge, and practicality; and moral *arete* (excellence) like the moral virtues. When describing moral character, a person is named "gentle" or "sophron," not "intelligent." The wise person is also lauded because he has a trained mental faculty. Any praiseworthy habit, trait or trained faculty is what is properly termed an *arete* (excellence, virtue).

~

Having isolated the highest good for human beings, *eudaimonia*, Aristotle approaches the investigation of this good by discussing its nature, its acquisition, and its complexity. *Eudaimonia*, often translated "happiness," is, on Aristotle's view, a stable state of the soul that expresses virtue. If this is so, at least a couple of questions arise. "What is this *virtue*?" and "How is this state of the soul acquired?" We should treat these questions in that order.

Aristotle, along with Plato, Socrates, and a number of other ancient Greek philosophers, are generally lumped under the heading "virtue ethicists." This is because the core of their ethical philosophical work tends to deal with the notion of the good life, the nature of the good, and the ability for human beings to acquire this good life and central to these questions are notions of what are commonly called virtues. The Cardinal Virtues are generally Bravery, Wisdom, Justice, Piety, and *Sophrosune* (often translated "moderation" or "temperance"). There are other virtues addressed by these philosophers, with Aristotle spending considerable space on lesser virtues like generosity, magnanimity, and the like. However, despite the general acceptance of the ascription "virtue ethics" to these philosophers, there is a reasonable view that suggests this is somewhat wrongheaded.

The crux of this view turns on a close examination of the word that is often translated "virtue." The Greek *arete* is not strictly translated "virtue." Strictly speaking, *arete* is most accurately translated as "excellence." While the notion of "virtue" clearly carries with it a connotation of excellence, it does not seem, at least from contemporary use, that virtue should entail excellence. Indeed, oftentimes, a person is described as virtuous who is precisely the one Aristotle excludes from the study of the highest good. For example, the naïve but gentle-spirited soul is often called virtuous because he is without taint from experience of the world itself. The notion of virtue has clearly been appropriated as a synonym for everything from chastity to purity of soul to wisdom. Clearly, this is not the way Aristotle (nor Plato) used *arete*. Further, one can imagine all manner of excellences that we would far exclude from "virtue." One might imagine an excellent computer programmer or an excellent carpenter and not conclude, in virtue of those particular excellences, that the programmer or the carpenter were indeed virtuous people. And one would hardly call the carpenter a virtuous carpenter if one was merely trying to say that he did excellent work. Thus, we can see that excellence, the most literal translation of *arete*, and virtue are different concepts, though they may overlap in places. Those holding this view argue that it is better, or at least more accurate, to describe Socrates, Plato, and Aristotle (along with Epicurus, and many others) not as "virtue ethicists" but as *eudaimonists*. This is reasonable given that each of them holds something like *eudaimonia* to be the highest good for humans and characteristic of the good human life. However, to call them all *eudaimonists* makes for an overbroad category head that does not make an very important distinction between Socrates, Plato, and Aristotle, on the one hand, and the Epicureans, the Stoics, the Pythagoreans, and the rest. So, while it is appropriate to call them *eudaimonists*, it is also appropriate to distinguish Socrates, Plato, and Aristotle from the rest by labeling them as "virtue ethicists." We can see why that label is appropriate by turning again to the very careful work of Aristotle surrounding the concept of *arete*.

There are many types of *arete* that a human being might possess. One might be an excellent carpenter or an excellent farmer or an excellent bureaucrat. These sorts of excellence are all dependent on a variety of things – for example, to become an excellent carpenter, one will clearly need opportunity to learn the craft from others more accomplished, the tools that will enable one to practice the craft, and the ability to think through a project, understanding the ways in which the various pieces will be attached to apply the craft in appropriate ways and build a house that will not tumble in the first strong breeze. Without these conditions being met, it is impossible for a person to develop into excellence as a carpenter.

Since we would hardly call excellence in carpentry a moral virtue, it might be asked how the word *arete*, which properly describes the carpenter, can also be attached to a notion of virtue. To understand this distinction, it is necessary to look at another quite proper and truly Aristotelian use of *arete*; one that is intimately related to that last necessary condition of excellence in the carpenter – excellence in reason (or analysis or critical thinking).

Intellectual excellence is one of the most highly regarded states of human accomplishments. And, it is clear from Aristotle's arguments concerning the *arete* that is related to the highest good for human beings that *eudaimonia* is dependent, at least in part, on intellectual excellence. Thus, one might question the use of "virtue," then, as the proper translation of *arete* here. After all, one might have considerable intellectual prowess, perhaps even excellence, and yet not be virtuous. Here, Aristotle departs again from the view of Plato and Socrates, particular as regards the Epistemological Principle of Ethics. For Aristotle, the fact of possessing knowledge, and, presumably, even the ability to use that factual knowledge in a variety of elegant and creative ways, is not a sufficient condition for virtue. Here, it might be helpful to examine a four-fold division of human beings.

Here, again, we encounter the Aristotelian method of Collection and Division. That which is collected is the totality of human beings who are capable, theoretically, of virtue. At the top of the list is the person who is truly virtuous. To be sure, the *virtuous* person possesses intellectual excellence but also possesses something beyond that. We will return to the other necessary conditions for virtue momentarily. Suffice it to say, for the moment, that the virtuous person is the person who both possesses intellectual *arete* and acts in virtuous ways.

Aristotle continues the division of the collection of all human beings by focusing on the ways in which the parts of the soul interact. While Plato uses his example of a tripartite soul to discuss the excellence of a human character, Aristotle posits a soul with two parts, a rational part and an irrational one. The ways in which these two parts of the soul interact in any individual will ultimately describe the classification in which that person belongs. Like Plato, Aristotle believes that the rational aspect of the soul must be in control of the soul for the character of the person to be virtuous. However, there are many more subtle ways that these parts of the soul can interact besides the straightforward one of controller and controlled. In the *virtuous* person, the rational part rules the soul but not in a harsh or overbearing way. It need not be harsh or overbearing because the irrational or emotional part of the soul willing submits itself to the direction of the rational part. This circumstance is fairly rare, however, and the extent of control exercised by the rational part will differ in each of the categories of people that are below the *virtuous* category. The first of those subordinate groups is one in which the rational part is in control of the soul, but that control is not as total nor as gentle as the control exercised in the soul of the virtuous person.

This next sort of person, as Aristotle calls him, the *continent* person is the one in whom the rational part of the soul maintains control of the system but in which the irrational part of the soul is somewhat to considerably more unruly. The more tenuous control of the rational part of the soul in the continent person is directly related to two features. The first of those features is that in the soul of the continent person, the rational aspect is not as fully developed. That is, the continent person is one who may or may not possess intellectual excellence, though he may well act in ways that are morally required. This morally correct behavior is not product of an intellectual excellence that commends the behavior for its own sake. The second of the features is that the soul of the continent person possesses an irrational part that has not been properly or fully subordinated to the rational part through proper training and habituation. That is to say, while the continent person may act in morally correct ways because of some intention to follow the commands of the virtuous or to act in those ways that the virtuous person might act in similar circumstances, it is much more likely that that he acts in this way because the motivation for the action is a matter of fear of the disapprobation of the community or for fear of punishment or some other external motivating factor. It is not the inherent rationality of the action that compels the continent person to act. Because the continent person does not yet have the sort of will that is compelled by rationality and by virtue, he will only generally do the right thing. He will fail to achieve the virtuous action for any number of reasons – he does not completely understand it (that is, he does not possess intellectual excellence, but is merely competent), he is motivated by external fears or desires for rewards (rather than an internal sort of second nature that aims at the virtuous action), or because he is unable, due to weakness of will, to enforce the rational ends of his deliberations upon himself. For example, imagine that a student has the opportunity to spend a beautiful day at the lake or to spend it in class. The continent student will, for the most part, choose to spend the day in class rather than to go to the lake. This is so because he is either motivated by fear of doing poorly in the class should he miss regularly or by desire to be rewarded by an outstanding grade in the course. However, he will sometimes fail to make the correct choice because his desire to go to the lake overwhelms his rational deliberations or because he fails to realize that there might well be negative consequences to his missing class.

This brings us to the third sort of person, the *incontinent* person. The incontinent person is the one who generally acts in ways contrary to virtue. This is either because he does not understand the situation – he does not possess intellectual excellence, or perhaps even competence. The standard image of the incontinent person is the one who is overwhelmed by *akrasia*. *Akrasia* is most often conceived as "weakness of will," and Aristotle describes the *akratic* soul as one in which the irrational part of the soul has usurped the role of ruler of the soul from the rational part. Consider the following example. A person makes a decision to spend the afternoon studying for an exam that is upcoming the next day. He realizes that he must study in order to succeed and clears the afternoon to be able to do so. He knows that he wants to study. He knows he needs to study. He makes the decision that he is going to study. And, the next day, he wakes up and realizes that he never got around to studying. The day passed, despite the thinking and planning of the morning, without a single book being opened or essay being read. Reflecting on the lost afternoon, he might well say,

Section 4.4: Aristotle and the Human Function 159

"I got distracted" or "Something came up." He was incapable of driving himself, through force of will, to follow through with his decisions. This case of *akrasia* is one form of the incontinent person. Aristotle thinks it is but one, however.

The less well-known version of the incontinent person is the one who simply does not have anything resembling intellectual excellence. Driven by desires and wants, he may well simply try to rationalize why the actions that he wants are the right ones rather than evaluating the actions to determine whether or not they are, in fact, good. Alternatively, he may simply not understand all that is at stake and might well be incapable of arguing rationally from one set of premises to the next. Incapable of following a line of argument, he will fail again and again simply to understand the situation in which he finds himself and to know how to react properly to that situation. He might well become frustrated by his impotence to act correctly or he may tell himself and others that he meant for the result that actually occurred all along. In any event, this very disjointed reasoning will not provide any structure for the will or for the actions of the person. His actions will be quite unpredictable and his reasoning even more unexplainable.

As the Method of Collection and Division continues, one might expect a continued degradation of intellectual ability to continue into the fourth of the kinds of people. In one sense, this is true. Much like the incontinent person, the *vicious* person comes in at least two varieties. The first is a development of the less well-known incontinent person. This version of the vicious person is one who does not know the good or the evil, but actually mistake the one for the other. In a sense, he is like the continent person who wants to act virtuously, generally because of a desire to avoid negative consequences or to receive benefits of behaving in ways endorsed by the community. It is important to note that the rational part of the soul has subordinated the emotional or irrational part of the soul again, here, but that the rational part is not exhibiting excellence. It is because the rational part of the soul completely mistakes the good for the evil that he will act always in ways that produce vicious results. He might well be surprised that his actions are not well received because he is confident that he has acted positively. This person might well be capable of following a line of argument from premise to conclusion, but he begins with precisely the wrong premises and those, then, proceed directly to precisely the wrong conclusions.

The other version of the vicious person is person who demonstrates that intellectual excellence cannot be sufficient for virtue. In this instance of the vicious person, the rational part of the soul can distinguish between good and evil, can reasonably proceed from premises to conclusions, and chooses to embrace the evil precisely because it is evil. He understands the inherent goodness or viciousness of actions and acts precisely with this understanding to act evilly. An example of this person might well be the person of Glaucon's Challenge in Plato's *Republic* who, in being free from the possibility of societal sanction, acts in ways that are quite vicious. Even if one interprets this as behaving wholly on the basis of self-interest, it is not the case that this would alleviate the judgment that this vicious person behaves wrongly or justifies those actions. Thus, given that this person possesses true intellectual excellence and yet is the antithesis of virtue, it is clear that, at least on Aristotle's view, intellectual excellence is insufficient for virtue. Having examined the types of human beings that make up the population, we can turn now to the reason that, at least within the *Nicomachean Ethics*, it is appropriate to use the word "virtue ethics" to describe Aristotle's *eudaimonistic* system. The person who is truly excellent and who possesses *eudaimonia* has intellectual excellence, but he is also possesses moral excellence. As Aristotle writes, "The person with *eudaimonia*, then, can be understood as the one ... who throughout life maintains his excellent character. He will always be employed in *arete*, both in reason and in the actions that flow from the dictates of reason. Whatever befalls him, he will meet honorably and virtuously, and he will do all this because he is good indeed. He will do the right things at the right times in the right ways and for the right reasons." While he may not possess all of the virtues (Aristotle differs from Plato on the doctrine of the Unity of Virtues), he does possess the sort of excellence of character that issues in virtuous, or morally excellent, actions. Since "virtue" tends to refer to moral excellence, and since it is clear that Aristotle is offering an analysis of moral excellence of character, then it follows that we can properly name Aristotle's ethics "virtue."

Having examined the sorts of people encountered within the *polis*, and categorized them according to the relationship of the parts of the soul and the respective characters that the distinct kinds of relationship entail, an interlocutor of Aristotle's might well ask him how it is that a character can come to have this *eudaimonia* or state of the soul expressing virtue. That question will be discussed in considerable detail in the section that follows. However, at this point, it is important to import a doctrine that Aristotle develops elsewhere. One of the things that makes Aristotelian scholarship difficult is that he will sometimes merely allude to arguments that he has made elsewhere, clearly expecting that the reader will either know the allusion or will be able to supply the argument. This is the case in the *Nicomachean Ethics*. Aristotle makes all-too-brief reference to arguments he has made in other works, the fullness of which is somewhat critical to understanding the present arguments. One of those important, and imported, doctrines is the Four Cause Doctrine, elaborated in Aristotle's *Physics*.

One of the central topics in Metaphysics is the notion of *causation*, or perhaps, cause and effect. Socrates was accused of being a Natural Philosopher in part because he was thought to be looking for natural explanations for natural events. Rather than explore that notion, Socrates merely disclaimed the accusation – I am not Anaximander, after all. Not the most satisfying of discussions of the topic. Aristotle, on the other hand, would gladly accept the title Natural Philosopher and his treatment of the notion of *causation* is a good example of his attempt to understand the essence of any natural object by appeal to its natural causes.

This notion of causation is a topic to which Aristotle returns at length in a number of places from the *Metaphysics* to the *Politics* to the *Generation of Animals* to name a few. On Aristotle's view, there are four things that can legitimately be called a natural cause of a natural object. These are the Formal, Efficient, Material, and Final Causes (and hence, the Four Cause Doctrine).

Aristotle's use of the word "cause" to describe some of these causes is odd to the modern ear. Generally 21st century hearers of the word immediately imagine something like cause and effect; e.g., the bowling ball caused the pins to fall down. Aristotle uses "cause" this way also – this is the Efficient Cause. But, Aristotle has a broader use for the word and a broader agenda.

Aristotle's concern in specifying the four causes of any natural object is to analyze the *essence* of the thing. The essence of something is that property of the thing without which it would not be what it is. A formal example may look like this. The essence of E is R. If something does not have the property R, then it is not an E. Or, perhaps another, less formal example will help. The essence of my dog Bishop is "dog." If somehow Bishop no longer had the property of being "dog," then something rather fundamental has happened to Bishop. She is no longer what she had been. Whatever the essential properties of "dog" are, Bishop must have them, lest she is not a dog.

Each of the Four Causes is supposed to isolate a particular essential property of any natural object in question. The use of the modifier *natural* is quite important here. Only natural objects, as opposed to artificial objects, can have all four causes. The distinction between *natural* and *artificial* here is the following. A *natural* object is some entity that arises from the process of nature; e.g., a tree, a person, a dog. An *artificial* object is some object constructed by human beings; e.g., a ship, a hat, a ball. Thus, *artificial* refers to something that can be seen as the product of art (or craft), an artifact. Artifacts have Formal, Material, and Efficient Causes, but, on Aristotle's view, they do not have unique Final Causes. For example, some artifact could be constructed and have quite effective use as a paperweight or as a doorstop or as a projectile. Consider the following case. Suppose a company made a hand lotion and marketed their product to those consumers likely to desire a fragrant hand softening lotion. Suppose further that the lotion was discovered to be much better suited for warding off biting and stinging flying insects. In such a case, the company might well refocus their marketing efforts to position their product as a pest preventative with hand softening properties. Thus, to ask what the *natural end* of the product is would be to make a category mistake. As an artifact, it has no natural end.

It is important to make another distinction at this juncture; the distinction between an *essential* property and an *accidental* one. An essential property is a property such that if it is changed, then the object itself is radically altered.

Consider my dog, Bishop, again. If we were to paint her blue, while her appearance would change, she would still be a dog. Color, then, is an *accidental* and not an *essential* property. *Dog*, however, would be an example of an essential property (and is an example of a Formal Cause). Changing Bishop from a dog to some other animal, vegetable, or mineral is to change something *essential* about Bishop.

Let us examine each of the Four Causes in turn to see more clearly what work Aristotle has them do. There is a helpful method of coming to understand the essential property isolated by any particular cause with respect to any particular natural object. There is a set of four questions the answers to which correspond to each of the causes respectively. So, to isolate the Formal Cause of any natural object, we simply ask ourselves of the object, "what is it?" Take Bishop, for example. Bishop's Formal Cause is *dog*. Notice that if we alter the Formal Cause, changing it from *dog* to *rabbit*, we have fundamentally altered Bishop. No longer is she a dog; now she is a rabbit. It should be noted here that the Formal Cause of any particular natural object (e.g., Bishop) is the first abstraction from the Primary Substance level of the Category tree. So, having found Bishop (a particular dog) on the Category tree, we can move up one level of abstraction and discover that the name that applies to all objects that share the same essential property with Bishop is *dog*. Thus, the Category map can show be used as a tool to rather quickly isolate the Formal Cause of any particular object.

The second of the four, and likely the most familiar to modern ears, is the Efficient Cause. The Efficient Cause merely isolates the cause of which the natural object under consideration is the effect. So, for example, if we were to ask the question "what made it?" of Bishop, upon finding the answer we would then know the Efficient Cause of Bishop. This is rather straightforward. The Efficient Cause of Bishop is two-fold; that cause is Bishop's biological parents. If the two dogs that came together to create Bishop had never encountered each other, Bishop would not have existed. Thus, Bishop's biological parents are essential to Bishop and thus are an essential property and not an accidental one. Changing them would change what Bishop essentially is.

The third of the four causes is also reasonably straightforward. The Material Cause is the essential property that we can isolate within any natural object by asking of that object "of what is it made?" As the name *Material* suggests, this cause or essential property refers to the actual stuff that comprises the object. So, we might conclude that that which comprises Bishop is flesh, where the word "flesh" refers to all those parts of Bishop that are tactile. If we changed the stuff of which Bishop was made into something like, for example, lime jello, then we would have again changed something absolutely fundamental about Bishop. Thus, the stuff of Bishop is an essential property of her, on Aristotle's view.

Section 4.4: Aristotle and the Human Function

This, of course, brings us to Aristotle's Final Cause. The Final Cause feature of the Four Cause doctrine is easily the most difficult of the four and one of Aristotle's more controversial doctrines, in general. It raises more troubling questions more quickly than any of the other three "causes" – Formal, Efficient, or Material. This is in part because of a lack of clarity regarding "cause"; particularly as it relates to the Final Cause. To isolate the Final Cause of any natural object, we might ask a set of seemingly different questions, all of which are supposed to have the same answer. We might ask, "what is its purpose?" or "what is it for?" Thus, is the Final Cause a reason, an explanation, or some indication of design by an outside agent? To address this question, it is important that we understand that when speaking of a Final Cause, Aristotle is not speaking of something like "cause and effect." If he were, then the Final Cause would be the same as the Efficient Cause and it clearly is not. Thus, we must keep in mind that Aristotle uses the notion of a Final Cause to isolate a particular *essential property* of the thing. It might be even more helpful if we return to the Greek that underlies the notion of the Final Cause. The Greek behind the notion of Final Cause is *telos* or "end." Just as Aristotle begins the *Nicomachean Ethics* with an analysis that leads to an understanding of the proper end of human action, *eudaimonia*, here Aristotle is isolating the metaphysical *telos* of a natural object.

The Final Cause is a window into the Aristotelian notion of *natural teleology*. The view is that a *telos* or a *function* or an *end* is something toward which all natural objects point. For example, the *telos* or *function* of an acorn is to become an oak tree. An acorn is a very good example of a natural object whose final cause is both obvious and easily confused. If one were to ask what the proper end or function of an acorn is, there are two answers that seem to spring immediately to mind. The first of these is that the natural function of an acorn is to become an oak tree. The second is that its function is to become squirrel food. While both of these are ends of acorns, to be sure, only one is its natural end. This illustrates a very important distinction. The acorn has within it the power to become an oak tree. Thus, it is the acorn's own power or capacity that tends toward the oak tree. On the other hand, becoming a squirrel snack is something that is external to the acorn; it is something done *to* the acorn, not done *by* the acorn. The *telos* of any natural object, then, is that which is within the object's natural power to do, not something that is done to the object by something external to it. All natural objects possess a natural *telos*. The issue that is important within the *Nicomachean Ethics*, indeed, that is essential to the entirety of the Aristotelian ethical project, is isolating the proper natural function, not of acorns or dogs, but of human beings.

What is the human *function* or *telos*? Before we can identify that function, we must first specify a bit more clearly what sorts of options are available. There are many things that human beings do. We sort mail, we build buildings, we write books, we ski, we play hopscotch. However, none of these can be the *human* function. For something to be an essential property of humans it must be part of what it is to actually *be* human. Thus, it must be something that *all* humans do. So, have collected together all of the things that human beings do, we first divide from those things only the things that *all* humans do. The human function must be *common* to all human beings.

At the same time, there are many things that all humans do that are nevertheless not candidates for being the *human* function because they are also things that other natural objects do. Indeed, Aristotle's Function Argument, advanced in brief in the *Nicomachean Ethics*, is an attempt to isolate the thing that *only* humans do from the list of things that all humans do that many other things also do. That is to say, the human function must not only be *common to humans*, it must also be *unique to humans*.

With these criteria in hand, we can now turn to the Function Argument itself. The Function Argument is an argument from elimination that first collects all those things that are common to humans and then pares away those things that, while common to humans, are also shared by other natural objects and therefore not *unique* to humans. The first of these is *nutrition*. The nutritive or vegetative action of human beings is fairly simply the process of taking in sustenance, of processing that sustenance to produce energy and the like, and growth. However, while this is common to humans, it is not unique to humans because plants also engage in this practice. The second human commonality is *sense perception*. A seemingly distinct human activity is the act of perceiving the world around us through the five senses. However, with only a little review, it becomes clear that humans are clearly not alone within the animal kingdom when it comes to sense perception. The vast majority of animals do this as well and thus sense perception is not unique to humans either.

Having eliminated all of the human activities that are common to humans but not unique to them, Aristotle believes he has isolated the Final Cause of human beings. The *telos* or function of a human being is *reason*. Aristotle essentially coins the commonly heard phrase used to describe human beings – *rational animal*. On Aristotle's view, only human beings possess the power of reason. While this may be controversial to modern ears, especially as we survey the vastness the animal kingdom and the intricacy with which so many of our animal cousins interact with the world and behave in ways that seem to express a certain amount of rational ability, it is also the case that even if other animals have a capacity for reason that they do not reason *as a human being* does. While cats or dogs may have a rational faculty, it is clear that they would reason, insofar as they do, as a cat or as a dog reasons. And, these reasonings themselves would be distinct as Fluffy reasons *qua* cat while Bishop reasons *qua* dog and neither have any idea what it would be like to exist as the other. So, too, human beings are incapable of understanding what it is to be a dog. At the same time, this suggests that while other animals may reason, and by hypothesis, some may even reason more effectively than humans, it is also the case that no other animals reason *as humans*. Thus, the human function is to reason as human beings reason.

Given that *eudaimonia* is a state of the soul expressing virtue and that virtue is a matter both of intellectual and moral excellence, then it becomes reasonably clear that Aristotle has developed the view that the avenue toward *eudaimonia* is to function *qua* human excellently. Since the human function is reason, then, only reason, done excellently, will be the path to virtue, and ultimately, *eudaimonia*. As Aristotle says that this human function, reason, is not merely something possessed but something that issues in action, it will be important to understand how that reason is developed and how character is shaped such that intellectual excellence and moral excellence can together become second nature to a human being. In the section that follows, we turn our attention to the acquisition of virtue through the power of the human function. Before we move forward, however, it will be helpful to examine another Aristotelian argument concerning the life of virtue.

Aristotle's view of the human function and its excellence is reiterated as Aristotle engages in yet another instance of the Method of Collection and Division. Oftentimes, people will speak of a "way of life" or a "way of living." Often, people will even refer to this "way of life" incorrectly as a "philosophy of life." This is not a foreign notion to Aristotle. Indeed, as he surveyed Athens, he took note that the majority, if not the totality, of the citizenry lived their lives as if directed toward a particular objective. For some, this was the Highest Good; for most, it was some other object. Since a person is a natural entity, it is not surprising that people will tend toward an end just as all other natural objects do. However, unlike acorns which do not possess the capacity to reason, human beings will often use (or misuse) the natural function to aim at ends other than the Highest Good. Generally speaking, Aristotle thinks that the objects at which human beings aim their lives can be grouped into four categories – Wealth/Money, Sensation, Honor, and Contemplation. To isolate which of these sorts of life is the sort associated with the life of the Highest Good or the life of virtue, Aristotle again turns to an argument from elimination.

The Life of Wealth/Money is simply straightforwardly dismissed. There is little argument other than to say that it is safe to dismiss this one. One can, with a bit of imagination, understand why Aristotle so quickly eliminates this way of life. Wealth is an extraordinarily transient thing. A person can be quite wealthy one day and shockingly poor the next. While most to not suffer such radical shifts of fortune, it remains true that wealth, whether in small or large amounts, is a transient thing. Aiming one's life at something so fleeting and ephemeral as monetary acquisitions is to insure that one will never have a truly stable life. Failing to have anything resembling stability in one's life will necessarily result in a lack of stability within the state of the soul. If one does not have a stable state of character, then it is impossible that one will possess *eudaimonia* which is a stable state of character. Thus, the Life of Wealth/Money is safely eliminated from the candidates for the life of virtue.

Turning to the Life of Sense-Perception, we find a very similar result; although Aristotle takes a bit more time in dismissing it. The Life of Sense-Perception is a life directed toward the experience of pleasures. Here, the difference between *eudaimonia*, often translated as "happiness" and pleasure is employed again. Aristotle does not eschew pleasure. However, he argues that pleasure is not a stable experience either. From common experience, it seems rather clear that pleasure is a fleeting thing. One might be quite elated one moment and quite depressed the next. Even if one moved from one pleasure to the next, a life directed at such a goal is a life that exposes the soul to the constant potential of drastic reversals of fortune. Further, the Life of Sense-Perception can be marked by a gradual dulling of pleasure so that the agent needs greater and greater experiences to kindle the same spark. Thus, in addition to being unstable, the Life of Sense-Perception is also one that is directed, controlled, and compelled by objects external to the soul of the agent. This will entail a rather complete lack of control relative to shaping and crafting the soul *by* the person. Thus, since it is both an unstable life and one dominated by forces external to the person, the Life of Sense-Perception is eliminated as well.

The Life of Honor is a life that is often confused with the life of virtue because *honor* is seen as a beneficial and positive thing. Unlike pleasure, honor is elevated by the community as worthy of praise. Honor, or high reputation, is considered fine and noble. However, a brief reflection on the nature of honor will quickly reveal that it too fails as a candidate for the life of virtue.

Honor, or reputation, is only partly dependent on the sort of character the person of high repute is. Many are the people who have great reputations and turn out to be unworthy of them. Indeed, thinking back to those questioned by Socrates – "all those with a reputation for wisdom" – is sufficient to show that reputation is not a function of the character of the person, but rather is a matter of the community's perception of that person. Thus, one who lives his life in pursuit of reputation is shaping his actions based in large part on what he perceives to be the wants and desires of the community in which he is rather than on what is actually right. As communities are notoriously fickle, one who is greatly honored today might well be greatly despised tomorrow. Thus, the pursuit of honor is also a life that is inherently unstable and largely beholden to forces external to the person, himself. Thus, the Life of Honor is eliminated.

Having eliminated all of the potential candidates for the life of virtue except one, the Life of Contemplation, the careful reader will anticipate this conclusion. Indeed, Aristotle holds that the Life of Contemplation is the life of virtue. He has a positive argument for this conclusion, apart from the negative argument from elimination that has been presented heretofore. Contemplation, obviously, is a matter of the function of the rational part of the soul. The most common conception of a contemplative experience is one in which the person is thinking, deeply and seriously about some subject or other. This is, indeed, central to the life of virtue and the Life of Contemplation is the life of excellence in the practice of reason. As it is a matter of the excellence of the human function, it must be the life of virtue.

It should be noted that contemplation, as Aristotle conceives it, is not a matter of simply thinking deep thoughts. To reason effectively is not merely to be capable of providing an analysis of some situation or other, it is also a matter of being able to act in those ways that are consistent with the reasoning of the virtuous person. Thus, the virtuous person is not one who merely considers a number of actions and through the powers of analysis identifies the action that is the right course to take, she is also the person who actually takes the action. Thus, the Life of Contemplation, far from being an exercise in Ivory Tower mental gymnastics, is rather a life in which the person does the right things at the right times in the right ways and for the right reasons. Thus, the life of virtue is a rather complex thing and one which involves the practice of virtuous acts, not merely the thinking about them. How that life of virtue is acquired is the topic of the next section.

Guided Reading Questions:
1. What is the highest human good, according to Aristotle
2. Why is it not nutrition?
3. Why is it not sense perception?

Logic Blurb
Law of Non-Contradiction

One of the first principles of formal logic is the Law of Non-Contradiction. Simply put, the Law of Non-Contradiction holds that it is impossible to hold any two propositions that form a contradiction as true at the same time and in the same respect. That is, if one has two propositions, "Bozo is a clown" and "Bozo is not a clown," then only one of these propositions can be true. If one knows that the proposition "Bozo is a clown" is true, then, in virtue of knowing that it is true and that it is a contradictory proposition to "Bozo is not a clown," then one knows that the second proposition is necessarily false.

This is one of the most important principles of formal logic. Any argument that includes contradictory premises or that has a conclusion that contradicts one of its premises is a false argument and is rightfully dismissed. Further, any set of propositions that entail contradictions can themselves be described as contradictory. One of the examples of propositions which do not seem at first contradictory but which, on analysis of their implications, turn out to be would be the two propositions that comprise the Euthyphro Problem. As we discussed in that section, the notion that "X is holy because the gods love it" and notion that "the gods love X because it is holy," are contradictions although at first glance they seem simply different.

The foregoing discussion should not be taken to suggest that no one would put forward and strenuously defend contradictory arguments. Indeed, one need only pay close attention to the arguments that swirl around on television, in coffee houses, and the like to notice people holding, with heartfelt fervor, to contradictory propositions. On Aristotle's view, those who hold contradictory propositions to be true, even after having been shown that they are contradiction, are not suitable interlocutors for argument. He thinks that anyone who insists on holding contradictory views cannot be convinced they are in an impossible position simply through argument and will not profit from a rational discussion of the contradictory position in which they find themselves. In one of his less charitable moments, he labels those who insist on holding contradictory beliefs to be true, and thus violating the law of non-contradiction, as artichokes.

Section 4.5: Aristotle and Virtue

Nicomachean Ethics, The Acquisition of Virtue

Since *arete* (excellence) has two sorts – intellectual and moral – we can see how they are developed. Intellectual *arete* arises from teaching and requires experience and time. Moral *arete*, on the other hand, is a matter of custom (ἐθος – *ethos*) and, thus, has a slightly different name (ἠθος – *ethos*). No moral *arete* is a matter solely of nature. Training cannot alter nature. A stone naturally falls down. It is quite impossible to train it to behave differently even if one threw it into the air thousands of times. Similarly, fire will never move downward. Thus, the moral excellences (virtues) are not counter to nature nor are they natural. At the same time, nature makes them possible, provides within human beings a disposition toward them, and it is this disposition that can be trained.

Virtue is acquired through practice. This is the same with all of the arts. We learn by doing. If we are to become carpenters, we practice carpentry; if we are to be harpists, then we practice the harp. Similarly, one becomes just only through practicing justice (or doing just acts) and so to with *sophrosune* and bravery. Similarly, the opposite traits or vices come from the same sorts of actions. If one practices carpentry well, one will become a good carpenter; if one practices carpentry badly, one will become a bad one. The virtues are the same. It is only through interaction with people that justice (and injustice) can be practiced; and only by facing danger and training to react rightly to fear can one become brave. It is also the same with our appetites and desires. If one behaves rightly when the spirit of anger is called forth, one can develop gentleness while behaving wrongly will result in an ill-temper. Simply put, acts of a certain sort develop characters of the same sort. Thus, we must insure that we act rightly – at the right time, in the right ways, and for the right reasons – because character is variable and arises from those actions.

In actions like this, both excess and deficiency are destructive. Obviously this is so with regard to health. If one exercises too much or too little, strength is destroyed. If one eats too much or too little, again health is destroyed. However, doing the appropriate amount of exercise and eating the right amount of food will bolster health and preserve it. It is the same with *sophrosune*, with bravery, and with all the other moral *arete*. The one who always runs in fear, never facing it, is a coward. The one who is immune from fear but always stands and fights, he is foolhardy. The one who engages in all the possible sorts of pleasure is profligate; the one who avoids them all has no sense. Thus, bravery and *sophrosune* are destroyed by excess or deficiency and only maintained through a moderate way.

One develops strength through exercise and diligent work. At the same time, the strong man has a greater ability to perform exercise and work. It is the same way with moral *arete*. *Sophrosune* is developed through restraint from pleasure and the *sophron* one is the one most able to resist. Again, the same with bravery. He who has habituated himself to overcome danger becomes brave and is most capable of facing future dangers. Moral *arete* is entwined with pleasure and pain. Often, pleasure motivates a person to act crassly while pain causes us to avoid the high road. It is like Plato said, a person must be raised from birth to see pleasure and pain in the right ways and proper things. This is the meaning of good education.

There are those who define moral *arete* as a sort of blank or accepting state, a kind of apathy. This is completely wrong. Even a balanced soul must be qualified by the actions that arise from it with regard to proper or improper means, timing, place, and so forth.

Heraclitus said that the struggle against rage is difficult and to fight pleasure harder still. Moral *arete* is analogous – concerned with that which is difficult and the more difficult, the greater the triumph. So, virtue and the science of virtue is a matter of pleasure and pain. The one that acts properly is the good person, the one who does not is bad.

We say that something is *sophron*ly done when is it done as the *sophron* person would do it. However, the person who does the *sophron* thing is not himself *sophron* unless he, too, has the soul of the *sophron* person. Thus, only by doing just things does a person become just, but he is not just simply in virtue of having done some just things. At the same time, failure to do just things entails that the person is not just.

Oddly, rather than engage in this sort of approach, most people rush to theories and speculations and fancifully imagine that they are philosophers, thinking this will be the avenue to goodness. This is like a sick person who pays very close attention to whatever his physician says but then does whatever he wants instead. This approach to philosophy will no more produce a healthy soul than that sort of care would result in a healthy body.

So, what is moral *arete* or virtue?

There are three qualities of the soul. There is passion, powers or capacities, and habits (which are dispositions that have been trained). Therefore, virtue must be one of the three. The passions are appetites – things like anger, fear, confidence, jealousy, desire, hatred, love, sympathy – anything that is attended by pleasure or by pain. A capacity is the ability through which the passions press upon us – the ability to become enraged, for example, or to be overwhelmed by sympathy. A habit is trained with respect to being well guided or ill guided with regard to emotions.

The virtues are not emotions. The vices are not either. A person is not called "good" on the basis of his emotions, but only because of virtues. Praise and blame are not assigned in virtue of emotions – a person isn't blamed for being angry or fearful but for the *way in which* he is angry or fearful. Again, praise and blame are assigned because of the virtues, or vices. Anger and fear may happen with no choice or contemplation on our part; virtues are the result of deliberate choice (or, more exactly, contemplation is required for virtue). Finally, it is said that our emotions move us, but we do not say of the virtues that they move us, but rather that we are guided or disposed by them to act in this way or that. Since moral *arete* is not emotion nor a mere capacity or power, then it can only be a habit.

If something is excellent, then that excellence will describe both the condition of the thing and the manner in which it performs its function. For example, excellence of an eye causes both the eye and its functioning to be good. If this is true universally, then, the true excellence of a human being will be excellence of that habit that both makes the person good and causes the person to perform his function excellently. Let us now investigate the nature of this virtue.

Given any quantity, we can have too much of it or too little or a proper amount; and this can be either an absolute matter or one relative to the needs of a particular person. By "proper amount," is meant a mean – something between excess on the one hand and deficiency on the other. The absolute mean is the midpoint between excess and deficiency, equal distance from both. This is the same for all things. The mean relative to a particular person, however, is that neither too much nor too little for that person. This will not be the same for all persons or things.

For example, suppose that ten is too much and two is too little. By arithmetic we discern that six is the mean, equidistant from both endpoints. However, suppose that ten pounds of food is too much but two is too little. From this, we cannot conclude that his trainer will require him to eat six pounds – that might still be too much. The same is true in all athletic events. So, we can conclude that the one who has mastered an activity knows what is too much and what is too little and avoids them and know what the proper mean between them is and chooses it. It follows, then, that moral *arete*, as an excellence so like the others, must aim at the mean.

Thus, moral *arete* covers emotions and actions where excess and deficiency are both wrong and the mean is right. Virtue is a trained habit borne of deliberate choice. The chief characteristic of that choice is its moderation – attaining the mean for the particular person, and that mean is determined by reason. This reason is reason as the good person would determine it and it is moderation as it is between excess and deficiency. Both of these are vices and fail to reflect the proper course in emotion or in action. This reason discerns the mean amount and directs the person toward it.

It is insufficient to speak only in generalities about things of this nature – about virtue and vice. It is necessary that we see how the theory is applied; that is, how the several virtues and vices are in practice. Let us examine bravery. The middle way between fear and foolhardiness is bravery. Excess in this does not really have a proper name (this sometimes happens) but we can call it foolhardiness or recklessness. The one with a deficiency of bravery is a coward. The same is true of giving away money. The moderate way is generosity. The one who gives everything away is a spendthrift; the deficient one is a miser.

It is enough that we have shown that moral *arete* is the mean between excess and deficiency and how that might work – navigating between two vices on either side and focusing on the mean in both emotion and action. Given this, it is quite difficult to be good. Find the middle in all these things is hard, indeed. Just as many cannot find the precise center of a circle, so, too, many cannot navigate the mean between excess and deficiency. Only the one with the proper knowledge can do so. For example, any person can be angry and any person can give away money. However, to do these to the right person, in the right amounts, at the right time, with the right things, and in the right way is not something that many can do. It is not easy. This is why doing the right thing is so very rare and is thought noble and is highly praised.

This is our outline and sketches out the manner by which we can best find the mean. It is hard, especially in particular instances. It is difficult to know with whom to be angry and why and how long. At times, the public praises those who fall short (calling them gentle) and at others praises those who exceed the mean (calling them manly when they show harshness). But this is clear. Regardless of public sentiment, the middle character is, at all times and in all cases, the one worthy of praise.

~

In the relatively short space of the opening sections of the *Nicomachean Ethics*, Aristotle has made considerable progress toward developing a very complex and sophisticated theory of ethics. So far, he has identified the Highest Good for human beings (*eudaimonia*), the science of the Highest Good (politics), and the qualifications of the student of the Highest Good. He has argued that *eudaimonia* is the stable state of the soul expressing virtue and begun to put forward a theory of virtue that will be more fully addressed here. He has also laid the foundation for understanding how the acquisition of virtue is possible – it is a matter of *arete* of the soul, both intellectual and moral – and he has examined the nature of the human soul, arguing that the way in which the part of the soul interact will be described as a matter of the sort of character possessed by the person whose soul it is. Thus, we have the four-fold distinction among human beings – virtuous, continent, incontinent, and vicious – although this four-fold distinction admits of considerably more variety that it would appear on first glance. And, Aristotle has argued that the human function, the excellence of which is what it means to be virtuous, is reason; something common to all human beings and at the same time unique to humans. From this view of the human function and its excellence, Aristotle eliminates all of those kinds of life or ways of life that aim at something other than the Highest Good through means of active reason.

With this framework in place, Aristotle now turns to the more delicate task of examining the nature of virtue itself and the acquisition of virtue. There are several necessary conditions that must be satisfied in order for a person to acquire virtuous character. The first of these is very simple. To have a virtuous character, one must do virtuous things. That is, a virtuous character will issue in the right sorts of actions in the right ways at the right times and for the right reasons. Here, it becomes clear that Aristotle's view involves a crucial distinction between virtuous actions and virtuous character. A person might do many, many good deeds. However, simply in virtue of this, we would not say that a person is good. It may be that he has all manner of motives for doing good things. For example, perhaps he is actually pursuing the Life of Honor and is merely doing things of which he knows that the community will approve because he knows that he will receive high marks and praise for doing them. He is not acting because he has the sort of character that issues in the right actions but because he is, at best, a continent person who comports his actions with those he knows to be the right ones but only because he will receive reward for acting rightly and fears a loss of stature for acting wrongly. Thus, while he may do the right thing at the right time and in the right way, he does not do so for the right reasons. So, merely doing many correct things is not sufficient to give a person the label, "good." At the same time, it is quite clear that one cannot be considered a virtuous person if one does not act at all or if one acts wrongly or in the wrong ways or at the wrong times. Thus, doing the right things is necessary for virtue, but not sufficient for it.

This brings us to the second necessary condition for virtue; the proper natural dispositions. The question of whether character is fundamentally a matter of nature or nurture is not a new question. Indeed, Aristotle takes up that very issue in the *Nicomachean Ethics*. This is another place where doctrines and principles Aristotle develops elsewhere must be imported to fully understand the view he advances here. The scientific view developed by Aristotle is essentially the foundation for scientific inquiry into the structure of the natural world from his day until well into the 17th century C.E. Thus, for nearly two thousand years, Aristotelian science is the order of the day for scientific investigation. Central to that scientific model is the Aristotelian notion of *natural teleology*. A special case of natural teleology is the Final Cause, the *natural telos* or *end* or *function* of any natural object. A broader understanding of natural teleology is that there exists within each objects certain tendencies or capacities that are activated by circumstances. These capacities express necessary features of the makeup of the object in question and cannot be overcome by external impositions. Thus, Aristotle writes that a rock will tend to fall and that no matter how many times one tries to train a rock not to fall by throwing it into the air, those attempts will be futile, fruitless, and foolish. The rock naturally tends to fall when in a situation where it is not supported or kept from falling by some outside force. It can never be the case that the rock can be taught or convinced to act outside of its nature. So, nature, at the very least, provides constraints outside of which it is impossible for an object to act.

Given this natural mandate, one might suspect that Aristotle would conclude that human beings naturally tend toward virtue or are naturally predisposed toward the good. This is not the case. At the same time, it is not the case that Aristotle thinks virtue is wholly a societal construct. However, Aristotle has a much more subtle view. His view involves a distinction between colloquially named "nature" and "nurture." All human beings possess a certain set of capacities as a matter of nature. Reason, for example, is one of these. It is clear that a person reasons with greater efficiency and perspicacity as an adult than as an infant or toddler. That natural capacity or disposition toward reason is activated throughout the life of the person and developed to greater or lesser extent. However, the fact of the innate capacity is not seriously questioned. The upshot of this view is that for a person to be able to develop a particular virtue, he must have the innate dispositions within the soul whose goal is that virtue.

This is not nearly so strange a view as it might initially seem. Consider the example of an infant who clearly does not yet possess the ability to speak any language at all. If that infant were to grow up in an English-speaking society, the language the child will grow to speak is English. If the child were to grow up in a Mandarin-speaking society, then the child will learn to speak Mandarin. Which language a child learns to speak is reasonably clearly a matter of the educational environment in which the child grows. It is not the case that some children are hard-wired for speaking English while others for French while still others for Mandarin. However, the fact *that* a child can learn a language points to something innate in the structure of the human mind, a capacity that is possible to activate into the knowledge of a language. If a child had no language faculty, either because of trauma or some other irregularity, no amount of training, whatever the particular language, will activate a capacity that is nonexistent. Similarly, as a child who possesses a rather standard capacity for language learning ages and develops, she will lose the ability to acquire complete fluency in other languages. For example, a child who grows up speaking only English will, sometime after the age of six or so, have fixed the language into which she will grow and all other languages have, for the most part, become truly foreign. While she may gain proficiency in another language which she begins to study at a much later date, the language learning faculty will have become focused around a single language making fluency in a different one all but impossible. There are exceptions to this, of course. Many children grow up in multi-lingual

Section 4.5: Aristotle and Virtue

environments and as a result develop fluency in a number of different languages from an early age. This is not so much an exception to the capacity/activation model as it is a demonstration of the fluidity of the capacity and its flexibility at accommodating several different languages at one. The more pertinent exception would be someone who is simply extraordinary at acquisition of language. An individual might have such a robust capacity for learning languages that she is always capable of adding to her linguistic repertoire. To be sure, such a person would be exceptionally rare. However, even in this rare case, the converse is true – without the innate language-learning capacity, no language would be learned. Thus, the proper natural dispositions are required for the development of many of the abilities that serve to help people to prosper.

One should not think that Aristotle leaves the notion of physical requirements for development of character at the level of innate intellectual or rational dispositions. Aristotle thinks that there are physical attributes that will make development of character more or less likely, more or less possible. On Aristotle's view, a person who is more physically attractive will have a better chance of developing a stellar character than one who is less attractive or who is deformed in some way. While one might readily want to cast aspersions at Aristotle's view here, arguing that virtue should be independent of such fatuous features as physical attraction, he thinks that, upon a survey of the actual practices of people, the more attractive or physically fit a person is, the more likely he or she is to have the opportunities to interact with others, to receive benefit from them, and to activate the innate dispositions he or she may have for virtuous character.

In one sense, while this may seem rather odious, in another it seems very much akin to contemporary understandings. For example, a person who was fully grown and only a bit under five feet tall is quite unlikely to play professional basketball. A person who is extraordinarily clumsy is unlikely to become a prima ballerina. And a person who cannot seem to speak without suffering horrible pangs of anxiety is unlikely to succeed and flourish in a profession that requires public speaking. While it might be noted that none of these has anything to do with the development of character, it should likewise be noted that each of these has to do with a physical attribute or lack thereof, and further, and more importantly, each of these physical attributes or lack thereof directly contributes to the way in which the person is perceived in society, and as a result, to the number of opportunities that the person will have to interact with, receive benefit from, and perform for others. This analysis points to a third important necessary condition for the acquisition of character – opportunity.

Related to opportunity is a fourth necessary condition, practice. Aristotle holds that certain dispositions are required for the acquisition of virtue, but that those dispositions will lay fallow, or worse, atrophy and disappear without practice. On Aristotle's view, it is impossible to have a virtuous character without actions that are themselves virtuous. Good character is not merely a matter of possessing a certain set of dispositions and a considerable number of facts and a prodigious analytical ability. Virtue must be practiced; it must be habituated. It is the life of active reason (contemplation) that is the life of virtue and a life of action must, of necessity, be active. However, if one is completely without opportunity to practice, or is presented with merely a limited number of opportunities to practice a particular virtue, it is not merely unlikely that he will acquire it, it is, on Aristotle's view, impossible.

This view is not that divergent from at least contemporary language about virtue, or, for that matter, about the acquisition of any craft or art. Great athletes are said to be "in their element" when in the midst of their competition. Great teachers and great soldiers and great computer scientists are all at home within their particular excellences, even if they are completely befuddled in other social or professional settings. Indeed, we sometimes say that a person who has a remarkable feel for some particular practice has a *second nature*. This is precisely the sort of phenomenon that Aristotle is concerned to express about virtue. The truly virtuous person, the person whose character is truly excellent, has a sort of second nature; one that has been overlaid upon the dispositions of the first nature and has come about through the diligent and rational activation and perfection of those dispositions. Thus, the person has become different from those who are merely competent. This sort of second nature is the difference, then, between the truly virtuous person and the merely continent one. So, we have come something like full circle. The first necessary condition of developing an excellent character through the acquisition of virtue was to engage in virtuous action. We have now see that necessary conditions for engaging in that action are the proper sort of natural dispositions, opportunity, and practice. It might do well to consider one of the virtues Aristotle uses as an example of the acquisition of virtue. In this consideration, other necessary conditions for the acquisition of virtue will become apparent.

Let us consider one of the virtues Aristotle examines as an exemplar of the acquisition of virtue, *generosity*. Before giving full attention to this virtue, it is important to note that Aristotle means something slightly different by "generosity" than its common contemporary connotations. We often speak of someone who is generous with praise or generous with her time or generous with his hospitality. However, Aristotle limits the notion of generosity to the giving away of material possessions, particularly money. Thus, a person might be quite giving of her time and energy and effort to some cause or another, but Aristotle would not call this *generosity*. It is important to note that he would not label it a vice or that he would think it bad at all. Indeed, it may in fact be a virtue. However, in an effort to avoid the confusion that always attends equivocations, Aristotle is quite restrictive in his definitions of the virtues. Thus, the virtue of generosity is a matter of being generous with money.

If it is the case that certain external goods are necessary for the acquisition of virtue, with the virtue *generosity* the identity of those external goods is likely to be quite clear. For a person to practice the Aristotelian generosity, she must have money to give away. Since the only way *generosity* can become second nature is through practice and since the only way in which one can practice the giving away of money is to have money to give, then it is clear that one of the external goods necessary for the development of this virtuous character trait is the monetary wherewithal to give. Let us consider, then, the person who has the right sorts of natural dispositions – that is, he has a natural propensity or capacity to develop a generous character. Further, let us suppose that this person has considerable personal wealth, such that he can not only practice sufficiently to develop the virtue but can continue to practice it after having developed it. Aristotle holds the very sensible view that one does not cease a Life of Contemplation (or active reason) simply in virtue of having acquired a virtue because to do so is to allow the slow process of atrophy to begin. Thus, the person has the natural dispositions toward generosity, the financial wherewithal to practice, and further, let us suppose that he has just the right number of opportunities and of just the right sorts so that he can practice. In virtue of all of these conditions, it is still possible that virtue itself might be far outside our well-positioned person's grasp. This is because we have yet to identify what, in fact, the generous *actions* are.

Identifying the right thing to do at the right time is quite a difficult task. Suppose Brent is presented with a person who is in need of five dollars within the next minute or so. Suppose further that Brent has all of the dispositions and wherewithal to act generously. Let us suppose still further, however, that he does not know what the right thing to do. He is perplexed concerning how much money he should give, he is not at all certain that this is the right time to give money or even that giving money in this situation is the right thing to do. Here, the importance of excellence with regard to the human function, reason, is all the more obvious. Brent must size up the situation and accurately discern what the right thing to do is. Supposing that the right thing to do is to give money, he must evaluate and arrive at the right amount to give and the proper way in which to give it. If he were to give the person $4.95, he might well have acted in a way that was not generous, but cruel. If he were to give the person $1000, he might well have gone far beyond the dictates of generosity and into foolishness. This pair of circumstances points to the difficulty of discerning the right thing to do at the right time in the right way and for the right reasons. On either end of the generous action, there is an entire gradation of actions that are closer and further from the right one. The right action, the virtuous action, lies somewhere between an excessively generous act and a deficient one. This mean between excess and deficiency is commonly referred to as *The Golden Mean*.

On Aristotle's view, the virtue always lies at the mean between excess and deficiency. The excessive act and the deficient one we will call by virtue's opposite name and call them *vices*. Let us consider again the virtue *generosity*. If generosity is about giving money away – at the right times, in the right ways, and for the right reasons – it should be reasonably easy to identify the vices associated with it. For example, if generosity, the virtue, lies between excess and deficiency, then we can simply ask what would be the excess of the action and the deficiency of it and thereby identify those actions that are the related vices. If one is deficient, we would call that person miserly. So, *miserliness* is one endpoint. The miser is not merely one who saves and does not give away, he is one who hordes money, even taking no pleasure in spending it for his own wants and desires. On the other hand, if one is excessive in his giving, he will soon find himself unable to give any more because his financial wherewithal is gone. This person is *foolish*. Between miserliness and foolishness, then, lies the virtue *generosity*.

It is important to recognize that when Aristotle speaks of the Golden Mean as the mean between excess and deficiency, he is not specifying the *midpoint*. It might well be that the midpoint is the Golden Mean in some particular circumstance. Only through careful analysis, however, will the agent be able to discern whether that mean is closer to deficiency, closer to excess, or in the exact center. For example, suppose one were to take in no liquids whatsoever. Within a few days, this deficiency of fluid would result in dehydration and ultimately death. Such a result would be a negative one, and likely a vicious one. In a similar way, suppose one were to ingest one hundred gallons of water in a single day (or that one tried, at any rate). A similar result would be the outcome – not dehydration, to be sure, but sickness and death. Again, this is a vicious result. However, if one were to suppose that the Golden Mean lay at the midpoint between deficiency and excess here, then one would suppose that the proper thing to do would be to attempt to ingest fifty gallons of water in a single day, an attempt that would conclude in exactly the same way that the attempt to drink one hundred would. Instead, the proper fluid intact is much closer to the deficiency pole, on this model. In a similar vein, consider again the case of Brent and the beggar who asks for five dollars. Let us suppose that the person truly needs the money, needs it immediately, and that Brent has both the dispositions and the money to make the gift. To give nothing would be consistent with miserliness, the deficiency of the virtue. To give one thousand dollars would be to act as a foolish spendthrift, the excess of the virtue. To give five dollars would be the proper action and, as in the case of fluid intact, is much closer to the deficient action than it is to the excessive one.

Let us consider a different example, then; one closer to the excessive pole. One of the Cardinal Virtues is *courage*. As Aristotle has offered a definition of generosity that is rather restricted, so, too, he offers a definition of courage that excludes many things that modern readers of Aristotle might well consider courageous. For example, consider the person stricken with a terminal illness who nevertheless fights doggedly against the disease and is an inspiration to all around her. Aristotle would consider that fight a good fight and indeed would view her actions as praiseworthy. They are not, however, actions that ought to be named "courage," on his view. In an effort, once again, to avoid equivocal names, Aristotle restricts the virtue of courage to actions on the battlefield. The courageous person is the one who knows when to fight and when to flee and acts accordingly.

To identify the virtue, *courage*, let us first specify its opposites. The person who is deficient in courage is easily named – a *coward*. The person who has an excess of courage is less easily named, but we shall call him *reckless*. The coward is the person who feels fear in the midst of battle and allows that emotional pull to flee to overcome the rational part of the soul and he flees. Succumbing to fear, he runs when he should fight, hides when he should stand firm, and sneaks away when he should be launching himself into battle. The reckless person, on the other hand, is the one who, against overwhelming odds, rushes pell-mell into battle. He is not ignorant of the danger surrounding him and he also, perhaps, feels fear. However, he is unable to understand that there are times when the right course of action is to withdraw and fight later rather than to waste oneself in a foolhardy assault. While epics and odes may be composed in his honor, Aristotle would not consider him to have behaved virtuously.

The courageous person, on the other hand, is one who feels fear, to be sure. A battlefield is a fearsome place and the truly fearless are often the reckless, endangering not only themselves but their comrades. Rather, the courageous person feels fear but does not allow that fearful state to sway him from what he should do. There will be times when the proper action of the courageous person is to withdraw, to act, that is, in a way consistent with what the cowardly person would do. However, more often, the courageous thing to do might well be to face ones enemies, even though there is some fear. The courageous person is not controlled by fear, nor by the lust for battle, but by rationality, excellently implemented. Some times he will withdraw. Perhaps more often he will fight. Knowing the proper thing to do in any given moment will require considerable analytical prowess on the part of the rational agent. Hence, again, the importance of reason to the acquisition of virtue is shown and reason is seen, again, as absolutely necessary for the development of an excellent character. Indeed, reason, done excellently, is the only path to virtue, and ultimately, *eudaimonia*.

Before leaving the work of Aristotle to move forward toward the end of the Ancient period and the beginning of the Medieval, it is important to note one last feature of Aristotle's virtue ethics. While the virtuous action lies at the mean between excess and deficiency and while that mean may differ from one moment to the next, one should not suppose that Aristotle is advocating some form of relativism. Relativism, indeed, is diametrically opposite of Aristotle's view. For Aristotle, in every moment, there is some action that is the right action. It is as much a feature of the natural world as the human function is. For one person, the proper action on the field of battle would be to withdraw while for another, in precisely the same situation, the proper action would be to fight. However, in each case, the person is different and that difference is a feature of the actual world. So, in one case, a ten-year old with a bad back and severe vision impairment and a battle-tested, excellently conditioned soldier might find themselves on a battlefield. Let us even suppose that both have the requisite rational ability to assess the situation, the proper natural dispositions toward courage, and even a bit of training. However, for one, the proper action will almost always be to retreat while for the other, the proper action will likely very rarely be retreat. But, this difference is one rooted in the features of the situation; which is to say, features of the actual world. Thus, there is, on Aristotle's view, a definite and objective right thing to do, although there may be many, many wrong things to do. These are all features of the natural world and thus are completely independent of what one might want to be the case. They simply are. Determining what that right thing to do is is a function, then, of excellence of reason and excellence in reason will reveal the objective, natural end of excellence of character, of virtue.

Guided Reading Questions:

1. How is virtue acquired?
2. What is *happiness*?
3. Aristotle says that it is okay that the definitions in the field of ethics are not precise, but only a sketch. Why?

Logic Blurb
The Argument from Elimination

One of the most powerful argument forms is the Argument from Elimination. It is the rare philosopher who does not depend regularly on it for advancing a view. Simply put, the Argument from Elimination is an approach in which one first lists all of the possible solutions for a given problem and then, singly or in groups, eliminates all of the possibilities until but a single option remains. The Argument of Elimination makes use of the *disjunctive "or"* to separate the various possibilities, or competitors, from each other. For example, consider that for some problem there are four potential answers, *A* or *B* or *C* or *D*. An excellent example of an Argument from Elimination is Descartes's *Causal Argument for the Existence of God*. In brief, he notes that his idea of God must have some cause and the possibilities are that it was caused by him, caused by some other person, or that it is a natural part of any human mind. He then argues that the first two options cannot be true. Therefore, the third one must be. In this example, we see that the Argument from Elimination is an indirect proof. It offers no direct support for its conclusion other than the fact that it is the only competitor left standing. Thus, the argument proceeds as each competitor is considered and discarded until but one remains.

There is very little requirement beyond these two. First, the competitors have to be truly distinct. If two of the competitors are the same, only worded differently, or very closely related in some way or other, then it might well be impossible to eliminate either of them. Thus, each competitor should be completely distinct – something that the disjunctive "or" forces.

The second requirement of the Argument from Elimination is that all true competitors be included. Consider Plato's arguments in the *Crito*. There, he examines two arguments about Socrates's fate – that it would be unjust for him to escape and that it would be unjust to stay. We can see that a portion of the Socratic elenchus is actually an Argument from Elimination. By showing Crito that his view (that it would be unjust for Socrates to stay in Athens and be put to death) is false, it follows that it would be unjust for him to leave. However, suppose we were faced with a rather more mundane situation. Suppose we are told that we must either (a) drive to the city or (b) fly or (c) bicycle. Then, the argument proceeded, eliminating (a) and (b). In virtue of this, we should bicycle. However, the careful reader might notice that these are not truly the only competitors. The list is not exhaustive. Indeed, perhaps walking or traveling by mule-cart is to be preferred even over bicycling. Thus, for an Argument from Elimination to truly command assent to its purported conclusion, the list of distinct competitors set off by the disjunctive "or" must be exhaustive.

Another example of the Argument from Elimination is Aristotle's Function Argument. There are three possible candidates for the Human Function – Nutrition and Growth, Sense Perception, and Reason. Since the first two are eliminated because they are things that humans share with others, one is left to conclude that the human function is Reason. Like the Argument from Analogy discussed earlier, the Argument from Elimination is a nearly ubiquitous tool in the critical thinker's toolbox.

Chapter 2 – Medieval Philosophy

Section 5: The Advent of Medieval Philosophy

The history of philosophy is generally divided into at least three periods, although there is considerable difference of opinion with regard to whether there are more than three. The three receiving widespread consensus are the Ancient, Medieval, and Modern periods.

Several measures can be used to argue the distinction between periods in the history of philosophy. If we hold that philosophy, historically speaking, is an ongoing conversation in which questions are asked, theories advanced, and positions refined in a cumulative sort of way, then we would expect that shifts in emphasis would be not only commonplace, but universal. However, major shifts in the approach to philosophy would be rare. By thinking of philosophy as consisting in three major branches, all with distinct, yet interrelated questions at their centers, we can isolate the major shifts in the history of philosophy and also account for the more subtle, more nuanced differences that make up the practice of philosophy in every period. In this way, important, if perhaps overly general, distinctions can be made in ways that will aid our investigations.

Philosophy is traditionally, and appropriately, divided into three broad subcategories – Metaphysics, Epistemology, and Ethics. These branches are interrelated, yet distinct. Metaphysics (theories about the actual world), Epistemology (theories of knowledge), and Ethics (theories of human conduct) correspond to the "big questions" with which we have worked throughout the text thus far.

As we have seen in the foregoing section, the entry into the "big questions" for the Ancients was through the question of human virtue. Thus, ethics was the doorway for the Ancients and the branch of philosophy emphasized. It was clear that this approach led immediately to questions of metaphysics and epistemology as Plato advanced a Theory of Forms, explored the difference between true and false beliefs, and spent considerable time demonstrating the relationship between the nature of the actual world and human perception of it. These explorations, however, were always in the pursuit of an understanding of the good life, human happiness (*eudaimonia*), and human excellence or virtue (*arête*). Similarly, Aristotle's in-depth discussions of grammar, causation, functions, and categories all serve to make clear his own ethical commitments. Thus, for the Ancients, the emphasis is ethics, although not to the exclusion of the other branches.

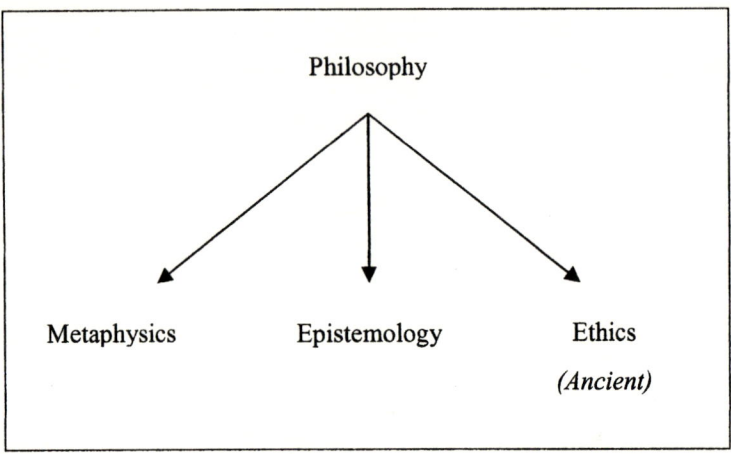

The pivot from the Ancient period to the Medieval one is generally considered to take place in the person and work of St. Augustine, bishop of Hippo and Doctor of the Church. The Medieval period is known particularly for the developments made in logic and metaphysics. For example, the Ancient philosophers were not particularly concerned with arguments about the nature of God, nor did they worry much about arguments for God's existence. Plato and Aristotle make references to the divine, but share a much greater affinity for the natural philosophers like Thales and Heraclitus than for the theologians who populate the canon of Medieval philosophy. St. Augustine, with his arguments concerning the nature of God, the nature of evil, and Original Sin, turned the focus of the philosophical conversation from one centered on human beings to one centered on God. To be sure, the role and nature of humanity is a matter of great importance to Augustine, but the starting point has changed. Rather than the Protagoras-like "Man is the measure of all things" that is common to Ancient philosophy, Augustine shifts the starting point to God. Humanity is understood as radically dependent upon, and subordinate to, God; thus, it is important to understand the nature of God and the secondary nature of humanity that is contingent upon God. Thus, Medieval philosophy is marked by a shift in emphasis, from ethics to metaphysics.

Section 5: The Advent of Medieval Philosophy

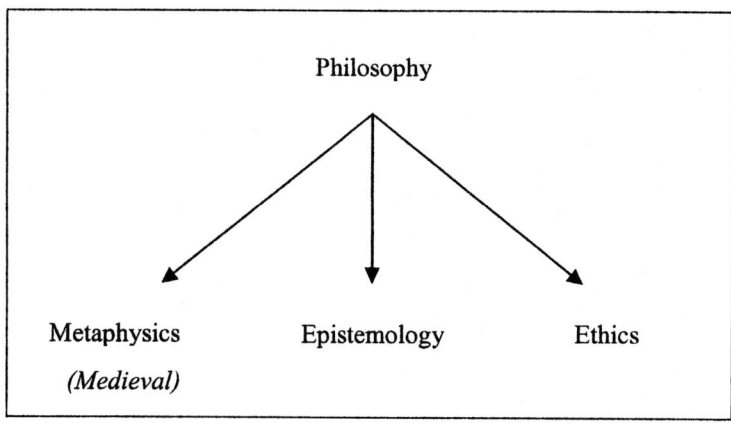

The significant historical events that contributed to the shifts in philosophical emphasis will be addressed at the beginning of the next period, the Modern. Likewise, the philosophical shift from Medieval to Modern philosophy will be addressed in greater detail there as well. However, it is appropriate here to discuss that shift briefly. As the Ancient emphasis was on ethics and the Medieval emphasis on metaphysics, the Modern emphasis was a question of knowledge, or epistemology. The dominant assumption that characterized the Medieval world, philosophically and otherwise, was that the world as it actually existed was represented to the human mind fairly precisely through the function of human perceptions. That is, the world was as it appeared to be. The rejection of this assumption in the Modern period set in motion a trend to explore the nature, scope, and limits of human knowledge. If the world was not as it appeared, then a question of knowledge of that world becomes a central concern. Thus, the shift that marks the transition from Medieval philosophy to Modern philosophy is a shift in emphasis from metaphysics to epistemology.

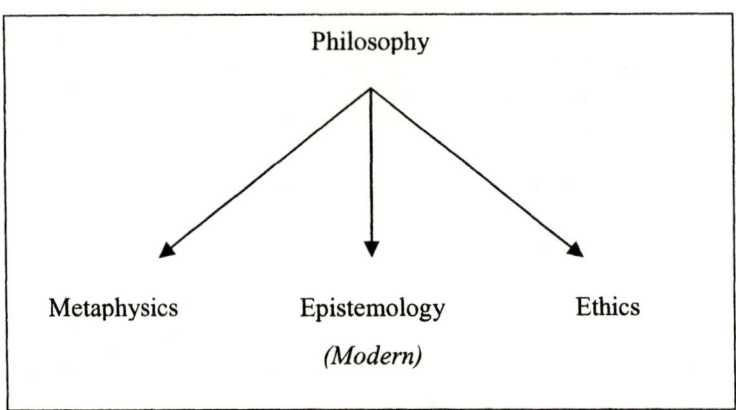

Whether there have been other periods in philosophy is a matter of considerable debate. Some argue that the philosophical traditions after Kant (that is, 19th century) and after the turn of the century (that is, the 20th century) are separate periods, distinct from the Modern period. It is clear that the content of many "Post-Modern" views is significantly different from the views of those of Descartes, Hume, Kant, and Wollstonecraft. At the same, the questions of human knowledge, meaning, and reference that characterize the work of Jacques Derrida and Michel Foucault (among the Continental Tradition) and Ludwig Wittgenstein and Bertrand Russell (among the Analytic Tradition) still reveal an emphasis on epistemology that is characteristic of the Modern turn. Thus, for the moment, it is generally best to suppose that the history of philosophy can most accurately be divided into Ancient, Medieval, and Modern periods, and to hold the question of a possible fourth period division, and how it should be described, in abeyance.

Returning then to the Medieval turn, we encounter questions of metaphysics taking center stage. Those questions, particularly having to do with the nature of reality and the nature of God, are questions grafted onto the preceding work of the Ancients. St. Augustine uses Platonic concepts to describe these new questions and to formulate answers to them. Thus, the discovery that Augustine's notion of God would be essentially the Platonic Form of the Good, and that the City of God in Augustine's *City of God* would resemble closely Kallipolis in Plato's *Republic* should come as little surprise. So, to, St. Anselm's Ontological Argument's dependence on a definition is remarkably similar, in sensibility, to Plato's own emphasis on the Priority of Definition. St. Thomas, on the other hand, adopts a method very nearly identical to the Aristotelian empiricism, particularly the method of Collection and Division, to argue in his *Summa Theologica* that God must exist and that God is the intelligent designer of all things. Central to Thomas's Five Ways are the Aristotelian causes from Aristotle's Four Cause Doctrine. Thus, while there is a distinct shift of emphasis in the approach to the big questions of philosophy from the Ancient to the Medieval period, the Medievals do not break from their ancient moorings.

Section 5: The Advent of Medieval Philosophy   187

Thus, while the philosophy of the Medieval period clearly does not abandon or differ essentially from the philosophical conversation of the Ancient period, it definitely marks a transition in emphasis as metaphysics comes to the fore. This relationship between the Ancient and Medieval periods is evident, to greater or lesser extent, in the other central metaphysical questions of the Medieval period.

Some of those other distinctly metaphysical questions, apart from the existence of God, are characteristic of Medieval philosophy. One of the particularly virulent arguments that takes center stage in Medieval philosophy from time to time is, at first glance, a recapitulation of the argument between Plato and Aristotle concerning the ontological status of universals and particulars. While Plato gave universals (the Forms) ontological priority, Aristotle took the opposite view. Within the Medieval debate, however, the argument ranges far afield of the differences between the Ancient originators of the debate. St. Augustine and St. Anselm, descendents of Plato, are clearly *Realists*; St. Thomas belongs to the *Nominalist* camp. Yet, none of the three is particularly remarkable for their contributions to this argument. Instead, a Franciscan, William of Ockham is perhaps the premier philosophical voice of the period, both in his ability to distinguish between the two camps (and the relevance of their philosophical views) and in his argument that the Nominalist understanding of ontology is to be preferred. It is in this argument over the ontological status and primacy of universals and particulars, that *Ockham's Razor*, perhaps his most famous contribution to the history of ideas, is particularly evident in its use.

Ockham's Razor finds use in evaluations of the arguments for the existence of God, as well; arguments that seek to establish something about the nature of God and of reality. Ockham even defends a position that sees a later evolution in the work of the Modern philosopher, Immanuel Kant, arguing that attempts to prove God's existence by means of philosophical tools will ultimately be insufficient. Another legacy of the Medieval period that grows from the arguments for God's existence but eventually has little to do with theology at all, necessarily, is the argument surrounding the notion of free will. St. Augustine's theodicy depends for its efficacy on the notion that human beings are capable of exercising a will that is inherently free; hence, his view is often called a *Free Will Defense*. Boethius, on the other hand, takes up the argument concerning freedom and determinism from the perspective of reflections on the nature of Divine Foreknowledge and whether such ultimately impairs human freedom. This is a special case of the debates that surround the notions of human freedom and causal determinism, which in the Medieval and early Modern period often center around the nature of God and the nature of reality and which in the later Modern period become matters of the relationship between science and the will.

Thus, the central metaphysical questions that are the hallmarks of the Medieval period, though often tied to religious themes within the period, have considerable influence on later philosophical reflections, unmoored from those religious underpinnings. Questions around the ontological status of universals and particulars, the Law of Parsimony (variations on Ockham's Razor), and the conflict between freedom and determinism are among the most common questions in the course of comprehensive philosophical conversation.

Section 6.1: Reading St. Augustine

St. Augustine of Hippo is easily one of the most important theologians and philosophers of the Western world. It is nearly impossible to overstate Augustine's influence on the doctrine and theology of the Roman Catholic Church. So important were Augustine's conceptualizations of the nature of God, the nature of humanity, the relationship between the two, the structure of the world, and the proper life of the Christian that his influence on the theologians responsible for the Protestant Reformation was similarly unmistakeable. Indeed, Augustine's work is so important that it forms the demarcation of the first great shift in philosophical inquiry and so marks the shift from the Ancient to the Medieval period.

To be sure, there were several factors that play a significant role in fundamentally altering the world view of the West. The importance of the fall of Rome on the way in which people conceptualized their universe is hard to overstate. To move from an understanding of the world that was influenced by the orderliness and security of Rome to one marked by uncertainty, politically and economically, caused a reevaluation of the nature of humanity and the world in which humanity lived. Rather than the Ancient view that "man is the measure of all things," the fall of Rome and its influence on culture caused a shift away from a more humanist sort of understanding of the world toward a more supernatural or metaphysical view; from looking first to understand humanity before trying to understand humanity's place in the world to looking to the nature of God, and secondarily, then, to understand humanity in light of that view of God. Thus, many of the early controversies of the Church center not on questions of the nature of humanity, but on the nature of God. Into the turmoil of the fourth century, C.E., arises a brilliant intellect from northern Africa who will formalize many of the fundamental doctrines of the Christendom and become the foremost early medieval Doctor of the Church.

It is not without a bit of controversy to place St. Augustine as a Medieval philosopher. As a follower of the Neo-Platonist tradition, he has strong affinities to the Ancient period, and particularly to Plato. His distaste for Greek notwithstanding, Augustine's work is so marked by a reliance on the philosophical concepts of Plato that it has been said that Augustine has baptized Plato. For this reason, Augustine has sometimes been considered the last of the great Ancient philosophers. However, as we will see, the differences between Plato and Augustine are really quite striking, and not solely dependent on the fact of the birth of Christendom that comes nearly at the midpoint between these two philosophers. Augustine is a Platonist; of this there is no doubt or controversy. But, Augustine is not an Ancient philosopher.

While the Ancient philosophers approached the big questions within philosophy from the avenue of exploring the nature of the good human life, and thus from the ethics branch of philosophy, Medieval philosophy is marked by an approach to those questions that involves speculations about the very nature of the universe, particularly God, and then seeks to understand the role of human beings within that more primary understanding. Thus, the Medieval philosopher approaches the big questions from the metaphysics branch of philosophy, making ethical and epistemological questions contingent on those metaphysical commitments. This shift is never seen more clearly than in the work of St. Augustine. His *Doctrine of Original Sin* and the depravity of humanity in relation to the perfection of God is paradigmatic of this shift of focus. For this reason, St. Augustine stands as the first of the great Medieval philosophers, rather than the last of the great Ancient ones. Augustine's conceptions of the Perfect Nature of God and the imperfect and fallen nature of humanity are the touchstones for all philosophical ruminations about God and humanity that follow. Philosophers following Augustine cannot help but deal with Augustine, whether they find themselves in agreement with him or compelled to point out perceived flaws. Finally, Augustine's answer to a newer problem is perhaps one of his most lasting contributions to popular arguments about God and trouble; about "why bad things happen to good people." In his Free Will Defense theodicy, Augustine argues that all evil is contingent upon the fall of humanity and thus the responsibility of human beings, not a perfect, omnipotent, omniscient, and benevolent creator.

The Neo-Platonic influence, and by extension, the influence of Plato on Augustine is probably most clearly seen in his work *City of God*, excerpts of which follow in the next section. Here, Augustine envisions two cities; one of which the perfect or ideal city, formal and beautiful in the heavens and the other, a wretched, fallen place marked by mere shadows or reflections of the beauty of the eternal and perfect city. The reader who thinks she notices echoes of Kallipolis, the Ideal City of Plato's *Republic* would not be mistaken. Thus, in many ways, the *City of God* is Augustine's appropriation of Plato's attempt to discuss the nature of humanity in relation to the nature of God. Reading Augustine in light of Plato's work can be both helpful and distracting. One should not conclude that Augustine necessarily agrees with Plato in the particulars of the Ideal City; only that the metaphysical structure of the universe is such that Kallipolis and the City of God occupy the same plane – perfect, eternal, and immutable. Thus, Augustine would concede that Plato's metaphysical vision is accurate, complaining primarily that the particulars within that universal vision are skewed, and perhaps badly so.

In *Confessions*, which leads off the discussion in the section after *City of God*, Augustine makes a contribution beyond philosophy and theology, and like Aristotle before him, offers a contribution to literature. Augustine's *Confessions* is generally conceived to be the first true autobiography and as such should be approached by the careful reader as such. In it, Augustine rehearses his dissolute life while expressing an unwavering arc to the work – the perfection of God, the depravity of humankind, and the necessity of God's action in saving humanity from its fallen state.

The pathos of Augustine's *Confessions* and the convictions of his *City of God* are outgrowths of a life of spectacular highs and equally spectacular nadirs. Augustine was born to a Christian mother and pagan father in 354 C.E. His mother, Monica (later herself canonized), refused to have Augustine baptized as an infant, even though he was quite sickly and not initially given long to live. This was not on account of some notion that he must later make a "decision" for himself as this was not a widespread doctrinal belief until after the Protestant Reformation nearly a millennium later. Instead, it was the product of a belief that since one could be truly baptized only once, one should wait before experiencing this salvific act. Monica, like many third century Christians in North Africa, held the view that any sin committed after baptism was unpardonable. Thus, to save Augustine from the fires of hell that would surely await him if he were forced to live his entire life without the possibility of removal of his sins through baptism (since it would have already been done), Monica gambled that Augustine would survive his infirm childhood.

Whether Augustine would have been subject to eternal judgment had he been baptized earlier rather than later is matter perhaps best reserved to third and fourth century theologians. What is clear is that the majority of his early life was as dissolute as a life of considerable gifts, both monetary and intellectual, could be. Augustine was profligate. He had remarkable intellectual gifts and turned those to the study of law and rhetoric, first in Carthage near the present-day city of Tunis, and ultimately in the capital of the Empire, Rome. He became quite accomplished and had all the attendant opportunities of a successful, rich, and powerful young man could be, ultimately appointed to the position of chief professor of rhetoric for the city of Milan. Yet, he records that he was profoundly unhappy. Indeed, Augustine had, perhaps, too many opportunities. So beset was he by all of the opportunities before him – for employment, for entertainment, for education – that he felt enslaved and ensnared. He writes that he felt he was in absolute bondage, unable to truly live because of the many demands, temptations, and alluring options, both good and unsavory, that were presented to him.

In the midst of this bondage of the will, Augustine took a lover and the two of them had a son. He also fell in with a religious sect known as the Manicheans. The Manicheans held a dualistic theology. On the view of the Manicheans, a good God or principle of light and an evil God or principle of darkness were in constant warfare. Creation had come about when the darkness attacked the light, shattering it and imprisoning spiritual sparks within the base flesh. This knowledge was considered secret and held in trust within the group of initiates. This rather simple and violent dualism seemed to explain many of the facts of the universe to Augustine; like, for example, the existence of evil, the existence of good, and the feeling of conflict within himself that manifested in the bondage of his will. If two great principalities were at war, this would explain the deeply conflicted nature of his internal struggles.

Soon, his mother Monica decided that it was time for Augustine to return home and settle down. She arranged a marriage for him to a local girl of about thirteen years of age. Augustine left his longtime mistress and their son and returned home and married at the behest of his mother. This, however, did not answer the turmoil that continued to plague him. Neither were the answers of the Manicheans ever completely sufficient for him and he began to question them more and more. In his continuing search, he returned to Rome and came under the influence of a priest, Ambrose. Ambrose led him to the NeoPlatonists and the NeoPlatonic understandings of the universe – particularly, that the Forms or the Good were truly real while evil was illusory, a shadow of true reality. This seemed somewhat more sophisticated to Augustine and prefigures many of his own ruminations on the nature of Good and evil. Baptized by Ambrose, Augustine left the Manicheans and began to investigate the views of the Church. Augustine felt that the grace of God had rescued him from a dissolute life and that for once he was truly free. The paradox of that freedom was that it came about only because, as Augustine understood it, God's grace eliminated many of the opportunities that were presented to him. Thus, by narrowing his options, Augustine felt actually free to act. This freedom, a product of grace, is a hallmark notion within all of Augustine's work, work that was ongoing even as the Roman Empire began to crumble.

Augustine was elevated to the position of Bishop of Hippo, a bishopric in Northern Africa, on the frontier of the Roman Empire. As the empire began to crumble, Augustine found himself in a city besieged by invading Vandals. In 430 C.E., Augustine died, but his legacy as one of the most influential theologians and philosophers of the Common Era was secure.

Section 6.2: St. Augustine, Doctor of the Church

Confessions

Book II

4. O Lord, theft is certainly and surely punished by you in accord with the law written upon the heart. That law is enduring, unalterable by human sin. Indeed, any thief would find it unbearable to be stolen from; even if the first thief is quite wealthy and the other completely destitute. But, I was all to happy to steal. It was not from poverty or from lack of anything, except, of course, for a lack of any feeling of justice. Indeed, it was from greed and from a love of sinning. That which I stole was something of which I had more than enough. In fact, I did not even want the thing itself, just the stealing, the doing wrong. Very close to our vineyard was a pear tree. It was overloaded with fruit, but the fruit was very poor – it was ugly and tasted foul. One night, very late, a gang of hoodlums, myself included, stole the fruit – shook it from the tree and hauled it away. It was one of the games we played, late at night. Even though we didn't plan to eat them, even if we had, we took far more than we could even try to eat. Instead, we made merry throwing them at swine. I don't remember if we ate any or not, the fun was in the stealing.

Look at me, O God, at my heart. It was this heart upon which you had mercy, even when I was at the nadir of my existence. Let that heart tell you why I sinned, why I, without any reason, did evil. It was only my taste for it, my love of sin that made me do what was wrong. That evil that is in me is horrible, but I loved it dearly. My own fallenness, damnation, and failings were things I adored. It wasn't the object of my wrongdoing but simply the wrongdoing itself. My soul was vicious. It sought to keep far from your care and protection because that way it could seek its own demise, it could chase after disgrace, not for the pleasure in the shameful actions, but for the committing of them alone.

Book VII

5. I was searching for the root of evil, but my search was lacking because I could not even see the evil in the process I was employing. In my imagination, I envisioned the whole of creation; the vast sweep of the universe, things seen and unseen. In my imagination, I conceived of all of the elements of the cosmos, every body, every tree and animal, and I thought of the universe as simply the

composition of all of those entities. This seemed huge to me, massive in every way. Then, I envisioned you, O God, encompassing all of this, surrounding it and infusing it with your very self. And, I said to myself, "Ah, here God is – completely, totally and utterly good and perfect and everything he has made is good as well. He surrounds everything and yet infuses all things with Himself."

"Only, where, then is evil? How did it come to be? Did it sneak into the world? Did it grow? From what? Could it be that evil does not truly exist? Then why do we fear it? Either evil exists and it is evil that we fear or fear is itself the evil."

"If God made everything and God is perfectly good then how does evil appear? God is the greatest good, far superior to anything else that we might call good; these are lower goods. However, if God, the creator, is good and the creation, made by the good God is also good, then from whence comes evil?"

These thoughts tormented me and I mulled them over and over in my mind. I was filled with fear that I might die before I discovered the truth of the matter. Yet my heart laid hold of faith and held it dear. Though I questioned deeply, I never surrendered the faith I have from you.

City of God

Book XII

1. In the last book, we saw the founding of the two cities, at least insofar as angels were involved. Having done that, we now turn to the genesis of humanity and see the founding of those cities insofar as it involves those rational creatures who are mortal. Before this, let us return to angels and make some comments that will be important in showing that it is not odd or inappropriate to speak of a society that includes both mortal and eternal creatures.

There are good angels and bad ones. These contrary dispositions develop not from God, the Creator of all things, but rather to the contrary choices and decisions made by the separate angels. Some were faithful while others looked to themselves. Life in God's eternal truth and love is a matter of choosing. So, some enjoy the good and blessed while others devolve into pride, deceit, and envy. … Nothing, save God, can cause any rational being happiness.

Their nature is so lofty, so high, that even though it is susceptible to change, it can achieve blessedness by being attached to the unchanging and ultimate goodness that is God. If the nature of an angel does not achieve blessedness, it is because that nature fails itself. This would be a perversion of that nature, and like all such perversions or imperfections, it will be detrimental to itself. Thus, the thing that truly separates good and bad angels is not something about the nature of an angel, but rather is on account of an imperfection. However, even this flaw is not blamed unless we are offering praise for the entirety, thus, even a flaw points toward the perfection of a thing. Consider blindness. Blindness is called a defect. By calling it a defect, we also say that it is contrary to the nature of the eye and that the nature of an eye is seeing. Similarly deafness points to the nature of the ear – to hear. Thus, the failure of an angel to achieve a union with God is the flaw that points out the nature of the angel – to be united with God. ... The failure of bad angels to remain connected to God is proof enough that they were blessed with a good nature at the outset.

2. The digression to speak of angels was done because I find it necessary to prevent the objection that could be offered – that those human beings who have fallen away and become apostate received a different sort of nature than angels. Since God is the ultimate being, and because God *is* (recall the words *I am that I am* [Exodus 3.14]), and because God is unchanging, then it follows that God instilled "being" into all that was created and that all that was created was created from nothingness. Some things have received more "being" (*essentia*) than others. This, then, establishes an order in nature that is hierarchical, from the highest (those receiving the greatest *essentia* to those receiving the least). Thus, there is no nature, except one that does not exist, that is contrary to God's nature, or the highest nature, which created all of the other natures that have *essentia*. The proper opposite of existence or that which is is nonexistence or nonentity.

3. From Scripture, we know that opposition to God defines those who are enemies of God. However, this opposition is not on account of the nature of those opponents, but on account of sin. God is unchanging and impossible to harm; all harm done is done to they who oppose God. It is not that their nature opposes God, but that an injury in that nature that does.

It is undeniable that God is perfectly good. Therefore, an absence of goodness stands opposed to God in the same way that evil stands in opposed to good. In virtue of this, one might encounter some perfectly good thing that is wholly without defect; the converse cannot be found. An absolutely evil thing can never be found. Even a nature that was marred at the very beginning by some evil can only be evil to the extent that this injury, flaw, or defect exists. Insofar as they retain naturalness, they retain goodness, evil insofar as they are defective.

6. Let us consider an example. Imagine two men who are completely equal, both physically and mentally. Suppose that they each gaze upon a woman of singular beauty. In gazing upon her, the will of one is moved toward lust and the other not. Why, then, did one will become evil and the other not? It cannot be the case that the simple beauty of the woman caused one will to become evil. Both saw her in the same way. Similarly, it cannot be the flesh because the flesh would have corrupted the other also. Perhaps the mind? Yet, again, given their equality, if one were moved in this way and the mind was the cause, then the other would have been moved in the same way. Could we say that the Devil whispered temptation and he consented to this allure? So, why would he give this consent? We must add something to our example. Just as they are equal physically and mentally, let us imagine that the temptation of each is the same as well; one consents and one resists. Our conclusion will be quite clear. One was

unwilling to fail in purity, one was willing. Yet, how might this be explained? No matter how clearly we look, there is not an obvious cause. Could we say that the man made his will evil? How is this possible since his nature was good and was authored by an unchanging and good God?

Let us sum up – we have a man who gives in to temptation and one who does not; the beauty is perceived equally, and prior to gazing upon the woman, both men are mentally and physically identical. Evil does not come from the fact that the man has a nature. The evil comes that the nature was fashioned from nothing.

7. We must, then, find the efficient cause of evil wills. Given that the effect is a defect, then the cause must similarly be a defect, like trying to hear silence of see darkness. Thus, the efficient cause is a deficiency or deficient cause and the blame attached to an evil will originates when the one falls. We have some grasp of silence and darkness, but only as privations – of sound and of light – not as positive things, but as absences or lacks.

Suppose someone asks me to tell him what I do not know – there can be nothing profitable in trying to learn from me that which I do not know. Thus, darkness is not "seen," it only happens when the eye fails to see; silence is not a sound, but a not being heard.

8. Among the things that I know is that God is in no ways deficient. As perfect being, it is impossible for there to be any defect within God. However, things created out of nothingness may well be deficient. There is an inverse relationship between being and goodness; the more of the former a thing has, the less deficient. All evil is therefore voluntary. As a result of a defect within the will, if some will becomes evil it is because it wanted to become so and willed it to happen. Thus, punishment is just because the evil is voluntary and not necessary. So, for example, the sin of greed is not a product of some deficiency in the gold, but rather of a desire in the will of the man who desires it wrongly. So, too, all of the sin in the soul is of this sort; loving or desiring inappropriately, expressing a flaw in the will.

~

As our attention turns to St. Augustine, the first of the great Medieval philosophers, it is appropriate that our first question should be one of the most important and enduring philosophical problems of the period. While many philosophical reflections of the preceding era address questions pertaining to the nature of humanity as the first object of understanding, St. Augustine's work approaches philosophy in a three-fold manner. This three-fold approach can be summarized by a trio of questions: What is the nature of God? What is the nature of humanity? What is the nature of the relationship between the two?

It should not be assumed that these three approaches are held as of equal importance. Clear primacy is given to the former. Indeed, in fine Medieval form, speculations on the nature of humanity and of God's relationship to humanity are completely dependent on the commitments expressed in answering the first of the three questions. Having specified an understanding of the nature of God, all other matters will have dependent form – thus, the understanding of the nature of humanity will, necessarily, be dependent on the understanding of the nature of God. This will, in fact, circumscribe the possibilities for conceptualizing issues like human freedom and the role of humanity in evil, for example. Before these matters can be taken up, however, we must first attend to a view of the nature of divinity.

While not a question that particularly concerned Classical philosophers, the view of the nature of divinity was of foremost concern as the creedal formulations of the Christian faith were developed during the organizational centuries of the Church. In the first three centuries of the Church's history, the canon was solidified, orthodoxy was sifted from heterodoxy and heresy by means of councils and controversies, and the doctrine of the Church was expressed in the work of the great Doctors of the Church and within the first creeds of the Church.

Among the foremost Doctors of the Church, or authors and defenders of Church doctrine, was St. Augustine. To understand his contribution to Church teaching and to philosophy, it is necessary to set his views of the nature of God into their proper context. From the Apostle's Creed to the Council of Nicaea and the Nicene Creed and in many tracts, letters, treatises, and apologies, God's nature came to be understood as one that expressed certain properties or qualities. Thus, God is understood as *omniscient* (that is, all-knowing, or in possession of all knowledge), *omnipotent* (all-powerful), *omnibenevolent* (possessed of a perfect will that always expresses good volitions or intentions), *omnibeneficent* (always acting in good ways), *eternal* (existing outside of time or existing in such a way that all of time is possessed within God), *infinite* (without beginning or end), and the *creator* of all things that exist with the exception of God. So, the God of the Medieval Church, in general, and St. Augustine, in particular, is the omniscient, omnipotent, omnibenevolent, omnibeneficent, eternal, infinite, creator of all that exists.

With this understanding of God, then, certain apparently intractable issues arise straightaway. What of the existential problems of death? Of pain? Of evil? St. Augustine comes to these questions through reflecting on his own experiences, his own theological journey, and his philosophical commitments. In the *Confessions*, St. Augustine goes to considerable lengths to plumb the depths of his own motivations and to understand his desires and his will. Easily the most famous of his examples of his misspent youth is the story of the pear tree. He and some friends, all of them thugs, hooligans, hoodlums, and ruffians, raided a pear tree near the fields of St. Augustine's family. It was late at night and they had been out looking for trouble to cause and doing so purely for the sake of causing trouble. They stripped the pear tree of its fruit, which St. Augustine points out was not at all good. It was ugly and did not taste good at all. They did not steal the pears because they needed pears – indeed, St. Augustine writes that he had an abundance of fruit and so there was no need.

They did not steal the pears out of spite for the farmer whose pears they were. They did not steal the pears for any other reason than the stealing. It would have been the same had the pears been plums or olives or apples. It was not the pears, but the act of stealing itself, that was the pleasurable experience. In fact, St. Augustine does not even seem to remember whether or not they ate any of the pears at that time or not; but he does remember taking them and throwing them at pigs, thus tormenting another creature with their ill-gotten gain. In this experience, St. Augustine realizes that it is the evil that is attractive and he wonders from whence this evil comes given that God is in no way evil.

St. Augustine goes further in the *Confessions* in his description of God than the list of characteristics commonly associated with God by philosopher/theologians. The list – omnipotent, omnipresent, omnibenevolent, eternal, infinite, creator of all that exists – is a standard, but fairly dry list. It does not rule out the possibility that this creative deity is wholly unconcerned with humanity or at the very least, disinterested. The portrait of the relationship with God that St. Augustine paints in the *Confessions* is a very different one. To be sure, the list is still true, but the way St. Augustine describes God in the process of expounding upon those properties reveals a depth of feeling and connection that is not readily apparent in the stale recitation of the list of properties. To be sure, God is omnipresent, but St. Augustine describes God as infusing all of creation with God's very presence. This is more than simply "being everywhere at once." Instead, God is thought to be completely and intimately related to all that exists. That presence is not simply in the midst of all that exists, but also surrounding all existent things. This is more than simply bounding them on all sides, but St. Augustine conveys a sense of deep care, almost an embrace rather than a sterile fencing in. Thus, the God of St. Augustine's *Confessions* is a profoundly caring God, deeply concerned with all that God has created and called "good."

This deeper and more intimate portrait of God serves to exacerbate the problem. If God is so deeply connected to God's creation, creating everything good from the fountain of God's own goodness, then how can evil come to be? Did it sneak in? Did it arise from the goodness of God's creation? Is evil some *thing*? Or is evil nothing? St. Augustine's encounter with the pear tree is sufficient cause for him to think that there is something deeply and profoundly wrong. While the robbing of the pear tree may seem like a mischievous prank, St. Augustine sees it differently. He was taken, not by the object but by the act of doing something wrong. Thus, whether it is stealing pears or some other wrongdoing, the very act of doing something wrong is the source of St. Augustine's youthful pleasure. He labels this *sin* and sin is wrong and evil. So, on the one hand, we have a good and powerful and caring God who creates all things good and on the other hand, we have clear and present evidence of evil. How can these two seemingly incommensurate hands be true?

In this question and in Book VII of *Confessions* included here, St. Augustine frames the problem that has come to be known as the Problem of Evil. While the *Confessions* makes the depth of the problem clearly and poignantly, the clearest Augustinian response to it is not in the *Confessions*, although he does allude to it there. Rather, St. Augustine's clearest assessment of the Problem of Evil and his proposal for a solution to it is in his weighty tome, *The City of God*. Before turning to the Augustinian solution, let us formulate the question as clearly as possible. The pernicious dilemma that is the Problem of Evil can be expressed as a series of propositions, all of which are supposed to be true, but which, taken together, seem to be incommensurate. Generally speaking, the list of properties of God is taken as a single proposition, but we will separate them here to clearly illustrate the possible ways in which the problem can be attacked and which of those possibilities St. Augustine employs.

The Problem of Evil
1. God is good.
2. God is omniscient (all-knowing)
3. God is omnibenevolent (of infinitely good will)
4. God is omnipotent (all-powerful)
5. God is omnipresent (everywhere)
6. God is the infinite creator of all that exists.
7. Evil exists.

The problem should be quite straightforward. If God is omnipotent, then God has sufficient power to enact anything God wills to be the case. If God is omnibenevolent, then God always wills the good in any and all situations. If this is so, then when John sets out to murder Tom, John acts against God's will and against God's power. However, since God would not will that John kill Tom, indeed, would will that John not kill Tom, then if John kills Tom, this would suggest that God is not truly omnipotent. On the other hand, if we hold that God is indeed omnipotent, then if John kills Tom, this must either be in accord with the will of God or at least not opposed to it. Thus, God would not always will the good. The incommensurate nature of the propositions poses a quandary.

To address this quandary, St. Augustine offers a *theodicy*. The word *theodicy* comes from two Greek words – *theos* and *dike* – meaning God and justice. Thus, a theodicy is a justification of the goodness of God given that there is evil in the world. The Augustinian theodicy has come to be known as a *Free Will Defense*. This means that, ultimately, St. Augustine sees the origin of evil within the human will, thus making human beings responsible for evil rather than God. However, before he can come to this conclusion, he must first do some heavy metaphysical lifting, particularly with respect to the understanding of the nature of God, the human nature, and the nature of evil.

To understand the nature of evil, it is first necessary that we consider the ontology of holes. This may seem an odd place to start, however, the importance of this digression will become clear. If we consider a hole and ask, "Does a hole exist?", it would certainly seem clear that it does. For example, a Kenny could step in a hole and twist his ankle. If we asked Kenny if the hole exists, he might well think we had become addled to ask such a silly and obvious question. "Of course it exists," he might say, "after all, I just stepped in it and I couldn't very well have stepped in something that doesn't exist!" However, if we consider the matter a bit further, an oddity within the reality of holes becomes apparent. A hole, it seems, exists differently from, say, a tree. The tree defines its own boundaries, it exists independently of other entities, and it has physical extension. A hole, on the other hand, does not exist independently. While we might say, "I stepped in a hole," it is clear that what is meant there is that "I stepped in a hole *in the ground*." A hole is always a hole *in something else*. Thus, it does not establish its own boundaries, it does not exist independently of the entity within which it is, and it does not have physical extension. A hole does not take up space; rather, it is an absence or a privation. Thus, a hole is not a *something*; it is a *nothing*.

With this understanding of the ontology of holes, we are ready for the first step of the Augustinian theodicy. The first thing to understand is the nature of evil. Evil is not a something; it is a nothingness. So, evil is a hole, not a physically existent thing. If we understand this, then the first premises of St. Augustine's *Free Will Defense Theodicy* will be as follows:

Statement	Justification
1. Evil is not a physical thing	1. Nature of Evil
2. Evil is a hole or an absence of a lack.	2. Implication of (1)

From (1) and (2), it follows that we can conceive evil separately from the good things that God has created. It is not in the power of God to create evil (as a physical object), but God could quite easily and perhaps justifiably create in such a way that there were interstices. That is, God could create something that was only as large as it is, not any larger. So, one might imagine that God could create the human will as a sort of Swiss cheese. Every part of the will that has actual existence is good because God creates nothing that is not good. But, God could well leave gaps and thus provide for the will to fill those in itself – either in ways that comport with the will of God or not. In this way, God does not abrogate God's own freedom but at the same time creates a space for the operation of the free human will to self-determine. This being the case, the rest of the *Free Will Defense Theodicy* proceeds apace.

3. Evil always consists in the malfunctioning of something that is in itself good. (e.g. like a disease).	3. From (1) and (2)
4. Human beings are given freedom of will by God.	4. Nature of humanity
5. Human beings can utilize that freedom in good ways or in evil ways.	5. Nature of humanity

Here, St. Augustine shows further evidence of his shift from an Ancient worldview to a thoroughly Medieval one. He takes the nature of God, and thus the metaphysical nature of reality, as his starting point. From there, an understanding of human nature is derivative from, and dependent upon, the nature of God. Since God acts creatively to provide for the human operation of the will, the operations of that will have consequences, the responsibility for which lie completely with the acting agent's will. Thus, we have the following two claims that depend for their justification on the nature of the human will and its activity. It should be noted that St. Augustine holds the view that the human will cannot act in any truly good ways apart from the grace of God. This is an implication of the Augustinian doctrine of Original Sin. Given that humanity is in a fallen state and thus wholly bound by the inherent failings of the fallen will, only God can overcome those failings to enable that will to will rightly. Thus, when St. Augustine holds the view that when an agent acts in good ways, he is acting under and because of the grace of God, he is merely extending his understanding of Original Sin to cover all actions that a free and willing agent might make. If the will directs in bad ways, then the responsibility lies completely with the agent. This is because the human will cannot help but act in bad ways because it is corrupt from the outset, an inheritance from the human condition. So, the human will may act freely prior to the imposition of God's grace, but it will always choose to act in pursuit of evil pleasures rather than in accordance with the will of God. After the infusion of God's grace, the will can act in accord with the divine will. Thus, we have the next two claims in the Augustinian theodicy.

6. If in good ways, then it is by the grace of God and reflects the health of the will.	6. Original Sin
7. If in bad ways, then it is the responsibility of the human agent and	7. Original Sin

> reflects the disease in the will of that agent.

The upshot of this argument is that ultimately, evil is not a physical thing and because it is a privation or a lack that exists within the human will, it is a nothingness that nevertheless corrupts that will. This corruption lies in the will acting on its own volition and apart from the direction of God. If this is so, then evil things that occur within the world are not the responsibility of God, but rather are the fault of human beings and we have that encapsulated in St. Augustine's conclusion:

> 8. Therefore, evil is the fault of human beings and not of God.   8. 1-7

Perhaps the most interesting thing about St. Augustine's theodicy is that it accepts all of the premises, but in fact suggests that there is an equivocation between (6) God is the infinite creator of all that exists, and (7) Evil exists. In (6), the word *exists* does not mean the same thing it does in (7). In the former proposition, *exist* designates a physical existence, indeed, all of the things that have actual substantial existence, either physically or spiritually/mentally. In the latter, *exist* designates a dependent state of existence; a state that supervenes on the type of existence specified by the same word in (6). This equivocation, on one interpretation of St. Augustine, renders the Problem of Evil a pseudo-problem. To say that it is a pseudo-problem is to say that is not really a dilemma but merely a failure to be clear in one's terms. Clarity there will make the problem dissolve. This *free will theodicy* became the dominant approach to the Problem of Evil from the Medieval Catholic Church through the contemporary Catholic and Protestant incarnations of the faith.

Despite its dominant position within the theological doctrines of the Church, Catholic and Protestant, the Augustinian theodicy has not been without its detractors. One of those was the German philosopher and theologian, Friedrich Schleiermacher. On Schleiermacher's view, we must start with the understanding that God is omnipotent and omnibenevolent. These are two of the characteristics of God that Schleiermacher rightly takes as unassailable and non-negotiable for St. Augustine. It seems, though, that the following proposition, "God would create flawlessly," follows directly from the omnipotence and omnibenevolence of God. Thus, God would not create entities that possess holes which could cause all manner of grief later. If these are true, then there are only two options to explain the presence of evil. Either, creation went wrong spontaneously or the ultimate responsibility for evil belongs to God. In the former case, Schleiermacher wants to rule out the spontaneous devolution into evil because this would suggest that creation is somehow out of the control of God.

This would deny the omnipotence of God, which St. Augustine cannot do and would not accept. In the latter case, responsibility for evil would lie with God because to omnisciently create with the great holes into which the human will can wander, causing all manner of mischief and grief is to fail to will the good. Consider this example. If a parent knowingly places his child in a room where there is apple juice and radiator fluid and allows the child to pick whichever the child will freely pick, it seems rather clear that the parent bears responsibility if the child makes a tragic choice. We assume that the parent has the power to stop the child from picking the antifreeze (else the analogy would fail). Thus, if the parent possesses the power and does nothing, then we could reasonably conclude that the parent was not benevolent. Thus, if we deny that creation spontaneously went awry (and thus uphold the omnipotence of God), then, on Schleiermacher's view, we are left with denying the omnibenevolence of God. Thus, the presence of evil, physical or non-physical, along with the assumption of the omnipotence and omnibenevolence of God form a trio of incommensurate propositions. If this is so, then persuasive as it is, the Augustinian theodicy would ultimately fail as a justification of God.

Whether the Augustinian theodicy ultimately succeeds or fails, what is abundantly clear is that St. Augustine shifts the philosophical conversation and the emphasis within the branches of philosophy. The first question is no longer about the nature of humankind, but rather about the nature of God and reality. From this metaphysical standpoint, St. Augustine radically re-envisions the big questions of philosophy and straightforwardly confronts some of the difficulties that arise (e.g., the Problem of Evil). St. Augustine's legacy is not only as one of the Doctors of the Church, but also as the conceptual touchstone that all philosophers who follow him much address. The early Modern philosophers, like René Descartes and G. W. F. Leibniz owe much of their work to formulations put forward originally by St. Augustine. As the Modern period shifts the emphasis within philosophy to epistemological questions, the notions of human nature, the human will, and the ontology of dependent and independent existence form the backdrop against which all of those questions of human knowledge are explored.

Guided Reading Questions:
1. What is the Problem of Evil?
2. How does St. Augustine solve the Problem of Evil? What is a theodicy?
3. Why can St. Augustine be called the first great Medieval philosopher?

Logic Blurb
The Appeal to the Crowd

"If everyone jumped off a cliff, would you jump off, too?" This is a time-honored response of parents. Little Johnny wants to go a party. His parents tell him that he cannot go. He responds, "But everyone else will be going." This is a common example of the *appeal to the crowd*. Presumably, Little Johnny's argument is that in virtue of the fact that everyone else will be going to the party, he should be allowed to go as well. Let's suppose further that his parents explained more of their reasoning for not allowing him to go. Suppose they felt that it would not be good for him to go. If his response were something like, "Well, everybody else thinks it's a good thing to go," he would have repeated the error. Indeed, we can imagine just such a scenario – a party that *everyone* is going to (and let us assume that Little Johnny is not falling victim to hyperbole, but is right that indeed, everyone besides him will be in attendance), and further that everyone who is going thinks it is a good, beneficial, and morally upright thing to do. Neither of these reasons, even so solidly construed, *entail* that Johnny should be allowed to go. His parents might even amend their initial response to say, "If everyone jumped off a cliff, and thought that it was the right thing to do, would you jump off, too?" Such a response points out precisely the difficulty with the argument from *appeal to the crowd*. Simply because a large group of people or an intimate group of friends believes a certain proposition does not make the proposition true. While this seems an obvious point, it is nevertheless a common rhetorical tactic and one that the careful critical thinker will meet with much the same response as Little Johnny's parents.

Section 7: Boethius, Medieval Metaphysician

Consolation of Philosophy

Book 5, Chapter 2:
"Philosophy": Let us say that chance shall be understood as the result of some random event, independent of any causal chain. I am convinced that chance does not exist, it is a word of meaningless sounds, with only one possible worth – demonstrating the issue before us now, and in the negative. There is no possibility of randomness as long as God controls things. We know that nothing can come from nothing. The ancients accepted this, although the scope of its application was limited to those objects but not to the causes. This principle is the foundation for all of their reasoning. For something to have no cause is for it to have come from nothingness. Given that this is impossible, then it is impossible that randomness, and thus chance, to be anything truly existent.

"Boethius": So, nothing can be called "chance," then? Perhaps there is something that "chance" means but that a common person would not know?

"Philosophy": Well, Aristotle defined in well in *Physics*.

"Boethius": How?

"Philosophy": "Chance" is something that, while done with a particular intention, causes something other than the intended consequence to happen; or, alternatively, certain happenings, which have unexpected causes, are encountered. Consider this example. A man digs in his field. His intention is to cultivate the land in order to plant and bring about a harvest. Instead, while digging he encounters a pile of gold buried there. It is commonly said that this was a chance happening, but it is clear that it is not a random one or one that originates from nothing at all. There are causes that led to the gold being buried in that field where it was found. It was not the intention of the one who buried the gold nor of the one who dug it up that it would be uncovered. It was a coincidence. Chance, then, is something unexpected, but still caused, a coincidence, not a random event. The cosmos is ordered. It is an inevitable causal chain. That chain of causes originates from God and puts all things where they belong at the right time.

"Boethius": Having listened with care to what you have said about chance, I must ask whether or not, in the midst of a causal chain, the will is free. Or, perhaps, the soul is in bondage to this fateful series of causes.

"Philosophy": The will is free because it is impossible for a nature to exist that is both rational and not free. Any entity that naturally has at its disposal the use of reason, must necessarily also possess the capacity for making judgments. The judgments are the source of decisions and the capacity must reside within the rational nature to apply the resources at its disposal to discriminate between the desirable and the undesirable.

At the same time, all entities do not possess this freedom. For the divine will, judgment, will, and desire are all pure, clear, and effective. On the other hand, the human soul, though free, is also lacking in freedom. When it is aligned with the divine will, the human will enjoys greater freedom; when apart from that divine will, its freedom is restricted. Those without reason are completely enslaved and darkness and ignorance binds them utterly. Embracing the passions, t he condition is worsened progressively and because this is a matter of the agent's own choosing, he is enslaved precisely because of his freedom. God witnesses this completely and at once, immediately seeing all things. Having foreseen this in God's providential nature then affords to each its own destiny.

Chapter 3:
"Boethius": I am not even more confused.
"Philosophy": Why? Although I suspect that I know.
"Boethius": Here, then, is the dilemma. I perceive an endless and ultimately futile and hopeless war between the foreknowledge of God and the freedom of the human will. If it is the case that God knows all things prior to their advent, and not only the actions, but indeed, even the movements of the human mind, its planning and dreaming and desiring, then freedom of the will is simply impossible. This is because, given divine foreknowledge, there is a fixation of all that follows and not a single thing could escape that foreknowledge or happen in any other way than has already been foreseen by God who is wholly infallible. Since God's foreknowledge is infallible, and thus is certain, then things must necessarily happen as God has foreseen them. Any other happenings would be counter to the infallibility of God and God would not have certainty or perfection.

There have been several approaches to this dilemma, but I simply cannot agree to them. Generally, the main thrust is to say that the events do not happen *because* they are known by God beforehand. The view is, instead, that God knows what will come to pass because it is what will come to pass. Being foreseen does not constitute necessity. God simply only sees that which will happen. Thus, the dilemma is recast in this way. Is God and God's foreknowledge the necessary cause of the events or is the necessity of the events the cause of God's foreknowledge? But this seems to be the wrong question. Is the happening of future events necessary, whatever the causes may be, even with the supposition that it is not God's foreknowledge that it itself causal? Consider an example. A man sits. Therefore, the proposition that he is sitting is true necessarily. Also, if we know that the proposition that a man is sitting down is true, then it is necessarily true that the man is actually sitting. Necessity obtains in each case. The man is necessarily sitting and the proposition is necessarily true. However, we would not say that he is sitting down *because* the proposition is true. Rather, the proposition is true because it was preceded by the man's act of sitting down. Thus, the cause of truth is only from the action, although necessity is involved in both descriptions.

Let us apply this analogy to the matter of divine foreknowledge and the occurrence of events in the future. Even if foreknowledge sees events because those events will occur, their occurrence is not the result of having been seen. However, in either case, it seems human freedom is destroyed. If things happen because they are foreseen or if they are foreseen because they will happen, the result is the same; human freedom is compromised. It is absurd to suppose that events in time cause the foreknowledge of the Eternal. To suppose that God knows future events in virtue of the fact that they will occur is essentially the same as the claim that historical events are the cause of God's Providence. So, in the same way that when I know something, that something known must be necessarily true, if I *know* that something will happen, it will happen, of necessity. Thus, if something is known beforehand, it must occur, of necessity.

Chapter 6:
"Philosophy": It is commonly held that God is eternal. If we examine the nature of eternity, then we will have insight into the nature of God and the nature of God's foreknowledge. To be eternal is to possess, in one moment, the endless life, complete and perfect. Let us compare this to things that are not eternal, and thus are bounded by time. For something to live in the flow of time is for it to live in the immediate present. That immediate present proceeds from the past moment and into the future one. Nothing within time can encompass the whole of its life in one moment – it has departed yesterday and not arrived in tomorrow. Even immediate life is merely the progression from one moment to the next, passing through this one toward that. Thus, anything within time cannot be *eternal* which is to be *outside* of time. Aristotle, who conceived even the world to be an infinity, without beginning or end; however, it is not *eternal*. Only that entity that exists outside of time can hold the immense variety of existence into an immediate present. It will encompass itself completely, holding all of infinity within itself.

So, those who followed Plato and believed that the world had not beginning or end within time are wrong. This view would be to suppose that the creature is also eternal as the Creator is. There is a distinction between existing endlessly and existing outside of time and encompassing the fullness of time in a single moment. This latter is the nature of the divine mind. ... So, to follow Plato properly and make sense of the distinction he made is to hold that God is eternal but the world, infinite.

Because God exists in an eternal immediate present, God's knowledge is beyond the progression of time from past to present to future. God, in God's eternity, possesses the whole of timely existence in God's immediate present. Thus, God's foreknowledge is not knowledge of future occurrences, but rather knowledge of God's own immediate present. Divine foreknowledge is thus called providence instead of predestination because it views all things from on high rather than residing in time with lesser things.

("Philosophy" continues)

Suppose you were to say, but I change my mind about doing things. If I can do this, do I not thwart providence? After all, if I change something that was seen in the divine Foreknowledge, then I have thwarted it. My response to this would be that you can, indeed, change your mind. However, since God is eternal, the present truth Providence apprehends is not thwarted at all. One cannot escape the eye of a person who is present and watching you. And, God the eternal holds within God's immediate present all of the progression of time. Hence, one cannot escape the watchful eye of God, who is present to both the "change of mind" and the effect of that alteration. God anticipates all alterations and those are part of God's immediate present in which there is no movement or variation of time. God grasps the changes immediately and in God's present. It is not the complex notion of necessity – past, present, and future – you suggest, but the simple necessity of God's immediate present.

If this is so, then the human will is free and not violated by the foreknowledge of God. God perceives from above, beholds all things, and God's eternal knowledge is congruent with the future occurrences that are the results of our actions. Providence then distributes reward and punishment on the basis of that perfect knowledge. Thus, we are still commended to act toward virtuous things and avoid vicious ones knowing that all of our actions are immediately done in the immediate present of the perfect and all-seeing Judge.

~

Are human beings free to do what we want, or, are the actions of people determined by external (or internal) forces apart from human will? That is, are humans free or does determinism reign? Beyond this metaphysical question lie several other questions related to the other branches of philosophy. For example, how does one's view of the freedom/ determinism question affect ruminations on other matters – e.g., how ought one to assign praise and blame? If, for example, one is to assign blame for some action, does such an action not require the assumption of some level of freedom to choose between the blameworthy action and some alternative? This crucial metaphysical question is one of the several metaphysical emphases that Medieval philosophers, driven in part by their concern to understand the nature of reality itself, faced. One of the most intriguing approaches to this question is found in the work of Anicius Manlius Severinus Boethius (470-524 C.E.), particularly in his *Consolation of Philosophy*.

The intriguing approach of Boethius to the question of freedom and determinism lies in part in the way the rather unique, and yet extraordinarily perceptive way that the question is framed. Traditionally, the freedom/determinism dilemma is framed something like this. Either one accepts the *determinism thesis* or one accepts a *freedom thesis*. It is perhaps important here to specify clearly what these are in order to appreciate fully the subtlety of Boethius's approach.

The *determinism thesis* has several incarnations and representations, but all of them can be reduced to some variation of the following:

> *Determinism Thesis*: All effects have an identifiable and complete physical cause.

This representation of the determinism thesis amounts is particularly tied to Modern, rather than Medieval thought, but it is instructive to begin here. The thesis is understood to amount to something like this. For any event, e, there is a cause, c, that is responsible for e and that cause can be said to determine e. Thus, the cause of one billiard ball moving across the table is that it was struck by another billiard ball. It is not the will of the billiard ball that it be in motion, rather it is the imposition of an outside force upon the ball that causes it to move. One can envision all of the human process that we often consider to exemplify free choices and free acts as simply the culmination of a causal chain that supersedes any and all agent-directed choice in the matter. Thus, each action is merely the product of the physical process that preceded it which is the product of the physical process that preceded it and so on. Given this closed system of causes and effects, there is no place where one can see the independent will of the free agent intervening to alter the effects set in motion by the forces of the physical universe.

Those who reject the determinism thesis in favor of preserving a notion of human freedom generally hold something like the following:

> *Freedom Thesis*: Some effects are caused by the independent will of a freely choosing agent..

There are several subtle distinctions that it is important to keep in mind. First, the rejection of the determinism thesis is not to claim, necessarily, that *no* effects have identifiable and complete physical causes. The denial of a universal quantifier (All) is not another universal quantifier (None), but rather an existential quantifier (Some). Thus, if some person held that "all ravens are black," it would not be the responsibility of the person arguing with that proposition to show that "no ravens are black." Rather, he would need only show that "at least one raven is not black." Thus, a defender of the freedom thesis could hold that even the vast majority of effects are caused independent of human free choices. However, he would have to hold that at least some were caused by the agent's free choices themselves.

It is likewise important to note that the rejection of the determinism thesis is not a statement that some effects are randomly occurring. That is, one cannot support a notion of freedom by appealing to randomness as a denial of the determinism thesis. This is clear from the understanding of what it means for something to be random. If something is randomly occurring, that is just to say that it has *no* cause. If some effect or some event has *no* cause, then it cannot be the effect of an independent, freely choosing human will because that would be to say that the event is, in fact, *not* random. Thus, an appeal to randomness will not support a notion of freedom, although it would reject the determinism thesis.

Thus, it becomes clear that there are several possible perspectives on the freedom/determinism theses. One might hold determinism to be true and in that case reject a notion of freedom in human action; one might hold that determinism is false and that the freedom thesis is true; one might hold that both the determinism and freedom theses are both false (an appeal, for example, to randomness); or one might hold, perhaps, that the determinism thesis is true and that a different version of freedom is what is required to understand why there is the illusion of a dilemma rather than an actual one. This latter view is sometimes called *compatibilism*, expressing the view that determinism and freedom are compatible despite apparent conflicts to the contrary. The former view is sometimes called *hard determinism*. The first intermediate view is generally named *libertarianism* and the second has several names, but is usually understood as a simple and straightforward rejection of the dilemma altogether.

In *Consolation of Philosophy*, Boethius approaches this question, albeit from a slightly refined angle. Rather than approach the question in a way that would seem familiar to a modern scientist, well versed in the intricacies of Newtonian mechanics and its postulation of a universe of forces and collisions between unthinking molecules, Boethius wonders about the relationship between

Divine Foreknowledge and free human action. That this is a special case of the freedom/determinism dilemma is fairly straightforward. If one assumes that God is omniscient (which is to say, in this case, that God knows all things, past, present, and future), then is it also possible to say that human beings can act freely. That is, if God knows that John will choose to eat an orange for breakfast tomorrow, then is it reasonable to also say that John can choose not to eat an orange, but to eat a banana instead? In other words, does Divine Foreknowledge entail determinism?

Before turning to Boethius's solution to this question, it is important to set his work into its historical, philosophical, and theological context. Boethius, like St. Augustine before him, was deeply influenced by the philosophical traditions of ancient Greece. Unlike the deeply Platonic St. Augustine, however, Boethius saw close connections between the work of Plato and Aristotle and sought to develop his own philosophical views on the reconciled views of the two. Fairly early in his career, he set for himself the task of translating the complete and extant works of both Plato and Aristotle to the end of reconciling them. He never fully accomplished this task, but he did succeed in translating the Aristotelian *Organon* into Latin and providing some of the most insightful commentary into that work; commentary that remains relevant to the interpretation of Aristotle even to the present.

Behind this endeavor at translation and commentary, however, is the far more philosophically interesting intuition that Plato and Aristotle are far more alike than they are different. Quick readings and introductory texts tend to accentuate the differences between Plato and Aristotle, often painting a bright line between the "rationalist" Plato and the "empiricist" Aristotle. Such a distinction, while itself preserving an intuition about the broad differences methodologically between them, greatly overstates the case. Here, then, is an early and striking example of Boethius' philosophical insight and vision.

Easily Boethius' most famous work is his *Consolation of Philosophy*. At surface issue is Boethius' unjust imprisonment. Recalling Plato's account of Socrates' conversation with the Laws in the *Crito* as Socrates endured unjust imprisonment and faced death, the *Consolation* is Boethius' dialogue with Philosophy herself. In the role of the petitioner, Boethius bemoans the injustice of his sentence, the fickleness of fate, and the transience of happiness. Just as the Laws turn Socrates' complaints back upon him, so Philosophy recasts Boethius' questioning. The highest or ultimate good is not happiness, a good fortune, or any of the particular things of this world. True good lies only within God and as such is immune to the vagaries of fate, the whims of human power politics, and the caprice of worldly powers.

Let us now return to that early question of determinism and freedom. The central question that endures from the *Consolation* is the metaphysical and epistemological one of God's foreknowledge and human freedom. As suggested previously, this is a special case of the larger metaphysical topic of human freedom and causal determinism. Indeed, one of the most pernicious of all metaphysical topics is the juxtaposition of those two notions – human freedom in a causally determined world. This is even more troubling for Boethius because rather than an insentient natural world filled with mechanistic collisions between unfeeling bits of matter, Boethius's world is one in which the notion of an intelligent and creative God constantly preserves the created order. Thus, the question is not one of the rational human will intervening in physical processes to enact its desires, but rather the human will contravening the will of God in addition to those physical processes. If Boethius can solve the puzzle of divine foreknowledge and human freedom, then he will have given some potential solution to the less thorny problem of determinism and human freedom.

Stating the problem of divine foreknowledge and human freedom is rather simple. Boethius wonders how it is possible, if God knows before an action is performed or a course of action is chosen, what that action or choice will be, for that action or choice to be a free one. For example, if God knows that Boethius will eat an apple instead of an orange for breakfast tomorrow, does Boethius truly have the choice of eating the orange? Not only does this problem torment metaphysicians, it is one of the most troubling philosophical questions that plagues Christian theologians as it would seem to suggest that the fact of divine foreknowledge entails a lack of true human freedom. If freedom is eliminated, so, too, is responsibility, it would seem. Thus, it would seem truly unjust to hold one accountable for that over which he truly had no control, not even the control of choosing freely.

This dilemma was one that troubled St. Augustine, as well. To suppose that God was somehow in less than complete control or that human freedom somehow superseded that of God was anathema. Thus, St. Augustine argued that God, in God's grace, granted free rein to the human will, in a manner of speaking. As a result, he could argue that God was preserved from charges of being responsible for the evil in the world because that responsibility rested squarely upon the shoulders of human beings who acted, at least nominally, independently of the direct and active will of God.

St. Augustine's theodicy, however, does not pay particular attention to the matter of divine foreknowledge, concentrating instead on the issue of God's omnipotence and entirely holy will. But, Boethius recognizes the extent of the problem and that a solution to that problem will entail a subtle and thorough examination, not of God's power or will, but of the content of God's knowledge and the mode of God's existence.

In Book 2, Boethius argues that humans, as rational beings, must possess freedom as a necessary condition of rationality. It is an interesting interpretive matter to realize that the positive thesis that is advanced is not in the mouth of the character of the work who explicitly represents the author. That is, "Boethius" the character does not convey the argument of Boethius, the philosopher. Instead, "Philosophy" carries the argument and "Boethius" is the foil who asks the questions that pose puzzles for "Philosophy" to address. Thus, the title of the book has a double meaning. Not only is "Boethius" consoled by Philosophy while in prison, but Philosophy is seen as the discipline whereby the problems that perplex people of faith are addressed and remedied.

Boethius, in "Philosophy," turns to defend a version of divine foreknowledge that he considers possible in Book 3 and particularly, again, in Book 6. On Boethius's view, there is a critical distinction between two concepts that are generally conflated and confused one with the other. Often, people speak of something as *eternal*" when by *eternal* what is meant is *infinite*. Likewise, people will use *infinite* as a synonym for *eternal*. This confuses and obscures a critical distinction. Something that is *infinite* is something that has no beginning and no end. However, the proper opposite of *infinite* is *finite*. While it may be unclear that something that is infinite exists within space and time, it is quite clear that anything that is finite does. Something that is finite has a beginning and an ending, whether those can be identified conclusively or not. Finite things exist within space and time because what it means for something to be finite is for it to be bounded and that boundedness is spatial and temporal. Thus, infinity, in virtue of being related to finitude, must also exist within space and time. Since finite things have both a beginning and an ending *in time*, something that is infinite is understood to be without beginning and/or without ending, *in time*. This can be seen more clearly by imagining a series that has a definite beginning, but that extends without end and is therefore infinite; or, recalling Aristotle, one can imagine, for example, a regression from the present into the past that goes on without end, or an *infinite regression*. So, clearly, then, to call something either *finite* or *infinite* is just to say that it exists within space and time. On the other hand, to claim that something is *eternal* is just to say that it is not bounded by space and time, but exists outside of them or independent of them. While it may be difficult to conceive of such an entity, it may be clearer in an example.

Let us suppose that Cara is a finite human being. She has a past, she lives within an immediate present, and lives into an as yet unrealized future. That immediate present is quite instantaneous; it is not more than a fleeting moment, and then it passes into the past. All of her perceptions, sense, memory, imagination, etc., are present experiences; that is, she experiences the fragrance of a rose immediately; she experiences the memory of a fragrance of a rose immediately in the present; she anticipates the fragrance of a rose she sees but has not yet smelled immediately. While the content of the memory may be of a past experience (indeed, it is hard to conceive how it could be otherwise), the experience of the memory is in the immediate present. Thus, a finite human being, Cara lives in the present, has memories of the past and expectations of the future. For her, it appears as if she moves through time in a linear fashion – before, present, after. The same could be said for an infinite entity. Let us assume that Cara is not only a human being but that she is immortal, as well. She clearly has a beginning moment – that time when she was born. However, in virtue of being immortal, she has no concluding moment and thus, is an infinite creature. Nevertheless, she will still live in the present moment, and ever expanding past lying behind her and a neverending future ahead. For an *eternal* being, however, there is no distinction between past, present, and future; there is only the immediate present. Or, another way of expressing that is to say that the eternal being does not experience existence as a series of present events that pass into the past from the future. Instead, time is separate from the *eternal* being; the eternal being perceives all of time at once, past, present, and future in the immediacy of the eternal beings perceiving.

By making a metaphysical distinction between existence within time and space and existence outside of them, Boethius argues that God, as an *eternal* being, but not an *infinite* one, exists outside of time and space and therefore does not determine the actions of Boethius in the future but rather simply has passive knowledge of those actions. "Philosophy" says, "God the eternal holds within God's immediate present all of the progression of time." Thus, divine foreknowledge is not an active determinant of the future, but a passive viewing of it. God watches and watches the totality of temporal and spatial existence in the immediacy of God's perception, not in a linear progression from past to future. The model of Boethius, then, is that in existing outside of time and temporal progression, God apprehends the entirety of existence and all temporal variation in God's immediate present, or completely and at once.

How, then, does this not simply wave hands at the problem without actually resolving it? To say that God simply exists outside of space and time does not immediately seem address whether or not divine foreknowledge in point of fact predetermines the outcomes of events. "Boethius" raises this point and "Philosophy" has an answer. "Boethius" wonders about the event of changing his mind. Does that mean that God's foreknowledge is thwarted or that that which God perceives in God's immediacy is altered. On the view of "Philosophy," however, God merely receives this change as well, in God's immediacy. Essentially, the view is that God is every watchful. God anticipates the changes of mind because God knows the change and its effects immediately and without the progression of time from cause to effect. In other words, God experiences the "change" of mind instantaneously along with all of its consequents. Or, another way of viewing this is to say that God knows the mind, the "changed" mind, and the effects of the changed mind instantly.

One might reasonably conclude that Boethius has argued that the nature of God's perception entails that the changing of a human mind is an illusion. That is, Cara experiences her mind, experiences a change of mind, and acts in accord with that change. God, on the other hand, sees all of these in an instant. Thus, the initial state of mind, its change, and the consequences wrought by the change are, indeed, static within the eye of God. Change, then, is illusory and freedom as well. However, for Boethius, this metaphysical distinction is understood to preserve both the understanding of the nature of God as omnipotent, omniscient, and holy creator of all things other than God and human freedom. Humans are thus commended to direct their lives toward virtue and to understand their actions as existing within a dynamic system of change and flux, of cause and effect, of choice and consequence, all of which exist under the watchful eye of a transcendent deity who perceives the entirety of the system in God's immediacy. Whatever conclusions this solution has for the problem of divine foreknowledge and human freedom, and the broader problem of determinism and human freedom, the distinction between *infinity* and *eternality* is a critical one that is often sloppily elided within Medieval, Modern, and even contemporary metaphysics and theological discussions about the nature of God and the nature of humanity.

Guided Reading Questions

1. What is the freedom/determinism problem?
2. What difficulties for understanding human freedom does the concept of the foreknowledge of God cause?
3. How does Boethius argue that Divine Foreknowledge and human freedom are not incompatible?

Logic Blurb
Necessity/Contingency

The Medieval period is well-known for the strides in the subtleties and complexities of logical investigations. Taking the Aristotelian foundation of formalized propositional logic, two very important concepts – *necessity* and *contingency* – were elaborated. This is not to suggest that the Ancient predecessors did not use these concepts, but that their nuanced use is much more the product of their Medieval handlers. The notions of necessity and contingency are used to formalize the notions of that which is possible, that which is impossible, and that which is impossible not to be. For example, we say that a statement is *necessarily* false just in case it is impossible for that statement to be true. Similarly, we say that it is necessarily true just in case it is impossible for it to be false.

One of the strengths of these concepts is that they add a level of precision to our statements. For example, it might be true to say that Polly is a parrot. But, if we add that Polly is necessarily a parrot, we pick out something that is essential and unchanging about Polly. If Polly is a parrot, it is necessarily true that she is not a penguin and not only that, but it is also necessarily true that she never was a penguin nor will she ever be one. At the same time, it is only a contingent fact that Polly is in a zoo in Pennsylvania. She could quite easily have been on a pirate ship in the Caribbean. This is to say that it is possible that she is in one place and it is possible she is in another. That she is in one place or the other is not an essential or necessary property, but merely a contingent or possible one.

This brings us to a very important and oftentimes overlooked distinction. The opposite of a necessary truth is not necessary falsehood. That is, if we have a negation of the statement, "x is necessarily true," that negation cannot be rewritten as "x is necessarily false." Instead, to say that it is not the case that x is necessarily true is just to say that it is possible that x is false. It might well be possible that x is true, as well. If we were to say that it is impossible that x is true, we would then be saying that x is necessarily false.

For example, suppose we were to say that "Polly is a necessarily green." If we were to say that that statement was false, then it would not be the case that the new proposition would be "Polly is necessarily not green." Instead, it would be that "Polly is not necessarily green," the meaning of which would be that she may be green and she may not be green. That is, it is possible that she is and possible that she is not. Placement of the negation "not" is critically important here, obviously. On the other hand, if we were to negate a statement of contingency or possibility, then the result would be a necessary statement. Suppose we said that it is not possible that Polly is an elephant. The resulting proposition would be that "Polly is necessarily not an elephant." Thus, the notions of necessity and contingency add a new layer of meaning and texture to our logical analysis.

Section 8.1: Reading St. Anselm

St. Anselm, a Benedictine monk and, like St. Augustine, both a Doctor of the Church and a philosopher deeply indebted to the conceptual framework of Plato and his NeoPlatonic successors, was one of the most influential philosophic voices during the middle era of the Medieval Period. As a cleric in England, his life spans one of the most important geopolitical events of the Middle Ages, the Norman Invasion of the England in 1066 C.E. It is a testament to his influence, both spiritual and temporal, that he prospered both prior to the Conquest and after, rising to the post of Archbishop of Canterbury. Centuries prior to the dispute with the Church spawned by King Henry VIII which resulted in a division of the Church of England from its Roman Catholic roots, the position of Archbishop of Canterbury was not only the highest ecclesiastical authority in the British Isles, but among the highest within Catholicism. St. Anselm's moral and intellectual authority and prestige rivaled even that of the Papacy. However, it seems reasonably clear from the historical record that St. Anselm, again like St. Augustine before him, neither particularly sought his episcopacy nor did he seek higher appointment beyond it.

The influence of Plato on St. Anselm is evident in St. Anselm's approach to philosophical and theological questions. St. Anselm belongs to the Realist tradition that holds that universals (Platonic Forms, for example) have higher ontological primacy over the particulars of experience in the physical world. For St. Anselm, the best way (and perhaps the only way) to apprehend truth is by power of the rational mind, divorced from the deceptiveness that the senses introduce into human reasoning. Thus, as a Rationalist, it is not strange that he should see universals as having actual existence and as exemplifying the highest form of that existence. Further, that St. Anselm should envision God as the Form of the Good confirms again his Platonic and Benedictine commitments.

One of the key critical tools to understanding a philosopher's approach to the questions with which he or she concerns him or herself is an understanding of that philosopher's method. The approach that a philosopher takes to a question will often cast light on the broader philosophical project. Unlike many of his classical predecessors, St. Anselm actually sets out his methodological commitments explicitly. In one of his earlier works, *Cur Deus Homo* (Why God Became a Human Being), St. Anselm describes his method as "Faith seeking understanding." On St. Anselm's view, there is no real difference between theology and philosophy. His view is not quite that theology and philosophy are the *same* thing, but that they are so similar as to be impossible to disentangle one from the other. On his view, philosophy (Wisdom/Knowledge) makes clear the articles/doctrines of the faith. However, philosophy and theology are functionally equivalent; that is to say, either philosophy or theology can be used to arrive at the same conclusion. The proof for the existence of God is an excellent example. The method is reminiscent of Plato/Socrates. First, what is the definition of this word, "God"? What does it mean for something to "exist" or what is "existence"? Then, having arrived at a definition, what follows from it? Notice, however, that the impetus for the question was a religious one – the fool who says, "There is no God." So, on the one hand, there is a question that arises from a deeply spiritual moment, prayer and reflection on the Psalms, in this case; and on the other, an appeal to reason and philosophical reflection to make the faith commitment more clear. It is St. Anselm's deep commitment to the faith and its communication that is evident in both his vocation and his philosophical writing, a personal joining of faith and reason that exemplifies the method of inquiry that he commends as the proper method of undergirding the faith and understanding the world.

Relatively early in his career as a Benedictine monk, Anselm was given the role of teaching Christian doctrine to the novitiate – the new members in training of the Order of St. Benedict. Among his writings, explaining doctrinal issues from the incarnation to the relationship between theology and philosophy, is the *Proslogian*. Perhaps the most famous part of the *Proslogian* is the Ontological Argument. However, the *Proslogian*, and the Ontological Argument, had earlier incarnations in St. Anselm's work. Prior to penning the *Proslogian*, St. Anselm pondered the question of the existence of God in his work, the *Monologian*. There, his argument is long and winding, and extraordinarily complex. Presenting his brother monks with the work, it was met with rather resounding consternation. Essentially, the brother monks asked St. Anselm if, perhaps, he could revisit his ruminations and make the argument easier. Reflecting that the argument could indeed be sharpened, St. Anselm returned to his reflections and, nearly a year later, produced the final version of the *Proslogian*, in which appears what is likely the most insightful and deceptively simple Ontological Argument for the Existence of God in the annals of western philosophy.

Section 8.2: St. Anselm and the Ontological Argument

Proslogian

Chapter 2 – That God Exists

O Lord, the one who gives faith and understanding to the extent you know them to be helpful, help me as faith seeks understanding, to know that you exist as we believe. Faith believes that you are "that-than-which-a-greater-cannot-be-thought." (*aliquid quod maius non cogitari potest*)

Does anything have a nature like this? After all, the fool says, "There is no God." But even the fool would grant that hearing the words "that-than-which-a-greater-cannot-be-thought" he knows what the words mean. He would understand that there is something meant by these words even if he does not think that they refer to any actual thing. It is one thing to understand a definition of something and quite another to know that the thing defined actually exists. A case in point – the artist visualizes and understands what he has yet to paint. After the painting is completed, he has both the understanding he had prior to the painting and the understanding that the thing before him actually exists. It is clear, then, that even a fool has at least the understanding that "that-than-which-a-greater-cannot-be-thought" exists at least within the mind. This is because, upon hearing the phrase, he knows what it means. It thus is in existence in the mind (*esse in intellectu*).

It is not possible that "that-than-which-a-greater-cannot-be-thought" should exist only in the mind. If, "then that-than-which-a-greater-cannot-be-thought" existed only in the mind, then "that-than-which-a-greater-*cannot*-be-thought" is at the same time "that-than-which-a-greater-*can*-be-thought." However, this would be obviously impossible. Therefore, it is certain that "that-than-which-a-greater-cannot-be-thought" exists in the mind and in the world.

Chapter 3 – That it is not Possible to Think of God as Non-Existent

That God exists is so very clear it is not possible to think that "that-than-which-a-greater-cannot-be-thought" is non-existent. In the first place, it is possible to hold within the mind the notion of something such that the object of that idea cannot be thought of as non-existent. This is superior to something that can be thought of as non-existent. Further, something can be thought to exist that cannot be thought not to exist. Therefore, if "that-than-which-a-greater-cannot-be-thought" could be thought *not* to exist, then "that-than-which-a-greater-cannot-be-thought" is not the same as "that-than-which-a-greater-cannot-be-thought." This is contradictory and absurd. So, "that-than-which-a-greater-cannot-be-thought" so truly exists, then that it cannot even be imagined not to exist.

This, then, is you, O God. It is impossible to imagine that you do not exist. It is right that it should be this way. Indeed, if some mind could imagine some being above you, then the created would be above the Creator and would have dominion over it. This is another clear contradiction. Indeed, all things in existence, apart from you, can be thought of as not existing. Of all existent things, only you, Lord God, exist in the fullness of existence (*maxime esse*) and there exists no other in this way. Thus, all existent things, save you, have less reality than you.

So, why does the fool say that "There is no God?" There can be only one reason. He is a fool – irrational and dull. It is clear, to any rational mind, that you exist, and not only exist, but exist with greater reality than all other things.

Chapter 4 – How Might the Fool Say that which is Impossible

How did the fool say it? How could he express that about which he had no understanding? Or, how could he not understand that which he said?

Perhaps one understands a word one way when the word and its object are merely thought and in another way when the object itself is truly understood. One might confuse the words "fire" and "water" but it is impossible to confuse their natures if one understands them. So, it is impossible, if one understands the nature of God to suppose that God does not exist. It is possible for someone to confuse the word and to utter that "God does not exist," giving it some other meaning than its true one. God is "that-than-which-a-greater-cannot-be-thought." Anyone whatsoever who knows this or, at the very least, understands that this is the proper meaning of the word, can possibly think also that God does not exist. Thus, any one who understands that God is "that-than-which-a-greater-cannot-be-thought" cannot even entertain the idea that God is non-existent.

I give you thanks, O God, that which I believed first through faith, I now understand. Thus, even if I wanted to deny your existence, I would be unable to understand even the thought of that.

~

The fool says in his heart, "There is no God." Whatever could he mean? This question, from the Psalms (Psalm 14.1) inspired one of the most famous reflections of St. Anselm of Canterbury; reflections that came to be known as the Ontological Argument for the Existence of God. Prior to the Medieval period, proofs for the existence of a deity were almost unheard of. However, in the midst of the metaphysical turn that marks the shift from the Ancient to the Medieval period, certain debates arise that, while seeming esoteric in some ways to

21st century ears, are in fact quite important and raise particularly thorny issues for metaphysicians of the Medieval era. Among those controversies was an argument that carried over from the methodological commitments of Plato and Aristotle but which received both new life and greater importance in the hands of Medieval philosophers. The debate concerning the ontological status of Forms and particulars, especially the question of priority of one over the other, resurfaces with interesting implications for philosophical and theological debate. The debate is recast as an argument between the Realists (Platonists holding that Forms, or universals have real existence and ontological priority over particulars) and the Nominalists (philosophers who hold that universals are merely arbitrary and abstract names given to particular things). Given the considerable influence of Plato's work on the early Medieval period and given that questions concerning the nature of reality, and especially, the nature of God are dominant ones, it is not surprising that most of the early theologian philosophers of the Medieval period tend to belong to the Realist camp, conceptualizing God as the supreme universal. The Nominalist challenge to Realism, then, is a challenge not only about the ontological status of universals and particulars, but a challenge to the orthodox conceptions of God. As St. Anselm addresses "the fool," he is also staking out a position in the debate over the very nature of reality.

St. Anselm of Canterbury is a Platonist, in the tradition of St. Augustine of Hippo before him. A Benedictine monk, St. Anselm's wades into the Medieval Realism/Nominalism controversy firmly on the side of the Realists, with the understanding that the controversy is not tempest in a teapot, but that there are very important issues at stake. Among those issues are the nature of God and the nature of God's interaction with God's creation, in general, and humanity, in particular. Both St. Augustine and St. Anselm accept a Platonic hierarchy of ontology, with the Forms at the pinnacle and the physical objects and their representations at the bottom. Further, both posit a sort of hierarchy within the Forms, or universals, themselves. At the top of the hierarchy of universals is the Good. For St. Anselm, the nature of God is encapsulated in the notion that God is the Form of the Good.

If we recall the metaphysical and epistemological commitments expressed in the Platonic Divided Line and couple them with the Medieval shift toward emphasis on the nature of reality and, in particular, the nature of God, then it becomes clear what is at stake within the Realist/Nominalist debate. For St. Anselm, and St. Augustine before him, to say that God is the Form of the Good and that God is omnipotent, omniscient, and the creator of all that exists apart from God, is to make the claim that the true reality of the universe is that which is unseen, eternal, and immutable. This vision comports with all of the major creedal statements of the Church.

For a Realist, the universals (or Platonic Forms) have actual ontological status apart from any particulars in the world. The universal, "Chair," is just as real, or more likely, more real than any particular chair that one encounters. For the Nominalist, on the other hand, the only reason that we even speak of a general term like "Chair" is because we have agreed that all of these things on which we sit from time to time and which serve essentially the same function in our lives, these things we will call "chair." Thus, universals have not only dependent existence on the physical things of the world, but further their existence depends on the purely accidental and arbitrary way in which human beings decide on names for particular objects. Since we commonly call *that thing* "chair" and we commonly call *this thing* "chair," we deceive ourselves into thinking that there is some third thing, *Chair* that exists independently of our names for these two things.

St. Anselm's Ontological Argument proceeds from a Realist perspective; one that can be seen as a predecessor of the modern Rationalist tradition exemplified in Rene Descartes. The Rationalist conception of epistemology, for example, is that truths about the world can best be appropriated through the disciplined application of the mind, divorced from the senses and the deceptions that the senses can perpetrate upon the mind. Thus, rather than concerning himself with physical objects of the visible world, St. Anselm is concerned with the intelligible objects of the intelligible world. Indeed, his proof even begins in much the way one might expect a Socratic or Platonic one to begin, with a definition.

Before turning to the proof itself, there are some background assumptions that need to be spelled out so that the flow of the argument is clearer. Among the most important of those background assumptions is a metaphysical principle that has to do the discerning the ontological status of various forms of being. Here, St. Anselm's work harkens back to that of Plato and the Divided Line. There, it will be recalled, the *objects of thought* are an ordered in such a way that their ontological status is clear – the Forms have a greater level of reality than the mathematicals and those greater than the physical objects of experience and those surpassing the images or shadows caused by them. That relationship can be expressed as the Ontological Principle which can be rendered as follows:

> *Ontological Principle*: It is better to exist in the mind and in the world than to exist only in one or the other or to exist in neither.

While there is no argument in support of this principle, it is one that is both commonly held during the Ancient and Medieval periods and that captures a very straightforward prephilosophical intuition. This may be clearer upon reflection on the division of reality that the principle supposes. It is clear that this formulation that there are at most four potential definitions of "existence." These four possibilities are described below:

> 1. Something exists in both the mind and in the world.
> 2. Something exists in the mind, but not in the world.
> 3. Something exists in the world, but not in the mind.
> 4. Something exists in neither the mind, nor in the world.

That these are the only logical possibilities is clear. That they represent different definitions of "existence" is less so. However, let us evaluate each of them in turn and in so doing, it should become clear that the philosophical distinction comports with general prephilosophical intuitions about existence. To begin, it is clear that there are only three actual definitions or types of existence. To say that something exists in neither the mind nor in the world is just to say that it does not exist at all. Since non-existence is not a mode of existence (something made clear in St. Augustine's discussions of positive existence and negative existence), we can rule out the fourth category as a candidate for existence at all.

Evaluating the three types of existence, it seems reasonable to conclude that the first type (existence in both the mind and the world) is of higher desirability than the other two. Consider a one hundred dollar bill. To say that a one hundred dollar bill exists in the mind is just to say that we have an idea of it. However, it also seems clear that it is better to have a one hundred dollar bill in one's hand *and* to have the idea of the one hundred dollar bill in one's mind than it is to *only* have the idea in one's mind and have a pair of empty hands. Thus, existence in the mind and in the world, at least of the one hundred dollar bill, is to be preferred to its existence only in one's mind. Suppose, on the other hand, that a person had within his hand a rectangular piece of paper that was mostly green and white with a portrait in the center and numbers in various places on it and with a large number in the corner, but that the person had no comprehension that what is in his hand is a one hundred dollar bill. As far as he can tell, it is a piece of artwork or a sample of wallpaper or something of that sort. Perhaps he conceives it as a piece of scrap paper without any value at all. It is better, it seems then, to have both the one hundred dollar bill in the hand *and* the idea of it in one's mind than to have it *only* inone's hand. Thus, the intuition captured by the Ontological Principle seems reasonably plausible. St. Anselm's argument depends rather intimately on both the plausibility of that intuition and the principle of reality that encapsulates it.

With this understanding of the structure of reality and method of measuring the reality inherent in those things that exist, it is possible to turn now to the fool's statement and the proof that St. Anselm offers in response to it. To discern what the proposition, "There is no God" might mean, St. Anselm turns to the meanings of the words. The first and perhaps most obvious reflection is that it is imperative to understand the meaning of the word, "God." Only then can one understand what the fool is saying. Less obvious, but no less important, is the necessity of understanding the meaning of "There is" or "There exists." Here, the Ontological Principle is critical because it spells out precisely the various meanings of existence itself, and provides a framework for the meaning of "God" to be situated. Thus, with the Ontological Principle undergirding the understanding of existence, St. Anselm proffers a definition.

> Definition: "God" is "that than which a greater cannot be conceived."

The reaction to St. Anselm's definition of God is generally one that receives raised eyebrows if not outright dismissal. It is a very spare definition that does not comport with common, prephilosophical surveys of the nature of God or the meaning of the word "God." The definition seems, at first blush, to be wholly inadequate to capture what most orthodox religious adherents mean when they use the word "God." That is, it does not capture things that one would expect an archbishop and monastic of St. Anselm's stature to believe about God. Surely, he should hold a view of God that is more commensurate with the image of God captured in the great creeds of the church – omnipotent, omniscient, gracious, creator of all that exists – or something of that sort. Indeed, some would be willing to dismiss St. Anselm's argument in its entirety because they perceive the definition of God to be inadequate to what they mean when they use the word "God." This is even more likely when it becomes clear that St. Anselm is not using the definition as a backdoor way in which to convey those standard attributes of God into the argument. Indeed, the definition is simply what it is, a spare definition of God and one without the content that many might expect a theologian to hold.

Herein lies part of the genius of St. Anselm's style of argument. If he were confronted with this objection from a person of faith, a novitiate monk, for example, he would undoubtedly patiently explain that, yes, indeed, the definition is inadequate to communicate all of the complexity and fullness of the God of the Roman Catholic faith. However, there are at least two ways in which one could conceive of a definition being adequate – the first would be a matter of adequacy to communicate the fullness of the faith, the second would be a matter of adequacy to the issue at hand, in this case, proving that God exists. While it is necessary that the second is contained within the first, it is also the case that appeal to the first sort of definition, the full and complex definition, would be inadequate for a proof. Were he to build into his definition of God all of the fullness of the doctrines of the faith, the fool could simply respond, "This is not what I mean when I use the word, 'God'." At that point, St. Anselm's argument would be thwarted. Since this is not an actual debate with an actual person, for the argument to proceed, St. Anselm must put forward a definition of God that any person who might utter the proposition, "There is no God," or "God does not exist" would agree to. That is, he must put forward a definition with which any fool would agree. Such a definition is not the fullest possible, but rather the sparest. That is, it contains the minimum that one can mean by the word "God" and still be using the word correctly. Thus, to use the word "God," one must mean at least "that-than-which-a-greater-cannot-be-thought." Given this much narrower and weaker definition of "God," it is all the more impressive if St. Anselm can then answer the fool's heartfelt proposition and refute it.

Given this principle and the definition of God, the argument proceeds apace. If we assume that God exists only in the world and not in the mind, then the proposition would amount to meaningless sounds since the fool would not even know what he was saying. Further, and more importantly, if God did not exist in the mind, then God would not be "that than which a greater cannot be conceived" because one could conceive of an entity that existed both in the mind and in the world (an application of the Ontological Principle). Thus, God would not be God. This is a contradiction. Thus, the assumption that gave rise to the contradiction must be false. Thus, God must exist in the mind. The initial portion of the proof might be characterized as follows:

Statement	Justification
1. God is "that-than-which-a-greater-cannot-be-thought"	1. Definition of "God"
2. Suppose God does not exist in the mind	2. Assumption
3. Therefore, God is not "that-than-which-a-greater-cannot-be-thought"	3. Ontological Principle
4. Therefore, God is not God.	4. Substitution
5. Therefore, God must exist in the mind.	5. Contradiction, 2-4

However, one could not seriously suppose that the fool thinks that God does not exist in the mind. Indeed, if we suppose that this is a reasonable interpretation of the fool's statement, then it follows that we are supposing that the fool is merely uttering meaningless sounds, not merely meaningless to others, but meaningless to himself. However, since we have established that the definition of God is one to which even the fool would agree, then we cannot assume that he is uttering intentionally meaningless sounds. Indeed, the fool has an idea of God in his mind and insofar as he is using the word "God" correctly, then he must mean at least "that-than-which-a-greater-cannot-be-thought." Thus, God exists in the mind. Thus, when the fool says that "There is no God," what he is actually saying is that "God does not exist in the world." Part of the reason for being explicit about meaning here is that it makes it clear that St. Anselm has not played false with the argument, hiding one possible meaning of "existence" from the reader or from the fool. Indeed, he has not. Having demonstrated that God must exist in the mind, of the fool and of anyone who uses the word "God" properly, he turns to the centerpiece of the Ontological Argument, namely that God must necessarily exist in the world.

Let us then suppose that the proper assumption is that God exists only in the mind. Indeed, this must be what the fool means. If God exists in the mind, then the fool at least knows what his statement is supposed to mean; that is, the proposition "There is no God" is not simply meaningless sounds but a meaningful proposition – something like, "God does not exist in the world." With this assumption, if we apply the Ontological Principle again, we get the following result. God, who exists only in the mind, is not "that than which nothing greater can be conceived," because one can conceive of a entity that exists in both the mind and the world. Hence, once again, we have that God is not God. As this is a contradiction, we can safely conclude that the assumption that gave rise to it is false. Thus, God must exist in the world. By conjoining the two conclusions, we have that God exists in both the mind and the world.

---

6. Suppose God does not exist in the world.	6. Assumption
7. Therefore, God is not "that-than-which-a-greater-cannot-be-thought"	7. Ontological Principle
8. Therefore, God is not God.	8. Substitution
9. Therefore, God must exist in the world.	9. Contradiction, 6-8

The proof, having shown in the first part that God must exist in the mind and having shown in the second that God must exist in the world is not, therefore, complete. A final statement is necessary that conjoins the conclusion of the first and the second. Thus, appeal is made to the logical connector "and" and the two preliminary conclusions are conjoined into the final statement concluding the proof.

| 10. Therefore, God must exist in the mind and in the world. | 10. Definition of "and", 5, 9 |

St. Anselm's Ontological Argument is a brilliant example of a rationalistic approach to demonstration. It opens with a definition and a principle and proceeds deductively, completely independent of the senses and their potentially obscuring input, to its conclusion. It is both an elegant and a groundbreaking proof. Indeed, St. Anselm's version of the Ontological Argument, despite being

Section 8.2: St. Anselm and the Ontological Argument

one of the earliest formulations of a proof in this style, it is also probably the best example of its kind. It was recognized, during his lifetime, as an outstanding application of philosophical logic to the question of the existence of God.

However, while greeted with widespread acceptance by the theologians of the Church, St. Anselm's proof was not universally received as successful. A colleague of St. Anselm's, a Benedictine named Gaunilo, rejected St. Anselm's proof in a tract of his own entitled "Defending the Fool." Leaving St. Anselm's logic alone entirely and accepting, like St. Anselm, the Ontological Principle, Gaunilo turns his attention to the definition of God. Rather than arguing with the definition itself, an approach that would expose him to the difficulty of not using the word "God" properly, he instead puts forward a different sort of idea, not of God, but of a Perfect Island. If we conceive of the Perfect Island in this way, "that-island-than-which-a-greater-island-cannot-be-thought," then we can reframe St. Anselm's argument in the following way.

Statement	Justification
1. The Perfect Island is "that-island-than-which-a-greater-island-cannot-be-thought"	1. Definition of "God"
2. Suppose Perfect Island does not exist in the mind	2. Assumption
3. Therefore, Perfect Island is not "that-island-than-which-a-greater-island-cannot-be-thought"	3. Ontological Principle
4. Therefore, Perfect Island is not Perfect Island.	4. Substitution
5. Therefore, Perfect Island must exist in the mind.	5. Contradiction, 2-4
6. Suppose Perfect Island does not exist in the world.	6. Assumption
7. Therefore, Perfect Island is not "that-island-than-which-a-greater-island-cannot-be-thought"	7. Ontological Principle
8. Therefore, Perfect Island is not Perfect Island.	8. Substitution
9. Therefore, Perfect Island must exist in the world.	9. Contradiction, 6-8
10. Therefore, Perfect Island must exist in the mind and in the world.	10. Definition of "and", 5, 9

As before, the logic is impeccable and the argument flows from definition and an accepted principle to a deductively valid conclusion. However, the difficulty with the argument is readily apparent. If the God must exist as demonstrated by the Ontological Argument, then so, too, must the Perfect Island exist. Yet, the Perfect Island does not exist. This does not mean that people have not sought it. During the 15th century, when Christopher Columbus was looking for ships for his expeditions, he argued that one reason for acceding to his request was that it would enable him to look for the Perfect Island, or the Isle of Bliss. Similarly, when Captain Cook landed in Tahiti, he wrote that he had finally found the elusive Perfect Island. However well-meaning these explorers may have been, that they would go in search of the Perfect Island gives one an idea of how confident the general populace was in both St. Anselm's argument and the threat that Gaunilo's response posed to it. To find the Perfect Island would be to refute Gaunilo and support St. Anselm's argument all at the same time. However, this misses Gaunilo's actual critique.

The thrust of Gaunilo's critique, which later thinkers have recognized as truly devastating, is that there is a distinction between the ideas within the mind and the objects in the world that those ideas purport to resemble. Indeed, rather than the mind representing accurately and without variation the objects of the world, the ideas within the mind are completely separate from objects in the world. Thus, Gaunilo's critique of St. Anselm is that he actually is equivocating on the word "God" in his proof. In one sense, he means the idea "God" while in another he means the entity that corresponds to the word "God". However, because this distinction is blurred (or completely obscured) in the proof and yet is a critical distinction that actually carries the weight of the argument, the equivocation is fatal to the project.

Rather than acknowledge this difficulty, St. Anselm's response to Gaunilo's critique was to argue that an entity like God has a different sort of existence from entities like islands or mountains or rivers. Since islands, for example, have *contingent* existence, coming into being and ceasing to be, then they cannot be favorably compared to an entity like God that has *necessary* existence. That which has *necessary* existence cannot come into being or cease to be, it simply is. However, this tack is untenable because it, in fact, begs the question against Gaunilo. The conclusion that the Ontological Argument is supposed to establish is that God exists necessarily. Thus, St. Anselm cannot appeal to God's necessary existence to support the proof since the proof itself is suppose to conclude that God necessarily exists. Thus, the most that St. Anselm's Ontological Argument can be said to establish is that the idea of God exists in some mind or other and that the idea of God exists as a part of the world (likely because it exists in a mind that also exists in the world). This is clearly less that St. Anselm has in mind for the proof.

Whatever the difficulties St. Anselm's Ontological Argument ultimately suffers, it is clearly one of the most impressive arguments for the existence of

God proffered to date. It is a masterful example of logic and deduction and, even though it fails to establish its aim, it has the benefit of making very clear, even in the Medieval period, the distinction between the world of the mind and the physical world, showing fairly clearly (with Gaunilo's help) that the two worlds, while giving the impression of being closely related, are not nearly so closely tied as they appear. Instead, in an anticipation of the recognition within the Modern period of the radical distinction between the mind and the physical world outside the mind, St. Anselm's proof indicates not only that such a cleavage exists, but that any proof that depends on close resemblance of ideas and objects will meet the same fate as his Ontological Argument.

Guided Reading Questions:
1. How does St. Anselm define the idea of "God"? Do you find the definition adequate? Why or why not?
2. Why does he argue that "it is impossible to conceive that God is not"?
3. How does Gaunilo's critique challenge St. Anselm's Ontological Argument?

Logic Blurb
The Fallacy of the Excluded Middle

The *Fallacy of the Excluded Middle* is a pitfall of the Argument from Elimination. Sometimes called a *false dichotomy*, the Fallacy of the Excluded Middle presents an audience with a set of choices that intentionally or unintentionally excludes possible solutions. The unintentional commission is generally rectified by the simple inclusion of those choices previously excluded. The intentional commission, however, tends to have a different tenor.

Generally speaking, an intention *Excluded Middle* presents the audience with two choices, one of which is so horrible, frightful, absurd, or silly that it is rejected immediately. The result, then, is that the remaining choice, however onerous it may be, is perceived to be the only real choice. Imagine a patient given the options of a very expensive and painful operation to remove a hangnail, on the one hand, and sudden, but excruciatingly painful death, on the other. Obviously, even to the untrained eye, other options exist. Similarly clearly, the potential abuse of the false dichotomy, in its intentional form, is substantial. The reflective thinker will take pains to avoid the intellectual dishonesty that often attends the *Fallacy of the Excluded Middle*.

Section 9.1: Reading St. Thomas of Aquinas

St. Thomas of Aquinas, a Doctor of the Church like St. Augustine and St. Anselm, is largely responsible for the systematizing of Church doctrine and the foundation of the deeply reflective tradition of Catholic moral philosophy. The author of several works, including *Summa Contra Gentiles*, St. Thomas's unfinished magnum opus, the *Summa Theologica*, is among the most important philosophical works in the history of ideas. The *Summa Theologica*, whose title can be translated perhaps a bit too colloquially as "everything there is to say about the study of God and God's relationship to humanity," is an obviously wide-ranging text in which significant doctrines of church teaching and arguments for the underpinnings of the scientific curriculum of the fledgling Medieval university system are developed.

Among those arguments we find the development of the theory of Natural Law, a sort of grand unification theory that provides a philosophical foundation for disciplines from biology to politics by tying the particularities of each discipline to a metaphysical conception of the nature of reality that all must express in virtue of being attempts to understand truth. This metaphysical vision is deeply rooted in the metaphysical works of Aristotle. Indeed, it is particularly striking the extent of Thomistic adherence to the scientific project suggested by Aristotle's *Categories*. Readers of St. Thomas's work who are reasonably well-versed in classical philosophy might well be shocked to see how very closely St. Thomas's work is to that of Aristotle. In fact, to say that St. Thomas owes a debt to Aristotle is to significantly understate the matter. A more accurate claim would be that, even more than St. Augustine and his appropriation of Platonic and NeoPlatonic concepts and commitments, St. Thomas, in a sense, baptizes Aristotle and imports his work, in its extant entirety, as the framework for St. Thomas's own. The points of variance between Aristotle and St. Thomas, in one respect, are extraordinarily rare. Thus, one can fairly safely say that insofar as a doctrine or argument is to be found in Aristotle, its doppelganger can be found in St. Thomas.

This reliance on Aristotle marks a significant shift in the dominant academic world view of the mid- to late-Medieval period. For roughly the first seven hundred years of the Medieval period, Platonic metaphysics had been dominant, at least in the world of Western Europe. This is not to suggest that

Aristotle had no influence, but his extant works in the west were somewhat more sparsely preserved and distributed in the west than in the east where a greater portion of his work survived and occupied a place of higher esteem. Indeed, as we have seen so far, it was the Platonic influence on St. Augustine and St. Anselm and others that set the stage for philosophical and theological reflection during the early and middle Medieval period.

The influence of Aristotle began to widen during and immediately after the Crusades. Among the materials that made their way from east to west during these campaigns were many of Aristotle's works. The gradual integration of the Aristotelian concepts became exceptionally more rapid as St. Thomas essentially adapted the Aristotelian model and reinterpreted the vast majority of Catholic moral philosophy in its lights.

Like St. Anselm before him, St. Thomas was a member of a prestigious religious order and was responsible for the curriculum and education of the novitiate for that order. While St. Anselm was a Benedictine and ultimately ascended to the prestigious post of Archbishop of Canterbury, St. Thomas was a Dominican and remained within the general company of his order. With the serious and sober task of educating the novitiate of his Order, St. Thomas wrote voluminously and in a way that lent itself to addressing the many questions young men would have as they began their instruction. St. Thomas's most famous work, the *Summa Theologica*, is composed as an interrogatory treatise. That is, each new section is begun with a question that the argument that follows purports to answer. Often, a particular question and answer stands alone, independent of those before and after it. At other times, several sections will address a single topic, approaching it from a variety of angles all the while composing a single, layered argument.

This approach is quite pronounced in the section of primary text included in the following section. St. Thomas's Five Ways to Prove the Existence of God is often taken to be a set of five distinct arguments that each develops a similar conclusion. However, there are interpretive difficulties that arise if one views this most famous section of the *Summa* in this way; difficulties that I will argue can only be overcome by supposing that the five distinct proofs are, in fact, each part of a larger argument. Thus, one thesis of the examination of the work of St. Thomas will be that there are either six proofs (the five individual ones and the global one) or just one (the one global one with five individual pieces).

Section 9.2: St. Thomas, Doctor of the Church

Summa Theologica
Part 1, Question 2, Article 3

First Objection: It is apparent that God cannot exist. If two propositions are contraries and one of them is infinite, then the other must be utterly destroyed. Suppose that "God" means "infinite goodness." So, if God exists, then, because God is infinite goodness, it would be impossible for evil to exist. However, clearly there is evil. Therefore, God cannot exist.

Second Objection: If something can be explained simply, it is foolish to suppose that something far more complicated produced it. All observable things can be explained by principles other than God. All natural things are explained by a single principle – nature. All voluntary actions are explained by a single principle – the human will. Thus, the existence of God is superfluous.

On the contrary, God said, "I am that I am." Thus, in can actually be concluded (and I so answer the objections) that God's existence can be proven in five ways.

The first way in which God's existence can be proven we shall call the argument from motion. Clearly things move. If something is in motion, something else caused it to move. Motion is but the change from potential to actual, but only something actual can engage something in a potential state. For example, wood is only potentially hot. Fire, however, is actually hot. So, fire (actually hot) causes wood (potentially hot) to become actually hot. Something cannot be both potentially and actually the same thing at the same time. Thus, the same thing cannot both be in motion and be the cause of its own motion. If something is moving, and if it was put into motion by something else, this second thing, if it be motion, too, must have been moved by something else, and so on. However, if we suppose that this chain of moved movers goes infinitely backward, then there cannot be a first mover. However, it is clear that if there is not a first mover, then there cannot be things moved, as they would have to have been put into motion by this first mover. So, we conclude that there must exist some first mover that is not itself moved by some other thing. This unmoved mover is what all know as God.

The second way in which God's existence can be proven we shall call the argument from efficient cause. It is clearly observed that there are effects of causes, and, indeed, an order of efficient causes. However, nothing causes itself. If something caused itself, then it would have to be before itself, and this is clearly absurd. Again, it is impossible to have a chain of causes stretching back into infinity. Indeed, the first cause is the cause of the second and the second of the third and so on. If we suppose that there is no first efficient cause, there would be no second, third, and so on. This would entail that there are no causes at all, nor effects. Obviously, this is false. Since this is false, it must follow necessarily that there exists some first efficient cause. This first efficient cause is what all know as God.

The third way in which God's existence can be proven we derive from contingency and necessity. It is clearly observed that things we find in the world are merely contingent – they can be and they can not be. They come to be, they decay. However, if something is merely contingent, then there was some time when it did not exist (as it is not necessary). So, let us suppose that everything that is is contingent. If this be so, then there must have been some time when nothing existed (since existence of one thing is caused by the existence of some prior thing). But, if an some time nothing existed, then it is impossible that something could be generated. And, if this were true, then nothing would exist now. This is clearly absurd. So, it cannot be the case that everything that exists exists only contingently. There must exist some entity that exists necessarily. Further, there cannot be a chain of necessary things extending backwards into infinity, because that would suppose that some necessary thing caused another necessary thing to be. But, if something is caused to be, it cannot be necessary, but merely contingent. Thus, there must exist some being that exists necessarily and that holds this necessity within itself, and causes all subsequent contingent beings. This first necessary being is what all know as God.

The fourth way in which God's existence can be proven begins in the observable character of things. Some things are better than others, that is they have greater goodness, truth, and so on. But, we assign the property "more" and "less" because they resemble or they do not resemble some greatest thing. For example, we call something hotter because of its resemblance to the hottest thing; something truer because of its resemblance to the truest; as Aristotle wrote in the *Metaphysics*. The greatest of any kind of thing is necessarily the cause of all things of that kind. Fire, for example, is the greatest heat. It must, therefore, be the cause of all hot things. So, it must be the case that there is something that is the cause of all goodness, nobility, true, and every perfect quality. This greatest good thing is what all know as God.

The fifth way in which God's existence can be proven is derived from the ordering of the cosmos. It is clearly observed that many things have no intelligence of their own. These natural object, though, exhibit ends that we can also clearly observe. They act, or almost always act, in the same way again and again, and they do so to their best end. Given this, it is clear that it is not happenstance, but the product of some design by which they intend and obtain their proper natural end. However, if something does not have intelligence, it cannot possibly form an intention; that is, unless some other being, possessed of intelligence, guides and directs it. So, like an archer directs the arrow to the target, so there must exist some knowledgeable being who orders and guides all things for their natural ends. This governor of the cosmos is what all know as God.

Reply to First Objection: Augustine rightly said that "Because God is the Highest Good, He would not permit the real existence of evil in any of His creations, unless through His benevolence and omnipotence, He were to work good from it." So, because of God's infinite goodness, He could allow evil to be so that good might be derived from it.

Reply to Second Objection: Nature is guided to a particular end by the guidance of one who is above nature and orders it. Thus, all things that occur as natural ends must be the result, ultimately, of God, the first efficient cause. This is also true of things produced voluntarily by the human will. The will is contingent and mutable. Anything capable of defect and contingent must point back to the immovable and necessary. This has been demonstrated in this article.

~

However one reads the Five Ways to Prove the Existence of God, as five distinct proofs or as one proof with five identifiable subparts, one thing is abundantly clear. They are a particularly intriguing window into the thought and method of one of the most important contributors to the history of ideas in the western intellectual tradition. As alluded to in the previous section, St. Thomas employs his strict Aristotelianism to the argument(s) for the existence of God and in so doing, elevates Aristotelian metaphysics to the level (and perhaps beyond that) of the Platonic metaphysical conceptual framework that had been heretofore the dominant world view in Medieval philosophy. The implications of this elevation are fairly wide-ranging. While it clearly preserves Aristotelian influence in Western thought, it also begins to sow the seeds of internal intellectual conflict within the Church and the university system it founded. The empirical approach of Aristotle does not mesh easily or perhaps at all with the more rationalistic Platonic method. This incompatibility of method, which of necessity shifts the emphasis within doctrinal arguments in subtle but important ways, leads inevitably to the academic differences that are an important, if often overlooked, contributor to the Protestant Reformation.

In a similar way, it is with St. Thomas that the fissures that will ultimately lead to the radical specialization within the modern university begin to become apparent. Unlike St. Anselm who held that philosophy and theology were identical, or at the very least, so similar as to defy separation, St. Thomas views the disciplines differently. Theology, for St. Thomas, is the study of God's self-revelation to humanity through special, direct, or immediate means of scripture, revelation, and tradition. In other words, one can envision theology as almost a rationalistic enterprise the center of which is God's direct revelation, through one manner or another, to the heart and mind of the faithful. Philosophy, on the other hand, does not begin with special revelations to the faithful, but rather with observations of empirical evidence in the observable world followed by applications of reason to build arguments upwards, ultimately, to God. The significant shift from St. Anselm to St. Thomas can be seen with absolute clarity from the very first premise of their respective proofs. While St. Anselm begins with a definition of God that can be rationally considered apart from observation of the actual world, St. Thomas begins each of the five ways with an observation of that actual world. In this, it is clear that St. Thomas envisions the role of philosophy as that of appropriating evidence and, on the basis of that evidence coupled with Aristotelian logic, reasoning upward toward God. So, while philosophy and theology are related, they are clearly distinct disciplines, on St. Thomas's view. The wedge that separates the two in St. Thomas leads finally, and perhaps inevitably, to the modern separation of disciplines. While one might find philosophy of religion within a department of philosophy, one will be hard pressed to find the discipline of theology within one, and vice versa.

The careful reader of Aristotle might point out, at this juncture, that Aristotle is not known, particularly, for arguments for the existence of a deity, much less the Judeo-Christian one. How, one might wonder, can it be maintained that St. Thomas is a good Aristotelian and yet goes far afield of Aristotle? Here, then, is a part of the genius of St. Thomas. Where Aristotle has arguments and doctrines, St. Thomas adapts and baptizes them; thus, the university system and Scholasticism remains, until the advent of the New Science of Francis Bacon, Rene Descartes, and Isaac Newton, to be almost exclusively Aristotelian. But, Aristotle has little to say about philosophy, or, more properly, philosophical arguments whose conclusion is God. St. Thomas, to address these areas about which Aristotle has little or nothing to say, is presented with three options. The first would be to create, from whole cloth, new concepts and logical forms to advance his arguments. This *novelty* approach would not be in keeping with St. Thomas's temperament nor the tenor of his other work. A second option would be to adopt the work of St. Augustine and St. Anselm to fill this lacuna in the Aristotelian source material. That, too, is unacceptable, in no small part because it would entail introducing a significant inconsistency (NeoPlatonic rationalism) into his larger project. Having broken methodologically with that tradition in all other aspects of his work, it would hardly do to reintroduce it or ally himself with it here. The third option is the one St. Thomas employs. He adopts the Aristotelian toolbox of concepts and method and uses those tools to construct something novel and yet not innovative. That is, he offers arguments for new conclusions but those arguments are themselves deeply Aristotelian.

So, before turning to the proof(s) themselves, it is perhaps proper to revisit the Aristotelian toolbox that St. Thomas brings with him to do the work of constructing proofs for the existence of God. The first and most obvious of these is *method*. As Aristotle inverts Plato's ontology, believing that experienced objects have greater reality than abstractions and constructs his arguments beginning with observable particulars, so St. Thomas opens his proofs with observations and proceeds with Aristotelian syllogistic logic toward his conclusions.

In addition to a methodological framework, St. Thomas employs other Aristotelian tools – the *Four Cause Doctrine*, the *Principle of Infinite Regression* (also known as the *Principle of Vicious Regression*), and the *Doctrine of Gradations of Goodness*. We will explore each of these in turn.

Each of the Five Ways is a *causal proof*. That is, each begins with an observation and then asks of that observation (or of some part of it) what its cause is. Here, very clearly, we encounter the Aristotelian tool that, to mix metaphors, is the engine that drives each of the Five Ways. Aristotle's Four Causes, it will be remembered from the earlier discussion, are the *Formal*, the *Efficient*, the *Material*, and the *Final* or *Teleological*. St. Thomas's Five Ways are generally given the names *Motion*, *Efficient Cause*, *Contingency/Necessity*, *Gradations or Degrees of Perfection*, and the *Governance of the World* or *Teleological* or *Argument from Design*. As will be seen in the examination of each of the Five Ways that follows, one or more of the Aristotelian causes will play a significant role as justification for vital premises.

The next tool is the *Principle of Infinite Regression*, also known as the *Principle of Vicious Regression*. The significance of the alternative name for the Principle of Infinite Regression becomes clear in its usage. The Principle of Infinite Regression is fairly simple to state:

> *Principle of Infinite Regression*: If an assumption leads to an infinite regression, then the assumption must be false.

Aristotle employs this principle, without explicitly stating it, in the quest for the highest good in the *Nicomachean Ethics*. There, Aristotle argues that if the highest good were something that was desired for its consequences, or for something further, then the search for the highest good would be futile. This is because if it were desired for something further, the list of goods would be infinite – each pointing beyond itself to the next. The generation of an infinite regress is sufficient to eliminate the possibility that the highest good might be desired for its consequences. In the same way, the premise generating an infinite regress in any of the Five Ways will be similarly rejected. Since all infinite series of this sort serve to doom the premise that gives rise to it, the principle is sometimes known as the Principle of Vicious Regression.

The final Aristotelian tool in the St. Thomas toolbox is used in only one of the Five Ways. Again reminiscent of the *Nicomachean Ethics*, the *Principle of Gradations of Goodness* holds that the highest good, whatever it is, is somehow causal of the goodness of all other lower goods. Or, in another way, the highest good is the standard not only by which the lower goods are measured, but also the thing that makes them good insofar as they are. So, insofar as some lower good is related to the highest good, it is itself good and insofar as it does not, it is not. Thus, there is, ontologically speaking, a hierarchical order to all the particulars of the cosmos and this gradation is a function of how closely the lower goods approximate the highest good. With this toolbox in hand, St. Thomas is ready to tackle the task of proving the existence of God.

The outlines of the first two proofs are provided below. The careful reader will quickly note that the Proof from Motion and the Proof from Efficient Cause are extraordinarily similar. The similarities that these two share with the others are important, to be sure, but of the Five Ways, the first two have more in common with one another than any of the other possible pairings. Considerable scholarly ink has been spilt on the commonalities between these two. The primary question seems to be what could be the accounting for two proofs that for all intents and purposes seem identical. Let us first look at each of the proofs and then turn to the examination of their place within the larger framework of the Five Ways as a whole.

The Proof from Motion

Statement	Justification
1. Things move.	1. Observation
2. If X moves, it is because Y moves it. (Things do not move themselves.)	2. Efficient Cause
3. Either there is an infinite regress of movers or there is a first mover.	3. Exhaustive "or"
4. Suppose there is no first mover.	4. Assumption.
5. Therefore, there is no motion.	5. PIR
6. Therefore, there is no motion and things move.	6. Definition of "and", 1, 5
7. Therefore, the assumption that there is no first mover is false.	7. Contradiction, 1, 4-6
8. Therefore, there is a first mover.	8. Elimination, 3, 7

The Proof from Motion begins with an observation. Simply put, things move. One of the intriguing things about St. Thomas's proof, though, has little to do with the proof itself. The second premise is an early statement of the law of inertia. For St. Thomas, things move but do not move themselves. Thus, they must be moved by some force other than themselves. Neither do they cause themselves to stop. So, in other words, things that are in motion will tend to remain in motion and things at rest will tend to remain at rest unless acted upon by an outside force. Rather than attribute this early rendition of the law of inertia directly to St. Thomas, it is better to note that it is merely an application of the Aristotelian Efficient Cause to the observable phenomenon of motion. Thus, St. Thomas moves from the initial observation, by means of application of the Efficient Cause, to a question concerning the candidates for the role of cause of the motion observed.

Given that for something, x, to be in motion, there must be something, y, that moved it, St. Thomas is faced with the following options: either there is no first mover or there is. To say that there is no first mover is just to say that there is an infinite regress of movers. Thus, if we suppose that there is no first mover, then an infinite regress results. By application of the Principle of Infinite Regression, then, we can eliminate that assumption and are thus left with the conclusion that the supposition that there is no first mover is false. Therefore, there must be some first mover that is not itself moved by some other thing. Thus, this Unmoved Mover is the First Mover and we can conclude that the First Mover is God.

As we turn to the second of the Five Ways, one quickly notices that the Proof from Efficient Cause is strikingly similar to the Proof from Motion. Indeed, there is no difference whatsoever in the line of Justification and the only differences, at first blush, in the line of the argument itself is that "effects" is substituted for "motion" and that "cause" replaces "mover."

The Proof from Efficient Cause

Statement	Justification
1. There are effects.	1. Observation
2. All effects must have causes (Things do not cause themselves.).	2. Efficient Cause
3. Either there is an infinite regress of causes or there is a first cause.	3. Exhaustive "or"
4. Suppose there is no first cause.	4. Assumption.
5. Therefore, there are no effects.	5. PIR
6. Therefore, there are no effects and there are effects.	6. Definition of "and", 1, 5
7. Therefore, the assumption that there is no first cause is false.	7. Contradiction, 1, 4-6
8. Therefore, there is a first efficient cause.	8. Elimination, 3, 7

If one presupposes that St. Thomas is offering five distinct proofs for the existence of God, then one is faced with the interpretive difficulty of explaining the great similarity between the first two ways, a similarity that does not persist as the other arguments are advanced. It seems that the best interpretation of St. Thomas along those lines would be the conclusion that in order to demonstrate the model of argument that he will employ, he provides two examples of simple observation before turning to the third of the Five Ways, a proof that will involve three options in the eliminative argument rather than two. However, such an interpretation fails to fully appreciate the power of St. Thomas's argument or the difference between the two arguments that on reflection is relatively obvious. There is a change in the scope of the arguments from the first to the second proof. The relation of "motion" to "effect" is an example of the relation of part to whole. That is, a motion is a sort of effect, but may well not be the entirety of effects. That is, while motion is an effect (and indeed, all motions are effects), it may well be the case that not all effects are, in fact, motion. Thus, the scope of the second proof is broader than the scope of the first. The first proof concludes that God is the cause of things in motion but that does not demonstrate, necessarily, that God is the cause of all effects. The second proof, then, takes up where the first concludes and advances the argument to a new, broader level.

Here, again, we see the influence of Aristotelian method on St. Thomas's approach. If we recall the procedure by which Aristotle isolated the highest good, we will remember that it began as a collection of all of the possible things that could be called good and pared them down through successive steps until only the highest good remained. This division of the collection allowed Aristotle to focus more and more tightly on the outcome of the argument. St. Thomas reverses this process here, beginning first with a particular sort of effect, motion, before moving to include all effects. Thus, the argument encapsulated in the Five Ways establishes first that God is the cause of things in motion and then, widening the scope, that God is the ultimate cause of all effects. With this interpretation, then, the reader turns to the successive argument, the Proof from Contingency/Necessity, with the expectation that the scope will be widened further and that the proof, far from being a separate proof that is expected to stand completely independent of the others, in fact develops the conclusion of the preceding proofs. With this interpretation, we can see that St. Thomas is not merely arguing for existence as a property of God but also developing an argument for the various properties often ascribed to God.

With this expectation of both a proof for God's existence and an expansion of the understanding of the nature of God, we turn to the third of the Five Ways and immediately notice that it differs from the first two in some rather significant ways. Obviously, it begins in the same style, with an observation. In this case, it is not an observation of motion, but of a property that is different in kind. Among the effects in the universe are beings. Further, all of the observable beings encountered in the universe have contingent natures. That is, none of the immediately observable beings are necessary. We generally use the logical terms "necessity" and "contingency" to refer to statements or propositions. As matters of logic, they are descriptions of the truth value of those propositions. We say that some statement is *necessarily* true just in case it is impossible for that statement to be false. For a more complete discussion of logical necessity and contingency, see the Logic Blurb at the end of the preceding. Here, St.

Thomas applies this generally epistemological notion to these metaphysical arguments. A *necessary being* is understood as a being that must exist, of necessity. That is, if X is a necessary being, then it is not possible that X does not exist. This being the case, a *contingent being* is a being that might exist or that might not exist; or, that did not exist at some time and came into existence and may well cease to exist. Thus, the observation that there are contingent beings is quite straightforward. All humans are contingent, rather than necessary.

From the observation, St. Thomas proceeds in the same manner as in the first two proofs by employing both the Aristotelian Efficient Cause and setting up a proof by elimination by presenting an exhaustive list of potential causes of contingent beings. As with the Proofs from Motion and Efficient Cause, St. Thomas begins with noting that the possible ultimate cause of the contingent beings of his observation is something of like kind, namely another contingent being. Just as he looked among moving things for candidates for the cause of observed motion and for effects as candidates for candidates for the cause of observed effects, so here he looks first to contingent beings for the candidates for cause of the observed contingencies. Thus, two possibilities to be included in the exhaustive list are some first contingent being or the notion that no first contingent being exists. Let us consider these in turn.

If one supposes that there is no first contingent being, then one is immediately faced again with the Infinite Regression that eliminated the assumptions that there was not first mover and that there was no first efficient cause in the first two proofs. Thus, we can again rule out that possibility. However, we cannot immediately conclude, in virtue of eliminating the first assumption, that the second possibility is necessarily the end of the story. Indeed, let us suppose that it is. In other words, let us suppose that there is no first necessary being and that there is a first contingent being.

If we suppose that the regression ends with a first contingent being, we are forced to reflect upon the nature of contingent beings. What it is to be a contingent being is to be a being that is bounded or limited. Contingent beings come into being and, may, cease to be. Leaving aside any questions of immortality, the pertinent issue here is the notion of a contingent being coming into being. Since that is part of the nature of a contingent being, then we need consider that time during which there was but the one contingent being, the first of them. During that time, there would have been only the one thing in existence, that first contingent being. However, immediately prior to that contingent being coming into existence, there would have been nothing at all, absolute nothingness. Thus, if we consider that time when nothing existed, then we must conclude that there is no way in which the first contingent being itself could have come into being. The Latin here is sometimes helpfully direct. St. Thomas writes in another place, *ex nihilo nihil fit*, or, "out of nothing nothing comes." So, if we begin with the assumption that there is no necessary being and merely a first contingent being, then it follows that there are no contingent beings at all.

This is directly counter to the observation with which the proof began and as that observation holds that there are indeed contingent beings, then we must conclude that the assumption is false.

To conclude that the assumption that there is a first contingent being and no necessary being is false is not to conclude that there is no first contingent being. Indeed, the conclusion that there must be some necessary being to give rise to the first contingent being entails that there must exist that first contingent being. Thus, the Proof from Contingency and Necessity develops the two preceding arguments and we are now left with a proof for the existence of God that holds that God is the cause of motion (a particular sort of effect), that God is the cause of all effects, and that God is a necessary being, of nature, rather than a contingent one. Here, another of Aristotle's Four Causes makes an appearance. While the Efficient Cause is again a driving force in the progress of the proofs, the notion of the Formal Cause is at work here as the quite important distinction between the sort of things that contingent and necessary beings are is crucial to the completion of the proof. Here, then, is a case in which one can begin to see the broadening of the arguments (or argument) as it seeks to cast an ever wider net in the proof for God's existence.

The Proof from Contingency/Necessity

Statement	Justification
1. There are contingent beings.	1. Observation
2. All contingent beings must have causes (either contingent ones or necessary ones)	2. Efficient Cause
3. Either there is an infinite regress of contingent beings or there is a first contingent being or there is a necessary being.	3. Exhaustive "or"
4. Suppose there is no first contingent being.	4. Assumption.
5. Therefore, there are no contingent beings.	5. PIR
6. Therefore, there are no contingent beings and there are contingent beings.	6. Definition of "and", 1, 5
7. Therefore, the assumption that there is no first contingent being is false.	7. Contradiction, 1, 4-6
8. Therefore, there is a first contingent cause.	8. Elimination, 3, 7
9. Suppose that there is *only* a first contingent being (and no necessary being)	9. Assumption
10. Therefore, there was a time when there were no beings (prior to the existence of the first contingent being).	10. Formal Cause
11. Therefore, there are no contingent beings (*ex nihilo nihil fit*)	11. Formal Cause
12. Therefore, there are not contingent beings and there are contingent beings.	12. Definition of "and", 1, 11
13 Therefore, the assumption that there is *only* a first contingent being is false	13. Contradiction, 1, 9-11

14. Therefore, there must exist a necessary being.	14. Elimination, 3, 8, 13

Between the Proof from Contingency/Necessity and the last Proof, there is the Proof from Gradation or from Degrees of Perfection. This is widely considered to be the weakest of the five proofs for the existence of God. However, there are two very intriguing aspects of this proof, particularly if it is read as part of a larger effort that begins with understanding God as the cause of a particular sort of effect and concluding with the notion of God as the intelligent designer of the cosmos.

First, within this Fourth Way, we encounter another Aristotelian legacy. It will be recalled from the *Nicomachean Ethics* that Aristotle uses a sort of slope to visualize the search for the highest good. The Highest Good, something desired for itself but not desired for its consequences, is at the pinnacle, obviously. All of the other things that might be called "good" are named derivatively from the Highest Good. That is, all of the lower goods, both those desired for themselves and those not desired for themselves, are desired for their consequences, for something beyond themselves. This teleological aspect of all the lower sorts of "good" points to another interpretation; namely, that the lower goods are only good insofar as their proper aim (the good beyond themselves for which they are desired) is that Highest Good. Thus, one could interpret Aristotle as having envisioned an ethical system by which the Highest Good is not only the standard by which things are considered good, but also, in some sense, is the thing that causes the goodness of those inferior goods. That is to say, the goodness of the inferior "goods" depends, at least in some measure, on the Highest Good, the teleological end for the lower goods. That Aristotle then applies something like this model to actual existent things is fairly clear as well, as he delineates within the nature of human beings a hierarchy in which there are those capable of full virtue and those who are not, those who are, by nature, free and those who ought, by nature, to be slaves. His *natural teleology* informs not only his ethics but also his metaphysics.

St. Thomas adopts this *natural teleology* here and thereby foreshadows part of the argument that follows in the final of the Five Ways. Here, however, we see again the notion of the efficient cause applied to the proof to generate an infinite regress. The difference here is that St. Thomas conceives the Highest Good, in this case the metaphysical actual entity God, to be not merely the necessary cause of all effects, but also to occupy the position of ethical actual entity who is cause of all of the goodness of any and all effects, insofar as they are good. Thus, since there must be a Highest Good and it follows that God, as cause of all effects, must likewise be the cause of all goodness, we can judge, simply by observing a variation in the goodness of things we encounter, that God must ultimately exist.

The weakness of this approach is that it seems quite *a priori* to assign a variable "goodness" quotient to observable, existent things. To be sure, Aristotle is guilty of this rather rationalistic move himself, particularly with regard to the ontological status of, for example, women. However, St. Thomas takes the highly questionable empirical claim that there are degrees of goodness within the observable universe and reasons from it far beyond Aristotle's own claims. Without the Aristotelian contribution of the gradations of the nature of goods, descending from the Highest to the lower with the lower always pointing toward the Highest, this proof would fail to accomplish its end.

The second intriguing aspect of this proof is that it serves as a bridge from St. Thomas's first three proofs which each proceed from clearly observable features of the universe to his fifth proof which begins with the adoption of Aristotle's doctrine of the Final Cause an the attribution to that doctrine of observability. That is, St. Thomas adopts Aristotle's *natural teleology* and rather uncritically applies it both in the Proof from Gradation, within the middle of the proof, and the Proof from Governance of the World, at the very outset of the proof. Few, if any, modern empiricists would grant that the claim that inanimate things have natural ends is an empirically observable feature of the world. If one examines St. Thomas's Fifth Way apart from the others, however, one is forced to conclude that he begs the question with the very opening salvo of the proof. If, on the other hand, one interprets the Five Ways as one organic whole, then one can see how the Proof from Motion, which begins with a clearly observable feature of the world, can lead directly to the final conclusion that God is the intelligent designer of the universe. While criticism of the Thomistic project might well still focus here, it is at least demonstrably consistent within the broader project. Further, it shows quite clearly the extent to which St. Thomas depends on his Aristotelian toolbox to construct his arguments.

This, of course, brings us to the final of the Five Ways. The Proof from Governance of the World goes by many different names and has been incarnated in many different philosophical schemes since St. Thomas. Indeed, descendents of the proof continue to crop up within debates over the teaching of theories about the origins of human existence within various and sundry school districts even in the early parts of the 21st century. Few arguments have shown the subtlety and sophistication of St. Thomas's, however. Alternatively known as the Proof from Intelligent Design and the Teleological Proof, a version of the Fifth Way became part of the popular vernacular in the hands of 18th century philosopher and theologian, William Paley. Paley's Watchmaker Argument for the existence of God is essentially a pale and rather quick imitation of St. Thomas's. Paley's argument proceeds from an analogy. Given that a watch is a rather intricately ordered thing and that its order is imparted to it by the watchmaker, so to must the intricately ordered cosmos demonstrate, by inference, the delicate hand of the cosmic designer. Paley's Watchmaker Argument, though, suffers from a fatal and equally quick flaw. Recalling that for any analogy to hold, the related features of the argument must bear the same relationship to one another and that one cannot go beyond that relationship to introduce new items in one not found in the other, we can quickly discard Paley. As David Hume points out, the two relata that form the first half of the analogy – the watch and the watchmaker – are finite and that, at the very least, our experience of the cosmos is similarly finite, it is impossible, then, to impute infinitude to the presumably analogous designer of that cosmos. In other words, while the designer of the universe could be conceived as tremendously large, it would be impossible to suppose that designer to be infinite, based on the analogy itself. Hence, the Watchmaker proof fails to demonstrate its conclusion.

The failure of Paley's Watchmaker argument, however, points out a strength of St. Thomas's Fifth Way. The Watchmaker Argument fails because it appeals to an analogy that is ultimately unsupportable. St. Thomas's final proof does not appeal to an analogy, although the natural teleology of Paley's argument is clearly present in St. Thomas's. This final piece of the larger argument that is the Five Ways begins with the claim that inanimate things have ends. Here, we need to recall that St. Thomas follows an Aristotelian distinction that has fallen out of favor. By "inanimate" here, St. Thomas does not mean "without life." He simply means to designate, as did Aristotle, that there are objects in the world which do not possess the ability to move themselves. So, plants, for example, are inanimate on this interpretation. Whatever the case, this is a semantic matter than can cause confusion but does not affect the argument itself.

Let us consider the example we first considered in the discussion of Aristotle's Final Cause. An acorn has as its natural end the oak tree that it has the power to become. However, a necessary condition of possessing a natural end is the ability to tend toward that end, or to form intentions the goal of which is that natural end. Thus, it would be necessary for the acorn to form the intention to become an oak tree. It is commonly granted that intelligence is a necessary condition of intention formation. If this is so, then it would seem to follow that inanimate things cannot possess natural ends because they do not possess intelligence. Thus, the acorn could not form intentions because it does not possess intelligence and because it can not form intentions, it must be without a natural end. However, this is counter to the observation with which this proof began and therefore there must be some explanation for the possession of ends by inanimate entities. Suppose we assume, however, that inanimate things do not have ends, as would seem to follow from the requirement that intention formation requires an intelligence that acorns do not possess. As this would contradict the observable evidence, this assumption must be rejected. Thus, the only explanation for the end possessed by the acorn is that there must be some external entity who possesses both intelligence and the capacity to form intentions for acorns and to implant that intention into the acorn. By extension, since all natural objects have ends well before they are able to form intentions toward those ends, the relationship of this intelligent designer must be the same whether the object for whom the intentions is formed is an acorn or a human being. Thus, there must exist some intelligent designer who is the author of the natural ends of all things.

The Proof from Governance of the World
(Proof from Design, Teleological Proof)

Statement	Justification
1. Inanimate things have ends.	1. Observation
2. To have an end, it is necessary to form intentions.	2. Final Cause
3. To form intentions, it is necessary to possess intelligence.	3. Definition of "intention"
4. Inanimate things do not possess intelligence.	4. Observation
5. Therefore, either inanimate things do not have ends or some intelligent being intends on their behalf.	5. Modus Tollens (1-4) *or* Exhaustive "or"
6. Suppose inanimate things do not have ends.	6. Assumption
7. Therefore, inanimate things have ends and do not have ends.	7. Definition of "and", 1, 6
8. Therefore, the assumption that inanimate things do not have ends is false	8. Contradiction, 1, 6-7
9. Therefore, some intelligent being intends on their behalf.	9. Elimination, 5, 8

St. Thomas's Five Ways present the reader with clear insight into the shift from Ancient to Medieval philosophy (that is, from the shift from addressing the big questions of philosophy by approaching them from ethical claims to approaching them from metaphysical ones). The Five Ways also reveal the fairly common medieval practice of appropriating conceptual frameworks from the ancients, particularly Plato and Aristotle, and reconfiguring those frameworks to construct wholly new arguments concerning the nature and structure of the cosmos. Whether one reads St. Thomas's Five Ways as a single argument, as has been suggested and argued here, or as five independent arguments, the lasting influence of the work is indisputable. In many ways, St. Thomas's work is rightly considered the pinnacle of Medieval philosophical investigation. There are other philosophical contributions within the period, but no other Medieval philosopher is so able to systematize such a breadth of argument – metaphysical, ethical, epistemological, theological.

Guided Reading Questions

1. List and briefly describe the five ways to prove the existence of God, according to St. Thomas.
2. What are Aristotle's Four Causes?
3. How are the proofs connected to the causes? That is, how does Thomas use Aristotle's Four Causes in his Five Proofs?

Logic Blurb
The Universal Quantifier and its Negation

All ravens are black. All bachelors are unmarried. All roads lead to Rome. All even numbers are real numbers.

The use of the word "all" here signifies what is technically known as a *universal quantifier*. The *universal quantifier* is an exceptionally important mathematical, logical, and philosophical tool. Often, one wants to know if some property or quality is universal to some population or other. For example, one might inquire whether the property of having three legs is universal, or common, to all stools. Such an inquiry would not take long as it would quickly become apparent that not all stools have three legs.

So, how many non-three-legged stools would we need to discover to determine that not all stools have three legs? Only one. The discovery of a single four-legged stool would be sufficient to negate the claim that "all stools have three legs." An important aspect of the negation of the universal quantifier is found here. When one negates a universal quantifier, one does not get another universally quantified statement. Thus, the negation of "all ravens are black" is *not* "no ravens are black." Similarly, the negation of "all roads lead to Rome" is *not* "no road leads to Rome." Presumably the discovery of a road that led from Hearn community to Antoine community would not entail that it is no impossible to get from anywhere to Rome. Instead, the negation of a universal quantifier is an *existential quantifier* (see next logic blurb for a more complete discussion of the *existential quantifier*). In this case, it would be "there is a road that does not lead to Rome" or "there is a raven that is not black." To refute a universally quantified statement, it takes but one counterexample.

Apart from the negation of the *universal quantifier*, the foregoing examples point to a difficulty in using the *universal quantifier* in empirical arenas. To use the *universal quantifier* in empirical sciences is an exhaustive process, literally and figuratively. To use it, one must be able to assess each and every possibility. So, if one were to try to demonstrate that all ravens are black, one would have to find every single raven, past and present, and show that it is indeed black. In this way, one would exhaust all the possibilities of refutation by collecting every possibility and checking it off. This would literally exhaust the field. Clearly such a process would also exhaust the researcher, as well. Indeed, such an exhaustive cataloguing is likely practically impossible as one would always wonder if all of the ravens had actually been located and noted to be black.

The negation of the *universal quantifier* and the difficulty of using it in empirical arguments might mask its philosophical importance. When one claims that something is universal, it is the same as saying that it is common. Thus, carbon is common to all organic objects and DNA is common to all living organisms. One common use of the *universal quantifier* is to pick out some essential property of some kind of thing. For example, Aristotle uses the *universal quantifier* to isolate what he takes to be the essence or function of human beings. Recall from our examination of the *Nicomachean Ethics* that there are two criteria for some property being considered as the function of human beings. Those two criteria are that it must be unique to human beings – that is, only human beings have the property – and that it must be common to human beings – that is, all human beings have the property. This latter criteria is an expression of a *universally quantified* statement. For Aristotle, the *universal quantifier* is used negatively to isolate essential properties. If some quality is truly an essential property of humans, for example, it must be common to all humans, or universally present among them. If it is not, then it cannot be an essential property. So, along with its counterpart, the *existential quantifier*, the *universal quantifier* is a crucial tool in the critical thinking toolbox of the reflective philosopher.

Section 10: William of Ockham, Ockham's Razor

Summa Logicae

We earlier said that there are names of primary and of secondary intentions. Ignorance of this significant distinction within language has occasioned a great many errors. Thus, it is important to distinguish between primary and secondary intentions.

In the first place, there is something within the mind that represents something else. The relationship is similar to this: something that is written and the utterance of it. But, the utterance, primary in respect to the writing is itself secondary with respect to the representation in the mind. As Aristotle said, these utterances are "marks of the mind's passions."

The thing that is in the mind is itself a representation of some other thing. In this way, we construct a mental proposition from components in the same way a vocal proposition is constructed of utterances where those utterances are sometimes intentions with the mind, or concepts within the mind or passions within the mind. All of these are like what Boethius named them in his commentary, "understandings" (*intellectum*). Now, the components of mental propositions are understandings (*intellectibus*), but these understandings are not themselves intelligent minds, but rather these are representations before the mind, things that are signs of other things. Thus, mental propositions are composed from these things. Whenever a person speaks some proposition, the proposition is first formed in the mind as a mental proposition. This mental proposition is not linguistic. It is clear that many people create mental propositions that they cannot express because the language they have is insufficient to express it. So, we can name the components of mental propositions, *concepts, intentions, similiarities,* and *understandings.* (*conceptus, intentiones, similitudines et intellectus*)

However, within the mind, what is this representation? There are a variety of opinions. There are those who call these representations fictions of the mind. Others call them acts of intelligence or understanding that have purely subjective qualities. And, of course, there are still others who say that it is merely an act of understanding. On behalf of this final group, there is the principle that it is futile to do with many things what it is sufficient to do with but a few. (*frustra fit per plura quod potest fieri per pauciora*). Everything that can be preserved by supposing that the representation is distinct from the act of understanding itself can also be preserved by supposing that the representation is merely an act of understanding. Given this, one need not suppose anything more than the act of understanding itself.

~

Much as the opening of the Medieval period is subject to some scholarly controversy, so, too, the end of the period is somewhat sketchy. It will be recalled that there is some debate concerning the work of St. Augustine, whether it should be counted as part of the conclusion of the Ancient period or among the first of the Medieval. So, too, there is a similar, if more attenuated, difficulty in clearly demarcating the transition from the Medieval to the Modern. To be sure, René Descartes is almost universally considered the Father of Modern Philosophy, but it must be recognized that there were clearly trends and threads in the work of philosophers of the later Medieval period that were drawn together in Descartes's own work. As Newton said explicitly of his own work, Descartes's work stands on the shoulders of great thinkers who preceded him. William of Ockham is such a figure.

Rather than raising questions about whether we should date the opening of the Modern period in the history of philosophy some two centuries earlier than general consensus places it, it is perhaps better to note that William of Ockham is simply one of the Medieval philosophers most akin to their Modern successors. The arguments for placing Ockham in the Modern period are rather sparse. Almost all of which turn on an interpretation of the text included here, and more precisely, upon a particular passage of that text. Ockham's Razor, sometimes mistakenly identified with the Law of Parsimony, is among the most effective tools of the empirical philosopher, whatever scientific discipline she may occupy. Simply put, Ockham's view is that, in the course of offering an explanation for observable events, one should not introduce more than is strictly necessary. So, for example, suppose there are two competing views of how it is that the concepts in our mind come to be. In the first view, there is the belief that there exists a concept in our mind, an actual object in the world, and an act of understanding, independent of both the concept and the actual object by which we come to have a representation in our mind (the concept) of the object. Thus, there are, at least, two distinct sorts of entities – the concept and the actual object (along with the implied assumption that the two are reasonably closely related). It is this sort of model upon which St. Anselm's Ontological Argument depends – the assumption that the idea within the mind and the object represented by the mind both exist and that the relation between them is perfectly preserved such that the idea faithfully represents the actual object. This rationalistic view is punctured somewhat by Gaunilo, and rejected altogether by Ockham.

The second view is that there is merely the act of understanding within the mind. Such an act implies nothing further about the actual world and need not depend on the existence of objects outside the mind for its explanations. Thus, there are simply the concepts within the mind or the act of understanding itself. On this view, there need to be assumed only one set of objects, namely the concepts of the mind themselves. Thus, there are fewer actual objects presupposed and thus a sparser metaphysical scheme. It is this view that Ockham's Razor is employed to support. Given that there are two metaphysical schemes, both of which are explanatorily complete (that is, they account for all of the observable evidence), then it is unnecessary to explain with a multitude what can be explained with a simplicity. In other words, the greater complexity of the first system serves as a reason to reject it. Because the first system requires the philosopher to suppose an ontology that is perhaps an order of magnitude larger than the second, the second is to be preferred.

Ockham's Razor has been reformulated in a number of ways since Ockham. There are metaphysical formulations and epistemological formulations that both keep quite close to Ockham's own view. Ockham's formulation in the *Summa Logicae* is actually less well known than some of the successive formulations. Ockham's Razor has two famous formulations within his own work, one of which is from the text included here. It is as follows:

Ockham's Razor (epistemological form): It is futile to do with many things what it is sufficient to do with but a few. (*frustra fit per plura quod potest fieri perpauciora*)

This formulation of the Razor has a distinctly epistemological flavor to it as it is most clearly applicable to propositions and explanations. To be sure, one can imagine that the "things" to which Ockham refers are actual entities, but that requires a bit of finesse. Instead, it is likely better to appeal, for metaphysical matters, to Ockham's other formulation, which we shall call the *metaphysical form*.

Ockham's Razor (metaphysical form): Unless necessary, multiplicity is not to be assumed. (*pluritalis non est ponenda sine necessitate*)

Despite the variety of forms of the Razor within Ockham's own work, perhaps the most famous version of it is found nowhere in his work. That "entities should never be multiplied beyond necessity" (*entia non sunt multiplicanda praeter necessitatem*) is the most commonly explicated form of the Razor, but is the work of a later scholar. Let us call this, then, the *popular form*. The identity of the author of this version is the matter of some scholarly debate and no consensus.

As mentioned previously, Ockham's Razor is sometimes confused with the very similar Law of Parsimony. The Law of Parsimony, distinct but related to the Razor, has a more epistemological feel to it. It can be written fairly simply:

> Law of Parsimony: Given two theories that account for the evidence, the simpler theory is to be given preference.

The similarity of the Law of Parsimony to both of the forms of the Razor found in Ockham is clear. Careful reading of all three, however, shows the different scope of each. While there is both an epistemological form and metaphysical form of the Razor, this distinction is actually a matter of emphasis; both of them are fundamentally ontological. That is, both forms suggest that a minimum of *actual objects* should be presupposed. If one need but only a few objects for explanatory power, one should recognize that the use of further assumed objects is meaningless or hazardous. At the very least, those assumed objects are beyond the realm of observation. Recalling the two examples, the first view supposes at minimum two kinds of objects while the second view makes do with only one. As only one kind of object is actually experienced (the concepts within the mind) by the perceiving mind, the second sort of objects are merely additive and unnecessary. Thus, they are ontologically superfluous.

The Law of Parsimony, on the other hand, is clearly a matter of epistemology. The scope of its application is theory and hypothesis. If we recall one of the unofficial charges against Socrates, this scope becomes clearer. Socrates was charged with being a Natural Philosopher. A Natural Philosopher, as has been shown previously, is an investigator who seeks to provide natural explanations (or theories or hypotheses) for natural events. A second alternative would be to put forward an explanation that depended on the supernatural. Faced with the observable world, a Natural Philosopher is likely to advance a natural hypothesis while others might advance an hypothesis that has as a central explanatory device the will of a deity. For example, one thinker might put forward a Theory of Evolution to account for the existence of the variety of existent objects while another might appeal to Creationism. One of these theories is a natural one while the other is a supernatural. The Law of Parsimony is not concerned, directly, with the objects inferred by the two theories, but rather with the theories or hypotheses themselves. In an evaluation of the two theories *as theories*, the Law of Parsimony would require that the natural theory is given preference over the supernatural one as it is the simpler hypothesis.

The applications of the Law of Parsimony to scientific investigations are abundantly clear. Suppose a scientist is in her laboratory and trying to decide between two competitive hypotheses, both of which explain all of the data from her experiments. Let us suppose that one of the hypotheses is reasonably straightforward while the other is breathtaking in its complexity. Unless there is some piece of data of which the second hypothesis gives account while the first does not, then the first is to be preferred. That is, since both are explanatorily adequate views, the simpler view is given preference over the more complex. Indeed, not only is the Law of Parsimony helpful to the advance of the scientific method, it is one of the hallmarks of the advance of science. Some of the shoulders upon which Newton stands are those of William of Ockham.

In addition to a kinship with the scientists and mathematicians who radically altered the view of the world in the centuries following Ockham, he has considerable affinity to the empiricists of the early Modern period as well. This is particularly clear when one considers the empiricists of the British Empiricist movement – Locke, Berkeley, and Hume. Further, it is even clearer when one turns to Hume. One of Hume's more controversial claims is that belief should always be apportioned to the evidence at hand; that is, belief should go no further nor assume nothing beyond that which is within the observable record and that which is necessary to account for the observable evidence. Thus, the Humean view can be seen as a direct descendant of Ockham's Razor and the Law of Parsimony. If the two are accepted, then any speculative system that relies on principles and concepts that extend beyond the observable evidence, even if those principles or concepts are matters of deeply held faith, should be recognized as violations of the of both which together require that the explanation of the observable evidence account for it, but not amplify it, either by supposing the existence of objects not in evidence or by introducing unnecessary complexity to explanatory theories.

It is not only the scientific and empirical kinships with later thinkers that causes some to suppose that Ockham belongs among the Moderns. In a foreshadowing of Hume and Kant, Ockham also argues that it is not possible to *prove* that God exists. While this view clearly did not endear him to papal authority, it should also be recognized that as a Franciscan, it is unlikely that Ockham would hold the view that God does not exist. Rather, Ockham argues that the sphere of faith and the evidence gleaned from personal experience of faith, on the one hand, and observable, empirical evidence that is public and available to all, on the other, are actually completely separate realms. Belief in God is a matter of faith and theology, not science and philosophy. Indeed, as God would be a sort of universal, and thus, in principle, beyond the observation of the human mind, it is impossible to marshal evidence for either the proposition that God exists or that God does not exist. One might, by faith, belief one over the other, but one should not confuse belief with that which can be demonstrably proven. The reality of God is forever beyond the reach of scientifically verifiable knowledge. Thus, in a manner that prefigures the work of Immanuel Kant, perhaps the most important of the Modern philosophers, Ockham argues that the existence or non-existence of God is beyond proof.

For these reasons, it is sometimes proposed that Ockham should be seen as an early Modern philosopher, or at least a proto-Modern philosopher. However, this takes these views out of context and, while each clearly has an analogous counterpart in the work of undisputedly Modern philosophers, they are also part of a larger system that approaches the big questions of philosophy in a thoroughly Medieval way. Indeed, Ockham comes to these his views by participating fully in the very Medieval debate over the status of universals and particulars.

One of the uses of the Razor is to simplify metaphysical claims. The very modern sounding conclusions that Ockham reaches concerning proofs for the existence of God, scientific evidence, and hypothesis testing all spring as consequent metaphysical views; views he defends in a Nominalist tradition. The Medieval debate between Realists and Nominalists is a debate that sounds thoroughly pre-modern. Which sorts of objects have the greatest ontological status – universals or particulars? Another way of putting it is to ask which is more *real*. Within the early centuries of the Medieval period, when the Platonic approach held sway and NeoPlatonists dominated philosophy and theology, the accepted worldview was that universals (conceptual descendents of Platonic Forms) were the truly real things. Hence, the view that universals are real and particulars encountered within the everyday world are less so came to be known as Realism. On the Realist view, the universal *Chair* is more real than any particular chair because it is eternal, indivisible, immutable, and wholly independent of the vagaries of human perception and its limitations.

The Nominalists, on the other hand, take their name from the position that they hold relative to those universals. On the Nominalist view, the word *Chair* is simply a name that is given to a set of particular group of similar objects. As a name, it is completely dependent not only on the particular objects that it names but also on the social conventions that are agreed upon such that these particular objects are called *chairs* rather than *gophers*. There is nothing inherent or essential in the particular object commonly called a *chair* that makes it like the other things commonly so called. Indeed, there is really on *this object* and *that object* and it is purely an accidental feature of human language and perception that we choose to give the same name to both *this* and *that*. On this view, universals are not only stripped of their ontological primacy, but they cease to be conceived as having any reality to them at all.

The Razor is not exclusively employed to dispatch the Realist view, although it is part of Ockham's arsenal. Indeed, the Law of Parsimony is perhaps a greater tool in that debate. Ockham employs the two together to argue on behalf of the Nominalist tradition, a tradition that is resurfaces in the scientific empiricism of David Hume, among others. On Ockham's view, supposing that universals have existence apart from the particulars of which they are abstractions is to add entities to the metaphysical space without those entities actually doing any work. He argues that it is perfectly reasonable to address only the particulars of human experience – the individual objects that are all commonly, but non-essentially, called *chair*, without any recourse to imperceptible objects or abstractions. If a theory is adequate to account for the various objects, their relations, and their properties without recourse to imperceptible objects, then supposing those objects exist is a tenuous assumption at best. Worse, supposing that those objects beyond human perception have somehow *more reality* than those actually experienced seems fantastical, on Ockham's view.

Since the entities are superfluous, supposing that they exist entails a bloated metaphysics that makes understanding the world more complicated rather than less. Since the objects are superfluous, assuming that they have a greater ontological status, that is, more reality, to them than perceived objects is a notion beyond the grasp of reason. As a result, the Realist view is, on Ockham's view, simply incoherent.

Thus, Ockham's Razor and the Law of Parsimony are rigorously applied to all Realist metaphysical opponents in a manner; cleaving them one after the other from the field of competition. In this way, it is a metaphysical counterpart to Hume's *Epistemological Principle*, which Hume uses to such devastating effect on the Modern Rationalist counterpart to the Medieval Platonists against whom Ockham jousts. Again and again, Ockham assesses competitor theories and asks of them whether or not they multiply entities beyond that which is necessary to explain human perception and the world perceived through the senses. His insistence on simplicity, both of epistemological explanation and ontological suppositions serves as a springboard from which he argues for epistemic humility with regards to proofs for the existence of God, analytical rigor with respect to competitor scientific hypothesis, and critical rejection of, to his mind, the bloated ontologies of Realists, inherited from their Ancient predecessors. In these arguments, Ockham helps to set the stage for the Scientific Revolution that, along with the upheavals of the Protestant Reformation and the Renaissance brought the Medieval period to a close and ushered in the Modern.

Guided Reading Questions
1. In what ways does the work of William of Ockham anticipate the later arguments of Modern philosophers?
2. What is Ockham's Razor?
3. How does Ockham argue that it is not possible to prove that God exists?
4. How are the Law of Parsimony and Ockham's Razor related?

Logic Blurb
The Existential Quantifier and Its Negation
Having treated the *universal quantifier* in the preceding section, we turn our attention to its counterpart, the *existential quantifier*. The nature of the *existen-*

tial quantifier is quite simple. It is a statement of existence, particular rather than universal in scope. For example, one might say, "There is a baseball team known as the Cardinals." Demonstration of the truth of the existentially quantified statement is straightforward. To show that the claim is true, one need only produce a single baseball team with that name. There might well be hundreds, but the demonstration of any existentially quantified statement requires only that at least one exist.

The negation of a *universal quantifier*, as we have seen, is not another *universal quantifier*, but rather an *existential quantifier*. So, the negation of "All ravens are black," is not "No ravens are black," but rather, "There exists at least one raven that is not black." In a similar way, the negation of an *existential quantifier* is not another *existential quantifier*, but rather a *universal quantifier*. So, if we were to negate the existential statement, "There is a non-black raven," we would get the proposition, "There are no non-black ravens." But that is the same as saying, "All ravens are black."

This approach is commonly used in philosophical arguments as an assumption that begins a strand of the argument. For example, one might say, "Let us assume that there is a triangle the sum of the measures of whose interior angles is less than 180°." Through the course of the argument (probably in the application of the definition of a triangle) that assumption will be shown to be false and its negation true. The negation would be that there is not a triangle the sum of the measures of whose interior angles is less than 180°. Thus, the negation of the existential assumption is the universally quantified, "The sum of the measures of the interior angles of all triangles is 180°." So, as the complement of the *universal quantifier*, the *existential quantifier* takes its place in the philosopher's logical toolbox as an important analytical tool.

Chapter 3 – Modern Philosophy

Section 11: The Birth of the Modern Era

Rene Descartes is commonly called the "Father of Modern Philosophy." Such monikers are not given lightly. Indeed, Descartes's work, particularly his *Meditations*, mark a fundamental change from the method and aims of philosophy in the Ancient period and subsequent Medieval period. While it is surely too strong to claim that philosophy itself changes with Descartes, it is not at all inaccurate to say that the emphasis in philosophical investigation shifts rather dramatically. The philosophy of the Ancient Greeks emphasized questions of human nature, the good life, and way in which the good life might be achieved. The Medieval period was marked by concerns in expansion of Ancient principles into areas not considered by the Ancients, particularly questions concerning the existence and nature of God, sin, and evil. The Modern period, beginning arguably with Descartes, is characterized with a particular concern for understanding human knowledge; what it is, whether it is possible, and how it is acquired. Metaphysical concerns are similarly emphasized, although in a somewhat attenuated manner relative to the Ancients. Significantly, though, ethical concerns are pushed to the margins of the mainstream philosophical discourse. This is surely a departure from the approach of the Ancients.

The epistemological shift from the Medieval period to the Modern period may be seen best in the rejection of a fundamental and generally unquestioned assumption of the Medieval worldview. Behind the work of St. Anselm and St. Thomas, and underlying the empirical approach of the Thomistic/Aristotelian sciences, was the assumption that the actual world was very much like, and perhaps exactly like, the world as it appeared in perception. This assumption, unlike much of the Ancient world, survives the fall of the Roman Empire generally intact. The geopolitical upheaval that was the fall of Rome was the cataclysmic historical event that roughly coincided with the shift from the Ancient to the Medieval world. The repercussions of the fall of the empire reverberated throughout the western world, and considerable shifts in the way the world was understood were the result.

Following the fall of Rome, the Roman Catholic Church emerged as the dominant political, intellectual, and spiritual power of the Medieval period. The university system was created under the auspices of the church, primarily for the training of clergy, for fairly comprehensive roles from the local parish through the upper echelons of the church hierarchy. Given this, it is not at all surprising that the education, the scientific exploration, in addition to art and music were generally related, in one way or another, to church structure, and by extension, to church authority. The scientific worldview was an adaptation of Aristotle's empirical work, translated through St. Thomas. The Scholastic picture of the world preserved the intuition and unexamined assumption that the actual world was very much like the perceptions of it. Differences in individual perceptions of the world were taken to be the fault of the individual perceiver. That is, the world was a single thing perceived in a singular way. Deviation from that perception was not the fault of the created and ordained order of things, but rather the fault of the one who "misperceived." Thus, when Copernicus brought forward a scientific worldview that suggested that the planets, including Earth, revolved around the sun, rather than the sun and the celestial bodies revolving around the Earth, he was summarily chastened and forced to recant. This gives an indication of the scope of the authority of the Church, but more importantly, indicates the authority of the objectivist world view that was inherited from Aristotle but molded to fit the Medieval experience. Epistemologically speaking, given that the world was as it appeared to be, truth was understood to be an objective fact, independent of the perceiver. Thus, if an apple was red, the person who perceived it as some color other than red was objectively, and obviously, wrong. Truth, then, was an absolute, irrefutable relationship; and a relationship that was preserved in the Scholastic treatises that dominated the sciences. Authority, dependent on truth, was similarly absolute and unquestionable.

A revolution, at least as devastating to the common view of the world, was in the making in the rise of a new scientific approach, exemplified by Copernicus, Francis Bacon, Galileo, Rene Descartes, and Isaac Newton. This view radically called into question the authority of the Church and the authority of the received view of the world. All these scientists took note of the fact that perceptions are notoriously unreliable things. What one person sees in one way, another will see in a different way. A common experience is that of, for example, seeing a person some distance off and being sure that he is a dear friend of close acquaintance. After coming closer, it is recognized that the person is actually someone whom the person does not know at all. It is not that the identity of the person changed, but rather the perception of him was altered by circumstances – first he was far away, then he was close by.

Beyond the obvious errors to which perception is susceptible, the revolution reverberated throughout the structures of power, secular and ecclesiastical. If the perceptions of the world did not reveal the inner nature of the world, then the authority based on the assumption that the world was as it appeared was similarly undermined. Within the 16th century, two challenges arose to that "objective" authority. In 1517, Martin Luther nailed his *95 Thesis* on a parish door in Wittenburg and thus the Protestant Reformation, the most significant challenge to the authority of the Church to date was begun. That movement spiraled into the fracturing of the Church into literally hundreds and later thousands of denominations, all competing to advance their own visions of the world and the role of humanity within it.

Along with the upheaval within the ecclesiastical realm came a similar upheaval within the intellectual one. Michel Montaigne, born in 1533, translated the work of an Ancient Skeptic, Sixtus Empiricus. That work, *Outlines on Pyrrhonism*, took the fallibility of sense perception to advance a devastating critique of the notion of a theory of truth based on infallible perceptions of the natural world. Indeed, Montaigne and the new skeptics argued that it was impossible to know anything with anything resembling certainty. The implications of this view were drastic. If certain knowledge was impossible, then so, too, were moral and legal codes based on "certainty" or "objective" knowledge. The authority of the Church and the establishment over the secular and intellectual lives of the people was toppled. However, with that toppling came the apparently inevitable conclusion that not only were perceptions relative, but so, too, was all knowledge, either scientific or moral. Such relativism was a devastating challenge to both Church and scientific authority, and the reliance on Metaphysics that marked the Medieval period came to be seen as untenable, in the best case, and impossible, in the worst. The Copernican Revolution in the sciences and worldview was as devastating, in its own way, as the Fall of Rome had been. And, as questions of metaphysics were marginalized, the questions of human knowledge (epistemology) came to the fore. The era of Modern Philosophy had begun.

Into this turmoil, Rene Descartes sought to find a middle course between the radical relativism of the Skeptics and the similarly strongly held objective authoritarianism of the Scholastics. The profound difficulty that Descartes faced, though, was that he agreed with both groups. That is, the new science that the Skeptics took as justification for their rejection of objective truth was precisely the new science for which Descartes sought to defend and establish a foundation. Yet, the notion of objective truth and certain knowledge, common to the Scholastics, is also his own view. Thus, he was faced with arguing that the "skeptical" new science was superior to the old science of the Scholastics, but that in adopting the new science, one was not committed to the relativism about knowledge.

The *Meditations* is a challenging text for several reasons. First, its style is different from the other forms of philosophical investigation that we have discussed to this point. We encounter a similar problem of strengths and weaknesses of the style. For example, while dialogues and notes and treatises have their own peculiar strengths and weaknesses, so the *Meditations*, too, has attendant strengths and weaknesses as a style. One of the primary strengths of the meditation style is that it is reasonably familiar to anyone who has ever tried to organize his or her thoughts on paper, reflecting on all of the possibilities available, and trying to sift through those options to arrive at an acceptable conclusion. Another strength of the style is the way in which it invites the reader to follow the thought process of the author as he explores the landscape of his own mind. The meditation style shares weaknesses with the dialogue style. Both styles tend to be difficult to write well. Thus, only the best writers give us meditations or dialogues that actually seem to function as meditations or dialogues. At the same time, those that function well bring with them the possibility of becoming lost in the rhythm and flow of the prose. Because they do not present us with arguments in a point-by-point, premise-by-premise fashion, it can be more difficult to discern what the arguments actually are. A distinct weakness of the meditation style is that it is so personal in tone that, unlike a dialogue that invites the reader into a conversation, the meditation seems to keep the reader out of one. Descartes goes to great lengths to avoid this latter weakness. Rather than publishing the *Meditations* alone, he sent them to several of the leading philosophic minds of the day. Those that responded with objections to the work had those objections published alongside the *Meditations*. Thus, Descartes presents the reader not only with a set of meditations, but with a set of objections as well. As a result, the reader is drawn into the philosophical conversation of the topics with which Descartes is especially concerned.

As discussed already, Descartes is supremely concerned with establishing a foundation for the new scientific world view. He writes in the *First Meditation*, "I became confident that, at least once in my life, all this must be stripped away if anything firm and stable was to be built within science." This puts him directly at odds with the very group to which he appeals to publish his work, namely the Scholastic intellectuals who run the educational system. At odds with them because his view of the physical world comports more closely with that of the Skeptics, Descartes is also at great pains to argue that the Skeptics have it wrong as well. Thus, in many ways, however, Descartes sets out to refute both the major philosophical traditions of his day. In arguing that the Skeptics are ultimately mistaken, Descartes will argue that the mind and the body are two completely distinct substances. The legacy of Cartesian dualism, the Mind/Body Interaction problem resonates through fields from philosophy of mind to psychology well into the 20th century. The other purpose that Descartes claims is at the heart of his meditative efforts is a demonstration that God must necessarily exist. Reminiscent of his rationalistic forebear, St. Anselm, Descartes's proof, in the *Third Meditation*, critically involves a definition as the foundational element. Discovering these last two purposes is somewhat easier than identifying the former two. Given to writing long titles, Descartes's title for the *Meditations* is actually, "Meditations on First Philosophy in which the necessary existence of God and the separation between the mind and the body is demonstrated."

In an interesting aside, Descartes claims in his *Preface to the Reader* that, in the course of demonstrating that God exists and the mind and the body are distinct, he will show that the soul is immortal. He says that having shown the existence of God, he will show that the soul does not perish when the body dies. However, nowhere in the *Meditations* does he treat this stated purpose. Considerable speculation has attended this rather glaring oversight. One might conclude that Descartes simply did not think that it was possible to complete this proof with the premises established. At the same time, one could argue that the existence of God and the distinction between the mind and the body are sufficient ground to then argue that the mind, an immaterial and indivisible substance, is eternal while the body, a divisible, material substance, is not. In any case, Descartes leaves this purpose unfulfilled.

As Descartes approaches the *Meditations,* then, he has five discernible purposes. He sets out to establish a firm foundation for the new scientific world view and thereby refute the entrenched Scholastic view, to refute the Skeptics (in particular, Montaigne), to demonstrate that the mind and the body are distinct substances, to demonstrate the necessary existence of God, and to prove that the soul is immortal. Regardless of the ultimate success or failure of Descartes's efforts with regard to these purposes, like Augustine before him, Descartes's work is so revolutionary that it can be taken to mark a shift in the very approach to philosophy. While Augustine marks the transition between Ancient and Medieval philosophy, Descartes ushers philosophy from the Medieval period into the Modern.

Section 12.1: Descartes, Method of Doubt

*Meditations on First Philosophy
in which the Existence of God and
the Real Distinction between the Mind and the Body
are Demonstrated*
First Meditation - Those Things that may be Doubted

It has been many years since it dawned on me that many of the beliefs I had always assumed to be true were actually false. Given these many falsehoods, I knew that the principles built on them were all questionable as well. I became confident that, at least once in my life, all this must be stripped away if anything firm and stable was to be built within science. This effort will be earnestly directed to the end of disposing all those doubtful beliefs. I am also convinced that I should not accept as true anything that is doubtful to any degree; only those things that are beyond doubt (that is, that are certain) should be accepted as true.

So far, everything that I have accepted as the most trustworthy and true are things that I have received from my senses. However, the senses are deceptive; and prudence suggests that we ought not trust those things that deceive us, even if that deception be but once.

At the same time, it seems clear that the senses deceive us about small things or things far off (that is, those things that we cannot scrutinize closely). But does it not seem as if some things presented by our senses are beyond doubt? For example, I sit here before the fire. I am wearing my nightgown and holding a scrap of paper. Are these not my hands? Isn't this my body? To deny these, would I not be called insane, possessed of ill spirits like those who claim royalty when they are peasants or that claim they are cucumbers?

However, I must accept that I am human and that as a human I must sleep. When sleeping, I dream – and thus, see myself in all manner of fantastical situations, no less incredible than those of they whom we call insane. More to the point, I have dreamt that I sat here before the fire, in circumstances exactly as these are. Yet, in those moments, I was in fact in bed asleep. I hold up my hand, and I see my hand before my eyes and I have had exactly the same perceptions of my hand when I was asleep. I am amazed by the coincidence, so amazed in fact that I can almost convince myself that I am currently dreaming, so close are the perceptions.

Suppose, then, that I am dreaming. Suppose all these perceptions of my hands and eyes and head are dreams. Suppose even that I do not have hands or a head or any body at all. Even with these suppositions, it is still the case that I perceive these objects (whether asleep or awake). It would seem, then, that even if I am dreaming, these things that I perceive must exist in some sense or other. Further, if these things exist, then so, too, must other things that they themselves make necessary.

Within this category of objects, we might include everything that is physical in nature, that has a body, that takes up space – in other words, anything with extension. We might suppose that fields like physics, astronomy, and medicine that have as their objects things like hands, heads, etc. (that is, things that have parts) are subject to the same doubt as their objects. However, some sciences are about those things that do not have parts, that are simple. Among these would be arithmetic, geometry, and other mathematical sciences. These have as their objects the most general sorts of things. And whether or not I am asleep, it certainly seems that two plus three is five, that a square has four sides, and that these are impossible to doubt.

However, there exists a belief in a God who is in essence omnipotent and who created everything that exists. What reason, then, might I suppose that all that appears to me is not designed by God to appear as if they exist when in fact they do not? Or, at the very least, that they do not exist as they appear to me? Instead of supposing that God, who is good and the source of truth, deceives me, let us suppose instead that there is some evil genius who also has great power and is malignant indeed. Suppose that this evil genius employs all his powers to deceive me at every turn. Thus, I should suppose that everything external to me, the entire external world (sky, air, earth, color, shape, sound) are no more real than the illusions of my dreams. While this may seem quite impossible, these are the suppositions that I will make as far as I am able to do so. Thus, if anything may be the product of the deceit of this evil genius, I will withhold belief from that thing.

This is an exhausting task. It is so difficult that even without my consent, my mind drifts back to the ordinary flow of life. When this happens, I find myself again surrounded by those beliefs based on doubtful principles. I shall rest so that exhaustion does not bring back darkness and extinguish the light of reason.

~

René Descartes, much like Socrates, understood that false beliefs are the antithesis of knowledge and that, far from being a mere hindrance to the acquisition of knowledge had to be stripped away entirely. Unlike Socrates, who was without false beliefs and possessed of few true ones, Descartes seems to think that both sorts are likely mixed together within his own mind. So, while Socrates went about entering into dialogues with his fellow Athenians to disabuse them of false beliefs and perchance to acquire knowledge for himself, Descartes turns his own questioning inward, meditating upon what he finds within his own mind.

He recognizes from the outset that whatever true beliefs he might possess are compromised by the false ones that grow alongside them like weeds among the flowers. However, so complicated is the mixing of true and false that it is impossible merely to uproot the false. Indeed, he is not at all certain he could identify which were which. Since making mistakes at this endeavor will compromise the entire project, Descartes decided it would be better to employ the method of one of his rivals and in using the skeptics' Method of Doubt to strip away everything that could possibly be subject to doubt. In so doing, Descartes likely jettisons true beliefs along with the false ones. However, if it turns out that there is something that is beyond doubt, something that is indubitable, then he will have established a foundation on which to reclaim discarded beliefs and to build new ones.

By appropriating the Skeptics' method, Descartes sets up the ultimate argument against them in the only way possible. If employing doubt, Descartes comes to discover an indubitable proposition, then the Skeptics, who hold that no such proposition exists, will be refuted. Descartes sets about to strip away false beliefs and explore the possibility of the existence of some indubitable proposition by structuring his own version of the Method of Doubt into three stages, each more devastating than the last. Ultimately, Descartes employs a radical skepticism that is even more virulent than the staunchest skeptic.

Stage one of the Method of Doubt is a fairly simple and straightforward observation. Many times, our senses deceive us. For example, when one looks out from the beach at a blue lake, the water appears blue. However, if one took a glass of water from the lake, it will not be blue. Or, in another way, one of the most common experiences is that of seeing an old friend from across a long distance only to recognize that it was not even a person we knew upon coming closer. So, simply put, our senses, at least on matters of people and objects far away, deceive us.

But many of the things our senses communicate to us are not about matters far away. Many, if not most, are about objects and people that are close by. Surely the confidence in the veracity of our senses would be high. Descartes recognizes this himself. He writes, "But does it not seem as if some things presented by our senses are beyond doubt? ... Are these not my hands? Isn't this my body? To deny these, would I not be called insane, possessed of ill spirits like those who claim royalty when they are peasants or that claim they are cucumbers?"

This brings us to the second stage of the Cartesian Method of Doubt, the Dream Hypothesis. Consider, Descartes seems to say, how often dreams are so real that it is hard to discriminate between whether the dream was about something real or just a dream. Descartes points out that, "For example, I sit here before the fire. ... I have dreamt that I sat here before the fire, in circumstances exactly as these are. Yet, in those moments, I was in fact in bed asleep. I hold up my hand, and I see my hand before my eyes and I have had exactly the same perceptions of my hand when I was asleep."

One common objection is that most dreams are quite fantastical. Indeed, most are completely unreal that they would never be confused with the waking world. However, this is not the issue. For Descartes, even a sliver of doubt was sufficient to scuttle a claim to indubitability. It is not important that every dream seem real, but only that one dream seem so very real. If even one dream has had that quality, then it is in principle impossible to rule out the possibility that this moment, real though it may seem to our senses, is another instance of such a dream.

Surely casting doubt upon the senses would be sufficient doubt to employ for pursuing Descartes' mission. Yet, these first two aspects – recognizing the lack of reliability of the senses with regard to far off things and the Dream Hypothesis casting doubt on all the senses, even of those things close at hand – are only the beginning. The most radical element of Descartes' Method of Doubt is yet to come.

Suppose there exists some evil genius or evil demon, perhaps even God, is practicing deception on him. If, indeed, some being of infinite powers set its mind to toying with us such that no sense perception or any inference from a sense perception were true, would there even be confidence in the existence of an external world. The only things that may exist is the Demon and Descartes; or, by extension, the individual with whom the Demon is practicing deception.

At this point, the three-fold Method of Doubt has called into doubt all those things that can be doubted. Descartes has employed a doubt even more radical than the most skeptical of the skeptics. As the *First Meditation* closes, it is an open question whether anything can survive the onslaught of Cartesian doubt.

Guided Reading Questions

1. What are Descartes' purposes for writing the Meditations?
2. What is Descartes seeking?
3. What must he put away to find it?
4. What is the method he feels will be useful in his quest?
5. What sort of things can be doubted? Do you agree? Why or why not?
6. What does the Dream Hypothesis call into doubt?
7. What does the Evil Demon Hypothesis call into doubt?

Logic Blurb
The Fallacy of Opposition

One of the most common arguments that surfaces during the midst of acrimonious partisan debate is the fallacious *argument from opposition*, or Fallacy of Opposition. It is a reasonably straightforward argument and its flaws are quickly noted. Nevertheless, it continues to rear its head.

The Fallacy of Opposition is akin, in some ways, to the *ad hominem* and *appeal to emotion* arguments that will be discussed later. Simply put, suppose that Kenny and Nicole do not like each other at all. Forced by fate to be in the same class together, they almost delight in taking opposing views. Thus, if Kenny said, "The sky is blue," Nicole would argue that it is not, simply because she holds the view that if Kenny believes it, then it cannot be so. Thus, the argument from opposition suggests that our opponents, whatever position they actually hold, can never be right. Obviously, this is a fallacy because, much to our chagrin, there are times when our opponents are, in fact, right. Although, hopefully not very often.

Section 12.2: Descartes and the Nature of the Mind

Second Meditation - The Nature of the Human Mind

In yesterday's mediation, I was so full of doubt that those doubts persist into today. Further, I have not discerned a rational by which I can answer those doubts. It is as if I am in deep and turbulent water and cannot find a firm place to put down my feet. However, I shall continue the effort and pursue the course from yesterday to its end. I shall discard any notion about which it is possible to have any doubt at all. Like Archimedes who from a single established point as fulcrum could move the world, so, too, I shall demand at least one immovable place from which to find that which is certain. Where might that point be? Could it be that there is no such place, that nothing is certain?

Perhaps there is something certain. After all, is there not a God who causes the idea of God in my mind? Can I assume this, however? Could it not be so that I myself have created this idea in my mind? So, what of me? Surely I exist? However, yesterday, did I not deny the senses, the body, and even the possible existence of the external world? Didn't I suppose that there was perhaps a being of such great power and malignancy who always used the greatest cunning to deceive me? Let it be so. Indeed, let him deceive me as much as he wants, indeed, as much as it is possible for him to deceive me. Even then, he can not cause it to be the case that I do not exist. If I am deceived, then it must be the case, without a single doubt, that I exist. [*cogito ergo sum*] I am, I exist, is a necessarily true proposition.

But, if I exist, I am confronted with the question of what it is that I am. Before I began these meditations, I concluded that I was a human being. What is that? Perhaps a rational animal? I cannot say this because I would then have to be able to say what it is to be an animal – and this I have not yet discerned. What, too, is meant by *rational*? Each of these questions would lead to even more difficult ones. Then, I thought I had hands, arms, all of the things that comprise the body. A *body* is something that takes up space, occupies a particular position, and fills that place such that nothing else can coexist there with it. A body is that which can be touched, seen, heard, tasted and/or smelled (*tactu, visu, auditu, gustu, vel odoratue percipi*).

Since I can suppose that there is a deceiver of great and diabolical power using everything at his disposal to deceive me, is it possible for me to say that I have any of these properties that attach to bodies (taste, touch, etc.)? It certainly seems that none of them are necessarily parts of me.

So, what is it that I am? I am a thing that thinks (*res cogitans*). And what is that? A thing that thinks is a thing that imagines, doubts, affirms, denies, and perceives. It is clear that the one that doubts is in fact me. To add anything else would be superfluous to being more precise than this. Thus, with clarity and distinctness, I know the answer to the question, "what am I?" I am a thing that thinks.

If this is so, I should free the mind to consider again those things that I discarded before – those things that appear to me through the senses. To begin, I will think on those things that seem easiest – the bodies touched and seen. Suppose I have a piece of wax. It seems to have sweetness from the honey (as it is recently from the hive), it has a particular odor, size, shape, all those things that the senses portray to me. However, suppose I take the piece of wax and hold it over a flame. Soon enough, there is no smell – it has evaporated, the smell has been altered, so, too, the color, shape, and indeed all those sensible qualities. Continuing to hold it to the fire, the wax even changes from solid to liquid and becomes too hot to hold. Everything sensible about the wax has changed and yet it remains the same wax. Of this there can be no doubt. So, what was/is the piece of wax? It was not the smell of flowers nor the sweet taste nor the shade nor the shape of the comb. To be precise, if we remove all those things about the wax that are changeable, then we will know the essence of the wax. Nothing, then, is left save that it takes up space (*extension*), is flexible, is changeable. But, are flexibility or mutability essential to wax. Indeed, one can imagine all manner of changes to shape and size and flexibility and still think it is the same bit of wax, whether it be a square, a triangle, or some other figure into which I have molded it. As I think about the wax, I come to see that the essence of the wax can be perceived only by the mind and not the senses. To perceive the essence of the wax is not to experience its color or taste or shape or through any faculty of imagination the many colors, tastes, or shapes into which the wax could be made. Rather it is solely through the grasp of the mind (*inspectio*) – though this may be obscure and confused (*imperfecta esse potest et confusa*) as it was at the first quite clear and distinct (*clara et distincta*) as it is now.

If I consider the wax thus, stripped as it were of all its external aspects, then certainty may obtain. While I may still have mistakes (*ineptum*) in my thinking, it is completely clear that I am absolutely incapable of perceiving it at all without a human mind. If I think the wax exists because I can touch it, then it follows that I exist. If there is any other cause – my imagination, or whatever – that convinces me that the wax exists, then the same conclusion obtains. And to the extent this is true about wax, it is true of all other things that are outside of me.

So, I have returned to the conclusion held previously – that bodies are not understood by the senses but only by the mind (*solo intellectu percipi*). However, it is difficult to replace long held opinions, false though they may be, with new knowledge. Thus, I must meditate upon this conclusion at length and so reshape my memory that I may pursue this course further.

~

Having finished his *First Meditation* the previous day, Descartes returns to the Method of Doubt. Descartes has followed the skeptic's path to the brink itself – everything that can be doubted has been. Indeed, it is an open question whether or not doubting everything that can be doubted is equivalent to doubting everything. If it is, then the Skeptics, whom Descartes wants to refute, are right. If not, if there is something that it is impossible to doubt, then Descartes has accomplished at least one of his objectives for the *Meditations* – namely the refutation of the Skeptics.

The Method of Doubt has allowed Descartes to strip away all ideas that have even a possibility of doubt. Thoughts about colors and sounds, thoughts about all sense perceptions, even thoughts about the existence of an external world have all been cast aside. The terrain has been cleared for rebuilding a system of knowledge, but first, Descartes must discover if there is anything that has survived the radical application of doubt that he has employed. Descartes first supposes that God, as the source of ideas, must be certain. But, he then abandons this because, even though he had exempted God as a deceiver, an evil, manipulative genius in the Evil Demon portion of the Method of Doubt, he recognizes that this was arbitrary. Thus, it is not impossible that God could be deceiving him.

This recognition, that even God could be deceiving him, however, leads Descartes to discover the first thing that must be certain and without doubt. Suppose Descartes is being deceived; indeed, suppose he is being so deceived that he has been led to think that he is part of a world in which there are people and colors and sounds and all the rest when all that truly exists is Descartes himself and whatever evil power is deceiving him. No matter how badly Descartes is being deceived, it must be the case that Descartes himself exists. In order for some person to be deceived, he or she must exist. It is clearly impossible to deceive someone who does not exist. Thus, Descartes confidently exclaims, "Indeed, let him deceive me as much as he wants, indeed, as much as it is possible for him to deceive me. Even then, he cannot cause it to be the case that I do not exist. If I am deceived, then it must be the case, without a single doubt, that I exist." And, thus, the first certainty has been established (and in so doing, the Skeptics have been refuted). Descartes exists. His proclamation of his existence is perhaps one of the most famous statements in all of philosophy – I think, therefore, I am; or in Latin, *cogito ergo sum*.

Descartes has only begun to rebuild that which has been eliminated by the Method of Doubt. Having established that he exists, Descartes now sees the next questions that must be answered. If he exists, what is it that he is? This is fairly clear and fairly straightforward. Since he is a thing that can be deceived, and since being deceived is a kind of thinking, then Descartes must be a thinking thing. The name given to thinking things is "mind." Hence, Descartes exists and is a mind. On the basis of this, Descartes concludes that there is at least one substance in the universe; Mind. However, even if Descartes senses are deceptive and all that exists is Descartes and the deceiver, there appear to him to be other objects in the world, things that do not think at all; things like chairs and tables and trees. These objects, should they exist, take up space (that is, they have *extension*) and do not think. Thus, if they exist at all, they must be wholly different from minds since minds think. Thus, a second substance can be conceived – namely, Body. The substance, Body, though not demonstrated to exist yet, must be an extended, non-thinking thing. Since Descartes is a mind, Mind can be conceived as a thinking, non-extended thing. Thus, Descartes can conclude that he exists, that he is a mind, and that he is not a body.

By showing that he is a mind and not a body, Descartes has shown that the two fundamental substances that comprise the existent things of the universe are distinct. There are minds and minds are completely different from bodies. Given this, Descartes has achieved yet another of his purposes; namely that minds and bodies are distinct. To give an example of this, Descartes employs one of his most famous examples. Consider, he says, a piece of wax. The wax seems to have all manner of properties – it is a particular size and shape, it is sweet, it has a particular color and odor. However, if the wax is heated, it melts, its shape changes, its color changes, it ceases to be sweet or to have an odor. Rather, it becomes different in all of its particular qualities, except that it continues to take up space, albeit in a different form than previously. If we then ask, "What is the piece of wax?" we are asking what its essential property is. It is clear that it is not color or shape or taste or smell that comprise the essence of the wax. Indeed, the only thing that remains unchanged is that it continues to have extension. Thus, the essential property of wax is Body, an extended, non-thinking Substance. This conclusion is not achieved through the function of sense perception – sense merely perceives first one thing with several properties (sweet, golden, etc.) and then another thing (tasteless, white, etc.). There is no reason, obvious to sense perception, that there is only one thing rather than two. Only the mind can apprehend that the perceived properties are separate from the thing itself, that it is wax regardless of its taste or its color or its smell. Now, this mental apprehension may not be exact; after all, it is still a matter of reflecting on sensory input which is naturally confused and obscure. However, the existence of bodies, separate from the perceived qualities, is now clear and distinct to the mind.

Within this meditation are the first, nascent threads that will eventually become Descartes' Theory of Truth; a theory that will be much more fully developed in the *Third* and *Fourth Meditations*. However, to lay the groundwork for that theory, it is important to look again at the first bit of certain knowledge that Descartes acquires. Thus, we return to the *Cogito*.

There is some disagreement in the scholarship of Modern Philosophy concerning the structure of the *Cogito*. It is fairly clear that at times, Descartes uses the *Cogito* as if it were an argument; and it is obviously in argument form as it is presented here. I think, therefore, I am. However, there are at least three possible structures that have been proposed for this most famous of Descartes's sayings. Each is important for work that Descartes does later in the *Meditations*, so it is safe to conclude that he at least thinks that all three of these forms are appropriate.

The first form, and perhaps the one most closely tied to his Theory of Truth, is the Direct Intuition Form. A direct intuition is like a flash of insight; an "ah ha" or "Eureka" moment that brings with it such absolute clarity that there is no way doubt could encroach upon it. It seems this is the way in which Descartes conceives of the *Cogito*, at least at the outset of the *Second Meditation*. As he ponders the possibility of being in the hands of a devious and deceitful power intent only on tormenting him with illusions and chimeras, it dawns on Descartes that he must exist. Like a lightbulb inside his head suddenly coming on, Descartes sees that he must exist in order to be deceived. In one fell swoop, he instantaneously intuits that "I think, therefore, I am!" There is such clarity and distinctiveness to the idea that it is impossible to doubt it. That clarity and distinctiveness that is characteristic of the direct intuition is the standard by which Descartes will judge other ideas to determine whether they, too, are beyond doubt. Now that he has discovered one piece of certainty, and the character of that certainty is clarity and distinctness as opposed to obscurity and confusion, he will apply the test of that character to other ideas. If they, too, are clear and distinct, then they will be the same kind of idea as the *Cogito*, and thus must also be beyond doubt.

Before Descartes can develop this notion into a full-blown Theory of Truth, he must first, he thinks, show that God exists and is not deceiving him. However, to do that, he must explore other forms of the *Cogito* and from them, glean the logical forms that will allow him to argue for the existence of God in the *Third Meditation*. This brings us to the second form of the *Cogito* and the first form that is actually an argument form. The second form of the *Cogito* is the Simple Inference. A simple inference is called "simple," not because it is easy or because it is unimportant or trivial. Rather, a simple inference is called "simple" because it has only one premise and that one premise entails the conclusion. In the case of reading the *Cogito* as a simple inference, the premise is "I think." From this premise, the conclusion follows: "Therefore, I am." Thus, given the indubitability of the statement, "I think, therefore, I am," the simple inference form of argument is one that Descartes can use in other places under similar circumstances.

While the direct intuition and the simple inference are each powerful in their own rights, they do not carry with them all that Descartes will need. Instead, Descartes needs to construct from this insight an analogue to the Aristotelian syllogism that will allow him to explore much more complex systems of premises and conclusions on the way to showing the existence of God and rebuilding his knowledge from the ground up. To see how that might be done, we can look at the *Cogito* as a complex inference. By "complex" here, we mean only that it has more than one premise, and therefore is not simple. The complex inference form of the *Cogito* needs another premise that is not found immediately in the *Cogito* itself. However, the additional premise is a formal one and therefore not a matter of difficulty for the proof itself. The complex inference form of the *Cogito* goes like this:

Major Premise: Thinking requires a thinker. (supplied formal premise)
Minor Premise: Descartes thinks.

Conclusion: Therefore, Descartes exists.

In this way, we see that the *Cogito* can fit into the *modus ponens* form of the Aristotelian syllogism. Since this is the case, Descartes must have available to him the full power of Aristotelian logic, as the *modus ponens* form is logically equivalent to the *modus tollens* form and from there can be transformed into all the required complex inference forms of formal logic. Having shown that the mind and the body are distinct, laid a nascent foundation for a Theory of Truth (and with it, perhaps, a foundation for science), refuted the Skeptics, Descartes is ready to move to a much larger project; namely, the demonstration of the existence of God.

Guided Reading Questions:

1. Why does Descartes think he exists even if he is being deceived?
2. What does Descartes discover that he is not?
3. What is Descartes?
4. According to Descartes, what things are true?

Logic Blurb
The Appeal to Authority

Two friends were arguing over the outcome of a presidential election. George insisted that Thomas Dewey would be taking the oath of office as the new President of the United States. Al was incredulous. How could George believe such a thing? To support his own claim, George brandished a copy of the Chicago Tribune which trumpeted the headline "Dewey Wins." Al was not persuaded, continuing to believe that Harry Truman had pulled out a narrow win.

Section 12.2: Descartes and the Nature of the Mind

George's argument is a good example of an *appeal to authority* and indicates one of the inherent dangers in such an approach. Even if one appeals to a real authority, that voice could well be wrong. The *appeal to authority* is often a rhetorically convincing argument simply because it marshals to its cause a person or entity (e.g., a newspaper) that is respected, well-known, and/or personally compelling. It is this persuasive power that makes the appeal to authority so appealing. However it is fraught with difficulty, especially if one's aim is to get at the truth rather than merely to persuade one's interlocutors. The Socratic questioning of all of those with a reputation for wisdom underscores this point. In his questioning, it became clear that those questioned were not authoritative at all because despite their reputation, they were unable to answer the important questions. This is a straightforward demonstration of the perils of the appeal to authority. If the authority appealed to is in error, then the argument fails straightaway. Being thought an authority in no way entails true beliefs about matters even within one's supposed realm of expertise.

A further difficulty with appeals to authority is not necessarily widely recognized. This difficulty becomes perhaps most apparent in religious debate; but it is by no means limited to this realm. Within religious arguments, appeal is often made to the sacred text or texts of one's tradition. This, however, illustrates the difficulty. Suppose one's interlocutor does not belong to the tradition. Suppose he/she belongs to a different one entirely, one with its own sacred text. How might one establish the authoritative standpoint of one's own text over against the other? Simply put, without begging the question or being circular, it is impossible. Thus, however persuasive an appeal to authority might be, critically it is little more than a rhetorical flourish and inadequate for serious philosophical inquiry.

Section 12.3: Descartes and the Existence of God

Third Meditation – The Existence of God

I shall now ignore all my senses and even wipe away from my mind all the images of bodies. At the very least, I shall consider all these images illusory. Having done this, I shall think and focus closely upon myself to improve my understanding of my nature. I, myself, am a thing that thinks *(Ego sum res cogitans)*. This much is clear. And, this is about all that I know. However, I wish to know much more, about not only myself but about whether there exists anything at all further. So, I ask myself, what conditions must some perception meet in order for me to accept it as certain, as true. The condition I take as the standard is that anything clearly and distinctly perceived [*by the mind*] is true *(omne esse verum, quòd valde clare et distincte percipio)*.

Before, however, I have thought things true and been convinced of their certainty only to have them proven false. What sorts of things were these? These were all the objects that I perceived by means of my senses – earth, sky, stars, etc. But, I know that these are doubtful because I may very well possess a nature that is susceptible to deception. While I have no particular reason to suppose that God is deceiving me (in fact, I do not yet even know if such a Being exists), the basis of my doubt rests completely on the quite tenuous foundation of this small metaphysical possibility. Thus, I must discern whether or not God exists and then, further, whether or not God has a nature that could practice deception – that is, does God exist and is God a deceiver. Without knowing the answer to these questions, any certainty beyond what I already possess is likely impossible to obtain.

All of my ideas seem to spring from one of three sources – they are innate, or adventitious, or created by me. Since so many of the ideas presented to me clearly originate from beyond me – noises, light, heat – I might be led to suppose that all ideas are of the adventitious sort.

Without my consent, certain ideas press upon me – I feel heat, for example. This idea arises from a sensation that is not caused by me whatsoever. It seems to make sense that that which is represented to me represents its own character rather than that of something else.

At the same time, when I investigate whether this reason carries force of reason to convince me, I understand that there is simply a force that drives me to suppose that an idea must resemble the object of that idea in some meaningful way. This is not the natural light of reason that gives me this connection. And these are quite different – the force of nature and the natural light of reason. The former is already called into doubt. The latter is the way in which truth and falsity are discerned. If this be the case, it seems clear that it is, then it is also the case that I have no reason to suppose such a relationship between idea and external object. Further, I have reason to suppose that the relationship indeed does not obtain. Take the sun, for example. I have within myself two ideas of the sun and these two ideas are completely different. The first, and the one based on my sense perception, suggests to me that the sun is quite small. This idea is adventitious. The second idea is that the sun is many multitudes larger than the earth. This idea has its cause in astronomical foundations. Those foundations are derived from other ideas that exist within my mind. The natural light of reason leads me to understand that the first idea is not the product of the second, nor the second from the first.

If we then consider those notions that perhaps arise from myself, it seems quite clear that there are those that represent substances and those that represent qualities. It seems quite clear that the former are more real than the latter. Further, an idea like God (eternal, infinite, omniscient, omnipotent, unchanging, and intelligent creator of all things save God – *æternum, infinitum, omniscium, omniptentem, rerumque omnium, quæ præter ipsum sunt, creatorem intelligo*) certainly contains more reality than those ideas that exhibit finite substances.

One principle that is clear by the natural light is that within an efficient cause there must exist at least as much reality as there is within the effect. If this were not true, from where would the excess reality (that not received from the total and efficient cause) present in the effect come? Similarly, something that exists cannot be the effect of non-existence, and that which is less perfect cannot generate that which is more perfect.

I have many ideas. Some represent animals, some angels, some inanimate objects, and at least one that represents a God with all of the characteristics enumerated above. All of these ideas, save one, can be conceived as originating outside of me or from within me by the admixture of several other ideas. Nothing within these ideas is so great that I am incapable of conceiving its origination within my imagination. Indeed, when I investigate them, as I yesterday investigated the wax, I find little if anything about them that is clear and distinct.

Some, however, do seem to represent something clear and distinct. These, too, may have originated with me. For example, let us take a rock and suppose it to be a substance (or something capable of independent existence). While I am a thinking, non-extended thing, a rock takes up space and is thus extended and does not think. Between these two ideas – a thinking, non-extended thing and an extended, non-thinking thing – there is the height of difference. Each of these ideas, then, would seem to represent differing substances.

What of God? By God, I mean an intelligent substance (a mind), that is infinite, independent, omniscient, omnipotent, and the cause of everything that exists. (*Dei nomine intelligo substantiam quandan infinitam, independentem, summe intelligentem, summe potentem, et a quâ tum ego ipse, tum aliud omne, si quid aliud extat, quodcumque extat, est creatum.*) However, these qualities are so great that the more I meditate upon them, the more I understand that the idea whose qualities these are could not have originated within me or within any finite source. I could not have such an idea without it being implanted within me from something of at least as much reality as the idea possesses. It is thus the only conclusion that God exists and exists necessarily.

Indeed, were my knowledge to grow and expand as rapidly as possible, it seems scarcely likely that it could ever become infinite itself. However, I do in fact conceive God as infinite – so perfect that no improvement can be made. Since the object of an idea cannot be generated by something that is lesser, and indeed, only potential, then it must be concluded that this infinite God exists.

How, then, do I come to have this idea. It is not generated by my senses nor from within my imagination. The conclusion that the idea of God must therefore be innate follows, just as the idea of myself. The argument is essentially this – I am not the kind of thing that could conceive the idea of God; yet that idea exists in my mind. Thus, this God, who possesses all these characteristics that I perceive the idea to have, must likewise exist. In this light, it is clear that such a being could not possibly be a deceiver or evil in any way. Thus, by the natural light, I perceive that all deception, all falsehood, all doubtfulness must arise from some defect.

~

Having employed radical skeptical doubt to strip away false beliefs and having concluded that he indeed exists in the previous two *Meditations*, Descartes turns to the daunting task of proving the existence of God in the *Third*. Prior to Descartes, there were many attempts to prove the existence of God, the most original and philosophically interesting of which have been explored in detail earlier in this text. St. Anselm's rationalistic proof, beginning with a definition and proceeding apace to deduce from that definition and other accepted postulates and axioms that God must exist, may at first seem to be most compatible with Descartes' own philosophical leanings. As rationalists, it would not seem odd that their separate proofs might have numerous points of similarity. However, one difference is striking, in part because it points to an affinity between Descartes' proof and the Five Ways of St. Thomas.

St. Thomas' Five Ways, a hallmark of the empiricist method of approaching philosophical questions, would seem to be as different from Descartes' proof as it is from St. Anselm's. Yet, at first glance, Descartes' proof in the *Third Meditation*, would seem quite similar to St. Thomas' Proof from Efficient Cause. Descartes proof, like the Proof from Efficient Cause, is a *causal* proof; that is, it is a notion of "cause and effect" that is the engine that drives them both. However, while they seem to have a similar view of "cause and effect"; i.e., every effect has a cause, this is about all the two have in common. St. Thomas' proof is exemplary of the empiricist tradition, beginning with observations and reasoning from the concrete and particular toward the more abstract and general. This avenue is not open for Descartes thanks to the radical skepticism of the Method of Doubt. All Descartes has available to him are ideas, the things that populate the mind. In his introspective examination of the cause of these ideas, Descartes' proof is exemplary of his own rationalist tradition. While his rationalist approach aligns his proof with that of St. Anselm, the points of contact between Descartes and St. Thomas are of some philosophical interest. Again, Descartes walks a middle line between those philosophical positions that have been staked out before, bearing some resemblance to each, but at the same time, presenting a completely novel approach. Descartes's proof is truly original; different in substantive ways from all of the proofs of God that have preceded it.

Rather than beginning with a definition as St. Anselm does, Descartes begins with the idea of God that he finds within his mind. Here we encounter the first striking difference between St. Anselm and Descartes' proofs. St. Anselm's "that-than-which-a-greater-cannot-be-conceived" is a very spare definition, formal, and empty of all content. Because of this, the definition is starkly different from traditional conceptions of God. On the other hand, Descartes' idea of God is much closer to that traditional notion. As Descartes surveys the ideas that are before his mind, he notes that the idea of God is an idea of a being who is "an intelligent substance (a mind), that is infinite, independent, omniscient, omnipotent, and the cause of everything that exists." From this idea, Descartes does not then deduce what must follow from it, as St. Anselm does. Rather, Descartes works in the other direction. He asks himself where he possibly could have gotten this idea; that is, how the idea came to be in his mind.

To Descartes, it seems as if there are three possibilities for the origin of the idea of God that he has. The idea could be *adventitious*, it could be *imaginative*, or it could be *innate*. An *adventitious* idea is an idea that one receives from somewhere outside of oneself. For example, suppose John wakes up one morning after having missed the outcome of the baseball game the night before. When he arrives at work, he asks Jane how the game came out. She tells him that their favorite team had won by a score of 4-2 in 12 innings. At this point, John has the idea within his mind that his favorite team won the game the preceding evening by a score of 4-2. Before Jane told him this, he did not have this idea. Hence, the idea came from Jane and entered his mind, that is, it has ventured out from one source (literally *ad-venture*) to arrive in a second. Thus, Descartes supposes that the idea of God could be similar. It could be that the idea is adventitious and that he received the idea from some other person.

This does not settle the question however. The idea could be *imaginative*, as well. An imaginative idea is an idea that is created by, for example, John himself. Of the three sorts of ideas, this is probably the easiest to grasp as it is both fairly common and carries a name that is familiar to most. While the experience of *adventitious* ideas is reasonably common, the name *adventitious* is not. However, the creative process of imagination is easily as common and the name *imagination* is common in usage. Imaginative ideas are simply those that are made up, that are created by the individual himself. These ideas result in inventions, innovations, and advancements of all sorts. The light bulb, the car, and the computer are all the fruits of particularly vibrant imaginations. Descartes allows the possibility that the idea of God could be similar to imaginative ideas of this sort, the product of a very fruitful mind.

It seems that this would exhaust all of the obvious possibilities. After all, to suppose that ideas are created within the human mind and that others come from outside the mind would seem to account for all of the ideas possessed within the human mind. Descartes leaves open the possibility that there might be a third sort of idea, an *innate* idea. This seems fantastical on its face. An *innate* idea is an idea that is within the mind but does not come from outside the mind nor is it created by the mind. Rather, an innate idea is part of the structure of the mind itself. A mind possesses an innate idea, if it does, simply in virtue of being a mind. "Innate" means in-born or part of nature. That is, the innate idea is part of the very nature, the very architecture of the mind. In reality, this is somewhat similar to the Platonic notion of Forms, all of which are innate and recalled or recollected over time and through diligent reflection. Descartes does not have the stronger Platonic view that all true ideas are innate; rather, Descartes simply leaves open the possibility that some ideas are innate. Thus, at the outset of the proof for the existence of God, Descartes recognizes that within his mind there is an idea of God and that that idea could have originated in three ways; that is, it could be *adventitious*, it could be *imaginative*, and it could be *innate*.

Before turning to the proof itself, it is important to take note of a background assumption that is unspecified at the outset of the proof, but which is present and at times utilized within it. This principle we will call the *Law of Conservation of Ontology*. The Law of Conservation of Ontology is straightforward.

> Law of Conservation of Ontology (LCO): There can be no more reality in the effect than was present in the cause.

The thrust of this can perhaps best be seen in example. Suppose Luis has a two-litre bottle of water. It will be impossible for Luis to get more than two litres from the bottle. He can easily get less simply by pouring only a bit of water from it, but he cannot get more. The bottle cannot produce more water than it can hold. Similarly, if some thing, A, causes another, B, then B can have, *at most*, the same amount of reality that A has; though it is also possible for it to have less. Let us look at another example. Luis and Inola have a baby girl, Christina. Clearly, they are the cause of Christina. Christina is no more real than her parents, and she is no less real than her parents. It would be impossible for her to be more real, and it would be counterintuitive to view her as less real. Instead, Christina and her parents possess the same ontological status. Having established that Descartes has an idea of God, that there are three possible originations of that idea, and that the idea of God can have no more reality than its cause, Descartes is ready to turn to the proof. To this point, the proof can be formalized in the following way.

Statement	Justification
1. There exists an idea of God (an infinite, independent, omniscient, omnipotent mind that is the cause of everything that exists).	1. Idea of "God"
2. The cause of the idea of God must have at least as much reality as the idea itself.	2. LCO, Efficient Cause
3. The idea of God must be *imaginative, adventitious*, or *innate*.	3. Exhaustive "or"

Descartes' proof proceeds then by process of elimination. Let us consider first whether the idea of God could be imaginative. For the idea of God to be imaginative, it must have been created by Descartes within his own mind. For this to be the case, Descartes must be able to conceive of a being who possesses all the qualities possessed in the idea – that is, a being that is infinite, independent, omniscient, omnipotent and the creator of all. Thus, Descartes, a finite being with a finite mind, must originate an infinite idea of infinite being. This is a straightforward violation of the Law of Conservation of Ontology (LCO) because a finite entity (Descartes) is said to have created an infinite entity (the idea of God). As the finite cannot create the infinite, then it is not possible that the idea of God is imaginative. We can add this result to our formal proof as follows.

4. Suppose the idea of God is *imaginative*.	4. Assumption
5. Therefore, a finite being must have created an infinite entity.	5. Implication of 4
6. But, this is a violation of the Ontological Causal Principle	6. LCO
7. Therefore, the idea of God is not *imaginative*.	7. 4-6

Since the idea of God cannot be imaginative, perhaps it is *adventitious*. For the idea of God to be adventitious, it must be that Descartes received the idea

Section 12.3: Descartes and the Existence of God

from some other person, or from some other feature of the natural world. For example, in St. Thomas's proofs, he begins with observations of that natural world and reasons, ultimately, that God must be the cause of that world. Other, more romantic thinkers, have argued that by looking upon the beauty of the world, that the world itself communicates the existence of God. In all of these cases, the idea of God that Descartes has within his mind would be an adventitious idea, created by some feature of the finite, natural world and communicated to Descartes. Here, however, we encounter the same problem encountered with the supposition that the idea of God was an *imaginative* idea. If the idea of God is *adventitious* and, as such, created by some person or object and communicated to Descartes, then an infinite idea has once again been created by something finite. Once again, this disparity of ontological status is impossible; that which is finite cannot create that which is infinite. Therefore, the idea of God cannot be an *adventitious* idea. This can be formalized as follows.

8. Suppose the idea of God is *adventitious*.	8. Assumption
9. Therefore, a finite being must have created an infinite entity.	9. Implication of 8
10. But, this is a violation of the Ontological Causal Principle	10. LCO
11. Therefore, the idea of God is not *adventitious*.	11. 8-10

So, since it has been shown that the idea of God cannot be *imaginative* nor can it be *adventitious*, then it must be the case that the idea of God is *innate*, since these are the only possibilities for the origin of the idea itself. Though at the outset there was some question whether or not *innate* ideas were even plausible, it turns out that each of the other kinds of idea simply cannot carry the weight of the idea of God. Since there are but three possible options for the kind of idea that the idea of God is, and since it cannot be either of the first two (*imaginative, adventitious*), then it must be, by process of elimination, the third (*innate*). Upon reflection on the idea of God, Descartes asks what sort of being could be the cause of the implantation of the idea of God within his mind. Given the Law of Conservation of Ontology, only a being that is an infinite, independent, omniscient, omnipotent, and creative mind. Such a being is what is meant when the word "God" is used. Since such a being must exist in order to cause the idea of God in Descartes' mind, then God must exist. The last part of the proof is formalized as such.

12. Therefore, the idea of God must be *innate*.	12. Elimination
13. Only an infinite, independent, omniscient, omnipotent mind could cause the idea of an infinite, independent, omniscient, omnipotent mind.	13. LCO

14. Since Descartes has the *innate* idea of an infinite, independent, omniscient, omnipotent mind, such a being must have caused Descartes to have it.	14. LCO, Efficient Cause
15. Therefore, God must exist in order for Descartes to have the idea of God that he has.	15. Efficient Cause

Having concluded that God exists and is not a deceiver, Descartes can continue, in the next *Meditation*, to develop the theory of truth that will undergird much of his reconstruction of the ideas that he cast aside through the Method of Doubt. He will return to the proof of the existence of God briefly in the *Fifth Meditation*, but this proof suffices, on Descartes' view, to establish that foundation for the certainty in the sciences that he has been seeking. Thus, as the *Third Meditation* closes, Descartes has refuted the Skeptics, shown that the mind and body are distinct, demonstrated the existence of God, and established a foundation for the sciences.

Before we turn to Descartes' development of his theory of truth and, with it, his theory of knowledge, it is first important that we revisit the proof as we have done with St. Anselm and St. Thomas before. The first of the three criticisms that seem most problematic for Descartes is that he makes an errant assumption at the outset of the proof that ultimately dooms it. Simply put, Descartes never really questions whether the idea that he has of God is an accurate reflection of the object of that idea. That assumption is, in some ways, a very understandable one given his rationalist method. However, the confident conclusion that the idea within the mind accurately represents an object outside the mind is predicated on both the success of the proof and the underlying assumption that the world of ideas represent objects in the actual world. Descartes has acknowledged the weakness of this assumption himself with his Method of Doubt. However, the assumption is so deeply ingrained within the methodological approach of rationalism that it is understandable that Descartes would fail to excise it completely; understandable, but nevertheless a difficulty for his project.

The second criticism of Descartes's Causal Proof is an adaptation of Hume's critique of St. Thomas's Proof From Design. Descartes truly has no idea of infinity or of omnipotency, only of much larger than he and much more powerful than he. If it is impossible for the finite mind to create an infinite idea, then it is similarly impossible for that same finite mind to comprehend what is meant by an infinite idea. Descartes reasons from the existence of his finite mind to the existence of an infinite mind, but finitude and infinity are different not simply in degree, but in kind. That is, they are fundamentally different things. Thus, the best Descartes could conclude from the starting point of his own finitude is some very large, potentially immensely powerful being, but it would be impossible to conclude that the being is infinite. Thus, Descartes is mistaken about the content of his idea. He uses words like "omnipotent" when instead he means, albeit unconsciously, "immensely powerful."

For the third criticism, let us assume that the idea of God actually is an infinite one. Descartes' cause is still without aid. Underlying the proof is the assumption that a finite human mind cannot create an infinite idea. However, suppose that a teacher like Socrates approached a young man and asked him whether or not he could develop an infinite idea. When the young man said that he could not, suppose that Socrates asked him if he knew what the sum of $1 + 1$ was. "Sure, it would be 2," the young man would remark. Suppose, then, that Socrates further asked him the sum of $2 + 1$, and then, $3 + 1$, and so on. After establishing the progression of adding one to the sum of the preceding addition, Socrates could then ask whether or not there was some end of this arithmetic progression. Perhaps the young man would at first think that there is, but he would soon come to conclude that indeed, there was not. At this point, the young man has an idea whose object is an infinite series of the counting numbers. Now, whether or not he created this idea himself (an *imaginative* idea) or it was one he received from Socrates (an *adventitious* idea), it seems clear that the idea was not an *innate* one.

As the *Third Meditation* closes, Descartes has offered a proof for the existence of God, one which he takes to successfully meet the requirements of his objective stated in the full title of the *Meditations*. To develop this proof, he has first shown that he exists, that he is a mind and not a body, and that the skeptics who suppose that nothing can be known with certainty are wrong.

One of the most significant contributions to the practice of doing philosophy is Descartes' publication of the *Meditations*. Descartes recognized that his views would not be universally accepted and that it was possible that he had gotten some very important piece of the puzzle wrong. Thus, rather than simply assume that the *Meditations* were clear and irrefutable, he engaged some of the most thorough and respected philosophers of his day to read the material and offer their comments and objections. Several of them obliged. Rather than discard the objections as misguided, Descartes had them published right alongside the *Meditations* themselves, including with them a set of replies to the objections. So significant were some of the criticisms that Descartes took great pains to refer the objectors not to the first three *Meditations* where the views were initially developed, but to the latter three where Descartes can be seen as developing the views again and explaining them in greater detail. The genius of this approach is that it provides the reader with the feel of entering into a philosophic discussion with the great minds of the day and reminds the reader that philosophical questions are not generally settled in a matter of pages or days or conversations, but that they require serious engagement and a willingness to receive and thoughtfully address criticisms.

Certain objections that were raised to Descartes' work had to do with the notion of the separation of the mind and the body that is at the center of the work in the first three *Meditations*. The strongest of these objections was not made by one of the "professional" philosophers to whom Descartes submitted the *Meditations* for comment. Rather, the most direct and substantial critique of Descartes's metaphysical dualism was made by one of his correspondents, Princess Elisabeth of Bohemia. Her criticism of Descartes's work led, in some scholars' views, to a reworking of the *Sixth Meditation* in order to provide a response. In Section 12.5, we will address her view and Descartes's response; a response, incidentally that casts a different light entirely on the purposes of the *Meditations*.

Guided Reading Questions:
1. How does Descartes's idea of God differ from St. Anselm's definition of God?
2. What are the characteristics of God, on Descartes's view?
3. What are the possible causes of the idea of God?
4. How does Descartes argue that God must exist?

Logic Blurb
The Fallacy of Irrelevancy

Suppose two friends are having an argument. Alex and Mollie are arguing about whether or not they should fly to New York City or drive. Alex, who loves to drive, says that driving would be best. Mollie, who hates to drive, says flying would be better. Suppose, as a justification for the claim "We should drive," Alex says, "But, I like to eat sushi." On the face of it, this statement has no bearing on the matter at hand. The "reason" is no more convincing upon further review than it was at first blush. Alex has given a completely irrelevant reason to support his claim that they should drive.

It seems reasonably clear that Mollie would not be convinced of much of anything based on such a *non sequitur*. However, suppose the reason instead was something like, "But I like to drive." This, at least, is related to the topic at hand, and may very well convince Mollie to accept the claim that they should drive. However, it is not clear that the "I like to drive" claim has any more relevance to whether or not they actually *should* drive. All manner of reasons could be marshaled here – the cost of fling, the distance, the length of time of the two modes of transport, convenience, and perhaps others. However, the aesthetic desire3s of the two need not be considered relevant factors.

Let us consider a more controversial case. Fred says that the existence of God is to be rejected because a survey of some of the two-bit charlatans who claim divine inspiration as a method of bilking money from the easily persuaded or because of great atrocities committed by followers of a given religious faith. Even if we grant, as we must, that such atrocities, large and small, have been committed and that indeed, history is littered with them, they are all irrelevant to the question of the existence of God.

Arguments of that sort are notoriously compelling because they inspire emotional responses that are in keeping with the conclusion we are supposed to embrace. Risk, reward, and present personal likes and dislikes can all be compelling psychological reasons for rejecting or giving assent to some proposition or other. For this reason, the critical thinker will learn to separate the relevant reasons to hold a view from the irrelevant ones, no matter how rhetorically persuasive.

Similarly, suppose one took the opposite view and argued that God must necessarily exist and that believe in God was required because otherwise, the unbeliever would suffer eternal and untold torment. While this might seem quite a compelling case for belief – avoidance of suffering – it is, in actuality, neither a case for belief nor for existence. Since the belief would supervene on the existence of a particular sort of deity, then the promised torment is presumably an argument for existence. But, potential reward or punishment is wholly distinct from the matter of existence and so is irrelevant.

Section 12.4: Descartes and the Theory of Truth

Fourth Meditation: Truth and Falsehood

I now see how to move from the clear conclusion that God exists and contemplations of God to thoughts about the other things in the world. Firstly, I know it is not possible for God to deceive me because fallacies and deceptions are evidence of imperfections (which are foreign to God). They are signs of weakness and evil; qualities not found in God. Secondly, I recognize that a part of me is the faculty of making judgments concerning the true and the false. Since all my qualities I received from God, and because God will not deceive me, then it follows that it is possible that I have received nothing from God that will guide me into falsity (provided I employ it properly).

When I meditate only upon God, I find no causes of falsity or error. When I return to think about myself, I discover many errors (obnoxiously innumerable). If I question these two discoveries, I note that I have two notions – a real and positive (*realem et positivam*) idea of God and a negative idea of nothingness. I, then, exist between these infinitely distant notions; between God and nothingness (*inter Deum et nihil*); between existences and non-existence. Nothing within me that depends upon God leads me to error (*defectum*). However, since I participate also in nothingness, I am not surprised that I fall into error. Thus, error is not something infinite and real, possessing positive existence, but is simply an absence or a defect, not attributable to God. Since it be not required that God provide me with an infinite faculty of judging truth, but rather a contingent and finite one, then the source of deception arises not from God but as a consequence of my own finite faculty.

At the same time, error is not simply negative. It is an absence (*privatio*) of some knowledge that it can be said I should have. When focusing on myself and my errors more closely, I discover that those errors have two concurrent causes – the faculty of thought and the ability to think and choose voluntarily (or will). By thought or intellect, I mean the perception (*percipio*) of ideas about which I can make judgments. About this there is no error, precisely speaking. Though there are many objects that perhaps exist, if the idea of these ideas does not exist in me, it is not properly said to be a privation or something of which I am destitute (since these do not properly belong to my nature anyway). It is simply the case that I do not have these ideas.

If I regard again the faculty of thought, I discover that it is quite small and considerably limited. At the same time, I can conceive of an idea of another faculty that shares this nature (that is, thought) and that is much greater, even to the extent of infinity. Of the faculty of will, when I reflect on it, I note that it is not limited in anything like the same way, that in fact, it is quite large. The power inherent in this will is simply that we can either act or not act (say "yes" or say "no"; pursue or reject). These actions, which do not seem to be determined by any power external to our own will, but framed instead by our own thought is what freedom consists in. To have freedom is not to necessarily maintain an impartial relationship to those things between which I choose. In fact, the very fact of being lured by one, either because I clearly perceive truth and goodness in it, or because God implants this lure within me, suggests that this act is all the more free. Thus, divine grace and the natural light increase freedom rather than compromise it.

So, where do my errors come from, then? They have but a single cause. I do not restrain my will (it has a much greater scope than thought). The limits of my understanding are not those to which I control my will. Instead, my will pursues things that are beyond my thought, beyond my understanding. Since the will does not care of such things as the limits of thought, it stumbles into error, and thus, sin, because it does the false and not the true.

The only reason for error is privation. However, this does not mean that God consents to this. Error is not something that exists, it is not an object (if it were, God as the sole creator would be responsible as cause of error). However, there is no imperfection in God. From God, I have received the ability to choose or to refuse things, particularly those that are clearly and distinctly perceived. So, the imperfection lies with me – I misuse my freedom and I make all manner of judgments about things I perceive in confusion and obscurity. I have the ability to refrain from such judgments, to remain steadfast and never make judgments about anything that is not clearly and distinctly perceived.

Thus, provided I rein in my will and keep it within the bounds of my knowledge, and further that I make no judgments about those things not clearly and distinctly perceived, I can avoid deception. Every clear and distinct perception is indeed something and something must come from something and not nothing, then it can be understood that it comes from God. God could only be the cause of error if we were to make a considerable contradiction because God is perfect and infinitely so.

Fifth Meditation: The Essence of Material Things; Revisiting the Existence of God

Many questions remain. So far, I have discovered how to come to knowledge of the world. But, if I move from the thoughts about the idea of some thing and knowing that God exists, I have also discerned that everything that can be said to be something and not nothing depends on God (who does not deceive me). From this, I know that all things I clearly and distinctly perceive are not only true, but necessarily true. Nothing can be marshaled against me to cause me to doubt these truths now. Thus, my knowledge is certain. Further, this certainty persists to all those things I have demonstrated in other contexts (truths of geometry, for example).

So, I now see that all of science depends on knowledge of God. This is so because before I knew of the existence of God, I had no certainty about any other existent thing. Now that I have come to understand that God exists and is not a deceiver, I know also that I have within me the faculty of perfect knowledge as well.

By the time the *Third Meditation* closes, Descartes has already offered arguments in support of the four of the five purposes that he sets out for the *Meditations*. Since the proof for the fifth, the immortality of the soul, goes wanting in the *Meditations*, it might reasonably be asked of Descartes why in fact there are six *Meditations* rather than simply three. Whatever answer Descartes himself might give for this structure, it is clear that he revisits topics from the first three throughout the final three. The *Fourth Meditation* finds a further treatment of his theory of truth, along with elaborations that strengthen it as a foundation for the burgeoning New Science. The *Fifth Meditation* holds a second argument for the existence of God, one that, as it happens, depends in large measure on the proof that went before it in the *Third*. Finally, in the *Sixth Meditation*, Descartes attends to the problems that arise from the demonstration that the mind and body are distinct substances. At least some of his treatment of the Interaction Problem in the *Sixth* can be interpreted as an attempt to answer some of the critics from whom Descartes solicited responses to his work.

Descartes's Theory of Truth, the skeleton of which was developed in the *Second Meditation*, is an integral feature of his theory of knowledge and, in virtue of this, an integral piece of his foundation for the New Science. The aim of founding knowledge upon an immovable, Archimedean point was satisfied in the clarity and distinctiveness of the *cogito*. It is this sort of precision that Descartes demands of all knowledge. Thus, the relationship between certainty (and with it the rejection of Skepticism) and truth (and ultimately knowledge) is something like this. If some proposition, p, is certain, then it is true and if p is true, then it is certain. This biconditional relationship between certainty and truth makes clear the importance of divorcing the mind from the information gleaned from the senses. The senses, and all information derived from them, are subject to the radical skepticism inherent in the Method of Doubt Descartes employs in the *First Meditation* in order to strip away all of the false beliefs that he knew to be present within his mind. It is perhaps helpful to revisit the thrust of the Skeptical Challenge that Descartes sought to refute in order to see how it is that the Theory of Truth is here developed.

Let us use again the Justified True Belief model of knowledge as a way to analyze both the Skeptical Challenge and the Cartesian response. Whatever justification might amount to and whatever the nature of belief might be, the heart of the Skeptical Challenge is found in the rejection of the possibility of absolute or objective truth. If truth is necessary for knowledge and if certainty is necessary, at least, for truth, then if it is the case that certainty is beyond our grasp, then, so, too, knowledge will be as well. Since the skeptics would hold that certainty is impossible, it would follow directly, then, that knowledge is impossible as well. Thus, any refutation of the Skeptical Challenge must address this rejection of the possibility of certainty. So, when Descartes, in the *Cogito*, comes to the conclusion that "I am, I exist is *necessarily* true" (my emphasis), he argues that there is at least one proposition that is not only certain, but is a necessary, and not merely contingent, truth. Thus, from the establishment of a certain proposition, Descartes both accepts the equation of certainty with truth and argues that such a sort of truth is possible because at least one necessary truth exists. From this, he starts to reconstruct his knowledge base; a process we have discussed previously. What is important to note here is the nature of this sort of necessary truth.

All knowledge is *of* ideas. That is to say, the objects that populate the human mind are ideas rather than physical objects. One could imagine an idea to be a sort of representation, perhaps, of some physical object – thus, the idea of a particular tree is a representation of that tree within the mind. Now, there are different types of ideas that exist within the mind. This is a different claim than the one that begins the proof for the existence of God in the *Third Meditation*. There, Descartes is concerned with the causal chain that gives rise to the ideas that populate the mind. Here, Descartes is concerned with the sorts of ideas there are. So, for example, one might talk of ideas that are founded in sense perception. An example of such an idea might be the idea of a particular color or a particular tree. The idea of that color or that tree is not an abstract idea, as such, but an idea that purports to represent an immediate particular of our experience. However, as such ideas are inherently tied to sense perception, they immediately fall victim to the radical skepticism of the Method of Doubt. Since all of the information arising from the senses is "obscure and confused" (*Second Meditation*), then it is not possible that these ideas should be thought of as certain, or as clear and distinct. Thus, since they are not clear and distinct, or not certain, they cannot be conceived of as true.

If ideas derived directly from sense perception are stricken as competitors for truth, then it seems that mental perceptions must be the true ideas if there are to be any. Many philosophers would argue that the only sorts of mental perceptions that exist are those that have their origins in sense perception. These sorts of ideas might be more abstract, say the idea of Color or the idea of Tree. Such ideas are not identical with any particular color or any particular tree, but they are abstractions of those particulars. However, Descartes would argue that these sorts of ideas also fall victim to the Method of Doubt. Because they are derived, albeit abstractly, from sense perception, these mental perceptions that depend on sense perception will share in the confusion and obscurity that mark sense perception. As such, these ideas cannot be the bearers of truth either.

One might reasonably ask if there are any other ideas that the human mind might possess. It would seem that the only ideas that can convey the sort of certainty Descartes requires for truth would be ideas that are mental perceptions that do not depend on the senses. However, one might cast about for what sort of idea might be a mental perception entirely divorced from sense. Fortunately, Descartes has already shown one. The *cogito* is independent of sense perception, at least on Descartes's view. Having employed the Method of Doubt to its fullest extent, anything that is left over will surely be independent of the senses which have been so thoroughly discredited in the early stages of the Method. Thus, at least the *cogito*, a necessary truth, and thus a certainty or clear and distinct mental perception, stands as an example of an idea that is independent of sense perception. Having shown one idea to be certain: a clear and distinct mental perception (by which is meant a mental perception independent of sense perception), Descartes has refuted the Skeptics and advanced a Theory of Truth that can serve as part of the foundation for the New Science.

One of the first questions that arises after Descartes advances a theory of truth is the challenge to give an account of human error and human deficiency, especially in light of the defense of the existence of God as an infinite, omnibenevolent, omnipotent, creator of all that exists that was offered in the *Third Meditation.* This characterization of God would seem to place Descartes squarely in the place that St. Augustine found himself in when confronting the question of nature of evil and the Problem of Evil. Indeed, Descartes depends, to a great extent, on the theoretical framework put forward by St. Augustine, although he does amend it somewhat to take into account the analysis of the human mind that has been advanced so far in this work.

Consider the opening of the *Fourth Meditation*. Descartes approaches his theory of knowledge, particularly as it relates to ideas, from yet another perspective. Rather than the *causal* distinction in the *Third Meditation* or the *truth* distinction in the *Second* that is expanded in the latter part of the *Fourth*, Descartes distinguishes between two kinds of ideas and thus makes an *ontological* distinction between sorts of ideas. On the one hand, there are *positive ideas*, by which Descartes means ideas that have as their object some actual existent thing. The example that he uses here is God, although he could well use the example of an actual tree. Some idea is a *positive idea*, then, if and only if it has as its object some thing that actually exists. On the other hand, there are *negative ideas*. A *negative idea* refers to some gap, hole, lacuna, or non-existence within some existent thing.

To explore this distinction, let us consider, then, the notion of a hole. When one considers a hole, it is impossible to take account of that hole without reference to the surrounding material in which the hole is. So, for example, to talk about a doughnut hole is necessarily to take into account the doughnut where the hole is found. If the doughnut in question did not exist, then the hole would not exist either. Thus, holes are not independently existent things, but rather are negations or absences within an existent thing. As such, they are not positive creations but rather gaps. So, one might well have a positive idea of God or a doughnut or the human will and a negative idea of the hole within the doughnut or the privation or lack or gap within the human will. Here, Descartes adopts the Augustinian notion of evil, which is to say, a *nothingness* and applies it to the notion of the ontology of ideas. The aim of this adoption is to discuss the occurrence of human error and the necessary results of human error. In this way, Descartes appropriates St. Augustine's *Free Will Defense* which was directed at preserving a particular metaphysical conception of the universe by establishing and preserving the notion of God as a perfect, infinite, omnibenevolent, omnipotent, and creative force with the notion that evil exists. Descartes takes this metaphysical distinction and explores it as an epistemological one; albeit, an epistemological one that results in the same sort of defense of God as put forward by St. Augustine.

As the old saying goes, "To err is human." However, Descartes argues that it is, in theory, possible for human beings to avoid errors. Since error is a defect or a lack or a hole, it is not strictly something that has positive existence. Thus, it should be possible for such defects to be avoided. How might this be done? For Descartes, error can be avoided by a very disciplined approach to knowledge and willing. The human will is an extraordinarily vast thing. That is, the human will, as judged by the number of wants and desires present within it, is immense. Descartes's will is no different from any other human will, in this respect. Many of those desires and wants are things about which Descartes has only confused and obscure mental perceptions. On the other hand, human knowledge is rather more sparse. Given that knowledge is a matter of clear and distinct perceptions, and thus a function of certainty, it will cover only a fraction of the wants and desires within the will. As such, to act on these desires would be to act outside knowledge. More than this, however, to act on that which is beyond clear and distinct perception is to expose oneself to error. The gap between the extent of the human will and the scope of human knowledge constitutes a hole in the human will. One can avoid error, then, by restraining the will to only those things about which there are clear and distinct perceptions and by acting only on those things about which there is certainty. However, such a prescription is rather onerous and exhausting. Without constant vigilance, of a sort that is likely impossible for human endurance, it is not possible to contain the will as it seeks to pursue its desires. Like the light and dark horses of Plato's chariot, the soul is driven by those desires and only the charioteer is capable of restraining them through thorough application of reason. On Descartes view, this charioteer would be governed by clear and distinct perceptions and insofar as he maintains absolute control of the team, it is possible to avoid errors. Such persistence is beyond human grasp, though. The human mind will tire and desire will run amok. Thus, while it is possible for human beings, theoretically, to avoid error, it is equally inevitable, given the weakness of the human mind and the strength of human desire, for that error to be avoided entirely.

So, while restraining the human will is part of the formula for avoiding error, there are other components as well. Avoidance of error is not merely a matter of keeping a tight rein on the desires and avoiding acting, perhaps entirely. Instead, humans must act. The imperative to act, in some way or another, exposes Descartes to the possibility of error again. However, if Descartes will reserve judgments on all things that he does not clearly and distinctly perceive and act only within the range of things that he does clearly and distinctly perceive, then he will avoid error here as well. Thus, the Cartesian project to avoid error is multi-faceted, involving a restraint of the human will and a commitment to act only upon those judgments about which there are clear and distinct perceptions.

An implication of this view is that only human beings, then, are responsible for error or for evil. Given that God is responsible only for those things that have positive existence (that is, that are not nothingnesses), then God is not responsible for error. As the author of clear and distinct mental perceptions, and thus, certainty and truth, God is the cause of truth. However, to act on the will that goes beyond clear and distinct perceptions is to choose to act beyond the scope of God's authorship; to embrace nothingness and non-existence rather than reality and existence. As such, Descartes can avoid error, and in Augustinian language, sin, by restraining the will, acting only on clear and distinct perceptions, and keeping his focus on God. Failure to attend to each of these rather difficult tasks will result in error, although responsibility for this error will be solely that of the human who acts outside of certainty and knowledge.

The *Fourth Meditation* gives way to the *Fifth* and to a new argument for the existence of God. This argument is a rehearsal of a version of St. Anselm's Ontological Argument that Descartes here offers for the purpose of making clear the conclusion of his own argument for God's existence in the *Third Meditation*, namely that God exists and is not a deceiving Evil Genius. With that conclusion in hand and having developed a complementary theory of error to further develop his theory of truth, Descartes is now ready to return to his commitment to the distinction between the mind and the body, a distinction that was recognized during his own career as perhaps the most challenging critique of the Cartesian project.

Guided Reading Questions:
1. According to Descartes, what is error?
2. Why is Descartes capable of error?
3. On Descartes' view, how can he avoid error?

4. What supports Descartes' assertion that everything he clearly and distinctly perceives is necessarily true?
5. Upon what does knowledge depend?

Logic Blurb
Begging the Question

"Well, the team has lost its last seven in a row, almost falling completely out of the pennant race. This just begs the question: What will the manager do to turn this team around?"

More and more in popular entertainment, political commentary, and analysis of the news, the phrase, "begs the question" is used in the sense represented in the imagined sportscaster commentary above. Unfortunately, this common usage has absolutely nothing to do with the philosophical fallacy of *begging the question*.

The philosophical meaning of question-begging is nothing like "leading to the question" or "causing us to ask." The "question" in question refers rather to the argument as a whole. Thus, when St. Anselm sets out to prove the existence of God, the question under consideration is whether or not God exists. The treatment of that question is a philosophical argument mean to establish a proposition that answers that larger question, either yes, no, or perhaps. In the development of that argument, there will be a set of premises that together are supposed to establish the conclusion.

Let us briefly consider a different example. Suppose two people are arguing whether the Kansas City Monarchs were the greatest team in the old Negro Leagues. John says that, yes, they were, and he sets out to argue for this conclusion. In the course of his argument, he asserts that it is simply obvious to anyone that the Kansas City Monarchs were the greatest. He has begged the question. Since the aim of the argument was to establish that they were the greatest, the assertion, as a part of the argument, that they were the greatest is out of bounds. If one assumes, as a premise, the content of the conclusion for which one is arguing, then one has begged the question. Presumably, Stan (John's opponent) did not hold the conclusion to be true. Thus, he would reject the proposition as a premise as well.

Let us return to St. Anselm's work. As was discussed in *St. Anselm – Proslogian*, critics of his argument have sometimes accused him of having begged the question against Gaunilo in his response to Gaunilo's defense of the fool. St. Anselm responded to Gaunilo's *perfect island* analogy by arguing that islands and God are different sorts of being entirely. Islands, he says, are *contingent* beings; they come into being and they disappear. Part of what it is to be an island is to be contingent. However, says St. Anselm, God is a *necessary* being. Thus, he argues that Gaunilo's argument fails because he confuses a contingent being with a necessary one. However, St. Anselm's Ontological Argument is supposed to *prove* that God is a necessary being. Thus, arguing that

Gaunilo's critique of his argument fails because God is a necessary being and an island is a contingent being is to beg the question against Gaunilo.

Sometimes, begging the question goes under another name – Circularity. If the conclusion supports a premise that in turn supports the conclusion, then the argument is circular and begs the question. Consider again St. Anselm's argument and his response to Gaunilo. In the first place, the ontological argument is supposed to establish that God is a necessary being. However, for the proof to overcome its critics, it must assume that God is a necessary being. Thus, God is assumed to be a necessary being in order to demonstrate that God is a necessary being. The conclusion of the argument depends on a premise, but that premise depends on the conclusion. This is an example of circularity and one can readily see how it and begging the question amount to the same logical error.

Section 12.5: Descartes, Father of Modern Philosophy

Sixth Meditation – That Material Things Exist and that the Mind and the Body are Distinct

The only question that now remains is the matter of the existence of material objects. From all that has been made clear thus far, I at least know that such things may exist. For example, those that are the objects of pure mathematics can be perceived clearly and distinctly and so must truly exist. God is perfectly capable of causing all these things clearly and distinctly perceived to exist.

Because I understand that all those things I clearly and distinctly perceive come from God and in the exact manner as I perceive it, this stands as sufficient evidence that I can clearly and distinctly perceive the one separate from the other. It does not matter whether or not I or any other could actually separate the two. God, in God's omnipotence, can separate all those things that can be clearly and distinctly perceived to be distinct. Given this, I return to the earlier conclusion that I am a thinking thing and conclude again that my essence is in this. Whether I have a body or not, and whether I am actually united with it or not, I have it as a clear and distinct perception of myself that I am a mind only and not an thing with extension. A body is an extended, non-thinking thing, and I possess my body but it is not part of my essence. I am distinct from my body and perfectly capable of existing without it.

I have a way of discovering the truth because with relative to all those things that are objects, God has instilled within me a capacity or faculty to correct the erroneous conclusions I may initially make. Since God exists and is not a deceiver, I am not given to falsehoods in those things that I clearly and distinctly perceive.

The nature that I have from God teaches me many things, among them that I have a body and that that body is affected when I experience pain and requires food when I experience hunger. It also teaches me that, in virtue of these experiences, I am not merely connected to my body like a sailor is to a ship – that is easily separable – but that I am so closely tied to my body as to be intermixed, comprising a unity of sorts. If this were not so, I would not feel pain when my body is injured. As the sailor notices the damage to the ship when he gazes upon it, so, if I were not something of a union with my body, I would only notice my wounds by sight. Indeed, I would have clear perceptions of these injuries were they apprehended solely by my mind. Instead, I come to this awareness by confused experiences – hunger, thirst, pain – and these are nothing more than confused modes of thought which arise from the union of mind and body.

Let us consider again the mind and the body. Between these there is considerable difference. The body is divisible and is always so. The mind cannot be divided; it is indivisible. When I think about myself as a thinking thing, I can perceive no divisions, no parts whatever. I clearly and distinctly perceive that I am a individual, complete in myself. The body, on the other hand, clearly is divisible into many parts, and them into further parts. While it appears that my entire mind is connected to the entire body, when a foot or some other part is severed, I understand that nothing has been removed or severed from my mind. The activities of the mind – willing, desiring, perceiving – cannot be called the parts of the mind because the mind is complete in each of these. This is not so of the body – I can easily imagine it divided and divided again. On these grounds, it is clear that the mind and body are completely distinct.

~

While Descartes puts forward several revolutionary and innovative notions during the *Meditations*, the primary contemporary criticism revolved around the striking implications of the *Cogito*. Known as the Interaction Problem, or, more often as the Mind/Body Problem, the structure of the criticism is straightforward. In showing that the mind and body are distinct, Descartes has argued that there exist two substances that comprise the entire universe – a thinking, non-extended one (the Mind) and an extended, non-thinking one (the Body). This dualistic metaphysics immediately raises a serious question and one that was among the most debated of the 17th century: If the mind and body are absolutely separate, with no points of contact, how is it that they interact? For example, if in one's mind, the notion to raise one's arm appears, how is it that the arm, which is completely separate from the mind and the thought within it, moves?

Before turning to the Mind/Body Problem and Descartes's attempts to propose solutions for it, it is important to take a moment to note what Descartes does not accomplish with the *Meditations*. Among the five stated purposes of the *Meditations* was the demonstration that the soul is immortal. Descartes does not address this purpose. There is no consensus as to why Descartes abandons this premise, an abandonment that is made all the more baffling by the fact that within the discussion of the nature of the mind and the body in the *Sixth Meditation*, an argument for the immortality of the mind/soul is available to him. One distinction between the mind and the body that is explored here is that the body is divisible. Because it is an extended thing, it can be divided, perhaps *ad infinitum*. Because it can be divided, it can decay. However, here Descartes need only appeal to Plato's argument for the immortality of the soul advanced in the *Phaedo*. The mind is indivisible. It is indivisible precisely because it does not have extension. Since the mind is indivisible, it cannot be broken into parts. Since it cannot be broken down, it cannot decay. Since it cannot decay, it cannot perish and if something cannot perish, it is immortal. This proof is available to Descartes precisely because of the conception of the mind that is developed from the *Second Meditation* and expanded in the *Sixth*. However, to the bafflement of scholars from his day to this, he leaves the argument unmade.

Moving from a bafflement to a fairly clear philosophical dilemma, we return to the difficult question of the interaction of wholly independent substances, the mind and the body. One of the universally accepted scientific principles was that there could be no causation at a distance. That is, if one billiard ball is on the table and the other is on the floor, it does not matter how much the first billiard ball moves on the table, it will never cause the one on the floor to move. Unless there is some point of contact, there can be no interaction. Thus, we can represent the Mind/Body Problem in the following way:

(a) Mind and Body are absolutely distinct, and thus have no points of contact.
(b) For interaction between two objects to take place, there must be some point of contact between them.
(c) Therefore, minds and bodies cannot interact.
(d) Yet, minds and bodies do, in fact, interact.

That the mind and body are distinct is one of the most influential of the Cartesian contributions. Within fields as diverse as literature and neuroscience, the relationship between the mind and the body is debated and great quantities of ink is spilt. This was the case among Descartes's contemporaries as well. One of Descartes's most praiseworthy examples that would be well adopted by current philosophers was his cultivation of comment and debate. Rather than publish *The Meditations* independent of comment or discourse, Descartes distributed early editions to several preeminent philosophers of his day. When several of them presented him with objections and points for clarification, he took seriously those objections, making some alterations to the primary text itself, but also authoring replies to those objections. He then published *The Meditations* alongside the objections and with his own replies to those objections. Thus, the stage was set for free-wheeling debate over the concepts, arguments, and principles advanced. The most hotly debated of those concepts and arguments was the distinction between the mind and body.

Benedict Spinoza would go on to argue that there really are not two substances, but that there is only one substance, God, and that mind and body are merely modes of that substance. Much later, reductionists would argue that there is no true distinction between minds and bodies, but that the mind is merely a function of the physical processes of the brain. Among the most intriguing of the Cartesian contemporaries who address this mind/body interaction problem are the Occasionalists, and particularly, Nicholas Malebranche. The Occasionalists argued that the mind and the body do not, in fact, interact. To conceptualize the Occasionalist metaphysics, one could imagine the universe as a very complex film strip. Each cell or frame of the film is a particular occasion, and, obviously, each of these frames is completely static, with no motion within it. If one imagines God creating the universe one frame at a time, then motion, fluidity, and change are all illusory and God is the only true cause of anything. Thus, minds and bodies do not interact, but merely appear to do so. As, such, this would attack the Mind/Body Problem by denying (d) and arguing that minds and bodies only appear to interact, although, in fact, only God is a causal force.

The Occasionalists were a significant force within early Modern Philosophy. However, another early modern philosopher and mathematician pointed out a significant flaw in the Occasionalist conception. G. W. F. Leibniz argued that if the Occasionalists were right, then there would be some very unsavory conclusions about the nature and function of God. If, indeed, God is the only causal agent in the universe, recreating the universe one frame at a time at every moment or occasion, then only God can be responsible for evil, for tragedy, or for maleficence in the universe. This would stand in direct contradiction to the view that God is omnibenevolent and without evil. Simply put, if God is the only cause, then God is the cause of evil. This criticism is a fairly straightforward refutation of the Occasionalists, including Malebranche, who hold all of the views about the nature of God that Descartes holds – that God is infinite, eternal, omnibenevolent, omnipotent, intelligent creator of all that exists – and that God is the sole cause (as a way to solve the Mind/Body Problem). Thus, while Descartes holds all of these views about God, the appeal to the intervention of God as mediator between mind and body is ultimately unavailable to him. It is important to point this out because while Descartes believes that God is the creator of all that exists and that, even though it is impossible for humans to separate minds and bodies that the fact that it is possible to conceive of them separately that God could separate them, it does not follow from this that Descartes concludes that God is the only cause. Indeed, Descartes thinks that although Mind and Body are completely distinct, they do, in fact, interact. Within the *Sixth Meditation*, Descartes attempts to navigate this philosophical minefield.

The *Sixth Meditation* is different in several ways from the preceding five. Among those differences is a shift in tone from straightforward reflective introspection to the development of examples that illuminate earlier views and, in so doing, answer potential criticisms of those views. Thus, the *Sixth Meditation* is more outward looking and more like a traditional philosophical text than the others. The most striking difference is the several analogies that form the centerpiece of the *Meditations*. Anticipating the criticism of the Mind/Body distinction rooted in the accepted scientific principles of cause and effect, Descartes seeks to overcome those criticisms and to overcome the perceived Mind/Body problem by use of these analogies.

In his correspondence with Princess Elizabeth of Bohemia, Descartes laments that many of his critics simply misunderstand what the distinction between the Mind and the Body is supposed to consist in. Generally, this misunderstanding is a matter of trying to understand how these very distinct substance interact by conceptualizing that interaction as one between two bodies. So, for example, philosophers will speak of one billiard ball striking another as an example of the interaction between two substances. Princess Elizabeth is perhaps the most perceptive of the Cartesian critics, though Descartes thinks that her critique is of this sort. Such a criticism, on Descartes's view, misses the point. If one is trying to conceptualize Mind/Body interaction by appeal to the billiard ball example, then one is trying to understand Mind/Body interaction by appeal to interaction between two *bodies*. If Mind and Body are truly distinct, then this attempt is a category mistake, an error in which an analogy fails because the analogy confuses a distinction between two categories of things. Thus, Descartes argues that one must conceive of the interaction between two distinct substances of this sort by appeal to a relation between two other distinct substances. The most famous of these analogies is the Sailor and His Ship.

It is quite easy to conceive of a sailor and a ship as independent and distinct substances and at the same time recognize that there is no difficulty in conceptualizing their interaction. Thus, the analogy is as follows – the sailor is to the ship as the mind is to the body. That this analogy is compelling is fairly straightforward. The sailor clearly influences the ship and the ship, to a lesser degree, influences the sailor. So, too, the mind seems to fairly clearly influence the body and the body, to one degree or another, influences the mind. Here the analogy also captures something important about the nature of the interaction. As the sailor actively influences the ship, so the mind is understood to actively influence the body. The sailor steers the ship, giving it direction while the mind directs the arm to lift, the legs to move, and the body to walk. At the same time, the ship has a passive influence on the sailor. It does not form intentions nor does it actively influence the sailor. So, too, the body, through fevers or illness or some trauma affects the mind passively. It does not form intentions to affect the mind, but rather is passive and thus indirect in its influence. It communicates external perceptions to the mind rather than forming intentions. As such, it is clear that both the ship and the body are Body.

The sailor is obviously independent of the ship, as well. When arriving in port, one can easily imagine the sailor taking leave of the ship and walking into town. Having left the ship, one could also imagine the sailor deciding that the life of the sea is no longer for him, traveling to the farmland outside of town, purchasing a little plot of land, and settling down for a life of agriculture, never to return to the sea. Hence, the sailor is clearly independent of the ship. Descartes holds, then, that much as it is easy to conceive of the relationship between the sailor and the ship, independent and yet interactive, so, too, one should conceive the relationship between the mind and the body in a similar way.

Princess Elizabeth, among others, points out a lingering difficulty here, though. In any argument from analogy, the relata must bear a similar relationship to each other. Thus, for the argument to do the work Descartes hopes for it, it must be the case that the sailor and the ship bear the same relationship to each other that the mind and the body do. Let us examine that relationship again. The mind is a thinking, non-extended thing. The body is an extended, non-thinking thing. The ship is clearly a body as it is not a thinking thing and it is obviously extended, so that part of the analogy holds. However, if we look carefully at the sailor, it will become clear that the sailor is not actually a mind. Or, more to the point, the sailor is not *only* a mind. The sailor is a hybrid of mind and body, or a substantial union of mind and body. If this is the case, then Descartes has failed rather badly with this analogy. Any analogy is supposed to take some difficult or obscure relationship and, by means of a clearer relationship, give insight into the more difficult one. However, the sailor/ship analogy has actually done the reverse. Intending to clarify the difficulties of the relationship between the mind and body, Descartes has offered an analogy that involves not only mind/body interaction, but the interaction of a mind/body hybrid with a body. Thus, to truly understand the sailor/ship analogy, we must first understand how it is that a mind and body interact. But, this is precisely what the sailor/ship analogy was supposed to address. Thus, we are left no better off than when we began.

To finally address this difficulty, Descartes returns to a less explicit, but perhaps more accurate analogy. If we recall a portion of the title of the work, *Meditations on First Philosophy*, this analogy will become clearer. Descartes is widely and correctly considered one of the greatest mathematicians of the modern era and his contributions to geometry and algebra are undeniably significant. One of the influences on Descartes was the ancient geometer, Euclid. Euclid's *Elements* presents the foundational axioms and postulates of plane geometry. From the definition of a point and a line to the postulation of a parallel line, the *Elements* express the basic principles (or First Principles) of geometry. It is impossible to prove the basic axioms and postulates. They are simply stated as the groundwork and starting point for any further discussion within the discipline. Thus, while one would use the basic axioms and postulates to prove, for example, the Pythagorean Theorem, one could not similarly prove those basic axioms. Any axioms that could be deductively demonstrated (or proven) would thereby be shown *not* to be truly foundational axioms.

We can read Descartes's *Meditations* as advancing a similar sort of view for philosophy – that is, for all of the functioning of the human mind. So, we can interpret Descartes's work here as leading the reader to discovery or recognition of those basic or foundational axioms of human thought that are necessary for the development of any knowledge. As first principles (or First Philosophy), these axioms are beyond proof and must simply be accepted as fundamental assumptions in order to perform any intellection at all. Thus, like first principles in mathematics, there are first principles in philosophy and the *Meditations* is a method by which one can isolate these principles.

There are four axioms in the set of First Philosophy (or, as Descartes calls them elsewhere, Primitive Notions). The first three are rather straightforward. The First Primitive Notion is the notion of General Existence. The *cogito* reveals this axiom to the reader because the content of the notion is that there is something rather than nothing. The Second and Third Primitive Notion are discerned through the development of the distinction between the mind and the body. The Second Primitive Notion is the Primitive Notion of Mind. The Third Primitive Notion is the Primitive Notion of Body. Descartes's view is that whenever one is exploring the interaction of one body upon another (e.g., within the discipline of physics), one is operating under the purview of the Third Primitive Notion. So, too, if one is exploring the interaction of one mind upon another (e.g., the self-revelation of God to humanity). Here, then, we have the first three categories by which the world is to be understood. Notice, this supports Descartes's contention that those who seek to understand mind/body interaction by appealing to billiard balls, for example, are in fact using only that axiom of the Third Primitive Notion. The Third Primitive Notion is no more capable of explaining the interaction of things that are not bodies than the definition of a line is capable of explaining the Pythagorean Theorem. Indeed, if one supposes that there are only these three Primitive Notions, then it is ultimately impossible to explain mind/body interaction.

Reflecting on the *Meditations*, it becomes clear to the careful reader that Descartes is not nearly as exclusively a rationalist as perhaps it would appear on first blush. It is a matter of observation that the mind and the body interact. Given this, and the description of the Mind/Body Problem above, it would seem that Descartes needs a Fourth Primitive Notion. Indeed, he recognizes this as well and there is, in fact, a fourth. The Fourth Primitive Notion is the Primitive Notion of the Substantial Union of the Mind and the Body. Descartes notes that it is from the nature he has received from God that he knows that he possesses a body. Since God exists and is not a deceiver, he knows that the mind and body, while distinct, must interact. Thus, it is not possible for there to be only three primitive notions – one that addresses existence, one that addresses mind to mind interaction, and one that is concerned with body to body interaction. Thus, the Fourth Primitive Notion must be the one under which discussions of the mind and body interactively hybridized must be governed. Here, Descartes points out that there will be confused feelings that arise because of that interaction, but this was clear from the very outset when the Method of Doubt called all of the information gleaned from the senses into doubt and from the Theory of Truth which established that only clear and distinct mental perceptions could be relied upon for certainty. Thus, we can conclude that the *Meditations*, much like a careful treatment of mathematical principles, is an attempt to isolate those foundational principles, that *First Philosophy*, that must be taken as the grounding assumptions for deductive argument. From these principles, the edifice of human knowledge, particularly within the sciences, is to be erected.

Guided Reading Questions:

1. What is a mind?
2. What is a body?
3. Why are they distinct?
4. What problem arises from this argument that they are distinct?
5. How does Descartes use analogies to try to solve the Interaction Problem?

Logic Blurb
Division/Composition

The *Division/Composition* fallacy is a slippery argument, indeed. Suppose an author of incredibly popular children's books was told that her book was quite well done. From this, she might conclude that the person thought that every sentence of her book was also well done. After all, the total work was considered excellent, so surely every component of it was similarly excellent. This might very well not be the case. In fact, many author's will commit themselves to a Preface Paradox to avoid this *division* fallacy. The Preface Paradox is committed when the author says that he believes every sentence in his book to be true when taken individually, but because of humility or uncertainty, if asked whether or not every sentence in the book is true (taken as a whole), might well say, "no." This gets to an important recognition. Even if the total project is quite good, there may well be certain aspects that are shoddy or poorly done. So, from an assessment of the whole, one cannot make necessarily true inferences about the constituent parts.

In a similar way, suppose an author composed 100 exquisite sentences and lined them up one after another. If it were concluded that the book that was the result of the linking of those 100 sentences was also exquisite, one would have committed the composition portion of the fallacy. We can easily imagine an author who composed 100 sentences, each about a completely different topic. Running those sentences together, then, would yield little more than a list of sentences that, taken separately, are quite nice but taken together are incomprehensible. Thus, from the conclusion that the whole is good, we cannot make a similar inference to the constituent parts and from the foundation of exquisite parts we cannot infer a similarly excellent whole. To do either would be to commit the *division/composition fallacy*.

Section 13.1: Reading David Hume

A Treatise of Human Nature:
Being An Attempt to introduce the experimental Method of Reasoning into Moral Subjects

Rara temporum felicitas, ubi fentire, quæ velis; & quæ fentias, dicere licet.
(Rare are those happy times when one can think what one wants and express it.)

Volume I: Of the Understanding
Introduction

Nothing is more usual and more natural for those who pretend to discover any thing new to the world in philosophy and the sciences than to insinuate the praises of their own systems by decrying all those which have been advanced before them. 'Tis easy for one of judgment and learning to perceive the weak foundation even of those systems, which have obtained the greatest credit, and have carried their pretensions highest to accurate and profound reasoning. Principles taken on trust, consequences lamely deduced from them, want of coherence in the parts, and of evidence in the whole, these are everywhere to be met with in the systems of the most eminent philosophers, and seem to have drawn disgrace upon philosophy itself.

As science the science of humanity is the only solid foundation for the other sciences, so the only solid foundation we can give to this science itself must be laid on experience and observation. 'Tis no astonishing reflection to consider that the application of experimental philosophy to moral subjects should come after that to natural at the distance of above a whole century; since we find in fact that there was about the same interval betwixt the origins of these sciences; and that reckoning from Thales to Socrates, the space of time is nearly equal to that betwixt my Lord Bacon and some late philosophers in *England*, who have begun to put the science of humanity on a new footing, and have engaged the attention, and excited the curiosity of the public. So true it is that however other nations may rival us in poetry, and excel us in some other agreeable arts, the improvements in reason and philosophy can only be owing to a land of toleration and of liberty.

Nor ought we to think that this latter improvement in the science of man will do less honour to our native country than the former in natural philosophy, but ought rather to esteem it a greater glory, upon account of the greater importance of that science, as well as the necessity it lay under of such a reformation. For to me it seems evident that the essence of the mind being equally unknown to us with that of external bodies, it must be equally impossible to form any notion of its powers and qualities otherwise than from careful and exact experiments, and the observation of those particular effects, which result from its different circumstances and situations. And tho' we must endeavor to render all our principles as universal as possible, by tracing up our experiments to the utmost, and explaining all effects from the simplest and fewest causes, 'tis still certain that we cannot go beyond experience; and any hypothesis that pretends to discover the ultimate original qualities of human nature ought at first to be rejected as presumptuous and chimerical.

~

While David Hume's philosophical works are some of the most comprehensive ever, we will focus primarily on his contributions in two areas: epistemology and religion. Particular attention will be given to two primary texts, *A Treatise of Human Nature* (*Treatise*) and the *Dialogues Concerning Natural Religion* (*Dialogues*). Widely accepted as the greatest philosopher to write in English, Hume is also the subject of considerable misinterpretation. Many philosophers since Hume have seen in his work an overriding theme of radical skepticism, perhaps even more virulent than that of Montaigne and his group. He was similarly misunderstood during his lifetime, for example, clerics of the Scottish church referred to Hume simply as "the Great Infidel." Even his philosophical work was largely overshadowed by another of his pursuits – historian. Whatever else might be said about the philosopher David Hume, it cannot be said that he was not controversial, that he was not brilliant, and that he was not among the greatest thinkers in the history of philosophy.

Hume is the third of the great British Empiricists that arose in England and served as counterpoint to the rationalism of Descartes, Spinoza, and Leibniz (among others) on the continent. The empiricists that preceded Hume, John Locke (1632-1709) and Bishop George Berkeley (1685-1753), are to be credited with establishing the foundation of the empirical response to rationalism that Hume epitomizes. John Locke is perhaps best known not for his work on metaphysics, epistemology, and ethics, but political philosophy. His *Second Treatise on Government* forms the basis for such documents as the American Declaration of Independence and Constitution. His *Essay on Human Understanding*, however, questions the assumed scope of clear and distinct perceptions that Descartes argued are the foundation of true knowledge.

Following Aristotle, Locke denies that human beings are possessed of innate ideas at all. Rather, on Locke's view, all humans are blank slates upon which experience writes. Since all human knowledge is a matter of experiential authorship and since experience is fundamentally a matter of perception, it is impossible to have the sort of certainty that Descartes supposes exists. Similarly, Berkeley (father of the British Idealist movement) argues that all we can have anything approaching certainty about is the fact of our own perceptions. Beyond perception there is nothing more to be said about the world.

While Hume is rightly considered an empiricist, as this passage from the Introduction to the *Treatise* indicates. "'Tis certain," he writes, 'that we cannot go beyond experience." Like any good empiricist, the experience of the world is fundamental; basic to any scheme of explaining the world around us. However, while Hume is properly classed among the empiricists, in many ways, he is more like Plato and Aristotle and the philosophers of the Ancient period than like the empiricists of his own. That is to say, his empiricism is a matter of emphasis, rather than dogma. Hume, like the ancients, sought a balance between the experimental and the theoretical. To be sure, the experimental sets the limits of theoretical or abstract knowledge, but the rationalist intuition toward simplicity of principles and theory is present as well. The context of his assertion that we cannot go beyond reason makes this point clearly. He writes, "we must endeavor to render all our principles as universal as possible, by tracing up our experiments to the utmost, and explaining all effects from the simplest and fewest causes." However, lest one take this as an endorsement of the sort of experience-poor ruminations of one like Descartes, Hume offers a criticism that is directed at all those who hold to a strictly rationalist approach to philosophy – "any hypothesis that pretends to discover the ultimate original qualities of human nature ought at first to be rejected as presumptuous and chimerical."

Hume's *Treatise*, published in 1739-40 (when Hume was 28) is among the most influential texts in western thought. However, at the time of its publication, it was met with neither widespread acceptance nor scorn. Rather, it was greeted by indifference when there was any recognition at all. This response was particularly galling since Hume was certain that at least the religious community would be agitated by some of his seemingly shocking statements. Yet it was received not with a bang or a whimper, but with a yawn.

This was not the reaction to the *Dialogues Concerning Natural Religion*. Here, Hume examines the several attempts philosophers and theologians have made at proving the existence of God and systematically demonstrates the inadequacy of those attempts. Oddly enough, this was first published posthumously. Completed some years before his death, Hume decided against its publication until after his death. He left instructions for the executor of his estate, his good friend Adam Smith (author of *Wealth of Nations*), to publish the work. Speculation is that Hume felt the book would be scandalously received. Adam Smith apparently agreed. Following Hume's death, he flatly refused to publish the work or to be associated with it in any way. It fell to Hume's nephew to see the work published. As it happens, Hume was prescient. The book was scandalously received..

During his lifetime (and for some time after it), Hume was derided by the clergy of his home country (Scotland) as "the Great Infidel." At the same time, Hume has been called a skeptic, a proponent of faith, a sinner, and a saint. His work is credited by Immanuel Kant of awakening him from his "dogmatic slumbers." The influence of Hume on Kant and later the existentialist theologian Soren Kierkegaard, had profound influence on the practice of theology from that day to this. His ruminations on the nature of human knowledge, what we can know and how it can be known, shaped much of the scientific inquiry that has followed. His rejection of many of the arguments for the existence of God led many to suppose him an atheist of the first order. That such a rigorous thinker should be met with such widely divergent interpretations is some testimony to his influence. In the course of this section, we will strive to understand not only who David Hume was, but how his thought has shaped human intellectual pursuits since the 18th century.

More important than the *Dialogues* is the work that sparked no initial furor at all – the *Treatise*. Hume was not at all thrilled that the *Treatise* did not sell particularly well. In fact, so discouraged was he by its lack of reception that he turned to other pursuits (at least in his writing) for some time. Among those other pursuits was the history of England. So proficient was he at this endeavor that he was best known during his lifetime, at least popularly, as an historian rather than as a philosopher. Indeed, on his tomb is inscribed the following: "David Hume: An Historian of England." Thus, in the person of David Hume is the greatest philosopher to write in English and one who is counted among the greatest historians of the period as well.

After a period of years, Hume returned to the *Treatise* and reworked it. Books One and Two of the *Treatise* (Of the Understanding and Of the Passions) were reworked into *An Enquiry Concerning Human Understanding*. Published in 1748, this work is commonly referred to simply as the *First Enquiry*. Book Three of the *Treatise* (Of Morals) was similarly revised and published as *An Enquiry Concerning the Principles of Morals*. In similar fashion, this is commonly referred to as the *Second Enquiry*. This latter work Hume calls "unquestionably his greatest." This is pretty clearly not the case and so should serve as evidence that even great philosophers, at times, go astray. The *Treatise* is properly regarded as Hume's greatest work and most significant contribution to philosophy.

However, Hume's claim for the *Second Enquiry* is instructive in another way. It is now generally accepted that Hume wrote Book Three (Of Morals) of the *Treatise* first. That is, it is reasonable to suppose that Hume's primary concern was morality or ethics. If this is so, it suggests that this is the lens through which Hume's work ought to be interpreted. Rather than a secondary implication of certain metaphysical and epistemological concerns, it seems that Hume's moral intuitions are primary. Having explored morality, its foundations and practice, Hume is investigating what sort of things must be true about the world given the ethical views he finds plausible. Further evidence for this interpretive approach to Hume's work is found in the very title of the *Treatise* – "Being An Attempt to introduce the experimental Method of Reasoning into *Moral* Subjects" (emphasis is mine). That he should grant the title of "greatest" to an ethical work and, moreso, to a work that grew out of "Of Morals" is further evidence that Hume's project is ultimately about ethics.

Since Hume is not at all confident that we can have anything like the sort of certainty that Descartes supposes and since he straightforwardly calls into question the fundamental notions of substance and causation so common to philosophy, it has been asserted that Hume is a radical and thoroughgoing skeptic. Because Hume challenges many of the major tenets of popular religious belief, it has been claimed that he is a radical and thoroughgoing atheist. Whatever the truth or falsity of those claims, one claim is fairly certain. Hume was a natural philosopher (in fact, a natural philosopher of the sort Socrates was accused of being).

Naturalism, as discussed in earlier sections, involves the view that the human mind is inextricably part of the natural world and as such, ideas within the mind are developed in natural ways. Further, Hume holds that observable evidence must lie at the base of the things we claim to know and that truly rational beliefs are those that are apportioned to the evidence and no more. Thus, the naturalist is interested in the natural causes of natural events, first and foremost. Given this, it is likely that Hume is not, in fact, a radical skeptic; instead, it seems that he is quite skeptical of the many claims to knowledge that do not have groundings in that which can be observed. Simply put, there are five ways in which the human mind is connected to the world around it (and the world of which it is inextricably a part). These five ways are the five physical senses. In some sense, the senses are something like channels – anything that enters the mind through these channels can be known (at least has the capacity of being known). Anything that does not enter the mind through one of these five channels does not, in fact, enter the mind. That is, the mind is blind to anything that might possibly exist but that it cannot experience. Knowledge of the world is rooted in experience and can extend no further. That Hume supposes there are limits on the human intellect and the scope of human knowledge does not entail that he is a skeptic; rather it suggests that among Hume's goals is the advocacy of a kind of epistemic humility – that is, of not saying more than is demonstrable or claiming more certainty than is strictly possible. In this way, Hume is again similar to Socrates.

After establishing what he took to be the principles of ethics, he then set out to discover what sort of world it must be such that these principles of ethics were entailed. This, of course, required considerable attention to how it is that the human mind forms ideas and how those ideas become knowledge. If this is so, why the widespread view that Hume is a skeptic? To address that question, and the much more important questions about the nature of knowledge, how knowledge is acquired, and what sorts of things can be known, it is important to turn to the first pages of the *Treatise* where Hume makes a fundamental distinction; one to which we will return again and again. That distinction is between two species of perception – impressions and ideas.

Section 13.2: Hume and the Origin of Ideas

Treatise of Human Nature
Volume I: Of the Understanding
Part I. Of Ideas, Their Origin, Composition, Connexion, Abstraction, &c.

Section I. Of the Origin of our Ideas
All the perceptions of the human mind resolve themselves into two distinct kinds that I shall call Impressions and Ideas. The difference betwixt these consists in the degrees of force and liveliness with which they strike upon the mind and make their way into our thought or consciousness. Those perceptions which enter with the most force and violence, we may name *impressions*; and under this name I comprehend all our sensations, passions and emotions, as they make their first appearance in the soul. By *ideas*, I mean the faint images of these in thinking and reasoning; such as, for instance, are all the perceptions excited by the present discourse, excepting only those which arise from the sight and touch, and excepting the immediate pleasure or uneasiness it may occasion.

There is another division of our perceptions, which it will be convenient to observe, and which extends itself both to our impressions and ideas. This division is into Simple and Complex. Simple perceptions or impressions and ideas are such as admit of no distinction or separation. The complex are the contrary to these, and may be distinguished into parts.

The first circumstance that strikes my eye is the great resemblance betwixt our impressions and ideas in every other particular except their degree of force and vivacity; so that all other perceptions of the mind are double, and appear both as impressions and ideas. When I shut my eyes and think of my chamber, the ideas I form are exact representations of the impressions I felt; nor is there any circumstance of the one which is not to be found in the other. In running over my other perceptions, I find still the same resemblance and representation. Ideas and impressions appear always to correspond to each other. This circumstance seems to me remarkable and engages my attention for the moment.

Upon a more accurate survey, I find I have been carried away too far by the first appearance, and that I must make use of the distinction of perceptions into simple and complex to limit this general decision that all our ideas and impressions are resembling. I observe that many of our complex ideas never had impressions that corresponded to them, and that many of our complex impressions never are exactly copied in ideas. I can imagine to myself such a city as the *New Jerusalem*, whose pavement is gold and walls are rubies, tho' I never saw any such. I have seen *Paris*; but shall I affirm I can form such an idea of that city as will perfectly represent all its streets and houses in their real and just proportions?

I perceive, therefore, that tho' there is in general a great resemblance betwixt our complex impressions and ideas, yet the rule is not universally true that they are exact copies of each other. We may next consider how the case extends with our simple perceptions. After the most accurate examination of which I am capable, I venture to affirm that the rule here holds without any exception, and that every simple idea has a simple impression that resembles it; and every simple impression a correspondent idea. That idea of red that we see in the dark and that impression which strikes our eyes in sunshine differ only in degree, not in nature. That the case is the same with all our simple impressions and ideas 'tis impossible to prove by a particular enumeration of them.

From this constant conjunction of resembling perceptions, I immediately conclude that there is a great connexion betwixt our correspondent impressions and ideas, and that the existence of one has a considerable influence upon that of the other. That I may know on which side this dependence lies, I consider the order of their *first appearance*; and find by constant experience, that the simple impressions always take the precedence of their correspondent ideas but never appear in the contrary order. To give a child an idea of scarlet or orange, of sweet or bitter, I present the objects, or in other words, convey to him these impressions; but proceed not so absurdly, as to endeavour to produce the impressions by exciting the ideas. Our ideas upon their appearance produce not their correspondent impressions, nor do we perceive any colour, or feel any sensation merely upon thinking of them. On the other hand, we find that any impression either of the mind or body is constantly followed by an idea which resembles it and is only different in the degrees of force and liveliness. The constant conjunction of our resembling perceptions is a convincing proof that the one are the causes of the other; and this priority of impressions is an equal proof that our impressions are the causes of our ideas, not our ideas of our impressions.

To confirm this I consider another plain and convincing phenomenon; which is, that where-ever by any accident the faculties which give rise to any impressions, are obstructed in their operations, as when one is born blind or deaf; not only the impressions are lost, but also their correspondent ideas; so that there never appear in the mind the least traces of either of them. We cannot form to ourselves a just idea of the taste of a pine-apple without having actually tasted it.

There is however one contradictory phenomenon which may prove that 'tis not absolutely impossible for ideas to go before their correspondent impressions.

I believe it will readily be allow'd, that the several distinct ideas of colours which enter by the eyes, or those of sounds which are convey'd by the hearing are really different from each other, tho' at the same time resembling. Now if this be true of different colours, it must be no less so of the different shades of the same colour that each of them produces a distinct idea, independent of the rest. For if this shou'd be deny'd, 'tis possible, by the continual gradation of shades, to run a colour insensibly into what is most remote from it; and if you will not allow any of the means to be different, you cannot without absurdity deny the extremes to be the same. Suppose therefore a person to have enjoyed his sight for thirty years, and to have become perfectly well acquainted with colours of all kinds, excepting one particular shade of blue, for instance, which it never has been his fortune to meet with. Let all the different shades of that colour, except that single one, be plac'd before him, descending gradually from the deepest to the lightest; 'tis plain that he will perceive a blank where that shade is wanting, and will be sensible that there is a greater distance in that place betwixt the contiguous colours than in any other. Now I ask, whether 'tis possible for him, from his own imagination, to supply this deficiency, and raise up to himself the idea of that particular shade, tho' it had never been conveyed to him by his senses? I believe there are few but will be of opinion that he can; and this may serve as a proof, that the simple ideas are not always derived from the correspondent impressions; tho' the instance is so particular and singular, that 'tis scarce worth our observing, and does not merit that for it alone we should alter our general maxim.

This is the first principle I establish in the science of human nature – all ideas are derived from sensation and reflection.

Section III. Of the Ideas of the Memory and Imagination

We find by experience that when any impression has been present with the mind, it again makes its appearance there as an idea; and this it may do after two different ways: either when in its new appearance it retains a considerable degree of its first vivacity, and is somewhat immediate betwixt an impression and an idea; or when it entirely loses that vivacity and is a perfect idea. The faculty by which we repeat our impressions in the first manner is called the *memory*, and the other the *imagination*. 'Tis evident at first sight that the ideas of the memory are much more lively and strong than those of the imagination and that the former faculty paints its objects in more distinct colours than any which are employ'd by the latter. When we remember any past event, the idea of it flows in upon the mind in a forcible manner; whereas in the imagination the perception is faint and languid and cannot without difficulty be preserv'd by the mind steady and uniform for any considerable time. Here, then, is a sensible difference betwixt one species of ideas and another.

~

Section 13.2: Hume and the Origin of Ideas

So, how does the mind work? How is it that we come to have the ideas that we have? And which of our ideas are actually ideas and which are illusions? These are questions that Hume addresses from the very first page of the *Treatise*.

Hume's most important and most influential work begins with a development of a Theory of Perception that has, as one appealing feature, its ability to reasonably accurately explain the origins of ideas from the perceptions of the world. All of knowledge is borne in perception and, on Hume's view, *perceptions* are of two sorts, impressions and ideas. He refines this classification further, dividing both species of perceptions into two distinct types. The types of impression are sensation and reflection. The types of idea are memory and imagination. We will first address the manner in which Hume distinguishes impressions and ideas before turning to the manner in which he distinguishes sensation and reflection in the case of impressions and memory and imagination in the case of ideas. After discussing the Theory of Perception and the epistemological work Hume does with it, we will conclude this section by turning to one of the potentially devastating criticisms that Hume himself puts forward against his view.

Impressions and Ideas are clearly different. Indeed, Impressions have all manner of priority over Ideas. Among these are phenomenological, temporal, and, perhaps, most importantly, causal. The phenomenological distinction between ideas and impressions is fairly straightforward and is perhaps the most vividly demonstrated. Ideas are distinct from impressions because they appear to the observer differently. Impressions strike the perceiver with force and violence while ideas are, quite literally, "faint copies of ideas." An example here will be helpful. Suppose Kevin is a young boy who is quite curious. One day, he takes a bobby pin and, curious about the little holes in the wall, inserts the pin into one of the holes. Unbeknownst to him, the little holes are part of an electrical outlet. The resulting experience is impressive, in both senses of that word. It is rather a spectacular flash of light and at the same time, presses in on young Kevin. An impression is made on him. It is instantaneous and without thought. The impression of the experience is immediate. Years later, while discussing the experience with his philosophy class, Dr. Kevin points out that even as he thinks of this experience now, it still gives him a bit of a shiver up and down his spine. However, the idea of that moment with the bobby pin and the electrical outlet is not nearly so forceful and violent as the impression of it at the time. At the time, he was blown across the room and a permanent scar etched on his hand. Thirty years or so later, the idea (in this case, a memory idea), is still vivid, but it does bear the force of the impression that gave rise to the idea. So, it is clear, then, that impressions differ from ideas in this phenomenological way – they appear to the perceiver in quite different ways.

So, for Hume, the distinction between impressions and ideas is the same distinction that exists between experiencing something and thinking about it. On Hume's view, this purely empirical distinction is rooted in our experience of

Section 13.2: Hume and the Origin of Ideas 317

impressions and the ideas to which they give rise. Though this distinction is somewhat rigid and fixed in the simple cases of impressions and ideas, Hume recognizes that often it is more difficult to distinguish impressions and ideas. Allowance is made for those difficult cases, though such allowance in no way scuttles the general theory. As he writes in the *Treatise*,

> The common degrees of these are easily distinguished; tho' it is not impossible but in particular instances they may very nearly approach to each other. Thus in sleep, in a fever, in madness, or in any very violent emotions of soul, our ideas may approach to our impressions: As on the other hand it sometimes happens, that our impressions are so faint and low, that we cannot distinguish them from our ideas. But notwithstanding this near resemblance in a few instances, they are in general so very different, that no-one can make a scruple to rank them under distinct heads, and assign to each a peculiar name to mark the difference.

In other words, occasionally an idea will possess such great force that it will seem stronger than certain impressions. For example, the sunshine on a moderate day impresses itself upon the observer. But, if we consider the shiver up the spine inspired by the memory of the electrical outlet and bobby pin, we might well note that that memory idea has spawned an impression of its own and one that is more forceful than the passive experience of the sunshine. However, in the first place, it should not seem odd that ideas might carry with them some weight of their own. This seems a fairly straightforward result of our own experience. Secondly, however, Impressions have more than simply phenomenological priority over ideas. They have temporal and causal priority as well.

The example of the childhood trauma and the chills caused by the memory of it is an excellent one to demonstrate that although certain ideas may, in extremely special circumstances, carry a force and violence greater than some impressions, it is still impossible to conceive of them as prior to impressions. While the idea of the electrical experience causes an impression to arise that is greater than the impression of sensation of the sunshine upon the skin, the force and vivacity of the idea is not greater than the impression that gave rise to it. Further, and here we encounter a second type of priority of impressions to ideas, the impression of the electrical event is prior in time. That is, the impression is temporally prior to the idea that is the reflection of the impression. This seems fairly straightforward. The idea, as a faint copy of the impression, could not possibly occur prior to the impression itself. Thus, impressions have both phenomenological and temporal priority over ideas.

The third sort of priority is perhaps the most important and is connected to the first two. This third sort of priority of impressions to ideas is causal priority. Put in another way, impressions cause ideas; or, if an idea is anything other than chimerical, it is the product of an impression. Thus, we have a systematic justification for Hume's first stated principle of human nature, that all ideas are derived from sensation and reflection. Let us state that more formally.

> *Hume's First Principle of Human Nature*: All ideas are derived from sensation and reflection.

With this Theory of Perception and the analysis of the psychological origin of ideas of various sorts and the first principle of human nature, it also becomes clear that Hume has established a criterion for all claims of knowledge, for judging between true ideas and illusions. Since knowledge is always *of* ideas, then those ideas that are meaningful ones are only those that have been produced in a particular way. From the very first chapter of Hume's *Treatise*, it becomes quite clear that he is concerned with establishing the criteria under which claims of knowledge might be justified. That principle, in two forms, we will call Hume's Epistemological Principle. In its primary form, the Epistemological Principle would be written something like this: If there is an idea, then there must be a corresponding impression, or set of impressions, which give rise, either singly or jointly to the idea. Most often, this principle is shortened to "If there is an idea, then there must be a corresponding impression," however, it is important to recognize its first and more accurate formulation, particularly as we turn to discussions of the ideas of *substance* and *cause and effect* in later sections. For clarity's sake, we should state the first form of the Epistemological Principle.

> *Epistemological Principle*: If there is an idea, then there must be a corresponding impression, or set of impressions, which give rise, either singly or jointly to the idea.

Given the Epistemological Principle's statement as a conditional, it follows that its contrapositive should follow as well. Indeed, the alternative form of the Epistemological Principle is one of the most powerful critical tools that Hume uses in analysis of the work of other philosophers. The contrapositive of any conditional, *If p, then q*, is of the form, *If ~q, then ~p*. Thus, the contrapositive of the Epistemological Principle would be, "If there is no impression, then there is no idea." This, then, is the alternative form of Hume's Epistemological Principle.

> *Epistemological Principle (alternative form)*: If there is no impression, then there is no idea

This use of this principle to analyze our ideas and the work of other philosophers will receive considerable attention in the foregoing sections. Suffice to say here that it sheds light onto the larger Humean project, namely an analysis of human nature, the nature of human knowledge, and the justification of that knowledge. While Descartes, for example, seemed much more concerned with the nature of truth, often subsuming a view of justification within that theory of truth, Hume does much the reverse. Hume is particularly concerned with the justification of knowledge or claims to it. He returns again and again to the Epistemological Principle and the First Principle of Human Nature which underlies it. It is the touchstone that he will not surrender. Hume, the empiricist, holds consistently that human knowledge, insofar as it exists, is a product of experience.

It would be helpful to examine ways in which Hume's project might be addressed to certain immediately recognizable difficulties. With the recognition of the principle that justification for ideas must be tied, ultimately, to experience, let us turn to three potential difficulties. The first of these is commonly called the *Molyneux Problem*, the second is a matter of the development of the incredible complexity of the human mental architecture from such simple beginnings, and the last is the Missing Shade of Blue.

Since, impressions are understood to correspond to seeing, hearing, pleasure, pain, love, hate, etc. while ideas are the fainter images of these things which occur in thought, any conception of an 'idea' must have experience as its foundation. One example is the Molyneux problem which asks the question, "If a person born blind were to recover sight, would they be able to make a distinction without touch?" On Hume's view, the answer is a quite straightforward "No." Instead, the person so born would have to learn to make the distinctions which perhaps seemed innate to a sighted person. I say "seemed" because I think it would be consistent with Hume's view to argue that the sighted person herself learned to make the distinctions as well, though perhaps as such a small child she does not remember learning. Nevertheless, distinctions between ideas of this sort are learned, of necessity, if they are ever to be made at all, though the time of the learning is somewhat more contingent. Hume seems to think that this principle is needed in philosophy as a corrective measure and method of judgment between ideas. In the *Enquiry Concerning Human Understanding,* Hume writes

> When we entertain, therefore, any suspicion that a philosophical term is employed without any meaning or idea (as is but too frequent), we need but enquire, *from what impression is that supposed idea derived?* And if it be impossible to assign any, this will serve to confirm our suspicion. By bringing ideas into so clear a light we may reasonably hope to remove all dispute, which may arise, concerning their nature and reality.

In short, without an impression there is no simple idea corresponding to a philosophical term. Without the justifying impression, use of such vacuous philosophical terms is spurious. Thus, we see the immediate application of the Epistemological Principle within the realm of philosophical reasoning and the Molyneux Problem, although perhaps a bit counterintuitive in its solution, is seen to be a pseudo-problem, at best, for Hume.

Turning to the issue of the vast scope of the human mind, filled with intricate ideas which do not seem, in many cases, to be immediately traceable to originating impressions, we should not conclude that Hume thinks that there are merely initial impressions of sensation and reflection and the initial ideas that spring from them. Such an epistemological view would fall far short of explaining the quite complex ideas that populate the human mind. However, careful examination of Hume's actual view will show what has heretofore merely been alluded, that quite complex ideas may arise from impressions. Recall that impressions of sensation and impressions of reflection are distinguished as follows: impressions of sensation arise "in the soul originally, from unknown causes" while impressions of reflection are connected in some sense to ideas. Though distinct, these differing impressions are related. On Hume's view, impressions of sensation are understood to have their genesis in the soul. These impressions are registered in the senses and certain perceptions arise: heat, cold, pleasure, pain, etc. Copies of these perceptions are made in the mind and thus are simple ideas. These simple ideas remain after the initial experience which gave rise to the sensation has ceased. However, when the idea of the experience arises again in the soul, the person experiences new impressions that arise from the old: aversion, hope, fear. These new impressions are impressions of reflection because they are at two removes from the initial impression and yet retain much of the force and vivacity of that original impression. This recursive relationship of impressions can potentially give rise to a continued and potentially baroque series of impressions of reflection.

It should be of little surprise that ideas are closely connected to impressions of reflection on Hume's view. It is the simple idea, which itself is the copy of the initial impression which arose in the soul, that gives rise to an impression of reflection. The ability to repeat impressions within the soul is the faculty of memory. An idea of memory "retains a considerable degree of its first vivacity." For this reason, Hume understands ideas of memory to be somewhere between impressions and perfect ideas. Once an idea has lost all of its vivacity so that it can no longer produce impressions and is totally impotent to motivate the individual, then it is understood as a perfect idea. The ideas of imagination, which have lost all vivacity, possess a power not held by ideas of memory, however. Ideas of imagination are free to be conjoined in a variety of ways which represent the initial impressions in no immediately obvious ways. Ideas of memory, which still possess some of the vivacity of the originating impression, are tied to that impression in such a way that they are "without any power of variation." Thus, through the recursive nature of the Theory of Perception, ideas of amazing complexity can be constructed, leaving little doubt that Hume's view can, at least on the surface, explain that complexity.

Let us now turn to the more difficult of the three problems, the Missing Shade of Blue. Much philosophic ink has been spilt concerning the missing shade of blue "problem" that Hume mentions in the *Treatise* in *Of the Origin of our Ideas*. Indeed, Hume, himself, seems to realize that this problem poses at least a minor difficulty for his view. Hume states quite clearly that the imagination is not capable of generating the idea of pine-apple, for example, without having tasted it. Indeed, Hume makes the very strong assertion that it is a plain and convincing phenomenon that

> where-ever by any accident the faculties, which give rise to any impression, are obstructed in their operations, as when one is born blind or deaf; not only the impressions are lost, but also their correspondent ideas; so that there *never* appear in the mind the least traces of either of them.

He then raises the issue of whether or not an individual, by use of imagination alone, could fill in a shade of blue missing from a spectrum in which all the gradations in shade above and below the missing shade were present. It would seem that following Hume's view, one is committed to the conclusion that since ideas are only justified by their corresponding impressions and since the impressions and the correspondent ideas are lost when any accident prevents the original impression, then the missing shade of blue will remain forever out of reach of the individual who, though possessing every other color of the spectrum before her, has no impression of that particular shade of blue.

Interestingly enough, however, this is not the conclusion to which Hume feels himself committed. Rather, he thinks it a rather odd example and states that scarcely anyone would deny that the individual, by use of the imagination, could indeed supply the missing shade. Hume seems to think that the gradations of color, each moving into the next, would enable the imagination to construct a simple idea without a corresponding impression. Indeed, he says that this example amounts to a sort of proof "that simple ideas are not always derived from the correspondent impression." Given this result, then, it would seem logical for Hume to suppose that his programme of basing knowledge upon perception and understanding perceptions as of two types, impressions and ideas with impressions always preceding and giving rise to ideas, is in danger of faltering for want of a color.

Again of some interest, Hume does not take the missing shade of blue "proof" to be troubling. Indeed, he rather cavalierly dismisses it; "the instance is so particular and singular, that 'tis scarce worth our observing, and does not merit that for it alone we should alter our general maxim." Such a dismissal would seem to want for a reason and on Hume's view, there seem to be two.

There does not seem to be a strict atomism at the fundamental level of perception on Hume's view. Though perceptions are distinct, distinguishable, and separable, there are relations between ideas, even among simple ideas. If there were a strict atomism, Hume's project would be in danger because there would be no more relation between blue and green than between blue and white or between blue and green than blue and sour. However, in the *Appendix* to the *Treatise*, Hume notes that on his view there are indeed relations at the fundamental level of perception. "'Tis evident, that even different simple ideas may have a similarity or resemblance to each other; nor is it necessary, that the point or circumstance of resemblance shou'd be distinct or separable from that in which they differ. *Blue* and *green* are different simple ideas, but are more resembling than *blue* and *scarlet*."

However, these relations at the fundamental level of perception are not the only things that Hume can depend upon to explain away any difficulties arising from the missing shade of blue problem. This is so at least in part because the topics with which he will concern himself have nothing to do with the missing shade of blue or any idea which fills in a blank spot in a gradation of impressions. Among the topics covered in the *Treatise* are (1) Space and Time, (2) Causal Relations and Necessary Connexions, (3) Substance and Attributes, (4) Continued and Distinct Existence of Things, (5) Personal Identity, (6) Moral Qualities and Relations, and (7) Justice and Property. These ideas are not ideas supplied to fill in a blank spot in a graduated series of impressions. Indeed, there are no foundational impressions to form a graduated scale into which these ideas could be fit. So, the missing shade of blue "problem" is not a problem for Hume's larger programme because it deals with a qualitatively different sort of experience: the experience of gradations of impressions of sensation versus the absence of impressions entirely. Thus, whatever critique may be offered of Hume's project, Hume himself believes that the missing shade of blue is not the ground for such.

Perhaps he should, however. It seems straightforward that, given the Epistemological Principle, Hume should respond in the way that we suppose he would respond to the Molyneux problem; that is, to take the perhaps counterintuitive conclusion that it would be impossible to construct the idea of this missing shade of blue, in the imagination or elsewhere. Such an argument would be completely consistent with Hume's Theory of Perception and could go as follows:

Statement	Justification
1. If there is no impression, then there is no idea.	1. Epistemological Principle (alternate form)
2. There is no impression of the missing shade of blue.	2. By hypothesis
3. Therefore, there is no idea of the missing shade of blue.	3. Modus Ponens.

However, one is not limited to this manner of analysis. One can approach the question from the standpoint of the basics of the Theory of Perception itself. Let us suppose, for the moment, that the missing shade of blue is named "Blue 5." Let us also suppose that all the shades around Blue 5 have been perceived by some individual, Mary. Thus, Mary has had impressions of sensation of Blues 1 through 4 and of Blues 6 through 10, for example. As a result, memory ideas of Blues 1 through 4 and of Blues 6 through 10 have arisen. So, the impression of Blue 1 gives rise to the memory idea "Blue 1" and so forth. As memory ideas of simple impressions, these memory ideas will themselves be simple. Thus, Mary has simple memory ideas of "Blue 1," "Blue 2," and so forth. How, though, is the idea of "Blue 5" to arise. If Hume's answer in the *Treatise* is taken at face value, it arises from the imagination. As suggested by Hume, this seems consistent with the common sense view of the question. However, since the idea, "Blue 5," arises from the imagination, it is presumably constructed from some method of merging, in the imagination, "Blue 4" and "Blue 6" and through that merging deriving "Blue 5." As a result of this, however, "Blue 5" is not a simple memory idea, but rather is a complex imagination idea. Thus, even if the imagination were able to construct the idea of "Blue 5" and fill in the missing shade of blue in the mind, the idea would still be qualitatively different from each of its blue fellows. So, even assuming an imaginative approach to the difficulty, one fails to see, given Hume's Epistemological Principle and his Theory of Perception, how the idea of the missing shade of blue could be constructed, in the first place, or how, if constructed, it could be anything like the ideas of the other shades of blue that proceeded from impressions of sensation. Rather than give assent to the perhaps prevailing common view of the solution to the problem, perhaps it would have been more consistent for Hume to adopt the counterintuitive conclusion, one completely defensible from his own empirical analysis. Analysis similar to that employed here is employed by Hume, himself, when the conversation turns to topics of a more obviously philosophical bent in later sections.

Guided Reading Questions
1. What are the two species of perception? Describe their characteristics.
2. Which of the two species of perception has priority over the other? Why?
3. What is the Epistemological Principle?
4. According to Hume, can we have an idea of something if we have no impression of it?
5. According to Hume, do we have an idea of the "missing shade of blue" even though we have no impression of it? Why does he take the position that he does?

Logic Blurb
Theory of Knowledge

What is knowledge and how does one acquire it? Commonly, people are quite ready to claim to know all manner of things. Socrates encountered this as he examined all those with a reputation for wisdom. Descartes began his Meditations with a recognition that we potentially have many beliefs that are taken to be knowledge but in fact are not. Philosophers since Plato have understood that the ability to distinguish opinion from belief from knowledge is central to the pursuit of wisdom. So what differentiates a knowledge of some proposition, say "2 + 2 = 4" from a strongly held, albeit false belief, that "2 + 2 = 5"?

In Plato's *Theaetetus*, "Socrates" suggests a model for knowledge that has come to be the most widely accepted in epistemology. The model of knowledge is commonly referred to as Justified True Belief (JTB). Each of the aspects of the name refers to a necessary condition for a claim to knowledge. That is, for us to accept that a person knows p, it must be the case that p is true, that the person actually believes p, and that the person is justified in believing p. These conditions are perhaps best understood in example.

Suppose a friend says that he knows that "2 + 2 = 5." Under any reasonable interpretation of arithmetic, we know that this proposition is false. If we take "2" to represent that situation in which there are two objects, then we know that by taking a set of two objects and adding that set to another set of two objects, that the resulting situation is described by the word "4" and not by "5". Hence, the sentence "2 + 2 = 5" is false because it does not accurately describe the situation. Thus, it cannot be said that our friend knows the proposition because part of what it means to know something is to know it to be true. Since the proposition is, in fact, false, it cannot be known to be true. Thus, truth is necessary for knowledge.

The next condition for knowledge that we should examine is belief. This may be the most obvious aspect of the model. Suppose our friend came and said that he knew "2 + 2 = 5" but that he actually believes it to be false. So, we might ask, do you believe that "2 + 2 = 4"? And he would say, "Why, yes, I do." So, we are then presented with the situation of two propositions – "I know that '2 + 2 = 5' and I don't believe it" and "I believe that '2 + 2 = 4.'" Clearly such a situation is one that could not reasonably be called knowledge.

Finally, suppose our friend said that he knew "2 + 2 = 4" and we ask how he knew it (or why he thought it to be so). Suppose that his justification for his view was that last night a purple and green bird with yellow polka dots flew her space ship through his window and perched on his bedside table. From this perch, the bird whispered into our friend's ear that "2 + 2 = 4," and in virtue of this (and this alone), our friend believed it. It seems perfectly reasonable to suppose that while it is true that "2 + 2 = 4" and while it is clear that our friend believes that "2 + 2 = 4," he is not justified in holding that belief. In other words, the person who gives a brief, but thorough rendering of the principles of arithmetic in response to our request has provided a proper justification of the proposition while our bird-watching friend has not.

Section 13.3: Hume and the Association of Ideas

Treatise of Human Nature
Volume I: Of the Understanding
Part I. Of Ideas, Their Origin, Composition, Connexion, Abstraction, &c.

Section IV. Of the connexion or association of ideas

As all simple ideas may be separated by the imagination and may be united again in what form it pleases, nothing would be more unaccountable than the operations of that faculty, were it not guided by some universal principles. The uniting principle is not to be consider'd as an inseparable connexion. The qualities from which this association arises and by which the mind is after this manner convey'd from one idea to another are three – *Resemblance, Contiguity* in place or time, and *Cause and Effect*.

I believe it will not be very necessary to prove that these qualities produce an association among ideas and upon the appearance of one idea naturally introduce another. 'Tis plain that in the course of our thinking and in the constant revolution of our ideas, our imagination runs easily from one idea to any other that *resembles* it, and that this quality alone is to the fancy a sufficient body and association. 'Tis likewise evident that as the senses, in changing their objects, are necessitated to change them regularly and take them as they lie *contiguous* to each other, the imagination must by long custom acquire the same method of thinking and run along the parts of space and time in conceiving its objects. As to the connexion that is made by the relation of *cause and effect*, we shall have occasion afterwards to examine it to the bottom, and therefore shall not at present insist upon it.

The word *relation* is commonly used in two senses considerably different from each other. Either for that quality by which two ideas are connected together in the imagination, or for that particular circumstance in which even upon the arbitrary union of two ideas in the fancy, we may think proper to compare them. 'Tis only in philosophy that we extend it to mean any particular subject of comparison without a connecting principle. The ideas of the *philosophical* relation may be compriz'd under seven general heads which may be considered as the sources of them all.

1. The first is *resemblance*: And this is a relation without which no philosophical relation can exist; since no objects will admit of comparison but what have some degree of resemblance.

2. *Identity* may be esteem'd a second species of relation. This relation I here consider as apply'd in its strictest sense to constant and unchangeable objects; without examining the nature and foundations of personal identity.

3. After identity, the most universal and comprehensive relations are those of *Space* and *Time*, which are the sources of an infinite number of comparisons, such as *distant, contiguous, above, below, before, after,* &c.

4. All those objects, which admit of *quantity*, or *number*, may be compar'd in that particular.

5. When any two objects possess the same *quality* in common, the *degrees* in which they possess it form a fifth species of relations. Thus of two objects which are both heavy, the one may be either of greater or less weight than the other.

6. The relation of *contrariety* may at first sight be regarded as an exception to the rule, *that no relation of any kind can subsist without some degree of resemblance.* But let us consider that no two ideas are in themselves contrary, except those of existence and non-existence, which are plainly resembling, as implying both of them an idea of the object; tho' the latter excludes the object from all times and places, in which it is supposed not to exist.

7. All other objects, such as fire and water, heat, and cold are only found to be contrary from experience, and from the contrariety of their *causes* or *effects*; which relation of cause and effect is a seventh philosophical relation as well as a natural one.

~

With an understanding of the process by which ideas arise in the mind, Hume turns to a treatment of the way in which the human mind addresses those ideas. The mind is constantly linking ideas together by one means or another. Indeed, Hume argues that ideas are linked together by the imagination in two general ways, each of which encompass several distinguishable relations. So, after having shown that all ideas arise from initial sense perception, Hume turns to discuss the ways in which those ideas are then linked together, or associated.

The association of ideas is, for Hume, a critical piece of his own positive epistemological view as well as his negative, critical view of other, more rationalistic epistemological theories. Colloquially known as *Hume's Fork*, Hume's view is a theory of the association of ideas that is, at first, somewhat counterintuitive. If one were following the Cartesian intuition that knowledge must be certain to be worthy of the name "knowledge" at all, then most (if not all) knowledge is not. Whatever else it may or may not accomplish, Descartes's skeptical method in the *First Meditation* casts doubt on the senses and any ideas that are dependent on them. The Medieval assumption that the world, for all intents and purposes, was accurately reflected in human perception was effec-

Section 13.3: Hume and the Association of Ideas

tively refuted by Descartes; a refutation with which Hume does not disagree. Thus, if human knowledge requires certainty, and if Hume is right about the source of all ideas (in human perception), then human knowledge is impossible. The motivating proposition in this difficulty we can call "The Certainty Principle"; that is, if ideas are certain, they cannot be rooted in sense perception. This dilemma that follows from this principle can be represented formally as it is below. The Certainty Principle is one with which both the Cartesian rationalist and the Humean empiricist would agree; in the case of the Cartesian, it is a consequence of the doubts of the *First Meditation*, in the case of the Humean, it is a product of experience of the fallible relationship between sense perception and the ideas that reflect it.

Statement	Justification
1. Knowledge requires certainty with respect to the ideas known.	1. Cartesian rationalist assumption
2. If ideas are certain, they cannot be rooted in sense perception.	2. Certainty Principle
3. All ideas are the faint images of sense perception.	3. Epistemological Principle
4. Thus, no ideas are certain.	4. Modus Tollens
5. Thus, knowledge is impossible.	5. Modus Tollens

Indeed, for this reason, Hume has often been considered a radical Skeptic with regards to human knowledge. Such an interpretation of Hume is straightforwardly superficial and naïve. It is clear from Hume's own work that he thinks the human mind is capable of knowledge. Given this, Hume can address the Certainty Problem by simply denying the assumption that human knowledge requires certainty of the sort desired by Descartes. Thus, by rejecting the initial assumption – the Cartesian rationalist assumption – Hume is not bound to the conclusion that knowledge is impossible.

To reject the notion that certainty is a prerequisite for knowledge is certainly to make the acquisition and ascription of knowledge considerably more difficult. To address that difficulty, Hume turns to discuss the ways in which ideas are related to one another; or, the ways in which new ideas are imaginatively developed from basic ones. Hume's Fork divides the process of building new ideas (or relating basic ideas one to another) into Matters of Fact and Relations of Ideas. The second superficially counterintuitive aspect of Hume's view is found here. If one were to be asked which of the two, *Matters of Fact* or *Relations of Ideas*, is the place in which *certainty* would most likely be located, it is almost certain that the respondent would say, "Matters of Fact." Hume, however, locates *certainty*, or at least his description of it, under the heading *Relations of Ideas*.

While this is straightforwardly counterintuitive on first glance, upon reflection, with examples, it becomes much clearer. An example of a kind of discipline that would fall under the heading of *Relations of Ideas* is geometry. The objects of the study of plane geometry are points, lines, planes, parallel lines, etc. Each of these is an idea. In fact, each of these ideas are definitional ones that can be put together in myriad ways to demonstrate other ideas that are not basic assumptions. For example, one might take the Euclidean Elements that are the fundamental axioms of plane geometry and arrange them in such a way that the Pythagorean Theorem is demonstrated to follow from those axioms. Suppose a student was given the following problem in plane geometry.

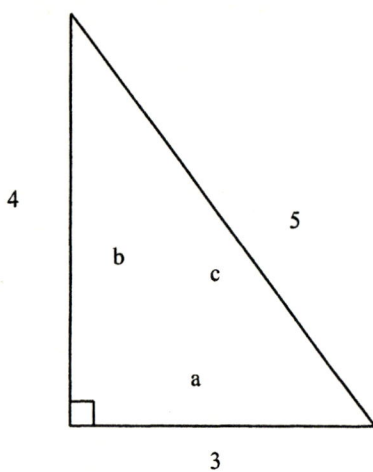

Pythagorean Theorem: The square of the length of the hypotenuse of a right triangle is equal to the sum of the squares of the lengths of the two shorter sides. Thus, $a^2 + b^2 = c^2$, where *a* and *b* are the shorter sides of the right triangle and *c* is the hypotenuse.

The student could then apply the Pythgorean Theorem, which is not itself a basic axiom of plane geometry, but rather is a theorem that is derived from them, to arrive at the answer "$c = 5$." However, suppose the student responded that the answer was "$c = 7$." Whatever the answer offered, it is either correct or incorrect, right or wrong, true or false. There would not be any room for variation here. This sort of precision is what is generally thought to be *certain*. Hume agrees.

However, it is important to note carefully that this *certainty* is not universal. The answer to the geometry problem is developed by putting the axioms of geometry and other theorems that have been shown to follow from them together. This is an exercise in relating ideas. Notice that the student has taken the ideas of "3," "4," "5," and the Pythagorean Theorem and arranged them in the proper relationship. Thus, by relating the ideas properly, the student comes to the correct answer. To relate the ideas improperly would likely result in the answer being incorrect. Thus, certainty can be thought to obtain in this case. However, to assume that *certainty* extends beyond this mental exercise is to assume something even more basic than the axioms of plane geometry. This exercise in relating ideas assumes that the axioms of Euclidean geometry actually correspond to the world in some way. This, however, we do not know for certain. In fact, it is the case that the universe is not Euclidean and thus, the axioms of plane geometry do not hold. This in no way affects the certainty of the student upon presenting his answer, "$c = 5$", but it does show that the practice of relating ideas in this way does not entail any close connection to the actual world. Thus, *Relations of Ideas* are relations that bear a great measure of certainty, but are not necessarily aligned with the experience of the world whatsoever. Notice that the conclusions of geometry, for example, follow from *axioms* not from *experience*. Thus, the axioms, as imaginative definitions can be related in ways that preserve certainty within the system defined by the axioms, but no further. Thus, the ways of linking ideas that can be described as *Relations of Ideas* preserve demonstrative certainty but have no necessary connection to the actual world.

Matters of Fact, on the other hand, are precisely the reverse. Again, this is seen best in example. If we imagine a chemist in her laboratory, we can envision her running a set of experiments, testing an hypothesis through repeated empirical trials. Let us imagine that each of the trials can be represented by t. Thus, we have t_1 and t_2 and t_3 and so on, through t_n. Tomorrow, she will go into the lab and conduct trial, t_{n+1}. We might be led to conclude that tomorrow's trial will have the same result as all of the preceding ones. However, it is clear from our experience of such hypothesis testing that this is not the case. Indeed, tomorrow's trial may be the one that defeats the hypothesis. Prior to the trial, it is impossible to know what the outcome will be. Further, given that no set of trials is universal, covering every single possible case, it is impossible to generalize to all cases from a finite set of trials. Thus, the sort of certainty that attends mathematics is markedly absent in the sciences.

At the same time, each of the trials is a particular experience of the actual world. That is, each trial is, itself, a fact of experience. These facts are neither true nor false; they merely are. Since each trial is a fact of experience, *Matters of Fact* are more closely aligned with the world. Thus, we are left with a category in which ideas are linked that is both closely linked to the world as it is experienced and, at the same time, fraught with uncertainty. It would have been ideal to have a third category, one closely linked to the world and imbued with the certainty of the mathematical sciences. However, experience reveals this is impossible. Thus, the human mind has before it ideas that are the images of basic sense impressions, ideas that are then linked one to another in the imagination either as *Relations of Ideas* or *Matters of Fact*, and, as a result, an impossibility of certainty with regard to those ideas, either because the ideas are not tied to the actual world (*Relations of Ideas*) or because they are highly particular and do not admit of universal generalization (*Matters of Fact*).

Rather than concluding that humanity is fundamentally incapable of knowledge, however, Hume's view provides the framework by which we can begin to understand not only what we know but how it is we come to know it. Hume's treatment of the association of ideas indicates a shift in emphasis in the Justified True Belief model of knowledge adopted, to one degree or another, as the basic model of knowledge by both Descartes and Hume. Descartes, as we have discussed, is centrally concerned with the notion of Truth. If ideas are clear and distinct, and derived in the way in which clarity is preserved, then Justification follows as a consequence. For Hume, however, this is not the case. Having rejected certainty as a criterion for knowledge, Hume must focus more on the Justification aspect of knowledge. Thus, for Hume, it appears that Justification is the central concern in the theory of knowledge, and that further, ideas that are developed or acquired in the appropriate ways are properly justified.

Justification is a matter of the generation of ideas, through the process of impressions producing ideas, and the association of those ideas in such a way that is appropriate to the relation. For example, an idea for which there is no impression is rejected and an idea that implies a level of certainty or a connection to the world that it cannot express is also cast off. How, then, do the ideas that originate in simple impressions link together in the mind to produce the more complex ideas that give breadth and depth to human thought and knowledge? To answer this question, Hume reflects at length on the philosophical relations.

The philosophical relations are relations that fall under the heading of *Relations of Ideas*. In the *Treatise*, Hume notes seven relations, although in his later work he treats only three. Even in the *Treatise*, it is clear that three of the philosophical relations occupy a tier above the others in importance. The first of these is the relation, *Resemblance*. *Resemblance* is a straightforward and absolutely foundational amenable notion. Ideas are connected in the imagination first by the resemblance that each has to the other. Without this relation, any other relation of ideas would be impossible. Hume writes of *Resemblance*, "this is a relation without which no philosophical relation can exist."

Resemblance simply refers to the fact that the human imagination moves from one idea to the next by taking note of the ways in which the two ideas have features in common. Further, the human mind is more likely to suppose that one idea is more closely or more distantly related to a second idea in virtue of the level of commonality between them. That is, if the two ideas resemble one another closely, the imagination supposes that the objects conveyed by the ideas are similarly close in relation. At the same time, if the two ideas bear little resemblance to each other, the imagination infers that the objects of the ideas also are barely related to one another, if at all. Thus, for example, the mind considers the idea "ink pen" and "pencil" and notes that there are many features the two have in common. Thus, the imagination moves to the idea that the actual ink pen and the actual pencil are also quite closely related. In fact, each is simply an independent object in the actual world and the grouping of them into a "similarity" relation is purely a product of the human imagination, and thus, an accidental property of the human perception rather than a necessary property of the world.

Another example of *Resemblance* cuts the other way. One might have the idea of a "car key" and the idea of a "small, thin, plastic card with a magnetic strip along the back." The imagination, noting that there is little in common between these two ideas might suppose that the objects referred to by the ideas are similarly completely unrelated. However, the object of the idea "plastic card" might actually be a card key and thus more closely related, at least in terms of function in the world, than the ideas appear at first blush. Thus, the philosophical relation, *Resemblance*, is the process by which the mind, through imagination, groups ideas into sets based on commonality between the particular elements of the sets and excludes from those groups those ideas where there is less perceived commonality.

The relation, *Identity*, is related to *Resemblance*. Two objects are said to be identical if they possess all the same features. *Identity*, however, is a difficult philosophical notion. Hume straightforwardly avoids the pitfall of *personal identity* by restricting the general use of the notion of *Identity* merely to is application to two objects bearing all the same properties. However, in restricting his discussion to this limited application here, he also anticipates the rather more important, albeit nearly impossibly complex, application of the philosophical relation to matters of personal or self identity. The difficulty with the philosophical relation, *Identity,* is most pronounced when it is a matter of *personal identity* that is under review. For example, how is it that we say that Ashli is the same person she was twenty years ago when it is clear that she is now taller, stronger, possessed of many more experiences, and holds nearly none of the beliefs that her four-year old self held? An ancient thought experiment, the Ship of Theseus example, gets to the heart of the identity matter. Suppose there was a ship that sailed into a harbor and made berth. Suppose further that each day, one and only one plank was removed from the ship. Each day, a different plank was replaced, such that from day to day, the ship changed only by that one board. After a considerable time had passed, the ship no longer had a single plank that it had upon its initial docking in the harbor. As the ship prepares to make sail, it looks exactly as it did upon its entry. However, not a single feature of the ship at the constitutive level (the stuff out of which it is made) is the same.

Is it the same ship that docked the in the berth? If it is, it would seem that a story must be told about how identity is preserved when there is not a single feature identical from one edition of the ship to the next. If it is not the same ship, at what point did it cease to be? After a single board was replaced? After half the boards were replaced? To make the matter a bit more pointed, let us consider a human being. The atoms within a particular human body are completely replaced gradually over a seven year period. That is, the person who was Maria seven years ago and the person who is Maria today have no atoms in common with one another. Thus, it would seem odd to say that she is the same person that she was. At the same time, it would seem odd to say that she is not identical to her earlier self in all of the ways that are important. While *Identity* can pose some pernicious philosophical problems, as a philosophical relation, it is a straightforward refinement of the philosophical relation, *Resemblance*.

The last two of the three most important philosophical relations are *Contiguity* and *Cause and Effect*. We will address the notion of *Cause and Effect* in a following section. Thus, we will close this section with a discussion of the relation, *Contiguity*. Simply put, *Contiguity* refers to the proximity two or more objects bear to each other. That is, two objects are said to be contiguous if they have a common border. For example, Vermont and New Hampshire are contiguous states. One can move from Maine to California by moving from one contiguous state to another. However, Alaska and Georgia are not contiguous, either transitively (Georgia to Alabama to Mississippi is an example of transitive contiguity) nor immediately (Oklahoma to Kansas is an example of immediate contiguity). The most important use of the philosophical relation, *Contiguity*, comes as Hume develops a notion of *Cause and Effect*. Since Hume's treatment of that notion is sometimes the ground by which he is given the label, Skeptic, it is important that we turn to it in the next two sections, first addressing Hume's critique of the philosophical notion of "substance" in 13.4, before applying a similar approach to the analysis of "causation," in 13.5.

Guided Reading Questions
1. What is a relation?
2. What are the six philosophical relations, according to Hume?
3. What is Hume's Fork?

Logic Blurb
The Slippery Slope/Fallacy of the Beard

The *Slippery Slope fallacy*, sometimes called the *fallacy of the beard*, is a commonly used rhetorical device, the error of which is sometimes difficult to pin down. The structure of the slippery slope is this. If one gives one's opponent even an inch, then one has started down a slippery slope on which one will forever be unable to regain one's footing and which will result in the person experiencing rather horrible consequences. Here is an example of a slippery slope fallacy. Tina tells John that he can borrow her car to go to the grocery store. Her friend, Melissa, leans over to her and tells her not to let him borrow the car. She says that if he gets to borrow the car, the next thing you know he will want money for it, and then he will want to borrow one of her bedrooms for a couple of nights and then he will take over the entire house, bank account, and social life. If given an inch, he will take not only a mile, but everything beyond that as well. Melissa is committing a slippery slope fallacy and hoping that Tina will slide to the bottom with her.

The fallacy is sometimes called the fallacy of the beard because rather than going down a destructive slope, sometimes arguments start from the bottom and build up. If a person has a single hair on his face, we would not say that he has a beard. If he had a second hair, we would still not conclude that he had a beard. The question becomes, how many hairs would it take for us to conclude that he has a beard. It is clear that there is not set number of hairs above which one has a beard and below which one does not. The fallacy is a result of trying to introduce specificity and precision into terms that are, by definition, lacking in specificity and imprecise. So, going down the slope or up the beard, the fallacy takes its victims from one step to the next without grasping the larger context into which the argument they are offering fits.

Section 13.4: Hume and Substance

Treatise of Human Nature
Volume I: Of the Understanding
Part I. Of Ideas, Their Origin, Composition, Connexion, Abstraction, &c.

Section VI. Of modes and substances
I wou'd fain ask those philosophers who found so much of their reasonings on the distinction of substance and accident and imagine we have clear ideas of each, whether the idea of *substance* be deriv'd from the impressions of sensation or reflexion? If it be convey'd to us by our senses, I ask, which of them; and after what manner? If it be perceiv'd by the eyes, it must be a colour; if by the ears, a sound; if by the palate, a taste; and so of the other senses. But I believe none will assert that substance is either a colour, or a sound, or a taste. The idea of substance must therefore be deriv'd from an impression of reflexion, if it really exist. But the impressions of reflexion resolve themselves into our passions and emotions; none of which can possibly represent a substance. We have therefore no idea of substance, distinct from that of a collection of particular qualities, nor have we any other meaning when we either talk or reason concerning it.

~

The work of Hume, perhaps more than any we have explored to date, illustrates how cumulative philosophy can be. Each section of Hume's work presupposes a thorough grasp of the preceding sections and builds upon those sections with little in the way of review of the previous work. Having established the proper genesis of ideas and the association or linking of those ideas within the imagination to form new ones, Hume turns to examine ideas that fail to exemplify this origination and/or linking. Central to this examination of false "ideas" is the treatment of a notion that plays a central role in the philosophical ruminations of thinkers from Aristotle to Descartes; namely, the "idea" of *substance*.

Aristotle, it will be recalled, goes to great length to class all particular objects in the actual world under the category, *Substance*, and to argue that primary substances (e.g., Socrates or Trigger) are more real than secondary substances (e.g., Human or Horse). A *substance*, on Aristotle's view, is any entity that has independent existence. Descartes argues that the universe is comprised of two fundamental substances, Minds and Bodies. These substances are independent, as well, of each other and of all other substances, save God. Indeed, most of the early Modern philosophers thought a great deal about the nature of substance, advancing positive arguments and criticizing rivals based on a supposed thoroughgoing understanding of substance and its various properties.

Hume's treatment of the notion of *substance*, like some of his other work, is at times counterintuitive, although in this case, the counterintuition is largely the product of straightforward prephilosophical acceptance of common use of a word, "substance," with little reflection on that to which the word actually refers. Hume recognizes perfectly well all the philosophical work the notion of *substance* is supposed to do. However, he is skeptical whether or not the notion can actually carry such a substantial load. In keeping with the epistemological approach heretofore employed, Hume wonders about the justification of the idea, "substance," itself.

If the idea, "substance," exists, that is, if it is a real idea and not simply meaningless sounds, then it must be produced like every other real idea. In other words, it must produced by impressions of which it is the image. Thus, if it is a real idea, then it must be either the image of an impression of reflection or the image of an impression of sensation. If we suppose that it is an impression of sensation, then we are compelled to as ask whether the impression that produces it is a color or a sound or a taste. As it happens, the idea, "substance," is neither the idea of a color nor of a sound nor of a taste nor of any other of the simple perceptions that fall under the heading *Impressions of Sensation*. We can represent this part of the argument in the following way:

Statement	Justification
1. If there is an idea of X, there must be a corresponding impression of X.	1. Epistemological Principle
2. If there is an impression of *substance*, then it is either an impression of sensation or an impression of reflection.	2. Exhaustive "or"
3. Suppose the impression of *substance* is an impression of sensation.	3. Assumption.
4. Therefore, the impression of *substance* must be a taste, sound, color, etc.	4. Theory of Perception
5. But, *substance* is not a taste, or a color, or a sound.	5. Observation
6. Therefore, there is not an impression of sensation of *substance*.	6. Contradiction, 4, 5

Section 13.4: Hume and Substance

Since the idea of *substance* is not the product of an impression of sensation, then if it is a real idea and not merely meaningless sounds then it must be the product of an impression of reflection. As was shown in the discussion of Hume's Theory of Perception, an impression of reflection is a composite reflection comprised of a set of impressions of sensation. Thus, an impression of reflection is a collection of sounds or a collection of tastes or a collection of colors or a collection of sounds, tastes, and colors. If this is so, then the idea of *substance* must arise from an impression of such a collection. However, if *substance* is not a taste, then it is not going to be a series of tastes either. Similarly with all the sense perceptions; if *substance* is not any one of them, then it is not going to be a collection of them either. Thus, there is no corresponding impression of reflection for the idea of *substance*. We can represent this formally as follows:

---

7. If there is an impression of *substance*, it must be an impression of reflection.   7. Elimination, 2, 6

8. Thus, the impression of *substance* must be a composite of impressions of sensation.   8. Theory of Perception

9. Thus, the impression of *substance* must be a composite of tastes, colors, sounds, etc.   9. Theory of Perception

10. But, the impression of *substance* is not a composite of tastes, colors   10. Observation

11. Therefore, there is not an impression of reflection of *substance*.   11. Contradiction, 9, 10

While it was recognized that the idea of *substance* must arise from an impression and therefore had to arise either from an impression of sensation or an impression of reflection, at the conclusion of the first two parts of the argument, it is clear that *substance* arises from neither of these. Since it is generated neither from an impression of sensation nor an impression of reflection, then it is generated from no impression at all. Since no real idea can be generated apart from a corresponding impression or set of impressions, then it follows that there is no real idea, *substance*.

---

12. There is neither an impression of sensation of *substance* nor an impression of reflection of *substance*.   12. Definition of "and", 6, 11

13. Therefore, there is no idea of *substance*.   13. Modus Tollens

---

However much work the idea of *substance* is thought to do for philosophers from Aristotle through Descartes, it is Hume's conclusion that all systems that depend on a notion of *substance* to work must necessarily fail. Indeed, the force of Hume's criticism is perhaps best captured in his condemnation of all speculative systems of thought that are independent of empirical foundation in sense perception at the end of Book 12 of *The Enquiry Concerning Human Understanding*. He writes, "If we take in our hand any volume--of divinity or school metaphysics, for instance--let us ask, Does it contain any abstract reasoning concerning quantity or number? No. Does it contain any experimental reasoning concerning matter of fact and existence? No. Commit it then to the flames, for it can contain nothing but sophistry and illusion." While Hume is known for making scandalously severe comments, he should not be read here as endorsing a program of book burning. Rather, he simply holds the view that uncritical acceptance of, and in fact, dependence on abstract notions that have no foundation in human experience are ultimately doomed because they depend on notions that cannot be known. As such, they are essentially meaningless castles built in the air, exercises in mental gymnastics, but nothing further.

The response to Hume from students of philosophy is often that substance must exist because there must be something that a pencil is or that a pen is or that a kangaroo is, apart from its sensible qualities. That is, given any object that appears to the senses, it must be the case that those sensible qualities somehow inhere in an imperceptible substrate or else the qualities could not be perceived. To this, Hume would reply that all that the human mind perceives are the perceptible qualities – the tastes, sounds, colors, etc.,– that comprise the particular object. Indeed, suppose we begin to eliminate the qualities one by one until there were no perceptible qualities left. All that would remain, on Hume's view, is empty space. Even if there were some imperceptible thing in which the perceptible qualities inhered, it would be beyond the ability of the human mind to have any idea of it. In virtue of being unable to form an idea of that imperceptible thing, it follows that it is impossible to know it.

Some might push further, using Descartes's example from the *Sixth Meditation* of the piece of wax that had flavor, colors, shape, smell, etc. After heating, the wax melted and upon cooling returned to solid form. In this form, the wax no longer had the rich golden color of the honeycomb, no longer had the sweet taste of honey, no longer held the previous shape. In short, it was an odorless, tasteless, pale blob. Yet, still, it was wax. Does this not entail that there is something independent of the perceptible qualities that is the wax?

However, if we reflect carefully on that example, it is clear that throughout the transformations that the wax undergoes, it is still colored (first golden and then whitish), it still has shape (first the hexagonal shape of the honeycomb, then the blob-like shape into which it has hardened), it still has a taste (first honey, then waxy and bland). At no time was the wax itself imperceptible. While it is true that at each point in the transformation it remained wax, it is also true that all along the way, it remained perceptible. Eliminating all of the perceptible qualities at any stage in the process would have had the result of eliminating the wax. Thus, at least, Hume's view entails that knowledge of anything beyond that afforded through the senses and those ideas comprised of the things afforded by the senses is beyond the scope of human ideas and, thus, of human knowledge.

This result does not entail that Hume is some sort of radical skeptic. Indeed, it is not an indication that Hume thinks that human knowledge is impossible. It is, however, a limitation of the scope of human knowledge and an admonition to a level of epistemic humility that is not always present in learned circles. Hume clearly thinks human knowledge is possible and that even quite complicated ideas that are not immediately obviously generated from the senses can be known. However, the process of knowledge is a complicated one, fraught with peril for the uncritical eye. To demonstrate how very critical, complicated, and common-sensical ideas can be known, we will turn to a discussion of the philosophical relation, *cause and effect*, in the next section.

Guided Reading Questions

1. What does Hume say about substance? Where does the idea of "substance" come from?
2. Are there such things as "substances"?
3. Compare and contrast this position with the position of Descartes.

Logic Blurb
Induction and Epistemic Humility

Suppose we know that Sweetie is a cat. Further, suppose we know that all cats are felines. In virtue of these two propositions, we know that Sweetie is a feline. Formally, that argument could be represented like this:

> Premise: All cats are felines.
> Premise: Sweetie is a cat.
> Conclusion: Sweetie is a feline.

This sort of argument is a *deductive argument*. The conclusion of a *deductive argument* follows directly from the premises; some logicians have said that the conclusion of a *deductive argument* is *contained* in the premises. *Deductive arguments* proceed from general principles or premises ("All cats are felines") and some specific ones ("Sweetie is a cat") to other specific or particular conclusions ("Sweetie is a feline"). *Deductive arguments* convey a level of necessity. That is, if the premises are true, the conclusion is inevitable.

On the other hand, arguments from *induction* are considerably different, though they sometimes are mistaken for deductive ones. Rather than general principles, *inductive arguments* begin with a series of particularities. For example, we might notice that Sweetie is a cat and is black, that Fuzz is a cat and is black, and that Tipper is a cat and is black, and that every other cat we have in the house is a black cat. From this, imagine that Kat (a little girl who lives in the house) comes to believe that all cats are black. The argument could be represented like this:

> Premise: Sweetie is a black cat.
> Premise: Fuzz is a black cat.
> Premise: Tipper is a black cat.
> Conclusion: All cats are black cats.

It is quite clear that such an argument fails to ultimately support its broad conclusion. Suppose someone who lived next door had a cat named Miles who happened to be gray. Thus, all cats are not black cats despite the fact that every cat Kat had experienced was, indeed, black.

Inductive arguments always move from specific or particular instances or observations to more general or abstract conclusions. As in the example, the conclusion, "All cats are black cats," goes beyond what is contained in the premises. All that is contained in the premises is that every cat encountered to this point (before Miles crosses our path) is a black cat. It has simply been our good fortune to encounter so many black cats, although perhaps it would lead to unreasonable conclusions like the one above. Because the conclusion goes beyond what the evidence will support, the careful thinker will recognize that the force of the argument is limited by this limitation in scope.

The *inductive argument* illustrates yet another aspect of the relationship between the *universal quantifier* and the *existential quantifier*. Properly deductive arguments involve some broadly construed proposition, most often a universally quantified one. Thus, if all cats are felines, then any particular cat will necessarily be a feline as well. On the other hand, *inductive arguments* consist of a series of existentially quantified statements, but, however many there are, one can never construct a properly phrased universally quantified statement from them. No matter how many individual cats are observed, the universally quantified claim that all cats are black cats is beyond deductively certain proof.

This is not to suggest that *inductive arguments* are without use. Indeed, the value of *arguments from induction* is hard to overstate. All of the greatest conclusions of the natural sciences (physics, chemistry, etc.) are the result of inductive investigations, proceeding from individual observations and experiments to general statements of abstract concepts. At the same time, the inherent limitation of the *inductive argument* must be recognized as well. Many are the theories that have been falsified by new data that invalidated the inductive inference. Each of these falsified hypotheses is superseded by successive theories that accounted for the observable data and served as predictors for future observations that, in turn, set the stage for their own possible falsification and refinement. Thus, Scholasticism gives way to the New Science of Bacon, Descartes, and Newton which gives way to Einstein which progresses toward ever more clarity in understanding the physical universe. Our conclusion to be drawn from this process is that the reflective philosopher/scientist always excercises a bit of *epistemic humility*, endorsing the view of Alfred North Whitehead that "in philosophical discussion, the merest hint of dogmatic certainty as to finality of statement is an exhibition of folly." (*Process and Reality*, xiv)

Section 13.5: Hume and Causation

Treatise Of Human Nature
Volume I: Of the Understanding
Part III. Of knowledge and probability

Section VI. Of the inference from the impression to the idea
The idea of cause and effect is deriv'd from experience, which informs us, that such particular objects, in all past instances, have been constantly conjoin'd with each other: And as an object similar to one of these is suppos'd to be immediately present in its impression, we thence presume on the existence of one similar to its usual attendant. According to this account of things, which is, I think, in every point unquestionable, probability is founded on the presumption of a resemblance betwixt those objects, of which we have had experience, and those, of which we have had none; and therefore 'tis impossible this presumption can arise from probability. The same principle cannot be both the cause and effect of another; and this is, perhaps, the only proposition concerning that relation, which is either intuitively or demonstratively certain.

An Abstract of a Book Lately Published, Entituled,
A Treatise of Human Nature, &c.

'Tis evident, that all reasonings concerning *matter of fact* are founded on the relation of cause and effect, and that we can never infer the existence of one object from another, unless they be connected together, either mediately or immediately. In order therefore to understand these reasonings, we must be perfectly acquainted with the idea of a cause; and in order to do that, must look about us to find something that is the cause of another.

Here is a billiard-ball lying on the table, and another ball moving towards it with rapidity. They strike; and the ball, which was formerly at rest, now acquires a motion. This is as perfect an instance of the relation of cause and effect as any which we know, either by sensation or reflection. Let us therefore examine it. 'Tis evident, that the two balls touched one another before the motion was communicated, and that there was no interval betwixt the shock and the motion. *Contiguity* in time and place is therefore a requisite circumstance to the operation of all causes. 'Tis evident likewise, that the motion, which was the cause, is prior to the motion, which was the effect. *Priority* in time, is therefore another requisite circumstance in every cause. But this is not all. Let us try any other balls of the same kind in a like situation, and we shall always find, that the impulse of the one produces motion in the other. Here therefore is a *third* circumstance, *viz.* that of a *constant conjunction* betwixt the cause and effect. Every object like the cause, produces always some object like the effect. Beyond these three circumstances of contiguity, priority, and constant conjunction, I can discover nothing in this cause. The first ball is in motion; touches the second; immediately the second is in motion: and when I try the experiment with the same or like balls, in the same or like circumstances, I find, that upon the motion and touch of the one ball, motion always follows in the other. In whatever shape I turn this matter, and however I examine it, I can find nothing farther.

This is the case when both the cause and effect are present to the senses. Let us now see upon what our inference is founded, when we conclude from the one that the other has existed or will exist. Suppose I see a ball moving in a straight line towards another, I immediately conclude that they will shock, and that the second will be in motion. This is the inference from cause to effect; and of this nature are all our reasonings in the conduct of life: on this is founded all our belief in history: and from hence is derived all philosophy, excepting only geometry and arithmetic. If we can explain the inference from the shock of two balls, we shall be able to account for this operation of the mind in all circumstances.

Were a man, such as *Adam*, created in the full vigour of understanding, without experience, he would never be able to infer motion in the second ball from the motion and impulse of the first. It is not any thing that reason sees in the cause, which makes us *infer* the effect. Such an inference, were it possible, would amount to a demonstration, as being founded merely on the comparison of ideas. But no inference from cause to effect amounts to a demonstration. Of which there is this evident proof. The mind can always *conceive* any effect to follow from any cause, and indeed any event to follow upon another: whatever we *conceive* is possible, at least in a metaphysical sense: but wherever a demonstration takes place, the contrary is impossible, and implies a contradiction. There is no demonstration, therefore, for any conjunction of cause and effect. And this is a principle, which is generally allowed by philosophers.

It would have been necessary, therefore, for *Adam* (if he was not inspired) to have had *experience* of the effect, which followed upon the impulse of these two balls. He must have seen, in several instances, that when the one ball struck upon the other, the second always acquired motion. If he had seen a sufficient number of instances of this kind, whenever he saw the one ball moving towards the other, he would always conclude without hesitation, that the second would acquire motion. His understanding would anticipate his sight, and form a conclusion suitable to his past experience.

It follows, then, that all reasonings concerning cause and effect, are founded on experience, and that all reasonings from experience are founded on the supposition, that the course of nature will continue uniformly the same. We conclude, that like causes, in like circumstances, will always produce like effects. It may now be worth while to consider, what determines us to form a conclusion of such infinite consequence.

'Tis evident, that *Adam* with all his science, would never have been able to *demonstrate*, that the course of nature must continue uniformly the same, and that the future must be conformable to the past. What is possible can never be demonstrated to be false; and 'tis possible the course of nature may change, since we can conceive such a change. Nay, I will go farther, and assert, that he could not so much as prove by any *probable* arguments, that the future must be conformable to the past. All probable arguments are built on the supposition, that there is conformity betwixt the future and the past, and therefore can never prove it. This conformity is a *matter of fact*, and if it must be proved, will admit of no proof but from experience. But our experience in the past can be a proof of nothing for the future, but upon a supposition, that there is a resemblance betwixt them. This therefore is a point, which can admit of no proof at all, and which we take for granted without any proof.

We are determined by *custom* alone to suppose the future conformable to the past. When I see a billiard-ball moving towards another, my mind is immediately carry'd by habit to the usual effect, and anticipates my sight by conceiving the second ball in motion. There is nothing in these objects, abstractly considered, and independent of experience, which leads me to form any such conclusion: and even after I have had experience of many repeated effects of this kind, there is no argument, which determines me to suppose, that the effect will be conformable to past experience. The powers, by which bodies operate, are entirely unknown. We perceive only there sensible qualities: and what *reason* have we to think, that the same powers will always be conjoined with the same sensible qualities?

'Tis not, therefore, reason, which is the guide of life, but custom. That alone determines the mind, in all instances, to suppose the future conformable to the past. However easy this step may seem, reason would never, to all eternity, be able to make it.

This is a very curious discovery, but leads us to others, that are still more curious. *When I see a billiard-ball moving towards another, my mind is immediately carried by habit to the usual effect, and anticipates my sight by conceiving the second ball in motion.* But is this all? Do I nothing but *conceive* the motion of the second ball? No surely. I also *believe* that it will move. What then is this *belief*? And how does it differ from the simple conception of any thing? Here is a new question unthought of by philosophers.

When a demonstration convinces me of any proposition, it not only makes me conceive the proposition, but also makes me sensible, that 'tis impossible to conceive any thing contrary. What is demonstratively false implies a contradiction; and what implies a contradiction cannot be conceived. But with regard to any matter of fact, however strong the proof may be from experience, I can always conceive the contrary, tho' I cannot always believe it. The belief, therefore, makes some difference betwixt the conception to which we assent, and that to which we do not assent.

To account for this, there are only two hypotheses. It may be said, that belief joins some new idea to those which we may conceive without assenting to them. But this hypothesis is false. For *first*, no such idea can be produced. When we simply conceive an object, we conceive it in all its parts. We conceive it as it might exist, tho' we do not believe it to exist. Our belief of it would discover no new qualities. We may paint out the entire object in imagination without believing it. We may set it, in a manner, before our eyes, with every circumstance of time and place. 'Tis the very object conceived as it might exist; and when we believe it, we can do no more.

Secondly, The mind has a faculty of joining all ideas together, which involve not a contradiction; and therefore if belief consisted in some idea, which we add to the simple conception, it would be in a man's power, by adding this idea to it, to believe anything, which he can conceive.

Since therefore belief implies a conception, and yet is something more; and since it adds no new idea to the conception; it follows, that it is a different *manner* of conceiving an object; *something* that is distinguishable to the feeling, and depends not upon our will, as all our ideas do. My mind runs by habit from the visible object of one ball moving towards another, to the usual effect of motion in the second ball. It not only conceives that motion, but *feels* something different in the conception of it from a mere reverie of the imagination. The presence of this visible object, and the constant conjunction of that particular effect, render the idea different to the *feeling* from those loose ideas, which come into the mind without any introduction. This conclusion seems a little surprising; but we are led into it by a chain of propositions, which admit of no doubt. To ease the reader's memory I shall briefly resume them. No matter of fact can be proved by from its cause and its effect. Nothing can be known to be the cause of another but by experience. We can give no reason for extending to the future our experience in the past; but are entirely determined by custom, when we conceive an effect to follow from its usual cause. But we also believe an effect to follow, as we as conceive it. This belief joins no new idea to the conception. It only varies the matter of conceiving, and makes a difference to the feeling or sentiment. Belief, therefore, in all matters of fact arises only from custom, and is an idea conceived in a peculiar *manner*.

I have likewise omitted many arguments, which he adduces to prove that belief consists merely in a peculiar feeling or sentiment. I shall only mention one. Our past experience is not always uniform. Sometimes one effect follows from a cause, sometimes another: In which case we always believe, that that will exist which is most common. I see a billiard-ball moving towards another. I cannot distinguish whether it moves upon its axis, or was struck so as to skim along the table. In the first case, I know it will not stop after the shock. In the second it may stop. The first is most common, and therefore I lay my account with that effect. But I also conceive the other effect, and conceive it as possible, and as connected with the cause. Were not the one conception different in feeling or sentiment from the other, there would be no difference betwixt them.

With his rejection of the notion of *substance* because it does not arise from impressions, one might suppose that Hume would likewise reject the notion of *cause and effect*. After all, *cause and effect* cannot arise from an impression of sensation because impressions of sensation are simple and *cause and effect* is a complex notion, involving at least two ideas, that of a cause (which entails an effect) and that of an effect (which presupposes a cause). At the same time, *cause and effect*, like *substance*, is neither a series of tastes, smells, sounds, colors, etc. Thus, *cause and effect* is not the product of an impression of reflection either. Hence, it would seem reasonable, at least at first guess, to suppose that Hume lumps *cause and effect* along with *substance* into that heap that is to be committed to the flames.

This result would seem to put Hume in the very untenable position of rejecting a notion that seems quite fundamental to the experience of human beings. After all, if we have no real idea of *cause and effect*, then it makes little sense to study for an exam, since that will have no effect on the outcome of our education; to plant a crop in the spring, since there is no connection between the planting and the harvest; or to light a fuse, since there will be no reason to think it will lead to an explosion. If Hume's view is that *cause and effect* does not exist, then the charge of radical skepticism is right and the moniker, "Greatest Philosopher to Write in English," is misplaced. Fortunately, we need not come to this conclusion.

Hume is somewhat agnostic with respect to the notion of *cause and effect*; or at least how humans come to have knowledge of *cause and effect*. Yet for Hume, *cause* is of considerable importance. Hume maintains that knowledge of Matters of Fact depends largely upon *cause and effect*. Indeed, he writes in *An Enquiry Concerning Human Understanding* that "All reasonings concerning matter of fact seem to be founded on the relation of *Cause and Effect*." Further, it is only this relation that allows individuals to "go beyond the evidence of our memory and senses." Or as Hume writes, "we can never infer the existence of one object from another, unless they be connected together, either mediately or immediately. In order therefore to understand these reasonings, we must be perfectly acquainted with the idea of a cause."

Given that so much rests upon *cause* and *effect*, it behooves Hume to give some reckoning of how we come to know *cause* and *effect*. Obviously knowledge of *cause* and *effect* cannot arise from *a priori* reasonings on Hume's view. Neither can such knowledge arise from any abstract reasoning apart from experience itself. Instead, custom and habit form the foundation of knowledge of *cause* and *effect*. Hume conceives the cause/effect relation as one of three general principles by which ideas are associated. The others are *contiguity* and *resemblance*. These principles, while neither infallible nor sole causes of ideas and the unions of ideas, are nevertheless the three principles by which Hume understands the mind to conjoin distinct and separable ideas. Hume then endeavors to demonstrate how we may judge of causes and effects by setting out some general rules which are necessary conditions of the cause and effect relation. These briefly are (a) contiguity in space and time, (b) priority, (c) constant conjunction, and (d) necessary connection.

The imagination gives rise to a idea of *cause and effect* because we grow accustomed to seeing event B follow event A in time, we observe that event B never precedes event A, and we note that whenever A occurs, it is followed immediately by B. In another way, in our experience of events A and B, suppose we find them to be contiguous in space and time and constantly conjoined. Further, suppose we find that A always precedes B. From these empirically observable features, we become habituated to anticipating event B whenever we observe A and thus we expect B to follow upon it. However, the rule of *necessary connection*, that is that the same cause always produces the same effect is *not* empirically observable. Ultimately, Hume thinks it impossible to prove these causal connections.

Hume thinks a great deal of the difficulty in demonstrating the existence of *cause and effect* lies in the fact that events A and B can be conceived of independently in the mind. This is not an idea novel to Hume; for example, Descartes argued for such an independent conceivability relative to minds and bodies in the *Meditations*. But Descartes does not apply this principle to cause and effect. Hume does.

On Hume's view, event A does not include any notion of a cause, either as cause of itself or as cause of another. If it did, then it would not be completely conceivable independent of the other. But perceptions are separable, distinct, and distinguishable. Hence, they are conceivable independent of one another. Thus, the notion of cause cannot be inherent in the event or object itself. So on Hume's view, one cannot get cause and effect from analysis of the events or objects themselves.

Ultimately cause and effect reasoning rests upon experience. As a result, Hume seems to believe that eventually one comes to recognize that constant conjunction, however meager a notion of causation that may be, is all that there is. That is, there is no further explanation of cause and effect than constant conjunction. As he writes in the *Enquiry Concerning Human Understanding*, "As to the causes of these general causes [e.g. elasticity, gravity, etc.] we should in vain attempt their discovery; nor shall we ever be able to satisfy ourselves, by any particular explication of them. The ultimate springs and principles are totally shut up from human curiousity and enquiry."

With this view of cause and effect, then, it is not difficult to see how the impossibility of proving that the future will resemble the past follows. For Hume, induction rests upon a supposition of the uniformity of nature. That supposition itself rests upon the custom and habit that, in our imagination, give rise to an idea of cause and effect. However, we have no immediate experience (and hence no simple impression) of the cause/effect relation. Thus, there is no ground upon which to build a proof that past causal connections, that is connections which up until now have been only constant conjunctions, will hold in the future. It is not intuitively false to assume that these causal connections will hold, but neither can it be demonstrated that they must hold.

I return now specifically to the idea of *necessary connection*. Hume never denies that there is a real connection between cause and effect. However, he does deny that one is to find necessary connection in an instance of one billiard ball striking another and the second ball moving or in repeated instances of sufficiently similar sorts, for example. Given his understanding of causation as a general principle by which ideas are conjoined, albeit not infallibly nor necessarily, it is little wonder that Hume would not depend upon necessary connection for a doctrine of cause and effect. Instead, on his view, the mind is presented with distinct perceptions which in themselves possess no notion of cause. An idea of necessary connection must have at its base an impression. From an idea of necessary connection, if one were derivable from a particular impression, one would be able to tell with certainty which event would follow. In that sense, the second event would be dependent and inseparable from the first. But, each perception is separable, distinct, and distinguishable. Hence, there is no immediate impression from which the idea of necessary connection could arise. In another way, it is true that we may discover that certain events are constantly conjoined in time and space. We may further discover that each time we encounter then those events the circumstances of our encounter sufficiently resemble past ones. However, it is not possible from this constant conjunction of events to suppose the arising of a new idea, e.g. necessary connection. Indeed, since such an idea was not present in any particular events or their conjunctions, no such idea would arise from a regular series of those conjunctions. The idea of cause and effect, however, arises from the experience, "which informs us, that such particular objects, in all past instances, have been constantly conjoin'd with each other." That is, we become accustomed to anticipating the second object whenever we encounter the first. This constant conjunction and our habituated anticipation of events called "effects" form the general principle of association of ideas known as *Cause* and *Effect*.

Arising from experience, Hume must explain how it is that the notion of *cause and effect*, a complex idea, arises then from some impression or other, given that it must arise from experience. We are conditioned, through repetition, through custom, of experiencing a certain anticipation, namely that seeing the first billiard-ball moving toward the second, we will see the second move. That *anticipation* is itself a feeling, and thus an impression, is not at all clear, on first blush. However, one need only imagine a child, say four years old, on Christmas Eve to see a pure and undiluted anticipation that is itself an impression of such purity, of the force and vivacity that Hume attributes to *impressions*, that it is impossible to deny that it is anything other than a passion and thus possible impression of sensation. Now, the anticipation of seeing the second billiard-ball move when seeing the first in motion is not nearly so forceful and violent as the full-body anticipation of Christmas Eve watchfulness of the child, but the difference is one of degree, not of kind. Thus, we have an impression of sensation of anticipation that we have become accustomed to having; so accustomed in fact that it hardly seems an anticipation at all. However, were that anticipation not satisfied by the expected effect, we would react strongly, as if something were significantly amiss; the significance of our reaction would differ in proportion to the distance of the actual effect on the second ball from the expectation, in all likelihood. So, for example, if the second ball crumbled to dust or exploded, we would be aghast. That experience would then have an effect on future anticipations. Unsure what would happen when next we saw a billiard-ball in motion toward a second, we would experience a feeling, perhaps of uncertainty, perhaps of dread, that would make clear that, prior to the unexpected effect just experienced, we were, in fact, anticipating a particular result that was not forthcoming. As a result of that disappointment, we no longer know what to expect and so the quality of our anticipation is now more variegated. Even several repetitions of the usual cause/effect relationship might be unable to fully remove from our anticipation the possibility of an unexpected result. Thus, that feeling of anticipation becomes crucial to our assignation of the label "cause and effect" to the first billiard-ball striking the second and the second moving. Indeed, it is in this experienced feeling and the attendant experienced feeling of satisfaction (when the anticipation is satisfied by the expected effect actually occurring) that is the impression that gives rise to the complex notion of *cause and effect*.

So, while Hume's critique of the notion of *substance* serves as a devastating critique of Cartesian rationalistic metaphysics, his own Theory of Perception does not cripple his epistemology by either failing to explain the idea of cause and effect or by entailing that we have no such idea. Rather, the notion of cause and effect is a quite complex notion that is not lightly or easily developed. This quite thorough analysis of the idea, then, provides for a useful matrix not only for making assessments of cause and effect within our own ideas, but also as an empirical and critical tool for assessing claims of cause and effect within all scientific disciplines. To claim that A is the cause of B, whether it be in medicine, physics, sociology, or other discipline is to place the claim under the intense scrutiny of Hume's perceptive, penetrating, and at times, devastating analysis of the very notion of cause and effect.

Guided Reading Questions

1. On Hume's view, is it possible to have a simple idea of *cause and effect*? Why or why not?
2. How does Hume argue that we come to have the notion of *cause and effect* that we have? Would it fall under Relations of Ideas or Matters of Fact?

Logic Blurb
Post hoc ergo propter hoc

The Latin is translated "after this, therefore, because of this." This translation illustrates quickly and clearly the fallacy and the error that Hume tries to avoid with his careful analysis of the notion of *cause and effect*. The *post hoc* fallacy is extraordinarily common among the superstitious. Imagine a baseball player who had a steak sandwich and curly fries for lunch before a game in which he hit for the cycle, made a game saving catch, and scored the winning run. There are very few baseball players who, the lunch before the next game, would pass up the opportunity to have exactly the same meal. Since the extraordinary game came after the particular meal, he sees a causal relationship that is not there.

Similarly, suppose a student stayed up late studying for a final exam but, rather than simply going and taking the exam, he puts on his best suit and tie and takes the teacher an apple. If he gets a good grade on the exam, he is perhaps likely to think that the nice presentation of himself and the apple bribe had something to do with the final grade. He might even think that the grade had *more* to do with those irrelevancies than the studying itself. Thus, we would, in virtue of an invalid connection between two things, one prior to the other, conclude that one was the cause of the other when in point of fact they are completely unrelated. This is the danger of the *post hoc ergo propter hoc* fallacy.

Section 13.6: Hume and Religion

Dialogues Concerning Natural Religion

Cast: Pamphilus, Philo, Cleanthes, Demea

Part I (Setting: Cleanthes' library; The conversation begins with a question about the education of the young in matters of religious belief and reasoning.)

Philo {*Turning himself towards* Demea} And here we may observe a pretty curious circumstance in the history of the sciences. After the union of philosophy with the popular religion, upon the first establishment of Christianity, nothing was more usual, among all religious teachers, than declamations against reason, against the senses, against every principle derived merely from human research and inquiry. All the topics of the ancient academics were adopted by the fathers, and thence propagated for several ages in every school and pulpit throughout Christendom. The reformers embraced the same principles of reasoning, or rather declamation; and all panegyrics on the excellency of faith were sure to be interlarded with some severe strokes of satire against natural reason. A celebrated prelate too, of the Romish communion, a man of the most extensive learning, who wrote a demonstration of Christianity, has also composed a treatise, which contains all the cavils of the boldest and most determined *Pyrrhonism*. *Locke* seems to have been the first Christian who ventured openly to assert that *faith* was nothing but a species of *reason*, that religion was only a branch of philosophy, and that a chain of arguments, similar to that which established any truth in morals, politics, or physics, was always employed in discovering all the principles of theology, natural and revealed.

Philo: Don't you remember the excellent saying of *Lord Bacon* on this head?

Cleanthes: That a little philosophy makes a man an atheist; a great deal converts him to religion.

Philo: That is a very judicious remark too. But what I have in my eye is another passage where, having mentioned *David's* fool, who said in his heart there is no God, this great philosopher observes, that the atheists nowadays have a double share of folly, for they are not contented to say in their hearts there is no God, but they also utter that impiety with their lips, and are thereby guilty of multiplied indiscretion and imprudence. Such people, though they were ever so much in earnest cannot, methinks, be very formidable.

Part II

Demea: But lest you should think that my *piety* has here got the better of my *philosophy*, I shall support my opinion, if it needs any support, by a very great authority. It is Father *Malebranche* who, I remember, thus expresses himself. "One ought not so much to call God a spirit, in order to express positively what he is, as in order to signify that he is not matter. He is a Being infinitely perfect. We ought to believe that as he comprehends the perfections of matter without being material.... he comprehends also the perfections of created spirits without being spirit; that his true name is, *He that is*, or in other words, Being without restriction, All Being, the Being infinite and universal."

Philo: After so great an authority, *Demea*, as that which you have produced, it would appear ridiculous in me to add my sentiment or express my approbation of your doctrine. Nothing exists without a cause; and the original cause of this universe (whatever it be) we call God, and piously ascribe to him every species of perfection. But as all perfection is entirely relative, we ought never to imagine that we comprehend the attributes of this divine Being, or to suppose that his perfections have any analogy or likeness to the perfections of a human creature. Our ideas reach no farther than our experience: We have no experience of divine attributes and operations.

Cleanthes: I shall briefly explain how I conceive this matter. Look round the world: contemplate the whole and every part of it. You will find it to be nothing but one great machine, subdivided into an infinite number of lesser machines, which again admit of subdivisions to a degree beyond what human senses and faculties can trace and explain. All these various machines, and even their most minute parts, are adjusted to each other with an accuracy which ravishes into admiration all men who have ever contemplated them. The curious adapting of means to ends, throughout all nature, resembles exactly, though it much exceeds, the productions of human contrivance -- of human designs, thought, wisdom, and intelligence. Since, therefore, the effects resemble each other, we are led to infer, by all the rules of analogy, that the causes also resemble, and that the Author of nature is somewhat similar to the mind of man, though possessed of much larger faculties, proportioned to the grandeur of the work which he has executed. By this argument *a posteriori*, and by this argument alone, do we prove at once the existence of a Deity, and his similarity to human mind and intelligence.

Philo: What I chiefly scruple in this subject is not so much that all religious arguments are by *Cleanthes* reduced to experience. But wherever you depart, in the least, from the similarity of the cases, you diminish proportionably the evidence, and may at last bring it to a very weak *analogy*, which is confessedly liable to error and uncertainty.

If we see a house, *Cleanthes*, we conclude, with the greatest certainty, that it had an architect or builder, because this is precisely that species of effect which we have experienced to proceed from that species of cause. But surely you will not affirm that the universe bears such a resemblance to a house, that we can with the same certainty infer a similar cause, or that the analogy is here entire and perfect. The dissimilitude is so striking that the utmost you can here pretend to is a guess, a conjecture, a presumption concerning a similar cause.

{Cleanthes *gives his assent.*}

That all inferences, *Cleanthes*, concerning fact, are founded on experience; and that all experimental reasonings are founded on the supposition that similar causes prove similar effects, and similar effects similar causes; I shall not at present much dispute with you. Unless the cases be exactly similar, they repose no perfect confidence in applying their past observation to any particular phenomenon. Every alteration of circumstances occasions a doubt concerning the event. It is an active cause, by which some particular parts of nature, we find, produce alterations on other parts. But can a conclusion, with any propriety, be transferred from parts to the whole? Does not the great disproportion bar all comparison and inference? From observing the growth of a hair, can we learn any thing concerning the generation of a man? Would the manner of a leaf's blowing, even though perfectly known, afford us any instruction concerning the vegetation of a tree?

So far from admitting that the operations of a part can afford us any just conclusion concerning the origin of the whole, I will not allow any one part to form a rule for another part, if the latter be very remote from the former.

Part V

Philo: Now, *Cleanthes*, with an air of alacrity and triumph, mark the consequences. *First*, By this method of reasoning, you renounce all claim to infinity in any of the attributes of the Deity. For, as the cause ought only to be proportioned to the effect, and the effect, so far as it falls under our cognisance, is not infinite

Secondly, you have no reason, on your theory, for ascribing perfection to the Deity, even in his finite capacity, or for supposing him free from every error, mistake, or incoherence, in his undertakings. ... At least, you must acknowledge, that it is impossible for us to tell, from our limited views, whether this system contains any great faults, or deserves any considerable praise, if compared to other possible, and even real systems. Could a peasant, if the *Aeneid* were read to him, pronounce that poem to be absolutely faultless, or even assign to it its proper rank among the productions of human wit, he, who had never seen any other production? ...

In a word, *Cleanthes*, a man who follows your hypothesis is able perhaps to assert, or conjecture, that the universe, sometime, arose from something like design: but beyond that position he cannot ascertain one single circumstance; and is left afterwards to fix every point of his theology by the utmost license of fancy and hypothesis.

Part VIII

Philo: In such questions as the present, a hundred contradictory views may preserve a kind of imperfect analogy; and invention has here full scope to exert itself. Without any great effort of thought, I believe that I could, in an instant, propose other systems of cosmogony, which would have some faint appearance of truth.

All religious systems, it is confessed, are subject to great and insuperable difficulties. Each disputant triumphs in his turn; while he carries on an offensive war, and exposes the absurdities, barbarities, and pernicious tenets of his antagonist. But all of them, on the whole, prepare a complete triumph for the skeptic, who tells them that no system ought ever to be embraced with regard to such subjects. For this plain reason, that no absurdity ought ever to be assented to with regard to any subject. A total suspense of judgment is here our only reasonable resource. And if every attack, as is commonly observed, and no defense, among theologians, is successful; how complete must be *his* victory, who remains always, with all mankind, on the offensive, and has himself no fixed station or abiding city, which he is ever, on any occasion, obliged to defend?

Part X

Demea: It is my opinion, I own, that each man feels, in a manner, the truth of religion within his own breast; and from a consciousness of his imbecility and misery, rather than from any reasoning, is led to seek protection from that Being, on whom he and all nature is dependent.

And why should man, added he, pretend to an exemption from the lot of all other animals? The whole earth is cursed and polluted. A perpetual war is kindled amongst all living creatures. Necessity, hunger, want, stimulate the strong and courageous. Fear, anxiety, terror, agitate the weak and infirm. The first entrance into life gives anguish to the new-born infant and to its wretched parent. Weakness, impotence, distress, attend each stage of that life. And it is at last finished in agony and horror.

Were a stranger to drop on a sudden into this world, I would show him, as a specimen of its ills, a hospital full of diseases, a prison crowded with malefactors and debtors, a field of battle strewed with carcasses, a fleet foundering in the ocean, a nation languishing under tyranny, famine, or pestilence. To turn the gay side of life to him, and give him a notion of its pleasures; whither should I conduct him? to a ball, to an opera, to court? He might justly think, that I was only showing him a diversity of distress and sorrow.

Philo: And is it possible that after all these reflections, and infinitely more which might be suggested, you can still persevere in your anthropomorphism, and assert the moral attributes of the Deity, his justice, benevolence, mercy, and rectitude, to be of the same nature with these virtues in human creatures? His power we allow is infinite: whatever he wills is executed: but neither man nor any other animal is happy: therefore he does not will their happiness. His wisdom is infinite, he is never mistaken in choosing the means to any end, but the course of nature tends not to human or animal felicity: therefore it is not established for that purpose. Through the whole compass of human knowledge, there are no inferences more certain and infallible than these. In what respect, then, do his benevolence and mercy resemble the benevolence and mercy of men?

Epicurus's old questions are yet unanswered.

Is he willing to prevent evil, but not able? Then he is impotent. Is he able, but not willing? Then is he malevolent. Is he both able and willing? whence then is evil?

Part XI

Philo: In short, I repeat the question: is the world, considered in general, and as it appears to us in this life, different from what a man, or such a limited being, would, *beforehand*, expect from a very powerful, wise, and benevolent Deity? It must be strange prejudice to assert the contrary. And from thence I conclude that however consistent the world may be, allowing certain suppositions and conjectures, with the idea of such a Deity, it can never afford us an inference concerning his existence.

There seem to be *four* circumstances, on which depend all, or the greatest part of the ills, that molest sensible creatures; and it is not impossible but all these circumstances may be necessary and unavoidable.

The *first* circumstance which introduces evil, is that contrivance or economy of the animal creation, by which pains, as well as pleasures, are employed to excite all creatures to action, and make them vigilant in the great work of self-preservation.

But a capacity of pain would not alone produce pain, were it not for the *second* circumstance, viz. the conducting of the world by general laws; and this seems nowise necessary to a very perfect Being.

If everything in the universe be conducted by general laws, and if animals be rendered susceptible of pain, it scarcely seems possible but some ill must arise in the various shocks of matter, and the various concurrence and opposition of general laws; but this ill would be very rare, were it not for the third circumstance, which I proposed to mention, viz. the great frugality with which all powers and faculties are distributed to every particular being.

The *fourth* circumstance, whence arises the misery and ill of the universe, is the inaccurate workmanship of all the springs and principles of the great machine of nature. One would imagine, that this grand production had not received the last hand of the maker; so little finished is every part, and so coarse are the strokes with which it is executed. Thus, the winds are requisite to convey the vapours along the surface of the globe, and to assist men in navigation: but how oft, rising up to tempests and hurricanes, do they become pernicious? Rains are necessary to nourish all the plants and animals of the earth: but how often are they defective? How often excessive? Heat is requisite to all life and vegetation; but is not always found in the due proportion. One would imagine, that this grand production had not received the last hand of the maker; so little finished is every part, and so coarse are the strokes with which it is executed. Thus, the winds are requisite to convey the vapours along the surface of the globe, and to assist men in navigation: but how oft, rising up to tempests and hurricanes, do they become pernicious? Rains are necessary to nourish all the plants and animals of the earth: but how often are they defective? How often excessive? Heat is requisite to all life and vegetation; but is not always found in the due proportion.

On the concurrence, then, of these *four* circumstances, does all or the greatest part of natural evil depend. Were all living creatures incapable of pain, or were the world administered by particular volitions, evil never could have found access into the universe: and were animals endowed with a large stock of powers and faculties, beyond what strict necessity requires; or were the several springs and principles of the universe so accurately framed as to preserve always the just temperament and medium; there must have been very little ill in comparison of what we feel at present.

The true conclusion is, that the original Source of all things is entirely indifferent to all these principles; and has no more regard to good above ill, than to heat above cold, or to drought above moisture, or to light above heavy.

Part XII

{Demea *departs.*}

Cleanthes: Our friend, I am afraid, will have little inclination to revive this topic of discourse, while you are in company. Your spirit of controversy, joined to your abhorrence of vulgar superstition, carries you strange lengths, when engaged in an argument; and there is nothing so sacred and venerable, even in your own eyes, which you spare on that occasion.

Philo: I must confess, replied PHILO, that I am less cautious on the subject of natural religion than on any other; both because I know that I can never, on that head, corrupt the principles of any man of common sense; and because no one, I am confident, in whose eyes I appear a man of common sense, will ever mistake my intentions. You are sensible, that notwithstanding the freedom of my conversation, and my love of singular arguments, no one has a deeper sense of religion impressed on his mind, or pays more profound adoration to the divine Being, as he discovers himself to reason, in the inexplicable contrivance and artifice of nature. A purpose, an intention, a design, strikes every where the most careless, the most stupid thinker; and no man can be so hardened in absurd systems, as at all times to reject it. That nature does nothing in vain, is a maxim established in all the schools, merely from the contemplation of the works of nature, without any religious purpose; and, from a firm conviction of its truth, an anatomist, who had observed a new organ or canal, would never be satisfied till he had also discovered its use and intention. One great foundation of the Copernican system is the maxim, *That nature acts by the simplest methods, and chooses the most proper means to any end*; and astronomers often, without thinking of it, lay this strong foundation of piety and religion. The same thing is observable in other parts of philosophy: and thus all the sciences almost lead us insensibly to acknowledge a first intelligent Author; and their authority is often so much the greater, as they do not directly profess that intention.

These, *Cleanthes*, are my unfeigned sentiments on this subject; and these sentiments, you know, I have ever cherished and maintained. But in proportion to my veneration for true religion, is my abhorrence of vulgar superstitions; and I indulge a peculiar pleasure, I confess, in pushing such principles, sometimes into absurdity, sometimes into impiety. And you are sensible that all bigots, notwithstanding their great aversion to the latter above the former, are commonly equally guilty of both.

~

Hume's *Dialogues Concerning Natural Religion* was scandalously received. A group of clergy from his native Scotland simply referred to Hume as "the Great Infidel." So scandalous was the text thought to be that Hume himself did not have the work published during his lifetime and instead left instructions for his executor to have the work published. Adam Smith, Hume's dear friend and executor, also refused to publish the work as he agreed with Hume that the public reaction to the work would be quite negative. Neither Hume nor Smith thought the work wrongheaded nor inaccurate. Both, however, realized that given the sensitive nature of the topic that people would be likely misread and misinterpret the work. Indeed, many who might comment with the most vitriol would likely be the ones who did not read it at all. Such was the nature of religious debate in his era that any reflective work that seemed to question the biases and prejudices of popular religious dogma was generally tarred and feathered, at least figuratively, and occasionally literally. Given that Hume's *Dialogues* systematically rejects all of the proofs offered for the proof of God's existence up until his time, it is little wonder that he suspected the public reaction to his work would be less than positive.

Much of the reaction was born of a failure to read carefully Hume's work. Some of this may be genuinely accepted as a difficulty with the text itself. One of the strengths of the dialogue style of philosophic writing is that it allows the reader to enter a conversation and imagine herself overhearing the debate and to imagine interposing her own questions in the midst of the conversation. Since philosophy takes place best in the context of conversation, the dialogue, of all the written forms of philosophy, is perhaps the best at capturing this dynamic interplay of ideas and argument. However, this is not to dismiss the difficulties with the style. Indeed, several difficulties attend the dialogue style. First, if the dialogue is well written, it may be quite easy for the reader to become so lost in the literary elegance of the work that she loses the train of the argument in the midst of the give and take of the conversation. This malady can be remedied by close and repeated readings of the text. The second difficulty is more problematic. As an interpretive matter, there is a difficulty of deciding which character, if any, speaks for the author; in this case, Hume. This was a difficulty mostly avoided by Plato because there it was generally clear that Socrates was advancing the Socratic/Platonic view.

The kernel of the overwrought reaction to Hume's *Dialogues* was somewhat to be expected given that Hume does argue, at least in the voice of Philo, that every proof heretofore offered for the existence of God fails to accomplish that goal. It is clear that Hume's view is almost never carried on the voice of Demea, though there is some argument that Cleanthes, at least at times early in the *Dialogues* carries Hume's voice. The simplest interpretive device here is to assume that Hume's views are found predominantly in the voice of Philo and insofar as they are found elsewhere one would need to argue them in every particular case. If we take this interpretive mechanism then Philo's rejection of the proofs for the existence of God certainly seems to represent Hume's own philosophical reflections on the matter. Whether or not Philo's rejection of this speaks to Hume's "spirituality" is philosophically uninteresting, although there is a connection between Hume's argument here and his philosophical commitments elsewhere, a connection we will discuss further at the conclusion of this section. The reaction does, however, point out a fairly common logical error.

As was discussed in the section *St. Anselm – Proslogian*, one of the more common logical errors that is committed within religious debate is to presume that on the basis of disagreement with an argument that establishes some proposition p that one must in virtue of this belief $\sim p$. Thus, when Gaunilo argued that the Ontological Argument failed to establish that God exists, many concluded that Gaunilo must believe the contrary proposition, namely that God does not exist. Given that Gaunilo was a Benedictine monk, the error of this assumption is quite egregious and completely without merit. Hume, on the other hand, is not a monk and thus carries with him no presumption that he has a particularly noteworthy set of religion *bona fides*. Thus, as he argues in the *Dialogues* that not only does the Ontological Argument fail but that all of the arguments heretofore offered fail, it is hard for the incautious reader of Hume to keep in mind that simple rejection of an argument does not entail rejection of its conclusion.

Thus, Hume, like Gaunilo, may well believe in the existence of God and still maintain that the arguments to establish that conclusion fail to do so. Thus, one should not immediately conclude, on the basis of the arguments Philo advances, that Hume is a committed skeptic.

That being said, it is high time to engage the arguments Hume puts forward in the *Dialogues*. The first of the historical arguments for the existence of God to come before the interlocutors in the *Dialogues* is the Ontological Argument of St. Anselm. Indeed, Hume uses the Ontological Argument to open a critique of all of the arguments for the existence of God in the rationalist vein. Thus, Hume includes Descartes, Malebranche, and, to some degree, Leibniz in his opening dismissals. Hume inveighs against rationalist arguments by arguing that all of them are "declamations against reason, senses, every principle derived from human research." At first glance, this is an allusion to Hume's *Epistemological Principle* and betrays Philo as the primary voice of Hume in the dialogue. However, he departs markedly from his fellow British Empiricist, Locke, here. Locke, it is claimed, holds a very Anselmian view, that faith is a kind of reason. This seems an odd view given his empiricist leanings. The voice of Cleanthes seems a bit sarcastic, equating Locke with Bacon's famous line that a little philosophy makes a man an atheist while a great deal converts him to religion. This "faith seeking understanding" method led St. Anselm to advance his *Ontological Argument* and thus Philo takes up that argument himself, examining whether or not it succeeds to establish all it hopes.

The Epistemological Principle serves as the critical tool here. While Philo suggests that the fool is not particularly a formidable foe, the reference here is to Gaunilo's quite devastating critique of the *Ontological Argument*. Recalling that the argument of St. Anselm turned completely on a definition of the word, "God," such that either one meant by it at least that God was "that than which a greater can not be thought" or one did not use the word correctly, Philo points out that the fool is really thought to be doubly so – not only saying within his heart that God does not exist, but not even understanding that which he told himself.

If one applies the *Epistemological Principle* in defense of the fool, however, one quickly notes that the distinction pointed to by Gaunilo is actually a fundamental one that points to a fatal flaw in St. Anselm's argument. The distinction between the existence of some object in the actual world, whether it be an island-than-which-no-greater-can-be-thought or that-than-which-no-greater-can-be-thought, and the representation of the object in the mind is precisely the distinction that Hume's Theory of Perception exploits. While St. Anselm assumes that there is a direct correspondence between the two, the bold and determined Pyrrhonist will not be swayed at all. Given the flawed mechanisms by which the mind apprehends the world (e.g., the senses), it is impossible to suppose that the mental object (idea) accurately represents an the actual object (island, God) or that in virtue of being able to define a word would entail that the object referred to by the word had existence beyond the mental representation. While Hume does not suggest that Gaunilo is a skeptical Pyrrhonist, the conclusion is clear – while St. Anselm's argument might well seem convincing to one already possessed of faith, it will not sway someone who does not. Indeed, the skeptic might well ask what impression of sensation gives rise to the idea of God, concluding that there are at least sensory impressions of physical objects like islands while there do not seem to be such impressions of spiritual objects. Thus, the Ontological Argument fails to bridge the gap between ideas within the mind and objects of those ideas. At most, St. Anselm has shown that the idea of God exists within the mind and that, in virtue of the mind existing within the world, the idea of God exists within the world.

Demea engages the argument again to offer a further rationalist support for the existence of God. Citing Malebranche and the Occasionalists, he expands the Anselmian definition to something more like the Cartesian idea. What is important to note here is that while René Descartes's argument is a *causal* one, depending on the idea within the mind and inquiring after its cause, Demea furthers the Anselmian cause, proposing a definition and suggesting that the argument advance from there.

That Hume would appeal to the *Epistemological Principle* to clear the field of all fundamentally rationalistic proofs for the existence of God becomes clear here. He writes, "Our ideas reach no farther than our experience: We have no experience of divine attributes and operations." This is to say, we have no impressions of sensation of the divine attributes nor do we have impressions of reflection of them. Since there are neither impressions of sensation or impressions of reflection of the divine attributes, there is no valid corresponding idea of them either. Thus, even if some entity with all of these attributes were to exist, we would have no ability to *know* this because the evidence for such an entity would be beyond our capability of perception. For this reason, since all rationalist arguments for the existence of God proceed without regard whatsoever to the order of perception – from impression to idea and not vice versa – all of these arguments suffer a fatal flaw; the flaw of St. Anselm's collapsing of the distinction between the idea or representation in the mind and the supposed object of that representation outside the mind.

Cleanthes takes up the cause, turning from the class of proofs that would be labeled "rationalist" and putting forward a much more Thomistic/Scholastic empiricist approach. Here, we encounter perhaps the most common of the philosophical arguments for the existence of God, an Argument from Design. It is fairly clear that Hume has in mind the arguments not only of St. Thomas but of Hume's contemporary theologian, William Paley. Paley's *Watchmaker Argument* proceeds by virtue of an analogy. Given that there is order within a watch, a finely tuned object that is the product of design and careful construction, then when one perceives even greater order and fineness of construction within the world, one must conclude that, like the watch has a watchmaker, so, too, the cosmos must have a designer. This designer must be intelligent, infinite, and the creator of all that is. That is, there is a first Intelligent Designer who is the author of the universe.

Hume rejects this view, though not because the analogy itself is flawed. On Hume's view, the analogy is something like this:

> A watch is to a watchmaker as the cosmos is to an intelligent designer.

Hume's argument is more a matter of the scope of the argument. Since the Argument from Design is supposed to establish the existence of an eternal, intelligent, omniscient, and omnipotent Designer, it is important to analyze the analogy close to see if it can carry this weight. A watch and a watchmaker are both finite objects and given that the cosmos is finite as well, albeit much larger than a watch, the most that the analogy can convey is that there exists a quite large designer, but not an infinite one. Whether or not the designer is omniscient or omnibenevolent is a matter not so much of the Argument from Design, but of theodicies, and the Problem of Evil. Given that the universe though perhaps orderly in the manner of a watch, also includes pain, suffering, disease, and death. Thus, the author of an Argument from Design must necessarily address the Problem of Evil that the view of an intelligent creator juxtaposed with the presence of suffering in the world introduces.

While we have explored the Problem of Evil already (see St. Augustine – *City of God*), this is not the only historical theodicy. Indeed, one of the most famous treatments of the Problem of Evil is found in the work of German mathematician and philosopher, Leibniz. Leibniz, a rationalist like Descartes, has his cause taken up by Demea again.

For Leibniz, like Descartes and Demea, God is omniscient, omnibenevolent creator of all that exists. In the creative process, God contemplated many different possible worlds that God could actualize. That God contemplated many different possible worlds is not to say that God could actualize any possible world. To contemplate a possible world is to envision everything that is true about every single individual within that world. So, God contemplates what Leibniz calls the *complete concepts* of every possible individual. A *complete concept* consists of every single proposition that is true of a person, from the date of birth to the date of death to the color of hair to the cat(s) owned to the dinner consumed each and every night of that person's life. Prior to creation, God contemplated every possible world, a possible world merely being a conjunction of some set of possible individuals.

Some worlds are not possible, even for God, to create. Here, Leibniz parts company with Descartes who held that all things are possible for God. For Leibniz, to say that God could not create certain possible worlds is actually to say that certain worlds are not possible. For example, in contemplating the possible individuals for any number of possible worlds, it turns out that some possible individuals could interfere with one another, that is, individuals could fail to be *compossible*. For example, suppose there is a possible person, Mary, who, as part of her complete concept, gives birth to Elizabeth; and suppose there is a possible person, Elizabeth who gives birth to Mary. Mary and Elizabeth, though both possible people, are not compossible. In such a case, it is not possible to have a possible world in which are both these non-compossible individuals. Thus, God could not create a world in which existed two individuals who were not compossible. Such a world is not a possible world.

However, this is not to say that two individuals who are not compossible are not possible individuals. In the case of each individual, the individual is individually possible. That is, contemplated separately, or even in different possible worlds, the two individuals who are not compossible in the same possible world are individually possible or possible in different ones. It is possible that there is a possible world of which individual x is a part and it is possible that there is a possible world of which individual y is a part. In this case, the individuals are each individually possible but not compossible. Further, this conjunction of possibilities does not entail that there is a single possible world of which both individuals are a part. In the case where there is a possible world of which two distinct individuals are a part, the individuals are said to be compossible.

Leibniz argues that in the act of creation, God always acts for a reason. This is known as the *Principle of Sufficient Reason*. Given that God acts for a reason, there must be some standards which God employs. Among those standards that follow from the omnipotence and omnibenevolence of God is the *Principle of the Best*. When deciding which possible world to actualize, God employed this principle and actualized the best of all possible worlds. It is this creative process that forms the foundation of the Leibnizian theodicy.

Leibniz takes it as a given that there is pain and suffering in the world. Indeed, he makes a distinction between types of suffering – moral and natural. Natural suffering is that suffering that takes place as a result of natural disasters; e.g., volcano, earthquake, etc. Moral suffering is that which takes place as a result of human agency; Cain kills Abel, for example.

The Problem of Evil, in a shortened form from the section *St. Augustine – City of God*, consists in propositions that seem to be incommensurate. So, to say that God is omnibenevolent, that God is omniscient, that God is omnipotent, and that evil exists seem to be contrary; that is, they cannot all be true at once. Unlike St. Augustine and Descartes, who argue that evil is not an actual, positive substance, but rather a hole or a privation, Leibniz does not consider the ontology of evil, but rather the experience of it. This experience, of death and pain, is clearly a real experience, and as part of the complete concept of the individual who experiences it, it is clearly something that God has contemplated. Not only that, God has acted within God's power and created a world in which that person experiences that pain. Thus, God's omnipotence is preserved, but doubt is cast on God's omnibenevolence. If God always wills the good, why create a world in which pain and suffering exist; why not create a world of untold bliss?

God's creation through the *Principle of the Best* is the way in which Leibniz thinks God's omnibenevolence is preserved. If God created the *best of all possible worlds*, then the presence of suffering in this world is merely an indication that the other worlds God contemplated were either deficient in goodness or were logically impossible worlds. So, God's omnibenevolence is preserved because even though pain and suffering exist, it is the world that, out of all of the infinity of worlds God contemplated at the moment of creation, is the best in terms of its goodness.

In *Process and Reality*, Alfred North Whitehead calls Leibniz's *Best of All Possible Worlds* argument an "audacious fudge." Here, Whitehead expresses the general sentiment captured by Hume in the voice of Philo, suggesting that Leibniz has not played completely fairly with various propositions that comprise the Problem of Evil. Demea, taking up Leibniz's case, imagines a scenario in which a person is dropped into the world and is shown the great sufferings of the world and also its pleasures. As an objective observer, he would conclude, says Demea, that on balance, the latter outweigh the former, and further, that this world, taken from among all those possible, exhibits the greatest proportional difference between the pleasures of the cosmos and its distresses.

Philo is not persuaded. Hume, through Philo, offers a devastating critique of the Leibnizian theodicy by granting some of the propositions upon which Demea, Leibniz, Descartes, and St. Augustine, for example, insist. Granting omnipotence and omniscience, "his power we allow is infinite... his wisdom is infinite," he seems to reject omnibenevolence. However, this is merely an entrance into showing that the omnibenevolence of God, the omniscience of God, and the experience of evil is the world are incompatible. In perhaps Hume's most famous quip, he has Philo say, "Is he willing to prevent evil, but not able? Then he is impotent. Is he able, but not willing? Then he is malevolent. Is he both able and willing? Whence, then, is evil?"

Unwilling to conclude his argument with a quip and determined to explore the notion more fully, Philo explores circumstances under which evil might arise within the world. While he considers four of these, it is the last that is the most telling. It is the case that occurrences like heat and rain are necessary for the growth of plants and animals. IT is also true that too much heat and excessive rain can result in precisely the reverse – the death of plants and animals. So, if heat is required, but not always found in the right sort of amount, and similarly rain is found, but at times results in mudslides and devastation, then is it not the case that these defects are directly the responsibility of the one who created the system in this way? If this is so, and if we observed a building in which such defects were present, we would conclude that it had to be the work of an incompetent builder. By analogy, Philo concludes we are led to the same conclusion by the observation of pain and evil and of deficiencies and excesses in requisite features of the world.

At this point, Demea departs from the conversation and Cleanthes is somewhat unwilling for it to continue. "Your spirit of controversy," he says, "carries you to strange lengths when engaged in an argument. Is there nothing so sacred and venerable, even in your own eyes, which you spare on that occasion?" Philo's response is illuminating. In the immediate sense, it serves as an opening to examine the last of the sorts of arguments for God's existence that we will consider here. We will turn to that momentarily. In a more philosophically interesting sense, it serves to address the question with which we began this section, namely, is Hume a skeptic? Philo offers that, with regard to the question of natural religion, he is less cautious than on other matters. This is so because he claims that the person of principle and of common sense will not be deceived by the argument to suppose that his intentions are malicious. Rather, Hume tries, in the field of religion, to introduce the same sense of *epistemic humility* that he has tried to introduce in other fields of human inquiry – science, metaphysics, epistemology, etc. Defenders of religious doctrine, on his view, too often claim too much and in so doing are often the very source of the pain and suffering, in themselves and in their fellow citizens of the world, that the Problem of Evil laments. Thus, the careful reader of Hume ought not conclude that he is a skeptic, necessarily, with regard to the *existence* of God, but rather that he is a skeptic of the many claims made *about* God and the entailments that are thereby foisted upon the public.

Indeed, despite Hume's dismissal of the Argument from Design, the response of Philo to Cleanthes "spirit of controversy" rejoinder is illustrative of Hume's own view. Here, Hume concludes the *Dialogues* with a very subtle and telling distinction. On the one hand, Hume holds that much of religious discourse and belief is little more than vulgar superstition built on superstitious absurdity. On the other, there is what Hume describes as *true religion*, which is a matter of belief, not proof, and which strives to eliminate assent to superstitious notions. Indeed, he admits of a "peculiar pleasure" in debunking these. Intriguingly, Hume does not tend to demonstrate that the superstitions themselves are false directly, but rather he takes them at face value and by logically extrapolating their implications from them, he shows that the views, no matter how deeply professed, nevertheless entail absurdity or, sometimes, impiety. However, one should no more conclude from this that Hume is himself a skeptic than one should conclude that Gaunilo was. Indeed, Hume, in the voice of Philo, suggests that he is compelled by scientific investigations to hold something like a belief in some "first intelligent author," though this belief is the result of the work of astronomers and scientists not that of devout laity and clergy. Indeed, he turns Ockham's Razor to support this view, although it is the maxim from the Copernican system that is his formulation. That view, that "nature acts by the simplest methods, and chooses the most proper means to any end," tends to establish something like a foundation for religious belief. It should be noted that Hume still withholds the notion of "proof" from religious belief, in part because epistemic humility seem to demand it and in part because all of his foregoing arguments have shown that the proofs offered to date have failed to *demonstrate* the existence of God. Thus, while the *Dialogues* were met with a vitriolic response from many devout individuals, their failure to read carefully Hume's work suggests an intellectual dishonesty on their own part. Again, as in his scientific, metaphysical, ethical, and epistemological argument, Hume seems at most to advocate for a sort of humility with epistemological claims about religious belief. This is not the position of a skeptic, but rather that of a thoughtful and reflective philosopher who is concerned with truth and wisdom rather than bombast and superstition.

Guided Reading Questions
1. How does Hume argue that the Ontological Argument fails?
2. How does Hume argue that the Argument from Design fails?
3. What is Hume's ultimate view of proofs for the existence of God and of the existence of God, itself?

Logic Blurb
Jumping to Conclusions

Suppose Socrates makes an argument for the proposition, p. Suppose further that Plato demonstrates that the argument for p fails to prove p. Does this entail that Plato believes $\sim p$. Does the refutation suffice as a proof for $\sim p$? Simply put, no and no. It may be the case that Plato believes $\sim p$; it could be that he believes p but thinks the argument Socrates advances to be insufficient support.

On the basis of Socrates' argument and Plato's refutation, we have no idea about Plato's own positive views. Similarly, the *Dialogues* serve as demonstrations that the proofs fail. It is not clear that they do much to settle the question of Hume's positive beliefs. In fact, Hume concludes the *Dialogues* with a passage that has been taken by many scholars to suggest that Hume would find an argument from design to be rather convincing, although not rising to the level of proof. However, because the *Dialogues* systematically and thoroughly reject and refute all of the arguments offered to support the existence of God, he is sometimes labeled an atheist or, as the Scottish clergy did, "The Great Infidel." Both are entirely too quick as evaluations and unfair as interpretations of his work. The quickness and the lack of fairness stem from the ease with which people jump to conclusions based on insufficient evidence.

Section 14.1: Reading Immanuel Kant

An action has moral value if and only if it is done from reverence for the moral law and not admixed with any other cause, either a desire or a consequence, actual or hoped for.

(Groundwork)

    The work of Immanuel Kant is widely noted for its dense and difficult language and composition. However, it is even more widely acclaimed for the contributions made to the philosophical conversation, and indeed, to the quest for knowledge and understanding of the world, the human mind, and the nature of morality. Very few thinkers have the distinction of being inescapable. It is rare that the contributions of any person are so singular, so paradigm-shifting that they become required reading for future generations; that to truly grasp anything that follows them, one must become familiar with them. Kant is among these few. All serious conversations about the nature of reality, the structure and workings of the mind, and the behavior of human beings must include treatment of the work of Kant. Whether his work is accepted or rejected or some combination of the two, it is the case that it cannot be ignored if serious inquiry is to be made. Kant is a touchstone for all who come after.

    This is not to say that Kant is independent of all who came before him or that his work is so original that it cannot be seen in the context of the development of ideas. Indeed, Kant was a humble and gracious man who clearly gave credit for the influences on his own views. Of David Hume, for example, Kant writes that it was Hume that awoke Kant from his "dogmatic slumbers" and caused him to re-evaluate and broaden his own conceptions of the world. Here the contribution is easy to elaborate. As discussed in the preceding chapter, Hume took some pains in his *Dialogues* to refute all the proofs for the existence of God that had been offered to date. What he does not do is to show that it is impossible to prove God's existence. That fell to Kant, a devout Pietist. Kant, in advancing from Hume's view, built upon that which had been done before him.

    While the speculation about God and the nature of God is perhaps the easiest point at which one can see the groundbreaking work of Kant developing work of others prior to him, it is neither the only one nor the most important.

Perhaps the most important contribution of Kant, and one that lies at the heart of all of his work, is an intuition that takes into account the work of Sir Isaac Newton, G. W. F. Leibniz, and the incredible advances of the 16th, 17th, and early 18th, century in the sciences.

Prior to the Scientific Revolution marked by the advent of the scientific method, little progress had been made in understandings of the nature of the world and what progress had been made was made in fits and starts. Superstition and religious commitments hampered the growth of scientific knowledge. Those who dared to question the accepted worldview, like Nicolas Copernicus and Galileo Galilei, were harshly criticized, forced to recant their discoveries, and, in some cases (e.g., Giordano Bruno), burned at the stake. Even after the maturing of the Reformation made the climate a little less threatening, philosophers like René Descartes found it expedient to couch their speculations and arguments in forms palatable to the powers in charge of the Church and the Academy. However, as the scientific method was embraced, the breadth of knowledge of the world increased almost exponentially, gathering speed and, as a result, contributing to greater and greater increases in every field from manufacturing to medicine. The rapid advances of the natural sciences within the 17th and 18th century were breathtaking, greater and swifter than any period prior.

At the heart of these advances was a move from superstition and magical views of the world to regular and scientific ones. This move captures an intuition that the universe exhibits a regular and predictable structure, a particular order that can be called the "Natural Law." We must be careful here not to confuse the phrase "Natural Law" as it refers to the underlying physical structure of the universe with the use of the phrase as it refers to things like Newton's First Law of Motion, for example. Here we encounter an example of a very important Kantian distinction, one between metaphysics (or the way the world actually is) and epistemology (or how humans perceive and come to have knowledge of the world). Kant recognizes that it is fundamentally impossible to know how some object is, in itself. The object in itself (or the *ding an sich*) is something independent of the various perceptible qualities. So, simply put, it is impossible for Jennifer to know what it is like to be John, and vice versa. Although she may know that John is six feet tall, has brown eyes and brown hair, and has a winning smile, and while she may know many of the things that he has done over the course of his life and have heard him tell stories of things he yet wants to do, she cannot know what it is to *be* John. It is even clearer, then, that it is impossible for Jennifer to know what it is to be, say, a cat or a ferret. This points to two further distinctions of epistemological grasp of the actual world. For example, while we use the word "know" to refer to both a complete understanding of some subject and to a working acquaintance with it, there is a very important distinction between these two things. Given Kant's native language, German, it is considerably easier for him to avoid this distinction In German, to know something completely in all of its particulars is expressed by the verb, *wissen*. Let us call this knowledge of the first type. To be aquainted with some topic or person or object is expressed by the verb, *kennen*. Let us call this knowledge of the second type. Thus, we can describe the inability to know something as it is in itself (the *ding an sich*) as a failure to have knowledge of the first type. Thus, we may be acquainted we a cat (knowledge of the second type) despite the fact that it is impossible to understand what it is to be a cat (knowledge of the first type). Making clear this distinction and avoiding the pitfall of confusing the two types of knowledge is essential to understanding the difference between the Natural Law and expressions of it. It is to this distinction that we now turn.

To call, say, the Law of Gravity a "Natural Law" is to use Law here to refer to a statement, formula, or expression that is itself referring to something beyond itself. That is, there is an aspect of the physical structure of the universe that is gravity, then there is the Law of Gravity that refers to that aspect as it describes the perceptible and testable effects of gravity. Thus, when we use the phrase "Natural Law" carefully and exactly, we are referring to the actual physical structure of the universe itself. Hence, Newton's First Law, for example, that for every action there is an equal and opposite reaction, is an expression that seeks to point us to a feature of the universe that is separate from the expression itself. In other words, there is the actual aspect of the world and then there are the things that are said about it. When we use the phrase "Natural Law," we are making reference to that actual physical structure of the universe.

Understanding the Natural Law is the hallmark of the advances of the physical sciences in the 17th and 18th centuries. From Copernicus to Newton and beyond, there was a Revolution in that understanding. On the shoulders of these giants, Kant adds a further contribution. The intuition that provides a lens to understanding the work of Immanuel Kant begins with his deep and careful understanding of the ways in which the physical structure of the universe is understood. From that, Kant notes that while understanding of the world itself has made great strides, the moral sense or the understanding of the mind, will, heart, and action of human beings has not made similar strides. He concludes that perhaps the reason that understanding of the moral sense, or perhaps, moral structure of the universe has not kept pace with the growth of science is that it is held back by precisely the same sorts of superstitions and prejudices that once held science at bay. And, the prejudice most to blame for this, he thinks, is the judgment that morality is wholly unlike science; that while there is perhaps a moral structure to the universe, it is completely dissimilar from the physical one. Stripping away these superstitions and prejudice is central to Kant's work on human knowledge and morality. Indeed, Kant proceeds from his key intuition, that there is a Moral Law and this it is ontologically equivalent to the Natural Law, to argue that similar progress in morality is both possible and, further, absolutely obligatory.

We can represent Kant's intuition in the following way:

> The Natural Law and the Moral Law are ontologically equivalent

Another way of putting it would be to say that the Natural Law and the Moral Law are the same kind of thing. Now, it is important to be quite careful here and not to fall into the error of misunderstanding the nature of the equivalency. Kant is not saying that the Natural Law and the Moral Law are the *same* thing. For example, it is not his view that gravity is an aspect of morality. Such would be a rather odd view. Instead, Kant's view can be understood this way. Given that there is a regular physical structure of the world that expresses necessity, universality, and objectivity, we can expect that the moral structure of the world will also be regular and express the same sort of necessity, universality, and objectivity. Thus, while the Natural Law and the Moral Law are not the same thing, they are similar.

If the Natural Law and the Moral Law are similar, then perhaps if we approach understanding the Moral Law in ways similar to our approach to the Natural Law, we will make similar progress in understanding, as well. If science had advanced through the Copernican Revolution, perhaps, the understanding of morality, too, could have its own Copernican Revolution. To that end, in the *Groundwork*, Kant explores the structure of the Moral Law, supposing that it possesses the qualities of the Natural Law, although the aspects to be explored are not gravity, force, and motion, but will, duty, and motive. In the *Critique*, Kant examines the nature of human knowledge, demonstrating how we can go beyond what he takes to be the merely reactive stance of strict empiricism to a progressive view of science and morality. This will involve an examination of the nature of perception, truth, and categories of knowledge (*a priori*, *a posteriori*, and the Kantian contribution here, the synthetic *a priori*). With the lens of the Kantian intuition about the equivalency of the Moral and Natural Law, the very dense and complex work of Immanuel Kant becomes somewhat more accessible.

Section 14.2: Kant and the Good Will

Groundwork of the Metaphysics of Morals
Chapter 1: From Common Sense Morality to Philosophical Morality

The only thing that can be called "good" without any qualification at all is the good will. Mental power, humor, bravery, persistence, and perseverance are termed good, but they are only relatively so. Each of these can, in its own way, cause considerable harm if employed by a will that is not itself good. Material possessions are similar – power, money, reputation, health, and even what is commonly called "happiness" – each of these, if not controlled by a good will, can lead to arrogance. Only the good will, through maxims governing actions, can subdue each of these and direct it toward the end of reasonable people.

Several things aid the good will, but these things are not themselves independently valuable. In every case, a good will is presupposed when they are called good. Thus, their value is constrained by the limits of the will. Because of these limits, these things cannot be called good without reservation. Restraint, self-control, peaceful disposition – all these are constituents of a valued character. However, despite the many endorsements of the ancients, there are aspects that prevent us calling them absolutely good. Without the good will and its maxims governing actions, even these states of character can be corrupted. A true villain might possess restraint, control of himself, and an abiding calm. These qualities would make him even more vile and dangerous.

First of all, a good will is called "good" not because of consequences or utility, but rather by the fact of its good willing. That is, the good will is good in itself. Reason alone cannot direct the will toward those things that are sufficient to satisfy our desire. Reason has but one true function – the production of a good will that is not called good merely because of some further aim, but good in itself. That will, the good will, is not merely a good; it is the ultimate good. As such, it provides the bounds for all other things called "good." To explain this concept, and note that it is a concept shared by the most vulgar mind, the concept of *duty* must likewise be examined.

To discuss *duty*, we first rule out all those things that are clearly not part of duty, even if they are useful. We also eliminate actions that are consistent with duty but which originate from self-interest or desire or disposition. The difference between these actions and actions from duty is sometimes difficult to discern, important though it is. It is especially difficult to detect when it is consistent with duty but arises from personal dispositions or biases that lead to it. For example, it is consistent with duty for a shopkeeper to charge his customers only that which is appropriate and to neither charge them more or deal with them fraudulently. All effective (and prudent) shopkeepers have a single price for a single item and a child can purchase it for the same price as an adult. Though the shopkeepers deals honestly with the public, we cannot say that he has acted out of a sense of duty or from maxims of truthfulness. It is his own interest that is the source of his actions. It is far too much to suppose that it is from a sense of benevolence that he deals fairly with his customers.

It is a duty to keep one's life. However, independent of duty, all people, by their very being, feel compelled to do so. Thus the maxim that one must preserve one's life is of no internal merit and has not moral implications – that is, it is not an ethical principle nor does it possess ethical content. Beneficence is a duty and some people are such that they naturally feel great sympathy and take pleasure in doing good for others, experiencing some measure of self-satisfaction in this. However attractive such characters are, and however much the actions seem consistent with duty, they are completely without moral value.

Secondly, any action done from duty has moral value arising out of the maxim that determines it. It does not depend on outcomes, but purely upon the simply principle of willing. The end or consequence of an action cannot impart any moral value whatsoever.

Thirdly, there is a consequence of first and second. Duty is the necessity of an act, not from consequence but from a reverence for the moral law. I may feel some affection for an object or other, but not reverence, because the object is not an act of willing. Only that which is the ground of will and not the effect of it can be an object of reverence. Thus, the moral law alone is fitted for reverence and sufficient to be a directive. Any action truly from duty must be done independent of any desire or wants. Thus, all that remains before the will is the objective moral law and the subjective feel for the law.

An action has moral value if and only if it is done from reverence for the moral law and not admixed with any other cause, either a desire or a consequence, actual or hoped for. What is this law that is the determinant of the will? This alone – the general form of the law (since every other possibility has been ruled out) that can be expressed by the following formula: "Act only on that maxim that one can at the same time will to be universal law." Nothing is contained in this save the general necessity of law. This will serve as the principle that determines the will or else we must abandon the concept of duty.

Let us look at an example – may I, perhaps in the midst of great hardship, make a promise while at the same time determined to act contrary to that promise. Though this may be prudent, one can see immediately that it would not conform to duty and to the law to promise falsely. If I leave the principle of duty, my action is evil. If a prudential maxim, however, is departed, it may or may not be evil; at most it will be seen that I have acted in some way that is not immediately conducive to my self-advantage. To decide whether false promising is consistent with duty, let us ask the following: can the maxim be willed to be law in a broader system of universal moral law? This would be impossible. Were I say that it is fit for universal law, others could (and indeed, ought to) act accordingly; each returning to each other in the same way with false promises. If this maxim, to promise falsely, were law, it would be inherently self-destructive and fundamentally inconsistent, and thus, unfit to be considered universal law.

~

It is not unusual that the first questions for one concerned with understanding the nature and structure of ethics would about "goodness." What is the good? Why this and not something else? How is the word "good" properly used? These questions were ones treated by Aristotle in the *Nicomachean Ethics* and it is no surprise that Kant, in the midst of his Copernican Revolution in the field of morality, would address these straightaway. Kant's title for this chapter is instructive. Like Aristotle and Hume before him, Kant understands his task to be taking a survey of the common sense moral views of his time and place and from that collection, coming to a conclusion about the nature of morality itself. Unlike his empiricist predecessors who employed this approach, however, Kant does not suppose that the truth about morality is to be found in the common sense moral intuitions of his time. He does not rule out the possibility, but he does not suppose that it must be the case. Thus, to move this project along, he follows Aristotle and investigates the use of the word "good" to determine what its proper use is in the realm of ethics.

The word "good" is generally an adjective, a word used as a qualifier. For example, we refer to a "good sandwich," a "good toaster," a "good movie," and a "good person" in much the same way. However, it is also clear that in each of those cases, something different is meant by the word "good." In all of the cases, different though they may be in the particulars, there is something in common as well. Namely, each of those objects is called "good" for some reason external to it. That is, there is some conditional or qualification that makes the thing good. We call something a good sandwich because it meets our aesthetic tastes or it fills us up. We call a toaster good because it toasts bread well. We may even call a person good because we see the actions he or she does and attribute goodness to those actions. In each of these cases, however, the word "good" supervenes on some other feature of the object (that is, it is dependent on something besides the object itself). Thus, these would be things called good, with qualification.

For Kant, all of these are improper, or at least sloppy, uses of the word "good," if we mean to connote anything resembling moral goodness. The use of the word "good" as a moral qualifier is only truly good if it is ascribed without qualification. Turning back to the four objects that might be described as moral, all of the reasons that the objects, except the person, would be called "good" is matter of some qualification or other, some consequence that is found beneficial. Indeed, many of the reasons we might call a person "good" are similar. We might see the actions a person does and on the basis of these call him good. He might call a person a good friend because she is unfailingly loyal to us even when we are probably pretty sure we are in the wrong. A person might be called "good" because he or she is particularly attractive or intelligent or well-spoken. On Kant's view, almost all of the reasons for calling a person a good person are inaccurate or irrelevant to morals. A person who is unfailingly loyal might, in fact, do rather despicable things on our behalf, and so cannot be called morally good. A person of great intelligence might use that intelligence for good or bad ends and so even intelligence cannot be called "good" without qualification. And a set of actions is scant reason to call a person good. Consider the following example.

>John is a pharmacist. He truly dislikes Phil. Indeed, he despises Phil. However, Phil does not know this and, further, neither does anyone else. Phil is stricken with some malady or other and goes to his doctor. The doctor prescribes a medicine for him and Phil goes to John's pharmacy to have it filled. John sees this as his opportunity to rid himself of this thorn in his side. Rather than filling the prescription properly, he goes into the back and fills it with what he is sure is a poison that will kill Phil. With a smile and genial manner, lest Phil suspect something, John even gives Phil a discount on the drugs. Phil goes home, takes the misfilled prescription and, rather than dying, is cured of his disease, and beyond that, is cured of things he did not even realize were a problem – everything from athlete's foot to male pattern baldness. He goes on to live a long and healthy life.

Clearly, the consequences of John's action have been beneficial – at least to Phil. And an outside observer might well conclude that John has done a good thing, and in virtue of thinking that John has done a good thing, conclude that John is a good person. It would be an untenable position, at best, if our ethical reflections were to conclude that John is a good person. Indeed, we need to be able to isolate the nature of John's character and the consequences of the action, concluding perhaps that John is a villain and his actions had positive consequences.

Conversely, let us revisit John and Phil and this time suppose that John does not dislike Phil. Indeed, suppose that they have been friends for years and the last thing John would ever do is to jeopardize his friend's health. Presented with the prescription, John goes through all the procedures to make sure that the prescription is the right one, that there should be no adverse drug interactions, and that the pills he places in the bottle are precisely the right sort and numbers as dictated by the prescription. Phil takes the prescription home, takes the first pill, and drops dead. Clearly, we do not want to conclude that John is a bad person on the basis of consequences beyond his control and clearly not intended. Thus, the morally relevant feature of both examples is not the consequences of the action, but rather the motive or intention of John. In this latter example, Kant would still not ascribe "good" to John because his actions sprang from a motive of friendship and loyalty. However, if we re-imagine the example yet again, this time supposing the John acts, not from friendship, but because he recognizes the good thing to do, does his duty to the best of his ability, and intends to act because it is the moral thing to do, then we can, with Kant, call John's action a good action.

Through these examples and the rejection of almost all of the reasons the word "good" is ascribed to actions and people, we come to the Kantian position. For Kant, the only thing that can be called good, without qualification, is the good will. Motives and intentions are at the heart of morality and those reside in the human will. Hence, the centerpiece of Kant's ethical theory is an analysis of the will and the motives that reside within it.

If we return to the fundamental Kantian intuition, namely that the Moral Law and the Natural Law have the same ontological status, then we can situate his view about the good will in the broader picture of the relationship between the structure of the universe itself and the nature of ethics. Kant writes that the good will, "through maxims governing action can direct all of the qualified goods" – intelligence, bravery, wealth – "to the end of reasonable people." Perhaps it would be best to step back and view the entirety of the relationship of the relationship between the Moral and Natural Law, at least in broad strokes, to see how these maxims both express the Moral Law and direct actions of individual human agents.

Using the supplied diagram will be of use, although it is important to walk through it carefully. The first portion captures the Kantian intuition of morality. This is not merely a claim about ethics, nor a claim about physics. Rather, this is a metaphysical claim that has to do with the structure of the universe itself. In the same way that the structure of the universe exhibits a physical order, so, too, there is a moral order. For Kant, then, metaphysics and ethics are intrinsically related. That there is a clear relationship between the two is captured in perhaps one of the most famous summation of a Kantian view. It is often said, and attributed to Kant, that "ought implies can." Although a very abbreviated notion, this is clearly consistent with Kant's more complex view and is explored in more a formal way in the Logic Blurb attached to this section.

Proceeding from that intuition, then, it makes sense that one should look carefully at the aspect of the intuition within which the greatest progress has been made toward understanding. Thus, given the rapid advance within the realm of science, it behooves one to examine how that advance has proceeded and, more particularly, what has made that advance possible. The character of the physical structure of the universe has at least three interconnected constituent characteristics. That is, the physical order of the universe is universal, formal, and objective. In other words, whatever the structure of the universe, it is universal, or it obtains in all places. Features like gravity, mass, force, momentum, etc., are not local phenomena. Although their measurements vary, the features themselves are necessary parts of the physical universe, and thus are intrinsic to it.

Similarly, the physical order is formal. The expressions of the Natural Law are most easily recognized in formulae of varying complexity. Perhaps the most recognized is the Einsteinian "$E=mc^2$." This formula is not itself the Natural Law, but merely an expression of it. As a formula, it is completely formal. That is, it has no content and is not considered particularly useful in a practical way until some specific measurement is specified. Thus, while it describes a relationship between matter and energy, until one or the other values is supplied by the circumstances of a particular experiment, the formula is completely devoid of content. Looked at in another way, gravity is a universal feature of the physical order of the universe. However, the force of gravity varies depending on the mass of the objects in question. Thus, a person might jump quite high on the moon and be quite incapable of such heights on Earth. It is not the case that gravity differs, but rather the variables that are expressed in the formula in the practical situation differ. Since gravity is described by a function of the masses of the objects in question, changing those objects will change the observed phenomena, but must not be taken as altering the nature of gravity itself. That nature is constant.

Finally, the Natural Law is objective. Simply put, this is to say that the Natural Law is not relative. One should not take this as a rejection of Einsteinian relativity as this is not the sense expressed by "objective" or "relative" here. Instead, objectivity here means that the Natural Law is independent of the perceptions of it or the opinions about it. For example, suppose Jane decided that she would walk from the top of one tall building to another, directly and without aid of a skybridge or some other help. Suppose further that she decided to do this because she believed that she was somehow exempt from the Natural Law. Or perhaps, she believed she had seen someone else achieve such a feat and wanted to repeat it. In either case, the universe does not care whether she thought herself exempt or thought she had perceived its possibility. She would meet the end met by all others who attempted such a feat. The structure of the universe being what it is, and being independent of the perceptions and beliefstates of the observer, Jane would fall from the first building in accordance with the formulae for gravity and acceleration that express the physical order of the universe. Thus, the central characteristics of the Natural Law are that it is universal, formal, and objective. And, more to the point, those propositions that are thought to be expressions of the Natural Law must reflect the same characteristics within them.

Can the same be said for the Moral Law? If, indeed, it can, as the Kantian intuition would suggest, then it should be the case that expressions of the Moral Law must similarly be universal, formal, and objective. One of the first objections that might be directed at this view is that, from experience, it certainly seems that while the Natural Law exhibits a cause/effect structure such that an attempt to defy gravity, for example, results in rather unpleasant consequences for the perpetrator, a similar cause/effect structure does not seem to obtain for those who would attempt to defy the Moral Law. Here, Kant might reply that one ought look more carefully at the cause/effect structure of the Natural Law before coming to such a conclusion too quickly. For example, the person who seeks to defy the Natural Law by walking from the top of one building to another will meet with rather unpleasant consequences rather quickly. At the same time, the person who jumps from an airplane flying at several times the height of the building will also meet rather unpleasant consequences (assuming no parachute or that it does not open). However, the time differential between the two is clearly different. From the attempted defiance to the consequence of crashing into the ground in the first case to the second, the interval between them is different and depends, not on changes in the nature of gravity or the expressions of the Natural Law, but upon the consequences of the attempt itself. In a similar way, the time differential between the consequences of an attempted defiance of the Moral Law in one case might be greatly different from another. In this way, the Moral Law and the Natural Law might be said to exhibit the same structure, only different in circumstances.

Kant's view also serves as a rejection of the notion that ethics is a matter of relativity. Indeed, as the physical order of the universe takes no heed of the opinions and perceptions of those caught within it, so, too, the moral order of the universe is independent of the opinions of those within it. Thus, while there may be many different views about what one ought to do or how one ought to live, the existence of those differing views is in no way reflective of the actual moral order of the universe. For example, people in different cultures may believe all manner of things about why apples fall downward. In one case they might say that there is within the apple the intent to go down. In another they may say that gravity acts upon the apple. However, the actual physical structure of the universe, however different the descriptions may be, is identical in both places. So, too, two different cultures may have quite different views about the nature of the status and role of women or about war or any number of other ethical matters. However, on Kant's view, there is a single moral order to the universe and at most one of the two differing views is accurate. Both may be inaccurate. That is, given that they are contraries, at most one is true. In this, the moral order of the universe is completely objective, independent of the views about it.

Kant's intuition also captures a deeply held view of morality that is almost timeless, the intuition that moral prescriptions should be rule-like. From at least Hammurabi (and, in truth, from much before), human beings have attempted to codify moral codes. Each of these codes is comprised of a set of propositions that are universal (they apply to all, no one is above the law), objective, and, indeed, formal. For example, the proposition "Do unto others as you would have them do unto you" is such a proposition. However, that it is purely formal is not really in question. It is subject to interpretation given changing circumstances. For example, does the proposition hold directly when one's person, one's house or one's nation is attacked? Does it hold the same way in all of those circumstances? Great religious thinkers of many traditions have argued that while the basic propositions that are supposed expressions of the Moral Law are applicable in all circumstances (that is, they are universal), they results they entail might well be different in each set of circumstances. Thus, for the world-class heart surgeon, the admonition to treat her patient as she would hope to be treated in similar circumstances would entail that she perform the bypass surgery to the best of her skill. At the same time, if an auto mechanic were faced with the same situation, in an operating theater with a patient in need of a bypass, the admonition would entail that she not touch the patient at all. Changes in circumstance (or new variables inserted into the formula that the proposition expresses) change the moral requirements for those involved without in any way altering the proposition or formula itself. Thus, Kant's intuition about the ontological similarity of the Moral and Natural Law seems to hold for the characteristics of the two. For this reason, Kant's view is described as a Deontological theory of ethics. It is called "deontological" because the rules or formulae derive from the structure of reality, that is, they are "of ontology" or "from ontology." Thus, the second section of the diagram, or why the characteristics of the two (Moral and Natural Law) are the same, is explained.

Turning our attention again to the analysis of the Natural Law, it is important to discern how the propositions that are taken as expressions of the Natural Law are distilled. The scientific method is a method that requires extensive experimentation. In the laboratory, experiment after experiment is performed, controlling all manner of environmental conditions so that the particular question under examination can be examined in as isolated and unadulterated setting as possible. From these experiments and from the experiments of past scientists, hypotheses are formed. These hypotheses are provisional expressions of some feature of the Natural Law. After development of an hypothesis, the hypothesis is subjected to more testing and experimentation. This experimentation leads to refinement of the hypothesis and the process begins again. Throughout this process, statements or propositions that express some relationship of features of the physical structure of the universe are put forward. A similar process attends the development of statements or propositions that express the moral structure as well, although there are a couple of very obvious and quite critical differences.

Perhaps the most obvious difference, to this point, between the Moral and Natural Law has little to do with the order itself, but rather with the way the two are apprehended. This is an epistemological matter and points to some limitations in the ways in which human beings might come to grasp the Moral Law, perhaps, at the same time, explaining the lack of progress in this arena relative to its complimentary one. In both cases, it is impossible to know the *ding an sich*-ness of the structure of the universe, moral or physical. However, it is possible for the acquaintance knowledge of each to more closely approximate or reflect the in-itself knowledge. Within the realm of knowledge of the physical structure of the universe, investigators can perform identical experiments in controlled settings again and again. Unfortunately, such an option does not exist for those investigating the moral structure of the universe. Within the ebb and flow of life, no two moral situations are exactly the same. As a result, it is impossible to replicate a setting to experiment with the various options that may be available to discover which results in the best outcome. Similarly, given the time differentials between cause and effect in the moral setting, it is all the more impossible to perform replicable experiments.

Fortunately, there is a brand of experiment that is available to the moral investigators. While physical experiments are not an option, thought experiments are. To that end, Kant discusses several common situations or cases as a way of beginning a conversation about the proper expressions of the Moral Law. As cases are examined and turned over and again in the mind, hypotheses develop. These hypotheses can then be placed in new contexts with different variables and difficulties or refinements will be suggested and then incorporated into the proposition. Thus, though the method of developing the expressions of the Moral Law are different from the method within explorations of the Natural Law, in both cases, it is through experimentation and refinement that the expressions of the structure of the universe are derived.

Having discussed the first three parts of the diagram and the nature of the analogy between the Moral and Natural Law, we will turn to the expressions of the Moral Law, in particular, in the next section.

Guided Reading Questions
1. What is the relationship between the Moral Law and the Natural Law?
2. According to Kant, why is a good will good?
3. What sorts of actions have moral worth? What sorts do not?
4. What is duty?

Logic Blurb
The Appeal to Ignorance
Gaunilo calls St. Anselm's Ontological Argument into question. David Hume demonstrates that all of the arguments for the existence of God up until his time had failed. Immanuel Kant proves that it is impossible to prove or disprove the existence of God. All of this is to say that someone might well conclude that she does not know whether or not God exists. If Tiffany argues that it is clear that God does not exist because no one has been able to prove that God exists, she has committed the *appeal to ignorance* fallacy. Indeed, even if she takes the Kantian line and argues that it is impossible to prove that God exists, it does not follow from that that God does not exist. Simply put, one cannot justi-

fiably claim that one's view is the right one simply because no one has managed to refute it yet.

In a similar fashion, suppose that Pat argues that since no one has disproved the existence of God, and that Kant has even shown that it is impossible to disprove that God exists, then God must exist. This is an appeal to ignorance in the other direction. Simply because an argument has not been disproved to date does not mean that it is impervious to refutation. So, the moral to the *appeal to ignorance* fallacy is simply this – knowledge cannot be founded upon ignorance.

Section 14.3: Kant and the Metaphysics of Morals

Groundwork of the Metaphysics of Morals
Chapter 2: From Common Sense Morality to a Metaphysics of Ethics

Thus far, we have examined *duty*, and have noted that it is present in common, everyday actions. However, simply because it is seen there does not mean that it is an *a posteriori* concept based solely on experience. To the contrary, when the common morality is surveyed, a great number of disputes, many justified, are given to us from experience. Even in those cases where an action seems to arise solely from duty, it is quite impossible for experience or observation to convince us absolutely that it is so. Thus, it is impossible for experience and observation to conclude, on its own, that any action has moral worth. Indeed, there have always been those thinkers that deny the existence of internal intentions of duty altogether. These generally ascribe the actions seemingly from duty to be *grounded* in self-love.

The views of those who reject the idea of objective morality as absurd are aided in no small measure, if it be claimed that *duty* is merely a notion derived from observation *a posteriori*. To do so is to grant them certain victory. However, the question is not whether or not actions arise from insight *a priori*. Even if no actions ever arose from this source, that is not the issue. The matter is this: can reason, independent of experience, issue legislation and state what ought to be?

What might be said of this law, except in those instances and by those who deny morality entirely? The law must be universal in scope, valid and applicable objectively and of necessity, not merely contingently or imaginatively. As such, it is limited not to human beings but applies to any intelligent being.

It could not be worse for ethics to be defended by those grounding it on examples/experience. An example must be compared to some principle to know whether or not it is a reasonable example or an example at all. But, this means that the example cannot generate the principle by which it must be judged. Similarly, imitation is foreign to ethics. An example may only encourage ethical actions, but the moral legislation of which it is an example must come first and it is a perversion of example and of reason to reverse them.

After a science is properly grounded and first principles established, it is good to evaluate common sense morality. This is how it is done here. This means grounding ethics on its proper ground – metaphysics. Clothing it then in common sense will disseminate it broadly.

It is clear that ethical notions originate and are grounded in reason *a priori*. This is true for both the uneducated and the wise. Ethical notions cannot be demonstrated or grounded in *a posteriori* experience. It is this *a priori* status that provides their lofty positions as the ultimate practical principles of life. Adding *a posteriori* intent only weakens their power. It is objectively necessary, even for the practical living of life, to deduce the moral law from reason alone. Only like this can we purge ethics and refine it till it is a pure philosophy and thus fit to be the ground of a metaphysical science.

The whole of the world acts in accordance with laws. Only an intelligent being can act in accordance with a representation of the law. If reason is necessary to deduce action from law, then it is also true that the will itself is nothing more than practical reason or common sense. If reason determines the will, then the actions arising from that will are objectively and subjectively necessary; if the will is distracted and so not in harmony with the moral law, then the action is objectively necessary and subjectively contingent. The representation of any universal principle, related to the will, is a directive of reason. The expression of that principle as a formula is an *imperative*.

And imperative is always in terms of "should" or "ought." Both the perfect and imperfect wills are governed by the absolute moral law. The nature of the perfect will, however, will always comport to this law and as such is not directed by it.

An *imperative* is only a formula, without content of its own. As such, it shows the relation between the moral law and the imperfect will.

There are, strictly, two sorts of *imperatives* – the Hypothetical and the Categorical (although there is often mention of a third, the Prudential, which is a subset of the Hypothetical). The *Hypothetical Imperative* directs the will to those actions conducive to some further desire, as a means to some other end. The *Categorical Imperative* directs the will of necessity to those actions that are of moral command and with no regard whatsoever to consequences.

Every maxim concerning action expresses the action as something good. If the goodness of an action is dependent on its consequences alone, it is *hypothetical*; if it is good in itself, *categorical*.

The Hypothetical Imperative is purely relative; something good because of what it brings about. The Categorical Imperative, on the other hand, expresses an action that is necessary and objectively so.

There seem to be two sorts of Hypothetical Imperative and but one Categorical Imperative. So, it would be helpful to examine the three in turn. Firstly, let us consider the ability a person has to accomplish this or that desire he possesses. Within the will, there are as many maxims as there are objectives contained within them. Each maxim is required to bring about the end it contains. The end expressed in a particular maxim need be neither good nor rational, it

Section 14.3: Kant and the Metaphysics of Morals 387

simply exists and expresses simply the conditions necessary to accomplish it. Both the physician and the assassin concoct their potions to do their respective ends, the physician to heal and the assassin to poison and kill. These hypothetical imperatives have in common that they are both the imperatives of practice or craft.

Secondly, all human beings share an end. This end we can name *happiness*. It is a hypothetical imperative that one must serve or seek to accomplish that which is in one's self-interest. This hypothetical imperative we name prudential because it involves a choice as a means to an end, and this end is the personal happiness or advantage of the individual.

Finally, there exists an imperative that we shall name the Categorical Imperative. We give it this name because it specifies a course of action independent of all personal aims. This imperative is a matter of the form of an action. Whether an act can be thought good is actually a matter of the form of the motive that activates it, whatever the result. Only this imperative can be termed "moral."

It is fairly simple to note the differences between the three commands of the imperatives. We can aptly term them Rules of Practice, Rules of Prudence and the Moral Law. IN this last case, it is rightly called Law because only Law is without exception, wholly objective, and universally necessary. Rules express a sort of necessity, but only one that is conditioned or qualified, wholly or in part subjective, and contingent on other factors. Only the Categorical Imperative is an expression of absolute necessity, and as such, a Law. The first are matters of practice, the second matters of pragmatism, and the third is moral; that is, ethical.

~

The move from a survey of the moral intuitions of the common, prephilosophical sense to a disciplined analysis of those intuitions to determine the truth about morality that was begun in chapter one of the *Groundwork*, continues in the second. The distinction here is that Kant makes a further restriction within his title and the work that follows, isolating the relationship between the nature of ethics with a metaphysics of ethics. Here, the Kantian intuition about the nature of the Moral Law becomes even clearer. It is a metaphysical claim that the Moral Law and the Natural Law have equivalent ontological status. Having already discussed the characteristics of the Natural Law and their counterpart characteristics of the Moral Law in the previous section, we need merely explore them further here.

On Kant's view, the Moral Law has a measure of *a priori*-ness. That is to say, the propositions that are expressions of the Moral Law cannot be the result of careful and controlled laboratory experiments. Given that each moral situation is unique, there cannot be a series of replicated experiments from which to derive a hypothesis that will serve as a working theory until it can be refined with further experimentation. In this way, the natural sciences carry a heavier load of *a posteriori* character. That is, the propositions that are expressions of the Natural Law have their origin in experience than in speculative reason. Given that such is not possible for the expressions of the Moral Law, we are left with experiments of a different sort.

The experiments that give rise to the expressions of the Moral Law are very akin to experiments within disciplines like mathematics; which is to say, it is quite odd to call them experiments at all. In mathematical reasoning, first principles of systems are put forward and explored through means of proof. Euclidean Geometry, for example, has fundamental axioms and postulates which are then used to develop theorems and proofs that are logically necessary because they are deductively sound. Mathematics is not strictly *a priori*, because the mathematician has considerable experience with numbers, relations, definitions, proofs, mathematical systems, and the like. However, it is *a priori* in the sense that the conclusions are not subject to confirmation through experimentation, but rather bear a measure of logical necessity simply in virtue of being deductively certain. It is an analogous sort of reasoning that attends the understanding of the Moral Law and expressions of it, called Imperatives. What Kant does here is to examine all those propositions that people advance as being part of the Moral Law and, through *a priori* analysis (which is to say, not themselves subject to experimentation). That analysis is possible because the Moral Law, itself, as part of the structure of the universe, carries with it the characteristic of being necessary, and not contingent. Thus, though the one investigating the nature of the Moral Law may well begin with things from experience (the survey of common moral intuitions, for example), she is not bound to them and her speculations will, if deductively sound, be found necessary, and not contingent.

While expressions of the universe's physical order may be called laws of nature or theories, expressions of the moral order are called Imperatives. The word "imperative" is little used in common parlance in the way Kant uses it anymore. A generation ago, it was common to hear a person say something like, "It is imperative that we get to town on time," for example. Now, rather than "imperative," someone is likely to use a different word like "must" or "should." With regard to ethics, this evolution of language is actually helpful. An imperative of action involves a sense of must or should. Given the formulation of most moral admonitions, "should" is perhaps the most common directive; that is, most admonitions take the form, "You should do thus and so."

However, the word "should" is also used in a variety of senses, some of which are properly moral and some of which, though at times given the appearance of being moral directives, are, in fact, not part of the moral fabric of the universe. Kant recognizes this as well and provides a very helpful analysis of the sort of "shoulds" that are like to be encountered, isolating the only sort that is truly moral. The three types of imperatives or "shoulds," Kant describes are the Hypothetical Imperative, the Prudential Imperative, and the Categorical Imperative. We shall take each of these in turn and assess to what extent it is a competitor for consideration as the Moral Imperative.

The Hypothetical Imperative is perhaps the first and easiest to distinguish. An example might make its nature and use clearest. Suppose a faculty member approached a student in the Student Center and told the student, "You should study for that Particle Physics final exam." An outside observer might reasonably analyze that imperative in the following way. Under what circumstances is it true that the student should study for that exam? First of all, if the student is actually taking Particle Physics, then it might be reasonable to conclude that, yes, indeed, she should study for her final in that course. Second, supposing for the moment that the student is in that class, it would be imperative for her to study for that final if she has a desire to do well in the course. However, suppose the student was not in the course, or, if in it, has no desire to succeed. In either of those cases, then, the student does not feel the weight of the imperative because the imperative does not have any force. Thus, there are at least two conditions that must be met in order for that expression of an imperative to actually pertain to the student. What we have here is an hypothetical situation in which only that student who has an interest in experiencing a certain consequence need do those things that will bring the consequence about. An Hypothetical Imperative, then, is one that is highly particularized. Only those people who want some particular conclusion or other are bound by the conditions required to bring that conclusion to being. As a result, those expressions of "should" which fall under the heading of Hypothetical Imperative cannot be candidates for true expressions of the Moral Law because they fail in the very first test, the test of universality. They fail also to express objectivity, as they are completely relative to the individual at hand and his desires. Also, the Hypothetical Imperative is not necessary, but rather is wholly contingent on the individual who either feels its weight because he wants the promised result or does not because he does not.

The Prudential Imperative is explicitly mentioned in the included excerpt as it pertains directly to one of Kant's most famous examples, the example of false promising. However, an easier example may serve our purposes for now. Suppose that a young man has been told by his parents that his room must be cleaned or he will face dire consequences. Suppose further that his parents ask him, by phone, if he has cleaned his room. Knowing that he should have cleaned it by now and that he has, in fact, not done so, he is faced with the prospect of lying to his parents or telling them the truth. Let us also suppose that his parents will not arrive home for several hours and that there is plenty of time for him to clean his room prior to their arrival. The Prudential Imperative would direct the young man to lie to his parents in this situation, precisely because it would be the "prudent" thing to do. By doing so, he would avoid the potentially negative consequences of telling the truth to his parents and buy time for the cleaning of the room. However, given that this is both imminently self-interested (and thus not objective) and wholly contingent on the desire to avoid punishment, it cannot survive as a candidate for the Moral Law either.

Only the Categorical Imperative can be considered to be an expression of the Moral Law. The Categorical Imperative, in its most basic form, is actually given in chapter one of the *Groundwork*. It is as follows:

Categorical Imperative (basic form): Act only on that maxim that one can at the same time will to be universal law.

Kant discusses other forms of the Categorical Imperative, although he takes them all to be derivative of the basic form. The most commonly quoted form of the Categorical Imperative is one of these derivative forms and is as follows:

Categorical Imperative (second form): One should act, toward the humanity present in oneself or in another, as an end in itself and never as a means solely.

Whether or not the derivative forms of the Categorical Imperative can actually be reduced to the basic form is of some interest within modern scholarship. However, it is of little issue for Kant, himself. For Kant, all of the forms of the Categorical Imperative capture the universality, formalness, objectivity, and necessity characteristic of the Moral Law. We will address some of the particular propositions that Kant takes to be expressions of the Categorical Imperative later in this section. Before turning to those, however, it is important that we situate what Kant says about maxims within the framework of the Moral Law developed thus far.

Kant says that the Categorical Imperative is to govern all truly moral motive or maxims of action. Perhaps, then, it is important to understand how maxims of action become motives or intentions. A brief, perhaps overly so, examination of a common theory of the relationship between intention and action will be helpful here. While this view is not strictly attributable to Kant, it is helpful in situating his own view.

All human beings have desires for all manner of things – food, shelter, leisure, etc. Those desires which have an object external to the person can be called immediate desires. So, for example, when hungry and faced with a panoply of options for satisfaction of that hunger, we might have several immediate desires: a desire for a hamburger, a desire for a salad, a desire for a steak, a desire for a banana split, and on and on. At the same time, we may have all manner of other immediate desires at the same time: a desire to write a letter, a desire to study for an exam, a desire to spend the day lounging at the lake. All of these desires reside within the human will and each of these desires pulls the will, straining to move the agent to satisfy each of them. At the same time, it is impossible to satisfy each of our immediate desires. They are in competition and often satisfying one will entail necessarily thwarting another. Thus, we must, through some mechanism, evaluate those desires and choose from among them which will motivate us to action. This is, we must do this if we are to be reflective. On the other hand, as Plato pointed out in his Charioteer Analogy, a human being could simply be in thrall to these immediate desires, seeking to satisfy whichever is stronger at any given moment. Such a person is perhaps the paradigm of an incontinent, weak-willed, and likely immoral agent.

Any action on the part of an agent is the product of some desire or other. Indeed, we can say that whichever desire ultimately motivates us to action is our true intention, even if, upon reflection, we would say that we did not intend to act in that way. For example, having been caught turning in a paper in which every word was copied from some other source (that is to say, having plagiarized our assignment), it would make little sense to say that we did not intend that action, even if we recognize that such an action is wrong and unworthy of actualizing. Thus, all actions are the product of a desire becoming a motivating intention, even if we would, upon reflection, wish that we had not acted in that manner.

Some of these desires are conscious, some may be unconscious, but all carry the power to motivate a person to action. The action is a consequence of some intention that expresses a desire. Given this, it is important to understand how a desire becomes an intention. Suppose that a person has several competing immediate desires, not all of which can be satisfied. If there were not some further set of desires within we would be buffeted and, ultimately, devastated by the relentless crush of incompatible desires. Instead, within the will exists another set of desires which do not have as their object something external to the person, but rather have as their object an immediate desire. We shall call these desires *secondary desires*. Secondary desires are desires that have the following form, "I desire to be the sort of person motivated by this particular immediate desire." Or, for example, take the person who is hungry and is presented with several options, many of them quite unhealthy, for satisfying the desire. There are several immediate desires, obviously. However, there are also several secondary desires, perhaps even one for each immediate desire. One secondary desire might be, "I desire to be the sort of person who is motivated by a desire to eat the healthy salad." Another might be, "I desire to the be the sort of person who is motivated by desire to eat the quadruple bacon cheeseburger." By analyzing our secondary desires, we can turn one of them into an intention. Suppose our secondary desire concerning the desire to eat the salad is selected. Then, when we eat the salad, we can trace the action (eating the salad) back through an immediate desire (to eat the salad) selected for motivation from among many competing immediate desires by the secondary desire (to be the sort of person motivated by the desire to eat the salad). That secondary desire we call an immediate intention.

It should be noted that there is another level of analysis available here. There is a deeper set of desires as well. Let us call these the *reflective desires*. These are of the sort, "I wish to be such and such a sort of person." So, for example, the reflective desire at beneath the secondary desire that becomes the immediate intention is the desire of the sort, "I wish to be a healthy person." That reflective desire is a matter of character. It is the basis for the discrimination between the secondary desires. It may be the case that, with regard to the immediate desires, the desire for the quadruple bacon cheeseburger is much stronger than the desire for the salad. However, we need not succumb merely to the strength of immediate desires. It may even be the case that the secondary desires would result in our eating the unhealthy option. However, with some effort, we are able to conform our actions, not to either our immediate or even our secondary desires, but to our reflective desires. In these cases, this reflective desire, when it issues ultimately in action, is the intention. It is this state of the agent's will, in which the reflective desires are the motivating intentions, that moral evaluations can be made. Here, reason plays a central role. Kant writes, "If reason determines the will, then the actions arising from that will are objectively and subjectively necessary." Reason will sift through the immediate desires, the secondary ones, and the reflective ones, analyzing which are compatible with the Moral Law. If pure reason is the power that discriminates between the various desires, eliminating those that are incompatible with the Moral Law and endorsing those that are compatible with it, then the actions that are the products of this will will carry objective necessity, because they will conform to the necessity of the Moral Law, and they will carry subjective necessity, because they will be the product of a desire that becomes intention and motivates the agent to the actions.

All desires can be expressed as a maxim. That is, every desire can be expressed as a statement of action. For example, the desire for a steak can be expressed in the following way, "When hungry, one should eat a steak." These maxims, clearly, are unfit to be considered part of the universal law because they are highly particularized and carry no level of logical necessity with them. Thus, maxims constructed from immediate desires cannot be moral maxims and cannot be expressions of the Categorical Imperative.

Maxims that describe the secondary desires and the reflective desires are more likely candidates for being expressions of the Moral Law. To be sure, many secondary desires will fail to express maxims appropriate for universal law for the same reason that immediate desires do – they are often highly particularized and contingent on the agent. However, one of the most famous examples of a maxim that might be considered for universal law is one of these secondary desires.

Suppose Tim is in need of money and has no source of gaining the funds except through borrowing them. However, since he has no revenue streams of his own, he will be quite incapable of repaying the borrowed money. Thus, he knows he cannot repay the money, but he also knows that merely asking for money, without the promise of repayment, will prove futile. So, he formulates the intention within his will that he should ask to borrow money and, knowing of his inability to repay, he should ask to borrow the money, promise to repay it, while having no intention of actually doing so. Thus, we have the problem of false promising. Is it morally permissible to promise falsely; to, in this case, ask to borrow money with the promise to repay and the intention not to repay. The maxim expressed here would be something like this, "in the midst of great hardship, I will make a promise while at the same time determined to act contrary to that promise."

It can be noted that this maxim will fail to meet the requirements for expressing the Moral Law because it fails to encapsulate the Categorical Imperative. That is to say, it is impossible to reasonable will that such a maxim should be the Moral Law. To suppose that such a maxim could be the Moral Law would be to suggest that everyone, when in the midst of hardship, should make borrowing requests with false promises of repayment. If we tried to imagine a world in which such a maxim was followed by all, one can scarcely envision human civilization at all. If everyone acted on such a maxim, within moments all vestiges of trust, commerce, and human interaction would be compromised. Such a maxim is inconsistent with the development or preservation of human society. Thus, it is scarcely possible to universalize such a maxim. As such, it fails to express the Moral Law. However, the failure of the maxim of false promising points to a possible alternative competitor for expressing the Moral Law. Suppose we negate the false promising maxim such that we have the following, "In the midst of hardship, I will only make a promise of repayment when I can have certainty of fulfilling the promise." Such a maxim seems to meet the various criteria for expressing the Moral Law.

How, then, is such a morality possible. Recall again the Kantian description of the good will and its function, "Only the good will, through maxims governing actions, can subdue each of these and direct it toward the end of reasonable people." While reason sifts through the various desires, it is important to note the way Kant characterizes the function of the good will. It, with the help of reason, *subdues* the desires. For Kant, becoming a moral person is not a matter of easy attendance to a set of convenient or comfortable rules. Rather, moral actions are more likely to be quite difficult and to run directly counter to our strongest immediate desires, and even our stronger secondary desires. Only actions done from duty, borne of reverence for the Moral Law, will be moral actions. This means that morality cannot be a matter of self-interest, nor can it be a matter of disposition. Rather, a moral life is a life of struggle and discipline that involves shaping the will until it conforms to the universal, necessary, and objective Moral Law.

Guided Readings Questions:
1. What is the formula for moral action, on Kant's view?
2. What is the difference between *a priori* motives and *a posteriori* motives?
3. What is a Hypothetical Imperative? Give an example.
4. How is a Hypothetical Imperative different from the Categorical Imperative?

Logic Blurb
The *a priori/a posteriori* Distinction

Among the most important distinctions within epistemology is the *a priori/a posteriori* distinction. For René Descartes, for example, all certainty, and thus all true knowledge, has is *a priori*. That is, it is deduced from first principles that are known independent of empirical experience of them. Thus, "I exist" is known *a priori* since it is known purely by operation of the mind and wholly independent of any set of experiments that could possibly verify it. So, all true knowledge comes *prior to* experience that might confirm that knowledge. On the other hand, David Hume excludes the possibility of the existence of *a priori* knowledge. Since all knowledge is of ideas and since all ideas are the product of impressions of one sort or another, then all knowledge is the produce of experience. Because it *follows after* our experiences, knowledge is always *a posteriori*.

Immanuel Kant gets in between the rationalist Descartes and the empiricist Hume with a notion of a *synthetic a priori*. The "synthetic" part of the *synthetic a priori* is very much the product of experience. For example, one might well experience the addition of columns of numbers again and again and again. In this, one might well discern that there is a relationship between the numbers and the concept of addition. However, one would know that this number theory is independent of any of the particular additions or subtractions that one might employ. Indeed, it is primitive to the additions and subtractions themselves and even though the discovery of the principle is posterior to the addition experiences, those experiences also reveal to the careful mathematician that the principle is prior to the actual additions. Thus, experience reveals a relationship that is, itself, independent of and prior to the experience itself. This is an *a priori* notion. Thus, the field of mathematics allows Kant to support a notion of a *synthetic a priori* that is a sort of hybrid of the rationalist and empiricist strains of epistemology.

Section 14.4: Kant and the Categorical Imperative

Groundwork of the Metaphysics of Morals
Chapter 2: From Common Sense Morality to a Metaphysics of Ethics

It is a complicated matter to explain how/why the *Categorical Imperative* is possible. Despite difficulty, it is the sole question that demands of us an answer. We cannot come to that answer through hypothetical examples nor from suppositions since these represent singular instances and not necessary expressions of universal Law. Examples will never remove the doubt that the imperative is of hypothetical rather than of categorical sort. Two propositions serve to make this point. "You shall never promise falsely," is clearly an imperative that is universal and not particular. On the other hand, "do not make false promises because to do so will ruin one's reputation," is not. Rather, it expresses a Hypothetical Imperative.

Given this, any investigation of the Categorical Imperative must proceed *a priori* from the outset. This is clear. Only the Categorical Imperative is Law. The others may express principles of one sort or another, but they cannot be Law. Only an imperative not tied to given ends, that is universal and without qualification or condition and that, therefore, gives no options to individual wills; only such an imperative has the essence of Law.

The Categorical Imperative is, however, simple in form and singular: *Act only from that maxim that one can conceive to be universal law.* All other imperatives of duty are derivative from this. ... The formal concept of Nature is that structure of seamless and constant laws that determine the order of things. Because the *moral* imperative has this same character, the Categorical Imperative can be written as "Act only from that maxim that one can conceive to be a universal law of Nature."

Examples of common notions of duty can here be examined to illustrate this formation of the Categorical Imperative.

1. Imagine a person beset by all manner of troubles. Suppose he has come to the end of his tether, so sickened is he by life and its unrelenting grind. If he considers suicide, he would first meditate and ask if the maxim that would produce such an action would be a reasonable universal Law. The maxim would be: "If life is perceived to be more filled with misery than happiness and thought likely to continue in that way, he is to end his life." We then have this question:

Is it possible that such a maxim could be reasonably imagined to be a Natural law? Suppose it were. It is immediately clear that if this were part of the structure of Nature that life would be destroyed and would perforce devolve into chaos. Thus, it follows that such a maxim cannot express Natural Law and, in fact, is repulsive to the ultimate demand of duty.

2. Imagine a second person in need of money so that he must borrow. Suppose further that he knows he cannot pay back the money. At the same time, he knows that if it is known he cannot repay that he will be unable to borrow any money. Nevertheless, suppose he decides that his maxim will be something like this: "Whenever I am impoverished and incapable of repayment, I shall promise to repay even though I know that I will not." This is again, like the first, a principle of self-love. Such a principle, when imagined as Natural Law, however, is hard to imagine. Where would such a principle stop? Indeed, if it were adopted by all, it would quickly become apparent that it entails a contradiction of itself. If it were adopted by all, then the very notion of a promise would be destroyed.

Here, then, are some duties that can grow out of the proper formula of morality. An intelligent being shall be able to reasonably universalize the maxims of his actions. This is the Moral Law as regards intentions. Certain acts cannot ever be conceived as expressing the Moral Law and these are properly rejected. Some actions are indeterminate, neither compulsory nor forbidden. The first kind of action expresses obligatory duties, the latter have more latitude. However, in both cases the actions and duties are dependent on the simple and singular principle of morality proffered earlier.

This investigation has been followed to the following conclusion: if the notion of duty carries any weight at all, they must be expressed as laws, and these as Categorical rather than Hypothetical Imperatives. We have, as well, found the formula for the Categorical Imperative. We should be able to develop that formula to cover every particular duty; if such duties exist, that is. However, to this point, we have not demonstrated that such imperatives exist *a priori*, or that some law, independent of all variables, commands absolutely, or that obeying this law amounts to duty.

It is clear that this proof must, of necessity, avoid the thought that it could be deductively shown by appeal to particulars of human nature. Duty must be unconditional. Any intelligent being must be bound to its constraints. Since it is sufficient to induce obligations on all intelligent beings, then it will, necessarily, extend to human beings. Those commands derived from the particularities of human experience might well be maxims for action, but they fail as Law because they are subjective – something we very well want to do – but they are not objective.

In fact, to add an *a posteriori* aspect to moral duties would in no way ever improve the duty, no matter how high-minded it appears. Rather, it will compromise the purity of the principle. The value of the good will consists in this alone – that the principles are universal, abstracted from all particulars, and completely independent of any external aspect whatsoever.

This is the question to put to any maxim/principle of action: Is the principle obligatory to each and every intelligent nature; is it such that it could be raised to the level of a Law in the Moral Law? If it is, then it must be intimately tied, *a priori*, to the notion of an intelligent person's will. The only way to demonstrate this tie is to engage in metaphysics, particularly, the metaphysics of ethics.

We think of the will as possessing the capacity to order itself in accordance with expressions of certain laws. This is a capacity possessed only by rational agents. The foundation of the self-direction of the will is an *end*; and if it is a rational end, then it must be available to all rational entities. The thing that conveys the mere possibility of actions toward an *end* is called the *means*. The desire with the agent to act is called the *source*, and external foundation or rule is called the *Law*. Therefore, there is a clear difference between internal desires or subjective ends, the foundation of which are subjective sources and external or objective sources which are expressions of Laws and which apply to all rational beings.

All rational entities, human or otherwise, are ends in themselves. A rational agent is never to be used merely as an instrument or tool for some purpose by any other rational will, or even by his own. Instead, a person must consider his existence, as an end in himself, whenever acting. And, he must consider every other Intelligence, in the same way, as an end in itself. Any existent thing, external to us, that has an existence independent of our rational will but dependent on nature are valuable only relatively. These things are properly considered instrumentally valuable, or as means to some end beyond themselves. For this reason they are called *objects*; but any Intelligence or rational being is a *person*. As such, he is an end in himself. The foundation of our principle, then, is this maxim – One should act, toward the humanity present in oneself or in another, as an end in itself and never as a means solely.

We must now investigate whether or not this second formulation comports favorably with the first.

Let us first consider duty as it relates to the humanity within ourselves. Consider the man who wishes to commit suicide. The question that pertains here is whether or not the action expressed by his maxim is consistent with the reality of the humanity that is an end in itself and not a means only. The person who, from great anguish, chooses to terminate his physical life is treating himself as a means, using himself instrumentally to bring about comfort and ease until his life ends. However, humanity is not an *object* but is an end in itself. It is not something that can be addressed as a single entity, but rather as something universal, that must be treated at all times and in all circumstances as an end and not a means. Thus, it is not permissible for me end my life, and terminate my humanity, by killing or deforming it.

Having first considered duties to self, we turn then to duty toward others. Consider the person who makes a promise falsely. It is clear that this person treats his neighbor instrumentally or as a means. He is not thought of as an end in himself, but merely as something to be used or to be abused. The one who is abused in this way could not possible endorse such treatment of himself. False promising, then, is anathema to the principle that humanity is to be treated as an end in itself. This is even clearer when we imagine it applied to individual freedom or personal property. In these situations, it is absolutely clear that the one who trespasses the principle has not seen the victim as anything other than a means to some end rather than as an end.

The view that every rational being is an end in itself is not an empirical matter arising from experience or from observation. This is clear from the fact that it is a universal matter and from the fact that the humanity of people is not a subjective end or instrumental end but is itself the objective end of humanity. The other ends that humanity may have may well limit humanity and these arise *a priori* as well. But the foundation of all laws of action is derivative from the objective rule and from the universal nature of the objective rule which makes it appropriate for being considered Law, such that it is congruent with the first form of the Categorical Imperative.

Given this formulation, any maxim that is not congruent with this universal nature of Law is rejected. This universal law is within the will itself. Thus, the will makes it so that the adherence to the universal law is not a matter of being subjected to its rule outside of the will of the agent, but rather is a matter of self-rule. Since the person is himself the author of the principle from within his will, he can be understood as the proper subject of his own sovereignty.

The Categorical Imperative, in this universal form, expresses the uniformity within human actions that is analogous to the uniform series of events that occurs in the physical world. It is expressed as Categorical because without this expression, we could not then comprehend Duty. When the will is postulated as the ultimate Law, it is apparent that it is disinterested. Since it is not built on interests, self-interest or the interest of others, it is clear that the Categorical Imperative is the only imperative that is unconditional, or universal.

It becomes clear now why all attempts to understand the structure of ethical theory and action have failed so utterly. Some saw that morality is objective, a matter of duty and Law; however that bondage was seen as external rather than the recognition that we have here that each person is bound by the self-authorship of the universal law, that part of the very nature of humanity is to function as universal law-maker, and thus that the law to which a person is subject is the law that he himself authors. If regarded as merely subject to some law, whatever the source, then it follows that adherence to the law is a matter of self-interest – either positively luring the agent or restriction. In this case, the maxim *cum* imperative that directs action is that of a foreign power and thus it is a conditional, or *hypothetical* matter. This is contrary to the most basic perspective of the Categorical Imperative, namely that it describes *autonomy* of the human will, rather than *heteronomy*, which is the nature of every principle of action or directive of duty that is not consistent with the first form of the Categorical Imperative.

All rational beings are equally under this Law, "one should act, toward the humanity present in oneself or in another, as an end in itself and never as a means solely." Ethics is then a matter of evaluating action to the universality of this Law. This Law, however, is encountered by all rational beings and grows out of the principle within the several, single wills to avoid acting in any way that cannot be expressed as a universally formulated maxim. That is, to act at all times such that one can imagine that one is converting one's own maxim of action into a universal Law.

The centerpiece of the very human self-determination is *autonomy*. This is the centerpiece of the nature of any rational being. ... The *autonomy* of the will is just that state of a will by which it is a law unto itself. Thus, to select those maxims individually that may be elevated to the state of Natural Law is the *principle of autonomy*.

Chapter 3. From a Metaphysics of Ethics to an Investigation of the Functions of the Will *a priori*

The will is a form of causation that is the sole reserve of rational, living agents, proportional to their rationality. *Freedom* is a feature of causation by which those agents cause events independent of external determinants. This is in direct contrast to the notion of the causation of physics. Within that realm, external determinants are the sole influence on events and the events that are effects are completely caused by those external forces.

Thus, we understand *freedom* in a negative way, although this is not at all helpful for providing us with a grasp on the nature of human willing. However, beginning in this way, we can progress to a positive conception of freedom more effectively. Since all causation communicates, of necessity, an expression of Natural Law, in which the prior causes necessarily give rise to their effects, the conception of *freedom*, independent though it is of the Natural Law of physics, is not, at the same time, independent of being understood to express Law. Instead, *freedom* is simply a different form of causation and it expresses Law that is appropriate for it and that, in comparison, preserves the difference in kind from physical Law. If this were not so, then freedom would be a complete illusion. Within physics, causation is heteronomous, external to the event or the effect. Freedom of will, rather, is *autonomy*. The autonomous will self-determines and causes from within itself, independent of externalities.

Freedom must be assumed as a property of the will of all rational beings

We cannot merely suppose that the will is free. We can only call our will free if we have enough grounding to ascribe freedom to the will of every rational entity. The Moral Law is our Law only insofar as we are rational beings.

Therefore, the Moral Law must be the Law of others insofar as they are rational as well. Further, since a notion of *moral freedom* (of freedom of the will) can only arise out of a notion of *freedom*, that *freedom* must reside as a property of any and every rational being's will. Thus, any and every being that can act under the notion of *freedom* must be understood as practically *free*; or, in another way, we must envision those beings who can act within this notion (e.g., all rational beings) as being *actually free*. As a result of this view, we understand that rationality must consider itself as the sole author of the principles of action that guide it, completely separate from external forces: thus, rationality is imbued with *practical reason* to understand itself as *free*; in another way, a will of any rational being can only be the will of *that* rational being if freedom is a presupposition.

That freedom *is inseparable from the notion of Ethics*

Having demonstrated the dependency of the very notion of *ethics* to that of *freedom of the will*, we must now show how it is that freedom actually exists within human nature. So far, we have only seen that freedom must be presupposed if we understand ourselves as rational beings who are, in some large degree, responsible as causes of our own actions. ... It certainly seems that there is an inescapable circle here. If we must assume that we are free in order to understand how it is that we stand under the Moral Law and turn then to suppose ourselves standing under this Moral Law precisely because we have imputed freedom as a property of our will, then it seems a circle. But, freedom and self-authorship of the Moral Law are both necessary conditions for true autonomy as opposed to heteronomy. For this reason, it is not a circle but rather a set of bi-conditionally related ideas. For example, in mathematics, we might well discover two fractions to be equal despite the fact that they have different denominators. We know them to be equal because they express the same measurement.

There remains one escape. Let us ask whether or not we perceive ourselves differently or the same when we perceive ourselves acting freely and when we perceive ourselves as acting with a causal chain presented to the senses. We know that there is a difference between the way things *appear* to us and the nature of the *thing in itself* (*ding an sich*). As soon as we understand this distinction, then it clearly follows that there must be something, at the base of any phenomenon, that is not itself a phenomenon. This basic thing is the *thing in itself*. We cannot ever apprehend it directly; we can only know it by its affectations on us. This is a clear distinction between a person and the world that can be known through thought – the *intelligible world* and the *visible world*. Something may well appear to the senses in several ways, mutable and varied, while retaining a single foundation that is immutable and self-identical.

We tend to think of ourselves as part of the *visible* or *sensible world* when we are evaluating ourselves in virtue of our sense perceptions; however, when we evaluate ourselves in virtue of the spontaneousness that we express within the will, we think of ourselves as part of the *intelligible world*. However, of this latter world, we do not have knowledge. Thus, humanity understands itself as standing apart from the rest of the world, and perhaps even from itself (to the extent that we are influenced by the *sensible*): the separating feature is the power of reason. Thus, we see ourselves as two-fold and thus subject to two sets of Law. In the one sense, there is the heteronomous subjection of the agent to physics and the necessity of Natural Law; in the second, as part of the *intelligible*, wholly independent of physical influences, the sole determinant of which is reason. It is only possible for a rational agent to appear to itself as apart from physical causation through the idea of *freedom*; but *autonomy* is inextricably linked to that notion of freedom. This, then, is intimately connected to the notion of morality. And morality is at the base of all of the action of every rational being just as the Natural Law is at the foundation of all phenomena. Thus, regarding ourselves as contained within both the *sensible world* and the *intelligible world*, we avoid the circle that seemed to suggest that we built *autonomy* on *freedom* and *freedom* on *autonomy*. Understanding ourselves as free, we are part of the *intelligible* world where the Moral Law and *autonomy* operate; and when we understand ourselves as obligated, we are bound in both the sensible and the intelligible.

How is the Categorical Imperative possible?

Every rational being sees itself as being both a rational being, and thus part of the *intelligible world*, and as something subject to mechanistic causes within the physical world. The Categorical Imperative is seen as possible because the notion of *freedom* by which I understand myself as part of the *intelligible* or *Noumenal world*. The Noumenal World contains not only its own metaphysical grounding, but also that of the Phenomenal World. This is because even though I am a phenomenon and part of the sensible world, I cannot but conceive of myself as free, and thus a rational being, and as such, subject to the foundational Moral Law which makes possible the autonomy, rather than heteronomy, of the will. Because of this rationality, the Moral Law of the *intelligible world* obtain immediately and, in virtue of this, the Categorical Imperative. and the actions that express the maxims and duties contained therein. Thus, when we say *ought* and *should*, we express a necessity similar to physical necessity, in this case the necessity of the will and the Moral Law, as a part of the *intelligible world*. Thus, while existing in both worlds, the *sensible* (physical, Phenomenal) and the *intelligible* (rational, Noumenal), a rational being must recognize the authority of the intelligible.

Everyone regards both his will and himself as free. This derives not from observation. At the same time, it is necessary that we also conceive of every event as determined by Natural Law. But, this idea is not one from observation either, rather simply from the idea of necessity. So, reason is in a dialectic. Freedom is at odds with physical necessity, or so it appears. For reasons of speculation, the mind finds the path of physical necessity in the *sensible world* to be smooth while the path of freedom more narrow and difficult. Thus, even the most gifted philosopher is incapable of arguing himself from a notion of freedom. As a result, there is the foundational intuition that there is no contradiction between Natural Law and freedom; both are considered regulators of the actions of rational beings. Reason can not surrender either – cannot eliminate from the mind the notion of the Natural Law nor rid itself of the notion of freedom.

We can now answer the question of how the Categorical Imperative is possible. The only ground on which the imperative may be founded is *freedom*. To the extent that the necessity of this postulate can be comprehended, it is sufficient for practical reason, the core commitment of which is the authority and truth of the Moral Law.

~

A cursory reading of Immanuel Kant's *Groundwork* is sufficient to communicate the complexity and intricacy of the work. As we have walked through this dense work in a somewhat more careful way, the profound importance of it has begun to come to the fore. American philosophers C. S. Peirce and William James wrote extensively on the structure of the human mind, envisioning the mind as an incredibly complicated web of beliefs in which each idea is framed by the others within the mind, gaining meaning from contextualization within the particular mind of the particular individual. Abstracting any single idea or belief from that web of concepts to try to examine it as an independent notion is to fundamentally do violence to that idea and to entail an inevitable *mis*understanding of that notion. This is because the meaning of any belief or idea is partially a matter of the other ideas and beliefs it influences and the beliefs and ideas that influence it; those other ideas and beliefs to which it is connected. A truly subtle and perceptive philosophical system is in many ways the same sort of thing. It is generally impossible to abstract some particular philosophical notion completely from the context in which it is meaningful – its influences and its contributors. One notable difference from a standard web of beliefs that comprises a human mind is that a philosophical system will generally be somewhat more orderly, with many of the connections between ideas more or less explicit and considerably less subconscious than their counterparts in the prephilosophical mind. Kant's philosophical reflections constitute a system of considerable complexity and interconnection. However difficult it is to isolate notions for investigation, it is crucial that we do so; at the same time, it is equally crucial that we continue to relate those ideas back to the philosophical framework of which they are a part.

It might be helpful to briefly review the foregoing work. The foundational insight that the Moral Law and the Natural Law have the same ontological status allows Kant to craft a system that makes some of the thorniest issues in ethical theory somewhat clearer for the reader armed with the fortitude to read carefully and diligently. From this foundation, Kant then develops the important distinction between formulations of the notion of "should" or "ought." The Categorical (or moral) Imperative and its non-moral counterparts, the Hypothetical and Prudential Imperatives provide a critical model that can be applied to intentions and actions as a measuring stick to determine the praiseworthiness or blameworthiness of those intentions and actions. Turning to this section of the *Groundwork*, the rather artificial abstraction of ideas that has been our model so far collapses and a glimpse of the intricacies of Kant's work is gained. We will begin to pull together the several threads that have been developed into a couple of different forms, separate them again, and reform them.

While Kant says in the foregoing sections in which the Categorical Imperative is developed that it is impossible to argue for a set of ethical foundational principles by appeal to examples, it is with examples that this section begins. It needs to be clearly understood that Kant is not reneging on the earlier claim. The examples that Kant offers here are not offered as a method of arguing *for* the Categorical Imperative, but rather as examples, as illustrations of the breadth of the principle. These examples, illustrating Kant's ethical commitments, also serve to rule out a clearly non-Kantian interpretation of his work. Given that he argues that the Moral Law is self-authored within the will of the autonomous, rational agent, one might conclude that Kant is an advocate of some sort of relativism – each agent self-authors the Moral Law for him/herself. Given his fundamental intuition that the Moral Law and the Natural Law are ontologically equivalent, this interpretation is fatally flawed. While a physicist might well author the Einsteinian "$E=mc^2$" on his own, it in no way suggests that physics is an exercise in relativism. Ethical relativism is inherently self-interested; that is, the maxims constructed will be imagined by the agent to be beneficial to him/herself in some fashion. The Moral Law is independent of individual interest and unchanged by individual reflections on it. Thus, self-authorship of the Moral Law within the will of the agent is not an exercise in writing a set of ethical standards that are wholly individualized and non-universal. Here, Kant's examples bear this philosophical commitment out and thus serve as corrective illustrations of his view rather than as supporting argumentation for those principles themselves.

While Kant offers four examples, we will look at only two (and, as it happens, the two most famous). The first of these involves the question of suicide, the second of making false promises. We will also discuss, briefly, a critique of the second example.

Tom is miserable. He is convinced that only by committing suicide can he end the suffering that his life has become. Every day grinds into the next, unrelenting, and he is absolutely convinced that each will continue in this fashion. His inability to overcome this grinding misery fuels his conviction. Let us even suppose that he is correct. Kant asks whether or not, given this unbearable existence, if Tom might well be justified in coming to the conclusion that killing himself is his only avenue of release and acting upon that conclusion. In other words, can the maxim that "If life is perceived to be more filled with misery than happiness and thought likely to continue in that way, he is to end his life" be elevated to the status of universal Law and thus permitted, and perhaps, obligatory under the aegis of the Categorical Imperative?

While one might well analyze this dilemma from the perspective of the first and primary formulation of the Categorical Imperative, the second is more obviously applicable, at least initially. "One should act, toward the humanity present in oneself or in another, as an end in itself and never as a means solely." If we apply this formulation to the situation, it is immediately clear that Tom's conviction that suicide is an appropriate action to commit in his situation is flawed, and thus, not wholly rational, on Kant's view. If Tom were to kill himself, he would be treating the humanity within himself as a means; in this case, as a means toward ending the suffering that he is experiencing. However, it entails a contradiction for violence towards oneself to be, at the same time, beneficial for oneself. That is, it cannot be reasonably concluded that by killing himself that Tom is acting toward the humanity within him as if it were anything but some instrumental means to an end, rather than as an end in itself.

Rather than applying the second formulation of the Categorical Imperative, let us apply its primary form. Here, we ask whether or not Tom's maxim could be elevated to the level of universal Law. The first and only test that need be applied to Tom's maxim is whether or not that maxim can be universalized to all of humanity. Let us suppose that it can be universalized. It becomes clear almost immediately that there is an inherent contradiction in universalizing this maxim. To universalize the maxim is to say that all people, when perceiving that life bears more misery than joy and that the condition will likely persist, *ought* to end that life. In other words, with precisely the same level of necessity that obtains when contemplating gravitation's act upon a falling rock, one should end one's life in accordance with the maxim. Such a universalization would soon result in the destruction of humanity itself. Given this result, we can safely conclude that Tom's maxim is not fit for universal Law. Further, we can conclude that the objective Moral Law is not, then, altered by the subjective conditions facing Tom; thus, while his reflections on his dilemma will be highly individualized, the actions that are morally permissible in his situation are not relativistic.

Turning to the second example, Kant turns from reflecting on an individual contemplating an action in which the agent is the sole actor and the sole effect to an action that has consequences beyond the actor himself. Scott is in need of money. He knows that he does not have the wherewithal to repay anyone who would loan him money, but he also knows that if he says that he cannot repay when he asks for the loan that it is highly unlikely that he will actually receive the loan. So, he concludes that he must lie about his intentions, claim that he will repay the loan, and all the while, know within himself that he will not. Thus, the maxim under which he acts is something like, "Whenever I am impoverished and incapable of repayment, I shall promise to repay even though I know that I will not."

Here, again, we have a self-interested principle rather than a universal one. Indeed, the failure of Scott's maxim to be fit for universal Law is quickly discerned. Let us suppose that we universalized the maxim. In that case, we would say that whosoever was in need of money and without the ability to repay, ought to lie to one who would loan him money and by false pretense secure the loan. Rather quickly, whenever a person was approached about the loaning of money, she would lack the trust to enter into such a contractual relationship. Without trust, human interaction becomes untenable and once again, humanity is devastated. Thus, this principle of self-interest also fails to be an appropriate expression of the Moral Law.

Many scholars extend the false-promising example to cover all instances of lying, arriving at a maxim that is something like this, "One should never lie," or, "One should always tell the truth." It is not clear from the *Groundwork* that Kant would have held this strong a principle, but it might be a reasonable inference from the false-promising example. Here, Kant might well be subject to a critique that could be devastating to the project. Let us suppose that the maxim for examination is "One should always tell the truth." It seems clear that such a maxim survives the universalizability test. One can, without contradiction, imagine such a principle applying to all people.

However, let us consider a counterexample. Suppose Socrates has been falsely, and maliciously, convicted of a crime and sentenced to death. Rather than submit to the wrong-headed conviction, he flees the city, only to be pursued by a mob of pitchfork and torch-wielding vigilantes. Upon arriving at Plato's house, he asks for Plato to be hidden and Plato hides him in a closet in the back room of his house. Some time later, the mob arrives at Plato's house and asks whether or not he has seen Socrates. If he is operating under the anti-lie maxim suggested, he would find himself obligated to reveal the whereabouts of his hidden guest to the end that Socrates unjust sentence is carried out and an innocent man is put to death.

Given this rather odious conclusion, we might conclude that Kant's ethical view, however founded on the revolutionary notion of the ontological equivalence of the Moral and Natural Law is nevertheless fatally flawed. Indeed, if we consider this example, we might well conclude that rather than an obligation to tell the truth in every situation, there is actually a moral obligation to lie, at least under certain circumstances. Or, perhaps, to adopt a version of the anti-lie, pro-truth-telling principle of St. Thomas, roughly translated as "One should always tell the truth to those worthy of hearing it."

An objection to this latter maxim might be that it is much more complicated than the rather simple, "One should always tell the truth." However, this would not be a reason to suppose that Kant would not hold the more Thomistic view. Indeed, if it is the case that the Moral and the Natural Law are ontologically similar, then one might reasonably conclude that expressions of the Moral Law are likely to be at least as complex as expressions of the Natural Law. Thus, the Moral science is likely to require at least as much intense deliberative work as the most complicated branch of physics.

To shed further light on Kant's own views here, it is illustrative to examine why the false-promising maxim fails, not only from application of the first formulation of the Categorical Imperative, but also from the second. If one applies the second formulation, it becomes clear that Scott is not treating the humanity within his lender as an end in itself, but rather as merely a means to his own self-interest. Because his maxim fails to treat his lender's humanity as an end at all, it is clear that the principle of self-interest contained within that maxim fails to be fit for universal Moral Law.

The false-promising example is often interpreted as committing Kant to the view that something like the maxim contained in the colloquially named "Golden Rule" is an apt formulation of the Moral Law. While Kant is a deeply committed Christian, it does not follow from that or from the false-promising example that he is committed to such a view. Let us first recall that the Golden Rule expresses the maxim that "one should always treat another as one would prefer to be treated himself." While it would seem to be clearly universalizable and so to pass the first test, it ultimately fails to be fit for universal Moral Law, at least in this form. This becomes apparent through counterexample.

Let us consider a person, Ann, who envisions herself as completely independent of all other people, wanting no help from any other person. Let us suppose that there is a situation in which another person, Phil, needs help from someone and let us add that Ann is particularly qualified to render that help, and further that she is the only person available with those qualifications. When faced with this situation, Ann might consider the maxim expressed in the Golden Rule, decide that in a similar situation, she would not want aid, and therefore not render the aid that is need and that she is uniquely qualified to provide. This example demonstrates how the maxim expressed by the Golden Rule can, in fact, be an inherently self-interested maxim. Thus, for all that the Golden Rule might well work in most situations, given that it fails in even one, it fails to be universalizable.

From the examples and reflections on them, we can begin to sense the complexity of the moral system for which Kant argues. However complex it may be, however, there is one glaring and strikingly simple requirement that must be satisfied for the system to be palatable in any form. Kant's moral philosophy, and indeed, any system of ethics, or, more generally, any system that assigns praise and blame, depends for its very coherence on the notion that freedom obtains in the universe. Given the mechanistic understanding of cause and effect within physics, there seems to be little, if any, room for free actions of agents. The freedom/determinism dilemma was anticipated by the Medieval philosophers (e.g., Boethius) and it is one with which Kant must deal. Beyond this dilemma are several others. Indeed, there is an entire class of philosophical problems that can be expressed as contrary pairs of concepts. These dichotomous pairs are known as *antinomies*. Kant explores these dichotomies in considerably greater depth in his *Critique of Pure Reason*, but it is evident from his discussion of the freedom and determinism here that he has them in mind in the *Groundwork* as well.

An *antinomy* is a notion, concept, or proposition that is beyond the possibility of deductive proof. So, for example, the proposition that "there exists a necessary being" turns out to be of this sort. With regard to this particular proposition, Hume has already addressed it at some length in his *Dialogues Concerning Natural Religion*, in which he showed that the common proofs offered to his day for God's existence each failed to demonstrate that existence. Hume's *Dialogues* had great influence on Kant who wrote that Hume had awakened him from his dogmatic slumbers. Part of the genius of Kant's work is that he moves beyond Hume's own view to a stronger one. While Hume showed that all of the proofs to his day had failed, Kant demonstrates that not only had all proofs failed, but that they would always fail. In other words, that it is impossible to deductively demonstrate that God exists.

This is not a new idea. Boethius had held something similar, arguing that notions about God were the proper realm of faith and not of deductive argument. Indeed, Hume's own limited conclusion anticipates Kant's stronger one. Kant's argument is rather straightforward. Anything that might count as evidence for an inductive proof for the existence of God (a proof in the empirical vein of St. Thomas's, for example), will never be able to point, conclusively, beyond the physical world of which it is a part. So, an appeal to the beauty or order of nature can point no further than the realm within which it is, namely the physical world. Further, given that there are infinitely many possible explanations for the evidence, explanations that cannot be ruled out without question begging or circularity or dogmatic *ad hominem*, the deistic explanation is merely one possibility among several.

Any proof that approaches the proposition from the rationalistic side is likewise eliminated. At most, any rationalistic proof (of the sort St. Anselm or Descartes advance) is completely dependent upon unargued axioms and postulates. While deductively certain, within the scope of those axioms, the axioms can simply be rejected and no argument can establish them (else they are not axioms, but theorems). Thus, there is no deductively certain foundation from which to argue for the proposition. Thus, since it is impossible to demonstrate inductively or deductively that "there exists a necessary being," we can conclude that the proposition is an antinomy, something without proof.

It is important to note a logical consequence of any proposition being shown to be an antinomy. If any proposition is demonstrated to be beyond proof, then its contradiction must likewise be beyond proof. If it were not, then a logician could simply assume the contradictory principle, demonstrate it to be either true or false, and in virtue of syllogistic inference, demonstrate that the original proposition is either false or true. So, any proposition shown to be beyond deductive proof entails that its contradiction is also. Thus, since it is impossible to prove that "there exists a necessary being," it is also impossible to prove the contradiction, "there does not exist a necessary being."

Among the other dichotomies within the class of antinomies are *freedom/determinism* and *finitude of space and time/infinity*. Kant's Moral Argument suggests another – *immortality/mortality*. Often, interpreter's of Kant suppose each of the antinomious pairs to be discrete from the others. So, arguments will be made about freedom and determinism, independent of the existence of God or the infinity of space and time. However, Kant's Moral Argument, to which we will turn briefly, suggests a different interpretation. That is, Kant not only pairs the antinomies, but also understands them to be related beyond their contradictions. As Kant considers other antinomies, he pairs them in such a way that one can imagine two columns, each with one of the pair. So, we can interpret Kant as also holding a view that can be expressed in terms of the graphic below:

Set A	Set B
Freedom	*Determinism*
Infinity of Space/Time	*Finitude*
God exists	*God does not exist*
Humans are immortal	*Humans are mortal*

Before examining the relationship that Kant sees between each of these sets, it will be important that we examine the first antinomy – *freedom/determinism*.

There is some debate whether or not *freedom/determinism* is actually an antinomy at all. Some would argue that all of the available evidence points to the conclusion that the *determinism* thesis is true and that *freedom* is an illusion. Newtonian mechanics and the vision of a causally determined, regular physical universe does not seem to leave much room for the free operation of agent choice. If the universe is a collection of atoms (or smaller physical particles) that translate energy from one to another through collisions between them, then does not seem to be any place for the will of the free, rational agent to impose its choices on that unfeeling, insentient physical world. Thus, there are those who argue that the evidence presented from science conclusively demonstrates that the Determinism Thesis – "All effects have an identifiable and complete physical cause" – is true. In virtue of the truth of the Determinism Thesis, the notion that the human will is free is either completely false (Hard Determinism) or true, but in a very limited way (Compatibilism).

Kant rejects the initial statements of the argument. On his view, it is not the case that all evidence points toward the *determinism* conclusion. He grants that all of the *physical* evidence does, indeed, support that view; however, *physical* evidence is not the sum total of the evidence under consideration. Kant imports a Platonic distinction here. For Plato, there were two distinct realms – the *visible world* (or the sensible/perceptible world) and the world of the Forms (or the *intelligible world*). While Kant reintroduces the Platonic distinction, he does so without the Platonic ontological conclusions. Where Plato argued that the Forms or the *intelligible world* has ontological priority over the *visible world*, Kant's fundamental assumption (that the Moral Law and the Natural Law are ontologically equivalent) commits him to the view that there is no ontological priority of either over the other. If the *visible world* and the *intelligible world* are ontologically equivalent then, the evidence from each is also of the same status. Thus, if evidence from one were at odds with evidence from the other, to prejudge the conclusion in favor of one set of evidence over the other is to either beg the question or to reason in an *ad hoc* fashion. The evidence from the *visible world* does, on Kant's view, tend to support *determinism*. On the other hand, we cannot ignore the evidence from the *intelligible world*. If that evidence comported itself with the evidence of the *physical world*, then we would have the result that there is no antinomy at all because *determinism* would be supported and *freedom* banished. However, the evidence is not congruent.

Kant argues that we tend to imagine ourselves as part of the *visible world* when we considering ourselves as physical objects with particular senses. However, this in only one of the ways in which we envision ourselves. We also see ourselves as spontaneous and rational beings. Because human beings, and indeed, all rational beings if such rational beings apart from humans exist, sees themselves as rational beings. In virtue of this, all rational beings see themselves as part of the *intelligible world*. While the Natural Law obtains within the physical realm, the Moral Law obtains within the intelligible one. There are two avenues of argument that are now available to Kant. The first is the notion of the perception of ourselves as rational beings, the centerpiece of which lies deliberative choice, the necessary condition of which is freedom. The second is the understanding of the very structure of the Moral Law itself. Let us treat this in order.

On Kant's view, it is impossible for a rational being to consider him/herself wholly causally determined. While the *visible world* is heteronomous, external forces colliding and determining the actions of physical elements within it, it would be impossible to conceive of oneself *qua* rational being as wholly determined by heteronomous forces. That is, it is inconceivable that one could choose to act as though one were completely determined. Indeed, the very notion of choosing to act as if the universe was a wholly determined entity contains within it a rather straightforward contradiction. Thus, every rational being is bound to twin necessities – the necessity of the Natural Law in the *visible world* and the necessity of the Moral Law in the *intelligible*.

This brings us to the second line of argument, the structure of the Moral Law itself. Since the Moral Law and the Natural Law are ontologically equivalent and neither supersedes the other, then those things that are logically necessary for the Natural Law and/or the Moral Law to obtain must also be given. This brings us to one of the most famous apophthegm's attributed to Kant, "Ought implies can." Let us call this the Deontological Principle and render it formally in the following way:

Deontological Principle: If a person, p, ought to do y, then p can do y

---

.The importance of the "Ought implies can" principle is straightforward, although the exact meaning is subject to rather subtle interpretation [See Logic Blurb following this section]. To make the claim that someone ought to do some action, a, implies, at least, that it is possible for the person to actually do a. At the same time, if it is impossible for a person to do b then it is not the case that we can reasonably say that the person is obligated to do b. Thus, we have the following set of related syllogisms.

Direct Statement	Justification
1. If p ought to do y, then p can do y.	1. Deontological Principle
2. p ought to do y.	2. Categorical Imperative
3. Therefore, p can do y.	3. Modus Ponens

Indirect Statement	Justification
1. If p ought to do y, then p can do y.	1. Deontological Principle
2. p cannot to do y.	2. Observation
3. Therefore, p ought not do y.	3. Modus Tollens

In the Direct Case, we can say that the justification for (2) is the Categorical Imperative since the reason that we can say that a person is obligated to some action or other is that it issues from a self-authored will that is compatible with the Moral Law and expresses a maxim fit for universal Law. The connection, then, to the ontologically valid obligation, *ought*, and the natural or intellectual possibility of the action specified by that obligation is clear. In the Indirect

Section 14.4: Kant and the Categorical Imperative

Case, the justification for (2) may well simply be the fact that the person cannot do y. This may be because he is constrained in some way or that it is simply physically impossible for anyone to do y.

A more important implication is borne out here, though. In addition to saying that a person can do y and meaning that it is a physical possibility, we must also mean that the person *actually can do* it. That is, if the universe is completely causally determined, then it is reasonable to conclude that, given two apparent options, only one of them is a real option, the other is not. Since it is a matter of the deterministic universe which of the two options will in fact be taken, it is also a matter of that universe that the other will not. Thus, it is outside of the rational will of the agent whether he will take the first or second option. Thus, his freedom is abrogated.

As a result of this, we can conclude with Kant that the practice of assigning praise and blame is a matter of making claims about the moral character of actions selected by the rational agent. To assign praise or blame is only rational if the person could indeed choose between the praiseworthy and the blameworthy. Thus, to say that some actions are compatible with the Moral Law and others are not is to say that the Moral Law requires moral freedom – the freedom to choose between two morally valid options. But, a necessary condition for moral freedom is actual freedom. That is to say, if moral freedom exists, it entails that actual freedom does as well; moral freedom supervenes on actual freedom. However, the existence of actual freedom entails that the Determinism Thesis is false. Thus from the rational experience of the Moral Law we have the evidence from the *intelligible world*, which stands in contradiction to the generally accepted testimony of evidence from the *visible world*.

The conclusion of this argument is not, then, that the evidence from the *visible world* is to be discarded, any more than the continued experimental data from the sciences results in the discarding of the evidence from the *intelligible world*. Instead, the conclusion is that the two principles, *determinism* and *freedom*, are, in fact, opposite and each, alike, beyond deductive proof (or, even inductive proof). Thus, we have the first antinomy pair – *freedom/determinism*.

Given that neither can be demonstratively proven, the rational agent is then left to make a decision. One set of the antinomies must be granted as axiomatic for rational thought and conclusions to be reached. Just as Descartes argues as Euclid had argued before him that there must be a set of First Principles that are themselves without proof, so Kant suggests that there are actually two sets of such first principles. Or, more properly, that there are two sets of related principles, each of which can form the basis of a philosophical system, and only one of which can be appealed to as first principles at any given moment. Thus, the rational agent, surveying the antinomies, is left to wonder which set is the set that one ought to accept as the basic postulates or assumptions of thought.

Kant does not suggest that proof is possible, but that the rational agent must choose to live *as if* one set or the other is the case. Turning to Kant's Moral

Argument for God is helpful in understanding which set Kant argues is the set that must be adopted. Having argued that it is impossible to prove God's existence or God's non-existence, it is a misunderstanding of Kant to suggest that his Moral Argument is a deductive argument for God's existence. If it were, it would straightforwardly contradict all he has demonstrated so far. Instead, the proper interpretation of the Moral Argument is that it is an argument that demonstrates the interrelations between the separate sets of antinomies and that supports making the assumption of one set over the other.

The foundational interpretive assumption for our work with Kant is his view that the Moral Law and the Natural Law are ontologically equivalent. Let us call this the Framework Principle.

> *Framework Principle*: The Moral Law and the Natural Law are ontologically equivalent.

From this, let us assume that, in virtue of this principle, that *freedom* obtains. If the Moral Law and the Natural Law are truly ontologically equivalent, then there must be something within the Moral Law that functions analogously to the cause/effect relation within the Natural Law. From this, we can conclude that those things that have moral value should have effects similarly and those that are morally wrong will also bring repayment in kind. If, indeed, this sort of Moral Law of logical consequences comports with Natural and logical consequences, then we are faced with a difficulty. Suppose a person lived a truly villainous life, and yet one that was marked with great pleasures and benefits, never feeling the consequences of the evil actions born of ill intent and a villainous will prior to dying peacefully in his sleep at a ripe, old age. Similarly, suppose a person lived a truly good life and yet was seen as a villain, punished horribly, and beset with all manner of ill consequences in spite of good intent and generous and virtuous will. Essentially, this example is a form of Glaucon's Challenge – suppose one person, truly unjust, is thought to be just and receives all the rewards of the just while another, truly virtuous, is thought the opposite and suffers accordingly. How might we maintain that the Moral Law and the Natural Law are ontologically equivalent if the Moral notion of moral causes and effects does not obtain in an analogous way to the notion of natural causes and effects?

Simply put, if we have selected the related concepts, *freedom, infinity of time and space, God exists,* and *immortality*, then we can answer this challenge, albeit in a way rather different from Plato's response. Beginning with the Framework Principle and choosing the *freedom* thesis for our living *as if*, we can answer the challenge in this way. Since the Moral Law and the Natural Law are ontologically equivalent and since it follows from the assigning of praise and blame that we must assume that rational agents can act on freely chosen options, then if we are to follow this line of reasoning to conclude that those choices have consequences to be experienced by the chooser in an analogous way to the effects that are the consequences of physical causes in the *visible world*, then we must also assume, as one of our philosophical First Principles, that there is an infinite space/time continuum within which those consequences play out and that the lives of rational agents do not end with the physical cessation of the body. If the will of the rational agent is immortal and given an infinity of time, the necessary consequences of actions, moral or natural, can play themselves out. If time/space were finite, then there would be no way to preserve moral or physical necessity in causes and effects. This is so because if time were finite, however long it might be, there would be some final instant. Those events occurring in that final moment would be identical to other events that were causally efficacious, but those events occurring in the final moment would not be. Hence, they would be causes without their necessary effects. So, too, with moral causes. Thus, if we begin with the notion of the similarity between the Moral and the Natural Law, it entails that we live *as if* we are actually free, and, subsequently, as if we are morally free. Such moral freedom coupled with the moral analogue to physical cause and effect entails that we must also life *as if* space and time were infinite and *as if* rational beings are immortal. With these fundamental assumptions in place, it follows, then that one need also assume an author and preserver of such a universe. Thus, it is reasonable to begin with the additional assumption that God exists.

The intricate web of concepts that comprise Kant's philosophical system is breathtaking in its perception and complexity. Kant so deftly handles the interconnections between metaphysics, epistemology, and ethics that it is rather shocking that any ethicist could ever suppose that ethics could be a field divorced entirely from metaphysical and epistemological tendrils, or they from the influence of ethical commitments. Kant's penetrating analysis of human knowledge and the fundamental metaphysical assumptions about the structure of the universe form the starting point for his Copernican Revolution in ethical theory. That deontological view is so essentially sound that Kant's work becomes inescapable for all those philosophers who follow him. Whether his work is generally accepted, generally rejected, or amended in some fashion, it is the case that all philosophical speculations concerning ethics, metaphysics, and/or epistemology, from his day forward, have been required to wrestle with Kant's own work. Such is the influence of one of the premier philosophical voices in the history of ideas.

Guided Reading Questions
1. How is the Categorical Imperative possible?
2. What are the antinomies and how are they related?
3. Why is Freedom important for autonomy?

4. How does Kant argue that Freedom exists in human nature?
5. What is the distinction between the Phenomenal World and the Noumenal World?
6. How does Kant argue that the existence of God ought to be assumed?

Logic Blurb
Deontic Logic

To this point in our discussions of logic, we have examined syllogistic logic, formal and informal fallacies, and modal logic. Immanuel Kant connects these logical systems to a novel formalization of logical concepts, the logic of morality or *deontic logic*. While the modal systems introduce concepts of possibility and necessity to basic first order predicate logic (e.g., the logic of syllogisms), *deontic logic* introduces notions of *obligation, permission,* and *forbidden*.

Kant's most famous expression of a deontic concept is the notion that "ought implies can." This is to say, if one has an *obligation*, the fact of that obligation implies that it is actually possible for the person to fulfill it. If it is impossible, for whatever reason, for the person to fulfill the action, then the action cannot be an obligation. While Kant did not, himself, outline a formalized semantics for deontic logic, there is a logic of morality that undergirds his deontological moral theory. We can tease out the meanings of the deontic concepts fairly quickly and the resulting notions can be formulated as follows.

Something is *forbidden* just in case it is not permitted. Consider the act of false promising. False promising is not permitted, which is just to say that it is forbidden. An *obligation*, interestingly enough, is defined in terms of *forbidden*. We call something an obligation if it is forbidden to do its opposite. Thus, we ought to do those things that we are forbidden not to do. So, some action is *permitted* if it is not forbidden. An act is *obligatory* if the agent is not permitted not to do it. And, an act is *forbidden* if the agent is not permitted to do it.

As is clear, these concepts are all closely interrelated. Kant takes the foundational or primitive notion to be *obligation*. Obligation carries a sense of necessity and thus, as a representation of the Moral Law (which is ontologically equivalent to the Natural Law), it has priority over the other two. That the Moral Law is fundamental to Kant's moral logic is clear from his view of the concepts of good and evil. Without the Moral Law, good and evil are without definition. In the *Critique of Practical Reason*, he writes, " 'good' and 'evil' are defined in terms of the moral law and must have the moral law as the foundation; they are only defined after and in terms of the moral law." So, it is clear that Kant not only uses *obligation* as the primitive deontic notion, but connects it to the modal logic of the Natural Law – the concept of *necessity* is primitive to the concept *obligation*.

The deontic concepts of obligation, permission, and forbidden form the basis, then, for a logic of morality that is similar in structure to the formal logic that is the basis of metaphysical speculation and epistemological justifications. In virtue of these concepts, the nature of ethical demands and the Moral Law are representable in formal and symbolic ways. This provides the analytical tool for the ethics much like the ones employed by the metaphysician and the epistemologist.

Section 15: Mary Wollstonecraft, Forgotten Philosopher

Vindication of the Rights of Women

Introduction
After considering the historic page, and viewing the living world with anxious solicitude, the most melancholy emotions of sorrowful indignation have depressed my spirits, and I have sighed when obliged to confess, that either nature has made a great difference between man and man, or that the civilization, which has hitherto taken place in the world, has been very partial. I have turned over various books written on the subject of education, and patiently observed the conduct of parents and the management of schools; but what has been the result? a profound conviction, that the neglected education of my fellow creatures is the grand source of the misery I deplore; and that women in particular, are rendered weak and wretched by a variety of concurring causes, originating from one hasty conclusion. The conduct and manners of women, in fact, evidently prove, that their minds are not in a healthy state; for, like the flowers that are planted in too rich a soil, strength and usefulness are sacrificed to beauty; and the flaunting leaves, after having pleased a fastidious eye, fade, disregarded on the stalk, long before the season when they ought to have arrived at maturity. One cause of this barren blooming I attribute to a false system of education, gathered from the books written on this subject by men, who, considering females rather as women than human creatures, have been more anxious to make them alluring mistresses than rational wives; and the understanding of the sex has been so bubbled by this specious homage, that the civilized women of the present century, with a few exceptions, are only anxious to inspire love, when they ought to cherish a nobler ambition, and by their abilities and virtues exact respect.

My own sex, I hope, will excuse me, if I treat them like rational creatures, instead of flattering their *fascinating* graces, and viewing them as if they were in a state of perpetual childhood, unable to stand alone. I earnestly wish to point out in what true dignity and human happiness consists--I wish to persuade women to endeavour to acquire strength, both of mind and body, and to convince them, that the soft phrases, susceptibility of heart, delicacy of sentiment, and refinement of taste, are almost synonymous with epithets of weakness, and that those beings who are only the objects of pity and that kind of love, which has been termed its sister, will soon become objects of contempt.

The education of women has, of late, been more attended to than formerly; yet they are still reckoned a frivolous sex, and ridiculed or pitied by the writers who endeavour by satire or instruction to improve them. It is acknowledged that they spend many of the first years of their lives in acquiring a smattering of accomplishments: meanwhile, strength of body and mind are sacrificed to libertine notions of beauty, to the desire of establishing themselves, the only way women can rise in the world--by marriage. And this desire making mere animals of them, when they marry, they act as such children may be expected to act: they dress; they paint, and nickname God's creatures. Surely these weak beings are only fit for the seraglio! Can they govern a family, or take care of the poor babes whom they bring into the world?

Chapter 1 – The Rights and Involved Duties of Mankind Considered

The rights and duties of man thus simplified, it seems almost impertinent to attempt to illustrate truths that appear so incontrovertible: yet such deeply rooted prejudices have clouded reason, and such spurious qualities have assumed the name of virtues, that it is necessary to pursue the course of reason as it has been perplexed and involved in error, by various adventitious circumstances, comparing the simple axiom with casual deviations.

Men, in general, seem to employ their reason to justify prejudices, which they have imbibed, they cannot trace how, rather than to root them out. The mind must be strong that resolutely forms its own principles; for a kind of intellectual cowardice prevails which makes many men shrink from the task, or only do it by halves. Yet the imperfect conclusions thus drawn, are frequently very plausible, because they are built on partial experience, on just, though narrow, views.

Going back to first principles, vice skulks, with all its native deformity, from close investigation; but a set of shallow reasoners are always exclaiming that these arguments prove too much, and that a measure rotten at the core may be expedient. Thus expediency is continually contrasted with simple principles, till truth is lost in a mist of words, virtue in forms, and knowledge rendered a sounding nothing, by the specious prejudices that assume its name.

That the society is formed in the wisest manner, whose constitution is founded on the nature of man, strikes, in the abstract, every thinking being so forcibly, that it looks like presumption to endeavour to bring forward proofs; though proof must be brought, or the strong hold of prescription will never be forced by reason; yet to urge prescription as an argument to justify the depriving men (or women) of their natural rights, is one of the absurd sophisms which daily insult common sense.

The civilization of the bulk of the people of Europe, is very partial; nay, it may be made a question, whether they have acquired any virtues in exchange for innocence, equivalent to the misery produced by the vices that have been plastered over unsightly ignorance, and the freedom which has been bartered for splendid slavery. The desire of dazzling by riches, the most certain pre-eminence that man can obtain, the pleasure of commanding flattering sycophants, and many other complicated low calculations of doting self-love, have all contributed to overwhelm the mass of mankind, and make liberty a convenient handle for mock patriotism. For whilst rank and titles are held of the utmost importance, before which Genius "must hide its diminished head," it is, with a few exceptions, very unfortunate for a nation when a man of abilities, without rank or property, pushes himself forward to notice. Alas! what unheard of misery have thousands suffered to purchase a cardinal's hat for an intriguing obscure adventurer, who longed to be ranked with princes, or lord it over them by seizing the triple crown!

Such, indeed, has been the wretchedness that has flowed from hereditary honours, riches, and monarchy, that men of lively sensibility have almost uttered blasphemy in order to justify the dispensations of providence. Man has been held out as independent of his power who made him, or as a lawless planet darting from its orbit to steal the celestial fire of reason; and the vengeance of heaven, lurking in the subtle flame, sufficiently punished his temerity, by introducing evil into the world.

Chapter 9 – Of the Pernicious Effects which arise from the Unnatural Distinctions Established in Society

From the respect paid to property flow, as from a poisoned fountain, most of the evils and vices which render this world such a dreary scene to the contemplative mind. For it is in the most polished society that noisome reptiles and venomous serpents lurk under the rank herbage; and there is voluptuousness pampered by the still sultry air, which relaxes every good disposition before it ripens into virtue.

One class presses on another; for all are aiming to procure respect on account of their property: and property, once gained, will procure the respect due only to talents and virtue. Men neglect the duties incumbent on man, yet are treated like demi-gods; religion is also separated from morality by a ceremonial veil, yet men wonder that the world is almost, literally speaking, a den of sharpers or oppressors.

There is a homely proverb, which speaks a shrewd truth, that whoever the devil finds idle he will employ. And what but habitual idleness can hereditary wealth and titles produce? For man is so constituted that he can only attain a proper use of his faculties by exercising them, and will not exercise them unless necessity, of some kind, first set the wheels in motion. Virtue likewise can only be acquired by the discharge of relative duties; but the importance of these sacred duties will scarcely be felt by the being who is cajoled out of his humanity by the flattery of sycophants. There must be more equality established in society, or morality will never gain ground, and this virtuous equality will not rest firmly even when founded on a rock, if one half of mankind are chained to its bottom by fate, for they will be continually undermining it through ignorance or pride. It is vain to expect virtue from women till they are, in some degree, independent of men; nay, it is vain to expect that strength of natural affection, which would make them good wives and good mothers. Whilst they are absolutely dependent on their husbands, they will be cunning, mean, and selfish, and the men who can be gratified by the fawning fondness, of spaniel-like affection, have not much delicacy, for love is not to be bought, in any sense of the word, its silken wings are instantly shrivelled up when any thing beside a return in kind is sought. Yet whilst wealth enervates men; and women live, as it were, by their personal charms, how, can we expect them to discharge those ennobling duties which equally require exertion and self-denial. Hereditary property sophisticates the mind, and the unfortunate victims to it, if I may so express myself, swathed from their birth, seldom exert the locomotive faculty of body or mind; and, thus viewing every thing through one medium, and that a false one, they are unable to discern in what true merit and happiness consist. False, indeed, must be the light when the drapery of situation hides the man, and makes him stalk in masquerade, dragging from one scene of dissipation to another the nerveless limbs that hang with stupid listlessness, and rolling round the vacant eye which plainly tells us that there is no mind at home.

I mean, therefore, to infer, that the society is not properly organized which does not compel men and women to discharge their respective duties, by making it the only way to acquire that countenance from their fellow creatures, which every human being wishes some way to attain. The respect, consequently, which is paid to wealth and mere personal charms, is a true north-east blast, that blights the tender blossoms of affection and virtue. Nature has wisely attached affections to duties, to sweeten toil, and to give that vigour to the exertions of reason which only the heart can give. But, the affection which is put on merely because it is the appropriated insignia of a certain character, when its duties are not fulfilled is one of the empty compliments which vice and folly are obliged to pay to virtue and the real nature of things.

Let me return to the more specious slavery which chains the very soul of woman, keeping her for ever under the bondage of ignorance.

The preposterous distinctions of rank, which render civilization a curse, by dividing the world between voluptuous tyrants, and cunning envious dependents, corrupt, almost equally, every class of people, because respectability is not attached to the discharge of the relative duties of life, but to the station, and when the duties are not fulfilled, the affections cannot gain sufficient strength to fortify the virtue of which they are the natural reward. Still there are some loopholes out of which a man may creep, and dare to think and act for himself; but for a woman it is an herculean task, because she has difficulties peculiar to her sex to overcome, which require almost super-human powers.

A truly benevolent legislator always endeavours to make it the interest of each individual to be virtuous; and thus private virtue becoming the cement of public happiness, an orderly whole is consolidated by the tendency of all the parts towards a common centre. But, the private or public virtue of women is very problematical; for Rousseau, and a numerous list of male writers, insist that she should all her life, be subjected to a severe restraint, that of propriety. Why subject her to propriety—blind propriety, if she be capable of acting from a nobler spring, if she be an heir of immortality? Is sugar always to be produced by vital blood? Is one half of the human species, like the poor African slaves, to be subject to prejudices that brutalize them, when principles would be a surer guard only to sweeten the cup of man? Is not this indirectly to deny women reason? for a gift is a mockery, if it be unfit for use.

Women are in common with men, rendered weak and luxurious by the relaxing pleasures which wealth procures; but added to this, they are made slaves to their persons, and must render them alluring, that man may lend them his reason to guide their tottering steps aright. Or should they be ambitious, they must govern their tyrants by sinister tricks, for without rights there cannot be any incumbent duties. The laws respecting woman, which I mean to discuss in a future part, make an absurd unit of a man and his wife; and then, by the easy transition of only considering him as responsible, she is reduced to a mere cypher.

But what have women to do in society? I may be asked, but to loiter with easy grace; surely you would not condemn them all to suckle fools, and chronicle small beer! No. Women might certainly study the art of healing, and be physicians as well as nurses.

They might, also study politics, and settle their benevolence on the broadest basis; for the reading of history will scarcely be more useful than the perusal of romances, if read as mere biography; if the character of the times, the political improvements, arts, etc. be not observed. In short, if it be not considered as the history of man; and not of particular men, who filled a niche in the temple of fame, and dropped into the black rolling stream of time, that silently sweeps all before it, into the shapeless void called eternity. For shape can it be called, "that shape hath none?"

Business of various kinds, they might likewise pursue, if they were educated in a more orderly manner, which might save many from common and legal prostitution. Women would not then marry for a support, as men accept of places under government, and neglect the implied duties; nor would an attempt to earn their own subsistence, a most laudable one! sink them almost to the level of those poor abandoned creatures who live by prostitution. For are not milliners and mantuamakers reckoned the next class? The few employments open to women, so far from being liberal, are menial; and when a superior education enables them to take charge of the education of children as governesses, they are not treated like the tutors of sons, though even clerical tutors are not always treated in a manner calculated to render them respectable in the eyes of their pupils, to say nothing of the private comfort of the individual. But as women educated like gentlewomen, are never designed for the humiliating situation which necessity sometimes forces them to fill; these situations are considered in the light of a degradation; and they know little of the human heart, who need to be told, that nothing so painfully sharpens the sensibility as such a fall in life.

Mary Wollstonecraft's voice is one of the first voices of women philosophers generally added to the canon of the Modern Period in Western Philosophy. I have called her the Forgotten Modern Philosopher because her inclusion into the canon is only a very recent thing, an inclusion that is still somewhat controversial. Yet, many of those philosophers who come after her and are universally accepted within the canon of Western Philosophy bear considerable impression of her influence upon them. This is particularly true of John Stuart Mill, but the heroines of the Suffrage Movement owe much of their very persuasive arguments to this much lesser known 18th century philosopher.

The absence of women's voices in the canon has come to be understood to be by no means on account of a lack of depth, sophistication, and/or creativity. Rather, contemporary scholars have come more and more to understand the significant loss to philosophical inquiry that resulted from the arbitrary exclusion of the voices of women philosophers. Wollstonecraft's until recent exclusion is a clear case of this arbitrariness and the attendant loss. Her most famous work, *A Vindication of the Rights of Women*, which followed her lesser known work, *A Vindication of the Rights of Men*, by two years, is a powerful criticism of the social, political, economic, and educational oppression of women and a compelling argument for the full inclusion of women in the public arena. It should be noted that *Vindication* precedes Mill's *Subjection of Women* by four decades and the granting of the franchise to women in the United States by 120 years.

Wollstonecraft was a direct victim of the suppression of women's voices. Despite the demonstration of a tremendous intellect from a very early age, she was excluded from "proper" English education and society. Without much formal education, she worked mainly as a writer and an editor, which is itself a testament to the breadth of her self-taught learning. Even with such impressive contributions to the arena of philosophical discourse, she has been, until recently, best know for the work of her daughter, Marry Wollstonecraft Shelley, author of *Frankenstein*.

Wollstonecraft's lack of educational opportunities during her formative years was never far from her mind or her writings. She argues, in *Vindication*, that the subjection of women and the relegation of women to second class status, or worse, tied exclusively to hearth and home, is the direct result of women's having been systematically denied the opportunity of education. As a proto-feminist, Wollstonecraft is sometimes marginalized by the very feminist movement that owes much to her. This is probably due to the fact that she concedes that the women of her era are, in fact, inferior to men in the area of intellect. This marginalization is unfortunate because it reflects a very naïve reading of her work. She is not suggesting that the fact of intellectual inferiority is in any way a natural or essential feature of women. Instead, it is an accidental property of English society, a property caused by male oppression through the denial of education to women. Having been excluded from the opportunity of education, it is small wonder that a person so denied might, as a result, be uneducated. While this denial of educational opportunity will not entail a lack of education, it will tend, in a large population organized under such a system, to produce precisely that result as a common feature of the group thusly denied. Simply put, being a woman did not render one inferior; being systematically denied the opportunity to develop one's intellectual capacity tends to render one less intellectually capable. Since the education actually widely available to women was solely focused on passive aspects of beauty and servility, one should not express surprise that this is the general result. An alteration in the system would result in women having not only educational opportunity, but also in the rightful assumption by women of equal political and social rights.

Before turning to her analysis of the systematic suppression of women, societal and personal, let us fastfoward a few decades to the much better known work of one of the recognized philosophical giants of the 19th century, John Stuart Mill. There are five central arguments within Mill's *Subjection of Women* leveled against those who would argue that women are naturally, socially, physically, emotionally, and rationally inferior to men. His thesis, advanced at the very outset of the book and thus inescapable for anyone who would even begin to peruse it, is quite simple and direct:

> The object of this Essay is to explain as clearly as I am able the grounds of an opinion which I have held from the very earliest period when I had formed any opinions at all on social or political matters, and which, instead of being weakened or modified, has been constantly growing stronger by the progress reflection and the experience of life. That the principle which regulates the existing social relations between the two sexes---the legal subordination of one sex to the other---is wrong itself, and now one of the chief hindrances to human improvement; and that it ought to be replaced by a principle of perfect equality, admitting no power or privilege on the one side, nor disability on the other.

In other words, the subjection of women is morally, politically, socially, naturally, rationally, and experientially wrong and the consequence of this evil is the weakening, and perhaps ultimate destruction, of the entirety of civilization.

While such a description sounds quite cataclysmic, it turns out that Mill's arguments are successful, despite their being offered nearly two centuries ago. In short, he wins. At least, on the theoretical plane, that is. However, before complete credit is offered to Mill, it is necessary to take a step back and reevaluate the genesis of critical aspects of his views. Indeed, many of his arguments have their beginnings in the work of his predecessor, Mary Wollstonecraft. Let us turn to her arguments which prefigure so many of his arguments.

Vindication opens with an elegant statement of one of the abiding philosophical questions concerning education and character development. Is character a matter of nature or nurture? That is, are we simply born a certain way and given those birth characteristics thus incapable of being shaped by the application of education; or are human beings blank slates upon which education and experience write? Most sophisticated philosophical treatments of this question come down somewhere in the middle, noting, as Aristotle did, that there are certain natural predispositions within any person and these predispositions are then either activated or thwarted by the environment within which one lives.

One philosophically interesting question here is the mixture of nature and nurture that each theoretical framework presupposes. There is, it seems, a gradation presumed by work in this area. If one holds that nature is dominant and is dominant to a significant degree in determining the character of a person, then one would tend to suppose that nurture plays a smaller, complementary role, tweaking certain features of character rather than forming them. On the other hand, if one holds that nurture is the dominant feature in character formation, then one would likely hold something more akin to the blank slate view of human nature. Thus, as greater emphasis is supposed on the one hand, lesser will be entailed on the other. This inverse proportion relationship is characteristic of most careful reflection on this question.

Interestingly enough, the societal presuppositions of Wollstonecraft's day imply an interesting position on the nature/nurture question. Rather than supposing that this inverse proportion relationship obtains, it tends to imagine a maximization of both. At least with regard to women, it is presumed that their nature is so fixed and dominant in determining the character of women that they are suited only for domestic pursuits and for *women's virtue*; characteristics like beauty, for example. Further, it is supposed that they are primarily suited for a single role (although it is a role that has multiple requirements): wife/mother. Thus, nature so fixes women's character that no amount of nurturing can elevate her above childlike fealty to her father and then husband.

Given this view, one would expect the philosophical underpinnings of the societal oppression of women to suppose that nurture/environment is superfluous, at best. Given that nature so firmly establishes the character of women, there would be little reason to have societal strictures (nurture/environment) that served to shape that character. Or so it would seem. Yet, again and again the legal system sets forth and establishes guidelines to proper behavior, to proper ambition, to proper place. Thus, there is the view that there needs to be a comprehensive educational structure in place that ensures that women will learn both their place and contentment with it. This view would seem to entail that women's nature is moldable and mutable rather than rigidly fixed. Thus, the two views are in direct opposition to each other, both reinforcing the societal prejudice that women are "weak beings" and properly subject always to their male overlords.

On this view, both nature *and* nurture are both maximally determinant of women's nature. That such a view is straightforwardly specious is reasonably clear. Given the inverse proportion relationship between nature and nurture, the societal view of women's inferiority is incoherent on its face since it presumes that nature and nurture are not inversely proportional. Will Mill will later point out this inconsistency, Wollstonecraft both points it out decades earlier and with greater clarity and shaper cut. "Men," she writes, "employ their reason to justify prejudices." She takes the incoherence of the social philosophy to be not one of ignorance or neglect, but rather of intentional injustice. Indeed, she thinks that men do, in fact, recognize the incoherence of the social practices and "philosophical" arguments that parallel them, but because of "intellectual cowardice," do nothing about it or act only in half measures. Justice is sacrificed to "expediency" and to a position of partiality, privilege, and power that they do not wish to surrender. "Vice," she writes, "skulks," and a "set of shallow reasoners are always exclaiming that these arguments prove too much."

Wollstonecraft's analysis of the social, political, and economic systems and the inherent disadvantages that women found in them during her era has more and more widely recognized as one of the clearest and most cogent of philosophers of the late 18th century. The substance of her view is incontrovertible. The systems within Europe, monarchy, democracy, authoritarian, etc., were all, in her words, "partial." That is to say, they gave great advantages to men over women, in general, and to a small subset of men, in particular. The insidious oppression of the working class and of women, the misery produced there, is obscured from the general public view by a variety of veils. For example, the allure of riches with all of the trappings of wealth – these tend to mask the manner by which the wealth was accumulated. The general public chooses to ignore issues like slavery, which is hidden, generally, from common sight, because of the glitter of the benefits society gains. On Wollstonecraft's view, the allure of wealth and the enjoyment of benefits often is sufficient to inure the beneficiary to the suffering that may well have given rise to those enjoyed products, services, and social status.

Slavery is one of the examples that Mill employs later, declaiming the slavery practiced in the United States at the time and making an analogy from the justifications offered in the United States for slavery to the justifications offered both in Britain and the U.S. for the subjection of women. Here, again, Wollstonecraft's argument prefigure Mill's. While Mill argues that slavery and the subjection of women injure the character of the oppressor, Wollstonecraft focuses more on the damage to the character of the oppressed, particularly the oppressed who either refuse to acknowledge their oppression or   She argues that women often accede to their oppression, either from fear or from a misguided sense of security found in that capitulation. Given that their entire livelihood depends on the whim of the men in their lives, Wollstonecraft finds that women will often turn on one another, becoming mean and spiteful and intensely competitive. For the scraps tossed from the table, they will at once be fawning with "spaniel-like affection" towards their patron and victimize those under their power with cunning and selfish regard for their own position. Such actions are antithetical to virtue, whether public or private. Indeed, Wollstonecraft argues that under such an oppressive system that so systematically impoverishes the character of the oppressed, it will ultimately be impossible for women to develop even the virtues required for best caring for others. Thus, the very system that legislates that women remain within the home and that sees them as fitted by nature only for marriage and motherhood also makes it impossible that they should be good wives or mothers as it shrivels the character of those oppressed.

Another overlooked contribution of Wollstonecraft is her influence on the philosophy of class and class struggle found in Marx and Engels. One of her sharpest critiques revolves again around the allure of wealth and the power of the trappings of wealth, even in moderate amounts, to cause those who possess it to obscure their own vision of the world and the inequities that support the status quo. She writes, "what unheard misery have thousands suffered to purchase a cardinal's hat." That the social, political, and economic systems significantly disadvantaged a majority of people is incontrovertible. That for the most part, this system maintained itself on the backs of slaves and terrifically underpaid working men and women is similar straightforwardly accepted by scholars of the period. The system of partiality was ingrained in the worldview of those with power. She writes further, "such has been the wretchedness that has flowed from hereditary honours, riches, and monarchy, that men of lively sensibility have almost uttered blasphemy in order to justify the dispensations of providence." In other words, even those educated men who should know better have seen the bounty they possess as somehow a marker of their own intrinsic worth, rather than the ill-gotten gain of a system of oppression. When questions have arisen, it has not been uncommon for those in power to even credit God and the providential grace of God for their high standing, and by extension, to note in the low standing of others the disfavor of the deity. Thus, when philosophical argument and legislation prove specious to justify the ongoing system of gross inequity, many turn to argue for it by suggesting that such a structure flows from the will of God.

Class inequity is near the center of Wollstonecraft's analysis of the power relationships and the abuse of power that are characteristic of the social, political, and economic systems of the day. Each class "presses on another" in its effort to acquire greater and greater wealth, thinking that in the acquisition of that wealth that other honors will follow. Here, not only is the class struggle analysis of Marx prefigured, but also a position is implied for an argument that was centuries later.

One of the central questions facing Marxist feminists is whether or not women, *per se*, constitute a class in the Marxist sense. While it is clear that the working class proletariat – the factory assembly-line workers or miners, for example, constitute a class because of their common social and economic settings as well as their singular identification with a particular economic role – it is less clear that women do. Those who would argue that women do not constitute a true class would point to the exceptional variety of roles played by women. They are wives, daughters, mothers, friends, lovers. Some play these roles within the bourgeois and others within the proletariat. It is unclear, then, on this account that women would constitute a class.

However, Marxist feminists would respond that women do, in fact, constitute a class. While the trappings of economic status differ – the bourgeois woman may have expensive clothes and live within an expansive manse while the proletarian woman lives in a tenement and dresses in poor quality, cheaply made clothes – this difference in appearance masks a more fundamental similarity. That is, women are defined by the roles that they play and those roles are inherently subordinate ones. Some women may become coopted to the bourgeois agenda, again through the crushing of the character. She writes, "Women are in common with men, rendered weak and luxurious by the relaxing pleasures which wealth procures; but added to this, they are made slaves to their persons, and must render them alluring, that man may lend them his reason to guide their tottering steps aright." An example might be a queen or wife of a captain of industry who, rather than seeking solidarity with her sisters in similarly precarious states, turns to cunning, meanness, and selfishness in order to preserve her perch.

Here, Wollstonecraft's influence and her status as, at the very least, a proto-feminist is exceptionally clear. Not only is it clear from her analysis that women constitute a class, but the pressures upon and exploitation of that class is almost paradigmatic of all class oppression. She argues that there exists a "specious slavery which claims the very soul of woman, keeping her forever under the bondage of ignorance."

This bondage of ignorance claim points toward the solution that Wollstonecraft sees as absolutely necessary less the "preposterous distinctions of rank" ultimately lead to the decay of the character of the society and the men and women who populate it. Since it is in the interest of society for each individual to attain virtue, with public virtue originating from the private sphere, then it is absolutely necessary that women be given educational opportunities to this point denied them. If women are similarly educated, exposed to the full breadth of human knowledge, as men regularly are, then Wollstonecraft argues that the resulting intelligence base of women would be greatly increased and that, as a result, society would be improved. By eliminating the inherent injustice perpetrated by an incoherent system of partiality, the characters of individual men and women would be inoculated to the disease of oppression and the allure of its ill-gotten gain. Far beyond simply the elimination of negative influence on society and the souls of men and women, full educational opportunities for women would lead them to the study of politics, philosophy, and economics. The system in which highly educated men and women worked together would be one in which greater benevolence obtained, the character of society would be made more just, and improvement would be seen in politics, the arts, education, the sciences, and, indeed, in every aspect of humanity's common life.

Wollstonecraft's most important work was lightly regarded during her life and was read rather sparingly from all accounts. However, despite its limited circulation, the profundity of the arguments within it, the sharpness and accuracy of the analysis, and the plea, nay, demand for equal education for women as a means for the advancement not only of women but of all of society had influence far beyond what one might imagine from some limited a distribution. Philosophers like Mill and Marx take up many of the threads of Wollstonecraft's thought, reworking parts and adding emphasis in others to sharply criticize the grinding economic and social structures of 19th century Europe, economic and social structures that were fundamentally unjust and which crushed body and spirit. It is hard to overstate the influence Wollstonecraft had on later political movements, like the Suffragists in England and the United States, and although she is sometimes marginalized by contemporary feminists, it is largely because she is still less widely read than her work deserves. As one of the forgotten philosophers who happen to be women, it is long past time that her work was placed in the canon alongside others whose work she influenced.

Guided Reading Questions:

1. Why does Wollstonecraft argue that women have been seen as inferior to men? What is her suggested remedy?
2. How does later feminists address Wollstonecraft's work in their own work?
3. What is the role of education in women's liberation, on Wollstonecraft's view?

Logic Blurb
The Pro-Con Fallacy

The *Pro-Con Fallacy* is actually a form of an argument that has a proper and valid form as well. The valid form of the Pro-Con argument would go something like this. Suppose two friends are arguing and Little Red Riding Hood says to Rapunsel, "There are a multitude of reasons that we should go to grandma's house this weekend. There are also many reasons that we should not. Upon weighing the two sets of reasons, I conclude that the pros of going to grandma's house this weekend outweigh the cons." While Rapunsel might not be convinced, the argument is at least a clear and open one. Red and Rapunsel may well have different weightings for the different reasons for going and not going, but all of the reasons are on the table to be considered. The fallacious form of the Pro-Con argument is similar in that Red would offer reasons for going to grandma's house, but would not offer any of the counter reasons. She would simply say, "There are a multitude of reasons that we should go to grandma's house; therefore, we should go to grandma's house." It may well be the case that the reasons for not taking the trip far outweigh the reasons for taking it. However, since Red has not provided a space for the introduction of any counter reasons to her conclusion, she would argue that the conclusion must hold. Since only one side of the pro-con debate has been aired, any conclusion would be fallaciously premature.

Chapter 4 – Middle/Late Modern Philosophy

Section 16: The Fragmentation of Philosophy

With the death of Immanuel Kant in 1804, the Early Modern period comes to a close and the incredible diversity of the Middle Modern period begins. Some scholars see the 19th and early 20th century as the close of the Modern period, one that is superseded by the Post-Modern era. Rather than chase that particular rabbit, it is perhaps better to consider the period on its own, as a clear continuation, albeit one with great innovation, of the Early Modern period. Just as Descartes marks a clear turning point within the history of philosophy, so Kant marks that turning point within the Modern period. Philosophy became more and more fragmented and there was greater and great specialization with the halls of academia. Given this fragmentation/specialization, only two of most important thinkers of the period are given the title "philosopher" although each is clearly pursuing a philosophical project.

John Stuart Mill, Karl Marx, Charles Darwin, and Sigmund Freud all left indelible marks on Western thought. In every case, these four thinkers would have been labeled "philosopher" in an earlier age; Mill's works are fabulously comprehensive, ranging from economics to politics to history to ethics, Marx would be counted among the social/political theorists, Darwin would be numbered with the Natural Philosophers and Freud among those concerned with philosophy of mind and psychology, moral and otherwise. In short, each of these thinkers is within one or more of the traditional veins of philosophy. A cursory reading of the contributions of Plato and Aristotle would suffice as demonstration of this point.

The fact that the discipline of academic philosophy pays scant attention to Darwin and Freud, tepid attention to Marx, and focuses almost entirely within Mill's work on his political and ethical views is a telling indication of the fragmentation of philosophy into specialized disciplines, a fragmentation that began, in many ways, in the Medieval period and was so thoroughly culminated in the Modern that the disciplines psychology, history, physics, and biology are seen as almost entirely separate from the discipline. This fragmentation has the negative result of isolating investigations into the several distinct fields of study from all the others and, in virtue of that, from the broad context that is intrinsic to the meaning of those investigations. Thus, Athens and Jerusalem have much to do with one another; so, too, biology and history, physics and psychology, ethics and politics. Looking at Mill and Marx, in particular, in this chapter is a way of both beginning to contextualize many of the contributions to human understanding, because these two are illustrative of the synthesis of the fragments of human inquiry into a coherent, if controversial system of conceptualizing human knowledge, critically reflecting on human nature, and proposing insightful commentary on the human condition. In this way, both of these philosophers are descendents of the ancient philosophical tradition of Plato and Aristotle.

While this section of the text focuses on the two thinkers generally acknowledged within and without the philosophical community as "philosophers," the legacy of the others ought not be ignored. In every case, their legacy is controversial and wide-ranging; Mill's somewhat less than Marx, Freud and Darwin scandalous in vastly different ways. Freud is now generally considered almost exclusively within circles of psychological scholarship, although his analysis of the nature of human desires, motives, drives, and mental states is clearly both influenced by the work of Ancient philosophy and influential on fields of inquiry far beyond psychology. For example, few images so grip the popular imagination as Freud's tripartite description of the human mind – the *Id*, the *Ego*, and the *Superego*. While this is not the forum for a full-blown discussion of these concepts, it is interesting to note that Freud saw his own work as a continuation of the Platonic notion of the tripartite soul, with the Freudian categories overlaying their roughly analogous Platonic counterparts, the *appetite*, the *spirit*, and the *reason*. It is important to note that the general consensus of scholars of both psychoanalysis and Ancient philosophy that Freud misreads Plato rather badly and that the only reasonable analogy between the three systems is between the *Id* and the *appetite*.

This failure to read clearly the work of ancient philosophers is common within the 19th century. While there was a significant revival of classical scholarship in the century, it was also quite normal to read into those ancient texts a prefiguring of one's own view. Thus, Plato becomes a ancient Freudian, an ancient fascist, an ancient feminist, and an ancient anti-evolutionary. Given that it is clearly impossible for Plato (or Aristotle) to be all things to all people, it is important to read the 19th century interpretive work of the ancients with an understanding that the interpretations are likely to be quite skewed. At the same time, it is also instructive to recognize that the philosophers of this period understood quite well the perceptiveness of their ancient counterparts, appeals to authority and prooftexting notwithstanding.

Like Freud, the work of Darwin was met with skepticism, acceptance, and scorn, indicating both its originality and perceived threat to the commonly accepted world view. Like the Socratic sojourner in the Cave, his work was not always particularly welcomed. However, Darwin's careful categorization of animals discovered on his journey on the *H.M.S. Beagle* is eerily reminiscent of Aristotle's. Both thinkers traveled far beyond their normal geography and in so doing, found themselves privy to the unique perspective of encountering entire species of flora and fauna completely unknown to them previously. This perspective then allowed them to observe and carefully analyze their observations with fairly little bias. Following those observations to more and more generalized concepts, Darwin radically reshaped the way in which human beings understand themselves in relation to the rest of the world. For the natural philosophers among the Pre-Socratics and for Aristotle, human beings are natural objects, just as trees and birds and rocks are. However, while Aristotle (and his successors) saw great differences between humans and the rest of the natural order, Darwin's work demonstrated just how very small that distinction is; a conclusion that is born out again and again with further analysis and finer studies within the natural sciences. The notion that human beings are both natural objects and not fundamentally separate from other natural entities rather drastically recasts the philosophical inquiry into the nature of ethics, the nature of human understanding, and the very understanding of the world itself. Thus, the work of both Freud and Darwin has important consequences for those exploring the branches of philosophy – ethics, epistemology, and metaphysics.

Section 17.1: Reading John Stuart Mill

Reading John Stuart Mill is both reasonably easy and deceptively complex. His most famous work, *Utilitarianism*, had its first run in publication as a newspaper serial. Like the works of Sir Arthur Conan Doyle and Charles Dickens, among others, Mill's work was first published in newspapers/news magazines. As such, Mill wrote carefully for that particular audience, with easy cadence and considerable readability. It is often supposed that Mill sacrifices philosophical sophistication for readability. Hopefully, it will become clear that this is not so. Mill is an exceptional intellect, gifted as well in his ability to contribute to the philosophical conversation by including a broad range of people in the conversation. Ease of read is perhaps the least of Mill's contributions. Clarifying the doctrine of utilitarianism is a considerable effort. However, perhaps Mill's most important work, although not his most famous, takes up the odious practice of rendering women as second class citizens, or worse. His devastating critique of patriarchy in *The Subjection of Women* is one of the fundamental and pivotal works in the progress of women toward equality – in right to vote, in social relations, in business, and ------. We begin first with an examination of his *Utilitarianism* and then, *Subjection*. The clarity of his rendition of Utilitarianism is critical to placing it in the context of theoretical ethics from Plato forward.

Contrary to Aristotle, Jeremy Bentham and John Stuart Mill see pleasure and happiness as one and the same. Perhaps a bit of amendment is needed here. Happiness is not strictly the same thing as pleasure, even for Bentham and Mill. The opposite of pleasure is pain. For someone in great pain, the alleviation of that pain, even if it were not accompanied by pleasures, would be much more pleasant than the suffering. Hence, happiness is understood by the utilitarians to be pleasure and/or the absence of pain.

So, if the good is happiness and happiness is pleasure and/or the absence of pain, then a person, if she wishes to do what is right, will seek to maximize the one (pleasure) and minimize the other (pain), at least for herself. How does she know what things are pleasant and which are painful? These are personal experiences of things in the world. For example, suppose Jill finds that eating a hamburger is a pleasurable experience. Further, suppose that she is also fond of french fries. If Daniel asks her which she likes more, he is really asking which she finds more pleasurable. It is not strange to think that she could tell him, "I like the hamburger more than the fries." He could follow up the first question with another, "How much more?" While this is a more difficult question, it does not seem an unreasonable one. Presumably, Jill could quantify her pleasure, at least relative to the burger and fries – "I like the burger twice as much as the fries." Or, in the same situation, suppose the burger cost $5 and the fries, $2. She could say something like this, the burger was worth every penny, but the fries were not worth two dollars. In that case, we could be even more precise in determining how much more she liked one than the other.

In fact, it is in just such accounting as this that utilitarianism finds its deepest and widest appeal, although not always under the name "utilitarianism." More commonly, it is called "cost/benefit analysis." For a company, costs associated with the development, production, marketing, and sales of a product can be called pain (after all, it is money leaving the pocket of the company) and revenues or benefits gained from the sale of the product can be called pleasures (after all, it is money coming in). Faced with two scenarios, one in which the cost outweighed benefit and one in which benefit outweighed cost, the choice would be clear.

Making determinations of costs and benefits or pleasures and pains can be a bit complicated. However, it does at least seem possible and quite intuitively pleasing. The difficulties seem to be determining what things are pleasant, which are painful, and how much pleasure/pain is involved. Once those issues are resolved, decision-making becomes straightforward. For example, suppose we have the following three choices for action – action A, action B, and action C. Further, suppose each of the actions is determined to have the following pleasure/pain distribution (where "+" stands for pleasure and "-" stands for pain.

$$A = + + + + + + + - - -$$

$$B = + + + + + -$$

$$C = + + + - - - - - - - -$$

Based on these features, action B is the clear choice because the differential of pleasure to pain is +4. Even though action A would bring greater pleasure, the balance of pain is greater as well; so great, in fact, that the differential is but +3. So, action B wins and is the choice that should be made.

Now, to be sure, there are other factors to be considered. Proximity and certainty, for example. Is the pleasure pay-off sometime in the future and somewhat uncertain for action B and the pay-off and certainty both closer and greater for action A. These features can, and on the utilitarian picture should, be factored into the decision. In this case, the smaller differential of closer and somewhat more certain pleasure may be to be preferred. Fecundity is another. That is, is the choice likely to breed more opportunities for pleasure down the road. If so, a smaller pleasure now may be selected over a greater one based on the prospects of even more pleasure in the future. However, all these along with the utility calculus itself seem very commonsensical. One could easily imagine turning over the pros and cons of a choice in one's head before deciding whether to do one thing or another. It is precisely this commonsensical appeal that makes utilitarianism so attractive.

Bentham, however, received quite a lot of angry and pointed criticism. His view was derided as a "swinish doctrine," or a doctrine fit only for pigs. It is not immediately clear that the criticism is misplaced. Bentham's Utilitarianism differs from Mill's later work in that Bentham focuses solely on the quantity of pleasure and/or pain involved in any give situation (making allowances for the factors of proximity, certainty, and fecundity, of course). If B brings a greater quantity of pleasure relative to pain than A, then B is to be preferred. The *quality* of the pleasures and pains is irrelevant.

Imagine a pig. Suppose the farmer puts a perfectly prepared 6 oz. filet mignon in one trough and a huge bucket of slop in the other. It is fairly clear that the pig, if restricted to one choice or the other, will choose the slop. And, on Bentham's view, so it should. Hence the criticism of Betham's Utilitarianism as a "swinish doctrine."

Mill goes to great lengths to avoid this fate. Indeed, one of his more famous quotes is that "It would be better to be Socrates dissatisfied than a pig satisfied." For Mill, it seems just as much a matter of common-sense to include *quality* in one's calculations as it does to include *quantity*. For example, given two performances of the same piece of music, in the first case by a high school marching band and in the second by a world-renowned professional orchestra, it seems reasonable to suppose that one could experience on as more pleasant than the other. Only, in this case, when we say "more pleasant," we need not be speaking merely of the quantity of pleasure derived from the experience. Instead, we might mean (and likely *do* mean) to be making a comment about the *quality* of the experience. Thus, Mill thinks that a true utilitarian is going to take into account both the quality of the pleasure and pain as well as the quantity. As a result, Mill's utility calculus is much more complex than Bentham's. While Bentham has but two variables and two operations, to maximize pleasure and minimize pain, Mill has four variables and two operations, to maximize the quantity of pleasure, to minimize the quantity of pain, to maximize the quality of pleasure and to minimize the quality of pain. However, simply by adding complexity, it is not clear that Mill has abandoned the common-sense foundation that makes Utilitarianism so appealing. In fact, the added complexity may indeed mean that Mill's view conforms with common-sense even better than Bentham's.

As appealing and useful as the view seems from the outset, it remains to be seen whether or not it can be proven to be true. Mill sets out to do just that in serial form in *Fraser's Magazine* in 1861. These serials were later compiled into a book called *Utilitarianism*. In the fourth installment of the series, Mill turns to address what sort of proof might be available for the Principle of Utility.

Section 17.2: Mill and the Principle of Utility

Utilitarianism
Chapter 4: Of what sort of Proof the Principle of Utility is Susceptible
(emphases in italics are not original to the text)

It has already been remarked, that questions of ultimate ends do not admit of proof, in the ordinary acceptation of the term. To be incapable of proof by reasoning is common to all first principles; to the first premises of our knowledge, as well as to those of our conduct. But the former, being matters of fact, may be the subject of a direct appeal to the faculties which judge of fact – namely, our senses, and our internal consciousness. Can an appeal be made to the same faculties on questions of practical ends? Or by what other faculty is cognizance taken of them?

Questions about ends are, in other words, questions what things are desirable. *The utilitarian doctrine is, that happiness is desirable, and the only thing desirable, as an end; all other things being only desirable as means to that end.* What ought to be required of this doctrine – what conditions is it requisite that the doctrine should fulfil – to make good its claim to be believed?

The only proof capable of being given that an object is visible, is that people actually see it. The only proof that a sound is audible, is that people hear it: and so of the other sources of our experience. In like manner, I apprehend, the sole evidence it is possible to produce that anything is desirable, is that people do actually desire it. If the end which the utilitarian doctrine proposes to itself were not, in theory and in practice, acknowledged to be an end, nothing could ever convince any person that it was so. No reason can be given why the general happiness is desirable, except that each person, so far as he believes it to be attainable, desires his own happiness. This, however, being a fact, we have not only all the proof which the case admits of, but all which it is possible to require, that happiness is a good: that each person's happiness is a good to that person, and the general happiness, therefore, a good to the aggregate of all persons. Happiness has made out its title as one of the ends of conduct, and consequently one of the criteria of morality.

But it has not, by this alone, proved itself to be the sole criterion. To do that, it would seem, by the same rule, necessary to show, not only that people desire happiness, but that they never desire anything else. Now it is palpable that they do desire things which, in common language, are decidedly distinguished from happiness. They desire, for example, virtue, and the absence of vice, no less really than pleasure and the absence of pain. The desire of virtue is not as universal, but it is as authentic a fact, as the desire of happiness. And hence the opponents of the utilitarian standard deem that they have a right to infer that there are other ends of human action besides happiness, and that happiness is not the standard of approbation and disapprobation.

But does the utilitarian doctrine deny that people desire virtue, or maintain that virtue is not a thing to be desired? The very reverse. It maintains not only that virtue is to be desired, but that it is to be desired disinterestedly, for itself. Whatever may be the opinion of utilitarian moralists as to the original conditions by which virtue is made virtue; however they may believe (as they do) that actions and dispositions are only virtuous because they promote another end than virtue; yet this being granted, and it having been decided, from considerations of this description, what is virtuous, they not only place virtue at the very head of the things which are good as means to the ultimate end, but they also recognize as a psychological fact the possibility of its being, to the individual, a good in itself, without looking to any end beyond it; and hold, that the mind is not in a right state, not in a state conformable to Utility, not in the state most conducive to the general happiness, unless it does love virtue in this manner- as a thing desirable in itself, even although, in the individual instance, it should not produce those other desirable consequences which it tends to produce, and on account of which it is held to be virtue. This opinion is not, in the smallest degree, a departure from the Happiness principle. The ingredients of happiness are very various, and each of them is desirable in itself, and not merely when considered as swelling an aggregate. The principle of utility does not mean that any given pleasure, as music, for instance, or any given exemption from pain, as for example health, is to be looked upon as means to a collective something termed happiness, and to be desired on that account. They are desired and desirable in and for themselves; besides being means, they are a part of the end. Virtue, according to the utilitarian doctrine, is not naturally and originally part of the end, but it is capable of becoming so; and in those who love it disinterestedly it has become so, and is desired and cherished, not as a means to happiness, but as a part of their happiness.

To illustrate this farther, we may remember that virtue is not the only thing, originally a means, and which if it were not a means to anything else, would be and remain indifferent, but which by association with what it is a means to, comes to be desired for itself, and that too with the utmost intensity. What, for example, shall we say of the love of money? There is nothing originally more desirable about money than about any heap of glittering pebbles. Its worth is solely that of the things which it will buy; the desires for other things than itself, which it is a means of gratifying. Yet the love of money is not only one of the strongest moving forces of human life, but money is, in many cases, desired in and for itself; the desire to possess it is often stronger than the desire to use it, and goes on increasing when all the desires which point to ends beyond it, to be compassed by it, are falling off. It may, then, be said truly, that money is desired not for the sake of an end, but as part of the end. From being a means to happiness, it has come to be itself a principal ingredient of the individual's conception of happiness. The same may be said of the majority of the great objects of human life- power, for example, or fame; except that to each of these there is a certain amount of immediate pleasure annexed, which has at least the semblance of being naturally inherent in them; a thing which cannot be said of money. Still, however, the strongest natural attraction, both of power and of fame, is the immense aid they give to the attainment of our other wishes; and it is the strong association thus generated between them and all our objects of desire, which gives to the direct desire of them the intensity it often assumes, so as in some characters to surpass in strength all other desires. In these cases the means have become a part of the end, and a more important part of it than any of the things which they are means to. What was once desired as an instrument for the attainment of happiness, has come to be desired for its own sake. In being desired for its own sake it is, however, desired as part of happiness. The person is made, or thinks he would be made, happy by its mere possession; and is made unhappy by failure to obtain it. The desire of it is not a different thing from the desire of happiness, any more than the love of music, or the desire of health. They are included in happiness. They are some of the elements of which the desire of happiness is made up. Happiness is not an abstract idea, but a concrete whole; and these are some of its parts. And the utilitarian standard sanctions and approves their being so. Life would be a poor thing, very ill provided with sources of happiness, if there were not this provision of nature, by which things originally indifferent, but conducive to, or otherwise associated with, the satisfaction of our primitive desires, become in themselves sources of pleasure more valuable than the primitive pleasures, both in permanency, in the space of human existence that they are capable of covering, and even in intensity.

But if this doctrine be true, the principle of utility is proved. Whether it is so or not, must now be left to the consideration of the thoughtful reader.

~

John Stuart Mill was a great admirer of Plato. On Mill's view, no other philosopher of antiquity so influenced his own philosophic endeavors as Plato. However, Mill regards all of Plato's positive moral arguments as wholly unsuccessful. He writes, "all valid arguments in favour of virtue, presuppose that we already desire virtue, or desire some of its ends and objects. ... But no arguments which Plato urges have power to make those love or desire virtue, who do not already: nor is this ever to be effected through the intellect." (*The Collected Works of John Stuart Mill*) From this sentiment, it should be clear that Mill's objection is directed at any view that would advance any positive argument on behalf of virtue. Not that virtue is a bad thing, or a vice. This would be a fairly straightforward contradiction. Instead, Mill recognizes that it is good, and that it is a *means* to the end of Happiness. However, virtue is not itself Happiness; but one of a variety of ways to it.

Whatever his views on virtue, Mill is not only an admirer of Plato, but he also considers himself a Platonist (although only in a limited way). This may seem strange since we have included Mill among the Empiricist tradition of England while generally considering Plato more of a Rationalist than an Empiricist. Partly, this serves to indicate again that the distinction between the Rationalists and the Empiricists is not nearly so sharp as many would make it. At the same time, it should suggest that we should read Mill carefully to find out precisely *how* he sees himself a Platonist since, at the outset, such a claim seems odd. Mill considers himself a Platonist only in the sense that he adopts what he considers to be Plato's "Socratic method." Mill focuses on one central feature of Platonic philosophy, almost to the exclusion of all else, especially (for example) the Theory of Forms. On Mill's view, the Platonic *elenchus* is perhaps the most powerful tool available to critical philosophy. He writes,

> The Socratic method, of which the Platonic dialogues are the chief example, is unsurpassed as a discipline for correcting the errors, and clearing up the confusions incident in the *intellectus sibi permissus*, the understanding which has made up all its bundles of associations under the guidance of popular phraseology. The close, searching *elenchus* by which the man of vague generalities is constrained either to express his meaning to himself in definite terms, or to confess that he does not know what he is talking about; the perpetual testing of all general statements by particular instances; the siege in form which is laid to the meaning of large abstract terms, by fixing upon some still larger class-name which includes that andmore, and dividing down to the thing sought – marking out its limits and definition by a series of accurately drawn distinctions between it and each of the cognate objects which are successively parted off from it – all this, as an education for precise thinking, is inestimable. (*The Collected Works of John Stuart Mill*)

However great a tool Mill takes the Platonic *elenchus* to be, it also seems a two-edged sword. On Mill's view, the "close, searching *elenchus*" vanquishes generalities, tests all general statements by reference to particulars, and lays siege to "the meaning of large abstracted terms." Even in his claim of Platonism, Mill is a radical empiricist. It is the particulars encountered in the world that are the basis of reality, not general ideas abstracted from them. Mill is quite dismissive of Plato's own views when they seem at all at odds with Mill's own rigorous empiricism. Lest anyone fail to note the distinction, Mill writes,

> I have felt ever since that the title of Platonist belongs by far better right to those who have been nourished in, and have endeavored to practise Plato's mode of investigation, than to those who are distinguished only by the adoption of certain dogmatical conclusions, drawn mostly from the least intelligible of his works, and which the character of his mind and writings makes it uncertain whether he himself regarded as anything more than po-

etic fancies, or philosophic conjectures. (*The Collected Works of John Stuart Mill*)

Among these poetic fancies and philosophic conjectures, one finds Plato's Forms. Suffice it to say, Mill clearly sees a need to distance himself from those aspects of Platonic philosophy that might give aid and comfort to the ontological status of abstract ideas. In his discussion of Plato, Mill goes so far as to discount the value or use of abstract objects at all, relegating them to the role of spurious props of religious and philosophical dogma.

True to the empiricism of Hume (although the point is consistent with Descartes' conclusions in the *Meditations* and Descartes is by no means an empiricist), Mill begins by claiming that the "questions of ultimate ends do not admit of proof." This claim is taken to cover both the first principles of knowledge and the first principles of conduct. Since deductive proof is unavailable for all first principles and since the Principle of Utility is claimed to be a first principle, then the proof must be something other than an ironclad certainty. This is not particularly troubling since any proof of a first principle will lack the feature of certainty. Take, for example, the foundations of Plane Geometry. The geometer does not set out at the outset to prove that any two points in a plane define one and only one line. This is an axiom that is posited from the first. Or, in another way, this (along with the other definitions, e.g., point, plane, parallel line) is assumed and shown, by means of intuition, to be plausible. This *plausibility principle* is what Mill thinks is applicable here. To his way of thinking, he must only show that the Principle of Utility is plausible (and perhaps, more plausible than any other competing principle of ethics related to the highest good).

So, in Chapter Four of *Utilitarianism*, Mill sets out to show that the Utilitarian Doctrine (or the Principle of Utility) is true; by which he means, plausible. To do this, Mill cannot use the models of deductive logic, at least not straightforwardly. Instead, Mill must resort to a proof from analogy. Before turning to the famous analogies that are the engine of the proof, we need to be clear about the thesis. The thesis is of Mill's *Utilitarianism* is:

[Thesis] The utilitarian doctrine is that happiness is desirable, and the only thing desirable, as an end.

It must be noted at the outset that Mill has two things to demonstrate here, and not one. The thesis can be subdivided into Mill's two conclusions as follows:

[Thesis 1] Happiness is desirable as an end, and
[Thesis 2] Happiness is the only thing desirable as an end.

Mill argues for [Thesis 1] before turning to argue for [Thesis 2]. The proof depends on an analogy that goes like this: "The only proof capable of being given that an object is visible is that people actually see it. The only proof that a sound is audible is that people hear it; ... the sole evidence it is possible to produce that anything is desirable is that people do actually desire it." This analogy can be represented as follows:

> visible : seen
> : :
> audible : heard
> : :
> desirable : desired

To avoid confusion, we separate the two premises that Mill incorporates into this single passage. For Mill, there are two analogies, though both are of the same type.

> [Analogy 1]   visible : seen :: desirable : desired, and
> [Analogy 2]   audible : heard :: desirable : desired

It does not seem prudent to assume that Mill is doing anything other than adding a second analogy for emphasis. "Audible" and "visible" clearly seem to refer to the same sort of thing; that is, bodily sensual experience. Further, if this is the case, then Mill has given two analogies, either of which would suffice for his purposes.

From here, the argument moves to a second analogy. Mill concludes the proof by making the connection between the desires of an individual and the general happiness. "No reason can be given why the general happiness is desirable, except that each person, so far as he believes it to be attainable, desires his own happiness." Thus, we have the following analogy.

> individual's own happiness : individual
> : :
> general happiness : general population
>
> Analogy 2

The relationship specified in the analogy is the relation of *desire*. Since an individual desires his own happiness, it is reasonable to suppose that the general population would desire its own happiness in the same way. If this is so, then the "general happiness," which is the "greatest good," is connected to the "general population," or "the greatest number." And, thus we have as our conclusion, the Principle of Utility – *the greatest good for the greatest number.*

Mill's detractors tend not to be quite so careful in their explication of Mill's proof or in their search for the most plausible reading of it. One example is the criticism of Samuel Taylor Coleridge. Coleridge dismisses the proof almost at its outset by simply pointing to what he takes to be a blatant equivocation on "desirable". There is something to Coleridge's complaint, although he does not actually expand the point into a full argument. The gist of the critique is this: The analogy fails because while audibility simply means "heard or capable of being heard" and visibility simply means "seen or capable of being seen", "desirability" has two meanings. The first is similar to audibility and visibility; e.g., "desired or capable of being desired." However, there is a second, fairly common use of the word "desirable" – "worthy of being desired." An example might help. It may be the case that a college student simply despises her roommates musical tastes. However, whatever claim she may make about whether the music is worthy of being heard, it is quite clear that if the music is playing, worthiness plays no part in *whether or not* it is heard. On the other hand, one may desire a triple-cheeseburger all the while recognizing that it is an unworthy desire. While Coleridge may be on to something, he does not make all of this distinction that it may be possible to make.

Another 19th century philosopher, Henry Sidgwick, is much more careful, however. Sidgwick is both a supporter of the Utilitarian project and a detractor of Mill's. But it is because of the great care Sidgwick brings to philosophy, seen as one of the most significant reformers of pre-20th century utilitarian theory. In addressing Mill's argument, Sidgwick focuses on the issue noted by Coleridge; namely the intuition that desirability is fundamentally different from both audibility and visibility. As we have noted already, audibility and visibility are tied directly to human perceptual equipment – ears and eyes. In both cases, the common sense view is that it is good to hear and it is good to see. The word "good" here refers to the functioning of a natural feature of the world – the human perceptions. "Desirability" seems different, though. For example, suppose a man and woman meet and fall in love. Suppose further that the man grew up eating rice at every meal; with gumbo, with jambalaya, even with ketchup. Imagine that the woman was not from a part of the world that eats rice often, if at all. As the couple begins to explore one another's tastes in food, they immediately discover that they have very different tastes. These different tastes; e.g., different desires, are not the function of natural perceptive equipment, but rather of upbringing, of exposure, of community. Rather than *natural* goods, these are *non-natural* goods. So, if Sidgwick is right, Mill has made a mistake – he has mistaken a *non-natural* good (desire) for *natural* ones (hearing and seeing). As such, the analogy would fail.

Sidgwick is not as well known for this criticism as he could be. One of his students, G. E. Moore, is generally given credit for pointing out this informal fallacy. Moore calls the mistake Sidgwick says Mill has made the *Naturalistic Fallacy*. Or, simply put, mistaking one sort of goods for another. Moore develops the argument a bit further, and though he is often given credit for the entire critique, he, himself credits his mentor, Sidgwick.

This Naturalistic Fallacy has generally been considered the gravest of the critiques Mill's view has to face. It isn't. This is, in part, because Mill may not have committed the Naturalistic Fallacy after all. While it is true that to mistake one kind of good for another, to make a category mistake, would be fatal for the argument, it is not clear that such a mistake has actually been made. It certainly seems to be the case that particular desires that human beings have are very different. Given any room full of people, the attempt to select pizza toppings, for instance, that are amenable to them all will be a daunting, if not impossible task. Indeed, if each person listed all of their particular desires, it is relatively safe to say that no two lists would be identical. Thus, it would seem that this is just more support for the Sidgwick/Moore critique of Mill. However, one might come to Mill's defense this way. Given this same room and these same lists, it seems reasonable to suppose that while each and every person may have a unique list, that at the same time, each and every person will have *a* list. That is, the particular desires of particular people may be different, but even so, the fact that each person could make a list of desires suggests that desire itself is a natural part of being human. Thus, *desirability* may be seen as a natural good. If this is so, then all three analogues are natural things and the analogy is preserved, at least for the moment.

There is another critic of Mill whose argument does not turn on possible equivocations within the analogies. Lord Alfred North Whitehead, whom we will discuss more fully in the last chapter, weighs in on the Millian proof in a rather powerful way. There are two aspects of Mill's proof that trouble Whitehead. The first has to do with the ontological status of the notion of the "aggregate of all persons," or, the "greatest number." The second has to do with the heart of the Utilitarian project; namely the calculus that sums happinesses and pains. Let's begin with the second concern first. Simply put, how do dissimilar happinesses become additive into one sum of general happiness? Presumably it makes sense to speak of the happiness that an Olympic athlete experiences when she triumphs in her sport and it makes sense to speak of the happiness that a graduate student feels upon the completion of his degree. But, is there a "happiness" that is the sum of these two individual happinesses that then the aggregate (in this case two) of persons can experience? It looks like the athlete experiences a happiness that cannot be shared with the graduate student, even if the graduate student went on to have success as an Olympic athlete himself. Similarly, the graduate student has a happiness that cannot be shared with the athlete, even if she completes her own graduate degree. The experiences of happiness are highly individual, indeed, exclusively individual things. Thus, it looks very unlikely that happinesses can be added together into some new amount of happiness. However concerned Whitehead is about the adding together of individual happinesses, he is willing to let that concern slide for the moment and for the sake of argument.

This brings us to the first concern; what is the ontological status of the "greatest number." Or, in another way, is there such a thing. Suppose that a greatest happiness could be accumulated by adding together all the individual happinesses. Is there then anything that would be the possessor of that happiness? If we grant that individual happinesses can be added into what Mill calls "the general happiness", then there must be some actual thing whose happiness this "general happiness" is. Recall the case of the grad student and the Olympic athlete. If we have summed their happiness into some new thing – the greatest happiness – then who has the greatest happiness? Does the grad student have it? No, because he has his own happiness. Does the athlete have it? No, because she has her own happiness. Thus, we are left with the conclusion that even if we could sum the individual happinesses into some big new happiness, there is nothing in the world that would possess it. Thus, it would seem that Mill's argument for the principle of utility ultimately fails.

Guided Reading Questions

1. What is the sole proof that can be given that something is visible?
2. What is the sole proof that can be given that something is audible?
3. What is the sole proof that can be given that something is desirable?
4. Why is the "General Happiness" desirable?
5. Why are first principles not susceptible to direct proof?
6.. What is the Naturalistic Fallacy?
7. Why does Sidgwick (and Moore) think Mill has committed the Naturalistic Fallacy?
8. How might Mill respond to the criticism that he has committed the Naturalistic Fallacy?

Logic Blurb
The Category Mistake

The Category Mistake is a quite easy error to commit. It involves a confusion in kinds or types of things. For example, suppose Mary decides to use a 2-iron to iron her clothes. Since a golf club is not the sort of thing with which one irons clothes, she has committed a Category Mistake. She has taken one kind of thing and mistaken it for an entirely different kind of thing.

While such a mistake may well be rather comedic and uninteresting philosophically, commission of Category Mistakes within philosophical arguments is rather common. One of the most common examples of a Category Mistake occurs within the field of ethics.

We know that the world is an amazingly diverse place, filled with a wide variety of cultures and peoples. Within that diversity is a breathtaking array of cultural norms, belief systems, and traditions. Within one cultural context, it might be quite acceptable, and indeed, considered morally required for all marriages to be arranged by parties other than the prospective bride and groom (e.g., parents). The sweep of human history has seen arranged marriage, rather than "marriage for love," as the norm. The practice of arranged marriage is still the moral norm within many contemporary cultures. Many cultures likewise restrict women from voting, from owning property, and even from the most rudimentary education. Often these views are defended by appeal to cultural standards, traditional practices, or customary beliefs. On the other hand, many other cultures hold that marriages should be entered by willing and loving partners making a commitment to one another, that women should have the right to own property, and that they should, no less than men, have a stake in the political process and access to the best educational opportunities available. These cultural differences are all observable facts about the world in which we live.

From this incredible diversity, this cultural relativism, there are those who would argue that there is a similar moral claim. That is, from the fact that many cultures hold that it is right to do contrary things, it follows that moral norms are as relative as the cultural practices themselves. In other words, it is not only the case that things *are* done differently in Rome, but that "when in Rome, one *should* do as the Romans do." The Category Mistake here is mistaking a fact about culturally different practices as justification for a theory of moral relativity. While a theory of moral relativism might be defensible, the mere fact of different cultural practices is not the sort of thing that could be used to defend it. That is, mistaking cultural relativism, an *is* (or empirically observable fact of difference), for moral relativism or for its justification (a system of *ought*, that is not necessarily empirically observable), is an example of a Category Mistake. It is an error to suppose that cultural relativism is the sort of thing that could be used as justification for moral relativism. This is a particularly slippery example, and one often born of a laudable commitment to tolerance and personal and societal humility. However, praiseworthy motives are insufficient justification for the Category Mistake.

Section 17.3: Mill and *The Subjection of Women*

The Subjection of Women

Chapter 1

1. The object of this Essay is to explain ... (t)hat the principle which regulates the existing social relations between the two sexes---the legal subordination of one sex to the other---is wrong itself, and now one of the chief hindrances to human improvement; and that it ought to be replaced by a principle of perfect equality, admitting no power or privilege on the one side, nor disability on the other.

2. The difficulty is that which exists in all cases in which there is a mass of feeling to be contended against. So long as opinion is strongly rooted in the feelings, it gains rather than loses instability by having a preponderating weight of argument against it. For if it were accepted as a result of argument, the refutation of the argument might shake the solidity of the conviction; but when it rests solely on feeling, the worse it fares in argumentative contest, the more persuaded adherents are that their feeling must have some deeper ground, which the arguments do not reach; and while the feeling remains, it is always throwing up fresh entrenchments of argument to repair any breach made in the old. And there are so many causes tending to make the feelings connected with this subject the most intense and most deeply-rooted of those which gather round and protect old institutions and custom, that we need not wonder to find them as yet less undermined and loosened than any of the rest by the progress of the great modern spiritual and social transition; nor suppose that the barbarisms to which men cling longest must be less barbarisms than those which they earlier shake off.

5. ... In the first place, the opinion in favour of the present system, which entirely subordinates the weaker sex to the stronger, rests upon theory only; for there never has been trial made of any other: so that experience, in the sense in which it is vulgarly opposed to theory, cannot be pretended to have pronounced any verdict. And in the second place, the adoption of this system of inequality never was the result of deliberation, or forethought, or any social ideas, or any notion whatever of what conduced to the benefit of humanity or the good order of society. It arose simply from the fact that from the very earliest twilight of human society, every woman (owing to the value attached to her by men, combined with her inferiority in muscular strength) was found in a state of bondage

to some man. Laws and systems of polity always begin by recognizing the relations they find already existing between individuals. They convert what was a mere physical fact into a legal right, give it the sanction of society, and principally aim at the substitution of public and organized means of asserting and protecting these rights, instead of the irregular and lawless conflict of physical strength. Those who had already been compelled to obedience became in this manner legally bound to it. Slavery, from being a mere affair of force between the master and the slave, became regularized and a matter of compact among the masters, who, binding themselves to one another for common protection, guaranteed by their collective strength the private possessions of each, including his slaves. In early times, the great majority of the male sex were slaves, as well as the whole of the female. And many ages elapsed, some of them ages of high cultivation, before any thinker was bold enough to question the rightfulness, and the absolute social necessity, either of the one slavery or of the other. By degrees such thinkers did arise; and (the general progress of society assisting) the slavery of the male sex has, in all the countries of Christian Europe at least (though, in one of them, only within the last few years) been at length abolished, and that of the female sex has been gradually changed into a milder form of dependence. ... It has not lost the taint of its brutal origin. No presumption in its favour, therefore, can be drawn from the fact of its existence. The only such presumption which it could be supposed to have, must be grounded on its having lasted till now, when so many other things which came down from the same odious source have been done away with. And this, indeed, is what makes it strange to ordinary ears, to hear it asserted that the inequality of rights between men and women has no other source than the law of the strongest.

8. If people are mostly so little aware how completely, during the greater part of the duration of our species, the law of force was the avowed rule of general conduct, any other being only a special and exceptional consequence of peculiar ties---and from how very recent a date it is that the affairs of society in general have been even pretended to be regulated according to any moral law; as little do people remember or consider, how institutions and customs which never had any ground but the law of force, last on into ages and states of general opinion which never would have permitted their first establishment. Less than forty years ago, Englishmen might still by law hold human beings in bondage as saleable property: within the present century they might kidnap them and carry them off, and work them literally to death. This absolutely extreme case of the law of force, condemned by those who can tolerate almost every other form of arbitrary power, and which, of all others presents features the most revolting to the feelings of all who look at it from an impartial position, was the law of civilized and Christian England within the memory of persons now living: and in one half of Anglo-Saxon America three or four years ago, not only did slavery exist, but the slave-trade, and the breeding of slaves expressly for it, was a general practice between slave states. Yet not only was there a greater strength of sentiment

against it, but, in England at least, a less amount either of feeling or of interest in favour of it, than of any other of the customary abuses of force: for its motive was the love of gain, unmixed and undisguised; and those who profited by it were a very small numerical fraction of the country, while the natural feeling of all who were not personally interested in it, was unmitigated abhorrence. ... I am showing how vastly more permanent it could not but be, even if not justifiable, than these other dominations which have nevertheless lasted down to our own time. Whatever gratification of pride there is in the possession of power, and whatever personal interest in its exercise, is in this case not confined to a limited class, but common to the whole male sex. Instead of being, to most of its supporters) a thing desirable chiefly in the abstract, or, like the political ends usually contended for by factions, of little private importance to any but the leaders; it comes home to the person and hearth of every male head of a family, and of everyone who looks forward to being so. The clodhopper exercises, or is to exercise, his share of the power equally with the highest nobleman. And the case is that in which the desire of power is the strongest: for everyone who desires power, desires it most over those who are nearest to him, with whom his life is passed, with whom he has most concerns in common and in whom any independence of his authority is oftenest likely to interfere with his individual preferences. If, in the other cases specified, powers manifestly grounded only on force, and having so much less to support them, are so slowly and with so much difficulty got rid of, much more must it be so with this, even if it rests on no better foundation than those. We must consider, too, that the possessors of the power have facilities in this case, greater than in any other, to prevent any uprising against it. Every one of the subjects lives under the very eye, and almost, it may be said, in the hands, of one of the masters in closer intimacy with him than with any of her fellow-subjects; with no means of combining against him, no power of even locally over mastering him, and, on the other hand, with the strongest motives for seeking his favour and avoiding to give him offence. In struggles for political emancipation, everybody knows how often its champions are bought off by bribes, or daunted by terrors. In the case of women, each individual of the subject-class is in a chronic state of bribery and intimidation combined. In setting up the standard of resistance, a large number of the leaders, and still more of the followers, must make an almost complete sacrifice of the pleasures or the alleviations of their own individual lot. If ever any system of privilege and enforced subjection had its yoke tightly riveted on the necks of those who are kept down by it, this has.

10. But, it will be said, the rule of men over women differs from all these others in not being a rule a rule of force: it is accepted voluntarily; women make no complaint, and are consenting parties to it. In the first place, a great number of women do not accept it. Ever since there have been women able to make their sentiments known by their writings (the only mode of publicity which society permits to them), an increasing number of them have recorded protests against

their present social condition: and recently many thousands of them, headed by the most eminent women known to the public, have petitioned Parliament for their admission to the Parliamentary Suffrage The claim of women to be educated as solidly, and in the same branches of knowledge, as men, is urged with growing intensity, and with a great prospect of success; while the demand for their admission into professions and occupations hitherto closed against them, becomes every year more urgent. ... How many more women there are who silently cherish similar aspirations, no one can possibly know; but there are abundant tokens how many would cherish them, were they not so strenuously taught to repress them as contrary to the proprieties of their sex. It must be remembered, also, that no enslaved class ever asked for complete liberty at once. ... There is never any want of women who complain of ill-usage by their husbands. There would be infinitely more, if complaint were not the greatest of all provocatives to a repetition and increase of the ill-usage. It is this which frustrates all attempts to maintain the power but protect the woman against its abuses. In no other case (except that of a child) is the person who has been proved judicially to have suffered an injury, replaced under the physical power of the culprit who inflicted it. Accordingly wives, even in the most extreme and protracted cases of bodily ill-usage, hardly ever dare avail themselves of the laws made for their protection: and if, in a moment of irrepressible indignation, or by the interference of neighbours, they are induced to do so, their whole effort afterwards is to disclose as little as they can, and to beg off their tyrant from his merited chastisement.

11. All causes, social and natural, combine to make it unlikely that women should be collectively rebellious to the power of men. Men do not want solely the obedience of women, they want their sentiments. All men, except the most brutish, desire to have, in the woman most nearly connected with them, not a forced slave but a willing one, not a slave merely, but a favourite. They have therefore put everything in practice to enslave their minds. The masters of all other slaves rely, for maintaining obedience, on fear; either fear of themselves, or religious fears. The masters of women wanted more than simple obedience, and they turned the whole force of education to effect their purpose. All women are brought up from the very earliest years in the belief that their ideal of character is the very opposite to that of men; not self-will, and government by self-control, but submission, and yielding to the control of other. All the moralities tell them that it is the duty of women, and all the current sentimentalities that it is their nature, to live for others; to make complete abnegation of themselves, and to have no life but in their affections. And by their affections are meant the only ones they are allowed to have---those to the men with whom they are connected, or to the children who constitute an additional and indefeasible tie between them and a man. When we put together three things---first, the natural attraction between opposite sexes; secondly, the wife's entire dependence on the husband, every privilege or pleasure she has being either his gift, or depending

entirely on his will; and lastly, that the principal object of human pursuit, consideration, and all objects of social ambition, can in general be sought or obtained by her only through him, it would be a miracle if the object of being attractive to men had not become the polar star of feminine education and formation of character. And, this great means of influence over the minds of women having been acquired, an instinct of selfishness made men avail themselves of it to the utmost as a means of holding women in subjection, by representing to them meekness, submissiveness, and resignation of all individual will into the hands of a man, as an essential part of sexual attractiveness.

13. ... what is the peculiar character of the modern world---the difference which chiefly distinguishes modern institutions, modern social ideas, modern life itself, from those of times long past? It is, that human beings are no longer born to their place in life, and chained down by an inexorable bond to the place they are born to, but are free to employ their faculties, and such favourable chances as offer, to achieve the lot which may appear to them most desirable. Human society of old was constituted on a very different principle. All were born to a fixed social position, and were mostly kept in it by law, or interdicted from any means by which they could emerge from it. As some men are born white and others black, so some were born slaves and others freemen and citizens; some were born patricians, others plebeians; some were born feudal nobles, others commoners and *roturiers*. A slave or serf could never make himself free, nor, except by the will of his master, become so. ... [D]iametrically opposite doctrines now prevail. Law and government do not undertake to prescribe by whom any social or industrial operation shall or shall not be conducted, or what modes of conducting them shall be lawful. These things are left to the unfettered choice of individuals. ... Nobody thinks it necessary to make a law that only a strong-armed man shall be a blacksmith. Freedom and competition suffice to make blacksmiths strong-armed men, because the weak armed can earn more by engaging in occupations for which they are more fit. In consonance with this doctrine, it is felt to be an overstepping of the proper bounds of authority to fix beforehand, on some general presumption, that certain persons are not fit to do certain things. It is now thoroughly known and admitted that if some such presumptions exist, no such presumption is infallible. Even if it be well grounded in a majority of cases, there will be a minority of exceptional cases in which it does not hold: and in those it is both an injustice to the individuals, and a detriment to society, to place barriers in the way of their using their faculties for their own benefit and for that of others. In the cases, on the other hand, in which the unfitness is real, the ordinary motives of human conduct will on the whole suffice to prevent the incompetent person from making, or from persisting in, the attempt.

14. If this general principle of social and economical science is true, we ought to act as if we believed it, and not to ordain that to be born a girl instead of a boy, any more than to be born black instead of white, or a commoner instead

of a nobleman, shall decide the person's position through all life. ... In all things of any difficulty and importance, those who can do them well are fewer than the need, even with the most unrestricted latitude of choice: and any limitation of the field of selection deprives society of some chances of being served by the competent, without ever saving it from the incompetent.

16. The social subordination of women thus stands out an isolated fact in modern social institutions; a solitary breach of what has become their fundamental law; a single relic of an old world of thought and practice exploded in everything else, but retained in the one thing of most universal interest; as if a gigantic dolmen, or a vast temple of Jupiter Olympus, occupied the site of St. Paul's and received daily worship, while the surrounding Christian churches were only resorted to on fasts and festivals. ... It raises a prima facie presumption on the unfavourable side, far outweighing any which custom and usage could in such circumstances create on the favourable.

17. The least that can be demanded is, that the question should not be considered as prejudged by existing fact and existing opinion, but open to discussion on its merits, as a question of justice and expediency: ... experience does say, that every step in improvement has been so invariably accompanied by a step made in raising the social position of women, that historians and philosophers have been led to adopt their elevation or debasement as on the whole the surest test and most correct measure of the civilization of a people or an age. Through all the progressive period of human history, the condition of women has been approaching nearer to equality with men. This does not of itself prove that the assimilation must goon to complete equality; but it assuredly affords some presumption that such is the case.

18. Neither does it avail anything to say that the nature of the two sexes adapts them to their present functions and position, and renders these appropriate to them. ... What is now called the nature of women is an eminently artificial thing---the result of forced repression in some directions, unnatural stimulation in others. It may be asserted without scruple, that no other class of dependents have had their character so entirely distorted from its natural proportions by their relation with their masters; for, if conquered and slave races have been, in some respects, more forcibly repressed, whatever in them has not been crushed down by an iron heel has generally been let alone, and if left with any liberty of development, it has developed itself according to its own laws; but in the case of women, a hot-house and stove cultivation has always been carried on of some of the capabilities of their nature, for the benefit and pleasure of their masters.

24. One thing we may be certain of---that what is contrary to women's nature to do, they never will be made to do by simply giving their nature free play. The anxiety of mankind to interfere in behalf of nature, for fear lest nature should not succeed m effecting its purpose, is an altogether unnecessary solicitude. What women by nature cannot do, it is quite superfluous to forbid them from doing. What they can do, but not so well as the men who are their competi-

tors, competition suffices to exclude them from; since nobody asks for protective duties and bounties in favour of women; it is only asked that the present bounties and protective duties in favour of men should be recalled. If women have a greater natural inclination for some things than for others, there is no need of laws or social inculcation to make the majority of them do the former in preference to the latter. Whatever women's services are most wanted for, the free play of competition will hold out the strongest inducements to them to undertake. And, as the words imply, they are most wanted for the things for which they are most fit; by the apportionment of which to them, the collective faculties of the two sexes can be applied on the whole with the greatest sum of valuable result.

~

John Stuart Mill is far better known today for his work, *Utilitarianism*, and his efforts to advance a consequentialist theory of ethics than for his much more detailed and thorough work, The Subjection of Women. Some fifty years after Mary Wollstonecraft's, Vindication of the Rights of Women, Mill's work picks up the thread of that work and, in a devastatingly thorough way, simply annihilates the justifications for political and social systems that subjugate women. In Subjection, Mill walks step by step through historical justifications used to prop up an inequitable system of political and social rights and opportunities, arguments marshaled by his contemporaries, and potential criticisms of his own egalitarian outlook, demonstrating again and again and with powerful and direct arguments of his own that the system is fatally flawed. His opening salvo is encapsulated in the unmistakably clear language of his thesis statement:

> The principle which regulates the existing social relations between the two sexes – the legal subordination of one sex to the other – is wrong in itself, and now one of the chief hindrances to human improvement; and that it ought to be replaced by a principle of perfect equality, admitting no power or privilege on the one side, nor disability of the other.

Not only is the principle of subordinating women wrong; that principle is the primary hindrance to the advancement of the human race. This is a dramatic and forceful claim, especially given the era – 19th Century England – and the deeply ingrained prejudices inherent in the social, political, and religious systems of the day. The arguments justifying second class status, or worse, for women date back to Aristotle, at least. However, in England, some of the most forceful arguments used to justify this practice were found in the philosophical work of Thomas Hobbes and the collected "conventional wisdom" of the day. We will look at Mill's address to each of these in turn. However, before turning to the particular arguments Mill levels against the defenders of the status quo, it is perhaps best to look at his analysis of the underlying force behind the preservation of it.

Mill recognizes that the system of subordination of women to men is a system that props up and facilitates the use of personal and corporate power. He writes, "Whatever gratification of pride there is in the possession of power, and whatever personal interest in its exercise, is in this case not confined to a limited class, but common to the whole male sex." His claim is not that certain, individual males (e.g., the aristocracy, perhaps) derive power from the exercise of subjugating women, but rather that the entire class of males enjoys a privileged status, relative to women, whatever the particular socio-political status of the male. That this was the case in 19th Century England is rather beyond dispute. Part of Mill's genius, though, was the recognition of the sources of this power and the lengths that those in power would go to maintain it.

Mill justifies is rather extraordinary claim that men, as a class, enjoy privileged status over women and that this status is essentially a matter of power in the following ways. It is fairly obvious, to any who would make an empirical survey of the use and preservation of power, that power is, itself, greatly sought after. Power, as an end in itself, is greatly desired. Further, those who have acquired power will go to great lengths, perhaps, even, to any lengths to at the very least maintain the power that they have, and, more likely, to try to enhance that power, gaining more and more as it is possible. With this in mind, one need merely to examine the relationships within which men and women find themselves; again, an empirical survey. As a general rule, men have considerable power over the women, particularly those in close proximity to them – wives, daughters, daughters-in-law, etc. Unable to own property, to divorce their husbands, or to inherit property, generally speaking, women depended upon men for their very lives, in many, if not most, cases. Given this rather quick but thorough empirical survey, it is reasonable to come to the conclusion to which Mill came; namely, that men, as a class, have power and exercise that power over women through their constant and continued subjugation.

The case of the subjection of women, as a class, to men, as a class, has a quite unique feature that separates it from the historical practices of subjugation of one group of people by another. However, it has many standard hallmarks of exercise, and abuse, of power. Mill notes some common practices of those with power. In the first place, those with power tend to desire its exercise over those who are closest to them, either in proximity or in relation. The exercise of power, while it can be done at quite a remove from the subjects of that power, is most satisfying, on Mill's view, when it is used locally, where its results can be witnessed and enjoyed immediately. According to Mill, the reason for this is obvious. If those closest to a powerful person demonstrate independence, to any degree, really, then that independence will inevitably interfere with his own wishes and desires. Since the attractiveness of power is, at least in part, a matter of satisfying one's own desires, having independence run rampant around one is a straightforward threat to power.

A second hallmark of the subjection of women to other subjugations is that the subjugated population is dispersed in such a way that immediate control may be exercised. The more the servant is either under constant surveillance, or feels herself under constant surveillance, the less likely is a successful uprising or revolution that will challenge or overthrow the status quo power structure, either locally or more broadly. That such immediate control exists, in this case, within the household, is evident from the ceremonial reification of the master/servant relationship. The wedding ceremony sees the ritualization of the power relationship. A daughter, who has lived under the kingship of her father for her life, or her brothers in the case in which her father has died, has her ownership rights transferred to her husband at the altar. She is escorted to the altar by her senior male relative and, after the priest (again a male) asks, "Who gives this woman to be married to this man?", her escort responds with, "I do." This vestige of the ownership rights of males to females is viewed as a quaint and generally meaningless echo of the past, one that is given little more weight than meaningless sounds. However, in Mill's day, and to a lesser extent it is preserved, it captures something of the worldview of both the oppressed and the oppressor. The woman is the property of one man who is transferred to the ownership of another. This level of direct control exemplifies this second hallmark of the exercise of power.

Both of these are true of the subjection of women, but they are also true of the historical subjections of other peoples. For example, the power of the master over the slave was exercised locally. Although it was exercised through the establishment of legal systems that regulated the practice and gave the use of power the appearance of national warrant, the actual exercise of power was local. Secondly, the watchfulness of the master/slave relationship is present as well. To be sure, there is a level of family-feeling within the man/wife and man/daughter relationships that does not exist within enslavement, but that does not give the lie to the ownership and close surveillance feature.

However much like other historical subjugations the subjection of women is, it exhibits one very unique feature that perhaps makes it both more total and more difficult to identify and root out. Because of the wide dispersion and because of the absolute dependence on the master for livelihood and sustenance, because of the educational indoctrination pointed out by Wollstonecraft and appropriated by Mill, and because of the sense of both dependence and gratitude instilled within the subject, on Mill's view, it is impossible, or at the very least, very improbable, that the subjugated could group together into a single force with which to be reckoned. That fundamental inability to garner sufficient power, personal or numerical, to "overmaster" those in power, women are left in the position of being forced to curry within themselves, "the strongest motives for seeking his favor and avoiding to give him offence," and, thus, become partners in their own subjugation and in the subjugation of their daughters.

Having provided an assessment of the situation in which women are systemically subjugated by men, Mill turns to address the arguments of those who would justify this system. We will first examine his argument against the philosophical justification, exemplified by Thomas Hobbes before turning to the "arguments" commonly put forth within the halls of power. For Hobbes, the patriarchal structure of the society, from its political machinery to the religious hierarchy, was the necessary, natural and inevitable outgrowth of the State of Nature. In the Hobbesian State of Nature, the theoretical state in which all of humanity dwelt before entering into social contracts for protection, was a state of war in which each person was at war with every other person. Without rules and regulations, in a state of complete anarchy, the stronger would take what they wanted from the weaker, and would continue to do so, until stopped. Left to their own devices, men and women would run roughshod over their fellows to the extent possible. The rules governing civil society grew out of this primordial state of war. In order to protect themselves from their fellows and from a life that Hobbes described as "solitary, -----, nasty, brutish, and short," men banded together and came to agreements whereby they would cede some of their absolute freedom for the security of a social contract in which their rights were, by and large, protected. The patriarchal system of top-down rule by a monarch of his country and of the man as king of his household was the logical progression of a progression in which strength was favored as a direct projection of personal power.

Mill, as a good empiricist, rejects the Hobbesian view for a number of reasons. First, and perhaps foremost, Mill rejects this view because in the same way that it fails to justify the rule of an absolute monarch, so, too, it fails to justify the rule of an absolute rule by the father of the family. 19th century England had long since rejected the Hobbesian justification of the notion of an absolute monarch and the royal family was well on its way to figurehead status, wielding no real power over the lives of their "subjects." However, the same men who saw their new liberty and would not cede it back to an absolute king, at the same time rested their own claim to absolute household authority upon the same footing. Thus, defenders of the patriarchy found themselves in the untenable position of rejecting rule over themselves while exerting the same brand of rule they themselves rejected over others. Such a system of inherent contradiction was fatally flawed, on Mill's view.

Mill also rejects the Hobbesian view for reasons of philosophical method. Here, Mill's empiricist commitments become even clearer. The Hobbesian social contract, founded on a theoretical State of Nature and an even more theoretical rise of civil society from it, was analogous to the Platonic thought experiment in the *Republic* in which the ideal society is grown from the family upward. This rationalistic enterprise was precisely the sort of thought experiment that empiricists rejected out of hand as being far removed from the actual workings of a political society comprised of actual human beings, rather than theoretical constructs. Thus, since the Hobbesian enterprise was a deeply speculative one, it suffers the same fate of all speculations concerning the natures of humanity and civil society; as it demonstrates little or no connection to the actual world as experienced, it is insufficient to justify the practical execution of so deep and pervasive a concept as patriarchal rule of the nation or family.

Section 17.3: Mill and *The Subjection of Women*

Having dismissed the class of rationalist philosophical arguments used most often to prop up the patriarchy, Mill turns to the arguments that might be construed to be within a more empirical vein, namely the views commonly expressed that purported to rest on experience. Generally speaking, these arguments tended to fall into three sorts. The first of these was that the patriarchal subjection of women is permissible, and perhaps laudatory, because women prefer this sort of system. Another way of putting it is that women like it this way. Given their preference, women prefer the role of subject to the role of master and naturally gravitate toward it. To this, Mill makes a strong and ultimately successful refutation. Upon surveying women, he concludes that indeed, the notion that women like the patriarchal suppression of their gender is straightforwardly false. Indeed, his argument proceeds at three levels, each of which is sufficient to refute the claim that women prefer subjection.

In the first place, some women clearly do not. While he does not cite Mary Wollstonecraft, in particular, he is clearly familiar with her work. Further, one needs but a single counterexample to refute a universal claim, and Wollstonecraft (along with her daughter, Mary Wollstonecraft Shelley) can serve as Exhibit 1 and 1a here. However, suppose that it is true that a few women reject the patriarchy, but for the most part, women support it or prefer it. Here, Mill's second argument is pertinent.

Supposing that the majority of women prefer subjection to equality, there is at least one equally compelling explanation for such a preference. Here, Mill depends again on the work of Wollstonecraft. He takes her explanation for why women are, in fact, suppressed and uses it as follows. He notes that to the extent that some women "willingly" submit, there is another potential, and compelling explanation for it. "The masters of women wanted more than simple obedience, and they turned the whole force of education to effect their purpose. All women are brought up from the very earliest years in the belief that their ideal of character is the very opposite of that of men; not self-will, and government by self-control, but submission and yielding to the control of others." Here, Mill essentially expresses the core of Wollstonecraft's *Vindication of the Rights of Women* in which she clearly and convincingly analyzes and critiques the very different natures of the education of men and women, a difference that sees women indoctrinated into not only accepting an inferior role in society, but into believing that such an inferior role is to be preferred. Given that this explanation is equally as plausible, if not more so, than supposing *a priori* that women prefer subjugation, it is reasonable to conclude that the claim of women's preference is misplaced.

The third tack taken in the rejection of the claim that "women like it this way," is that even supposing that it is the case that women do in fact prefer subjection to equality as a matter of an empirical survey of women, it does not follow from this that such a preference, or a system enforcing it, *ought* to be the case. Recalling here the work of Immanuel Kant, particularly in the area of deontic logic, Mill notes that simply because something *is* the case does not entail that it *ought* to be the case. For example, Mill points out that the slavery was still being practiced in the United States at the time. However, as the practice had been abolished in England by then, and since the English had criticized the practice in the United States, it was clearly not the case that the simple existence of the practice in fact justified that practice. Since *is* does not entail *ought*, then simply pointing to the supposed preference of subjection on the part of women did not, at the same time, justify that practice. Thus, any argument used to defend the notion that women preferred subjection to equality failed from the outset.

Having refuted one of the most common "empirical" arguments for the subjection of women, Mill turns to another. It was commonly argued, and had been argued since Aristotle, at least, that women possess a different nature from men and that in virtue of this different nature have different virtues associated with it. These differing requirements, or "women's virtue," included particular roles, usually involving hearth and home. The domestic roles in life were reserved for those suited to them; namely, women. The roles outside the home, in government, in business, in education, and the like, were reserved for those with a nature suitable to those roles; namely, men.

To address the claim that men and women having differing natures and thus differing roles prescribed by nature, Mill assesses the actual practices that surround this claim. On the one hand, those in power claim that women, by nature, are unsuited to certain roles and activities; that they are, for example, too delicate to work outside the home and too emotional to have a place in politics. On the other hand, legislation needs to be enacted, and often was, to enforce these roles. The thought was, apparently, that without such protective legislation, women would seek roles outside the home, perhaps in business or politics. Here, Mill points out the height of hypocrisy and, more telling, logical contradiction. If it is the case that women's nature is such that certain roles are beyond it, then nature is sufficient to insure that such roles are not taken up. On the other hand, if legislation is necessary to restrain women from certain roles, then it is not in their natures to be denied such. For example, it is quite unnecessary to pass a law that requires an apple, when detached from its branch, to fall to the ground. It is within the nature of the universe that the apple shall fall. Further, no amount of legislation contrary to that nature is sufficient to restrain it. Thus, if women have a nature that restricts them to certain roles, the legislation that seeks to do the same thing is wholly meaningless and redundant. On the other hand, if it is not women's nature that restrains them, then justifying the legislation by appeal to that nature is disingenuous, at best, and more likely wholly and completely dishonest.

Another example is pertinent here. Mill cites the work of a blacksmith. Nature is perfectly capable of restricting the role of blacksmith to those who have sufficient strength to swing the hammer and work the iron. That only a few men prove strong enough for the task is not an indication that they have a nature different from women (and from most men). It is merely a reflection of the strength of arm and back. If a woman should seek to be a blacksmith and prove incapable because of lack of strength, then nature has no need of legislation to restrict her from the job. On the other hand, if she should take up the hammer and prove strong enough, then legislation that she should not clearly cannot be based upon her nature, but rather upon arbitrary rules designed by the patriarchal rulers to restrict her, contrary to her nature. Either it is women's nature to be subject to men or it is not. If it is, legislation is unnecessary. If legislation is necessary, then it is not women's nature. Or, as Mill puts it, "What women by nature cannot do, it is quite superfluous to forbid them from doing."

Turning now to the third of the three general arguments made to justify the subjection of women, we find it to be something that one might expect of a utilitarian. The argument goes something like this. It is necessary, both for the survival of the species and for the survival of human civilization, that women bear children. Since women, the argument goes, will not willingly choose to perform this role unless they are compelled to do so, it is imperative, for the survival of civilization, that women be compelled to bear children. Perhaps we should call this the "Preservation of Society" argument.

To address this argument, Mill uses an argument from analogy, using as analogues both the practice of impressments of sailors in the British Navy and the practice of slavery in the United States. In the latter case, the argument went something like this. Our way of life depends on the production of sugar and cotton. We clearly cannot produce these ourselves and we cannot produce them in the quantity required without slaves. The slave would not willingly choose to engage in this practice. Therefore, for the preservation of our way of life, the slave must be compelled to do it. However, Mill points out that, at least in England at the time, slavery had come to be seen as a despicable practice and one which, if abolished, would indeed not lead to the destruction of society (although, it might well lead to the downfall of a society that rested upon it – but, this is not something that people of goodwill would be sorry to be rid of).

Historically, impressments had been the method through which the British Navy had met the requirements for enlistment shortfalls within its ranks. The argument went something like this. The homeland requires defense and the Empire requires a strong navy for that defense. Men will not willingly choose the life of hardship and deprivation and severe discipline characteristic of the British fleet. Therefore, men must be pressed into service against their will. However, Mill points out that this practice had been ultimately rejected as one of great barbarity. Further, the British fleet, by altering its tactics and disincentives for service, had, indeed, maintained its supremacy at sea without the barbarous practice of pressment.

By analogy, there is no reason to suppose that the lifting the barbarous practice of subjugating women to a patriarchal oppression would lead to the devastation of society or of the species. In fact, many women (perhaps not all, but a number clearly sufficient for the preservation of the society) will choose to bear children, not because they are compelled to do so, but because it is a choice they freely make. Such a system is much to be preferred, on Mill's view, to one in which the bearing of children is seen as a burden to be laid upon women who themselves are treated as little better than chattel.

Having argued that the "justifications" for the principle regulating "the existing social relations" fail to support that system and that the system itself is fairly straightforwardly unjust on its face, Mill turns in the next chapters, particularly in Chapter Four, to explore what benefits might obtain for a society that divested itself of such injustice. However, before turning to those benefits in the subsequent section, it is important to note another quite perceptive moment of Mill's. There is a rather pernicious oddity found in human beings. Despite Millian arguments that annihilate the foundations upon which the subjugation of women is based, it was several decades and considerable social agitation later that women got so much as the right to vote. Arguments against extending the franchise to women included all of these arguments that Mill had so thoroughly discredited years previously. And the right to vote did not prove a panacea for the advancement of the socio-political equality of women, a happy state that has yet to be achieved. While the present situation for women, in most western nations at any rate, is markedly better than in Mill's day, only the most obtuse would claim that full equality has been achieved; and only the disingenuous or the villainous would suppose that the lot of women worldwide is remotely that of men.

Why, given the thoroughness and success of Mill's arguments, does such inequality persist? Mill, himself, recognized that such would be the case and that the cause of equality would not be recognized soon or with ease. He had barely set forth the thesis before he pointed out that mere argument would not sway hearts and minds quickly. He writes,

> The difficulty is that which exists in all cases in which there is a mass of feeling to be contended against. So long as opinion is strongly rooted in the feelings, it gains rather than loses instability by having a preponderating weight of argument against it. For if it were accepted as a result of argument, the refutation of the argument might shake the solidity of the conviction; but when it rests solely on feeling, the worse it fares in argumentative contest, the more persuaded adherents are that their feeling must have some deeper ground, which the arguments do not reach; and while the feeling remains, it is always throwing up fresh entrenchments of argument to repair any breach made in the old.

Given that the prejudice against women's equality, and indeed, against women, was so pervasive and was so deeply rooted as well, successful argument, rather than overwhelming that sentiment, was more likely to cause it to retrench. Since it was not a matter of reasoning, but of intensely held feeling that propped up the system, such feeling could only be overcome over time and with great difficulty. However, some of the first steps were taken toward overcoming a repressive patriarchy by Mary Wollstonecraft and John Stuart Mill. Neither would live to see the fruits of their labors, but the benefit to their daughters and sons is undeniable. It is to those benefits, foreseen to some degree by Mill, that we turn in the next section.

Guided Reading Questions

1. What is Mill's thesis?
2. What is the "peculiar character" of the modern world?
3. What is the basis for the current system of men ruling over women?
4. How does Mill argue that it is improper to assume, on "general presumption", that certain people are not fit for certain things?
5. Why does Mill argue that nature and law are contrary, despite the fact that those in power use both to subject women to their power?
6. How does Mill argue that women should be given equal freedoms (discuss his responses to each of the arguments put forward by the opposition)?

Logic Blurb
The Fallacy of Misplaced Concreteness

While Mill likely does not commit the *Naturalist Fallacy* in his argument for the Principle of Utility, he does commit the Fallacy of Misplaced Concreteness. The Fallacy of Misplaced Concreteness is the Whiteheadian name for the rather common practice of granting to some abstract concept more concreteness than it truly conveys. For example, to suppose that the abstract notion of *chair* somehow has more reality than the particular instance of a chair is an example of the fallacy. Ultimately, the fallacy is a metaphysical mistake, confusing the ontological status of two or more objects of knowledge.

Mill's argument is an excellent example because his argument for the Principle of Utility commits the fallacy at two points. The analogy that Mill uses to drive the conclusion of his argument, that the individual's desire for the individual's own good is analogous to the general populace's desire for the general good, involves the Fallacy of Misplaced Concreteness in both parts of the more general related pair. While the analogy seems to hold, it ultimately does so only if both the aggregate of all people (the general populace) and the general happiness (greatest good) actually exist. The analogy does not depend on these abstract notions existing in the *same way* that individuals and their desires exist, merely on the existence *at all* of them. That is, they much carry some quantity of concrete reality with them as particulars of one sort or another. However, an aggregate of all people is merely that – a collection of individuals. To be sure, there is quite good scholarship that suggests that groups of people do form something like organic unities that act in ways that none of the individual members of the group would endorse on the individual level, the fact remains that aggregates of people are precisely that – aggregates of individual, accidentally conjoined people. The notion of a "greatest number" where "greatest number" refers to something independent of the individuals that constitute it is a transfer of a sense of concrete reality from individuals to the abstract group they comprise. That group does not have that sort of reality, and thus the concreteness is misplaced.

Further, the individual happinesses, as exclusively private and internal states, are simply not additive. Given that the individual happinesses cannot be summed into a general one, it is clear that such a summation of happiness (the general happiness) does not have any actual existence, but merely an abstract and theoretical one. Since Mill's argument depends on transferring a sense of reality from the individual to the group and from the individual's desires to the group's desire, it commits the fallacy of misplaced concreteness because in both cases, the ontology of the more abstract notion is considerably different from the ontology of its constituent parts. Indeed, in the final analysis, one of the abstract entities (the general happiness) has no actual existence at all. Thus, to suppose that the ontological status of one sort of object can be transferred without complication to a more abstract sort of object or idea is to commit the Fallacy of Misplaced Concreteness.

Section 17.4: Mill and the Benefits of Liberty

The Subjection of Women

Chapter 4

1. There remains a question, not of less importance than those already discussed, and which will be asked the most importunately by those opponents whose conviction is somewhat shaken on the main point. What good are we to expect from the changes proposed in our customs and institutions? Would mankind be at all better off if women were free?

4. To which let me first answer, the advantage of having the most universal and pervading of all human relations regulated by justice instead of injustice. ... Think what it is to a boy, to grow up to manhood in the belief that without any merit or any exertion of his own, though he may be the most frivolous and empty or the most ignorant and stolid of mankind, by the mere fact of being born a male he is by right the superior of all and every one of an entire half of the human race: including probably some whose real superiority to himself he has daily or hourly occasion to feel; but even if in his whole conduct he habitually follows a woman's guidance, still, if he is a fool, he thinks that of course she is not, and cannot be, equal in ability and judgment to himself; and if he is not a fool, he does worse---he sees that she is superior to him, and believes that, notwithstanding her superiority, he is entitled to command and she is bound to obey. What must be the effect on his character, of this lesson? ... Is it imagined that all this does not pervert the whole manner of existence of the man, both as an individual and as a social being? It is an exact parallel to the feeling of a hereditary king that he is excellent above others by being born a king, or a noble by being born a noble. The relation between husband and wife is very like that between lord and vassal, except that the wife is held to more unlimited obedience than the vassal was. However the vassal's character may have been affected, for better and for worse, by his subordination, who can help seeing that the lord's was affected greatly for the worse? Whether he was led to believe that his vassals were really superior to himself, or to feel that he was placed in command over people as good as himself, for no merits or labours of his own, but merely for having, as Figaro says, taken the trouble to be born. The self-worship of the monarch, or of the feudal superior, is matched by the self-worship of the male. ... Above all, when the feeling of being raised above the whole of the

other sex is combined with personal authority over one individual among them; break out towards all who are in a position to be obliged to tolerate them, and often revenge themselves upon the unfortunate wife for the involuntary restraint which they are obliged to submit to elsewhere.

6. The second benefit to be expected from giving to women the free use of their faculties, by leaving them the free choice of their employments, and opening to them the same field of occupation and the same prizes and encouragements as to other human beings, would be that of doubling the mass of mental faculties available for the higher service of humanity. Where there is now one person qualified to benefit mankind and promote the general improvement, as a public teacher, or an administrator of some branch of public or social affairs, there would then be a chance of two. Mental superiority of any kind is at present everywhere so much below the demand; there is such a deficiency of persons competent to do excellently anything which it requires any considerable amount of ability to do; that the loss to the world, by refusing to make use of one half of the whole quantity of talent it possesses, is extremely serious. ... there must be added, on the other, the benefit of the stimulus that would be given to the intellect of men by the competition; or (to use a more true expression) by the necessity that would be imposed on them of deserving presidency before they could expect to obtain it.

7. This great accession to the intellectual power of the species, and to the amount of intellect available for the good management of its affairs, would be obtained, partly, through the better and more complete intellectual education of women. Women in general would be brought up equally capable of understanding business, public affairs, and the higher matters of speculation, with men In the same class of society; and the select few of the one as well as of the other sex, who were qualified not only to comprehend what is done or thought by others, but to think or do something considerable themselves, would meet with the same facilities for improving and training their capacities in the one sex as in the other. In this way, the widening of the sphere of action for women would operate for good, by raising their education to the level of that of men, and making the one participate in all improvements made in the other. But independently of this, the mere breaking down of the barrier would of itself have an educational virtue of the highest worth. The mere getting rid of the idea that all the wider subjects of thought and action, all the things which are of general and not solely of private interest, are men's business, from which women are to be warned off---positively interdicted from most of it, coldly tolerated in the little which is allowed them---the mere consciousness a woman would then have of being a human being like any other, entitled to choose her pursuits, urged or invited by the same inducements as anyone else to interest herself in whatever is interesting to human beings, entitled to exert the share of influence on all human concerns which belongs to an individual opinion, whether she attempted actual participa-

tion in them or not---this alone would effect an immense expansion of the faculties of women, as well as enlargement of the range of their moral sentiments.

8. Besides the addition to the amount of individual talent available for the conduct of human affairs, which certainly are not at present so abundantly provided in that respect that they can afford to dispense with one-half of what nature proffers; the opinion of women would then possess a more beneficial, rather than a greater, influence upon the general mass of human belief and sentiment. ... influence of women over the general tone of opinion has always, or at least from the earliest known period, been very considerable. The influence of mothers on the early character of their sons, and the desire of young men to recommend themselves to young women, have in all recorded times been important agencies in the formation of character, and have determined some of the chief steps in the progress of civilization. ... The moral influence of women has had two modes of operation. First, it has been a softening influence. Those who were most liable to be the victims of violence, have naturally tended as much as they could towards limiting its sphere and mitigating its excesses. Those who were not taught to fight, have naturally inclined in favour of any other mode of settling differences rather than that of fighting. In general, those who have been the greatest sufferers by the indulgence of selfish passion, have been the most earnest supporters of any moral law which offered a means of bridling passion. ... The other mode in which the effect of women's opinion has been conspicuous, is by giving, a powerful stimulus to those qualities in men, which, not being themselves trained in, it was necessary for them that they should find in their protectors. Courage, and the military virtues generally, have at all times been greatly indebted to the desire which men felt of being admired by women ... From the combination of the two kinds of moral influence thus exercised by women, arose the spirit of chivalry: the peculiarity of which is, to aim at combining the highest standard of the warlike qualities with the cultivation of a totally different class of virtues – those of gentleness, generosity, and self-abnegation, towards the non-military and defenseless classes generally. ... Though the practice of chivalry fell even more sadly short of its theoretic standard than practice generally falls below theory, it remains one of the most precious monuments of the moral history of our race; as a remarkable instance of a concerted and organized attempt by a most disorganized and distracted society, to raise up and carry into practice a moral ideal greatly in advance of its social condition and institutions.

16. It would of course be extreme folly to suppose that these differences of feeling and inclination only exist because women are brought up differently from men, and that there would not be differences of taste under any imaginable circumstances. But there is nothing beyond the mark in saying that the distinction in bringing up immensely aggravates those differences, and renders them wholly inevitable. While women are brought up as they are, a man and a woman will but rarely find in one another real agreement of tastes and wishes as to daily life.

20. He who would rightly appreciate the worth of personal independence as an element of happiness, should consider the value he himself puts upon it as an ingredient of his own. There is no subject on which there is a greater habitual difference of judgment between a man judging for himself, and the same man judging for other people. When he hears others complaining that they are not allowed freedom of action---that their own will has not sufficient influence in the regulation of their affairs---his inclination is, to ask, what are their grievances? what positive damage they sustain? and in what respect they consider their affairs to be mismanaged? and if they fail to make out, in answer to these questions, what appears to him a sufficient case, he turns a deaf ear, and regards their complaint as the fanciful querulousness of people whom nothing reasonable will satisfy. But he has a quite different standard of judgment when he is deciding for himself. Then, the most unexceptionable administration of his interests by a tutor set over him, does not satisfy his feelings: his personal exclusion from the deciding authority appears itself the greatest grievance of all, rendering it superfluous even to enter into the question of mismanagement. ... Let him rest assured that whatever he feels on this point, women feel in a fully equal degree. Whatever has been said or written, from the time of Herodotus to the present, of the ennobling influence of free government---the nerve and spring which it gives to all the faculties, the larger and higher objects which it presents to the intellect and feelings, the more unselfish public spirit, and calmer and broader views of duty, that it engenders, and the generally loftier platform on which it elevates the individual as a moral, spiritual, and social being---is every particle as true of women as of men. Are these things no important part of individual happiness? ... No less large and powerful is their part, we may assure ourselves, in the lives and feelings of women. ... The love of power and the love of liberty are in eternal antagonism. Where there is least liberty, the passion for power is the most ardent and unscrupulous. The desire of power over others can only cease to be a depraving agency among mankind, when each of them individually is able to do without it: which can only be where respect for liberty in the personal concerns of each is an established principle.

21. But it is not only through the sentiment of personal dignity, that the free direction and disposal of their own faculties is a source of individual happiness, and to be fettered and restricted in it, a source of unhappiness, to human beings, and not least to women. There is nothing, after disease, indigence, and guilt, so fatal to the pleasurable enjoyment of life as the want of a worthy outlet for the active faculties. ... The injudiciousness of parents, a youth's own inexperience, or the absence of external opportunities for the congenial vocation, and their presence for an uncongenial, condemn numbers of men to pass their lives in doing one thing reluctantly and ill, when there are other things which they could have done well and happily. But on women this sentence is imposed by actual law, and by customs equivalent to law. What, in unenlightened societies, colour, race, religion, or in the case of a conquered country, nationality, are to some

men, sex is to all women; a peremptory exclusion from almost all honourable occupations, but either such as cannot be fulfilled by others, or such as those others do not think worthy of their acceptance. Sufferings arising from causes of this nature usually meet with so little sympathy, that few persons are aware of the great amount of unhappiness even now produced by the feeling of a wasted life. The case will be even more frequent, as increased cultivation creates a greater and greater disproportion between the ideas and faculties of women, and the scope which society allows to their activity.

22. When we consider the positive evil caused to the disqualified half of the human race by their disqualification---first in the loss of the most inspiring and elevating kind of personal enjoyment, and next in the weariness, disappointment, and profound dissatisfaction with life, which are so often the substitute for it; one feels that among all the lessons which men require for carrying on the struggle against the inevitable imperfections of their lot on earth, there is no lesson which they more need, than not to add to the evils which nature inflicts, by their jealous and prejudiced restrictions on one another. Their vain fears only substitute other and worse evils for those which they are idly apprehensive of: while every restraint on the freedom of conduct of any of their human fellow-creatures (otherwise than by making them responsible for any evil actually caused by it), dries up *pro tanto* the principal fountain of human happiness, and leaves the species less rich, to an inappreciable degree, in all that makes life valuable to the individual human being.

∼

With his devastating criticisms of the arguments proffered by the opponents of recognition of the full humanity of women, one might suppose that Mill would be content to abandon the field with a triumph. After all, all his thesis would seem to need by way of support is a systematic demonstration that the arguments *for* the subjection of women are all necessarily false. The first chapter of *Subjection of Women* handles that part of his argument exceptionally well. However, Mill is not content with merely a critical demolition of the arguments of his opponents. On his view, the negative argument is convincing, but insufficient to his larger purpose. To achieve the goal of widespread acceptance of the primary implication of his thesis, namely that given the fact that the subjection of women is wrong that there must be an intentional and thoroughgoing rectification of the legacy of that subjection, he must show not only that the subjection of women is wrong in theoretical terms (e.g., by showing the arguments of his opponents fail), but also demonstrate the practical gains to be experienced by society as a whole in the elevation of the status of women. This is a more difficult argument to make. However, given his utilitarian/consequentialist philosophical framework, he believes he can make the case and do so in a convincing fashion.

It would not be supposed that Mill underestimates the opposition. He is well aware of the difficulty that faces his arguments. Indeed, Mill seems more fully aware of the scope of the opposition than many, if not the vast majority, of his successors in the movement to support the notion that women, no less than men, are full human beings. Despite his arguments, it was nearly a century before women gained the right to vote and fairly strong arguments can be made that nearly two centuries after the publication of *Subjection* that women still fail to enjoy equivalent social, political, and economic status with their male counterparts. While there has been much debate over the cause of this painfully slow progress toward equality, Mill recognizes that the root of the problem is quite simple – power and the corruption of the character of the one who possesses and wields ill-gotten power to oppress others.

While the arguments of those opposed to the liberation of women have been dismissed, the broader thesis is still to be addressed. Those opponents might say, "yes, Mill, our arguments were faulty and perhaps our view that women should be subject to the will of men is unjustified, but we still think the world is better off that way than the way you suggest." As chapter four opens, Mill plainly takes up the challenge. He writes, "Would mankind be at all better off if women were free?" This is an intriguing question, made moreso by the fact that Mill clearly recognizes something that even many contemporary thinkers do not; namely that the word "mankind" is not actually a gender-neutral name for all of humanity, but rather in itself conveys a presumption of the superiority of men to women. To be sure, the common use of the word had two senses then, and to a lesser extent, now. To speak of "mankind" was to speak, in one sense, of all of men in the world; in the second sense, it was to speak of all of humanity. Equivocations in its use, however, are particularly powerful and convey an underlying assumption – to equivocate between the two uses of "mankind" has historically been to say that what is good for mankind *qua* all men is good for mankind *qua* all of humanity. It is true that Mill does not opt for more inclusive language, but he does recognize the equivocation and his argument attacks both prongs of it. In addressing the question of whether or not the liberation of women would be best for women, he argues that this liberation would be best for all of humanity and, perhaps counterintuitively, that it would even be best for the group who benefits most from the oppression of women, namely men.

The first advantage to the Millian vision is a shift in the structure of the centerpiece of human relations – namely the relation between husband and wife. Under the system of subjection, that relation is governed by injustice; the unjustified exercise of power that communicates privileges to one side (the man) and disadvantages to the other (the woman) for no reason, legal or natural. This exercise in injustice can have no result other than instilling resentments on the one hand and an unjustified sense of privilege along with an unrealistic perception of the world on the other. Take, for example, a boy, Scott, who grows up with the view that even if he is the worst example of a person whatsoever, ignorant, frivolous, unworthy in every way of his status in life. Even in such a case, Mill points out that he would likely feel not only that he is nevertheless superior to half of the population, but also that he has a *right* to that superiority. Even in those cases where he is completely supported by a woman who, through her own wisdom and practicality, guides him through life by the hand, he would still feel both superior to her and that he is superior *in virtue of being male*.

Mill makes the analogy of the common household, where the man's home is his castle, to the hereditary, divine-right kings whose tyranny England had overthrown and to which men would never again submit themselves. Ironically, the very power relations they have sought to overthrow, they seek to preserve when they themselves are the beneficiaries of it. Beyond the irony of the oppressed becoming the oppressor, there is the epistemological falsehood and attendant inaccurate metaphysical assumptions that come with this position of unjustified privilege. Because of the system, Scott perceives women to be his inferior, all evidence to the contrary. In virtue of this epistemological mistake, he also persists in holding an inaccurate view of the world, perpetuated throughout centuries from Aristotle forward, that women are ontologically inferior to men simply in virtue of being women. Persisting in a fundamentally flawed notion of the structure of reality cannot help but cause the web of beliefs that comprises the mind to be out of kilter. Since it is generally considered better to know what the world is actually like rather than to be deeply mistaken about it, the systematic subjection of women impoverishes the view of the world held by the one who benefits so unjustly from it.

However, whatever unjust benefits accrue to the man in this societal model, those benefits pale in the face of the detriment to his character because of the system. The divine right monarch, whether pharaoh of old or absolute monarch of the more recent past, holds himself, to greater or lesser degree, to not only be worthy of the position he holds, but also to be somewhat worthy of obeisance and worship by his subjects. This inevitably leads to a sort of self-worship, as well. At the same time, he lives in a world in which he is much more marginalized – he is a wage-earner or a business man or a salesman, perhaps. Because he lives in that world, he is subject to others and often rails against the injustice of their seemingly arbitrary decisions that profoundly affect his livelihood and his aspirations to higher ambitions. As a result, he is torn. On the one hand, he conceives himself as unquestioned ruler; on the other, he realizes that he is subject to the whims of others. The frustration and impotence of the latter relationship often causes the former relationship to be the outlet of those frustrations, and thus, Mill observes that men "often revenge themselves upon the unfortunate wife for the involuntary restraint which they are obliged to submit to elsewhere."

On Mill's view, this will necessarily have an effect that is corrosive of the character of the oppressive/oppressed man who exercises his "divine right" in the home and is subject to the whims of others outside it. This man desires power, exercises power wherever it is possible, and has power exercised over him by others. He is caught between a love of liberty and a love of power.

These two loves, Mill writes, are fundamentally antagonistic toward are each other. Intriguingly, the man who seeks liberty in his own affairs and power in his relationships is torn between the inconsistencies of liberty and power. The pursuit of power, particularly power *over* another necessarily entails the deprivation of liberty *from* that person. In this dehumanization of the oppressed, the character of the oppressor itself erodes as that inconsistency between power and liberty plays out. The only way in which this erosion can be avoided is by seeking liberty, for himself and for those whom he before would have sought to oppress. Liberty for each must be the principle endorsed, both for self and others. Only justice within power relations can avoid the corrosion of the individual soul.

While the current system causes entire systems of false beliefs and misperceptions of the world and causes a corrosion of individual character of those who benefit from oppressing other members of society, Mill argues that there are even greater positive benefits that will accrue to society as a whole than the simple elimination of the negative consequences of the oppressive system. The central positive benefit to be gained by the full inclusion of all of its members is the advance of a civil, just, and mature society. However quickly it has progressed through employment of a portion of the talents of a portion of the population, it will more thoroughly advance through the employment of the talents of the entirety of the population. Not only does it make no sense to arbitrarily exclude vast resources from a business, for example, it likewise makes no sense to exclude from society the vast reserve of intelligence, character, talent, and artistic gifts of women. The inclusion of women into the spheres dominated exclusively by men will not be an easy transition. In some ways, the advance of women might seem to pose a threat to the easy power of men and they would seem threatened by that advance. The insecurity inherent in the power relationship would tend to be exacerbated as that power was perceived to be eroding. However, Mill argues that the erosion of that power is a positive and though it might well result in competition, that competition would be mutually beneficial. He wrote that, "the widening of the sphere of action for women would operate for good, by raising their education to the level of that of men, and making the one participate in all improvements made in the other." This would entail an "educational virtue of the highest worth," albeit not without some upheaval. Despite the turmoil that might result as a matter of so radically altering the social structure, through providing open access to full educational, social, economic, and political participation to women, the society benefits more completely than in the alternate reality marked by their exclusion. The character, diversity, and justice of the society then provide a nurturing environment to all of its members rather than grinding down the one and corroding the character of the other.

Because men as a class and humanity as a whole would benefit from the liberation of women and because women clearly would benefit both from the liberation itself and from its benefits communicated throughout society, it is also clear that the subjection of women to men is not only wrong in itself but also wrong for its consequences. While Mill's argument, and those that come after it, are devastating to the justification of the status quo, the equality envisioned by Mill is still not fully realized.

Guided Reading Questions

1. How does Mill argue that all people, including women, should have suffrage?
2. What does Mill say about the role women play in the "moral cultivation" of humankind?
3. How does the subjection of women impoverish the character of men and women?

Logic Blurb
The *Ad Hominem*

Few rhetorical flourishes are more satisfying than a good *ad hominem*. Castigating one's opponent for flaws real or imagined can be powerfully persuasive in addition to being highly satisfying personally for those who have the unfortunate tendency toward *shadenfreude* (taking pleasure in others pain). Sarcasm, and implied *ad hominem*, aside, the use of the *ad hominem* is found most commonly in adversarial arenas, particularly in the world of politics.

Rare is the political campaign that does not cast aspersions on the character of its opponent. Imagine a campaign for the U.S. Senate in which the incumbent is a decorated war hero and dedicated family man. In this hypothetical campaign, imagine also his opponent taking to the airwaves to call the man a coward, an adulterer, and a liar. Such vitriol leveled at the incumbent is not unusual. The independent and objective observer of the race might well argue that the challenger has not played fair, and she would be right. However, fairness is antithetical to the *ad hominem* attack. Indeed, the fact that the *ad hominem* is quite common is evidence not of its validity as an argument form but of its effectiveness. Merely raising the specter of vice or unseemly behavior is often enough to sway uncritical and unreflective audiences.

What about those cases in which an argument for *p* is put forward by someone who truly is a scoundrel or morally deficient individual? One of the persistent questions in ethical theory is whether or not the character of an individual has any impact on the argument he puts forward. For example, does St. Augustine's misspent youth and abandonment of his long-term lover who bore him a son matter when one evaluates his arguments concerning the nature of God? This is a difficult question that is not easily decided. Thus, to call into question the character of the person making an argument is not always out of bounds. One might quite rightly condemn Augustine's actions during what he himself recognizes as a period in which moral virtue was the least of his worries or interest. At the same time, it is also reasonably clear that there is a distinction between his behavior then and his mature thought. Thus, as a matter of practice, the *ad hominem* is to be avoided because, at the very least, it is an argument form that introduces irrelevant claims into a debate.

Section 18.1: Reading Karl Marx

The Communist Manifesto

A spectre is haunting Europe – the spectre of communism. All the powers of old Europe have entered into a holy alliance to exorcise this spectre Pope and Tsar, Metternich and Guizot, French Radicals and German police-spies.

Where is the party in opposition that has not been decried as communistic by its opponents in power? Where is the opposition that has not hurled back the branding reproach of communism, against the more advanced opposition parties, as well as against its reactionary adversaries?

Two things result from this fact:

I. Communism is already acknowledged by all European powers to be itself a power.

II. It is high time that Communists should openly, in the face of the whole world, publish their views, their aims, their tendencies, and meet this nursery tale of the spectre of communism with a manifesto of the party itself.

To this end, Communists of various nationalities have assembled in London and sketched the following manifesto, to be published in the English, French, German, Italian, Flemish and Danish languages.

~

Misconceptions, misunderstandings, and outright falsehoods dominate the popular opinion of Karl Marx. The "argument" that the communist experiment failed with the fall of the Soviet Union is a specious one, founded on those misconceptions and misunderstandings. The fall of the crushing oppressiveness that marked the Soviet system was a benefit to the world in many ways. However, to suppose that the economic system of the Soviet Union would have been something that Marx in any way, shape, or form would have endorsed is to fundamentally misunderstand the Marxist project and the philosophical view of economics, history, and revolution that he put forward.

Part of the cloud of misunderstanding that surrounds Marx's views is attributable to Marx himself. His primary philosophical work that widely read by the public is propaganda, in the form of tracts and the *Communist Manifesto*, a work that is a joint project with Friedrich Engels and followed a groundbreaking meeting of communists of Europe in 1847. One common aspect of a piece of propaganda is to put forward the views of one's opponents in the worst possible light, creating strawmen to knock down and moving from *ad hominem* to *ad hominem* not so much as an attempt to refute the opposing views but to discredit their plausibility. Propaganda is intended to persuade readers of the truth of the author's view generally by means of demonizing the opposition and opposing views more than demonstrating the weaknesses of those views. For this reason, propaganda is rarely seen a reliable vehicle for philosophical argument precisely because it tends to so overdraw the opposing views that it casts doubts on the argument that it, itself, is supposed to advance.

Marx commits the strawman fallacy from time to time, to be sure, and does not shy away from *ad hominem*, but the *Manifesto* also contains very readable and important critical arguments that are distilled from his more comprehensive philosophical works. There is an important distinction to keep in mind as one turns to read the *Manifesto*. Marx's view has two components – one that is a critical analysis of the current (to him) political and economic system and one that describes what he takes to be the inevitable conclusion of that system in the future and the nature of the successor to it. Keeping these two components distinct is critical to understanding the importance of Marx for contemporary readers.

Before turning to Marx's vociferous critique of Capitalism, it is important to dispel the notion that the system that viewed Marx as inspiration and whose opponents demonized both the system and Marx was one that was itself Marxist. To put it simply, the "communist" system of the Soviet Union, while totalitarian and oppressive, was not at all consistent with Marx's vision of either communism or the revolution that would bring it about. Indeed, the economic system within the failed experiment that was the Soviet Union would likely have come under the same venomous criticism from Marx that capitalism did. The reasons for this are simple, but obscured in the haze of political rhetoric. Marx, in the preface to the *Manifesto*, astutely describes the political atmosphere of his own day. "All of the powers of old Europe have entered a holy alliance to exorcise this spectre," he writes. Those in power demonize their opponents with the epithet "communist." Those in opposition demonize those in power in similar ways. Marx draws from this political rhetorical reality the conclusion that *communism* itself is a "power." This conclusion is an example of a rhetorical weakness that sometimes permeates Marx's work. From the political reality that the word "communist" is bandied about by all sides as an *ad hominem* against their opponents, it does not follow that communism, itself, is a power. Indeed, it might well be questioned whether any of the political forces truly understand the content of the concept *communist* that they hurl about so freely. Because of the political haze of charge and countercharge, a similarity between the economic system of the Soviet Union and capitalist economies is overlooked and thus the Marxist critique of both systems is obscured. Indeed, in Marx, the western capitalist would an unlikely ally in the battle of ideology that marked the Cold War.

Like Descartes's use of skepticism to refute the skeptics, so the western theorist can appeal to Marx to reject the claims of the Leninist/Stalinist "communist."

To examine this rejection, it is first necessary to carefully analyze the players in both a capitalistic system and a Soviet style state economy. In a capitalist model, the ownership class owns and controls the "means of production." In this model, the working class is the productive class, actually laboring to produce the products within the means of production. All of the citizens, both the ownership class and the working class are then consumers of those products. Let us turn, briefly, then to the state economy model. In that model, the state owns and/or controls the "means of production." This is the essential difference between the standard capitalist picture. Rather than individuals owning and controlling the productive engine of an economy, with government regulation to one degree or another, the state owns and manages that engine. In both models, the workers actually produce the goods and all of those within the society are consumers of the goods produced. Thus, rather than misidentifying state-run economies as "communistic," it is more accurate to label them as another form of capitalism, and one that is particularly inefficient. So, rather than "communist," this model is more properly called "state capitalism."

If the state economy system of the Soviet Union and its various satellites is merely a version of capitalism, and a highly inefficient one at that, then any Marxist critique of the capitalist systems as they existed in western European nations of the 19th century would be doubly devastating of those systems. That state capitalism is the actual practice of state economies is rather clear and Marx's analysis would be quite critical of it.

To be sure, this is a rather controversial view and, on the face of it, runs contrary to Marx's own claims at the conclusion of the *Manifesto* where he writes,

> But let us have done with the bourgeois objections to communism.
>
> We have seen above that the first step in the revolution by the working class is to raise the proletariat to the position of ruling class to win the battle of democracy.
>
> The proletariat will use its political supremacy to wrest, by degree, all capital from the bourgeoisie, to centralize all instruments of production in the hands of the state, i.e., of the proletariat organized as the ruling class; and to increase the total productive forces as rapidly as possible.

However, careful reading of the text dispels the appearance of contradiction. For Marx, the transfer of capital to the hands of the state is not a matter of replacing a bourgeois oligarchy of captains of industry with a cabal of revolutionaries. In both of these scenarios, the worker has merely had one master replaced by another. Such is completely antithetical to the Marxist vision. For Marx, the free development of each person is the proper goal because only in this way will the free development of all be possible. By carefully noting that Marx does not mean a hierarchical, Politburo driven, totalitarian, authoritarian bureaucracy when he describes the *state* is ample indication that there is no great controversy in the supposition that Marx would reject Soviet-style state capitalism in the same breath as industrial capitalism. The Marxist state is the result of the working classes wresting control of their political and economic destinies by winning "the battle of democracy." Only then can a state, not of ruling elites, but of the entire proletariat be established. Or, a government of, by, and for the people, rather than the powerful.

This argument is not the only one that distinguishes Marx's vision from that of the commonly labeled *Marxist* one. Additionally, Marx would argue that those nations that attempted the "communist" experiment during the 20th century did so in direct violation of the natural laws of history that govern the progression of human development just as surely as the law of gravity, for example, governs the natural world. This developmental critique depends on an understanding of the Marxist philosophy of history and to this topic we now turn.

The scientific revolution, begun with the advent of Modern Philosophy (see René Descartes and the New Science) and the rise of empirical science with Isaac Newton, had broad implications for all of the academic disciplines. Darwin's application of the principles of the scientific method to biology influence all manner of the biological sciences, to be sure, but also the variety of the social sciences in ways he never anticipated. One of the notable convergences of modern science and the social sciences is Marx's philosophy of history with all of its political implications.

Marx's view of history is sometimes called a Materialist Theory, in the same way that Modern physics is often conceptualized as materialistic. This is because Marx appropriates the materialism of Newton, the New Science doctrine of cause and effect (in contrast to the Aristotelian/Scholastic one), and the physicalism of scientific explanation to explore history, its ebbs and flows, its patterns, and its "laws." In addition to the physicalism/materialism of the New Science, Marx also draws on the philosophy of history of Hegel and the Hegelian notion of the dialectic. A brief digression to examine the Hegelian dialectic is in order here.

Georg Hegel was a later contemporary of Kant and greatly influenced by his predecessor. Hegel was also greatly influenced by his reading of Plato. Within Plato's middle and later dialogues, he employs a distinctive method of argument which he labels the *dialectic*. (For a review of the Platonic *dialectic*, consult the *Reading Plato* introduction to that previous section.) Hegel draws upon that Platonic dialectic to formulate his own. Hegel's dialectic, although rooted, in his view, on that of Plato, is, in fact, distinctly his own. The Hegelian dialectic is deceptively simple and a powerful analytical tool. It proceeds in stages.

Let us take any proposition, or *thesis*. If it is a well-formed proposition, it will, of necessity, give rise to its opposite, or its *antithesis*. This pair of contradictory (or at least contrary) propositions will necessarily give rise to a third proposition that is a combination of the two initial propositions, in one way or another. This *synthesis* of the initial two propositions is not the end of the process because this synthesis now is the new *thesis* which will necessarily give rise to its *antithesis* and so on. This process grows ever finer and more precise, constantly refining and refining a proposition by application of its opposite until the proposition more closely apprehends the actual state of affairs in the world.

Hegel does not think that the *dialectic* applies only to describable propositions, however. Indeed, Hegel sees actual facts of the world, whether they be political, historical, biological, etc., give rise to their opposites. Thus, *being* gives rise to the antithesis, *non-being*, which in composition refines the understanding of what it is *to be*. The universe is then described as a series of dichotomous propositions (where propositions are understood to be any actual thing, whether statement or entity) and the conflict between them that gives rise to a novel new proposition. This process is a natural feature of the universe and as unavoidable as the natural laws with which the scientist is familiar. Thus, disciplines like history are to be seen as more scientific explorations than merely interpretive ones. The sweep of history is the sweep of ideas, of the progression from one historical reality to another in a never-ending march of novelty.

For Marx, as well as Hegel, history follows laws that are as regular and predictable as those that govern the falling of apples from trees. Thus, in the same way that a person who understands physics and the law of gravity will know when she sees the apple detached from the branch that it will fall, so too the person who understands history and its laws will know what comes next upon observing some history-making event. This can be seen clearly in analogy.

Physics	:	Laws of physics
	::	
History	:	Laws of history

Marx appropriates this philosophy of history and amends it slightly. The dialectical progression of history is a centerpiece of the theoretical groundwork that Marx sees as the supporting ground of the second component of his view, the culmination of the progression of history through the "inevitable" Communist Revolution. On Marx's view, the Communist Revolution is as inevitable as the falling of a stone dropped from great height. The motion of bodies is governed by natural law, so too is the motion of history Coupled with this philosophy of history, which we will explore in greater depth in the following section, is a theory of value that stands as the antithesis to the Market Theory of Value of capitalism. We turn now to a brief analysis of two competing theories of value, the Market Theory and the Labor Theory.

The Market Theory of Value is quite easy and straightforward. Suppose Adam has a factory that produces widgets. On the open and free market, let us suppose that he can sell those widgets for $10 each. He could clearly sell them for less, but let us suppose that the ceiling on widgets is the $10; that is, beyond that price, people will cease to buy his widgets and will look to alternatives to satisfy their need for them. Thus, the market sets the value of the widget at $10. However, Adam does not pocket the entire amount. Clearly there are costs associated with the production of those widgets. Among those costs, obviously, are the raw materials out of which the widgets are fashioned. Additionally, there are the wages paid to those who do the assembly itself. In other words, the production of the widgets has two requirements – natural resources and human resources. Each of these is roughly equivalent and treated in the same manner. The widgets are sold on the free market and the natural resources are purchased in the same way. The *laissez faire* capitalist would hold that the labor of the workers who assemble the widgets (the human resources) is also purchased on the free market. The wage earner's time and productive labor are commodified in such a way that they represent a fixed cost on the debit side of the ledger. Let us suppose that the raw materials can be purchased for $2 per widget and that a worker can assemble eight widgets an hour and is paid $1 per widget. Thus, at the end of the hour, eight widgets are assembled and the cost is $24 ($16 for the natural resources and $8 for the human resources). For the sake of simplicity, let us also assume that the cost of administrative overhead is $6 per hour. Thus, the total cost of doing business for that hour of productivity is an even $30. Given that each widget sells for $10, Adam clears $50 for that hour. The revenue minus cost equation expresses what Adam will call *profit*.

As simple as this conception of *value* is, it is not without some drawbacks that even one who rejects Marxist critical theory might well recognize. While we will address the particularly Marxist critique of the Market Theory in the following section, it may be helpful to point out one difficulty with this approach to *value* here. A difficulty with this conception is fairly clear. The market approach does not take into account what many take to be perhaps most valuable – namely, what goes in to the production of the widget. In part this aspect is discounted because it is devilishly difficult to quantify. Evaluating and quantifying the cost of producing a widget is hard calculate apart from appeal to market valuations. The cost of labor, for example, can itself be commodified – what price must be paid to get the widget produced. The individual worker's labor is understood as something sold on the market for what the market will bear. Thus, if two people are offering their labor for sale, and one will work for $1 per hour while the other offers to work for $1.50, the market then fixes the value of the labor at the lower price. Even if we assume that the cost of raw materials is constant (an unlikely event), the cost is still difficult to fix because the "labor market" is notoriously fluid. Daily, weekly, monthly fluctuations combined with regional disparities quickly added layers of complexity to the calculations. However, there exists a deeper reason for excluding this aspect from assessment of value. The resources required for production of the widget are excluded from estimation of its value because it is not understood by advocates of this approach as fundamental. The fundamental feature of value is the market valuation. Notice in the attempt to calculate the cost of production, the focus of that discussion was in terms of the market valuation of the *labor*. So, even if the calculations could be made, they are determined *in terms of* market valuations. Thus, the assessment of value, from a market perspective, is market driven because what the market will bear is basic to all other concerns or calculations.

The Market Theory is not the only competitor for understanding "value." Another approach is commonly called the Labor Theory of Value. The Labor Theory is a bit more difficult to conceptualize, although it might well be argued that this difficulty in conception is a direct result of the more commonly accepted Market Theory. A cursory examination of the two theories points to the key structural difference between them. While the Market Theory focuses on the value assigned to a product by the market itself, and thus, at the end of the production chain, the Labor Theory assigns value by assessing the work or labor that is required to make the product, and thus, focuses on the production chain itself. Simply put, the Market Theory assigns value by figuring what can be gotten out of the product while the Labor Theory assigns value based on what goes into the product.

To examine the Labor Theory, let us return to the widget example. To make the central tenet of the Labor Theory clear, let us suppose that the costs associated with everything but the wages of the laborers remain the same. The cost of the labor can be assessed in a variety of ways, but let us examine two. In the first case, we can ask what the value of the labor itself is worth, independent of the later sale price of the widgets. Thus, let us suppose that the labor is actually $3 per widget. Let us also assume that productivity remains constant and eight widgets are produced. Thus, we would have the following calculation of the value of the eight widgets.

Raw materials (@ $2/widget)	$ 16
Administrative overhead	$ 6
Labor (@$3/widget)	$ 24
Total	$ 46

If we evaluate the costs that go into the production of the finished widgets and base our value assignment there, then the value of the widgets is $46 and the value of each individual widget is $5.75. Since this is the *true* value of each widget, they should then be marketed to the broader public for this price.

The second method of assessing the value of the labor is to evaluate it relative to the market valuation of the widget. That is, if we suppose that the market would assign a value to each widget of $10, then we can simply take that total, subtract the value of the costs except for the labor costs and the remainder, then, is the value of the labor itself. So, on this model, then, we would have something like the following calculation.

Total	$	80
Administrative overhead	$	(6)
Raw materials (@ $2/widget)	$	(16)
Value of Labor	$	58

This method of assigning a valuation to labor is in some sense dependent on a market theory approach. That is, one uses the market valuation of all of the components of the product, including the final sale price of the product, to arrive at a valuation for the labor contribution to the product itself. Each of these approaches is fairly simple, although both have rather radical reevaluations of the capitalist enterprise.

The first thing that should be noticed is that whichever of the Labor Theory calculations one uses to assign value, the notion of *profit* evaporates. On the first view, the price of the widget is completely accounted by the cost of the components of the widget; on the second, the price of the widget sets the value of the components in proportion to that component's contribution to the production of the widget. Thus, the difference between *revenue* and *cost* is zero. As such, there is no notion of *profit* whatsoever on a Labor Theory.

The Labor Theory criticism of the Market valuations, then, is two fold. In the first place, the Market theory is thought to be hypocritical. The owner of the means of production, the bourgeoisie, must equivocate on the notion of *value*. To the worker, Adam says that the *value* of the production of the eight widgets is one number ($30) while to the customer purchasing the widgets, he says that the *value* is another number ($80). Thus, Adam essentially has two sets of books – one that deals with the value of the production and the second that deals with whatever the market will bear. To the Labor theorist, this seems straightforwardly hypocritical.

The second critique of the Market approach by Labor is that if we suppose that the widgets are actually worth $80, then the difference between what Adam receives for the widgets (revenue) and what he spends for the production of the widgets (cost) is *exploitation*. That is, if the widgets are actually worth $80, then the $50 *profit* is actually value extracted from the components of the production of the widgets without recompense. On the other hand, if the widgets are actually worth $30, then the $50 *profit* is value extracted from the customer who purchases the widgets and who is rather significantly overcharged. Thus, *profit* is either revenue minus cost (the Market Theory) or exploitation of the worker, the consumer, or both (the Labor Theory). The Marxist counterpart of the Market Theory of Value presents, at the very least, a sophisticated critique of that theory as well as a model for better understanding the ongoing difficulty between management and labor. Their two fundamentally incommensurate understandings of the value of products and the labor that is necessary for the production of those products seems to entail that the conflict between the two will be without comfortable resolution, and indeed, may be resolved only with revolution – either actual or conceptual.

Section 18.2: Marx and the Philosophy of History

Communist Manifesto
Workers of the World! Unite!

I. Bourgeois and Proletarians (By bourgeoisie is meant the class of modern capitalists, owners of the means of social production and employers of wage labor. By proletariat, the class of modern wage laborers who, having no means of production of their own, are reduced to selling their labor power in order to live. [Note by Engels - 1888 English edition])

The history of all hitherto existing society is the history of class struggles. (That is, all *written* history. In 1847, the pre-history of society, the social organization existing previous to recorded history, all but unknown. Since then, August von Haxthausen (1792-1866) discovered common ownership of land in Russia, Georg Ludwig von Maurer proved it to be the social foundation from which all Teutonic races started in history, and, by and by, village communities were found to be, or to have been, the primitive form of society everywhere from India to Ireland. The inner organization of this primitive communistic society was laid bare, in its typical form, by Lewis Henry Morgan's (1818-1861) crowning discovery of the true nature of the gens and its relation to the tribe. With the dissolution of the primeaval communities, society begins to be differentiated into separate and finally antagonistic classes. I have attempted to retrace this dissolution in *Der Ursprung der Familie, des Privateigenthumus und des Staats*, second edition, Stuttgart, 1886. [Engels, 1888 English edition])

Freeman and slave, patrician and plebian, lord and serf, guild-master and journeyman, in a word, oppressor and oppressed, stood in constant opposition to one another, carried on an uninterrupted, now hidden, now open fight, a fight that each time ended, either in a revolutionary reconstitution of society at large, or in the common ruin of the contending classes.

In the earlier epochs of history, we find almost everywhere a complicated arrangement of society into various orders, a manifold gradation of social rank. In ancient Rome we have patricians, knights, plebians, slaves; in the Middle Ages, feudal lords, vassals, guild-masters, journeymen, apprentices, serfs; in almost all of these classes, again, subordinate gradations.

The modern bourgeois society that has sprouted from the ruins of feudal society has not done away with class antagonisms. It has but established new classes, new conditions of oppression, new forms of struggle in place of the old ones.

Our epoch, the epoch of the bourgeoisie, possesses, however, this distinct feature: it has simplified class antagonisms. Society as a whole is more and more splitting up into two great hostile camps, into two great classes directly facing each other – bourgeoisie and proletariat.

From the serfs of the Middle Ages sprang the chartered burghers of the earliest towns. From these burgesses the first elements of the bourgeoisie were developed.

The discovery of America, the rounding of the Cape, opened up fresh ground for the rising bourgeoisie. The East-Indian and Chinese markets, the colonization of America, trade with the colonies, the increase in the means of exchange and in commodities generally, gave to commerce, to navigation, to industry, an impulse never before known, and thereby, to the revolutionary element in the tottering feudal society, a rapid development.

The feudal system of industry, in which industrial production was monopolized by closed guilds, now no longer suffices for the growing wants of the new markets. The manufacturing system took its place. The guild-masters were pushed aside by the manufacturing middle class; division of labor between the different corporate guilds vanished in the face of division of labor in each single workshop.

Meantime, the markets kept ever growing, the demand ever rising. Even manufacturers no longer sufficed. Thereupon, steam and machinery revolutionized industrial production. The place of manufacture was taken by the giant, *modern industry*; the place of the industrial middle class by industrial millionaires, the leaders of the whole industrial armies, the modern bourgeois.

Modern industry has established the world market, for which the discovery of America paved the way. This market has given an immense development to commerce, to navigation, to communication by land. This development has, in turn, reacted on the extension of industry; and in proportion as industry, commerce, navigation, railways extended, in the same proportion the bourgeoisie developed, increased its capital, and pushed into the background every class handed down from the Middle Ages.

We see, therefore, how the modern bourgeoisie is itself the product of a long course of development, of a series of revolutions in the modes of production and of exchange.

Each step in the development of the bourgeoisie was accompanied by a corresponding political advance in that class. An oppressed class under the sway of the feudal nobility, an armed and self-governing association of medieval *commune* (This was the name given their urban communities by the townsmen of Italy and France, after they had purchased or conquered their initial rights of self-government from their feudal lords. [Engels: 1890 German edition]   *Commune* was the name taken in France by the nascent towns even before they had conquered from their feudal lords and masters local self-government and political rights as the *Third Estate*. Generally speaking, for the economical development of the bourgeoisie, England is here taken as the typical country, for its political development, France. [Engels: 1888 English edition]):

here independent urban republic (as in Italy and Germany); there taxable *third estate* of the monarchy (as in France); afterward, in the period of manufacturing proper, serving either the semi-feudal or the absolute monarchy as a counterpoise against the nobility, and, in fact, cornerstone of the great monarchies in general -- the bourgeoisie has at last, since the establishment of Modern Industry and of the world market, conquered for itself, in the modern representative state, exclusive political sway. The executive of the modern state is but a committee for managing the common affairs of the whole bourgeoisie.

II. Proletarians and Communists

In what relation to the Communists stand to the proletarians as a whole? The Communists do not form a separate party opposed to the other working-class parties.

The Communists are distinguished from the other working-class parties by this only:

> (1) In the national struggles of the proletarians of the different countries, they point out and bring to the front the common interests of the entire proletariat, independently of all nationality.

> (2) In the various stages of development which the struggle of the working class against the bourgeoisie has to pass through, they always and everywhere represent the interests of the movement as a whole.

The distinguishing feature of communism is not the abolition of property generally, but the abolition of bourgeois property. But modern bourgeois private property is the final and most complete expression of the system of producing and appropriating products that is based on class antagonisms, on the exploitation of the many by the few.

In this sense, the theory of the Communists may be summed up in the single sentence: Abolition of private property.

We Communists have been reproached with the desire of abolishing the right of personally acquiring property as the fruit of a man's own labor, which property is alleged to be the groundwork of all personal freedom, activity and independence.

Hard-won, self-acquired, self-earned property! Do you mean the property of petty artisan and of the small peasant, a form of property that preceded the bourgeois form? There is no need to abolish that; the development of industry has to a great extent already destroyed it, and is still destroying it daily.

Or do you mean the modern bourgeois private property?

But does wage labor create any property for the laborer? Not a bit. It creates capital, i.e., that kind of property which exploits wage labor, and which cannot increase except upon conditions of begetting a new supply of wage labor for fresh exploitation. Property, in its present form, is based on the antagonism of capital and wage labor. Let us examine both sides of this antagonism.

To be a capitalist, is to have not only a purely personal, but a social *status* in production. Capital is a collective product, and only by the united action of many members, nay, in the last resort, only by the united action of all members of society, can it be set in motion.

Capital is therefore not only personal; it is a social power.

When, therefore, capital is converted into common property, into the property of all members of society, personal property is not thereby transformed into social property. It is only the social character of the property that is changed. It loses its class character.

Let us now take wage labor.

The average price of wage labor is the minimum wage, i.e., that quantum of the means of subsistence which is absolutely requisite to keep the laborer in bare existence as a laborer. What, therefore, the wage laborer appropriates by means of his labor merely suffices to prolong and reproduce a bare existence. We by no means intend to abolish this personal appropriation of the products of labor, an appropriation that is made for the maintenance and reproduction of human life, and that leaves no surplus wherewith to command the labor of others. All that we want to do away with is the miserable character of this appropriation, under which the laborer lives merely to increase capital, and is allowed to live only in so far as the interest of the ruling class requires it.

In bourgeois society, living labor is but a means to increase accumulated labor. In communist society, accumulated labor is but a means to widen, to enrich, to promote the existence of the laborer.

The Communist revolution is the most radical rupture with traditional property-relations.

Of course, in the beginning, this cannot be effected except by means of despotic inroads on the rights of property, and on the conditions of bourgeois production; by means of measures, therefore, which appear economically insufficient and untenable, but which, in the course of the movement, outstrip themselves, necessitate further inroads upon the old social order, and are unavoidable as a means of entirely revolutionizing the mode of production.

These measures will, of course, be different in different countries.

Nevertheless, in most advanced countries, the following will be pretty generally applicable.

    1. Abolition of property in land and application of all rents of land to public purposes.

    2. A heavy progressive or graduated income tax.

    3. Abolition of all rights of inheritance.

    4. Confiscation of the property of all emigrants and rebels.

    5. Centralization of credit in the banks of the state, by means of a national bank with state capital and an exclusive monopoly.

    6. Centralization of the means of communication and transport in the hands of the state.

7. Extension of factories and instruments of production owned by the state; the bringing into cultivation of waste lands, and the improvement of the soil generally in accordance with a common plan.

8. Equal obligation of all to work. Establishment of industrial armies, especially for agriculture.

9. Combination of agriculture with manufacturing industries; gradual abolition of all the distinction between town and country by a more equable distribution of the populace over the country.

10. Free education for all children in public schools. Abolition of children's factory labor in its present form. Combination of education with industrial production, etc.

When, in the course of development, class distinctions have disappeared, and all production has been concentrated in the hands of a vast association of the whole nation, the public power will lose its political character. Political power, properly so called, is merely the organized power of one class for oppressing another. If the proletariat during its contest with the bourgeoisie is compelled, by the force of circumstances, to organize itself as a class; if, by means of a revolution, it makes itself the ruling class, and, as such, sweeps away by force the old conditions of production, then it will, along with these conditions, have swept away the conditions for the existence of class antagonisms and of classes generally, and will thereby have abolished its own supremacy as a class.

In place of the old bourgeois society, with its classes and class antagonisms, we shall have an association in which the free development of each is the condition for the free development of all.

~

Although Communism was the spectre haunting Europe, rampant and unchecked capitalism was the tyrant that had Europe in its iron fist. Marx's criticism of the capitalism emerging from the Industrial Revolution echoes Charles Dickens' themes in *Oliver Twist*, and in turn is echoed by Upton Sinclair's *The Jungle*, and Tennessee Ernie Ford's *Sixteen Tons*. It is a portrait of economic power destroying societal structures and replacing them with a state of conflict between two antithetical groups – the Bourgeoisie and the Proletariat. However, this latest conflict between differing economic classes is but the most recent in a long line of class warfare. Indeed, on Marx's view, the history of society is a history of class struggle and conflict.

In this interpretation of the sweep of history, Marx appropriates the Hegelian philosophy of history and reinterprets it through the lens of economic antagonisms. Marx's philosophy of history is a materialistic, dialectical, revolutionary one. Let us treat each of these in turn.

The materialism of Marx's philosophy of history should not be interpreted as a matter of the popularly lamented "materialism" of modern society. That is, the materialism of Marx has nothing to do with the consumerist society and its press for more and newer and better gadgets. It has nothing to do with the acquisition of things. Instead, by *materialism* Marx means to appropriate to the study of history the same sort of scientific apparatus that is employed by the physical scientists in the tradition of Newton. In that picture, the universe is comprised of uncountably many extraordinarily tiny bits of matter. Pieces of matter mindlessly bang into each other at the atomic level and thus drives the live of the planet and all those things comprised of these tiny bits of matter. Thus, physics is a matter of understanding collisions of atoms and forces like gravity and momentum and friction. From these unthinking building blocks, the entirety of the universe is constructed. Because there is a regular and determinable order to these forces and collisions that can be understood with a sophisticated and careful theory of cause and effect, science progresses because those regularities can be approximated, tested, and evaluated. The understanding of the universe is that of a predictably regular and understandably place. It is this notion of materialism that Marx imports to his philosophy of history.

Marx takes investigations of the sweep and progression of history to be a science in the same way that physics is. Thus, it is a materialistic progression governed by discernible laws from which testable predictions can be made. Just as humans are caught in the causal nexus of physical laws and mechanistic physics, so, too, are humans caught in the causal nexus of the laws of history and its progression. Thus, while Marx does indeed put forward quite severe criticisms of the acquisitiveness of the modern capitalist state, the materialism of his philosophy of history is quite distinct from that drive for having more stuff.

Just as atoms collide and drive the universe, Marx takes the progression of history to be driven by conflict. The way in which he conceptualizes the violent nature of history's development is one of the places in which he appropriates notions from Hegel. In this case, it is Hegel's dialectic marked by the conflict of ideas, thesis, antithesis and the conflict between them that gives rise to a synthesis which in turn becomes the new thesis and so on. Marx uses this notion of the thesis, antithesis, synthesis, coupling it with an economic interpretation of societal interactions to develop the dialectical quality of his philosophy of history.

For Marx, each epoch in human history is marked by a sort of thesis. Whichever is the dominant economic power in a society plays that role. Thus, in Medieval feudalism, there were the feudal lords who reigned as the dominant power. Their power was not merely a matter of heredity or "royalty" but of economics, of wealth, of property. However, each thesis gives rise necessarily to its antithesis. Thus, out of the serfs grew the burghers and from these developed the first strands of the bourgeoisie. On Marx's view, the seeds of the destruction of an epoch are planted by the dominant force within it; thus each economical dominant class sows its own destruction by giving rise to a class in opposition. Thus, the merchant becomes the opponent of the feudal lord. As the markets demand greater choice and more variety, and as kings and countries spend themselves in war against each other, those twin forces cause the merchant class to become more and more wealthy. As the industrial revolution begins to dawn, only the merchant class has the capital to take advantage of the advances, creating factories, consolidating labor into single shops. The guilds that had fostered the development of individual trades and widely diversified the labor force are overthrown and labor is consolidated into a single, efficient body. The rise of the machine made the *modern industry* possible. So, the feudal thesis and its antithesis give rise to a new synthesis, and as the march of history proceeds, the modern capitalist becomes the dominant thesis of the modern era.

The last of the three characteristics, the revolution, is controversial, but completely consistent with the underlying philosophical foundation of Marxist analysis. The struggle between the thesis and antithesis could be imagined as a minor tension that is played out within a moment and gives birth to a synthesis that is truly a compromise between the two initial propositions. However, the sweep of history is not gentle or compromising. It is marked by warfare and overthrow. While one might theoretically imagine one epoch gliding gently into the next, the reality of observation is that cultural systems do not go gently into that good night. They grip power with an ever-tightening grip until it is wrested from them, most often with bloodshed and carnage. The oppressed, when they rise up in revolution, have almost never been merciful and accommodating to their previous overlords. This experience, replayed again and again in the course of history, is taken by Marx to be an inevitable feature of the struggle of class against class, and indicative of human nature that that which is oppressed, upon overthrow of its oppressor, becomes oppressive itself. In every era, then, the cry, "The revolution is coming" is an accurate one; the spiral of human history is one of progress, perhaps, but also of one revolution following upon another.

So, while Marx appropriates Hegelian concepts, his application of them to a truly Marxist philosophy of history is intriguing, and deceptively simple. Economics, almost exclusively, drives the dialectical, materialistic, and revolutionary sweep of history. All people and cultures are caught in the inexorable march marked by inevitable conflict. Critics of Marx, at least those who honestly engage with the Marxist view and do not simply dismiss a misunderstanding of Marx out of hand, have pointed out that the economic-centered view is perhaps too simple. Individual conflicts, whether between persons or nations, do not always seem to be a matter solely of economics. While it would be disingenuous to argue that some international conflict has no economic component, it would at least seem reasonable, *prima facie*, to suppose that some conflict was not *solely* economic. Individual conflicts, even more, would seem to involve many more causal factors than financial ones. While Marx would accept this latter point, and, perhaps, to some extent, even the former one, he would likely point out that while there might be countercurrents in the river of history, the river itself is economic. Thus, while two individuals might well be arguing over whether or not one neighbor ever returns the lawnmower or not, that argument is but a tiny countercurrent in a much, much larger context.

Turning from the metatheory of the laws of history and its sweep from one epoch to the next, we should look next at the application of Marxist analysis to the economic situation of the 19th century. The era of modern industry was unique in its particulars. Clearly, all eras are unique, but a bit of novelty was introduced by the class struggle that gave rise to the modern capitalist moment. In this moment, the class struggle itself was refined, and sharply so. While in preceding eras, there were a variety of classes, within the industrial capitalist era, Marx sees the gradual development of but two – the bourgeoisie and the proletariat – squaring off against one another in a truly epic struggle. This breaking down of class and consolidation of ancient arguments into two camps makes the struggle all the more revolutionary in its scope. An analysis of the modern capitalist industry will serve to make the intensity of this conflict clear.

As modern factories began to dawn and the agrarian model of the prior feudal system faded as the dominant model, more and more people began to flock to cities in search of work. The rural system had been broken and could no longer support the increasing demands of the market. As the immigration to the cities became exponential in scope, the major cities, like London, were fundamentally incapable of providing services for all of the new arrivals. There simply was insufficient infrastructure to support the vast numbers of people. The resulting city life was one of grinding poverty, horrific pollution, crime, and disease. One need spend only a bit of time in the back alleys and orphanages of Charles Dickens or the opium dens of Sir Arthur Conan Doyle to get a glimpse of the overwhelming sense of hopelessness and despair that festered in the hearts of the new major population centers.

In the midst of this, the factories needed workers. Since the cities could not provide the necessary infrastructure for the human resources necessary for business, business took this role on itself. Mill houses were constructed, generally all of the same floor plan, cheaply and reasonably efficiently. Since the people who would be working in the factories were incapable of making a down payment much less purchasing a house, even a cheap one, outright, industry rented to them. However, since they could not generally make the first month's rent, that money was fronted to them as an advance on their first paychecks. Thus, the family moved into a mill house on the company property. For "protection" from the crime-riddled streets, these mill house villages were often fenced in so that the entire community was an island in the metropolitan sea.

The newly hired (and newly indebted) worker would need to not only furnish the house and provide food and the like, he was also required to provide his uniforms for work. To provide for these needs, industries generally created company stores which doubled as company banks. Since the worker was newly hired, he was unlikely to have money to make these purchases and so again, would find himself receiving a loan against his wages. So, prior to his first day on the job, the new worker would actually owe his new employer quite a substantial sum of money, at least relative to the money he would receive for his work. Indeed, it is not unlikely that he would owe more money to the company than he would receive in his first pay period. To make the ends meet from one pay period to another, given that he starts in the hole, he would often have to take out greater loans. Even in those cases where he could begin to make some headway, he could not shop for better deals outside the industry compound. This is because rather than paying wages in the coin of the realm, each industrial complex tended to print its own company "scrip" which could only be used within the company store. Thus, the worker becomes a sort of indentured servant to the company. He lives in the company house, owes payment for credited items to the company store, and receives his wages from the company. He is a human resource and simply part of the set of resources that the company uses in order to produce its products.

On the Marxist analysis of this vignette of the class struggle, people and raw materials are treated alike – both resources, one a human resource and one a natural resource. On his view, this is one of the dehumanizing of the capitalist industrial system. It reduces humans to only that which is produced and then, through application of Market Theory of Value, alienates the worker even from that. That is, the worker becomes identified not with the product he produces but with merely his ability to do work. His contribution to the productive process is commodified and he is reduced to the status of wage-earner instead of creative and productive member of society. Marx would argue that the systematic devaluation of the worker's labor coupled with the disconnection that he will eventually and necessarily feel from that which he produces will result in not only in dissatisfaction with his lot in life, but with a deep feeling of alienation.

On Marx's view, any person's notion of self and self-worth is directly tied to that which he does. So, when Ryan says that he is a miller, it is a statement of identity. His place in society is related to that which he produces and given that it is a valuable part of the community's life, his image of himself is that of a valuable contributor to the life of the community. With the rise of the modern capitalist industry, the work is no longer differentiated into valued labors (e.g., miller, carpenter, cobbler) but unified into assembly line style work. This work is often tedious and repetitive and the worker is never truly identified with it because he is only a cog in the wheel that can be easily replaced. Indeed, workers who became injured or unable to work were quickly replaced. Thus, workers begin to see themselves as a faceless and identity-less resource that is employed in the work of the factory without true recognition of their contribution. Since any persons self-identity and self-worth is related, the worker comes to feel a sense of alienation from himself.

Whether or not Marx is right in the broadest scope of his analysis, he is at least in the right ballpark. While a person may well not be completely determined by what he does, it is also true that, at the very least, there is a sense of productivity and meaningfulness that derives from the sense of accomplishment and value that attends work. The cliché of the worker who merely does a job to get a paycheck and lives for his vacation and time off, seeing that which he does to acquire money as fundamentally separate from him is a cliché for a reason. Marx would say that it is a defense mechanism to prevent the grind of the experience of work as an easily replaceable part of a machine. The common feeling that one is not really oneself at work, but only truly alive away from the workplace is a symptom that Marx would argue supports his overall thesis.

On Marx's view, humans are distinguished from other animals in that we produce our means of subsistence. That is, we are what we are because of what we do. We create ourselves in the process of intentionally, or consciously, transforming and manipulating nature. In this, Marx enters the debate about the composition of human nature. While Aristotle argues that human nature is a matter of the human function, reason, and that humans are essentially rational animals, Marx concludes that human nature is really a function of the productive creativity that drives us to innovate. If Marx overreads human creativity in his conclusion that we are what we do, it seems at true that what a person does is at least partially constitutive of his character.

One of the products of the alienation that marks the character of the modern capitalist industry is that the workers, over time, come to realize that they are all alike. Whatever differences mark them from each other, the fact that they are viewed by the corporation as identical parts of the large machinery of the company comes to cause them to view themselves as a single sort of object. While the corporation views them as a corporate whole, human resources to be exploited to the profits of the company, the workers come to have what Marx calls a *class consciousness*. Class consciousness is a recognition that whatever difference distinguish the workers from each other – ethnicity, religion, family of origin, nationality, etc. – they are all "in this together."

In these two things – the development of a refined class conflict and the production of the class consciousness within the proletariat – are jointly the seeds of the destruction of the capitalist hold on the economy. Because labor and ownership are divided by their conceptions of one another – ownership views labor as "resource," labor views ownership as "oppressive" – there is little possibility, on Marx's view, that the coming revolution can be forestalled or that it will be anything less than a complete overturning of the capitalist system. The result of that upheaval will be, on Marx's view, a complete re-imagining of the notion of property itself. Having examined Marx's quite perceptive analytical analysis, let us turn to a considerably more controversial aspect of the Marxist philosophy – the concept of property and the notion of the coming revolution.

Perhaps the most controversial of the prescriptions advocated by Marx and the Communists is the abolition of private property. This has been taken to mean that Marx supports a view of complete elimination of private property, with the attendant notion that the state is then in ownership of property and that no person will own even the house in which they live. Everyone, then, is thought to receive exactly the same amount from an autocratic and distant government populated by bureaucrats. This is a very naïve and unsophisticated reading of the Marxist prescription and philosophy of property. It must be remembered that property was nearly completely in the hands of the bourgeoisie; the members of the proletariat owned nothing to start with. Thus, the redistribution of property was to reestablish equity within the economic systems. However, it is also clear that Marx advocates some very draconian measures that are overly idealistic. Let us look, for example, at the notion of distributing the populace over the country. While this seems an appealing way to alleviate overcrowding, it also seems to reflect a very naïve understanding of geography. One might argue that Marx is not committed to the *even* distribution of population over the possible land, but it is also clear that Marx seems to think that something approaching that sort of distribution is the ideal. Other radical notions populate Marx's prescriptions, although each is seen as a remedy for a failing of capitalism. The elimination of inheritances is a method by which wealth is kept from accumulating in the hands of a very few. On Marx's view, there were many who had, through no fault of their own, become incredibly wealthy. They had inherited property and wealth from ancestors who had created the wealth, but the heirs had neither the ability nor the vision of their forebears, choosing instead to enjoy the fruits of the labor of others with no efforts of their own to be productive. The progressive tax was also to redistribute wealth, as an interim measure. After the revolution, wealth would accumulate only by contribution of the worker to society. In the meantime, as long as profit was a feature of the economic system, that profit (or *exploitation*) would need to be redistributed to the workers. Obviously, these are quite radical notions, at least to the extent that Marx advocates them.

Other Marxist notions that are less exotic, in part because they have become features of contemporary society, are ideas like the free education of all children, the centralization of means of communication and transportation in the hands of the state, and regulation of banks by the state rather than by individual industry. One of the most important features of the development of modern democracies was the assumption by the state of the sole authority for printing legal tender. The printing of "scrip" comes to be restricted as counterfeiting and only the state has the authority to print money, stamps, and legal tender. The centralization of monetary policy and supply is a central Marxist tenet that has come to be one of the most widely accepted practices of contemporary capitalism, so ingrained in the market system that its Marxist roots are either overlooked or generally unknown.

In a similar fashion, the development of highways, railways, interstates, and transportation infrastructure is the now the domain of national and state governments rather than individual businesses and industries. The assumption of this responsibility by governments, a Marxist prescription, has also become so ingrained within the accepted and expected roles of government that is generally ignored that it has Marxist origins. To be sure, other social/political philosophers have also advocated such activities, but many of them have, rightly or wrongly, been tarred with the epithet, "communist."

Finally, one of the most common views advocated by philosophers of what was generally considered liberal stripes during the 19th and 20th century was the institution of free public education. Rather than a piecemeal educational system of private schools, trade apprenticeships, and no training at all for many (including women), Marx, Mill, Wollstonecraft and a host of philosophers argued that the only way in which society would finally advance toward civilization and equal justice for all was the systematic and requisite education of all children, male and female. This was an extraordinarily radical notion at the time as the only institution of sufficient size to institute such a system was government. All of these philosophers believed that the only way in which a democratic system could be truly achieved would be if all people not only had access to education but were expected, and perhaps required, to attend school. That is, government and society were thought to have a vested interest in an educated populace. The truth of this view has been born out again and again in the rapid economic and civic advancement of those nations in which education is widely available, and widely available to all.

One commonality of all of the Marxist prescriptions is the belief that the state, as an entity in the thrall of the wealthy capitalist, would never enact any of these prescriptions, even in an attenuated manner. For example, Marx never conceived that government or business would allow labor unions to endure. For years, he was quite right as union-busting was one of the first orders of business for business and government turned a blind eye to the abusive ways in which unions were broken. However, over time, labor unions became common and while there is still an adversarial relationship between management and labor, the fact of unions continued existence with the blessing of the state is a circumstance Marx did not believe possible. Similarly, progressive income taxes, pensions, Social Security in its various forms, and free and public education were things Marx thought could come about only through complete and violent revolution. While the arguments on the floors of Congress and Parliament and the like have been at times harsh and mean-spirited, these advances have nevertheless come about without the violence Marx saw as inevitable. Thus, perhaps it is best to conclude, with regard to Marx's philosophical analysis and prescriptions that his critical work is quite perceptive and important to explore more fully while his prescriptive work is a incomplete and overly pessimistic. This would be a much more sophisticated and perceptive treatment of Marxist theory than is generally admitted in popular treatments of Marx and Communism, yet it is also a more accurate and profitable one.

Guided Reading Questions:
1. What is the "spectre haunting Europe?"

2. Where did the "bourgeoisie" come from and what have they brought about?
3. What must the bourgeoisie have in order to continue to exist?
4. What gave rise to the "means of production?"
5. Who are the "proletariat" and how did they come to be?
6. According to Marx, what has the Industrial Revolution and the Division of Labor done to the workplace of the proletarians?
7. According to Marx, what is the only truly *revolutionary* class? Why?
8. What is the *reactionary* class? Why are they considered reactionary?
9. What is the *dangerous* class?
10. What makes the proletarian revolution different from every preceding revolution, on Marx's view?
11. What is the difference between the Market Theory of Value and the Labor Theory of Value.

Logic Blurb
The Appeal to Emotion

For the final logic blurb, it is appropriate that we should investigate the *appeal to emotion*. Marx's propaganda writings, of which the *Communist Manifesto* is but one, are excellent examples of appeal to emotion. As a rhetorical matter, all propaganda is, in one sense or another, an appeal to emotion. However, the opening lines of the *Manifesto* mark it particularly so. "There is a spectre haunting Europe…" The appeal to fear and dread is among the most effective appeals because the emotions tied to it are so strong. Just as propaganda is not always false, however, the appeal to emotion is not always employed in the service of a fallacious or sinister argument. The Marxist critique of the 19th century industrial capitalist abuse of the worker is accurate and sharp, perhaps made even moreso by the emotional tenor of the work.

However, Marx's work suffers from an overuse of the appeal to emotion. It is quite common to fall victim to the appeal to emotion, both being swayed by one and finding oneself using one. Imagine two friends, Henry and Kate, who are in complete opposition to one another on some matter or other. One could easily imagine the argument escalating until one or both of them are overcome with anger and simply snap, perhaps arguing that if Kate gets her way, then the universe itself will come to an end or if Henry gets his way then there will be an immediate apocalypse. The appeal to emotion is most often an appeal to fear or anger. However, some of the more famous appeals to emotion are to patriotism or sympathy. A mass appeal to send money and food to victims of a natural disaster can be such an appeal. In some ways, the *Declaration of Independence* involves such appeals. Again, the conclusion of an appeal to emotion is not invalidated by the use of an appeal to emotion, but the appeal to emotion is to be received with a skeptical eye. They can be exceptionally powerful when paired with other arguments that establish the facts of the case or the basis of the appeal. However, sometimes such support is unavailable and often, the appeal to emotion is made because the conclusion is unsupportable by any other means. In such cases, the careful and reflective philosopher will dismiss the argument as faulty.